VERMONT*S IRISH REBEL

Capt. John Lonergan

To Mike —
Some Irish history —
(Faugh a ballagh!)
(Clear the way!)
Liam McKone

VERMONT*S
IRISH REBEL

Capt. John Lonergan

IN THE AMERICAN CIVIL WAR &
THE FENIAN INVASIONS OF CANADA

BY
WILLIAM L. McKONE

BREWSTER RIVER PRESS

Published by
Brewster River Press
P.O. Box 460
Jeffersonville, Vermont, 05464

Copyright © 2010 by William L. McKone
All Rights Reserved. No portion of this book may be reproduced or transmitted in any form whatsoever, including electronic, mechanical or any information storage or retrieval system, except as may be expressly permitted in the 1976 Copyright Act or in writing from the publisher.

Requests for permission should be addressed to:

Brewster River Press
Attn: William L. McKone
P.O. Box 460
Jeffersonville, Vermont, 05464

email: WMcKone@StoweAccess.com

www.VermontsIrishRebel.com

Editor: Katherine Quimby Johnson
Book design: Carrie Cook
Production manager: Peter Cook

ISBN: 978-0-9826330-0-7 (hardback)
ISBN: 978-0-9826330-1-4 (paperback)

Printed by United Book Press, Inc.
www.UnitedBookPress.com
Baltimore, Maryland, USA

TABLE *of* CONTENTS

Foreword *by Vincent E. Feeney* — ix

Dedication — xii

Prologue — xv

PART I - IRELAND — 1

Chapter 1 – CARRICK — 3

Chapter 2 – CONQUERED — 21

Chapter 3 – OPPRESSED — 31

Chapter 4 – STARVED — 49

Chapter 5 – AWAKENED — 71

Chapter 6 – EXILED — 89

PART II - AMERICA — 105

Chapter 7 – VERMONT'S IRISH — 107

Chapter 8 – FENIAN BROTHERHOOD — 125

Chapter 9 – MILITIA MOBILIZED — 147

Chapter 10 – AWAITING ORDERS — 175

Chapter 11 – IRISH COMPANY — 195

Chapter 12 – PICKET DUTY — 227

Chapter 13 – CAMP LIFE — 257

CHAPTER 14 – FORCED MARCH	283
CHAPTER 15 – INTO BATTLE	297
CHAPTER 16 – FLANK ATTACK	311
CHAPTER 17 – RETURNING HOME	331

PART III - CANADA   351

CHAPTER 18 – FOSTERING IRISH NATIONALISM	353
CHAPTER 19 – FENIANS ARGUE STRATEGY	385
CHAPTER 20 – FENIANS INVADE CANADA	409
CHAPTER 21 – FRACTURED FENIAN EFFORTS	437
CHAPTER 22 – FINAL FENIAN FOLLY	467
CHAPTER 23 – GREEN FLAGS FURLED	495
EPILOGUE	521
AUTHOR'S NOTE	529
ACKNOWLEDGMENTS	533
APPENDICES	537
NOTES	549
SELECTED BIBLIOGRAPHY	569
INDEX	573

LIST of MAPS

19th Century Ireland	xviii
Carrick on Suir	2
Greater Carrick area	70
Northeast United States and Southern British North America	104
Early Irish Immigration into Vermont	117
Locations of Vermont Militia	146
Downtown Burlington, Vermont	165
District of Columbia and Northern Virginia	174
Towns with members in Emmet Guards and 13th Vermont	194
Second Vermont Brigade area	226
Second Vermont Brigade on the Occoquan	256
March to Gettysburg	282
Approach to Gettysburg	288
Deployments on July 2	296
13th Vermont in action, July 3	310
Pursuit of Lee and return march	330
Northern Vermont and New York with Southern Quebec	350
Border areas of Fenian activity	384
Fenian area of operations	408
Fenians cross the border	420
Burlington, circa 1866	436
Fenian operations, 1870	466
Area of operations on Vermont border, 1870	490
Battle of Pike River	494

13th Vermont at Gettysburg

FOREWORD

FOR YEARS HISTORIANS NEGLECTED the presence of the large numbers of Irish immigrants living in Vermont during the nineteenth century. Only recently has their story begun to come to the surface. Now, in this volume historian Bill McKone brings to light the life of John Lonergan, the single most important Vermont Irishman of his generation. Immigrant, Civil War soldier, Medal of Honor recipient, militant Fenian, and community leader, Lonergan's life weaves through the great events of the mid-nineteenth century Irish-American experience.

Because little is known of Lonergan's youth in Ireland, McKone several times traveled to Carrick-on-Suir, the County Tipperary town where the future Fenian leader was born in the late 1830s. Walking the streets of Carrick, visiting the sites that must have been familiar to Lonergan, and steeping himself in the history of the area, McKone investigated the cultural and ideological environment in which the future Fenian was raised. McKone particularly noted that the abortive rising of 1848 was centered in the Carrick area and that John O'Mahony, founder of the Fenian Brotherhood, was a neighbor of the Lonergan family. Throughout his biography McKone reminds the reader of the importance of these early influences on Lonergan's life, particularly on his later connection to O'Mahony. Lonergan's life as revealed by McKone serves as a thread that moves through the events and obstacles, successes and losses, experienced by many Irish immigrants in the nineteenth century: from being uprooted in Ireland, finding a new home in America, earning a living, being swept up in the

Civil War, participating in militant Irish nationalism, to the mundane issues of everyday family life.

A former military man himself, McKone is at his best describing Lonergan's military career. How a company of Irishmen that Lonergan recruited in the opening stages of the war was rejected for military service—possibly out of anti-Irish prejudice—and how, when President Lincoln put out a call in 1862 for a greatly expanded army, Lonergan again recruited among his Irish neighbors. This time the authorities, chastened by mounting casualties, welcomed his efforts. His militia unit, known as the Emmet Guards, became Company A, 13th Regiment, Vermont Volunteer Infantry.

Company A was made up of "nine months" men. Although Howard Coffin broadly covers the 13th in his *Nine Months to Gettysburg*, McKone is the first historian to follow their term of service in detail from the time they enrolled in the Union army until they were discharged in late July of 1863. He describes the daily life of the Emmet Guards as they built and tore down encampments, performed picket duty, and as they functioned as a shield between the nation's capital and General Lee's Army of Northern Virginia. The climax of Company A's nine months tour of duty was the Battle of Gettysburg, and McKone's telling of the role played by the Emmet Guards there is riveting.

But perhaps McKone's greatest contribution to Irish-American history is his description of the Fenian movement in the United States and the part played in it by Lonergan and other Irish Vermonters. Though Vermont was twice the mobilization point for Fenian invasions of Canada, once in 1866 and again in 1870, until now the role played by the Green Mountain Irish in both attempts has been largely overlooked. McKone corrects that omission, detailing the work of Lonergan and others in advancing the Fenian cause.

McKone has done his homework, visiting every location involved in the story in Ireland, America, and Canada. Besides consulting general works on Vermont history, the Fenian movement and on the Civil War, he gleaned through U.S. military records, the Fenian archives held by the Catholic University of America, the Gettysburg archives, the

FOREWORD

Canadian archives, and the holdings of the Vermont state archives and the Special Collections library at the University of Vermont. Through his efforts the career and accomplishments of a patriotic Irishman and a heroic American have now come into clear focus.

Vincent E. Feeney
Author of *Finnigans, Slaters and Stonepeggers: A History of the Irish in Vermont*

Although John Lonergan is the focus of this story, it is dedicated to the countless men and women who served the cause of Ireland's liberation. Lonergan left Ireland as a lad of eleven and never returned, yet he devoted years of toil and danger to restoring nationhood and independence to the land of his birth. Thousands of others made their own contributions to the effort, though their names are now lost to us. Perhaps Lonergan's tale can give us some insight into the lives of these unrecorded patriots.

Oh! shame—for unchanged is the face of our isle;
As truagh gan oidhir 'n-a bh-farradh!
That taught them to battle, to sing, and to smile;
As truagh gan oidhir 'n-a bh-farradh!

We are heirs to their rivers, their sea, and their land—
Our sky and our mountains as grand—
We are heirs—oh! we're not—of their heart and their hand;
As truagh gan oidhir 'n-a bh-farradh!

'Gainst England long battling, at length they went down;
As truagh gan oidhir 'n-a bh-farradh!
But they left their deep tracks on the road of renown;
As truagh gan oidhir 'n-a bh-farradh!*

From "The Lament for the Milesians"
by Thomas Davis, nationalist poet
1814-1845

* *As truagh gan oidhir 'n-a bh-farradh* —"What a pity that there is no heir of their company." That is, no men now compare with them.

John Lonergan (probably Brandon Militia, 1861)

First Lieutenant John Sinnott

PROLOGUE

GETTYSBURG, PENNSYLVANIA - AFTERNOON OF JULY 3, 1863

"BOYS, LIE DOWN OR YOU'LL SURELY be hit!" shouted First Lieutenant John Sinnott, rising up from the sheltering breastworks of fence rails as the fierce Confederate bombardment began to subside. Soldiers jumping to their feet for a better view of the battlefield were exposing themselves to enemy fire. Just as he warned the men to take cover, a fragment from a bursting shell struck Sinnott in the head and he himself fell, severely wounded. The Rutland schoolteacher had given his last order to the members of Vermont's "Irish Company."

His commander and close friend, Captain John Lonergan, had moved Company A, 13th Vermont Volunteer Infantry, forward with the other units of the Second Vermont Brigade when the rebel cannon had opened fire two hours earlier. The three Vermont regiments had found some shelter behind hastily built defenses along the small stream called Plum Run. The Green Mountain boys, with the 13th Vermont on the right, now hugged the ground a hundred yards in advance of the main Union battle line on Cemetery Ridge, the target of the enemy artillery barrage. Lonergan's men, mostly Irishmen, held the position of honor on the extreme right, the senior company in the oldest Vermont regiment present. As the shelling finally slackened, some men stood up to look for the anticipated rebel assault. Their curiosity had cost the life of Lonergan's second in command, born in County Wexford in Ireland and now lying unconscious on a hillside near Gettysburg.

When the cannon on both sides fell silent, the smoke cleared from the mile-wide valley separating the opposing forces. The Union soldiers grimly watched as Longstreet's Confederate units filed out of the woods to form by regiment, brigade, and division. These gray-clad soldiers—disciplined, well-organized, fully armed, and led with clear purpose—contrasted sharply with the first rebels John Lonergan had seen, years ago, when the 1848 uprising in County Tipperary had centered on his home town of Carrick on Suir. Then, the national leaders of the Irish rebellion had been indecisive, without any real plan, and their followers were mostly ragged, starving peasants armed with pikes, stones, and farm tools.

What had led these Irish officers from their new homes in Vermont to this deadly encounter hundreds of miles away? Why did men dedicated to freeing Ireland from its union with Great Britain risk their lives to preserve the Union of their adopted country? How had Lonergan's choices brought him to command these men, now placed at the extreme point of danger on this crucial battlefield of the war? To answer these questions, we must look across the ocean, to the town where Lonergan's life began.

PROLOGUE

Sinnott's hat with shell hole

Sinnott's grave, St. Bridget Cemetery, West Rutland, Vermont

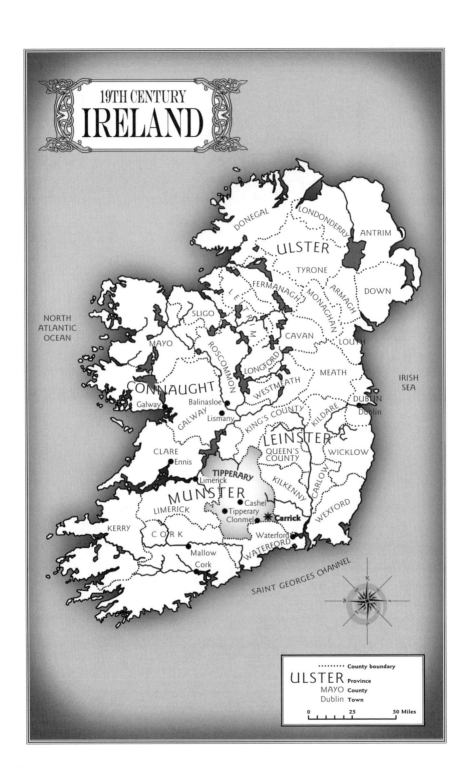

PART ONE

IRELAND

CLIFFS OF MOHER, WEST COAST OF IRELAND

To the West, beyond the setting sun,
lies Tir na nOg,
the Land of Eternal Youth.

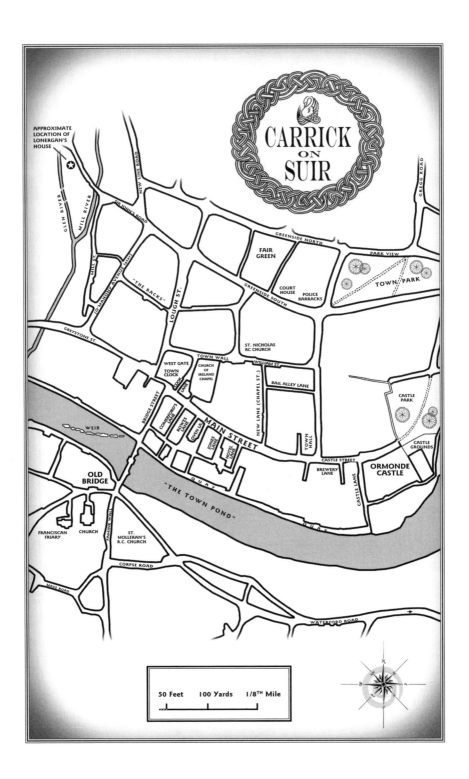

CHAPTER ONE

CARRICK

BORN INTO A WORKING CLASS Catholic family in 1837, the first year of Queen Victoria's long reign, John Lonergan began his life in circumstances a child was lucky to survive. Political, social, and economic conditions were already difficult for most Irish and about to collapse for many. Although the Penal Laws—imposed by the British during the past several centuries to regulate and restrict Catholic life and civil liberties—had been repealed, the majority religious group still faced great disadvantages. The years that John Lonergan lived in Ireland were marked by hardship, injustice, and revolution. Yet his childhood was infused with a magical sense of the land and the traditional beliefs of the people that continued as a part of everyday life alongside the established rituals of the Catholic religion. These early experiences combined to shape his later commitment to the struggle for restoring independence to his native land.

The corner of County Tipperary that John Lonergan called home still displays much of the rich heritage of Ireland. Stand in the middle of the old bridge over the Suir River at Carrick and study the surrounding hills and the town, the river and its valley. In every direction there are visible signs of the past, the history and beliefs that weave the story of the Irish into an endless Celtic knot. The river's flowing waters reflect the physical reminders of a repeated cycle of events—conquest, oppression, rebellion, and exile. When the schoolboy John Lonergan crossed this bridge in the 1840s, he breathed in the history of his country along with the faint salty tang in the air rising from the river below.

Beneath the bridge, the river ebbs and swells in the constant rhythm of the tides from the sea almost twenty-five miles away. Salmon, the fish of knowledge in ancient stories, swim here, while swans—the shape in which the children of Lir were enchanted for 900 years—drift in eddies along the shores. The hills on the horizon are home to the mystical "good people" whose fairy rings are still preserved in farmers' fields. To the west, the setting sun outlines Slievenamon, the "Mountain of Women." The towering hill is crowned with the huge cairn marking Finn McCool's tomb, an entrance to the fairy palace within the hill where Finn's mother dwelt.

THE BROAD VALLEY of the Suir River has long been known as the "Golden Vale," a notably fertile agricultural area producing an abundance of food. The village of Carraig na Siúire, whose name in the Gaelic means "Rock of the Suir," first appeared as Carraig MacGriffin around 1247. A cluster of dwellings and tradesmen grew up around the stronghold of the local Anglo-Norman lord at the time, Matthew FitzGriffin, part of the spreading control of the country by the newcomers.

These armored warriors built a network of outposts, square stone towers like those still standing on both banks of the Suir near the Carrick bridge. Norman lords made their homes in larger fortifications, including the Butlers' fifteenth century castle just downstream from the bridge. The Normans had established an administrative organization of counties based on the existing Irish kingships. Over time, many of these smaller "kingdoms" disappeared; the present county boundaries were set by the British kings in the sixteenth century. Carrick sits in the southeast corner of County Tipperary, close by the Lingaun River to the east that forms the border with County Kilkenny, while County Waterford lies to the south across the Suir.

A Butler built the Carrick bridge in 1447, the first structure to cross the river above the broad estuary where the Suir mingles with the Barrow and the Nore Rivers before joining the sea at Waterford. The stone arches span the water flowing between Carraig Mór and Carraig Beg, "big Carrick" on the north side in County Tipperary and "little Carrick" on the southern, County Waterford side. This bridge over the Suir also links the overland route between Munster and Leinster, two of the four ancient provinces, and for centuries the connection held strategic importance. The river itself gives Carrick access to the sea and the town developed into an important shipping point for sending the products of the region abroad, as well as supplying the larger town of Clonmel upstream.

The census of 1841 listed the population of Carrick Mór as 8,369.

CHAPTER ONE – CARRICK

OLD BRIDGE AT CARRICK ON SUIR

Together with the 2,680 on the south bank of the river in Carrick Beg, the area held 11,049 inhabitants, only a slight increase from the 1799 count of 10,863. The Irish, no longer owners of their native land, suffered in virtual serfdom under the ruling Protestant English. The parish of Carrick on Suir comprised "1,600 acres of chiefly arable land." In 1834, it was home to 7,128 Catholic and only 235 Protestant residents, but this small minority held all the power and most of the land.

A Protestant church, centrally located off the main street in Carrick Mór, was handsomely maintained through enforced contributions from everyone to the official Church of Ireland. Not until 1804 were the Catholics finally permitted to build St. Nicholas Church, "a plain, neat structure," outside the town wall on the site of an earlier thatched chapel. Near the church were also a monastery of the Christian Brotherhood and a convent of the sisters of the Order of Presentation. Carrick Beg—across the river and in a different parish, barony, and county than Carrick Mór—was served by both St. Molleran's Church and a Franciscan friary.

Because of its location, Carrick continued to develop as an important hub of transportation in the 1840s. "Upwards of £7,000" had been spent in previous years on improvements to navigation on the river and ships of 200 tons could now reach the quays in town. Before rocks were blasted to deepen the channel, lighters had to ferry cargo from Fiddown, a few miles downstream from Carrick. The wider navigation arch built into the old bridge and a towpath along the northern bank allowed for increased traffic upstream to Clonmel. The numerous watermen in Carrick developed a reputation for a feisty independence along with their own unique boats and garb. A knot used by them, the Carrick bend, is reproduced in the plasterwork of the manor house at the castle, testimony to the watermen's importance to the economy.

As seen by the land-owning establishment, expansion of the shipping capacity at Carrick for "exporting the produce of the surrounding district has had a most beneficial effect upon the general trade of the place." The effect of this "produce" leaving the country was less "beneficial" for the starving inhabitants of the area. Although exports did ensure employment for those in the shipping business and associated trades—including coopers like John's father, Thomas Lonergan, who crafted containers—the tenant farmers who produced the crops and livestock could not properly feed their own families.

A network of roads connected Carrick with Waterford, seventeen miles downstream, and Clonmel, thirteen miles upstream, as well as indirectly with Kilkenny to the northeast and with coastal towns to the south in County Waterford. Those who could afford the fare might travel by road in mail coaches and carriages, as well as the Clonmel-based innovation of the Bianconi private "cars."* Continuous boat traffic on the river, aided by the tidal ebb and flow, provided an alternative form of transportation and gave access to ships at the seaport of Waterford. Mail was delivered to the post office twice daily, but in 1848 there was not yet any telegraph service. The Waterford, Limerick, and Western Railway, incorporated in 1845, had opened the Limerick line as far as the town of Tipperary in May of 1848. The railroad would not reach Carrick until the station there opened in April of 1853, well after the rebellion that shook the area in the summer of 1848.

Daniel O'Connell, the "Great Liberator" who led the political fight against the anti-Catholic Penal Laws, also fostered nation-wide economic development when he founded the National Bank of Ireland in January of 1835. Within weeks, the first branch of the new bank opened on Main Street in Carrick on Suir as a safe place for the native Irish to do their banking. His choice of Carrick for the first branch is curious since it was not a major financial center or even one of the larger towns. Perhaps the location served

---

* An early and successful form of mass transit, these open horse-drawn carriages ran on a regular schedule at affordable rates.

CHAPTER ONE – CARRICK

to make a political statement, based more on the town's reputation for nationalism than any business rationale.

With an eye to Carrick's strategic importance and the inherently restless nature of the local Irish, British infantry were stationed in the old cavalry barracks on the north side of town. The constabulary, or police, had a "convenient barrack in New Street" as part of a network throughout the countryside. The officers were generally English, but the policemen themselves were Irish. To ensure that local loyalties would not interfere with their duties to uphold the higher authority of the monarch, constables were not allowed to serve in their own home county or that of their wife. A "new and handsome court-house" had been built on the green where fairs were held, next to the "bridewell" or jailhouse, a necessary part of the security establishment that maintained the "English garrison" in power. In this courthouse "general quarter sessions" were held for the district with petty sessions of the court every two weeks. A speedy trial could thus be expected, even if justice could not.

CARRICK PROVIDED SHELTER for the ruling class behind a town wall built in the medieval era. Early fortifications in Ireland had most often occupied hilltops, giving a natural advantage to the defenders.* Not until the Vikings founded the first towns as seaports were there large settlements in the lowlands, typically surrounded by stone enclosures. The Norman descendants of these seafaring conquerors continued this practice of protecting their new towns with walls, as well as building their castles and guard towers across the land. In the earlier phases of colonization, the English commonly enforced a curfew requiring the Irish to be outside the town wall at sundown. Large farms and estates in the countryside were usually built with defense in mind. High stone walls, built with the sweat of the conquered Irish, also enclosed these "bawns" to protect the owners and their property.

Certainly there was an obvious distinction between living, working, and worshiping inside or outside the town wall. A directory of towns in Ireland published in 1846 provides a view of life in Carrick and its environs during the years of John Lonergan's childhood. The town itself had spread beyond the wall and the description of Carrick in the directory clearly shows the contrast between the two worlds separated by the stone barrier. Banking, commerce,

---

* Throughout the island, the names of many places include the Gaelic *dun, lis,* or *rath,* all describing forts of varying sizes and types.

Sir John's Road, Carrick on Suir

education, and the better shops were found on the main street and the four short roads leading from it within the town wall. Shops of the trades and merchant stores occupied the riverside quay and the streets just outside the wall. The poor might find residence in cellars and servants' rooms of the houses within the town, but would more likely share a rough cottage outside the walls. The Lonergans lived on the outer fringe of the town on the road to Clonmel, an easy walk from their home to St. Nicholas, the Catholic church they attended.

In the eighteenth century, roads were generally built by local landlords who would take the initiative in providing a stretch at their own expense. If the Grand Jury of the county found that the road had been properly made, the builder could later be reimbursed. Sir John Osborne was responsible for improvements made to the road northwest out of Carrick through Mullagh to Ballydine Cross Roads. This main road followed the Suir River valley westward, continuing on to Killsheelan and Clonmel. Osborne's name survives in part for this stretch of the road out of Carrick, called "Sir John's Road." The only address given for the Lonergan family when they lived in Ireland is "Sir John's Road" without any further identification of their lodging. A cluster of rude cottages had likely developed in that area as housing for working men like Thomas Lonergan, perhaps with more than one family living in each.

The directory listings of the time provide some sense of what life was like on Sir John's Road. The category of "Nobility, Gentry, and Clergy" that heads the listings for Carrick includes two ladies living on Sir John's Road. Miss Matilda Herbert, an author who was the daughter of a clergyman, and Mrs. Sophia Manderville of this locally important family occupied "the Villa," a manor house. Though the Villa was located in the physical vicinity of the Lonergans' residence, socially it occupied another world.

The other listings for Sir John's Road indicate its true nature as a backwater for the poor. None of the thirty-one bakers, nineteen grocers, twenty-four shopkeepers, or even one of the twenty-five "spirit dealers" in the Carrick directory did business on Sir John's Road. No doctor, apothecary, or lawyer hung out a shingle there. Instead, the road was home to two dealers in corn (meaning "grain" in general) and a corn merchant, a pig merchant, a tanner, and one of the fifty public houses of Carrick.

There was also one cooper on Sir John's Road, William Cornan. Of the eighteen cooper shops in Carrick, seven were on Lough Street (now Kickham Street) leading past the town wall and west gate to the bridge and five were across the river in Carrick Beg. This concentrated the artisans making containers in an area handy to the quays for shipping. Most likely Thomas Lonergan practiced his craft as a cooper at Cornan's nearby shop on Sir John's Road. A number of coopers found employment in Carrick as the "principal trade now is in corn, butter, and provisions—the former is very extensive." A decade earlier the grain and butter trade of the town amounted to more than £360,000 each year, a very sizable sum. These craftsmen (Mary Butler in Carrick Beg was the only woman listed as a cooper) would be kept busy right through the famine years making firkins for butter, hogsheads for grain, and barrels for provisions. Such containers full of food were shipped in great quantities out of a country suffering widespread starvation.

Irish families without property left little behind them in Ireland in the way of written records. The documentation for the Longerans in Carrick consists of only a few records from the church.* The marriage of Thomas Lonergan to Mary Nolan is recorded at St. Nicholas' Church as taking place on November 3, 1835, with Edmund and Catherine Ryan as witnesses. Thomas at nineteen years old and Mary at only sixteen (based on their ages later given in U.S. census records) were close to the average age of marriage for the Irish working

---

* Scraps of the family's history before they fled the country were written down much later, but only a faint picture emerges of John's childhood years. Larger events in the area, including the famine and the uprising of 1848, undoubtedly left vivid impressions on his mind, yet their effect on John can only be inferred from his later actions.

class at the time—twenty for men and seventeen for girls. The general rule for age of marriage then tended toward "the poorer, the earlier." Their eldest son John was born on April 7, 1837 (some records give his date of birth one or even two years later) and baptised the following day at St. Nicholas for a donation of two shillings and six pence. Following John, the family recorded other births by baptism at the same church—Mary in 1841, Edmund in 1843, Ellen in 1846, right up to that of the third son. Named after his father, this child was baptized Thomas in 1848, not long before his parents left Ireland forever. Sponsors for these children at their baptisms were named Lonergan, Eagan, Ryan, Nolan, Hanson, and Walsh, all fairly common surnames in the area and indicative of intermarriage among these families.

THE PROHIBITION ON IRISH TEACHERS, part of the oppressive Penal Laws, had been lifted in 1782. Even so, a survey of education in Ireland by a British commission in 1826 found that with half a million students in schools, four out of five were attending the "hedge schools." Always short of cash, the Catholics in the countryside could pay an itinerant teacher with food and lodging. Still commonly called by the name they earned when itinerant teachers held illegal classes wherever they could, often in the hedge along the road, such schools were now more often sheltered under the roof of a house or barn. Students might attend them only sporadically, whenever they could and a teacher was available. The curriculum of these hedge schools would vary according to the teacher, but it likely included some Irish history presented in a light unfavorable to the current British rule. Usually the instruction would be given in Irish, an important contribution to preserving the language. With little in the way of a classroom or supplies, the teachers were replicating the role of the traditional keepers of Irish history, the poets who relied on their memory in the absence of a written language.

The childhood of Michael Doheny, later a leader in the 1848 rebellion and in the Fenian movement, reflects just such an education in South Tipperary. He was born in 1806 at the comfortable family farm near Fethard, not far from Carrick, but he could not be spared for schooling after his father died. Instead, the child worked on the farm and was taught to read by his mother. The family spoke both English and Irish and welcomed passing scholars who stayed and made their contributions to his learning. A cash crop from the farm was furze, sold to bakers to fire their ovens, and an old man was hired to cut the branches of this bush. As Michael worked alongside him, this peasant recited his "huge repertoire" of the *Scéalta Fiannáiochta*, the "traditional formal tales and poems of the Fianna, Fionn MacCumhail, Oisín," and others.

These stories were "the most popular literary fare of the Irish-speaking and bilingual populations of South Tipperary at the time," in part because many of the settings could be recognized in the local places around Slievenamon. By the age of ten, Doheny could recite the old storyteller's tales word for word. When he turned twenty, Doheny put down his farm tools and went to school in Fethard where the other pupils in his class ranged in age from seven to forty. He then tutored the children of a family in Cashel before studying law in London and he returned to Cashel as a lawyer in his thirties.

BY A STROKE OF LUCK for John Lonergan, Carrick had become home to the second of the Christian Brothers schools, founded there in 1805 and opened the following year.* The education of the poor was otherwise ignored by society until the National Schools were organized by the Education Act of 1831. The first such free school was not opened in the Carrick district until 1840. An unpopular provision of the National Board was the requirement that religious teaching and devotional practices be suppressed in the schools, all religious symbols put away except for one specified day a week. Meanwhile, the Christian Brothers continued with their "novel undertaking of educating what one might call the roughs and toughs without fee or reward from them or their parents." By 1841 Carrick had a total of twenty teachers, mostly in "pay schools," but six out of ten people in the area over twelve years old were illiterate.

In 1846, the Christian Brothers premises were described as "a very handsome building, in a delightful situation." In this school, 500 boys received a free "religious, literary, and scientific education" while "a certain number of the deserving are clothed, and have trades and situations provided for them." The nearby convent of the Presentation Sisters provided similar education for between 200 and 300 "poor girls" and John Lonergan's sister Mary may have

---

* The first Christian Brothers school had been established in Waterford in 1802 by a wealthy ex-merchant, Edmund Rice, to provide the benefits of literacy to the poor of the Irish towns. Mount Sion, the first institution founded, became the center of a network of Christian Brothers schools. Rice is credited with being fluent in Irish and the language was taught in the schools by native speakers belonging to the Christian Brothers order. Rice urged Thomas O'Brien, a wine merchant also from Waterford, to sponsor a school and Rev. McKenna of Carrick welcomed the project after it was refused by Clonmel.

attended this school. Although John had the benefit of classroom instruction only in his early childhood, it apparently gave him a sound basis for further educating himself after he left Ireland.

The operation of the Carrick school would have followed the standard Christian Brothers course of instructions. The routine began at nine o'clock with morning prayer and the lessons were punctuated with prayer as the clock struck each hour. At noon, "the Angelus and the Acts of Faith, Hope, and Charity were said." The end of the school day at three o'clock called for recitation of the Litany of Our Lady and other prayers before the boys were dismissed. In addition to this religious observance, boys sitting eight or ten to a long desk in the "lower room" were also taught the Catechism along with their reading, spelling, and writing. The religious education provided by the Roman Catholic Christian Brothers reinforced in John his sense of belonging to that church and he devoutly practiced the Catholic religion throughout his life.

In the higher classes, the instruction ran to practical subjects such as mathematics, drawing, and navigation. John left Ireland before he would have received such specialized training. The system provided for free libraries in the schools, even circulating books between them. Just what history was taught is not clear, but it seems to have concentrated on biblical and religious matters.

In keeping with the mission of caring for the poor, food and clothing were provided along with the education and religious instruction. Three tailors plied their trade in an upstairs room, mending the clothes of the poor as necessary and making new suits for boys about to be apprenticed to a trade. An important feature of the school was the bakery for feeding the students, a great incentive for attending school when so many were going hungry. In Waterford, three men worked at the bakery on the grounds and bread was produced daily for those in need. This food that the students received from the Christian Brothers would have helped John Lonergan survive the famine years.

DESPITE THE DIFFICULT TIMES, John's childhood held the comfort of a sense of belonging to family and community since he was part of an extensive network of relatives in the area. Lonergan is one of the old Gaelic names and earlier was the most common surname in that part of southern Tipperary. Many old graves of Lonergans are to be found at the ruined Ballyneill churchyard not far up the road from where John lived. The Nolans on his mother's side may have been later arrivals in the area, but would also have been well established by the time John was born. With clan connections to the farms of the countryside, his father's trade as a cooper (which probably gave him access to some provisions), and meals provided at the school, John likely was spared the worst of the famine. He grew into a robust and confident adult in America, so these hard years apparently had no lasting effects on his physical health.

His neighbors in the area often were not so fortunate during the famine period when "the death rate in Carrick rose so high that a special graveyard was opened in the Deerpark area." This Deerpark lies between Sir John's Road and the Suir River, on a large estate surrounded by a high stone wall and just up the road from where the Lonergans lived. The enclosure of fertile agricultural land, diverted from the production of food into a preserve for deer to amuse the landlord, provided an ironic final resting place for the casualties of famine. John would have witnessed the stream of funeral processions carrying the victims of disease and starvation to this graveyard, many of them no doubt people that his family knew and mourned. A desperate sense of injustice must have grown as the food that could have saved these poor Irish continued to be shipped down the Suir, destined for sale on the market to line the pockets of the already wealthy landowners. These proprietors commonly lived in England, far removed from the miseries of their tenants, and depended on the income from their holdings in Ireland to support their lavish lifestyle.

Sir John's Road in this area runs alongside the Glenn River, whose valley is known as *Glen na Phuca* or the Valley of the Fairy Horse. A boy with John's energy and boldness would surely have explored this wooded valley full of associations with ancient tales of the "noble people." A child familiar with the stories relating to the area could as easily accept the presence of fairy palaces underground as he could the existence of the manor house and wealth hidden behind the high wall of Deerpark, equally invisible to him. At least there was the possibility that at certain times of the year, particularly Samhain at the end of October, the gates to the otherworld of Irish legend might open to him. A mortal who spent a single day feasting in the fairy halls within the hills might find upon his return that a year, or even a hundred years, had passed in his own world since he left. The iron gates to Deerpark, by contrast, would never open for a poor Irish lad except as entry to a burial ground from which he could never return.

Much of the native Irish culture had begun to disappear by the mid-nineteenth century, the result of a deliberate effort by the English to stamp out any identity for Ireland other than that of a province of the United Kingdom. A "west Briton" mentality was promoted by a purposeful attempt to suppress the Gaelic language spoken by a majority of the population. This repression had a cumulative effect over the years. Still, Irish continued as the first language in many parts of the countryside with English used only when necessary to do business in the towns. John Lonergan no doubt had a foot in each of these worlds, living on the edge of town where the community used Irish among themselves, but attending school where the instruction was in English. In contrast to the hedge schools, Irish was taught in the officially sanctioned institution as a second language, as if it were a foreign tongue.

The Christian Brothers school operated on the sufferance of the authorities, so any official view of history presented to the schoolboys must have been slanted toward a British perspective. At home, Ireland's past would have been quite literally a different story, as Lonergan's elders recalled events that they had experienced themselves or learned from others. These incidents of living memory were no doubt recounted, in the Gaelic, against the larger background of Irish oral history that spoke of an independent and proud nation whose warriors had fought off foreign oppression. Dating back far before any written history of the island, heroic legends would have been retold with special fervor in the difficult years leading to 1848. Cuchulain, son of the god Lugh by a mortal woman, would be praised as the model of the solitary champion with his stirring warrior's death.

Tales of the Fianna, the warrior bands led by Finn McCool, were even more popular locally. The tradition of collective defense of the island by the Fianna involved close connections with nearby Slievenamon. The great cairn of rocks at the top of the mountain was said to be the tomb of Finn McCool; tradition still holds that a visitor should circle the cairn three times and place a stone upon it to honor his name. In the late eighteenth century and beginning of the nineteenth, the "Lays and Stories of the Fianna were the most popular literary form in prose and verse amongst the Irish speaking public." The poets composed this verse to be sung, their songs conveying the history of the time.*

---

* Details of the stories might vary with the singer and the chronology of any historic events could be bent to suit the tale, but a common thread of heroic action would be preserved. In the Western Isles of Scotland, even today "the art of singing the Fianna still survives."

CHAPTER ONE – CARRICK

AUTHOR AT FINN'S SEAT, SLIEVENAMON

The first people in Ireland, so the stories say, belonged to a small, dark race called the Fir Bolg. They were conquered by the Tuatha De Danna, (the people of the goddess Danu), a tribe that included many gods and goddesses with magical powers. This tribe was in turn vanquished, despite their powers, after bloody battles with the sons of Mil. These Milesians had sailed to the shores of Inisfail, the "Isle of Destiny," from the Iberian Peninsula and were also called Hibernians from this origin. The Celtic conquerors in seeming generosity granted the defeated Tuatha De Danna half the island, but it was to be the half that lies under the ground. So Lugh of the Long Hand led the people of Danu into the very hills themselves where they built their palaces under the ground, beneath the rings of standing stones. They were still present in the minds of men, however, and at times became involved in the affairs of mortals. Out of respect, they were called "the people of the hills" or "the noble people" and only the foolish would name them aloud as fairies.*

Lugh passed on his kingship to the Dagda, whose son the Bodb Dearg was in turn chosen to rule. The Bodb Dearg resided in "the Sidh of Femen," the mountain which is now called Slievenamon. From his palace there, he allocated the hills of Ireland as dwelling places for the other gods and

---

* The Irish *sidh* —pronounced "shee" and now spelled *sí*—first referred to the fairy palaces beneath the ground, then to the mounds and circles of stones above them, and finally to the people themselves. The word is now most widely known in the legend that the cry of a fairy woman, the "banshee," portends death in some noble families.

goddesses. Lir, the god of the ocean, was given a hill in County Armagh, but was angry at not being chosen the leader. To placate him, the Bodb Dearg offered one of his three sisters as a wife. When Lir's wife died leaving four young children behind, he was offered the choice of another sister. This stepmother was jealous of the children, however, and on a trip to visit the Bodb Dearg at Slievenamon she changed the children into swans. The swans were cursed to spend 300 years at each of three bodies of water and remain in that form until "a prince of Connaught marries a princess of Munster." By the time the swans had regained their human shape, the Children of Danu had all been driven under the ground and were remembered only as fairies.

In the reign of Conn, the *Ard Rí* or High King of Ireland at the end of the second century CE, the Celts are said to have founded the Fianna of Ireland, "a great standing army of picked and specially trained, daring warriors, whose duty it was to carry out the mandates of the high-king." In the Gaelic, the collective noun "Fian" means a band of warriors and the plural form for an army made up of such groups is "Fianna." The adjective referring to them is "Fenian," pronounced FEEN-ian.

Competitions were held for potential recruits at the great fairs, especially at Tara, Uisnech, and Taillte. Stringent tests ensured that only the best of the many candidates from among the sons of chieftains and princes entered the ranks of the Fianna. The Fianna were trained and ready for war when necessary, but at other times acted as a kind of national police patrolling the land. They roamed the island during the summer and fall, from the quarter-days of Beltinne to Samhain (May to November), camping in the open and living by the hunt. During the other half of the year, they were "quartered upon the people." In peacetime, there were three battalions of three thousand men each, expanded in time of war to seven battalions. Such a force of trained and loyal men ensured respect for the High King and his laws inside the country, while also giving pause to any invader considering an attack.

Legend says that Lugh, the leader of the Tuatha De Danna, had given his widowed mother in marriage to Tadg and they had two daughters. Muirne had married Cumhal (pronounced "Cool"), head of the Fianna of Ireland. Their son Finn (or Fionn) was therefore called "MacCumhal" (or "McCool"), that is, "son of Cumhal." When Cumhal was killed in battle, Finn's mother then took the king of Carrighe as husband and sent Finn away for his own

CHAPTER ONE – CARRICK

safety. He wandered the land and had many adventures, at one time living with the druid Finegas on the river Boyne to learn poetry.

Finegas, after watching the fish for seven years, at last caught the salmon of knowledge. From it, Finn learned the art of prophecy and he acquired further wisdom by drinking from the well of the moon belonging to the Tuatha De Danna. A member of that tribe had emerged from within the hill every Samhain for seven years in a row to burn the palace at Tara. Finn did a service for the High King by killing the arsonist where all others had failed.

In return for this act, Finn was made, like his father before him, chief of the Fianna of Ireland "in the time of Cormac MacArt", in the third century CE. Finn, a chief in his own right, had a sumptuous palace on the Hill of Allen in Kildare, the white fort made by his great-grandfather, Nuada of the Tuatha De Danna.

Wherever Finn went, his presence was marked by a banner that had a likeness of the sun upon it. In some stories, the flag was called the *Dealb-Greine*, the Sunshape, or in others the *Scal Greine*, the Sunburst. As Finn was the protector of a society that still gave primary reverence to this source of light and of life, it was fitting that this symbol was carried into battle by him. With the adoption of Christian belief, the Circle of the Sun was joined with the Cross to produce the unique Celtic cross. Down through the centuries since Finn's time, this sunburst flag would be identified with him and with Fenian warrior bands.

Finn took great delight in hunting for deer on Slievenamon and in hearing the voices of the hounds "east and west, from hill to hill" that were "sweeter than musical instruments and their faces outwards from the Suir." Finn required a new wife each year—no mortal women could sustain the relationship for a longer period—and he also hunted for his queens on the same mountain. With so many ladies eager to be chosen, the Fenian chief had the hopeful candidates race to the top of Slievenamon where he waited to embrace the winner. A flat rock at the summit is even today called *Sui Fionn* or Finn's Seat. Some say these contests for the prize of sharing a year with Finn are the origin of the name for Slievenamon, the "mountain of the women."

Life in the Fianna was not all hunting and feasting to the music of the harp, however. When the King of Lochlann brought his Norse to raid the island, the High King Cormac MacArt sent word from Tara for Finn to bring his warriors to drive off the invaders. Joined by "the reserve battalions of the Fianna, gathering from the four corners of Eireann," Finn defeated the foreigners. His grandson Osgar—the son of Oisin, "in turn himself the son of the mighty Finn"—killed the King of Lochlann in the combat.

After many such battles, the Fianna were destroyed when they put their pledge of loyalty to their leader Oisin, successor to Finn, above fealty to the High King. The Fianna supported the King of Munster, the son of Finn's daughter, against the son of Cormac, in a war between Irish factions. In a terrible battle at Gabra, Osgar died in single combat with the High King and all the Fenians were annihilated, but for two. Oisin survived the battle and then encountered Niamh, a fairy queen. They flew off together on her white horse to *Tir na nOg*, the Land of Eternal Youth, under the western ocean.

When Oisin finally returned to the world of men, he found that centuries had passed, St. Patrick had won over the land to the new religion, and the old ways were gone along with the Fianna. Disputing the saint's claim that "God is better for one hour than the whole of the Fianna of Ireland," Oisin tells "Patrick of the crooked crozier" that his staff would "be in little bits if I had Osgar with me now." Willing to cede authority only to a stronger power, Oisin explained, "If my son Osgar and God were hand to hand on the Hill of the Fianna and I saw my son put down, I would say that God was a strong man." To summon back the Fenian warriors, Oisin sought the great hunting horn of the Fianna hidden in the rocks of Slievenamon. His search was in vain and so all the Fenians disappeared into the mists of legend.

THESE STORIES OF THE FENIANS gathered on Slievenamon beneath the Sunburst banner of Finn McCool would have been among the tales told around the Lonergan's turf fire in the evening, as the sun set behind that very mountain close by on the western horizon. Then it would have been prayers and to bed for young John and his brother and sisters, probably in a corner of the same room that served as kitchen, sitting room, bedroom according to need. After hearing the stories praising the warrior bands of the Fianna, John as a boy might dream that he, like Finn McCool, could one day be the leader of such a Fenian group. Years later and many miles from Ireland, far away in America, this dream would become reality under a new Sunburst flag.

Before John could take his place in the ranks of a new Fenian army, however, he would undergo his own trials of exile and life-long separation from the land of his birth. He would be caught in the recurring tides of Irish history that would swell into a new wave of nationalism against old injustices, a wave that crested in rebellion. As a lad in Ireland, Lonergan saw first-hand the cost of foreign rule; as a man in America, he dedicated himself to making his homeland "a nation once again."

John Lonergan's devotion to his native land was strengthened by what he experienced during his youth when the forces of nationalism clashed with oppression in his hometown. To understand the terrible situation of 1848—when famine, despair, and rebellion brought death or exile to half the population of Carrick—the deep roots of Ireland's plight must be explored.

Norman tower on Suir River

CHAPTER TWO

CONQUERED

I RELAND'S GLORIES WERE FAR IN the past when John Lonergan attended school. The transformation of Ireland from a proud nation of warriors, once the richest country in Europe, to the down-trodden, impoverished, and starving people of 1848 resulted from centuries of military defeats and political oppression. Early invaders had at times gained control of the parts of the island, but they had then been absorbed into the society, becoming "more Irish than the Irish." In the final conquest, the Irish were dispossessed of their land, persecuted for their religion, and robbed of their nationhood. The British version of events might try to teach the benefits of Ireland's inclusion into a larger realm, but John could daily see in the sufferings of his conquered people the grim results of subjugation.

THE EARLY SETTLEMENT OF THE CELTIC tribes in Ireland had established the defining culture of the island. Forced westward from Central Europe by the pressure of other expanding cultures, the Celts found their final refuge on the islands nearest the setting sun. Beyond this lay only the realm of their afterworld in *Tir na nOg*. The Celts supposedly divided Erin into "five quarters"—the four provinces of Ulster, Munster, Leinster, and Connaught, plus the center at Tara where the High King ruled.

Lacking a written language, a highly trained class of poets, storytellers, and interpreters of the established law orally passed on Celtic history.* Generations of learned lawgivers bearing the title of Brehon preserved an advanced system of jurisprudence. Impartially applied to all, Brehon law bound king and peasant alike, though the "honor price" of fines for crimes

---

* Variations and contradictions are inevitable in an oral history. However, a general consistency was preserved in poem, song, and story down through the centuries.

depended on rank and wealth. In Celtic society, women were afforded equal rights and protection under these laws. The Celtic language and culture evolved over centuries in Ireland, and the Irish later embraced the religion of St. Patrick, the island's patron saint. Through this Celtic and Catholic heritage, John Lonergan acquired a sense of an identity apart from the ruling English.

As we have already seen, Vikings founded the first towns on the island in the ninth century and controlled the surrounding seas from ports such as Limerick, Cork, Wexford, Waterford, and particularly Dublin. Though Dublin became a great trading center, the High King continued to rule from Tara. The Vikings' shallow-draft dragon ships could also penetrate far up Ireland's rivers, including the Suir. Raids for plunder and later trading expeditions likely passed through the "Golden Vale," even beyond Carrick. The Vikings were fearsome warriors and astutely exploited dynastic feuds in Ireland. In many battles, Irish clans and Viking groups found themselves fighting as allies on each opposing side. Even the nearly constant conflicts did not destroy the major Irish kingdoms. With time, the Norsemen assimilated through intermarriage, alliances, and the exchange of children—known as fostering, such exchanges could extend the bonds of family or provide hostages.

At the close of the tenth century, Brian Boru consolidated power for his clan of the Dál Cais of Thomond. His court *file* or poet claimed that this dynasty in the west of Ireland descended from Finn McCool, though it was common practice for "the poet of every royal house to invent noble ancestors for their patrons." Brian defeated the Munster king in 978 and then made an alliance with the Vikings of Waterford. Brian hoped to gain control of Leinster and the Dublin Vikings, who resisted his expansion of power. On April 23, 1014, the Battle of Clontarf near Dublin brought Brian victory, as well as death in battle at the age of seventy-three. His descendants would proudly perpetuate his name as the O'Brien clan; even in 1848 the name retained its power to rally the people.

Previously the High King, as was the case with over one hundred lesser "kings" in Ireland, had held only limited power. The king did not make the laws, but rather was equally governed by them along with his subjects. Kingship was not hereditary since Ireland did not apply the principle of primogeniture; either the *tuatha*, or tribe, would select a new king or someone would seize power by force. The tribe also collectively held its land, not the local king

CHAPTER TWO – CONQUERED

alone. After Brian Boru, the throne of the High King became more powerful, resembling that of other European countries, and therefore more of a prize for which to fight. Ireland was still uniquely guided by its native Brehon law and also followed its own particular rules for the church.

This Irish approach to the organization of the church decentralized power in the religious community among the monasteries and ruling families, rather than directing it through a hierarchy of bishops and other officials. Pressure from Rome led to a more centralized system paralleling the concentration of temporal power. The synod at Kells in 1152 divided the country into thirty-six sees with archbishops installed at Armagh, Cashel, Dublin, and Tuam. Newly implemented policies for Ireland reduced the status of women in the church, abolished hereditary succession in the monasteries, and enforced celibacy among the clergy, bringing the Irish into conformity with Catholic practices elsewhere. The only English pope ever chosen, Adrian IV, issued a fateful papal bull in 1155. In this order, he authorized the King of England, Henry II, to invade Ireland to force compliance with Rome's dictates, including the dates on which holidays would be celebrated. At the time, Henry had more pressing concerns in France, but this papal bull served his purposes later when the Anglo-Normans launched an invasion of Ireland.

THE AMBITIONS OF DERMOT MACMURROUGH, who claimed kingship of the province of Leinster at the age of sixteen and aspired to be High King, brought him into conflict with the O'Connors of Connaught. MacMurrough had carried off the wife of O'Rourke, an ally of Rory O'Connor who had declared himself High King. MacMurrough fled to England after his main ally was killed by O'Rourke in battle in 1166. Seeking out Henry II in France for help in regaining his lost kingdom in Leinster, MacMurrough received the support of both the English king and the church. MacMurrough returned to Ireland and established a base in Wexford in 1169. The main Norman force of two hundred knights and a thousand men at arms came over from England the following year. Led by the Earl of Pembroke known as "Strongbow," they landed at Waterford, easily taking the city at the mouth of the Suir. From there, a conquest of Ireland began through force and alliances—Strongbow married MacMurrough's daughter within the year—as the mailed fist of the Normans crushed all opposition.

To prevent the establishment of an independent Norman kingdom under Strongbow, Henry II brought over a large force in 1171. His intervention in Ireland also carried the blessing of Pope Alexander III, successor to Adrian IV. A synod at Cashel reorganized the Irish church in 1172 to address the pope's additional grievances against it (such as eating meat during Lent). The English king achieved temporal power over all of Ireland in 1175 when Rory O'Connor signed the Treaty of Windsor. This gave Henry II control over that part of Ireland not already ruled by the Normans, who continued to tighten their grip on the country. O'Connor died in 1198, the last of the Irish High Kings. Rule over the island for the first time passed to a monarch outside the country, who now bore the titles of both King of England and Lord of Ireland. For the next seven centuries, Ireland's fate was to be in the hands of English rulers. A long succession of kings and queens demanded that the loyalty of old Gaelic families like the Lonergans be transferred from their local chieftains to this distant throne.

For hundreds of years the continuous intrigues and struggles for power in Ireland erupted from time to time into rebellions that were suppressed by force. Then, in 1515, Henry VIII ascended the throne of England with enormous and lasting consequences for Ireland. To destroy resistance to English rule, he reinstated enforcement of all previous laws against Irish culture, against marriage with the native peoples, against the use of the Gaelic language, and against every aspect of Irish nationhood. Then, when the pope refused to grant Henry a divorce, the king defied him by ending his first marriage so that he could wed Anne Boleyn.* After being excommunicated by the pope in 1533, Henry responded with the Act of Supremacy in 1534, making himself head of a new Church of England.

In 1536, Henry consolidated his role as worldly and spiritual leader, uniting England and Wales as one nation and also establishing by decree the Church of Ireland with himself as head. This created a state church in Ireland independent of Rome and the Roman Catholic Church was "declared null and void." The vast majority of the Irish, true to the Roman Catholic religion even after the synod at Kells, were now required to be loyal to both a foreign king and a church not their own. To drive home his temporal power over

---

* Daughter of the Earl of Ormond (and sister of one of Henry's earlier mistresses), many believed Anne was born in the Ormond family castle in Carrick.

CHAPTER TWO – CONQUERED

Ireland, Henry had an obedient Irish Parliament replace his title of "Lord of Ireland" with that of "King of Ireland." From 1542 until the Union of 1801, the king or queen of England thus claimed the right to wear two separate crowns. In the third quadrant of the royal coat of arms, the harp of Ireland was topped by a crown, clearly depicting the subservient status of the country for the many Irish subjects who could not read.

The nobles in Ireland were required to submit by acknowledging Henry as the King of Ireland and the "head of Church and State in Ireland," renouncing both their religion and Irish customs such as Brehon law. In return, Henry promised to grant them back their land and powers, but in fact rarely did so. When the old Gaelic families were robbed of their heritage, the lands were most often confiscated and then handed over to loyal English "planters" for exploitation.

Henry's daughter Elizabeth continued her father's policies during her long reign as queen, yet Ireland was never fully pacified or loyal to England. Even treachery like the massacre at Mullaghmast in 1577—when the Irish nobility of Leix and Offaly was invited to a banquet and then slaughtered—only served to strengthen opposition to English rule. The Catholic Irish looked to their co-religionists in France and Spain, long-standing enemies of the Protestant English, for help. The old Irish families made a last effort in the Nine Years' War of 1594–1603 led by the great Ulster clan, the O'Neills, and supported by a Spanish landing at Kinsale on the southern coast. Defeat this time led to exile of the Irish leaders. The "Flight of the Earls" in 1607 marked a major turning point in Irish history. Those lands still in the hands of the exiled Gaelic lords were forfeited to the crown. The Irish lands were given as reward to loyal English settlers and, particularly in Ulster, to Presbyterian Scots known as "Dissenters."

FESTERING RESENTMENT AMONG THE IRISH over their loss of land and power led to the Rising of 1641 in Ulster. The following year the Confederation of Kilkenny was formed amidst the turmoil of civil war in England. The Duke of Ormonde,* head of the old Carrick family of Butlers, served as the representative of King Charles I in Ireland. The Butlers had moved to Kilkenny and left their Catholic religion behind, accepting the Church of

---

* Irish spelling of many names varies over time and from place to place; for example, O'Neill often appears as O'Neil and O'Mahony as O'Mahoney, with most Gaelic surnames rendered into English in several versions.

Ireland as more advantageous for their ambitions. The Royalist military leader was Owen Roe O'Neill, who returned from exile after forty years of service in the Spanish army and was initially successful on the battlefield. The war dragged on as the king, the parliament, and the pope made shifting alliances. (O'Neill's death in November of 1649 as he attempted to unite forces to oppose Cromwell was long attributed to poisoning by the English, though it was probably due to disease.)

Victory for the Parliamentarians in England's civil war and the execution of King Charles in January of 1649 freed Oliver Cromwell to settle affairs in Ireland. He landed his New Model Army in Dublin in August of that year and lost no time in brutally crushing the supporters of monarchy and Catholicism, paying off his troops with confiscated land. The September massacre at Drogheda after the town had refused to surrender set the standard for Cromwell's operations. The city of Wexford under its military governor, Colonel David Sinnott,* resisted the New Model Army's march to the south until a traitor opened the gates of the castle. The town was then pillaged and its people put to the sword (much as "Old Model" armies had done in the past).

Cromwell's ferocious reputation caused many towns to submit without resistance as he campaigned down the eastern coast. However, he found Waterford defiant of his demand for surrender. Leaving it besieged, he continued on into the Suir valley in east Tipperary, taking Carrick and other towns. Tradition has Cromwell observing the fertile lands along the Suir from a hilltop and commenting "this, indeed, is a country well worth fighting for" (this same statement is also attributed to William of Orange on his visit to Carrick half a century later). After negotiating the capitulation of Kilkenny with Sir Walter Butler, Cromwell in April signed "Articles for the Protestant Party in Ireland" in Carrick, the former Butler stronghold.

Clonmel held out, the only town in the area still in Royalist hands, and there Cromwell suffered the worst defeat of his entire campaign. Under the command of Hugh O'Neill, a nephew of Owen Roe born in the Spanish-ruled Netherlands, Clonmel resisted even as the guns battered down the town walls. The attackers were lured into a killing zone—a cul-de-sac built behind a breach in the wall—and Cromwell lost over two thousand men. O'Neill escaped with his men to Waterford, the last major town to hold out against the New Model Army.

---

* Though no connection can be established, the colonel may well have been an ancestor of Lonergan's lieutenant killed at Gettysburg since John Sinnott also came from Wexford.

CHAPTER TWO – CONQUERED

The suffering of this prolonged and devastating war supposedly ended with a treaty signed in 1652. However, the hardships of the fighting only foreshadowed the misery the Irish felt as a result of the peace that Cromwell imposed upon them. "To Hell or to Connaught" was the motto under which the dispossessed were driven from much of Ireland into the west of the island, exiled abroad, or even sold into slavery in British possessions like Jamaica. After May 1, 1654, no Irish were to reside east of the River Shannon, being confined by law to the western province where it was grimly said that there was not enough wood to hang a man, not enough water to drown him, nor enough earth to bury him.

Many Irish were in fact forced to leave their homes for the West of Ireland. As a practical matter, however, the new landlords needed labor to make their holdings profitable and they could not import enough English or Scots to replace all the Irish. Most of the Irish, including the Lonergans, were therefore allowed to remain where their families had lived for centuries. These final confiscations by Cromwell resulted in a small Protestant minority owning three-quarters of the land in Ireland while the Irish were reduced to tenants.

THE BRITISH MONARCHY WAS RESTORED when Charles II was crowned in 1660, but matters did not improve for the Irish until the Catholic King James II took the throne in 1685. James set about a reform of government in Ireland to reverse the anti-Catholic measures—in 1687, the Earl of Tyrconnell, a Catholic, became Lord Lieutenant of Ireland—and powerful interests were threatened by his actions. When William of Orange was invited to England to lead the Protestant cause, the "Glorious Revolution" overthrew the "Jacobite" reign there.* James fled back to France, where he had lived for many years. This power struggle of continental dimensions was to be finally decided in Ireland when James returned, landing in Ireland at Kinsale in March of 1689. With him came Patrick Sarsfield, 1st Earl of Lucan, who had served in the king's army in England. Sarsfield had refused an offer by the new king, William, to act as his agent in Ireland. James was defeated by "King Billy" at the Battle of the Boyne on July 1, 1690, according to the old style Julian calendar. (After adoption of the Gregorian calendar in 1752, this became July

---

* From "Jacobus", the Latin form of James, this was often used to identify his supporters. The Dutch Prince of Orange, on the other hand, had his color adopted as a symbol by the Protestant Irish, still known as Orangemen.

12, the date still celebrated by Orangemen.) James once again sailed away for France, never to return. At Aughrim the following year, another victory for William decided the conflict.

Sarsfield, now commander of those forces still fighting on in Ireland, was besieged in Limerick, nearly the last stronghold of the Jacobites. Despite a daring raid on the Williamite siege train at Ballyneety that made him the popular hero of the war, Sarsfield was forced to sign the Treaty of Limerick on October 3, 1691. The military articles of this treaty allowed his forces to choose between transferring their allegiance to William or leaving Ireland for service in France with the Irish Brigade. Most of Sarsfield's troops chose to follow him to France in what was called the "Flight of the Wild Geese." King Louis XIV of France made Sarsfield a commander in Flanders where he fought with distinction until mortally wounded at the Battle of Landen on August 19, 1693. His last words are said to have been "Would it were for Ireland…." This devotion of the exile to the cause of Irish freedom served as an inspiration for later generations and his name was often invoked by nationalists, including John Lonergan, two hundred years after Sarsfield's death.

The civil articles of the Treaty of Limerick offered protection of property for the Jacobites who remained in Ireland, yet these provisions were broken almost before the ink was dry. Starting in 1695, harsh Penal Laws were imposed to crush the Catholic population into permanent submission to the "English garrison" that now controlled the country. Ireland still had its own Parliament, but it was a tool of the ruling English and totally compliant with the dictates of the English Parliament, which proposed all Irish laws.

The next one hundred years of institutionalized repression saw the Irish people reduced to the poorest peasantry in Europe, most of them tenant farmers with no rights to the land they worked. Catholics were excluded by the new laws from any opportunity to improve their lot through education or the professions. Still, no law erased the Irish language or the history that it passed on to new generations through stories and song. The legends of heroes like Finn McCool reminded the Irish of a time when they lived with prosperity and dignity, before the injustice done them by the English. Tales of past glories mingled with the harsh realities of John Lonergan's early years, convincing him that every Irishman had a duty to free his country from foreign rule.

CHAPTER TWO – CONQUERED

CLONMEL CITY GATE AMD WALL

Ormonde Castle, Carrick-on-Suir

CHAPTER THREE

OPPRESSED

WEALTHY PROTESTANT IRISH landowners, despite all the privileges that the system gave them, eventually raised a challenge to English rule of the island. Some Celtic chieftains who remained, even after the earls and the "Wild Geese" had fled the country, converted to the Church of Ireland to preserve their property and thus became part of the ruling class. The downtrodden Catholics, dispossessed of their land and crushed by the Penal Laws, might rage against their subjugation, but were without power or leadership.

Deprived of education and banned from professions, most Irish were reduced to bare survival as tenant farmers, but the growing towns and cities did offer opportunities for tradesmen and artisans. In John Lonergan's family, the skills of coopering were passed on from father to son. His forebears likely also supported their own families well enough by the same craft, despite bleak economic and political conditions. However, even steady work at the bench could not compensate for a deep resentment over being oppressed for their heritage and religion. Each generation of Lonergans probably nurtured in their children a rebellious attitude toward British rule.

Toward the end of the eighteenth century, the British Isles faced the threat of an invasion by France. As protection against the French, the Irish Volunteers were organized in 1778, replacing British troops withdrawn from Ireland to help put down the American Revolution. Expanded to some 80,000 men, these Volunteers developed into a political force outside the Irish Parliament system. A convention of the Volunteers held at Dungannon early in 1782 gained the right for the Irish Parliament to make its own laws for Ireland, though English patronage continued to control the Irish legislature. The leader of the Protestant "Patriot" party in the Irish House of Commons, Henry Grattan, even persuaded that legislative body to pass a

Declaration of Independence that was accepted by the English government.

Napper Tandy, inspired by the French and American revolutions to strive for true independence, formed the United Irishmen in 1791. Other upper class Protestants leading the United Irishmen organization included Wolfe Tone, Lord Fitzgerald, and Thomas Emmet. This "united" movement sought an alliance of all Irishmen, regardless of religion. (The goal of "union" among the Irish had nothing to do with any parliamentary union with England.) War broke out between France and England in 1793 and some concessions were finally made to the Catholics in the hope of reducing their discontent at English rule of Ireland.

With an eye to the aid France had given the successful American Revolution, Ireland's republican organizers likewise looked to that country for help. After an unsuccessful attempt to land French troops at Bantry Bay in the winter of 1796, a repeated effort to support the United Irishmen was planned for 1798. In February of that year, Lord Fitzgerald reckoned that he had over 250,000 men ready for an uprising, but the next month he was betrayed to the government by a member of his inner circle. The leaders in the Directory, the executive body of the United Irishmen that included Thomas Emmet, were arrested. Fitzgerald remained free for a time, but during his capture suffered wounds from which he died six weeks later.

Although the movement had been stripped of any national leadership by the arrests, isolated groups of United Irishmen rose up in the spring and summer. The king's troops moved against the rebels, who distinguished themselves from the loyal forces by wearing their hair cropped short. In a derisive reference to the insurgents' hairstyle, the cry "Croppies, lie down" was heard from the yeomanry across Ireland. The High Sheriff of Tipperary, a Fitzgerald who supported the crown, effectively broke the movement in that county with the severity of his floggings, hangings, and other repressive brutalities.

The major fighting took place in County Wexford where priests were among the leaders of the uprising. Lack of discipline and organization often turned these forces into no more than poorly-armed mobs. The advantage of some initial victories through sheer numbers of pikemen was too often lost when the rebels looted towns for drink. Uncoordinated actions in various parts of the island were each put down in turn. A few men rode over from the Suir Valley to join the rebels in Wexford, but Leinster waited in vain for Munster to rise up. On June 21, the main rebel camp at Vinegar Hill

CHAPTER THREE – OPPRESSED

was attacked by forces of the Crown. After a bombardment of the position by cannon, the uprising was crushed there with great loss of life among the disorganized peasantry.

United Irishmen had held councils of war in Clonmel and Carrick to plan for a rising in south Tipperary. Three to five thousand men were to attack Clonmel on July 26 when a signal fire was lit on the peak of Carrigmoclear, on the eastern slope of Slievenamon. The forests where Finn had hunted deer had long since been cleared from the top of the hill and the fire would be visible throughout the region, marking the place where the men of the countryside were to gather. Betrayed by a man in their ranks who set the signal fire ablaze before the leaders had intended, the rebels around Slievenamon were lured into a trap. At daybreak, hundreds of men found themselves atop the hill, leaderless and surrounded by forces that included regulars, yeomen, and Hessian mercenaries, along with English-officered Irish militia from other areas. The lament in Irish for this treachery "on the sunny slope of SlievenamBan" (the Gaelic spelling of the name) bitterly recalls the taunts from the king's well-armed men that they had little to fear from the rebels "with their pikes and spades" as weapons.

The slaughter that ensued at Carrigmoclear was followed by a rampage through the area, during which any signs of resistance to British rule were stamped out with deliberate ferocity. Men even suspected of rebel sympathies suffered flogging and "half-hanging" where the victim was repeatedly strangled into unconsciousness. A new form of torture called "pitch-capping" was widespread; a mixture of pitch and gunpowder or a paper bag of pitch was set afire on a man's head. Those directly implicated in the uprising were subject to prison, exile, or execution. Probably no Irish family in the area escaped without some loss of life, liberty, or property since those holding any land might have it confiscated. A pikeman captured at Carrigmoclear, one Daniel Norton, was executed by firing squad in nearby Mullinahone and his head placed on a spike in the castle wall there.

This sad affair on Slievenamon was just an aftershock of the uprising and had only a local impact. Lord Cornwallis, although defeated in the American Revolution, had been made viceroy and commander in chief in Ireland a few weeks after the rebellion began. He remarked on this "appearance of insurrection in Tipperary" in July as "significant, if of anything, of a return to normal unrest" in the quarrelsome county. During his childhood in Ireland, John Lonergan would probably have heard stories praising his immediate ancestors for contributing to this unrest.

Toward the end of August, too late to have any useful effect, the French sent a fleet to the west coast of Ireland. The British captured Wolfe Tone on a French ship off Donegal and jailed him in Dublin. After admitting his guilt and being sentenced to hang, he took his own life in the prison cell to become yet another martyr of the Irish struggle. In a popular ballad of the time, his sacrifice was symbolized by a new dawn for the country:

> See, Erin's song, yon rising beam
> The eastern hills adorning
> Now freedom's sun begins to gleam
> And break a glorious morning.
>
> Plant, plant the tree, fair freedom's tree
> Midst danger, wounds and slaughter,
> Erin's green fields its soil shall be,
> Her tyrants' blood its water.

This image of a sunburst through the clouds—harking back as it also did to the sunburst on Finn McCool's banner—was to become the identifying symbol of the republican movement. Along with the traditional harp and shamrock of Ireland, it would later be adopted by the Fenian Brotherhood in America for their flag.

The imprisoned leaders of the United Irishmen, Thomas Emmet among them, decided to cooperate with the government after the rebellion failed. They traded information on the organization for a promise that they could emigrate outside the British Empire. The prisoners were first moved to Fort George in Scotland and then released in 1802 to go to France. Thomas Emmet took ship from there to America and prospered in New York, becoming its State Attorney.

EVEN BEFORE THE 1798 UPRISING, British Prime Minister William Pitt had started working on a union of Great Britain and Ireland. The concept of a legislative union had been discussed in the past and Pitt could now use the rebellion to push through his solution to the Irish problem. The three hundred seats of the Irish Parliament were to be reduced to one hundred

CHAPTER THREE – OPPRESSED

seats in the Parliament in London. Sentiments about this action were divided among the incumbents in Ireland. Bribery, in the form of cash and peerages bestowed on some reluctant members, bought the necessary votes for the Irish Parliament to approve its own dissolution.

This dilution of Irish representation within a larger Parliament was greeted enthusiastically by many of the propertied class, who felt it solidified their hold on Ireland. Other Irishmen with more nationalistic feelings were strongly opposed to the loss of their parliament, rightly feeling that laws made in England would not promote the interests of Ireland. Most of the common people—the "men of no property" who made up the vast majority of the inhabitants caught up in grinding poverty—were less concerned with abstract issues of government than with survival.

The Act of Union came into force on January 1, 1801, and a red diagonal cross for Ireland was symbolically added to the British flag to create the current "Union Jack." The British flag featured the red cross of St. George of England superimposed on the diagonal blue cross of St. Andrew of Scotland. This pre-1801 flag was also called a "Union Jack" in recognition of the earlier merger of these two countries under a single king. The red diagonal cross is attributed to St. Patrick, but is not commonly recognized as a symbol for Ireland like the harp and the shamrock.

The English monarch now ruled over the United Kingdom of Great Britain (composed of England, Scotland, and Wales) and Ireland. The Prime Minister led the government at Whitehall as head of the legislative branch, the Parliament that made the laws. Ireland's interests within this Union were supposedly represented by its one hundred Members of Parliament (MPs). Many of the thirty-five seats allocated to the boroughs were the virtual possessions of wealthy landowners, the "rotten" boroughs. The former Irish Parliament building in Dublin's College Green no longer had a function. First used for art exhibitions, it was then sold to the Bank of Ireland in August of 1803.

The lord lieutenant in Dublin Castle continued to govern Ireland for the monarch, just as before the legislative union. Discussions took place as to whether the lord lieutenant was still a suitable position for Ireland, now that it was officially a province of the United Kingdom. A vice-regal representative should be no more appropriate in Dublin than in Edinburgh or Cardiff since Ireland's relationship was now the same as that of Scotland and Wales. Debate on this question persisted for decades, but the peculiar circumstances in Ireland made it expedient to retain the lord lieutenant's office as the effective head of government in the new province.

The lord lieutenant continued his direct political control of the country with some reduced powers. He would function within the limits of the policies agreed upon in the British cabinet while exercising considerable personal discretion to act as he saw fit. It could often take a week for instructions from London to reach Dublin, so he had to be empowered to make decisions on the spot as necessary. The chief secretary of the British cabinet handled Ireland's parliamentary business in London, with British interests taking priority over any concern for the Irish people.

Union transformed the Catholic majority in Ireland into a minority within the combined realm. The status of the Catholics within the kingdom had become a major issue in the first half of the eighteenth century. British policy toward the Catholics had reached a turning point favoring conciliation in 1795, but reaction to the rebellion of 1798 had hardened attitudes against concessions. Pitt resigned as Prime Minister on February 3, 1801, soon after the Union was formed. In part, this was to protest the rejection of his attempts at Catholic relief from the Penal Laws. The lord lieutenant of Ireland at the time, Lord Cornwallis, was replaced shortly afterwards.

THE LAST GASP OF THE UNITED IRISHMEN came in 1803 and marked the end of any effective Protestant support for Catholic Emancipation in Ireland. Robert Emmet, brother of Thomas, attempted his own rebellion after joining a reconstituted executive for the United Irishmen. Robert had been expelled from Trinity College for "holding radical political views" and then followed in his elder brother's footsteps. Robert had been in touch with the prisoners at Kilmainham jail in Dublin and while they were held in Scotland. In 1801, he went to France to resume contact with his brother and other rebels there. Robert returned to Ireland the following year and found another revolutionary conspiracy well under way.

War between England and France resumed in 1803 after the peace treaty of the previous year collapsed. This conflict seemed to create an opportunity for renewed efforts at a rebellion with French assistance. Thomas Emmet worked in France to procure arms, money, and officers from Bonaparte to support an insurrection in Ireland, though ultimately without success. Robert

CHAPTER THREE – OPPRESSED

claimed later that he held no hope of foreign assistance, depending instead on new technology such as rockets, mines made of wooden boxes full of powder, and pikes with folding handles. This last innovation seemed a good idea because it was difficult to escape notice when shouldering the usual eight-foot pike in the streets of an Irish town.

Robert Emmet had developed a good plan in concept, but it began to unravel when his store of explosives at the secret Patrick Street depot in Dublin exploded on July 16. The date for the rising had already been set for July 23 with the seizure of Dublin Castle to be the signal for the countryside. A proclamation of "a free and independent republic in Ireland" was printed and distributed on that date, but the operation itself was a total failure. On July 23, Emmet led into the streets just one hundred men armed with pikes and blunderbusses (wide-muzzled shotguns effective only at close range). Part of the mob encountered and piked to death the Lord Chief Justice, "a remarkably humane man."

Appalled by this unnecessary murder and the frustration of his plan, Emmet immediately called off the rebellion and sent word into the countryside for his supporters not to come into the city. Emmet was captured, tried, and sentenced to death in short order. The usual fate of traitors was imposed—he was to be hanged and beheaded, as well as drawn and quartered. Facing his death with dignity, Emmet gave a speech from the dock that still echoes among the Irish people.

Not denying his crime in the eyes of the English, he had but one request of the world, the "charity of its silence." He asked that "no man write my epitaph" and his "tomb remain uninscribed" until free Irishmen could openly respect his memory. His challenge rang out, "when my country takes her place among the nations of the earth, then and not till then, let my epitaph be written."

A scaffold was erected in Dublin's Thomas Street and on September 20, 1803, he was hanged for half an hour, then taken down and "in accordance with the judicial custom of the day, his head was cut off with a butcher's knife." Although Emmet has no tomb and his final resting place is unknown, he gained a prominent and permanent position among modern Irish heroes. The government clearly tried to prevent Emmet's grave from becoming a symbol for future resistance to English rule. As an abstract concept, Emmet's tomb became a rallying point for revolutionaries who formed the Emmet Monument Association a half century later. John Lonergan would also honor the memory of this martyr to Irish nationhood by naming his Vermont militia company the Emmet Guards, a clear statement of their dedication to the cause.

IF THE UNION OF 1801 were to succeed politically in merging Ireland with the United Kingdom, the plight of the Irish common people had to improve. Instead, the situation in Ireland grew steadily worse as an expanding population made competition for land ever stronger. Fields were divided and subdivided, with tenants holding leases through agents down to seven levels of remove from the landlord. Their tenuous hold on a farm, subject to eviction on the whim of the landlord or his agent, discouraged any improvements. The tenants were squeezed for rent on land that was barely enough to provide subsistence. Dependent to a fatal degree on the potato and short of cash, a family would often raise a pig in the cottage along with their children. Too valuable a product for the family to eat, the animal would be sold for money to pay the rent.

Feeding a population approaching eight million became increasingly more difficult as the land planted in crops was reduced. With growing frequency, landlords evicted the Irish peasant tenants in order to increase the land available for grazing more profitable livestock. The famine that had struck the poor repeatedly in the eighteenth century returned with even stronger impact in 1800, 1817, and 1822 as greater numbers of people tried to survive on shrinking amounts of farmland. John Lonergan's parents grew up under deteriorating economic conditions that ultimately led to the disaster of 1845–48.

The primary concern of the masses in the early 1800's was therefore not republican separatism or even religion, but the class distinctions in ownership of the land itself. Their need to control the basis for subsistence eventually fused with a sense of nationalism and a consciousness of an Irish identity. The growing number of emigrants abroad, particularly in America, voiced a bitter resentment of the situation in Ireland that could safely be expressed only outside British rule.

THE CAUSE OF CATHOLIC EMANCIPATION thrust Daniel O'Connell—born to a displaced Kerry family in Ennis, County Clare, in 1775—to the center of

CHAPTER THREE – OPPRESSED

the political stage in Ireland in the 1820s.* Catholics who could afford an education, denied to them by law in Ireland, often went abroad to Irish colleges in France and Spain. O'Connell was educated in France and observed first-hand the excesses of revolution, leaving that country on the day that Louis XVI was executed. He was called to the Irish bar as a lawyer on the very day in 1798 that Lord Fitzgerald was arrested for treason. In the aftermath of the uprising by the United Irishmen, O'Connell formed a lasting antipathy to armed revolution. Rather than choosing the path of rebellion, the clever new lawyer intended to use his barrister skills to achieve his goals for Ireland by legal means (such as the national bank he later established), and he frequently stressed his loyalty to the Crown. He would operate within the letter of the law, boasting that he could "drive a coach and six [horses] through any act of Parliament."

At a time when the ruling elite controlled all politics—a landlord commonly required those of his tenants who qualified for the limited suffrage to vote according to his instructions—O'Connell turned to organizing the masses. Since O'Connell was dedicated to restoring full rights to the Catholics by legal means, he had the support of both the church hierarchy and the people. His Catholic Association drew on the "penny a month" contribution from the common people that at times brought in a thousand pounds or more a week; the parish priests were the natural leaders of such a grassroots movement and commonly allowed the "Catholic rent" to be collected at the chapel gate the first Sunday of the month. O'Connell translated this support into political power when the Emancipation program's candidate won the 1826 election in Waterford, a staggering blow to the landlords. O'Connell, known as the "Great Liberator," was himself elected to Parliament from County Clare in 1828, the first Catholic to stand for election to Parliament in nearly 150 years. He then faced the hurdle of taking an oath in the House of Commons that required him to repudiate his Catholic beliefs and swear that the practices of the "Church of Rome are infamous and idolatrous." The Catholic Relief Act of 1829 abolished this requirement, but the Act had not gone into effect when O'Connell presented himself to the House. O'Connell refused to swear the oath and was not allowed to take his seat, so he returned to Clare to be re-elected unopposed. He then claimed his place in Parliament when the Act was in effect.

---

* The O'Connells had held the office of High Sheriff in County Kerry until the clan was transported to Connaught by Cromwell. The family was able to recoup its fortunes in County Clare.

Catholic emancipation was legally achieved on April 13, 1829—allowing access to education and the professions, and permitting the holding of public office—yet discrimination against Catholics continued in many ways. A new organization, similar to that for Catholic emancipation, was founded by O'Connell in 1830 with the goal of repealing the Union with Great Britain and restoring an Irish Parliament. When his anti-Union Repeal Association was immediately "proclaimed" and made illegal by the government,* O'Connell simply renamed it, repeatedly. When the weekly Repeal Breakfast was suppressed, O'Connell promised it would be followed by Repeal Lunches, Repeal Dinners, and Repeal Suppers, then by "A Body of Persons in the Habit of Meeting Weekly for Breakfast at a Place Called Holmes' Hotel."

While constantly reaffirming his loyalty to the Crown and his commitment to staying within the law, O'Connell could deftly also suggest that only his efforts were holding back the violence of revolution. He would point out that the United States of America—the "western boundary of Ireland"—had only three million inhabitants when it broke free of England and that there were eight million in Ireland. Unlike America, however, Ireland had no broad ocean between it and England, only the narrow Irish Sea. This proximity made intervention by the forces of the crown far easier and more effective.

A group of middle-class young men, equally divided as to Catholic and Protestant, formed a more radical faction within the Repeal Association. The core of these activists—consisting of Thomas Davis, John Blake Dillon, and Charles Gavan Duffy—founded a newspaper promoting their agenda that began circulation late in 1842. *The Nation* soon had the highest number of readers of any newspaper in Ireland. Most editorials were written by Davis, who was highly influential in creating a spirit of nationalism in Ireland that paralleled the search for a national identity taking place in many countries in Europe. Because his father was an English army surgeon who had married an Irish woman, Davis did not have the same deep roots in Irish culture as someone like O'Connell. Davis consequently made a more conscious and deliberate effort at promoting Irish nationalism and his poetry provided slogans like "a nation once

---

* Proclamations were used by the government to extend its powers and included the suspension of rights and prohibition of activities. Usually they specified a certain area, such as a county or region, where an activity was "proclaimed." The scope could range from declaring marital law to less drastic measures, for example, arrest for possession of arms, search without warrant, curfew hours, and the like.

CHAPTER THREE – OPPRESSED

again" and "trust ourselves alone." This emphasis on "we ourselves" (*sinn féin* in Irish) signaled a policy of rejecting the hope of foreign intervention to free Ireland, relying instead on the country's own resources.

O'Connell declared 1843 to be "Repeal Year" and a new membership card was issued for the Repeal Association. The green card depicted four key battles of Irish history in its corners. A flag with the symbolic sunburst occupied the center of the card, along with a shamrock whose three leaves were inscribed with Catholic, Dissenter, and Protestant. Drawing on the traditions of the Wild Geese, the Patriots of 1782, and the United Irishmen, he called for all Irish to join together to dissolve the parliamentary union. O'Connell did not reject the concept of the two crowns worn by the one monarch, however, and he continuously professed his fealty to the throne.

As part of his organization of the masses, O'Connell held a series of some forty "monster meetings" at locations selected for their historical significance. On August 15, around a million people—one out of eight on the island—gathered at Tara, seat of the Irish High Kings, to hear him urge Repeal. He next chose to speak to a huge crowd at Mullaghmast, "scene of the famous massacre of Irish chieftains in the time of Elizabeth," while the last meeting in the series was to be held at Clontarf, where Brian Boru had defeated the Danes.

The series of "monster meetings" had been well organized with "Repeal wardens" keeping order and an increasingly military atmosphere among the marching groups. The notice for the October 5 meeting at Clontarf was headed "Repeal Cavalry" and asked for volunteers to form troops of twenty-five horsemen each, led by an officer. The British government found this to have crossed the line of permissible actions and prohibited the meeting the day before it was to be held. O'Connell, with the support of his young allies on *The Nation* newspaper, chose not to invite bloodshed and called off the assembly. It was a tribute to the organization of the Repeal Association that word could be passed to the half a million people expected at the meeting and that they would obey, even increasing their contributions to "Repeal Rent." This level of efficiency and discipline would itself give the government cause for concern.

Despite the open and public nature of the Repeal Association and its activities, O'Connell and others were tried and jailed in 1844 on charges of "conspiracy." This action by the government alienated a wealthy Protestant MP, William Smith O'Brien. Only forty years of age, O'Brien had been an MP for many years, originally representing O'Connell's home district, the "rotten borough" of Ennis in County Clare. He had been educated in

England, as were most men in the Protestant upper class and some of the wealthier Catholics in Ireland. His mother's maiden name was Smith and some of the nationalist leaders thought that there was "too much Smith and not enough O'Brien" in him. However, he traced his descent from Brian Boru on his father's side and this lineage commanded respect. As a representative of the propertied and Protestant class, his support of the Repeal effort was invaluable, though he initially preferred some type of Federalism (along the lines of what was later called "Home Rule"). O'Brien's letter supporting Federalism was published in *The Nation*, even though the militant group associated with that newspaper was adamantly opposed to anything less than Repeal. Articles in the newspaper had even scolded O'Connell himself for any suggestion of compromise.

IN THE REPEAL ASSOCIATION, tensions increased as the more radical faction grew impatient with O'Connell's policy of renouncing the option of force to accomplish their goals. Like other nationalist revolutionary movements of the era, the group unwilling to rely on cooperation with the government was identified with youth and it became known as the "Young Irelanders." After Thomas Francis Meagher, a rising star in the nationalist movement at the age of twenty, gave his first political speech at a Repeal meeting in 1843, O'Connell had praised him with "Well done, Young Ireland." Perhaps O'Connell later used it as a scornful label for the rashness of youthful views, but the group adopted it with pride, particularly after Davis' death from disease in September 1845. The loss of the influential nationalist writer was a severe blow to the Young Irelanders and he was mourned by the country.

However, the death of one man was nothing compared to the discovery about that same time of "nearly universal rot in the potato." A blight—possibly brought over from the Americas as the potato itself had been—spread rapidly through Europe in 1844 and reached Ireland soon thereafter. Because the potato comprised the basic sustenance for the bulk of the rural population in Ireland, who were barely surviving even in the best of years, any loss of this crucial crop constituted a disaster with immediate consequences.

O'Connell, who had been released from prison after four months, had resumed his monster meetings in 1845 with successful tours of County Tipperary and the West of Ireland, always hotbeds of nationalism. The last of this series of meetings was in County Limerick in late October. On

CHAPTER THREE – OPPRESSED

October 25, *The Nation* predicted that at least half of the crop "on which millions of our countrymen are half-starved every year" had been destroyed. Political action now had to focus on pressuring the government to deal with widespread famine. Repeal was forced to take a back seat to survival.

While O'Connell believed he could gain the support of the new Whig government through his cooperation, the Young Irelanders were being taken in the direction of revolution by John Mitchel, who replaced Davis as the editor of *The Nation*. In his article describing how the new railways could be disrupted to prevent troop movements, Mitchel suggested that the rails would provide good material for pike heads. This drew a protest from O'Connell, still adamantly opposed to any violence.

O'Brien, humorously referring to himself as "middle-aged Ireland," initially tried to mediate between the Young Irelanders and O'Connell (as "Old Ireland"), but then began to gravitate toward the more revolutionary group. In April 1846, O'Brien refused to serve on the railway committee in Parliament to which he had been appointed and was given a month's imprisonment in Westminster, the first MP to be jailed by the House of Commons in 200 years.

By July 1846 the rift in the Repeal Association over the policy of cooperation with the government and an absolute prohibition of the use of force had become too wide to bridge. Failure of the potato crop in 1846 was universal and total, eclipsing the distress of the previous year, and action was imperative to alleviate the situation. An uncompromising rejection of force was laid out in "peace resolutions" proposed by O'Connell as a statement of Repeal Association policy. In reality, this step was meant to be a loyalty test for the Young Irelanders. O'Connell himself was not present at the crucial debate of the resolutions on July 27 and 28 because he was in England trying to strike a deal with the government for relief. His elder son, John, handled the deliberations and only succeeded in further alienating the Young Irelanders.

Meagher, famous already as an orator, pressed the abstract question of whether violence was ever justified in his "Sword Speech." He declared "I look upon the sword as a sacred weapon" and insisted that he would not "abhor the sword and stigmatize the sword" since its use was sometimes necessary. This was the final straw for John O'Connell. He announced that he could not tolerate Meagher in the Repeal Association with those views. In reaction to this ultimatum, O'Brien "abruptly got up and left, followed by Meagher, Mitchell, Duffy and other Young Irelanders." The split in the Repeal Association was complete and irreversible.

THESE DIFFERENCES IN ABSTRACT POLITICS were meaningless to the common people of Ireland who were dying in the thousands from starvation and disease. Some living on the coast were barely subsisting on a diet of seaweed, even as they watched ships sailing from every port to England with their holds full of the meat, grain, and other produce of their country. O'Connell agitated for relief by the government, drawing on the political credit he hoped had accrued from his cooperation with the Whigs. The economic thinking of the day ran against governmental intervention, however, especially when it was at the expense of the propertied class. Even in England there was no official relief effort for the poor; they were felt to be responsible for their own condition. Under the circumstances, prospects of official famine relief for the Irish were even less likely.

Many Irish refused to call the disaster a famine since food was available, yet denied to those who produced it. Instead, it was more accurately called the Great Hunger, *An Gorta Mór*. By whatever name, it was fatal to hundreds of thousands of Irish.

O'Connell was seventy-one years old and failing fast under the stress of the responsibility he felt to mitigate the effect of the famine. He warned the House of Commons that a quarter of the Irish would die unless they received aid. Within a few years, between death and emigration, Ireland's combined losses did in fact reach that level. Added to O'Connell's burden was the division in the Repeal Association that led the Young Irelanders to form their own organization.

The doctors warned O'Connell that his health required a warmer climate, a move most Irish would have been eager to make, given the prevailing conditions in the country. He could not, however, in good conscience take a vacation for his health, so he instead set off on a pilgrimage. He died en route to Rome on May 15, 1847. In accordance with his dying wishes, his heart was taken to that city in a silver urn while his body was returned to Ireland. O'Connell's supporters blamed the Young Irelanders for his death, at least in part, and refused to welcome them to his funeral. The Repeal movement became a bitter opponent of their new Irish Confederation.

WHEN THE YOUNG IRELANDERS CREATED their own organization after being expelled by the Repeal Association, the more militant group deliberately chose a name harking back to the last great armed Irish resistance to England, the seventeenth-century Confederation of Kilkenny. Under the leadership of O'Brien, the Confederation for Legislative Independence was organized by the Young Irelanders on January 13, 1847.

At the first meeting, Meagher spoke of the shipment of food out of Ireland, calling on O'Brien to warn the House of Commons of its destructive effect on the Union. He listed the "total export of provisions from the ports of Waterford, Cork, Limerick and Belfast, from 1 August, 1846 to 1 January, 1847: pork, barrels, 37,123; bacon, flitches, 222,608; ham, hogsheads, 1,971; beef, tierces, 2,555; wheat, barrels 48,526; oats, barrels, 543,232" and continuing on with similar figures for barley, oatmeal, flour, live pigs, cows, and sheep. Clearly, huge amounts of food were leaving the country while the people starved. At the cooper shop in Carrick, John Lonergan may well have helped his father make some of the thousands of barrels and hogsheads shipped from Waterford.

While the Young Irelanders had broken with Repeal mainly on the issue of cooperation with the British government rather than any theoretical use of force, they had yet to develop their own positive program of action for the Confederation. This new radical organization decided to establish Confederate Clubs around the country, each with a minimum of twenty members. By year's end only twenty-three clubs had been formed, four of them in Dublin. Some of the others had been organized in Great Britain, where the Irish population continued to swell with refugees from the famine.

A new political approach was clearly necessary to deal with the disastrous situation, so the Confederation passed a list of resolutions in an attempt to unite all classes, including the landlords. These resolutions included absolute independence from all English parties (as opposed to Repeal willingness to cooperate with the Whigs) and a declaration that the actions of the present government were insufficient for the growing calamity.

Proposals were being made outside the Confederation to bring the British Parliament's operations to a halt through legislative obstructionism and to upset the existing relationship with landlords by withholding rents. Such half measures drew the scorn of Mitchel, who soon withdrew from the Confederation and started his own weekly newspaper with the provocative name *United Irishman*. With no organization behind him, he wrote a series of militant articles that he hoped would help spark a spontaneous rebellion. Due largely to this appeal for violent action, the newspaper soon became the most popular in the country.

The leaders of the Confederation knew that the condition of the peasantry, which would form the rank and file of any such rebellion, was so desperate as to make a successful uprising impossible. Michael Doheny of Cashel, now a lawyer, pointed out that the church opposed rebellion and that the priests would therefore prevent the peasants from acting. He continued to warn against any uprising, "if the peasants do take to arms they'll be faced by England's disciplined soldiery and end as corpses on their native fields, or, if they did manage to have a local success, on the gibbet." He suggested with irony that they go to Skibbereen, hard hit by the famine, and reanimate the corpses there. O'Brien concurred that the Irish in their "present broken and divided condition" could not free themselves by force of arms. Even Meagher, despite his oration in praise of the sword, counseled caution.

The Young Irelanders were educated men and personally brave, but they lacked both a clear program and the ruthlessness that the situation demanded. Mitchel's rashness, the Confederation's caution, and Repeal's cooperation with the government were equally ineffective in easing the terrible condition of the masses as the fateful year of 1848 approached. Some key Confederation leaders spent the winter abroad for their health, as their comfortable positions in society allowed, while the people at home sank even deeper into misery.

As the daylight faded into short winter days, the hopes of many Irish for survival until the next harvest also dimmed. The parish priests might lead their flocks to spiritual salvation, yet could do little to keep them alive. A government indifferent to the sufferings of its citizens put protection of property before preservation of life. In this dark period of despair, men desperate to feed their families were prepared to take any action necessary, including revolution.

Thomas Lonergan likely was among the many that joined the Confederate clubs being formed in preparation for an armed uprising that would overthrow the callous British rule. Organizers were actively recruiting members for the clubs, sometimes with the approval of the local clergy. By spring, numerous new clubs had been formed in many towns and cities, particularly in the south. Meagher established a Confederation presence in Waterford, Doheny built up support in the Cashel area, and a remarkable leader, John O'Mahony, stepped forward to organize the Carrick region.

John Lonergan turned eleven years of age in April of 1848, perhaps still attending the Christian Brothers school in Carrick where he received food

CHAPTER THREE – OPPRESSED

along with his education. However, his mother had conceived another son during the winter and John, as the eldest child, may have been required to help support the growing family by assisting in the cooper's shop alongside his father. The dreadful scenes of starvation, disease, and dispossession that John saw during his childhood years must have had a lasting impact. Even after he was safely settled in America, he dedicated much of his life to the cause of Irish liberation.

St. Molleran's Church, Carrick Beg

Famine Wall and Plaque

CHAPTER FOUR

STARVED

MANY OF THE EIGHT MILLION people in Ireland suffered through the winter of 1847–48 just trying to stay alive. Issues of nationalism and legislative independence might determine the long-range fate of the nation, but for now the masses were concerned only about scraping together the next meal, fighting off disease, surviving one more day. Still the various Irish political groups could come to no understanding or plan of action that would achieve any short-term relief, much less a lasting improvement in the situation. As starvation and disease continued to rack the country, death and emigration reduced the number of poor until the Malthusian principles of population control began to take effect.

What limited assistance the government provided was ineffectual and usually required physical labor in return, lest the recipients become too dependent on handouts. At the Carrick Beg end of the old bridge over the Suir, a plaque in the high stone wall erected below St. Molleran's church reads: "This wall was built in 1846, a year memorable by the failure of the potato and the subsequent scarcity of food." Two years after that project provided employment for needy residents of the Carrick area, the "scarcity of food" reached a point that previously could not have been imagined. In the regions hit the worst by this man-made calamity, public works put starving Irish to building "famine walls" to no purpose and roads leading nowhere. Other countries, particularly Germany, had also been affected by the potato blight and the crisis added to a growing revolutionary spirit in much of Europe.

The Repeal Association continued to pursue constitutional action from its base in Dublin's Conciliation Hall and to reject any acts of force or bloodshed, but it went into a decline following O'Connell's death. The Catholic Church had benefited from the achievements of the "Great Liberator" and parish priests often urged support of his movement, even allowing collections at the churchyard gate. Dependence on the "Repeal rent" of pennies from the masses now worked against this political movement, since the poor could no longer afford even that modest amount. In this crucial year, despite the Repeal representation in the English House of Commons, cooperation with the Whig government had achieved virtually nothing to relieve the desperate conditions in Ireland. Some Repeal leaders accepted positions in the government and were stigmatized for this by Confederation spokesmen, who called them "place-beggars" who put their personal gain ahead of principle.

At the other end of the political spectrum, John Mitchel became ever more provocative in his *United Irishman*. The paper's motto quoted Wolfe Tone, claiming a dependence on "the aid of that numerous and respectable class of the community—*The men of no property*" (emphasis in original). Mitchel published deliberately inflammatory articles instructing people in such military matters as tactics for battle armed only with a pike or the care of swords and daggers. Even though these medieval weapons were hardly a serious threat to the Queen's army or the police, Mitchel's writings naturally drew the attention of the government. The first issue of the paper included contributions from Father John Kenyon, "the celebrated Parish Priest of Templederry" in County Tipperary, and Mitchel's friend, John Martin.

The Confederation meanwhile straddled the issue, still working within the law but ready to consider illegal steps should the circumstances dictate. The network of Confederate Clubs being organized throughout Ireland predictably had clusters in areas like Dublin and the south, but clubs were sparse or absent in much of the country, especially in less receptive regions such as Ulster. At first purely political, the clubs were beginning to take on a more military nature and were seen by everyone as the only possible focal points for any armed action.

As the Confederation gained in membership and political status, Meagher decided to run for Parliament in early 1848. Daniel O'Connell, Jr., had resigned his seat for Waterford in order to accept a position with the government, the kind of "place-hunting hypocrite" in the Repeal movement that the Confederates abhorred.* Meagher, only twenty-five years old, gave an

---

* Meagher was feuding with his father, once mayor of Waterford and now the senior MP, over this very issue. In 1848, the elder Meagher backed Costello, rather than his own son, and evened the score from an earlier election, when Thomas Francis had not supported his father's candidacy.

eloquent justification for his candidacy in his February 19 campaign speech in Waterford that harked all the way back to Strongbow's landing at the city in 1172. In opposing Repeal's candidate, Patrick Costello, the Young Irelander directly addressed his differences with O'Connell and the Repeal movement. Meagher drew a clear distinction between his revolutionary inclinations and the Repeal policy of accommodation, denouncing their "place-beggars" and "bigots" as the "worst enemies of Ireland."

The newspaper reported a "pugnacious front" shown by the "Carrick boatmen" in favoring Costello, yet even these opponents were moved by Meagher's "magnificent address." However, no matter how vocal such working class crowds might be for a candidate, they did not have the privilege of voting for him. Based on stringent property requirements, only some 700 out of a population of about 28,000 in Waterford were entitled to cast a ballot. Even if Thomas Lonergan supported the Confederation over any other political movement, he belonged to that class of "men of no property" who might contribute time or money to a cause, yet were denied the right to vote.

Meagher failed to gain the seat in Parliament that he sought because Repeal and Confederation divided the more progressive voters between the two movements. A third candidate, a "fossilized old fogy" representing the conservative elements who controlled the election, won with a twenty vote majority despite the widespread admiration for Meagher's impassioned speech.

Although 1848 had begun with a sense of the futility of relying on constitutional means and without hopes for any extreme actions, events in Paris that winter galvanized the Young Irelanders. News still traveled at the pace of the mail coach, but the abdication of the French King Louis Phillipe on February 24 was reported in Dublin before the month was over. Nationalist movements were developing in many countries in Europe and political events elsewhere were followed closely in Ireland.

France, an ally for Irish independence in the past, was the most important potential source of support for any rebellion. When news came that the king had been deposed and a republic installed with hardly a shot fired, it seemed to change the situation in Ireland overnight. Within the month, Irish enthusiasm for rebellion was further encouraged by similar revolts in Vienna, Berlin, Milan, and Venice. The reality of the situation in Ireland had not changed—the government was still strong, the people weak and divided—but the attitude now was that revolution might be a possibility after all. Bonfires appeared on the hilltops and the Confederate clubs displayed the French tricolor flag of red, white, and blue from their windows.

At the first meeting of the governing Council of the Confederation to be held after the successful French revolt, members agreed that within a year there would be either a restored national parliament or a revolution. During this March 2 meeting in the Music Hall on Abbey Street in Dublin, the editor of *The Nation*, Duffy, proposed that "a deputation be sent to France" to express the sympathy of the Irish people with their success.

WILLIAM SMITH O'BRIEN RETURNED from England to attend the next meeting of the council the following week. He called upon "all classes of their fellow-countrymen" to unite with them. Despite this invitation for the gentry to join the Confederates, O'Brien was the only Irish landlord present to "cast his lot with the people in this hour of trial." (Besides O'Brien, the only other landlord active in the movement was Mitchel's friend, John Martin, but he did not attend the meeting. Detractors scornfully said that the Confederation included a total of two landlords and two priests, meaning there was virtually no participation by these key elements of society.)

On March 15, at "the most important meeting yet held by the Irish Confederation" O'Brien extended his hand to the Repeal Association and asked for a joint meeting "of Old and Young Ireland" to congratulate the French people. Drawing on the French example, O'Brien called for "every lover of his country" to enroll as a member of a national guard if he was prepared to "preserve the state from anarchy" and "ready to die for the defence [sic] of his country." Meagher read an "Address of the Irish Confederation to the Citizens of the French Republic" praising their victory, to be sent on behalf of the Irish Confederation over O'Brien's signature. This address stated the Confederation's "firm resolve" that Ireland "once again be free and independent" through either constitutional action or "other efforts." O'Brien and Meagher, along with an Edward Hollywood, were deputized by the meeting to deliver the "Address of Congratulation" to the new French Republic.

However, the government had sent an official reporter to take notes at this meeting. His record of the statements made there was the basis for the charges of sedition filed the following week against O'Brien and Meagher. The "Aggregate Meeting" with the Repeal Association was first scheduled for St. Patrick's Day, but that conflicted with the Repeal ward meetings announced by Conciliation Hall for March 17. The "Great Meeting of Dublin Citizens" was therefore postponed until Monday, March 20. The gathering would take place "under any circumstances" despite the threat that it would be prohibited by the government, just as the Clontarf mass meeting had been in 1843. Fears of bloody suppression of the meeting by the police and the thousands of soldiers in the city proved unfounded. The meeting of some 12,000 to 15,000 people at the north wall of the city was orderly and concluded peacefully after many speeches. Upon adjournment, the "immense crowd proceeded down the quays" and "the multitude cheered most enthusiastically when passing Conciliation Hall." It then halted outside the Confederation committee rooms in Westmoreland Street where O'Brien and Meagher addressed the assembly from the windows.

The next day the government took action, filing charges against the two Confederation leaders for their "seditious" speeches—not of the previous day, but of March 15—and against John Mitchel for three "seditious" articles in the *United Irishman* newspaper. The three were required to report to the Police Office the following morning, March 22, where they each posted bail and were released. Escorted from the police station to the Confederation's Council Rooms in D'Olier Street by a huge cheering crowd, all three spoke to their supporters from the windows. Mitchel added fuel to the fire with his statement that "they have indicted me for 'sedition,' but I tell them that I mean to commit '*high treason*' [emphasis in original]." Meagher pledged that only his death would stop him from continuing his efforts to overthrow the government "which keeps its footing on our soil by sheer brute force."

Despite their inflammatory rhetoric, Meagher and O'Brien were allowed to travel to Paris at the end of the month as members of the Irish Confederation's deputation to meet with the new French Provisional Government. On April 3 the French President, Lamartine, received them and the Confederation's "Address" with a lukewarm statement of sympathy that refused any involvement in "internal disputes" of other countries. Apparently ignoring this official rebuff, O'Brien informed the United Irish Club of Paris, that the deputation had "seen and heard enough to feel assured that, were Ireland to demand assistance, France would be ready to send 50,000 of her bravest citizens to fight with her for liberty." O'Brien also claimed Ireland had friends in Germany, Belgium, Rome, and Spain, plus "numerous and influential ones in America." Already indicted for sedition and now seeking support from foreign powers, O'Brien and Meagher seemed intent on joining Mitchel in committing the more serious crime of high treason.

The Confederate Clubs in Dublin and other areas were rapidly expanding and becoming more organized as the belief grew in an impending armed revolution. The working class, particularly the more skilled artisans, made up the majority in most of the clubs. Some clubs drew in members from particular groups. The Student's Club was founded by men being trained in medicine, who then recruited students from other fields. Its secretary, John Savage, took the lead in calling for revolution and later played a key role in the armed operations in Tipperary. The Swift Club included two men over 75 years old who had fought in 1798 as United Irishmen under the "Harp without a Crown" and were active in enlisting recruits for the Dublin Confederates.*

Two days after the deputation had left for France, the clubs assembled to march for the first time "in semi-military order" to a meeting where Duffy repeated the call for an Irish national guard. Characteristically blunt in his own speech, Mitchel urged the crowd to "be prepared to rise" and to arm themselves. Rifles would be preferred, but if the club members could not afford the three pounds cost, they should procure "a sound ash pole, seven or eight feet long." An "enterprising hardware manufacturer" stepped forward to present Mitchel with a sample of his wares, an Irish pike head. This was "a shining, two-edged blade of polished steel, twelve inches long, with a sharp, strong hook, attached to a flanged socket" for mounting on the ash pole that Mitchel had recommended. At the time, possession of the pike head was not in itself an illegal act in Dublin, but when Mitchel displayed it to the audience it caused "a shout of exultation and defiance" to ring out in the hall. Within days, a brisk trade developed for "smiths and cutlers" producing these weapons "by hundreds and thousands."

---

* One of them, John Smith from County Cavan, fled the reprisals after the 1848 uprising with his son to the United States and they were "among the earliest enrolled members of the Fenian Brotherhood in New York." At the age of 89, Smith was to have a place of honor at the funeral of T. B. MacManus in New York in 1861.

CHAPTER FOUR – STARVED

To deal more effectively with the situation in Ireland, the British government introduced the "Crime and Outrage (Ireland) Bill" for the "security of the crown and government of the United Kingdom." This new "Treason-Felony Act" had provisions that converted what had previously been "seditious offenses" (for which bail could be posted and only brief imprisonment imposed on those found guilty) into felonies that carried a penalty of transportation for life. The standard for proving "treason-felony" was much lower than for high treason, which usually carried a sentence of death.

O'Brien had returned to London after his trip to France. He spoke out against the hurried passage of the Treason-Felony Act in the House of Commons on April 10, 1848, despite being shouted down by "violent bursts of yelling, which lasted fully ten minutes" from 400 other MPs. Rejecting charges of disloyalty to the Queen of England, he confirmed his "treason" of working "to overthrow the dominion of this Parliament over Ireland." He warned the House that the 10,000 police and 30,000 troops in Ireland would not be enough to suppress a rebellion if it came to one.

In sharp contrast to this rejection in the House of Commons, O'Brien was given a warm and enthusiastic welcome home in Dublin on April 15. The Music Hall was filled to "its utmost seating capacity" and decorated with flags hanging from the boxes and on the stage, where a man in "the ancient Irish national costume" of tunic and trews (breeches) was seated, harp between his knees. The other two members of the delegation that had traveled to France, Meagher and Hollywood, shared the stage with O'Brien.

At any dinner of this era, the custom included a series of toasts, starting with one to the monarch, and responses by designated appropriate persons. The first toast of the evening, "The Queen of Ireland," was reportedly received "respectfully" without any further commentary. The next toast, to "The People," drew a "spirited speech" in support of O'Brien by a renegade representative of the Repeal Association. This speaker clearly had repudiated the long-standing Repeal opposition to shedding "one drop of blood" to achieve independence. The situation in the country had obviously become so desperate that some supporters of Repeal were ready to consider force as the only solution.

The toast of the evening was to "Ireland's Uncompromising Patriot—William Smith O'Brien" and on this cue the harper played "Brian Boru's March" in recognition of the patriot's royal lineage. O'Brien was presented with a small green banner inscribed with his name and "Ireland's Truest Patriot." He then was given an "old banner of green silk," one of the original flags of the 3rd Regiment of the Irish Volunteers formed at the end of the previous century.

Meagher in turn handed the chairman of the event a flag on a staff surmounted by an Irish pike head. While he was in Paris, Meagher had been presented with this flag patterned after the familiar French tricolor and he now displayed it to the audience. Stating "I need not explain its meaning," he nonetheless did so: "The white in the centre signifies a lasting truce between the 'Orange' and the 'Green.'" His hope was that Irish Protestant (the orange) and Irish Catholic (the green) would join hands "beneath its folds" and that if it came to war England would again see the Red Hand of Ulster "upon that white centre." The new Irish tricolor had first appeared in early March in celebrations at Enniscorthy in County Wexford. This Paris flag may have duplicated that earlier color scheme, but its display in Dublin gave it almost official status as the nationalist banner, rivaling the traditional green flag of the past.

John Mitchel's response to the toast of the "Persecuted Patriots" was appropriately "plain as a pike-staff." He urged making the point of the argument using a pike, but reminded everyone that "firearms are indispensable." He waxed more eloquent about the new flag, though, citing two historic Irish victories under an earlier banner, "This magnificent Irish tri-color, with its Orange, White, and Green, dawns upon us more gloriously than ever Sunburst flashed over the field of Benburb, or blazed through the battle-haze of Contarf."

MEAGHER SERVED AS PRESIDENT of the Grattan Club—harking back again to the Irish Volunteers, the club bore the name of the Patriot Party leader Henry Grattan—in Dublin and upon returning from France his efforts were concentrated on arming and equipping its members. The club was made up mostly of "educated, well-to-do young men, who could afford to arm themselves with the most effective weapons attainable." Any member who could not afford proper arms and equipment had the cost covered by Meagher himself, so this group did not have to rely on the "eight-foot pike" that was the main weapon for many other clubs.

The Confederate Clubs in Dublin were obviously no match in arms or training for the 15,000 soldiers of the crown in the area. Any hope for action in the capital rested on the fact that many of these soldiers were Irish and "perhaps one-third of the garrison could be secured for the cause of Fatherland and Liberty." Recruiting these men would require a secret organization, however, and the Confederate Clubs were operating in the open, with their meetings regularly reported upon by government spies.

On April 29, the Sarsfield Club in Limerick held a banquet for the "Prosecuted Patriots" with O'Brien, Meagher, and Mitchel as the guests of honor. The festivities were interrupted by a mob of "Old Irelanders" who broke the windows of the building with stones in protest of Mitchel's presence. O'Brien himself was struck by sticks and stones when he went to the door to "remonstrate with the assailants" and he suffered cuts and bruises. This visit was supposed to be the first of a series to assess the readiness of the clubs in the south, but O'Brien returned to Dublin after the attack in Limerick to await his trial for sedition. Meagher continued the tour, accompanied by Duffy, editor of *The Nation*. Another dinner supporting the "Prosecuted Patriots" was to be held in Meagher's home town of Waterford on May 7. A large crowd of "enthusiastic nationalists" from Waterford was conveyed by "every vehicle attainable in the city" to meet Meagher and Duffy in Carrick the morning of the banquet and escort them to the city.

The two travelers arrived in Carrick about 11:00 AM and, since it was Sunday, went to Mass there. This is likely the first occasion where Meagher's path crossed that of young John Lonergan, who could well have attended the same service with his family. Only circumstantial evidence places John Lonergan on the scene at Mass with Meagher, but both were faithful Catholics and Carrick had only the one Catholic church. Meagher's attendance there would have provided an occasion for people to demonstrate their support of the "persecuted patriot." The famous orator would surely have been pointed out to John by his father, especially if Thomas Lonergan were active in the local Confederate Club by this time.

Records for the Lonergan family in Ireland are scant and the membership rolls in the Confederate Clubs were understandably not preserved (they might have sent those named to the gallows, prison, or exile). However, Thomas Lonergan fits the profile of a club member well. The old Gaelic families, like the Lonergans, tended to be nationalists and the artisan class to which Thomas belonged was politically active, supplying many of the clubs' members across the country. In addition, Carrick, always a hotbed of revolutionary spirit, formed an unusually high number of clubs for the size of its population. The leader in the area was John O'Mahony, from another old Gaelic family, whose farm was just down the road from John Lonergan's birthplace and home. O'Mahony would likely have first recruited reliable patriots from among the neighbors whom he knew and could trust.

Finally, the Lonergans' eventual emigration appears to have been motivated more by political than economic reasons; it likely resulted from participation in rebellion and the subsequent fear of prosecution. Anyone involved in organizing the uprising would certainly have been a member of a local Confederate Club and therefore known by O'Mahony, an ardent supporter of armed revolution. Presumably Thomas Lonergan passed this nationalist dedication on to his sons. John Lonergan clearly admired Meagher since he named two of his sons after the Young Irelander and would play host to this hero of his childhood in Vermont.

After Mass, Meagher and Duffy went to the hotel where the parish priest, Father Patrick Byrne, presented an address that was followed by speeches from the windows of the hotel. From there, "both gentlemen addressed an immense concourse of people, whom the news of their coming had attracted from both sides of the Suir—from the slopes of Sliabh-na-Mon [Slievenamon Mountain] on the Tipperary side and the valleys of the Commerahs [Commeragh Mountains] on that of Waterford. From end to end of the Island, no better fighting material could be found than was in Carrick on that day." The most resolute group was made up of Carrick boatmen who recently had opposed Meagher in the Waterford election, but were now his "devoted adherents."

Leaving Carrick for Waterford, a growing crowd accompanied Meagher over the bridge to Carrick Beg and along the road to Portlaw, the halfway point between the two towns. At Portlaw, the procession was met by "the congregated trades of Waterford with their bands and banners" and the last four miles into the city were like a "monster meeting" such had not been seen since 1843. Passing along the quay, Meagher pointed out a British warship moored there to remind his listeners that their country was being held by force and called for "Three cheers for the Green above the Red" to convey his message to the government. Both Meagher and Duffy spoke in the Waterford Town Hall that evening to urge the people to procure arms at once, remarks that were "carefully noted by two government reporters specially detailed for that purpose." The next day at a meeting of the United

CHAPTER FOUR – STARVED

Repealers of Kilkenny the two speakers repeated the message that "every true man" should arm "so as to be prepared for any contingency." They then returned to Dublin for Meagher to join O'Brien in waiting for the sedition trials of the two leaders the following week.

THE ATTENTION OF EVERYONE in Dublin was focused on the trial of O'Brien, set for Monday, May 15, when the government took action against the most outspoken of the nationalist leaders by arresting John Mitchel on Saturday, May 13. The Treason-Felony Act had essentially been crafted with Mitchel in mind and his arrest had been expected. However, no contingency plan existed for this anticipated event and the Confederates faced the question of what action to take in response, whether to leave the jailed Mitchel to his fate or to attempt a rescue. Only now did the leaders of the movement take a serious inventory of the resources available for armed action; they found them insufficient.

A brave showing of the Confederate Clubs was held on May 15 to escort O'Brien to court and a newspaper reported "at least ten thousand persons" marched in good order through Dublin. Sixteen clubs passed in review before O'Brien's lodgings in Westland Row, led by the Davis Club "headed by Thomas D'Arcy M'Gee" that "counted about five hundred fine young men, evidently respectable." Much was made in the accounts of the fact that "This was no Irish rabble," but rather "as fine a body of young men, of as manly bearing and respectable appearance, as were ever seen." The Swift Club of 620 members appeared next led by Richard O'Gorman, followed by Meagher's Grattan Club which, "augmented by the coalition of another club," numbered no less than 800 members. The president of the St. Patrick's Club, John Mitchel, was now behind bars in Newgate, the "Bastille" of Dublin, and the group was led by his brother William. Other clubs, most named for Irish patriots or towns, also paraded in the orderly procession to the Four Courts, where O'Brien entered for his trial. The clubs then marched to Newgate to demonstrate in support of Mitchel. When his St. Patrick's Club arrived in front of the jail, it was announced "This is the Felon's Club" and they "instantaneously uncovered and marched past in funeral pace," watched by Mitchel's wife, who was just leaving the jail.

O'Brien's trial for sedition lasted just one day and resulted in a hung jury, although they were locked up for the night and only dismissed the following morning when they could not reach a verdict. The process was repeated in Meagher's trial on May 16, as two jurors (one a Catholic and the other "an honest Protestant") would not agree to a guilty verdict even after the jury was kept overnight.

The Confederate Clubs repeated the process of accompanying Meagher to court and that evening demonstrated again in front of Newgate. This was too much for the Castle to tolerate and the Crown's representative, Lord Clarendon, issued a proclamation "forbidding such assemblages in future." The clubs defied this order on Sunday, May 21, when they held an "aggregate meeting" regarding Mitchel's situation, but this produced only a timid resolution against packing the jury for his trial to ensure conviction. Many club members wanted to attempt a rescue of Mitchel, but it fell to Meagher and O'Gorman to instruct them not to try such a desperate measure. The Council had asked the two leaders to assess the situation and they found the chances of success too low and the probability of extensive bloodshed too high. O'Brien himself had advised very strongly against action that would give the authorities a chance to crush the Confederation and could not save Mitchel.

The Treason-Felony trial was held on May 26 with Mitchel facing a jury carefully selected by the Sheriff to include not a single Catholic or any Protestant of doubtful loyalty. Duffy commented that the names of the jurors read "like a muster-roll of one of Cromwell's regiments." Mitchel knew that this stacked jury and the evidence against him predetermined the outcome of the trial. His defense was put in the hands of an aged former United Irishman, Robert Holmes. This was a deliberately symbolic choice, as Holmes was the brother-in-law of the martyr Robert Emmet. Holmes tried to argue that in advocating freedom for his country Mitchel was legally, but not morally, in violation of the new law.

This justification of his client's actions failed to exonerate him in the eyes of the jury and a guilty verdict was achieved in a single day. The sentence passed the next day, "transportation beyond the seas for a period of fourteen years," far exceeded what could have been imposed for mere sedition. Mitchel was defiant in the dock, expressing no regrets and saying he had done his duty. Scorning the packed jury that found him guilty, he said it was "a jury not empanelled by a sheriff, but by a juggler." Referring to the Roman who burned his hand before a tyrant with the promise of 300 men to replace him, he

CHAPTER FOUR – STARVED

called on those comrades present in the courtroom—Meagher, O'Gorman, Reilly—to continue the struggle. O'Brien had removed himself to Wicklow at this time, claiming he was still suffering from the injuries received in Limerick the previous month. That afternoon, on the fiftieth anniversary of the start of the 1798 rebellion, Mitchel was taken in chains directly from prison to a warship in Dublin Harbor. The *Sheerwater* immediately steamed out of the port to convey him on the first leg of his long journey to Van Dieman's Land (now called Tasmania).

WHILE THE CONFEDERATES WERE disappointed over standing by with folded hands and watching Mitchel be sent into exile, there had been no realistic hope of any rescue or of putting any effective pressure on the government to change the outcome of events. The decision by the Council to order the Clubs to avoid any outbreak of violence was understandable, although in later years "Meagher expressed regret for his action on that occasion." One of Meagher's first tasks was to justify his own role in restraining the clubs from action to save Mitchel. The transported Mitchel might usefully serve the cause as a martyr.

The Confederates increased their efforts to extend the organization of the clubs (doubling their membership in Dublin) and to arm the members. Steps were also taken to improve the operations of the organization by imposing secrecy and reducing the number of Council members to twenty-one. In the vote by secret ballot, it is interesting to note that O'Brien received only thirty votes—the same as Duffy, Dillon, and O'Gorman—while Meager and the Tipperary priest Father Kenyon tied for the most with thirty-one. Father Kenyon and Meagher were both being considered at that time for a tour of the United States to solicit funds. However, the priest shortly thereafter came to a "satisfactory understanding" with his bishop that ended his activities in the revolutionary movement.

Doubts were beginning to arise about O'Brien's leadership of the movement since, as a wealthy landlord, some Confederate leaders saw him as "nervously anxious about the safety of his class." It was decided that when O'Brien returned to Dublin he would, for his own protection, be given enough information "to keep good faith; not enough to create responsibility." While the Council made "preparations for active revolutionary work,"

O'Brien was responding to overtures from John O'Connell for merger of the Confederation and the Repeal Association.

The two organizations were to be joined together as the Irish League under terms worked out at the end of May. They hoped that this would broaden the appeal of the combined movement to include O'Connell's supporters, as well as gain the blessing of the church. Support for the Repeal Association had declined badly in the famine years, but O'Connell still insisted on its old principle that "direct incentives to war be avoided." The increasingly militant Confederate Clubs were to be kept separate from the Irish League organization, an arrangement the Church regarded with favor.

Just as the merger of Repeal and the Confederation was to be implemented, O'Connell announced that he was quitting public life. He blamed his retirement on the militant tone of O'Brien's letter announcing the agreement in *The Nation* on June 1. About this time, the Protestants had formed their own Repeal Association with goals similar to the Irish League. Government actions soon crushed any hopes that the Irish League could expand its base to include support by the Catholic Church or could join forces with its Protestant counterpart.

Mitchel's *United Irishman* had been suppressed in conjunction with his prosecution and for a while only *The Nation* was available to publish the nationalist views. The newspaper now also included letters of a militant nature like "Night Thoughts on the Bayonet." It was soon joined by *The Irish Felon*, successor to the *United Irishman*, with John Martin as publisher, and *The Irish Tribune* (a reference to Mitchel's speech from the dock) put out by Williams and O'Doherty of the Student's Club.

After five weeks of increased agitation by writers like James Fintan Lalor and Michael Doheny of Tipperary, John Savage and Thomas Devin Reilly of Dublin, and others of a revolutionary persuasion, the government cracked down. On Saturday, July 8, Duffy, Martin, and O'Doherty were arrested under the useful new felony law; Williams was taken into custody the next day. D'Arcy McGee, Duffy's assistant editor on *The Nation*, was picked up and charged with sedition the following week. Only four issues of *The Irish Felon* and three issues of *The Irish Tribune* had been published. The more established newspaper *The Nation* was suppressed on July 29. Duffy was brought to trial five times without the government securing a conviction and he was released after ten months. Meagher had written a letter from prison stating that Duffy was not responsible for what Meagher had published in *The Nation*. Williams also escaped being found guilty by the government's picked jury. Martin and O'Doherty were each sentenced to ten years transportation, although it took three trials before O'Doherty could be convicted.

THE THIRD MEMBER OF THE DEPUTATION that had traveled to France in March, Edward Hollywood, was also arrested in Dublin on July 12. The other Confederation leaders were outside the capital and had to be rounded up piecemeal. O'Brien, who had not spoken out in such clearly revolutionary terms as those being arrested, was left unmolested in Cahermoyle, his home in County Limerick.

Meagher had gone to visit O'Brien there, but they missed connections. Meagher then made a speech in nearby Rathkeale that became the basis for his arrest on July 11 in Waterford on the charge of sedition. The constable sent to collect Meagher from his father's residence was accompanied by a troop of the 4th Light Dragoons and three companies of the 7th Fusileers who carried sixty rounds of ammunition per man. The ringing of church bells brought a throng of people that prevented the troops from removing him. Meagher was informed that "messengers had been sent to Carrick-on-Suir, for the Clubs there organized" and that the clubs would be marching on Waterford within a few hours. Meagher sent a written order countermanding this action and convinced the crowd to allow him to go with the troops peaceably. He was taken to Dublin where he posted bail the next day and was scheduled to appear at the next Limerick assizes to answer the charge against him.

On the same day, Michael Doheny had a similar experience in his home town of Cashel in central Tipperary, when a mob also attempted to prevent his arrest. He was able to keep the violence down to fisticuffs only by assuring his rescuers that he would post bail in Roscrea and be released. The arrests of these two leaders in Waterford and Tipperary had "simultaneously fired the hearts of the two best fighting counties in Ireland." Meagher, Doheny, McGee, and others were all soon set free on bail and resumed their revolutionary activities.

While these government actions took place in early July, O'Brien was touring the south of Ireland, the area seen as most likely to support revolutionary action. He reviewed the Cork Confederate Clubs by moonlight and was encouraged to see some seven to ten thousand members, "many of whom marched past him in military order." Earlier, however, a letter in *The Irish Felon* had pointed out that, although numerous, the members of these clubs were for the most part poorly armed and that each club thought that the others must be better equipped and prepared for action ("Cork looks to Dublin and Dublin looks to Cork").

ENCOURAGED BY THE POPULAR RESISTANCE to their arrests in Waterford and Cashel, Meagher and Doheny staged a massive show of opposition to British rule soon after being released on bail. O'Brien, nominally the leader of the movement, seems to have been excluded from the leadership for this event, the initiative taken instead by the Confederate chiefs from Tipperary and Waterford. Inspired by O'Connell's monster meetings at locations significant for Irish nationalism, they organized a rally for July 16 atop the mountain of Slievenamon. The symbolic connection with Finn McCool and the Fianna, protectors of Ireland against foreign assault, was obvious to everyone. As Meagher's biographer observed, "Surely, no more appropriate spot could be found from which to recall memories of the past, or enkindle hopes for the future of their land."

The clear view in all directions from the summit also had several advantages: the strength of the assembled mass of people could be seen by everyone, the usual government reporters might be excluded, and discipline could be more easily enforced to avoid disorder. Drinking in particular was discouraged, as it had been at Repeal meetings, the slogan being "Ireland sober is Ireland free." Word of the meeting spread in time for delegations to come from some distance, so the plans must have been made days prior to the gathering on that Sunday.

The Confederate Clubs in the Carrick area were organized on a district level into a Central Board composed of the presidents of the various clubs, meeting in Carrick with Dr. A. O'Ryan as the elected chairman. Father Byrne was the "great originator and chief promoter of the movement in that quarter" and exercised the most influence over the Central Board. Other priests also took the initiative in South Tipperary as they "publicly told the people to form clubs, to make pikes, and many a one proclaimed from the altar that he would be with the people and lead them on the day of action." The Reverend Patrick Power, a native of Cappoquin across the Suir in County Waterford

CHAPTER FOUR – STARVED

and now curate in Ballyneill parish, persuaded Lonergan's neighbor, John O'Mahony, to "take the direction" of a club that the priest wanted to establish in Ballyneill. Building on this nucleus, O'Mahony, in his own words, organized "other rural clubs, all in the same district, of which I had the management, and our ramifications were extending widely through the district of which Carrick was the centre."

The "Carrick Green" where fairs were held, hard by the new constabulary building, was the rendezvous point for the clubs of the town and its vicinity on the day of the Slievenamon meeting. At daylight on that Sunday morning, the 200 soldiers stationed in Carrick and the police were at the ready and under arms in their respective barracks. To avoid any confrontation with the demonstrators, these outnumbered forces would remain confined to their barracks unless absolutely needed to restore order. The clubs formed up under their presidents and, "amid the wildest exclamations of delight and defiance from the townspeople," marched off for the mountain, following Sir John's Road past the Lonergan home. Thomas Lonergan most likely took his place in the ranks of a Carrick club that formed on the green. His son, John, at eleven years of age was not too young to walk the nearly ten miles to the top of the hill. Given his bold nature and the excitement of the day, it is easy to picture John joining the stream of people.

Crowds had choked the roads of Carrick long before the time set for the meeting, coming not only from the immediate area, but also from Waterford, Kilkenny, and even Cork and Wexford. Despite the intense heat of the mid-July day, it was estimated that some 50,000 people gathered around the "seat of Finn" at the top. The upper part of the hill was already black with people when a cheer arose "from base to summit" heralding the arrival of Doheny in the uniform of the 1782 Volunteers, leading 6,000 men from his district in middle Tipperary.

A system of relaying speeches had been developed for mass meetings and designated persons in the crowd would pass on what was being said to those beyond the range of the speaker's voice. Doheny spoke for an hour, urging his listeners to arm themselves even though County Tipperary was "proclaimed" and weapons therefore prohibited. He promoted the "utility of the club organization" and encouraged its expansion. Advising the people to stay calm and hold firm, not fearing the impending conflict, he concluded "amid a storm of enthusiastic cheers."

Meagher next appeared in a tricolor sash of green, white, and orange to address the "Men of Tipperary" making up most of the audience. He pointed to the land visible for miles around them as rightfully theirs, "yours by nature, and by God's gift," asking, "are ye content that the harvest of this land which you see, and to which your labor has imparted fruitfulness, should again be reaped for the stranger?" Though "the potato was smitten," the golden grain of the landlords' fields was still forbidden to them and ships bore it away from those who gathered it.

Many of those listening to Meagher had seen the weekly procession of laden barges down the Suir River under the protection of British troops. Filled with the region's bounty at the grain mills in Clonmel, the convoy would be accompanied by fifty cavalrymen, eighty infantry, and two cannon as it proceeded to Carrick. Such a formidable detachment was necessary to discourage any attempt to recover the food being stolen from the mouths of the starving Irish. Rage against this injustice fed their hearts, if not their empty bellies.

It was reported that Meagher displayed the new tricolor Irish flag when he declared his "ambition to decorate these hills with the flag of my country." He was followed by other speakers until the meeting ended about seven o'clock in the evening. Meagher and Doheny left the meeting for Waterford, but found in the Carrick market square a crowd of supporters from that city who had not been able to reach the meeting on Slievenamon. Some said they had been delayed and discouraged from attending by cautious priests. Doheny wrote later that "the Rev. Mr. Byrne" specifically was "foremost in this endeavour and actually dissuaded the people of Waterford, Carrick, and Wexford from proceeding to the mountain. These people all remained in Carrick...." The speakers were enthusiastically accompanied on their journey by this multitude, arriving in Waterford only at three o'clock in the morning.

After Meagher and Doheny had been arrested the previous week, the clubs in South Tipperary had agreed that they would offer resistance to any future arrests of club members, whenever and wherever attempts might be made. O'Mahony believed that was the resolve of all clubs and "well understood in all our clubs about Carrick" even if this had not been directed by "Headquarters." Early on the morning after the Slievenamon meeting, O'Mahony was roused from his bed by a messenger sent to his farm from Carrick "calling on me to arm my men and enter the town, for that the arrests

CHAPTER FOUR – STARVED

VIEW FROM THE TOP OF SLIEVENAMON

had commenced. I did so, had my club-men assembled, and we marched upon the town." This group from the Ballyneill area was determined to rescue the arrested Club members in Carrick, who might have included Thomas Lonergan. They were met by Father Byrne and others who thanked them for the prompt action, but explained that the magistrate, "terrified at the determined muster of the clubs," had released the prisoners. O'Mahony dismissed his forces, but "ordered the making of pikes to proceed and had guards placed on all forges to protect the weapons and the smiths."

Even the child John Lonergan, knowing how his people were mistreated by their British rulers, would have realized that the revolutionary tone of the Slievenamon meeting had dared to challenge the existing system. If he had not been able to climb the mountain and hear Meagher and Doheny speak, the excited talk around the family table and the neighborhood would have kept John informed of events. O'Mahony's march on Carrick the day after the gathering must have passed right by the Lonergans' home, a thrilling sight of armed Irishmen prepared to strike a blow for their country's freedom. John would soon carry such memories with him to America, where all things were possible.

Just two days after the mass meeting on Slievenamon, Lord Clarendon took another step to suppress the revolutionary movement; more areas in Ireland were "proclaimed" on July 18. The proclamation made the possession of arms in Dublin and a number of other counties illegal. This had already been the case in County Tipperary and other restive parts of the country, where "the possession of a percussion cap, or a pitch-fork with prongs of unusual length, was punished with twelve months' imprisonment." The measure created a crisis in the clubs and they debated whether they would allow themselves to be stripped of the inadequate arms that they had or take this as the signal for action. On July 19, a meeting of the Confederation Council—now constituted as part of the Irish League by the merger with the Repeal Association—after much discussion passed a resolution that the clubs should content themselves with "passive resistance" by not cooperating with the arms proclamation that required surrendering the weapons.

Many members dismissed the difficulties anticipated by their leaders and called for action. Stalwart Bob Ward, for example, had a reputation in the Confederation as "one of the most ultra disciples" of the doctrine of physical force and he had the build to back up his arguments. A Kilkenny man, Ward had served his apprenticeship as a saddle maker in Lonergan's home town, becoming a foster child of "Law-defying Carrick." When he moved to Dublin, he joined the Swift Club there, but showed little patience for the endless discussions and excuses for inaction. When O'Brien urged on July 20 that the club members only conceal their arms to prevent confiscation "because the people were not yet sufficiently prepared for a conflict," Ward lashed out in "a tone of passionate scorn." He exclaimed to his leader's face, "Not yet sufficiently prepared! There are some people who will *never* be prepared, fellows who—if the Almighty rained down rifles ready loaded from Heaven—would ask Him to send down angels to pick them up and fire them."

The Council met again on July 21 to create a small inner executive, a Revolutionary Committee of five. O'Brien was intentionally absent, having refused even to let his name be put in nomination and had removed himself to Wexford. Recognizing the need for leaders ready to take action, the Council elected Richard O'Gorman, Meagher, Dillon, McGee, and Devin Reilly, a

CHAPTER FOUR — STARVED

close supporter of Mitchel. Even these militants did not anticipate further government actions in the next few weeks and they reached a consensus that any uprising should be delayed until after the harvest. The rebels would then prevent the sorely needed food from being taken out of Ireland. Substantive reasons supported this delay; the starving peasantry needed to concentrate on survival, rather than revolution. However, this left the initiative totally in the hands of the government, which did not hesitate in its next move against the enemies of the Crown.

Events continued to swirl around Carrick as the Confederates finally attempted to raise the countryside. John Lonergan witnessed first-hand the difference between an irresolute leader like O'Brien, whose nerve failed him at the crucial moment, and a true Celtic chieftain like O'Mahony, as willing to shed his own blood as that of his enemies to free his country. The ordeal that the Lonergans shared with O'Mahony in Tipperary forged bonds of trust that they would later renew in America.

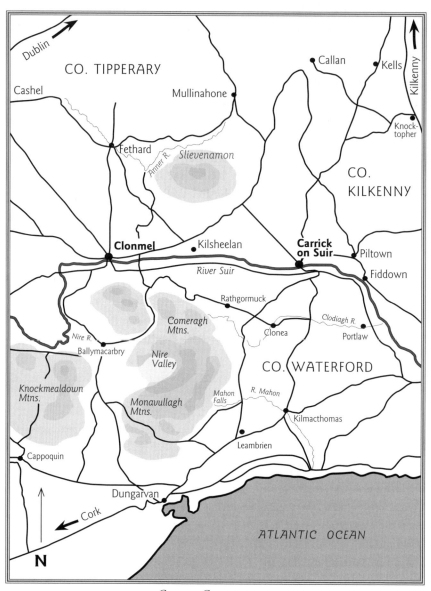

Greater Carrick area

CHAPTER FIVE

AWAKENED

THE YOUNG IRELANDERS APPEAR to have been consistently surprised by the government's actions against them, failing to anticipate events or to plan for likely contingencies. No strong leader took charge to make decisions and their reaction to each repressive measure by the representatives of the Crown was consequently debated at length. Mitchel had been transported without resistance, the capital and several counties proclaimed as rebellious, and the disarmed clubs prohibited from meeting. The final step to crush the incipient uprising was arresting those leaders still at liberty. To facilitate their imprisonment, the House of Commons had passed, without the least opposition, a bill to suspend *habeas corpus* in Ireland. The House approved this suspension on the very Saturday that the new Irish League formed its Revolutionary Committee. On Monday, July 24, the act was sure to be approved by the House of Lords as well and thus become law, at which point those arrested could be held without trial or bail.

Clearly the rebels could no longer consider postponing any armed resistance until after the harvest. The huge gathering on Slievenamon on July 16 and subsequent events in the Carrick area had demonstrated the people's readiness for action under resolute leadership. The Lonergans had observed first-hand the rebellious mood sweeping the countryside and it is highly likely that Thomas stood ready to do his part in any uprising, when the word was given. A firm decision by the new Revolutionary Committee could set the rising in motion by calling upon the Confederate Clubs to act before the leaders were arrested.

The British administration operating from Dublin Castle held a major advantage over those plotting against it; the officials were receiving good intelligence on anti-government activities. Their main source of information about the Confederate Clubs appears to have been a certain John Balfe, one of several hundred bodyguards assigned to accompany speakers. Balfe also served as the Confederate liaison with the English Chartist movement, which the Irish nationalists saw as a potential ally against the government. His duties as a bodyguard made him well placed to inform the Castle of the leaders' whereabouts and plans, though he was not a critical source of information. Most of the Confederate operations took place openly, despite their revolutionary purpose. James Dobbyn was also employed as an informer; he attended meetings and later testified against Meagher. The Confederates had finally realized that a revolutionary movement required both secrecy and clear decisions made quickly, without endless discussion. However, the creation of the five-man Revolutionary Committee on July 21 came too late to affect the course of events.

When Meagher received the news of the impending suspension of *habeas corpus,* he told his friend Pat Smyth, "There is nothing for us now, but to go out; we have not gone far enough to succeed, and yet, too far to retreat." O'Gorman, one of the five members of the Revolutionary Committee, had just left for Limerick to take charge of the uprising in "the patrimonial tribe-lands of his ancestral clan." Meagher, Dillon, and McGee convened at the Dublin headquarters without the fifth member, Devin Reilly, of the committee present. These three men held the fate of the nationalist movement in their hands, yet seemed unable to make practical decisions at this crucial point.

McGee was dispatched to Scotland, charged with raising a force of at least 2,000 Irish volunteers in Glasgow. He was to wait until notified by Dillon that an uprising had begun, then overpower Glasgow's garrison, commandeer merchant ships to transport his forces to the west of Ireland, and fight his way across the Shannon River to join the uprising in Tipperary. (McGee never received word of any rising to support, so he did not try to implement this impossible scheme, though he himself did travel from Glasgow to Sligo to foment rebellion in that area.) An emissary was also sent to France to solicit their help with the insurrection.

Meagher and Dillon embarked on the more reasonable task of finding O'Brien, the nominal chief of the organization. Agreeing that they had to get out of Dublin immediately to avoid arrest, the two men decided to seek out

CHAPTER FIVE — AWAKENED

O'Brien in Wexford.* Before leaving the Confederate headquarters, they told the secretary of the Council, Thomas Halpin, to inform the officers of the clubs, as well as the imprisoned Confederate leaders, of their departure and their "resolution of commencing the insurrection, if possible, in Kilkenny." They left instructions for the clubs in the Dublin area "to be in readiness to rise" when word of this action in the south drew troops away from the capital. A large map of Ireland was taken down from the wall and folded up for their travels, the only planning document for a national uprising.

NOTWITHSTANDING THE FUROR IN DUBLIN over the political developments, the two men were able to board a train unmolested and went to join Mrs. Dillon for dinner in a nearby village. After dining at Druid Lodge in Killiney, they went the two miles to Loghlinstown to take the coach for Enniscorthy. Two seats had been reserved in the name of Charles Hart, who accompanied them from Druid Lodge, "with a view to conceal our departure from the police, who were on the alert." They were the only "inside" passengers on the coach and Meagher later recorded his musings about the situation while making this trip, deciding that they could not have acted otherwise.

Proceeding overnight by coach to Enniscorthy on the Slaney River, they ordered up a carriage to take them on to Ballinkeele where O'Brien was staying. While the fugitive leaders waited, Meagher read to Dillon the "beautiful, noble appeal" written by Lalor for the last issue of *The Irish Felon*. Lalor's article ended prophetically with the questions "Who will draw the first blood for Ireland? Who will win a wreath that shall be green forever?" Leaving town in early morning with the unseasonable cold raising mists from the river, Meagher's eyes fell on "Vinegar Hill, with the old dismantled windmill, on the summit of it." The site of the major battle in the 1798 uprising that ended in a massacre of the rebels, the scene both sobered and inspired him. (Meagher later wrote "it is a bitter thought to me…more bitter, far, a thousand times, than the worst privations of prison-life—that, unlike those gallant Wexford men of '98, we have left behind us no famous field….")

Arriving in Ballinkeele, they roused O'Brien from bed to give him the news

---

*O'Brien was staying with an old friend, John Maher, near Enniscorthy after being invited down to visit some "mudlands then in process of reclamation in Wexford Harbour." At a time when the movement desperately needed firm leadership, O'Brien's actions were more in the nature of a landlord and civic reformer than a revolutionary.

of the suspension of *habeas corpus*. Dillon proposed that their only three options were to permit themselves to be arrested, to flee the country, or to "give the signal of insurrection." O'Brien held the view that he could not leave Ireland or surrender, as either action "would seriously compromise our position before the public." After all the brave speeches, it clearly was the time for action; Meagher assured him that they were "prepared to take the field with him that day." Returning to Enniscorthy in Mr. Maher's carriage, they discussed "different plans of operation" en route. Wexford was not the place to make a stand because very few Confederates had been enrolled from that county. No enthusiasm for rebellion could be expected from the Wexford men since the ruined windmill on Vinegar Hill stood as a mute reminder, even after the passage of fifty years, of an experience they would not wish to repeat.

THE CONFEDERATION LEADERS AGREED that their greatest chance for support lay in the area where the "three best fighting counties in Ireland"—Waterford, Kilkenny, and Tipperary—came together, in the triangle formed by Kilkenny city, Slievenamon mountain, and Carrick on Suir. O'Brien at first wanted to go to New Ross, but was persuaded that the town was untenable as a base because the British ships based on the Barrow River there could be easily reinforced by those on the Suir in Waterford.

Each point of the triangle chosen for the uprising had its own organizational advantages. Based on a newspaper report that the Confederate Clubs in Kilkenny had enrolled 17,000 men, O'Brien had scheduled the next meeting of the Irish League to be held there. Tipperary was home to both Doheny and Father Kenyon and the clubs were very active at Carrick, while Waterford was Meagher's base. To the southwest, Cork and Limerick would form a strategic reserve and McGee was supposed to bring forces in from the west coast. The concept—it can hardly be called a plan—was that a rising in the less heavily garrisoned south would draw enough forces away from Dublin for successful action in the capital. The leaders seemed oblivious to the fact that British reinforcements could easily be brought by sea to any Irish port, including Dublin.

In Enniscorthy that Sunday, Meagher and Dillon went to Mass while O'Brien spoke to the locals to determine their spirit and level of organization. He told his listeners to stand ready for any emergency, but did not "call them out to insurrection" before continuing on the trip. At around eight o'clock in the evening, the three travelers arrived in Kilkenny and met with Dr. Cane, the leader of the area clubs. Cane shocked them with the fact that there had been a misprint in the newspaper and only 1,700 members were enrolled in the clubs, not 17,000. Moreover, only one in four had weapons of any kind.

Kilkenny still seemed a possibility as a base for action because of its location and tactical considerations. The city streets were narrow and easily barricaded, the army barracks were outside the town, bridges over the Nore River could be demolished, and the railway from Dublin stopped fourteen miles short of the city. The intervening distance to the city could only be covered on narrow roads flanked by stone walls and high bramble fences, ideal for ambushes at close quarters by the insurgents. In addition, the Royal Agriculture Society was about to hold its annual cattle show in Kilkenny. This offered the prospect of noble hostages ("a couple of Earls, from half a dozen to a dozen Baronets, an odd Marquis") and fine dining on the prize cattle.

The splintered organization of the nationalist movement was woefully evident in the county. The Kilkenny clubs were United Repeal, not Confederate, and poorly armed. Kilkenny town itself was garrisoned by 1,000 infantry and two troops of cavalry behind walls, making the city impracticable as a base. The rebels hoped instead to raise forces elsewhere, in particular around Carrick, and then march upon Kilkenny and Clonmel, "both of which would be sure to fall into the hands of the national army."

The Confederates in Dublin were left behind in complete confusion because Halpin, the secretary, failed to direct the clubs to be ready to act when the uprising started in the south. The impending suspension of *habeas corpus* was generally known and prominent club officers were aware that the organization's leaders had left town to avoid arrest. The jailed Duffy did receive word from Dillon of his departure to find O'Brien and was able to communicate this to Martin, who was also in prison. Duffy advised other club officers—including Terence Bellew MacManus, Maurice Leyne, and Devin Reilly—to follow Dillon to Tipperary to support the stand to be made there.

An activist club member in Dublin, Michael Cavanagh, originally from Cappoquin in County Waterford, planned to join the rising in the south. However, he first sought instructions from Reilly as to whether to stay instead in Dublin and await action there. Reilly, the last of the five-member Revolutionary Committee still in the capital, had already decided to go to

Tipperary himself as recommended by Duffy. He asked Cavanagh to meet him at Doheny's house in Cashel where he expected to connect with O'Brien and his companions.*

Before departing Dublin, Cavanagh took two militant friends, one the outspoken Bob Ward with his Carrick connections and "rifles from Heaven," to his residence. They pulled up the floorboards in his bedroom to hide "a well-oiled musket, two full-mounted pikes, and the handle of a third." The head of the third pike was the weapon that had been presented to Mitchel at the April meeting of the clubs; before his arrest, Mitchel had in turn given it to Cavanagh. In a symbolic gesture, Cavanagh decided to bring the pike head with him to Tipperary, wrapping it in a handkerchief and placing a cork on the point so he could hide it in his vest.

Reilly had left the capital for Tipperary after placing Pat Smyth in charge of the Dublin clubs, but Smyth too pulled out for the south upon learning that he was about to be arrested. The largest concentration of Confederate Clubs—thousands of men armed, organized, and anticipating a call for action—thus idled, leaderless and bewildered, in Dublin. Even the secretary, Halpin, accompanied by Leyne, showed up in Carrick early the next week looking for "instructions for the Dublin Club-men." O'Mahony wrote later, "Poor Club-men of Dublin! Not a townland in Tipperary but was visited by some of them, in the vain search for an insurgent camp."

O'BRIEN, MEAGHER, AND DILLON traveled through Callan on Monday, July 24, where they encountered an enthusiastic crowd of about 900 people. The assembly promised them protection from arrest by the 8th Irish Hussars, who were also passing through the town. O'Brien fraternized with the troopers, raising three cheers from the crowd for the Irish Hussars. He then urged the people to arm themselves and to expect "a thousand Tipperarymen" to march on Kilkenny within the week. Unimpeded by the soldiers, the party continued on to Carrick, only stopping to change horses at Nine Mile House. After talking with the country people there to judge their mood and explaining "the business we were on," the threesome was encouraged by expressions of support for a rising. In terms of weapons, however, the locals considered themselves "armed well enough; if they hadn't guns, they had their hooks, spades, and

---

* Cavanagh later provided a detailed first-hand account of the events of 1848 in his biography of Meagher, published in America in 1892.

forks." They were willing to take the field using farm tools for weapons, just as they had in 1798. Against the forces of the crown, armed even better than fifty years before, this was clearly a formula for another disaster. Some of the listeners were sent off to raise the countryside in anticipation of the return of the rebels. All were urged to be ready to attack Kilkenny "before the end of the week." After dining at the public house, O'Brien's party raised cheers for "The Green above the Red" and continued on for Carrick.

Men digging in a field just outside Carrick told them that O'Mahony lived nearby and he was summoned to join the newly arrived leaders. O'Mahony soon appeared on horseback. The Young Irelanders, meeting him for the first time, were impressed with O'Mahony and described him as "one of the noblest young Irishmen" and a "true leader for the generous, passionate, intrepid peasantry of the South."

O'Mahony informed them that "the country all about Carrick, on towards Clonmel, and along the Suir on the Tipperary side was thoroughly alive and ready to take the field at once." He produced "a couple of leather-covered books" with lists of club members, the organization of sections, their captains, the number armed, and their spirit for a fight. O'Mahony showed great enthusiasm and was "strongly of the opinion we should commence that very night in Carrick" with the uprising. The week since the Slievenamon meeting had been spent in "most active preparations" and almost everyone in the area who "could buy iron for a pike-head" had been furnished with a locally-forged weapon. O'Mahony recounted the action of the previous week when the clubs had forced the release of their members, assuring the Confederation leaders that they would also be protected by the clubs. He offered the Young Irelanders an armed escort, which they declined.

O'Mahony watched them continue on into Carrick via Sir John's Road, encouraged by the promise of support by the clubs in the area. He then returned to his "pike-making" until he became impatient to learn what was going on and rode past the Lonergan's home into Carrick, where he "found the greatest excitement and enthusiasm." The visit of the Young Ireland leaders had drawn crowds into Carrick from the surrounding area, including numerous members of the local Confederate clubs. Thomas Lonergan was likely among these club members eager for action and John, now eleven years old, would probably also have joined in as a spectator of the exciting events.

O'Brien and his companions had arrived in Carrick "little more than half an hour" after parting with O'Mahony. There they found thousands of men who "thronged the streets," still unarmed while they awaited word from their leaders. The Young Irelanders held a meeting with the principal members of the Carrick Central Board of Confederate Clubs at Doctor Purcell's house on Castle Street, the eastward extension of Main Street that leads to the Ormond Castle. O'Mahony pushed his way through the crowds to join them. Among the local club presidents, he found "nothing but doubt and dismay" at the step they were being asked to take. Most of them just wanted to get O'Brien and his companions out of town. The club officers were asking O'Brien "Why had they come to that little town to commence the rising? Was Carrick able to fight the British empire? Were they—the leaders—rejected by everywhere else?"

O'Brien tried to conceal his disappointment at their timid response, explaining that he had come to Carrick because it was better organized than most places. He emphasized that "the thing should commence somewhere, and that Carrick seemed to be the place for such commencement." He did not expect "to engage Carrick single-handed against England," but wanted from them "a body of six hundred young men, armed with guns, and well provided with ammunition, and having sufficient means for self support, to guard him and his companions while they were raising the country." O'Mahony knew that the appearance of such a group would draw all the British forces in the area against them. Determined to begin fighting at once, he saw this approach to initiating the uprising to be "as suitable as any other—under the circumstances." As a theoretical guerrilla tactic, such a "flying column" moving around the countryside had a better chance of success than the defense of a static base against the more powerful British forces. However, only two members of the Central Board present "volunteered to form part of such a band" and the presidents of the other clubs were unable to commit any of their men.

O'Mahony suggested, "after much talk," that since the revolutionary leaders had done them the compliment of coming to Carrick "to make the first appeal to the country" they should remain overnight in the town to see if the requested guard could be raised. No one should question O'Brien as to why he was calling upon Carrick since "Our own boastings brought them to us." O'Mahony asked "Having declared ourselves willing to fight for any member of our body and proclaimed it loudly, what right had we to complain if the chiefs had taken us at our word?" It was agreed (reluctantly by some) that O'Brien, Meagher, and Doheny would remain in town that night guarded by the clubs brought in from the countryside and that "any hostile attempt from the garrison should be resisted." O'Brien and Meagher then addressed the "impatient crowd in the street" who in return gave them promises of defense to the death, if necessary. One can picture Thomas Lonergan among those shouting encouragement to the leaders, ready to fight, perhaps with young John next to him in the press of bodies filling the street.

With his usual oratorical skills and flowery rhetoric, Meagher later described the scene in Carrick that he saw from the window of the meeting room:

> A torrent of human beings, rushing through lanes and narrow streets; surging and boiling against the white basements that hemmed it in; whirling in dizzy circles, and tossing up its dark waves, with sounds of wrath, vengeance, and defiance;… wild, half-stifled, passionate, frantic prayers of hope; invocations in sobs, and thrilling wailings, and piercing cries to the God of heaven, His Saints, and the Virgin Mary; challenges to the foe; curses on the Red Flag; scornful, exulting, delirious defiance of Death… It was the *revolution* [emphasis in the original], if we had accepted it. Why it was not accepted, I fear, I cannot with sufficient accuracy explain.

No sadder commentary can be made on the indecisive nature of these leaders who had so stirred up the people to strike against their oppressors and then failed to act with resolve when the moment had clearly arrived.

IN CONTRAST TO THE LEADERS' reluctance to seize the opportunity at hand, O'Mahony left the meeting "for the distinct purpose of mustering the country clubs." Three times he was already in the saddle when he heard a noisy discussion spring up behind him. Three times he dismounted and returned to the meeting room to make sure that they were not changing their minds, only to be answered each time "in the negative." Father Byrne was not present at the meeting, but O'Mahony suspected that he had instructed the Central Board to avoid action. He now saw the club presidents, despite their earlier resolve to fight, creeping out of the picture. In his own words, "Some of them I know to have left the meeting that evening after I departed and never drew bridle until they put the sea between themselves and the enemy."

Finally satisfied that the leaders of the Young Irelanders would stay in Carrick under the protection of the clubs, O'Mahony rode off "to muster the country clubs from the Tipperary side of the Suir." He visited some clubs in the area, sent messengers to the presidents of those "too distant from me to see personally," and visited the "chief men of my own club." He found "enthusiasm and confidence" everywhere and took time for an evening meal before meeting his own men at the parish chapel at seven o'clock.

Ready to lead these forces to Carrick, he was met at the gate of his farm at Mullagh by a messenger from Doctor O'Ryan, head of the Central Board, saying "those for whose protection we were to meet had left Carrick" for Cashel and that he should not bring his men into town. Left in an "embarrassing position" with not only his own club, but also those others that he had called out, O'Mahony found that his men at the chapel had already been told to disperse by their parish priest, Father Morrissy. Four hundred men had gathered with "eighty guns and a goodly muster of pikes," all armed with some weapon, if only a farm tool or club. To prevent them from losing heart for the struggle, O'Mahony concocted a fortnight's delay in the rising, drilled the men until late at night, and dismissed them with the caution that they might be called out again the next day.

After visiting a friend, O'Mahony was headed home about twelve o'clock when he heard some firing and rode towards it. The Grangemockler men had responded to his summons and were headed for Carrick under Mr. Coughlan, their president, "at least one thousand strong." They had refused to believe the messenger sent by the Central Board and O'Mahony "had the disagreeable task of confirming the command they received." He "saw them home" and tried to keep up their spirits for the fight. It was daybreak before O'Mahony returned home, only to deal with a series of club leaders arriving from the more distant parishes to demand an explanation for the orders and the countermanding instructions that they had received when they were already on the march.

O'Mahony calculated that the scope of the response had been more than adequate for action then and there. He later wrote:

> From the reports I then, and afterwards got, of the numbers collected on
> the different roads radiating round Carrick, and comparing them with

what I saw myself of the two parishes mustered on the road that passed by my place, I have no doubt in my mind that between seven and eight o'clock on that night there were twelve thousand men, at least, (I made it at fifteen thousand) on [the] march for Carrick-on-Suir. Enough, surely, to commence the Revolution with—at short notice.

At dawn, Doheny arrived at his house and they rode around the area for some twenty miles, finding the people still preparing for battle. "Scarcely a house did we see that there was not a pike displayed; everywhere men were fitting them on handles, or sharpening them on the door flags [i.e. flagstones]." The pair encouraged the people to hold themselves ready for action: "but one man spoke against the rising, and he was soon silenced."

Upon their return to O'Mahony's house, they found Meagher waiting to tell them that O'Brien had gone to Cashel and he was himself on the way to Waterford to bring out his club, "some one thousand strong." O'Mahony was asked to collect what forces he could muster to help Meagher's men cross the Suir. The two Tipperary chiefs accompanied Meagher through Carrick Beg to Coolnamuck on the Waterford side of the river, where Meagher took a carriage to the city and Doheny left for Cashel. O'Mahony rode back into Carrick seeking either Father Byrne or Doctor O'Ryan. The doctor explained that all the local leaders, including Father Byrne and himself, were against the uprising as premature. Father Byrne thought O'Brien "must be mad" and that action had to wait at least a fortnight, until the harvest ripened. O'Mahony then checked in with the club leaders at the next level down and "met many of the mechanics" who were ready and eager for the call. (These "mechanics" were the artisans and skilled workers such as coopers, like Thomas Lonergan.) They told him "not to mind presidents or priests," but to come to them directly.

The day was spent preparing to assist the Waterford men in crossing the Suir with Meagher at their head. Instead of leading the expected column of armed rebels, Meagher returned to Carrick later in the day from his native city—alone. The chief men of his club had refused to act without the advice and consent of Father Tracy, who acted as "the Byrne of Waterford" in O'Mahony's words, controlling the clubs without presiding over any himself.

O'Mahony found the behavior of these priests inexcusable since they had fostered the organization of the clubs and then prevented them from being employed at the crucial moment. He attributed it to deliberate meddling in politics by the Church, which had never approved of the Young Irelanders in the same way that it had supported the Repeal movement. Meagher later rejected the idea that the priests had "betrayed" the movement since the priests as a group were, in his words, "actively and determinedly opposed to us" from the beginning.

Still ready to fight, O'Mahony proposed to Meagher that the two of them take charge locally. He would operate on the Tipperary side and Meagher would raise the countryside across the river in Waterford, each on their home ground. Meagher "declined to assume any independent command whatsoever" despite assurances that "the men of his native county would follow him enthusiastically." He preferred "to join O'Brien and share his fortunes—gloomy and disheartening as he felt them to be" and set off to find him in Cashel. Other supporters were also trying to find their leader while O'Brien moved from town to town in the hills raising hopes, if not forces. Each patriotic speech by O'Brien was met with enthusiasm from the downtrodden people, but this was soon dampened by the intervention of local priests, who discouraged any action.

By Wednesday, July 26, O'Brien and Dillon had been joined in the village of Mullinahone by Pat Smyth, Pat O'Donoghue, and Devin Reilly from Dublin. James Stephens, a twenty-five-year-old from Kilkenny employed by the railroad and not even a member of the Confederates, also reported for duty armed and ready to fight. After O'Brien's usual speeches, well-received by a crowd of several thousand that included the local police, the group spent the night in Mullinahone and awoke to find half of the previous day's audience had disappeared. Realizing that it was time for some tangible action to demonstrate his resolve, O'Brien entered the police station with Stephens and one other man to demand that the head constable and his five men surrender their arms to him. The head constable declined to surrender to such a small force, saying it would cost him his job and asking how then would he feed his family. Always too kind-hearted for the realities of revolution, O'Brien agreed to bring thirty men to meet the constable's requirement. While he was forming up the larger group, the police slipped out the unguarded back of the station and escaped with the arms and honor of the constabulary intact.

CHAPTER FIVE – AWAKENED

Anxious to take part in the action, MacManus had returned from his mission of raising support among the numerous Irish in Liverpool. He caught up with the group in Ballingary the next day as they entered a coal mining district in the hills of Slieveardagh. O'Brien climbed on to the chapel wall in the village to ask the people gathered there to protect him until the harvest came in, to respect property, and to join his group only if they could bring three days' provisions. O'Brien had on occasion paid for rations out of his own pocket, but his idea that a starving population could supply food for the rebels was far from realistic. Ever the cautious landlord, he insisted that there be no requisitioning of private property to support the rising. On Friday a troop of cavalry approached the travelers at the crossroads town of Killenaule west of Ballingary. Barricades were hastily erected on the main street under the direction of Dillon, Stephens, and O'Donoghue. When Captain Longmore brought his troopers right up to the first barricade, Stephens aimed his rifle at him. The captain asked permission of Dillon to pass through the town and the rebel refused to allow it, drawing wild cheers from the crowd that had assembled. O'Brien, however, agreed to let them go through if they promised not to arrest anyone and another opportunity for a tactical victory slipped away as the cavalry rode through unmolested.

Later that day, the wandering group was joined by Meagher, Reilly, Doheny, and O'Mahony. A council of war was held that evening in a public house to decide on further action. Doheny pressed for real revolutionary measures such as confiscation of landed property and "directing the people to live at the expense of the enemy." O'Brien, a member of the propertied class that such a policy would attack, still pursued the mirage of a bloodless revolt. Right to the end, he acted more in the spirit of the reformer O'Connell than the revolutionary John Mitchel, dooming the rebellion with his faint-hearted sensibilities.

O'Brien had already sent Pat Smyth back to lead the Dublin Clubs into action after they received word that the uprising was under way in the south. He then dispatched his other loyal lieutenants to continue to inspire the countryside and to monitor activity at the garrisons in the area. Meagher would return to Waterford where the rank and file of his club were still waiting, impatient to be led into the fray. Doheny was to keep an eye on Clonmel's sizable British garrison, while Reilly tried to rouse Kilkenny. O'Mahony had already demonstrated the readiness of his forces in the Carrick area to fight,

O'Gorman was working to bring out the people in Limerick, and McGee, who had left Glasgow, was active in the West. One bold stroke by O'Brien might still counter the efforts of the priests to calm the countryside and thus bring about a general uprising before the British could complete any redeployment of forces into the area.

THE FINAL OPPORTUNITY CAME on Saturday, July 29, when O'Brien took his group back to Ballingary, where he thought some miners were ready to fight. MacManus had ridden ahead and was reviewing the local forces, perhaps twenty men with guns and the same number carrying pikes, when word came of an advancing police column. John Kavanagh, member of a Dublin club, had come south through Kilkenny, where rumors had said the town of Callan was in rebel hands and O'Brien at the head of 20,000 men. Kavanagh reported seeing a column of police on the road, headed toward Ballingary. In fact, forty-six men of the constabulary from the supposedly rebel-held town of Callan arrived soon thereafter under the command of one Sub-Inspector Trant. Information was received of an even larger body of men approaching from Thurles and this brought about the decision to defend Ballingary. The rebels hastily erected a barricade on the main road and their meager forces armed with guns deployed behind slagheaps, while those men with only pikes and stones as weapons hid in the ditches.

The police formed a line of battle about 600 yards from the barricade and advanced to within one hundred yards of the obstacle when they suddenly turned to the right up a laneway off the road. The rebels pursued them to find that the constables had occupied a solid two-story house surrounded by a stone wall on the Boulagh Common at Farranrory. As the rebels spread out around the stone wall, neighbors informed them that the lady of the house, Mrs. McCormack, was away and had left her five children, all under ten years of age, at home. When she returned home to find her windows barricaded and half a dozen carbine barrels protruding from each, she appealed to O'Brien to save her home and children.

Accompanied by MacManus and two others, O'Brien escorted the widow through her cabbage patch to seek the children. He called out to the policemen to give up their arms, assuring them of no harm since they were all Irishmen. Some police reached out the windows to shake O'Brien's hand, but they refused to surrender or give up their arms and O'Brien gave them some time to reconsider. Reports vary on whether stones were then thrown at the house or even shots fired, but they agree that the police opened fire while O'Brien was about three yards from the house and the other rebel emissaries about seven yards away. The two men with MacManus dropped, one dead and the other wounded. MacManus fired to cover his retreat from the house with O'Brien and the howling widow. The well-disciplined police kept up a steady fire and Kavanagh fell with a serious wound. Outgunned and unable to dislodge the police, the rebel forces began to melt away. MacManus made an effort to smoke out the police, but saw that it was futile and led O'Brien away. Supposedly the two were the last men off the field.

Encountering a mounted policeman at the bottom of the hill, MacManus took his horse at gunpoint and placed O'Brien in the saddle to get him back to the village where he had left his rented carriage. Parting with O'Brien, MacManus went to locate the carriage in Ballingary. Upon returning, he found that O'Brien had already fled the village to avoid capture by a new force of one hundred police that had just arrived. When MacManus learned that Stephens—one of the few stalwart fighters—had been wounded, he rode off toward the shelter of Slievenamon.

Widow McCormick's House

The British press sneered at the fighting as the "Skirmish in Widow McCormack's Cabbage Patch" and the entire uprising in fact did show an almost comic-opera incompetence in the leadership. However, it also reflected the seething discontent of the Irish, who were barely surviving as a people under the crushing weight of British rule. Even though badly organized, the rising still shook the British government more than they cared to have the public realize; mocking the action at Ballingary served their purpose by downplaying its serious nature.

WITH CONDITIONS SO RIPE for revolution, how did the Young Irelanders manage to fail completely in their attempt at an armed uprising? Their own later reflections did not reach unanimous conclusions and certainly a number of factors must be considered. Broad support of the movement existed within the Confederate Clubs, but key elements of the society were not represented in them. The goals of the organization were seen as a threat by entrenched and powerful landowners. The revolutionary Young Irelanders also never gained the trust and support of the Catholic Church as O'Connell had done earlier for Repeal, when he won the Catholic hierarchy over with legitimate activities. Meagher wrote afterward that if even one out of twenty of the parish priests had responded to a general "call to arms," the vast majority of their flocks would have followed them, despite the disapproval of the other nineteen. Ulster remained outside the movement, as did most Protestants in the other three provinces. O'Brien himself represented the major exception in terms of both religion and wealth.

The resolve of the leadership is a key factor in any successful revolt and here the deficiencies are painfully obvious. Despite O'Brien's ability to inspire his followers with his personal courage and his status as a descendant of Brian Boru, he lacked the iron will needed to carry out a revolution. Patrick O'Donoghue, arrested for taking part in the fighting at Ballingary, wrote years later in prison, "A vicious man with the talents and prestige of O'Brien's name would have overthrown English dominion in Ireland." Meagher could orate with great eloquence, but he had neither the natural military ability nor the self-confidence to take the initiative, even when offered the chance. Mitchel, clearly the most ruthless of the rebel leaders, was confined to a prison hulk (a ship no longer seaworthy, used to hold prisoners) in Bermuda when he was most needed in Tipperary. Only a few men in the 1848 uprising showed determination, organizational skills, and a realistic understanding of the circumstances. Two of these outstanding fighters were O'Mahony and Stephens, the founders of the next revolutionary movement.

By the time the uprising was attempted, disease and starvation had ravaged the countryside for several years. Huge numbers of potential supporters had died or had left the country and many of those who remained were in a weakened condition, ill-fed, and essentially unarmed. Rage against injustice might give a starving man the strength to shove a pike into a soldier's belly, but no amount of anger could extend the weapon's reach to that of a musket. Still, O'Mahony's success in raising thousands of men in the Carrick region alone proved that many patriots, likely including Thomas Lonergan, retained sufficient health and determination to take up arms for the cause. (The heritage museum in Carrick displays two pike heads, clearly made in local forges, found hidden in the walls when houses were pulled down on Sir John's Road many years later.) Certainly the Lonergans, father and son, carried this dedication to Irish freedom with them to America for the next phase of the struggle.

Clonmel Court House

CHAPTER SIX

EXILED

Like every other aspect of this impromptu adventure, the rebels had no plan that would have helped them exploit a victory or cope with a defeat at Ballingary, so they all took to their heels independently. In the immediate aftermath of the skirmish—O'Brien himself called it an "escapade" that did not "deserve the name of insurrection"—police and troops moved into the area to restore order. The government forces had suffered no casualties and only a few rebels were killed or wounded in the fighting. Many local participants were arrested, but the leaders of the Young Irelanders all slipped through the net. In contrast to the consequences of the more serious unrest of 1798, widespread reprisals and executions were not added to the misery of the countryside. Even so, "whole families were left mourning and desolate, for many died in captivity and exile, others perished from long concealment in bogs and mountains." Isolated incidents of violence had also occurred in the west and southwest of the country. As word of the rout at Ballingary spread, the rebels elsewhere understood that there was no general uprising for their local efforts to support. The government had only to capture the leaders to put an end to the matter.

The British placed a price on the heads of the main instigators of the uprising, yet, despite the hardships of the times, not one was betrayed for the reward. The country folk gave shelter to the fugitives, who moved from place to place with only a vague destination in mind. O'Brien had been on the run for a week when he unwisely tried to return home to Limerick by rail on August 5 and was arrested at the Thurles station.* To prevent any attempt

---

* The story was told that O'Brien had approached an old woman selling apples at the station, offering her the chance to collect the reward for his capture. She had indignantly refused to sell out this Irish hero, even for the fortune of £500 on his head. He was arrested by a railway guard named Hulme and turned over first to the police, then to the military. Hulme did collect the reward, but was subjected to such scorn that he had to move away and change his name.

at a rescue, O'Brien was rushed out of the disaffected region on a train to Dublin on August 7.

O'Donoghue, fleeing Ballingary on horseback, had encountered Meagher coming back from Waterford, again without his club men. Joined by Leyne, the three set out through the mountains for Limerick where they hoped to make contact with O'Gorman. Recognized and given hospitality in the hills and glens, they avoided the army patrols and police checkpoints until August 12. The three were taken by cart into Thurles and quickly sent by rail to join O'Brien in Kilmainham jail.

Meanwhile, MacManus wandered the same hills looking for Meagher, once encountering a group of a thousand potential rebels armed only with some pikes and stones. Signal fires that he lit on mountain peaks were often answered by blazes from surrounding hills, each beacon an isolated groping in the dark for leadership. MacManus eventually made it to Cork city, where he was hidden by comrades. On September 7, he was in his cabin on an American ship about to sail for New York when the police, in a final search of the vessel, identified and arrested him.*

Other prominent rebels, including Stephens, O'Gorman, Dillon, Reilly, and Smyth, were more fortunate and managed to leave the country, mingling with the hordes of emigrants abandoning Ireland. Cavanagh and his two companions from Dublin went to ground in New Ross and Cappoquin, slipping away within a year for America. Edward Hollywood, down from Dublin looking for Meagher, searched in vain in Waterford, Carrick, and Cashel before escaping to France. This country, the old ally of Irish independence, also provided refuge for other rebels, who fled to Paris by various paths.**

Even after the leaders had scattered and many had been captured, O'Mahony and Doheny kept up the good fight around Carrick and Cashel. Each man operated in his home district in Tipperary to continue the armed

---

* Years later, the funeral of this hero of Ballingary would become a rallying point for revived Irish nationalism in America and Ireland.

** The *Kilkenny Moderator* had reported the death of Stephens from a gunshot wound received at Ballingary, lamenting the fate of the young man while holding him up as a warning to others. His burial was reportedly well attended in his home town. Several months later a rival newspaper announced that Stephens had written from Paris to a friend in Tipperary. The false report of his death had allowed him to escape via Bristol and London. Stephens had eventually joined Doheny, also hiding in England, for several weeks before they both made it to France.

struggle for a while longer. O'Mahony had been joined by John Savage and other survivors of Ballingary who had still not lost heart. Some Irish soldiers even deserted from the army and added to the forces that O'Mahony assembled in the hills around Carrick. Doheny soon despaired of the effort and wrote the government on August 12 to offer his surrender. He proposed giving up in exchange for a promise that other rebels would be allowed to leave the country, but no agreement was reached. Doheny continued cooperation with O'Mahony into the autumn, when he finally abandoned the uprising and fled Ireland.

Understandably, no lists of those participating in these treasonable activities are known to have been preserved by the clubs. O'Mahony was likely accompanied by some Carrick area club members when he went to Ballingary, but unless they were arrested no records have been found that would identify them. No evidence can be produced that Thomas Lonergan was involved in the skirmish there or in any of the later actions.

However, O'Mahony's return to the Carrick area would have given Thomas Lonergan the chance to join in local operations. The strong nationalist attitude of Thomas, as demonstrated by John's subsequent commitment to the cause, suggests that he would have supported the effort in whatever manner he could. Since Thomas was not arrested for any rebellious acts before he left the country, no court records exist to confirm his probable connection with O'Mahony. However, events afterward in America strongly indicate that such a connection did in fact exist in 1848.

Cavanagh later wrote glowingly of O'Mahony, favorably contrasting this effective, yet little known, local chieftain with the national reputation enjoyed by the distinguished politicians, eloquent orators, and brilliant writers of the movement. While O'Mahony fought on, the better known leaders were either hunted fugitives or imprisoned. At O'Mahony's call, the people "organized silently, armed themselves with such rude weapons as their way-side forges could supply, and depending on the neighboring farmers for provisions, abandoned home and family, and took to the hill-sides to prove their devotion to Liberty and Ireland." Taking advantage of their intimate familiarity with the Slievenamon area and the Comeragh hills across the Suir, these rebels stayed in the field for weeks after the Ballingary "escapade."

The end of August brought the long-awaited harvest, but no improvement in the desperate situation of the people, as food shipments out of the hard-pressed country continued. At this time, the authorities reported a "riotous assembly" at O'Mahony's farm in Mullagh, the settlement a few miles out Sir John's Road from Carrick. Since the farm's owner was "out" among the hills and unable to tend to his crops, his neighbors had gathered to harvest all his grain in a single day. Such a communal action served both to taunt the British and to show the district's respect for O'Mahony. A ballad was even written about "The Reaping of Mullagh," spreading the story in song.

The Lonergans were a family of coopers, not farmers, yet it is reasonable to suppose that they joined with their neighbors to lend a hand with the harvest in O'Mahony's fields. Since the Lonergans lived just down the road from the Mullagh farm, a sturdy lad like John could easily have done his bit to show the family's loyalty to the rebel chief. John's father may have been among those who had "abandoned home and family," hiding in the hills with O'Mahony, even though Mary Lonergan was heavy with child at the time and gave birth to her third son a few weeks after the harvest.

WHAT PURPOSE COULD BE SERVED in maintaining a small force of rebels in the area after the nation-wide effort had collapsed? As a lawyer, Doheny would have known that the "guests of the state" held in Kilmainham would be tried in a court where the offences took place. Since arms had been taken up against the Queen in Ballingary, County Tipperary, the trial would be held in Clonmel.

A strongpoint of British rule in the area, this walled town was always well garrisoned and additional troops were brought in to increase security for the trial. Doheny and O'Mahony kept the hope alive that the imprisoned leaders might be rescued once they were brought within reach. This idea was daring, perhaps recklessly romantic, but totally in character for these men and their devotion to the cause. John O'Leary later explained, "We meant to collect such men as we could gather in and about Clonmel, and expected to be joined by a much larger body of men from in and about Carrick and the adjacent parts of the county Waterford." This attempt at organizing the raid ended badly for O'Leary when, at the age of eighteen, he was captured with other plotters outside the town and thrown in the Clonmel jail himself.

While the groups planning the rescue awaited their chance, they carried out assaults on isolated police stations. These actions served as practical training for the men, weeded out any of the faint-hearted, and, with luck, provided the rebels with additional arms. The only way to obtain guns at this point was to take them from the enemy and the small constabulary stations presented the best opportunity. However, these solid station houses were built with defense in mind and could easily be held by disciplined police, even against greater numbers of attackers, who were usually poorly armed.

Around mid-September a series of raids took place under the leadership of O'Mahony and Phillip Gray, a railway clerk from Dublin. At Rathgormack on the eastern slope of the Comeraghs, a large force attacked the police barrack. This was followed by the capture of the station at the Aheny slate quarries north of Carrick. The Glenbower police station was well sited for control of the mouth of the deep and narrow valley through which the road ran south from Callan, forking there for Carrick and Clonmel. A determined attack here cost several rebel lives without gaining control of this important choke point for the movement of troops. The police also beat back an effort to seize the Portlaw station halfway between Carrick and Waterford.

THE FIVE STATE PRISONERS were brought down from Dublin to Thurles by rail on September 18, 1848, to stand trial in Clonmel before a Special Commission. They were charged with several counts of high treason; the court proceedings were set to begin three days later. The prisoners were allowed to furnish the rooms in which they were kept and could comfortably receive visitors, including family. Relatives of O'Brien attended the trial, but Meagher's father did not travel up the Suir from Waterford. He did provide his son with funds for a good lawyer, who also represented the less affluent O'Donoghue.

O'Brien's case was the first to be heard and began September 28 before a carefully selected jury. Cavanagh commented that the jurors all came from the English establishment that the uprising threatened, "Not a Milesian [Celtic] name on the list—all of the Cromwellian stock." The "farce of a trial" took nine days, though Cavanagh remarked that they "needed not *nine minutes* to make up their minds for a conviction." On October 8, the third day after the guilty verdict was returned, O'Brien was asked if he had anything to say as to why sentence should not be passed on him. In the tradition of Emmet and other martyrs, he gave a dignified speech from the dock:

My lords, it is not my intention to enter into any vindication of my conduct, however much I might have desired to avail myself of this opportunity of doing so. I am perfectly satisfied with the consciousness that I have performed my duty to my country; that I have done only that which, in my opinion, it was the duty of every Irishman to have done; and I am prepared to abide the consequences of having performed my duty to my native land. Proceed with your sentence.

Chief Justice Blackburne then put on his black cap and pronounced the sentence in the customary formula:

> The Sentence is that You, William Smith O'Brien, be taken from hence to the place from whence you came, and be thence Drawn on a Hurdle to the Place of Execution, and be there Hanged by the Neck until you are Dead; and that afterwards your Head shall be Severed from Your body, and Your Body Divided into Four Quarters, to be disposed of as Her Majesty shall think fit, and may God have mercy on your soul.

Earlier in Queen Victoria's reign, she had given up the tradition of disemboweling traitors while they were still alive and burning their entrails in front of them. Perhaps the monarch felt that the remaining measures—hanging, beheading, and quartering—were sufficient to prevent any repetition of treason.

Immediately after sentence was passed on O'Brien, MacManus was tried and predictably found guilty. O'Donoghue then faced a jury of "ultra-loyal Protestants" with the same outcome. Leyne was not brought to trial, either due to lack of evidence or because he was not a prominent figure in the rebellion. Sentencing of MacManus and O'Donoghue was deferred to a later date.

The Clonmel Courthouse was "crowded to its utmost capacity" when Meagher was tried on October 16 before another carefully selected jury. Knowing the outcome of the trial was predetermined, he nonetheless entered a plea of "not guilty." He then made a perfunctory objection to the fact that the jury list of three hundred names included only eighteen Roman Catholics. Charged with "levying war against the Queen" and "compassing the death of the Queen" despite his absence from Ballingary, Meagher was subjected to the same fiction of a fair trial and found guilty, although mercy was recommended because of his youth.

CHAPTER SIX - EXILED

On October 23, all three newly-convicted men were given a chance to speak before sentence was passed. His two comrades spoke only briefly, but Meagher took advantage of this last opportunity for an oration. Rather than pleading for his life in his address from the dock, Meagher expressed no regrets for what he had done and retracted nothing he had ever said. Although he addressed the court, his message was aimed at the Irish people and said in part:

> My lords, you may deem this language unbecoming in me, and perhaps it will seal my fate. But I am here to speak the truth whatever it may cost. I am here to regret nothing I have ever done—to retract nothing I have ever said, I am here to crave with no lying lip, the life I consecrate to the liberty of my country. Far from it; even here—here, where the thief, the libertine, the murderer, have left their foot-prints in the dust; here, on this spot, where the shadows of death surround me, and from which I see my early grave in an unanointed soil open to receive me— even here, encircled by these terrors, the hope which has beckoned me to the perilous sea upon which I have been wrecked, still consoles, animates, enraptures me.
>
> No, I do not despair of my poor old country, her peace, her liberty, her glory. For that country I can do no more than bid her hope. To lift this island up—to make her a benefactor to humanity, instead of being the meanest [poorest] beggar in the world—to restore to her her native powers and her ancient constitution—this has been my ambition, and this ambition has been my crime. Judged by the law of England, I know this crime entails the penalty of death; but the history of Ireland explains this crime, and justifies it. Judged by that history, I am no criminal—you (addressing Mr. MacManus) and you (addressing Mr. O'Donoghue) are no criminals. I deserve no punishment—we deserve no punishment. Judged by that history, the treason of which I stand convicted loses all its guilt, is sanctified as a duty, will be ennobled as a sacrifice.
>
> [Parentheses in original]

Meagher then "bid farewell to the country of my birth, my passion, and my death" and called on the court to pass their sentence. He closed his speech with the caution that "many judgments of this world" would be reversed when they stood before a higher tribunal where "a Judge of infinite goodness, as well as justice, will preside."

All three were then sentenced to death by execution in the same thorough manner specified for O'Brien. The condemned men were returned to their cells in the Clonmel jail "to await their doom as became the representative men of their brave old race." No rescue came from the rebels holding out in the hills as the prisoners sat contemplating their impending executions. Much attention had been drawn to the trials in the press and with "the gaze of the civilized world concentrated upon her" Queen Victoria "graciously" ordered the death sentence to be "mitigated to transportation for life." On October 26, the prisoners were given "official notification of Her Majesty's pleasure" that their lives were to be spared. The reprieve came only after Meagher, MacManus, and O'Donoghue had spent three days and O'Brien over two weeks expecting a grisly death. All four prisoners were returned to Dublin's Kilmainham jail on November 16 to await their exile. The removal of the prisoners from Clonmel jail at three o'clock in the morning, in the darkness of mid-November, put them far beyond the reach of any rescue attempt.

With no prospects for the situation improving and winter closing in on the mountains, the time had come for those rebels still at large in Ireland to save themselves for the future struggle. Doheny and O'Mahony, the last of the leaders holding out, had operated together on Slievenamon into September. Now they too laid down their arms and escaped the country. O'Mahony, according to one source, hid out for a while in a small cave near his home and then made his way to the southern coast at Dungarvan. From there he is said to have sailed on a "ship skippered by a brother-in-law of Fr. Byrne of Carrick" to Newport in Wales. He eventually reached sanctuary in France.

Even with their leaders in prison or in exile, groups here and there still held themselves ready for the call to rise up. Many of those rebels who could escape, however, followed the example of their captains by leaving Ireland. In their close-knit communities, they had no hope of concealing their participation in or sympathy for the nationalist movement, such as membership in the Confederate Clubs. Support of the nationalist movement by Thomas Lonergan would no doubt have been widely known among his neighbors and perhaps to the local authorities, as well. Under the circumstances, his best course led away from homeland and relatives, as difficult as that might be.

POLITICAL REFUGEES COULD SAFELY lose themselves among the tens of thousands still emigrating to escape economic hardships. Because little documentation was required or expected from the largely illiterate Irish, passage could easily be booked under an assumed name and someone could likely be found to vouch for an identity, even a false one. The British government appears not to have hindered rank and file rebels from leaving; after all, it saved the cost of a trial and transportation to the penal colonies.

The emigrants held no illusions about the finality of the step they were taking. It was common practice to hold what was generally called an "American wake" for those leaving; since very few emigrants would ever return to Ireland, only in the afterlife could those departing be sure of rejoining loved ones who stayed behind. In Tipperary these gatherings were called a "live wake" and no doubt the Lonergans were seen off by their friends and relatives in such manner.

It must have been especially painful to leave children behind, as the Lonergans did, while the rest of the family left Ireland forever. At the time, one or two members of an Irish family often traveled abroad in hopes of earning enough money to bring the rest of the family over at some later date. From United States census records of 1850, it appears certain that only Thomas and Mary with sons John and the infant Thomas came to North America together. The other children would have been placed with relatives, friends, or employers until they could eventually rejoin their immediate family.*

For whatever combination of economic and political reasons, Thomas Lonergan and part of his family disappeared from Carrick along with many others.** Whether or not Thomas had himself gone out with the rebels, he most likely had not decided to leave before the debacle of the 1848 rising. As a cooper, Lonergan's economic situation in the autumn of that year may not have been so desperate as to force the family to emigrate. The motivation for departing Ireland could have been more political or emotional—based on fear of prosecution, a refusal to remain under British rule, or a persuasive blending of the two.

The last scrap of documentation for the presence of this Lonergan family

---

*Although some of the other children, including Edmund, did later emigrate to Vermont, it is not certain that all of them did.

** The Carrick area suffered a disproportionate loss in population to death and emigration in this period. Barely five thousand souls were counted in the 1851 census, a reduction of nearly half from the previous survey. Overall, Ireland lost about a quarter of its population during the famine years. The two-fold rate of loss in the bountiful "golden vale" may have been a direct consequence of the widespread involvement of the area's residents in the uprising of 1848.

in Ireland is the baptismal record of their son Thomas, dated September 25, 1848. His sponsors at St. Nicholas' Church on the occasion were listed as Michael Nowlan (the maiden name of the baby's mother was spelled both Nolan and Nowlan in various documents) and Mary Walsh, a common surname in the area. Baptism usually took place soon after birth and this was presumably the case with the infant Thomas, born in the shortening days of autumn. It is at least possible that neither the mother nor the new-born child would have been strong enough for the ordeal of a trans-Atlantic crossing before winter arrived. In addition to this consideration, several other factors might well have delayed the departure of the family for some months.

ARRANGEMENTS HAD TO BE MADE for the passage itself and the funds acquired for the tickets. The Lonergans did not rent valuable agricultural land, so there was no landlord who, as was sometimes the case, provided passage money in order to clear the tenants from his land.* Emigrants typically sold off what possessions they could not take with them or borrowed money from friends and relatives who could spare it. The amount of cash that the Lonergans could quickly scrape together for their trip was probably very limited.

Fares on British ships sailing to other parts of the empire were significantly lower than those on American vessels crossing the Atlantic.** Each country restricted access to their ports, favoring ships under their own flag. This variation in cost was also due to different regulations under the Passenger Acts passed by the British and American governments. The U.S. allowance

---

* Many landlords cleared their estates in Ireland of unprofitable tenants by paying the fare and chartering the ships. Traveling as a group, these exiles at least had some familiar faces to accompany them to their new homeland, where they often settled together and reestablished their old communities. The subsidized fares required a pledge to settle north of the U.S. border, but few Irish felt bound by this promise. A great many of them who landed in the ports of British North America continued on to the United States at their first opportunity.

** The cost for a crossing increased in the initial famine period until the demand brought additional ships into the trade. At first any vessel that might survive the trip sailed from the ports, including Dublin, Donegal, Sligo, Galway, Limerick, Waterford, Westford, New Ross, Belfast, Londonderry, Tralee, Drogheda, Newry, Kilrush, Westport, and Youghal, directly to America. In the six worst years of the famine, some 5,000 ships carried emigrants away from Ireland. Initially the relief ships bringing food to the starving were pressed into service to transport passengers on the return voyage. By the late 1840s, American packets built specifically for the emigrant trade were carrying more than 400 at a time, some in private cabins, on faster and more comfortable trips.

CHAPTER SIX — EXILED

was for two passengers per five tons registered weight, while the British ships could carry an additional person at three passengers per five tons.

Typical fares per person in 1848 were two and a half to three pounds (about $10 to $15 in US currency) to Quebec and New Brunswick. Subsidized government fares of two pounds and less were intended to encourage a simultaneous reduction in the number of land-starved peasants in Ireland and an increase in the sparse population of the empire's enormous territory in North America. These favorable rates are further evidence that the Lonergans probably sailed for the British provinces, rather than the United States. (At the time of the famine, Canada did not exist as a country, although the provinces of Quebec and Ontario were commonly known as Lower and Upper Canada.)

The fare was supposed to include a minimum ration of food, set the first year of the famine at seven pounds of basic bread, biscuit, oatmeal, potatoes, etc. per passenger each week. Any additional food was to be brought aboard by the travelers. This standard was later changed to increase the amounts and expand the menu, but it was impossible to enforce and the supply of food and water remained questionable for many voyages.

While a passenger list was required for every voyage of each vessel, such surviving records are incomplete. No information has been found on the travel of the Lonergan parents and their two sons—when they left, on which ship, their port of departure, or where they landed—nor any documentation of the later travel of John's siblings to Vermont. The possibility that the parents used a different name for their trip adds to the difficulty in finding such records. Thomas might have concealed his identity to avoid any difficulties with British authorities resulting from the events of 1848.

The most direct route for the Lonergan's trip would have taken the parents and their two children by barge or boat down the Suir from Carrick to Waterford harbor. The pugnacious boatmen of Carrick had been vocal supporters of the uprising and were probably willing to help transport rebels fleeing the country. Waterford was home port at this time to nearly 250 ships and some forty different vessels sailed directly to North America from there during the Famine. In one week in 1846, ten ships left for Canada. While that pace slowed the next year to about three ships a week during the summer, in 1848 it increased again. The rapid development of steam navigation soon made it more economical to transfer passengers from southern Ireland to

Liverpool for travel across the Atlantic by steamer, rather than sailing vessel.

The Lonergans would have planned on a voyage that would last from six to eight weeks, depending largely on the weather in the sailing season. A winter crossing of the North Atlantic brought additional terrors to the usual weeks of misery. In the north, many ports on the Atlantic coast were often inaccessible during the winter because of ice. Some larger Canadian ports and the major access route of the St. Lawrence River might be frozen over for months. Leaving too early in the spring would risk the possibility of ice still blocking the northern ports and sailing too late in the summer brought the likelihood of storms.

Even when the ports were open, storms at sea could add days or weeks to the trip, and damage to a ship on occasion forced a return to Ireland for repairs. Any delay en route caused not only more discomfort on the crowded ships, but also the growing threat that the provisions would not hold out or that disease would empty many berths below decks.

Disease was a very real threat. Typhus, called "ship fever," was the main killer; the cramped and unsanitary conditions were ideal for its spread by the feces of lice and fleas. Even before the emigrants boarded their ships, they were often exposed to disease in the shabby boarding houses of the ports where they assembled for the voyage. Some effort was made to prevent those visibly ill from boarding, but no family would want to abandon a member and might conceal any disease so that everyone could make the trip together. Once at sea, there was no space to isolate a sick person. The standard berth was six feet in length, with each adult allocated a width of twenty inches (later expanded to twenty-four inches). In such close quarters, a highly contagious disease or one spread by parasites could infect practically everyone on board. The situation for most emigrants would have been a lot like facing the famine and pestilence back in Ireland, but with no privacy even for the dying, and with the added possibility of drowning.

The primitive medical care available and the weakened condition of many passengers combined to produce high mortality rates. Of the estimated 100,000 Irish who left for Canada, not always voluntarily, in 1847 perhaps 30,000 were struck down by typhus and only a third of them survived. Over 5,000 were given a burial at sea.

Considering the health of Mary and the infant Thomas, the Lonergan family may well have set out to sea in the early summer of 1849, about the same time as

CHAPTER SIX – EXILED

the Young Ireland leaders began their own voyage into exile. Since no passenger list has been discovered showing the Lonergan family's travel, their itinerary can only be surmised by working backward from their arrival in Vermont, probably in the last half of 1849. The most likely hypothesis is that they sailed from Waterford to Canada in the warmer months of that year and then made their way south to the United States, after the obligatory stop at a quarantine station.

ALL THE MAJOR ATLANTIC PORTS established quarantine islands to protect their residents from the influx of immigrants carrying disease, with varying degrees of success in avoiding fatal contagion. Strict health regulations were imposed, but enforcement was difficult in many cases. A large percentage of the Irish emigrants entering Canada made Montreal their intermediate or final destination. If the Lonergans traveled that busy route, the family was almost certainly subjected to a stay at the quarantine station some twenty-five miles downstream from Quebec City.

The Grosse Île station had been established in 1832 on an isolated small island in the wide St. Lawrence, in response to the appearance of Asiatic cholera in Great Britain the previous year. (The outbreak stemmed from a major epidemic in India in 1827. One of the costs of a world-wide empire, the British had found, was the spread of diseases by travelers among the countries under their dominion.) The British army built the first simple structures, including the Cholera Hospital for forty-eight patients.

Ships were held at Grosse Île for an average of six days, though many were kept for more than twenty days. Between 1832 and 1846, the facilities on the island expanded and individual graves were dug for the bodies of those who died. However, the black year of 1847 overwhelmed even these resources. Thousands died aboard the ships anchored at the island and in the hospitals on land. Long trenches were dug and the coffins piled three deep in mass graves. In 1847 alone, over 5,000 Irish were buried in this manner, unfortunates who had survived the long voyage only to succumb at this gateway to the New World. Of those who cleared (or slipped past) the quarantine station, further thousands were buried in Quebec City and Kingston as their strength finally failed them after the arduous journey, and 7,000 perished and were buried in Montreal. The Lonergans were lucky. All four travelers survived both their journey and any quarantine to arrive safely in Burlington, Vermont.

Even healthy immigrants were not always welcome in the United States or even in British North America. The waves of Irish arriving in America were seen as impoverished foreigners that Great Britain was dumping abroad and happy to be rid of them. Inevitably, outbreaks of diseases in the cities from time to time were attributed to the new arrivals. A strong anti-Catholic bias in many parts of the United States added to the antipathy felt by many Americans, particularly by the working class with whom these intruders would compete as cheap labor.

A warmer welcome would of course await those with contacts such as friends or family members to help them settle in their new home. Such hospitality might have been the exception for those traveling in the famine years, though any connections would have been sought out and developed where possible. No evidence has been found that the Lonergans were welcomed by relatives or even acquaintances upon their arrival in Burlington. However, the impoverished exiles in a strange land still found the strength to carve out a new life in America, even bringing their other children over when they were able.

A YEAR AFTER THE UPRISING of 1848 had collapsed in a muddle of indecision and vacillation, redeemed only by the resolute action of a few men, the nationalists were scattered across oceans and continents. The convicted leaders of the Young Irelanders were being transported into exile for life. Most of the fighters who had showed that they, unlike O'Brien, were willing to spill blood for the cause had fled the country or were in prison. Doheny, O'Mahony, and others eventually took ship to America, where they continued plotting against the crown in New York City, Boston, and other Irish emigrant destinations.

The four felons tried at Clonmel were held in Dublin's Richmond prison through the winter and spring. On July 9, 1849, they were removed for permanent exile from Ireland under the escort of fifty mounted policemen with pistols and carbines, along with three troops of the 6th Carabineers dragoons. At the harbor, under the loaded cannon of the British defenses and warships, the group of nationalist leaders was taken to a ten-gun brig, the *Swift*, for transportation to Van Dieman's Land. The prisoners were allowed on deck two at a time, so Meagher was able to watch the next morning as they sailed along the coast of his native Waterford past the estuary of the Suir River. He wrote later of his thought, "Will no one come out to hail

CHAPTER SIX – EXILED

me from Dunmore? I pass by, and my own people know nothing of it." The ship continued beyond the Bay of Tramore, past "the rock-bound coast by Bunmahon to Clonea" and on into the west until the last mountain top of Ireland sank from his view forever.

The lives of these exiles would intertwine over the next two decades as the struggle for the independence of Ireland from British rule took a new shape. Another generation of Irish patriots, including John Lonergan, would step forward to take up the fight. Tales of heroes in legend and history, told at work or around the table, would again weave their spell. First, though, Lonergan must find his way to a new home in the Green Mountains of Vermont.

Dun Brody, famine ship replica at New Ross

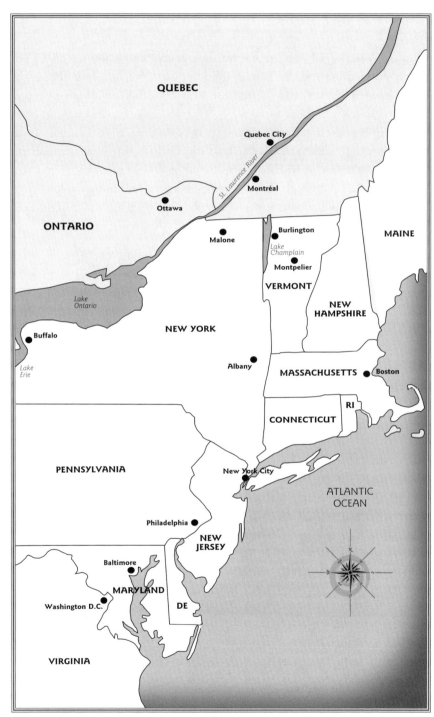

Northeast United States and Southern British North America

PART TWO

AMERICA

LAKE CHAMPLAIN, FROM BATTERY PARK, BURLINGTON, CIRCA 1880

*"When an Irishman takes a wife,
as he is sometimes liable to, does he therefore forget
his mother? America is the Irishman's wife,
but he does not forget his mother Ireland."*

– JOHN LONERGAN, ST. PATRICK'S DAY, 1870

Captain John Lonergan (probably fall of 1861 and likely from his carte de visite)

CHAPTER SEVEN

VERMONT'S IRISH

T HE LONG JOURNEY FROM IRELAND by the Thomas Lonergan family, whatever route they followed, ended in Burlington, Vermont. It is not clear why they made this small port town on the eastern shore of Lake Champlain their final destination. Most Irish who came to North America in the wave of emigration created by the famine conditions and the political turmoil of 1848 settled in the seaports or the major urban centers easily accessible from these entry points. Sometimes the choice was determined by personal connections with earlier emigrants, who might even have sent the necessary funds for the trip. Bewildered newcomers who lacked such contacts were commonly exploited by strangers at the dockside professing to assist them, usually fellow Irishmen who would steer them to the cheap boarding houses that had hired these guides. Often the travelers were simply unable to continue further—their bodies and purses exhausted—or they found a sense of refuge in joining the growing Irish communities. Many Irish never moved beyond the port cities where they gratefully set foot again on dry land, making their new lives wherever they landed.

The Lonergans continued beyond their initial point of debarkation after the trans-Atlantic voyage, presumably by water transport, since the railroads would not reach Burlington until the last day of 1849. Their route to Vermont most likely would have followed the St. Lawrence River to the Montreal area. For those with cash, Montreal provided easy access to the port of St. Jean on the Richelieu River, fifteen miles away, by coach or, after 1836, by railroad. From St. Jean, ships carried passengers to destinations along Lake Champlain or even further south. Destitute immigrants might have to walk for some part of their journey. However they traveled, the Lonergans probably reached Burlington in the summer of 1849.

Since other families had left Tipperary before them, perhaps the Lonergans had friends or relatives waiting to welcome them. Or perhaps this was as far as their money could carry them. Like the seaports of the Atlantic and Gulf coasts, most towns along the shores of Lake Champlain saw growing numbers of Irish arrive in the famine years. Often facing a hostile reception from the dominant and established Protestant Yankee residents, the Irish created their own communities bound together by culture, language, and the Catholic religion.

Although such social factors no doubt played a role in deciding where the Lonergan family settled, Thomas first of all had to ensure that he could earn a living for the four of them. He would have sought a suitable place to ply his coopering trade, since that skill would best provide for his wife and two sons in their new country. Not only would he be supporting his family in Vermont, he also needed to scrape together the money for tickets to bring over the children left behind in Ireland.*

When the Lonergans arrived, Burlington was a busy port and the largest town in Vermont, but still had only about the same number of residents as Carrick on Suir. The expanding community offered a good choice for their new home. Active shipping trade on Lake Champlain and the railroads under construction would offer Thomas steady work. Other Irish who had settled in the area provided a social network. The economic situation in this market town—the transportation hub for the local farming area, as was Carrick for south Tipperary—would have had a comfortable familiarity.

The landscape even resembles the corner of Tipperary that the Lonergans had left behind forever. To the west, the Adirondack Mountains rise across the lake like the Comeragh hills do beyond the Suir. True, Lake Champlain stretches far wider at this point than the Irish river and no bridge like that in Carrick could span the broad boundary between New York and Vermont, though many winters a sheet of thick ice may connect the two shores. Mount Mansfield towers in the distance on the opposite horizon, much as Slievenamon does near the Lonergans' former home, and in the 1840s sheep grazed bare hillsides like those around John Lonergan's birthplace.

---

* As an experienced craftsman, he was in a more favorable situation than many of the Irish, who came as dispossessed tenant farmers without the means to purchase land. Even if the immigrants were forced to accept low wages as laborers or hired hands on other men's farms, however, the danger of institutionalized starvation had passed. In sharp contrast to life under British rule, hard work in this land of opportunity held out a promise of prosperity denied the common man in Ireland.

CHAPTER SEVEN – VERMONT'S IRISH

Vermont also shares with County Tipperary a well-deserved reputation for a feisty attitude and an independent nature. The state's origin reflects bold action by strong characters with whom Irish rebels might easily identify, perhaps providing an intangible attraction for settling in Vermont. In the eyes of Irish nationalists, America stood as the model for forcibly breaking ties with the British throne. As with the strategic location of Carrick in southern Tipperary, opposing armies repeatedly passed through the important corridor of Lake Champlain in the recurring struggle to control the territory. The indigenous people were displaced by settlers whose monarchs then fought to claim the land, rebellious colonists rose up against distant kings, and campaigns moved north and south with changing fortunes and ambitions—the last battles in the area would involve John Lonergan.

EUROPEANS FIRST ENTERED THIS REGION when Samuel de Champlain explored south from the St. Lawrence River in 1609, on the route that the Lonergans likely followed almost two and a half centuries later to reach Burlington. Stretching over one hundred miles to the south, Lake Champlain is separated from Lake George only by a slim neck of land, giving access to the Hudson River that empties into the Atlantic. In this heavily forested and hilly region, such a water route offered the best path for exploration, trade, or war. Champlain found the territory that is now Vermont, defined by the lake on the west and the Connecticut River on the east, only sparsely occupied by indigenous tribes, mostly Abenakis.*

Along with Old World diseases and technology, Europeans also imported Old World conflicts into the area, as the French and British kings contested control of the vast territory. A fort built in 1666 at Isle La Motte in the northern end of Lake Champlain became the first permanent European settlement in the region and the site of the first Roman Catholic Mass celebrated there. England's "Glorious Revolution," which had brought disaster to Ireland at the Battle of the Boyne, echoed in the colonies as King William's War with France and Spain. The Treaty of Paris, which ended the Seven Years' War in 1763, ceded the French king's possessions east of the Mississippi River to

---

* Champlain recorded the Abenaki names of some Vermont rivers on his maps of exploration, including the Winooski or "Onion" River that enters Lake Champlain just north of Burlington. He is also popularly thought to have named "the Green Mountains" by describing the ranges of hills to the east whose rocks often have a greenish cast as "les Verts Monts."

Great Britain. New France, with its sparse European settlements of about 60,000 French, now belonged to the British ruler, together with his own more populous American colonies.

The royal grants that created British colonies in the New England region led to conflicting claims on the land and disputes about the boundaries of these grants. The area between Lake Champlain and the Connecticut River became known as the "New Hampshire Grants," but was also claimed by the governor of New York. Despite the questionable title to the land that they might purchase, settlers flocked to the frontier area of the "Grants" to buy land from speculators who had acquired large tracts. (Land in New York cost one hundred times as much and acreage in even more heavily populated Massachusetts sold for four hundred times the price in the Grants.)

In 1770, Ethan Allen and his relatives formed the Onion River Land Company—named for its Winooski River Valley holdings—to exploit the situation; they sold land despite their contested title to it. In resisting New York's efforts to enforce its own claims, Allen encouraged the formation of military companies called the Green Mountain Boys, (which became the traditional name for military units raised in the state of Vermont).

A larger conflict also threatened, however, as a spirit of rebellion against misrule by the distant British king swept through his American colonies. Allen and the Green Mountain Boys shrewdly saw this development as a chance to link their cause with a broader challenge to authority, an opportunity to become patriots for independence rather than mere outlaws in the eyes of New York's royal governor.

On May 10, 1775, Allen and Benedict Arnold led a force of eighty-three Green Mountain Boys to seize Fort Ticonderoga in New York, with its arsenal of valuable cannon. The military operation continued on into Quebec with an assault on St. Jean, but the rebels were repulsed. In September, Allen led one hundred men to attack Montreal, expecting to receive support from the largely French population. Quickly defeated when no popular uprising occurred, Allen was captured and sent to England, then held for a time on a prison hulk in Cork harbor on the south coast of Ireland.

In 1776, the British pursued the strategy of splitting the colonies in two along the water route from Montreal to New York. Although soundly defeated by superior British naval forces at the Battle of Valcour Island in October, Arnold delayed his opponents until the approaching winter forced them to retreat back into Canada. Early the following spring, General Burgoyne started south along the same corridor. By July the British had recaptured Fort Ticonderoga and chased the Americans from the area, although pursuit of the fleeing rebels was slowed by Seth Warner and his Green Mountain Rangers.

Burgoyne wrote that the Grants, thought before to be essentially an unpopulated wilderness, now "abounds in the most active and most rebellious race of the continent and hangs like a gathering storm on my left." (This description of a disaffected area sounds similar to later comments about Tipperary by his fellow general Cornwallis.) In August men from the Grants helped repulse a column of foraging German mercenaries at the Battle of Bennington (actually fought near Hubbardton, New York). His line of supply increasingly tenuous, Burgoyne suffered defeat at Saratoga, New York, and surrendered on October 16, 1777, a turning point in the American Revolution.

THE NEW HAMPSHIRE GRANTS formally adopted the name "Vermont" in June of 1777 as recognition of their "Green Mountain" identity and applied to the Continental Congress for statehood.* When Congress rejected the request, representatives from around the Grants convened at the Connecticut River town of Windsor on July 2 to organize their own country. The convention adopted a constitution modeled after the 1776 version of Pennsylvania's governing document, with a limited ban on slavery and protection of civil rights for Protestants (revised in 1786 to include all citizens). The Republic of Vermont then declared itself to be an independent nation and was governed as such for over a decade.

Ethan Allen returned from British captivity through a prisoner exchange in 1778 to find this new republic considering the annexation of bordering New Hampshire towns into a "Greater Vermont." Negotiations were also taking place on rejoining the British Empire as part of Canada. Allen met with a representative of the British army in Canada in the fall of 1780 and received the offer of a truce. The British hoped to split Vermont off from the other rebels and thus help secure the important Lake Champlain invasion route.

The Continental Congress was aware of Vermont's "Canada option" and even wrote a reverse version of the proposal into the Articles of Confederation, giving prior approval for Canada's membership in the Confederation if it

---

* Heman, one of the younger Allen brothers, was dispatched to make the case.

should apply. Inclusion of the territory of Canada into the United States arose repeatedly as an attractive idea in many American (and some Canadian) minds over the next century.

The war for independence ended with the Treaty of Paris in 1783,* yet New York continued to oppose statehood for Vermont, still disputing the status of the New Hampshire Grants. Only in 1790, after Vermont agreed to pay New York $30,000, were the land claims finally put to rest. On January 10, 1791, delegates from throughout the Green Mountains ratified the United States constitution, and on March 4 Vermont joined the union of the thirteen original colonies as the fourteenth state.

VERMONT'S MOST PROMINENT IRISHMAN of the revolutionary period was Matthew "Spitting" Lyon, born in County Wicklow near Dublin in 1749. He sailed to the colonies in 1765 and worked off his passage as an apprentice printer in Connecticut before moving into the Grants to found the town of Fair Haven, right on the New York border. An ardent Green Mountain Boy anxious to protect his investment in the disputed land, Lyon joined in the attack on Fort Ticonderoga and supported the rebel cause. His second wife was the daughter of Vermont's governor, Thomas Chittenden. Fair Haven became a thriving community with several businesses, including Lyon's newspaper, the *Gazette,* and attracted other early Irish settlers.

Chief spokesman for Thomas Jefferson's party in Vermont, Lyon was elected to Congress in 1796 where he earned his nickname by spitting on a fellow representative, Roger Griswold, a Federalist from Connecticut. (Later Griswold attacked him with a cane and Lyon successfully defended himself with fireplace tongs.) As editor of the *Gazette,* Lyon was the first person arrested under President Adams' repressive Alien and Sedition Act of 1798, one of only eighteen Americans indicted under the law. (Convicted of slandering the chief executive in his paper, Lyon was re-elected to Congress while serving out his jail time in Vermont.)

Lyon may have involved Governor Chittenden and Ira Allen, yet another

---

* Many American colonists had opposed the war, preferring the British monarchy to a republican form of government. Tens of thousands of these "United Empire Loyalists," encouraged by land grants of 200 acres per person, resettled in the provinces of Upper and Lower Canada (Quebec and Ontario). Along the border, they formed communities fiercely devoted to the crown, a bulwark against any encroachment from the south.

younger brother of Ethan, in plotting against the British crown. American adventurers and disgruntled French Canadians planned an assault up the usual invasion route through St. Jean for the summer of 1797, coordinated with a threat to Canada's Maritime Provinces by the French fleet. They hoped to create a new republic of "United Columbia" that would be a friendly and independent northern neighbor for Vermont. Chittenden appointed Ira Allen a major general and commander of the Vermont militia, then commissioned him to travel to France to buy arms for the state.* While returning from France on the ironically named *Olive Branch* with 20,000 muskets and two dozen cannon, far in excess of the requirements of the Vermont's militia, Ira Allen and the arms were seized at sea by the British.

Locked up in a British prison like his brother Ethan before him, Ira Allen was charged with supplying arms to the rebels in Ireland. Considered in the context of the French support of Irish rebels at the time—in 1798 French arms and troops were in fact landed in Ireland as part of the uprising of the United Irishmen—the British suspicions seem justified. The proposed expedition into Canada from Vermont appears to have been coordinated with the rebellion of the nationalists in Ireland; the proximity of the British possessions to Vermont made them a convenient target. Lyon, representing Vermont as a United States Congressman at the time, apparently intended to support the United Irishmen and their rebellion against British rule. With his influence as a representative to Congress and the governor's son-in-law, Lyon might have convinced Chittenden and Ira Allen to supply arms for the operation against Canada, the uprising in Ireland, or both.

Alternatively, perhaps Ira Allen had simply exploited his position as commander of Vermont's militia to act as an agent to supply the Irish rebels with arms directly, no doubt at a profit for himself. After a lengthy court case that bankrupted him, the charges in England were dropped. Soon after his return to Vermont, Ira Allen fled the state to escape his debts, staying for a time with Lyon who had moved to Kentucky.**

---

* On the way, Ira stopped off in England to seek funding for a canal project that would skirt the rapids on the Richelieu River and thus promote Vermont's trade with Canada to his own business advantage.

** Lyon apparently passed down a pugnacious gene—two of his grandsons fought as generals of opposing sides in the American Civil War. Hyland B. Lyon served in the Confederate army while his brother was the first Union general killed in Civil War action; Nathaniel Lyon, the commander of the Union troops at Wilson's Creek in Missouri, fell in 1861.

Vermont entered the new century as a state with a growing population. Over one hundred churches had been established by the turn of the century, none of them Roman Catholic. Legislation had been passed in 1783 to allow communities to tax residents to "erect proper Houses of Public Worship and support Ministers of the Gospel" with the intention of fostering the predominately Congregational and Baptist churches. This "Standing Order" resembled the forced support of the Church of Ireland, but the ties between church and state were abolished in 1807, before large numbers of Irish came to Vermont. The economy was also developing; trade with Canada via Lake Champlain and the Richelieu River increased as the most convenient outlet for Vermont's products, particularly lumber.

On the national level, however, relations with Great Britain continued to deteriorate to the point that the United States declared war on June 19, 1812. A protective battery of six large cannon emplaced on the high bluff over Burlington's waterfront was backed up by a garrison of 2,000 men. The influx of soldiers created a boom economy for the city and Burlington's only cooper employed ten additional men to meet the demand for government provisions.

In 1813, the United States made preparations for an invasion of Quebec via the established Lake Champlain–Richelieu River route. The British countered with a naval expedition in July that bombarded Plattsburgh, New York, and then Burlington, where 3,000 soldiers and 800 militiamen had assembled. The American victory over the British fleet at the Battle of Plattsburgh, in September of the following year, thwarted any campaign from the north and peace was signed between the two countries on Christmas Eve of 1814.

Despite an embargo, trade continued between Vermont and Canada even during the hostilities. However, when a canal from Lake George to the Hudson River opened in 1823, the commerce north from Lake Champlain all but disappeared. With this new access to the lucrative markets of the more populous south, by 1828 what had been forty vessels plying the lake increased to over 200.

Resentment of British rule was not confined to the American colonists or the Irish; the conquered French in North America harbored similar feelings. A nationalist uprising broke out in Lower Canada at St. Denis on the Richelieu River on November 23, 1837, in a rebellion led by the Patriote Party. British troops recovered from an initial *patriote* victory in Quebec to crush the ill-equipped rebels within a month, and hundreds of rebels were arrested. Others fled across the U.S. border to settle in the northwestern towns of Vermont, particularly in Alburg, Highgate, Swanton, St. Albans, and Burlington.

A second phase of the rebellion in early November of 1838 was suppressed largely by armed English volunteers and the movement collapsed with consequences similar to those experienced by the United Irishmen in 1798. Of the ninety-nine rebels condemned to death by courts-martial, a dozen leaders died on the gallows and the rest were transported to Australian penal colonies. Refugees from the conflict continued to expand the French-Canadian population of Burlington and the region. Based on their shared Roman Catholic religion and common experience with British oppression, the Fenians would later view the French in Canada as potential allies in military action against British rule, as Ethan Allen had hoped in 1775.

Not all immigrants from Canada were disaffected insurgents, however, since people shifted freely between Quebec and Vermont; only customs fees were collected at the border. Over the years, family kinships and business connections extended across the international boundary in regional relationships. Many early Irish immigrants to Canada eventually moved south into Vermont, often seeking out enclaves of their fellow countrymen.

ECONOMIC DEPRESSION IN IRELAND, the constant shortage of land and restrictions on its ownership by Catholics, and favorable descriptions of opportunities in America had encouraged bolder Irish to make the perilous journey even before the Famine. British government subsidies, including grants of land, provided financial incentives to bring needed settlers into the vast territory of Canada. Ships in the squared timber trade brought North American lumber to the British Isles and often returned with a cargo of Irish, depositing them in the Canadian Maritime Provinces, Quebec City, and Montreal. Frequently the Irish entering Quebec traveled on to the United States, where they foresaw better jobs and a home beyond the reach of the British crown. Cheap labor was in demand in America, although the Irish were commonly resented for undercutting the wages of unskilled American workers.*

---

* By the mid-nineteenth century, often a "Help Wanted" sign also warned that "No Irish Need Apply."

In Vermont, the earlier Irish settlers clustered for the most part in the northwest, as well as in the Castleton-Fair Haven communities. Significant numbers of Irish were found in the townships of Middlebury, Moretown, and Underhill, as well as in the Burlington and Rutland areas. One Bernard Brewin wrote from Underhill to his parents in County Leitrim in 1837, the year of John Lonergan's birth, to encourage his siblings to come to America, boasting that he owned a farm "and got a deed for ever of it," a level of stability impossible to achieve back in Ireland.

Fairfield in particular attracted Irish to a community that was founded by land-hungry farmers from County Louth. These Kirks, McEnanys, and Denivers were soon followed by Ryans, Carrols, Kings, and Connellys. In their wake came a surge of others, with Counties Louth, Meath, and Cavan heavily represented. This reflects the common pattern of "chain migration" where the initial trailblazers were later joined by others in the family or from the same area. Patrick and Catherine Howrigan from Clonmel, close by Carrick, first settled in Henryville, Quebec, before moving to Fairfield in 1849. These early emigrants from Ireland often brought the spark of nationalism with them and fostered the desire to see their homeland liberated from British rule; the Irish community in Fairfield would later play an important role in John Lonergan's life.

Almost all these Fairfield Irish were Catholic,* but lacking their own church until 1847, they availed themselves of the priests in the established French communities in Quebec. The parish priest from Chambly, just east of Montreal on the Richelieu River, would periodically make a circuit through Fairfield and other communities in northwestern Vermont to serve the Catholics in the area. Or the Irish could make the fifty-mile trip north when a priest was urgently needed. In Fairfield, it was well-known in the 1820s that Bridget Deniver and her sister walked to Chambly and back with Bridget's infant twins so that they could be promptly baptized in the church there.

The federal census in 1840, the last before the influx of Famine Irish, showed a small population of Irish (and likewise French-Canadians) in Vermont, although there were significant clusters in places like Burlington and the other towns mentioned above. The mostly Protestant Irish immigrants before the Famine period often came by choice, seeking opportunity. The

---

* North Fairfield by the early 1830s had a Baptist church whose pastor, Elder William Arthur, came from Ballymena, County Armagh. After some years in Canada, he had moved to Vermont, where his son, Chester A. Arthur, future president of the United States, was born.

CHAPTER SEVEN – VERMONT'S IRISH

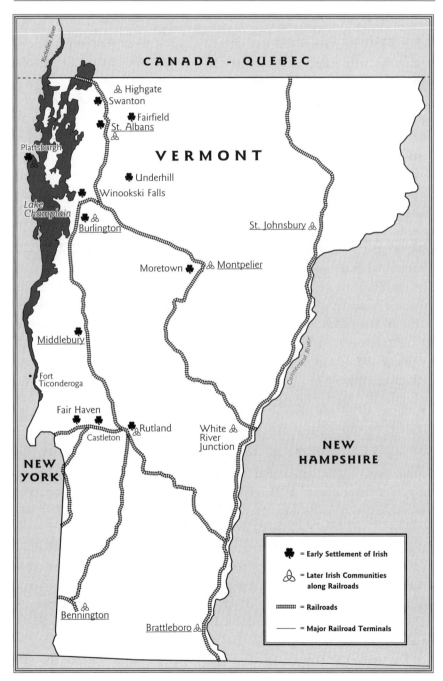

Early Irish immigration into Vermont

flood of Catholics fleeing the Famine came out of necessity, hoping to survive. Before 1850, the census did not include place of birth and only heads of households were listed; estimates based solely on Irish surnames no doubt seriously undercounted the actual numbers of Irish immigrants.

One of the largest ports on the lake, Burlington became the destination for many Irish entering the country through Canada. In Burlington, the Irish were concentrated along Water Street next to the lake as if clinging to their first foothold on arrival. The author Nathaniel Hawthorne, visiting Burlington in the summer of 1832, had been impressed with the setting and its relatively cosmopolitan nature, due at least in part to its connections with the nearby possessions of the British Empire. However, his comments were less favorable on a by-product of this proximity, the "great numbers of Irish emigrants" concentrated around the waterfront where they were "lounging" about the wharves and "swarming in huts and mean dwellings near the lake."

The busy waterfront Irish community offered work for craftsmen and unskilled laborers alike and the Irish also operated most small businesses in the enclave. Both hotels on the street, Hart's and Soregan's, were owned by Irishmen, as were the three grocery stores. The area remained an Irish neighborhood right until the end of the nineteenth century. Thomas Lonergan took up residence in this haven for the Irish, probably close to the spot where he first landed in the United States.

The Irish were clearly arriving in great swarms by boat at the Burlington docks because, about the time the Lonergans arrived, the town attempted to control the situation with regulations (undated, but issued "c. 1849"). The "indiscriminate importation and landing at this Port of foreign immigrants, subjects of Great Britain" in "large and crowded masses" presented "danger to the public health" and a financial burden to the town. Burlington therefore required the masters of all vessels to hold such persons, many of them "both paupers and diseased," on board until inspected by a physician and certified to be in good health. The captain of every ship, "whether steam or other vessel," who failed to abide by the regulations would "forfeit for each offence one hundred dollars." Although the regulations promised that "said penalty will be rigidly enforced," this probably had little success in holding back the flood of Irish into Burlington.

The decennial U.S. census in the summer of 1850 provides the first documentary evidence of the Lonergans in Vermont. This census, the first

CHAPTER SEVEN — VERMONT'S IRISH

to list place of birth and all family members, showed a third of Burlington's population to be Irish. Although the entry of August 30 spells the family name phonetically as it is often pronounced, Londargin, it clearly refers to John Lonergan's family. Thomas, age thirty-four, occupation cooper, and his wife Mary, age thirty-one, are listed with sons Thomas, one year old, and John, age fourteen [a year too old], all shown as born in Ireland. The Lonergans shared the house, no doubt as renters, with two other Irish-born families—the McAvoys and the Murphys, who worked as laborers—and some Canadian-born brick makers. A Canadian-born cooper named Bowie and his family lived next door in this thoroughly working-class neighborhood of immigrants.

Arrival of the Famine-era Irish coincided with a westward expansion in the United States that included the extension of transportation lines facilitating the movement of goods and people. Irishmen who landed at New England seaports often found employment on the railroad lines being built in the region, including Vermont.* In 1843, Vermont's General Assembly had authorized four railroads, including the Vermont Central, which connected the Connecticut River with Lake Champlain, and a line south from Burlington to Rutland.

While Burlington—population still only 7,585 in 1850—was too small to support a profitable passenger service on the Vermont Central, the shipment of lime propped up its operation, bringing the railroad line nearly $1,000 in freight fees per month. The output from expanded lime kilns would have produced steady work for coopers building the barrels and, along with the shipping on the lake, should have helped ensure employment for the Thomas Lonergan in his trade. Although much of the cargo of the canal boats and other vessels operating on Lake Champlain was handled in bulk, commodities such as apples were also commonly loaded in barrels of various sizes.

THE GROWING IRISH POPULATION in Vermont led to increasing hostility toward these immigrants. The presence of Irish laborers concerned a town father in Barnet, on the eastern side of the state; he called for assurances from the Connecticut and Passumpsic Railroad that they would all leave his area when construction of the line was completed. Workers sometimes did lay

---

* Elsewhere canals offered similar jobs, but the nature of Vermont's topography restricted canals to local by-passes of rapids on major rivers and some spurs off Lake Champlain.

down their tools at the end of the line and settled in places like Cork Alley in Winooski. Other Irish remained alongside the tracks they built, buried where they died.* The "Bolton War" of 1846 was sparked when Irish railroad workers there rioted for non-payment of wages. A company of militia was dispatched from Burlington, along with a priest, to pacify the Irish by force or persuasion. The conversion of some prominent citizens to the Roman Catholic faith—including the editor of the Burlington *Daily Free Press* newspaper and Fanny Allen, daughter of the iconoclastic Ethan—alarmed many Vermonters of Yankee stock. In 1847, an editor in Newbury called for all Catholics, including the increasing number of French-Canadians, to be expelled from the state.

Hostility toward Catholics was not restricted to the eastern states, but took on a nationwide scope. In reaction to the influx of immigrants—mostly Irish or German, in either case predominately Catholic—who entered the United States in the 1840s, the American Party was formed. Its members believed that the two established national political organizations, the Whigs and the Democrats, did not sufficiently oppose granting full rights to these newcomers. The existing American population of twenty million—largely Protestant, of British stock, and native-born—had to absorb almost three million mostly Catholic newcomers within a decade. A "nativist" backlash against the foreign-born sought to maintain control by denying or delaying citizenship and voting rights. The strong anti-Catholic prejudice of the movement was often not admitted openly. Instead, members of the American Party would profess to "know nothing" of such biases and the party became more commonly called the "Know Nothings."

George P. Marsh, a successful mill owner in Winooski Falls and later a United States ambassador, professed support of this movement in a letter to his friend Erastus Fairbanks of St. Johnsbury in April of 1855. While Marsh disapproved of the Know Nothings' trappings—the "foolish machinery of lodges & wigwams, sachems, oaths, secrets, and all the like silliness"—he again stated his support of their principles. Marsh reaffirmed his commitment of the past twenty years to the "repeal or at least restriction of the right of naturalization, and resistance to catholic commandments." He went on to express "In my judgment, our liberties are in greater danger from the political influence of Catholicism than from any other cause whatsoever."

---

* Playing on the British word for cross-ties, it was said that on some stretches of railroad every third "sleeper" was a dead Irishman.

CHAPTER SEVEN – VERMONT'S IRISH

Long-standing friends, Marsh obviously thought Fairbanks shared these anti-Catholic and anti-immigrant sentiments. Fairbanks' later dealings with John Lonergan would appear to confirm Marsh's assumption.

LIVELY ELECTIONS WERE HELD in Vermont each year for local and state offices, including that of governor, with eighty-two percent of eligible voters turning out in 1840. Newspapers openly expressed their party affiliations; in Burlington the *Daily Free Press* was a voice for the state's Whigs (and later for their successors, the Republicans),* while the weekly *Sentinel* editorialized on behalf of the Democrats.

In 1852, the question of slavery was approaching yet another crisis as a national issue when Erastus Fairbanks became the governor of a strongly abolitionist Vermont. A dour and wealthy member of the Congregational Church, who had been elected to the state legislature in 1836 as a Whig, Fairbanks had long provided leadership to the statewide temperance movement. His attitude toward drinking would cost him politically.

Prolonged winters, isolated communities, and ready access to materials for home brewing contributed to a perceived widespread abuse of alcohol that was loudly decried by the temperance movement that spread in the mid-1820s. By 1832, some 200 local temperance societies in Vermont boasted of more than 30,000 members fighting "demon rum" and the local hard cider. The June training of the state militia, required by law for all able-bodied male white citizens sixteen to forty-five years of age, was frequently cited by temperance advocates as one example of excessive use of alcohol. Gratitude toward the members of the militia was often expressed by treating the part-time soldiers to drink, usually strong spirits. Wags claimed that the only orders given to the cavalry in the annual training were "Mount, drink, fall off."

Fairbanks, a staunch advocate of abstinence, pushed a referendum on the absolute prohibition of alcohol through the legislature with a procedural vote; it barely passed 91-90. A statewide referendum approved Act 24, "Preventing Traffic in Intoxicating Liquors for the Purpose of Drinking" by only 521 votes out of over 44,000 cast, with the large population centers carrying the day over the rural areas. Although his narrow victory meant that Vermont officially remained "dry" for the next fifty years, Fairbanks lost his bid for

---

* The *Daily Free Press* is extensively used as a source in this book and hereafter will be cited as the *Free Press*.

re-election in 1853, largely in reaction to this ban on drinking. The law that prohibited trafficking was amended in 1853 to allow home consumption (as long as drunkenness did not result). In the event, it was only laxly enforced and apparently was overridden by local ordnances.

The following year the Republican Party was organized and the Whigs faded from the political scene. Vermont would be firmly controlled by the party of Lincoln for the next one hundred years. It would be some years before Fairbanks returned to office; when he did, his path would cross that of John Lonergan.

DEVELOPING INTO MANHOOD in the 1850s, John Lonergan was transformed from the child who had arrived in Burlington into a confident and assertive adult. Despite the hardships of his early years in Carrick, he grew up strong in body and spirit. Yet the horrors of the famine period must have left mental scars that drove him to dedicate his life to the liberation of Ireland.

As his son would write years later, John Lonergan's schooling by the Christian Brothers in Carrick had been "cut short by emigration." In Burlington, he had no opportunity to attend school during the day since he had taken up the tools of a cooper and "was at the bench helping to support a large family." (Mary Lonergan gave birth to children in Vermont in 1849, 1851, 1858, and 1864, the last when she was forty-five years old.) Still hungry for education, in his youth John "busied himself at night by studying and reading" after work "with the occasional assistance of a private teacher."

What would this young working-class Irish immigrant have studied? His penmanship in the few documents available displays a bold, but careful hand. These limited writings all show a high quality of grammar, spelling, and clarity of expression. Beyond these basics of education, likely mastered under the stern tutelage of the Christian Brothers, Lonergan might have directed his further studies toward knowledge that would aid him to serve the cause of Irish freedom. An understanding of history and the acquisition of military skills would have helped prepare him for his later leadership roles.

Few of those Irish who crossed the oceans ever returned to their homeland—the hardships and expense of such a voyage would not be repeated lightly—yet strong ties to family and birthplace continued. Letters were exchanged with those left behind and the reports on conditions in Ireland from personal correspondence and newspaper articles remained grim. Despite a slow process of assimilation, the Irish in America generally preserved both their identity and their resolve to change the situation in their homeland.

John Lonergan felt that even those who had escaped British rule owed continued loyalty to Ireland and should contribute to its liberation. Whether he came to this conviction from his own experiences, from the memory of events in the Ireland of his childhood, or was guided to the belief by someone else, he was a dedicated militant nationalist by the time he was grown. Perhaps he heard a steady discourse from his father at the family table or he might have spent time with other influential adults who awoke this passion in him. He might even have been selected by a mentor who saw in him the potential for leadership, much as the members of the Fianna were chosen to serve in the days of Ireland's glory.

Whatever the motivation, the result is certain. Lonergan embarked on a course of determined support for a military solution to the plight of his homeland. He must have had encouragement at home and in his community for a quest that took him away from his cooper's bench and eventually into battle. His involvement with the Irish revolutionary movement traced a path that led him into direct conflict with the authority of Vermont's governor at the outbreak of the American Civil War.

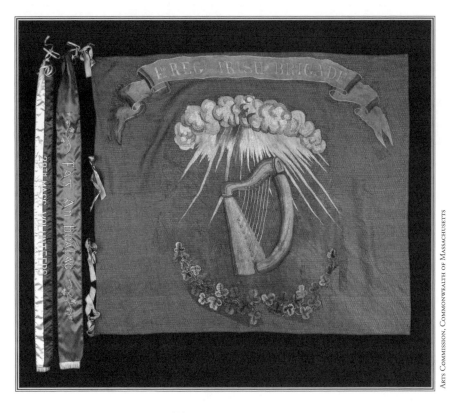

Typical symbols
of the
Fenian Brotherhood:
the Sunburst,
Uncrowned Harp,
and Shamrocks.

28th Massachusetts Regiment Flag
made by Tiffany & Co.
in New York City.

CHAPTER EIGHT

FENIAN BROTHERHOOD

FAMINE AND THE UNSUCCESSFUL uprising of 1848 had combined to clear most active rebels out of Ireland. As a consequence, Irishmen filled with bitter hatred of British rule were driven from their homeland to countries beyond the Queen's control. Many dedicated revolutionaries, including the Lonergans, took up residence in America where they could safely plan their next actions. In the United States, the Irish enthusiastically set about learning the art of war. As early as 1848, the exiles in New York organized into republican clubs that gave rise to units of that state's militia. These companies made up the uniformed forces that proudly saluted the liberated Young Irelanders on their arrival in New York in the early 1850s.

Militia units were raised within a given state and remained under the control of that state's governor unless federalized for national service under strictly defined legal limitations. A growing political force in New York, the Irish found that this militia system gave them the advantage of state sponsorship of their military units; commissions were issued by the governor for their chosen officers. When other nationalist organizations were established, their members were also encouraged to form official militia units to receive arms and training at the expense of the state.

Most of the immigrants to America, struggling to survive at the lowest rung of the economic ladder, strongly resented British rule of Ireland and the exile forced upon them. Various organizations were formed both to help the immigrants and to keep the spirit of rebellion alive, especially in the Atlantic port cities where the Irish congregated. In the South, ships carrying cotton to England returned with Irish passengers who formed similar enclaves. Even as many native-born Americans supported the Know Nothing movement, astute American politicians began to court the Irish vote, playing up to the immigrants' anti-British bias*

ALTHOUGH THE BEST-KNOWN figures of the 1848 uprising had been transported or imprisoned, some captains of the movement remained at liberty, in Ireland and abroad, to pursue their goal of making Ireland "a nation once again." This new generation of leaders saw clearly that they needed a much different approach from that of the Young Ireland movement. Where the Confederate Clubs had been openly organized, legal, democratic, and gentlemanly, the revolutionaries now recognized that secrecy, centralized control, and ruthless methods were required to achieve their purpose. The torch passed from the main nationalist spokesmen—O'Brien, Meagher, Mitchel, and others languished in British captivity—to the men who had done the actual fighting and were prepared to gain freedom even at the cost of lives. Those who had escaped capture after the collapse of the rebellion were mostly in exile, finding a safe haven in France or America. The scattered revolutionaries communicated as best they could, though the exchange of letters or personal visits entailed weeks of delay.

A few committed nationalists who had remained in Ireland even after the failure of 1848 formed secret groups that caused an aftershock the year following the uprising. In 1849 the potato crop failed again and widespread evictions of tenant farmers continued. In August, Queen Victoria made her first official visit to Ireland since ascending the throne a dozen years before; the ruling class of Ireland was delighted at the royal favor conferred by her visit and Cobh was renamed Queenstown in appreciation.** Most Irish, however, considered Victoria the "Famine Queen" for allowing such misery among her subjects and a plot was organized to seize her during the visit to Dublin.

Phillip Gray, whose uncle was hanged as a rebel in 1798, had joined John

---

* United States Senator Henry Foote of Mississippi in 1851 had put forward a motion to have the Young Irelanders freed from their exile in Australia and given asylum in America. President Millard Fillmore even instructed his Secretary of State, Daniel Webster, to work toward their release.

** The royal yacht carried the Queen to Dublin, Belfast, and Cobh harbor near Cork, probably the safest way for her to travel around Ireland. The name Cobh (pronounced "Cove") was restored by the Irish Free State in 1922, but the British retained control of the important naval base there until 1938.

CHAPTER EIGHT - FENIAN BROTHERHOOD

O'Mahony in the hills around Carrick after Ballingary and had taken part in the attack on the Portlaw police barracks in August of 1848. Gray and John O'Leary, a student at Trinity College, had led the effort to free the captured Young Ireland leaders during their trial at Clonmel, a plot that ended with O'Leary's arrest and brief imprisonment. Both these men continued their revolutionary activities in the south of Ireland, jointly creating secret societies whose members were bound by oath to establish an Irish republic. Gray and O'Leary organized a combined action in 1849 with Joseph Brenan and Fintan Lalor, both writers for nationalist newspapers, who led a similar movement in the Dublin area.

The "generalized simultaneous" rising planned for September 16 was "not only badly coordinated but also largely known beforehand to the authorities." Brenan led an unsuccessful attack that night on the police barracks at Cappoquin in County Waterford, the only armed action before the movement dissolved.* Lalor, in chronic bad health, was arrested and died in jail soon after he was imprisoned. O'Leary and Gray remained at large in Ireland, still conspiring against the crown, but Brenan fled to New York City and later moved to New Orleans.

GOOD HARVESTS EASED CONDITIONS among the drastically reduced population in the 1850s. Yet the overarching problem for the Irish peasant farmer remained his status as a renter, unable to own the land. The Tenants' League of North and South was organized to prevent the eviction of peasants and to obtain for them the right of occupation, if not ownership, of the soil they tilled. By 1852 the League had gained forty-eight of the Irish seats in Parliament. Despite the introduction of a land bill every year until 1858, no legislation reforming the system of ownership was passed. Any hopes for a radical restructuring to benefit the tenants faded when the Conservatives replaced the Liberal government in 1859.

This lack of progress by legal means renewed the rebel spirit in Ireland, which again took the form of secret societies. Many of the localized groups only revived the old "ribbon societies" in the countryside for action against the landlords; others pursued nationalist and republican goals. Through the police and its network of informers, Dublin Castle kept close track of various

---

* Brenan had also mobilized a group of 150 men for the abduction of Queen Victoria in Dublin, though the attempt was never actually made.

secret organizations around the country, yet at first the authorities did not recognize the actual revolutionary nature of the new "Phoenix" movement.

Phoenix members were required to take an oath renouncing any allegiance to the Queen and affirming their readiness to take up arms to achieve an independent republic. The origin for the underground network was the Phoenix National and Literary Society of Skibbereen, a village on the southwest coast that had been particularly ravaged by the famine. Jeremiah O'Donovan Rossa set up a reading room there in 1856 to provide the cover of "an open and legal, if nationally-minded, club for self-improvement." Some members proposed that it be named the "Emmet Monument Association," a clear reference to Robert Emmet's speech from the dock before execution ("let no monument be raised"). Rossa insisted on his own choice of "Phoenix," symbolizing a rising from "the ashes of our martyred nationality."

The Catholic Church in Ireland, the only country-wide organization with which the common Irish identified, held an ambivalent attitude toward the question of nationality. Once Repeal had removed the worst restrictions against Catholics, the church pursued only limited political objectives and in principle opposed any violence against authority. Two church leaders at the time took very different stands on nationalism. The Archbishop of Tuam, John MacHale, supported the progressive view that self-government could solve the Irish social and political problems while the more conservative Archbishop of Dublin, Paul Cullen, feared a return to the Penal Laws if the English were provoked.*

FAR ACROSS THE OCEANS, the leaders of Young Ireland were being held in penal colonies in Australia. In October of 1849—probably about the same time that the Lonergans reached Burlington, halfway around the world—O'Brien, Meagher, O'Doherty, O'Donoghue, and MacManus arrived in Van Dieman's Land. The convicted rebels were assigned widely separated areas of residence under a loose kind of house arrest called a ticket of leave. After being at sea for almost two years on both prison hulks and warships, John Mitchel, the first to be transported, joined them in April of the following year.

Many of those living in the penal colonies were Irish and the "state prisoners" enjoyed a certain elevated status among them as convicted rebels.

---

* Cullen, who had been at the Vatican during the revolutions of 1848, equated the anti-Papal actions of Young Italy in that country with the activities of Young Ireland.

CHAPTER EIGHT – FENIAN BROTHERHOOD

The Young Irelanders found willing hands locally to help them plot their escape. These countrymen cooperated when the Irish Directory in New York City, which included Michael Doherty, sent Meagher a letter proposing the rescue of O'Brien. In August of 1850, O'Brien's attempt at flight was prevented at the last minute; he was dragged out of the surf by a constable before he could board the boat sent out from the rescue ship.

MacManus had better luck. After a legal maneuver that challenged his imprisonment on a technicality, he was given a temporary release in February of 1851, during which he was smuggled on board a ship. He landed in San Francisco in June and established himself there in a growing Irish community that hailed him as a hero.

Meagher, despite his recent marriage (to the daughter of an Irish highwayman transported for life in 1818), did not hesitate to renounce his parole in February of 1852, slipping away after this formality. Leaving his pregnant wife to follow him later, Meagher was able to rendezvous with the same ship that had carried MacManus the previous year—thus the most flamboyant of the Young Irelanders escaped British custody. On May 15, the Boston *Pilot* reported Meagher's successful liberation, but he had changed ships in Brazil and so no one greeted him at the dock when he arrived in New York on May 27. The next day, however, there were wild celebrations, dinners, parades, and a serenade by the 69th Regiment, New York State Militia (NYSM).

O'Donoghue—who in the penal colony had published a newspaper called *The Irish Exile and Freedom's Advocate*—withdrew his own ticket of leave in December. He had problems getting away and only reached San Francisco in June of 1853; he soon continued on to New York.

The Irish Directory in early 1853 tried again to free O'Brien, sending Meagher's friend Pat Smyth—who edited a newspaper in Pittsburgh and now posed as the correspondent for a New York paper—to meet with him in Van Diemen's Land. John Mitchel, whose family had joined him in exile, urged a joint effort to bring out all the rebel prisoners. O'Brien refused to try again, even in the face of his sentence of transportation for life, and remained in exile. (His patience was rewarded by Queen Victoria the following year, when he was pardoned and allowed to return to Ireland.)

Mitchel, on the other hand, met with the district constables on June 8, backed up by a well-armed Smyth, to withdraw his own ticket of leave.

Mitchel anticipated boarding a ship within the week, but a series of difficulties prevented him from leaving until early August. He and his family finally reached San Francisco in October and then arrived in New York the last of November. The tremendous reception there included a parade in his honor and a thirty-one gun salute, implying that Mitchel was a head of state.

To the tune of "Garryowen," Irish militia units passed in review, among them a company of "Mitchel Guards" from the 9th Regiment NYSM, said to be the first Irish regiment raised in America. The marchers included Emmet Guards, Sarsfield Guards, Meagher Cadets, and other units with similar patriotic designations, named for historic or contemporary heroes. Another unit honoring the escaped felon, the "Mitchel Light Guard," had been organized as an independent company by Joseph Brenan, the leader of the attack on Cappoquin.

Brenan proposed that a new regiment, the "Republican Rifles," be formed around his company with Meagher made colonel in command. All the members of Brenan's company, other than the captain himself, were from Meagher's home county of Waterford. The expanded unit was organized as the 37th Regiment NYSM within months and marched in the St. Patrick's Day parade of 1854 as the "Irish Rifles" to ensure no doubt as to its identity. The creation and expansion of these nationalist-oriented military units demonstrated that the Irish in America were preparing to make the Irish state a reality by force.

Always the agitator, Mitchel began publishing a newspaper in New York, the weekly *Irish Citizen*, in January 1854. Further pursuing nationalist goals, he then founded an "Irishman's Civil and Military Republican Union" in April. Disappointed that no direct action was being taken against the British, at the end of the year Mitchel moved to Tennessee and began to integrate himself into life in the South, distancing himself from the Irish nationalists.

THE IRISH COMMUNITY IN PARIS provided refuge for many of the rebels who fled to the Continent when the Young Ireland uprising was crushed. The long history of Irishmen serving in the French army, coupled with the nearly constant hostility between France and England, made it a hospitable destination. Among the newly exiled combatants of 1848, two determined men united, despite their differences, in the single purpose of renewing the struggle. On the ashes of the Young Ireland movement, James Stephens and John O'Mahony joined forces to build a truly revolutionary base for armed action against British rule of Ireland.

Revolution had not been confined to Ireland in 1848 and these exiled Irishmen involved themselves in the French republican movement, gaining useful experience in developing a clandestine organization. Stephens and O'Mahony apparently fought side by side on the Paris barricades in the popular resistance to the 1851 coup by Louis-Napoleon that ended the French Republic.

Fluent in the Irish language, O'Mahony taught at the Irish College in Paris until he departed France for New York City in 1853, to reunite with Doheny and other rebels. Stephens also made use of his language skills in Paris, teaching English, working as a translator, and joining the staff of a French newspaper before he left France late in 1855.

After some time in London, an ailing Stephens continued on to Ireland the following year, unobstructed by the British authorities. Dedicated to independence for Ireland and a republican form of government, he embarked on an extensive walking tour of the country to judge the people's readiness to support these ideals. In 1856, almost the only nationalist movement that existed in Ireland consisted of the mild constitutional opposition of the Irish members of Parliament. The activist Phillip Gray's short-lived newspaper, the *Tribune*, had decried the absence of a sense of nationhood; Stephens confirmed this in most of his contacts. Despairing sometimes at the absence of a national identity, even in the most Irish province of Connaught, Stephens once mused bitterly, "Did Christ ever die for such a people?" His walk of nearly three thousand miles did restore his health and gave him ample time to consider the situation.

Influenced no doubt by his experiences in Paris, along with this survey of the conditions in Ireland, he determined that neither the upper class Irish nor the poor tenant farmers would provide the best material for an insurrection. O'Brien, who had returned from exile in 1854, told Stephens accurately that "the respectable people of the towns especially are quite indifferent to, if not hostile to, nationality" and that no reliance could be placed on that class (including O'Brien himself) for any revolutionary action. The tenant farmers were concerned with land, not nationality, and despite their numbers would be of little help in fomenting an uprising. As a result, Stephens concentrated his efforts on organizing the working class—men like Thomas Lonergan and his now grown son, John, who had joined his father at the cooper's bench.

During his walking tour of 1856, Stephens arrived in Skibbereen in May and made contact with Rossa and the Phoenix society there.* Stephens recruited the first members of his new revolutionary organization from among the Phoenix leaders, who in turn initiated others. Fintan Lalor early on had insisted that Ireland should be a republic, free of any monarch either foreign or native, and Stephens emphatically embraced this principle for his movement. This republican aspect was also essential to the other key factor of Stephens' plan, support by the Irish in America. Within a few months, groups of this new movement were formed in the southwest part of County Cork and military training began at night. The nationalists tried to verify the loyalty of their recruits and to conceal their activities, but the authorities nonetheless cracked down on them in December of 1856, throwing Rossa and some twenty other members of the Phoenix clubs into the Cork jail.

HOPING TO TAKE ADVANTAGE of Great Britain's distraction with the Crimean War, which escalated in 1854, Doheny and O'Mahony created the Emmet Monument Association in New York City. The choice of this name, originally considered by the Skibbereen Phoenix club, meant that any Irishman would recognize that the group was dedicated to revolution against British rule. Chapters of the Emmet Monument Association were formed in most cities with any sizable Irish community and many chapters recruited their members into companies of state militia symbolically called Emmet Guards.

The formula often quoted for timing any insurrection against British rule, "England's difficulty is Ireland's opportunity," seemed applicable in 1854. The Crimean War embroiled Great Britain, and her allies France and Austria, in a distant conflict with Russia. This appeared to create a favorable moment for revolutionary action, as British troops needed elsewhere were withdrawn from Ireland. The nationalists even made overtures to the Czar for his support, offering to open a second front against the British in Ireland that would aid the Russians. The Emmet Monument Association sent a

---

* Rossa claimed it was there that James O'Mahony of Bandon gave Stephens his popular name in Gaelic, *An Seabhac siubhalach*, the wandering hawk. This term, pronounced "shook shoolach," earlier applied to a "banned wanderer." This apparently to some degree confused the British police, who kept searching for a man named "Shook."

representative, Joseph Denieffe, to Ireland in 1855 to organize a rising there, promising that 30,000 men from America would land in the fall of the year. Denieffe met with Gray and others in Dublin, but the Crimean War ended in 1856 before any Russian aid could be obtained.

The many Irish in the New York City area included most of the leading figures of the nationalist movement, who remained true to the cause. However, one former Young Irelander in New York had a change of heart. D'Arcy McGee, who had fought at Ballingary in 1848, now decided that his future lay with the Canadian provinces.* In 1856, difficulty providing for his family led him to seek an invitation from the sizable Irish Catholic community in Montreal to establish a non-sectarian newspaper there, the *New Era*. The St. Patrick's Society was sufficiently impressed with McGee to urge him to represent the Irish Catholics in Montreal and in 1857 he was elected to the Parliament as an independent.

To the dismay of his electorate, McGee pursued some reform actions that did not favor the Irish and he worked for confederation of the provinces into a single country that would be part of the British Empire. The impetus for the creation of a unified Canada stemmed largely from a perceived threat of American expansion—popularized as the concept of "Manifest Destiny" that justified the annexation of neighboring territories—that might include the thinly populated expanse of British North America. In addition, intermittent and scattered sentiment in the provinces favored incorporation into the United States. In Quebec, former *patriotes* like Papineau, who had rebelled in 1837, supported the idea of American annexation, as did a minority of English in the Eastern Townships and some Montreal businessmen. However, in supporting confederation, McGee was pursuing the intention of the majority, who remained true to the British Empire and monarchy.

STEPHENS RETURNED TO DUBLIN from his walking tour at the end of 1856, a time when the Emmet Monument Association had lapsed into inactivity. O'Mahony had written Stephens that his disgust with Irish theatrics in America, what he termed "Yankee-doodle twaddle," had convinced him to give up the cause. Stephens was able to persuade him to revive his efforts in the United States based on developments in

---

* His defection from the nationalist ranks led to a fistfight with Doheny on a street in New York City.

Ireland and the plans for an effective revolutionary organization there.

In the autumn of 1857, O'Mahony and Doheny accordingly dispatched another representative from the Emmet Monument Association, virtually the final action of the declining group. Owen Considine carried the message to Stephens that he should establish a revolutionary movement with which the American Irish could cooperate. Stephens sent Denieffe back to deliver his response that financial support from America and a commitment of 500 well-armed men would guarantee Stephens bringing 10,000 rebels into the field. Of this number, he hoped for 1,500 carrying firearms, with the remainder relying on pikes, as in past centuries. Stephens claimed that within three months of being promised support from America he would be able to call up this rebel force upon twenty-four hours notice.

On January 6, 1858, Stephens declared himself the unfettered leader of the movement, taking on the title of Chief Organizer of the Irish Republic. Denieffe returned from America three months later (bringing only the £80 that Stephens had set as the absolute minimum monthly income) and that very evening the nucleus of the new movement was formed. On St. Patrick's Day, March 17, 1858, a meeting on Lombard Street in Dublin established a secret society dedicated to an independent and republican Ireland, with Stephens, Denieffe, and others swearing themselves into the organization. At this point there was no official name for the movement and it was referred to only as "our body" or "our organization" (similar to organized crime speaking of "our thing"). This worked to Stephens' advantage; in the government's on-going suppression of openly nationalist groups, his anonymous secret organization had not yet been identified as a revolutionary movement. Soon it was officially titled the IRB, which stood originally for "Irish Revolutionary Brotherhood," but was changed shortly thereafter to "Irish Republican Brotherhood" to emphasize the anti-monarchial nature of the movement.

Stephens applied his experience from the internationalist revolutionary activities in Paris, concentrating power in his hands while minimizing the risk of exposure. As the Chief Organizer or Chief Executive, Stephens was known as the "Head Centre" of the IRB. Below him, each of the four provinces of Ireland had a "V" or Vice-Organizer who was responsible for the Circles in his area. The Centre of an "A" level Circle held the rank of colonel and would command a regiment through his nine B-level captains. Each B in turn controlled nine C's or sergeants, each with nine D's (privates) reporting to them. In theory, this would isolate any potential exposure by restricting the members' knowledge of the organization at every level, so that arrest or the inevitable penetration by police informers would not result in the destruction of the entire network.

Committed to the violent overthrow of the British rule of Ireland, the IRB from the beginning was an illegal, oath-bound, and secret organization. Any one of these aspects was enough to draw the disapproval of the Catholic Church; taken all together, the nature of the IRB soon drew the opposition of that one institution that was truly national in scope. Individuals within the church hierarchy might be supportive of the goals of the IRB, but the nationalists had to reckon on overcoming an absence of support by the church and even on outright opposition to their revolutionary organization being preached from the pulpit.

IN PARALLEL WITH THE CREATION of the IRB, O'Mahony, Doheny, and others redirected their energies in 1858 into establishing an affiliated movement in America to replace the moribund Emmet Monument Association. While Stephens had to maintain secrecy within the British Empire, the Irish nationalists could operate openly in the United States. Even so, a hierarchy similar to that in Ireland was chosen with the same designation of chapters as "circles" led by "centres" and letters for the levels. Although distant from the headquarters of the American organization in New York City, Vermont formed one of the first circles in the country. This perhaps resulted from a close and continuing relationship between O'Mahony and Thomas Lonergan, formerly neighbors in Carrick. In the light of later developments, it seems likely that John Lonergan, now a man of twenty-one, could be counted among the early recruits to the movement.

Gaelic scholar that he was, O'Mahony returned to the heroic legends of Finn McCool in selecting a name for the branch based in America. He saw his modern band of warriors as the equivalent to the *fiana* that guarded Ireland under Finn and so described them as the Fenian Brotherhood. (Eventually both the American and the Irish wings of the movement were commonly called Fenians.) At a time when many of the Irish still could not read, leaders like O'Mahony knew the value of visual symbols and therefore he carefully chose the identifying Fenian emblem. The sunburst of Finn's battle flag was combined with an Irish harp—the absence of a crown atop the harp signified Ireland's liberation from rule by the British (or any other) monarch. These symbols appeared on Fenian flags and documents, often accompanied by wreaths of shamrocks and Gaelic inscriptions. Every Irishman would know that such a banner was dedicated to the freedom of a republican Ireland.

Difficulties arose almost immediately in coordinating the actions of two related movements separated by the Atlantic Ocean, in part because of the strong personalities of their leaders. Stephens, a working class republican, demanded subordination of the American Fenian Brotherhood to his command, giving him control over both branches. Though he accepted it to benefit the cause, this arrangement rankled O'Mahony, who was eight years older than Stephens and "a man proud of his name and of his race." The seeds of dissention were sown early on and would eventually lead to factional disputes and later outright ruptures in the movement. Signs of mutual suspicion were apparent as early as the summer of 1858, when Stephens, believing the Fenians remiss in providing funds to his effort in Ireland, insisted on touring the United States to raise money.

In addition to drumming up financial support, Stephens also hoped to encourage recruiting for the joint venture by enrolling those more famous rebels of 1848 who lived in America. In six months of touring, Stephens gathered only £600 in contributions and failed to enlist either Meagher or Mitchel to the cause. Perhaps Meagher, profiting from his status as the leading Irish nationalist through a series of speaking tours, did not want his position threatened by a more successful revolutionary movement (although he did later join the Fenian Brotherhood). Mitchel contributed $50, along with some useful letters of introduction, when Stephens visited him in Knoxville, but he would not come out publicly in support of this new effort.

The fund-raising tour, moreover, caused bad blood when Stephens collected money in the name of a "Fair Trial Fund" to defend the arrested Phoenix club members, but then diverted it into the IRB. The familiar problem of any united Irish effort splintering into factions threatened the attempt at coordination between the IRB and the Fenian Brotherhood. O'Mahony had supporters in Ireland who disapproved of Stephens' management of affairs and Stephens in return was backed by Fenians in America who were dissatisfied with O'Mahony's leadership. This lack of cohesion ultimately resulted in disruptive fights over the leadership of the Fenian Brotherhood.

Predictable British efforts to penetrate both branches of the movement succeeded in keeping the crown authorities well informed of their activities through disloyal members.

After the arrest of the Phoenix club members in Cork at the end of 1856, Stephens thought it unwise to return to Ireland from the United States; the Chief Organizer of the IRB traveled instead to Paris. He wrote O'Mahony a letter from there on April 6, 1859, which in part dealt with the need for revising the oath required of recruits to "our body." Potential members were concerned about the anti-Church tone of the oath and the repercussions of opposition by the Church, though Stephens claimed "numbers of the people would accept the worst—that is, threatened damnation—rather than be false to the cause of Ireland!"

O'Mahony had expected the bearer of the letter, John O'Leary, to make a fund-raising circuit of the United States, but Stephens declared him unsuitable for the task and instead directed O'Mahony to undertake "the working tour through the States." Stephens gave instructions in detail on how to forward the money gathered and also found it necessary "to tell—nay, command—you to procure clothes suited to the climates" and suited to impress the people he would encounter. Stephens even went on to state, "I give you three months to accomplish your work." One can imagine that such parental scolding from the younger man was not welcomed by O'Mahony. Stephens also required frequent communication from O'Mahony to O'Leary, who would be handling affairs back in New York, an arrangement not much to the liking of the American branch leader.

The prospects for any armed insurrection in Ireland would be greatly improved if it were timed to take advantage of concurrent problems for England. Absent any war, Stephens took some hope in political events, writing "next to a European war, a general election is about the best thing…for us. And the enemy—God increase their difficulties!—shall have the European war to boot! Oh! If all your transatlantic talk should turn out other than the vilest driveling, this very year shall see the Sunburst in the old sacred Isle!"*

A letter that O'Mahony wrote at almost the same time (April 4, 1859) to William Sullivan, a Fenian supporter in Ohio, outlines developments in the American organization. It shows the scope of the effort to organize the Irish throughout the United States, though unwarranted optimism at times

---

* Stephens signed this April 6 letter as "Innisfail," meaning "Island of Destiny," a pseudonym he used along with "James Kelly" and others.

creeps into O'Mahony's assessment of the situation. He alerts Sullivan to the anticipated arrival of O'Leary (Stephens' orders for O'Mahony to make the tour had not yet been received) and reassures him as to the stipulations in the oath that members would take. Realistically facing the situation, O'Mahony wrote, "We must calculate upon a certain amount of opposition from some of the priests." He wanted to avoid any "collision with them openly" and emphasized "Our association is neither anti-Catholic nor irreligious. We are an Irish army, not a secret society."

Citing a recent visit by the secretary of the Belfast Arms Club, O'Mahony waxed enthusiastic about the reported "20,000 stand of arms" the Ribbonmen held in Ulster and their determination "to join the Phoenixes, as they call them." The Ulster connections with England and Scotland also suggested to O'Mahony that they "could cripple England, by attacking her at home in her large towns" and thereby force a quick peace.

Closer to home, O'Mahony could more reliably record that "the organization is extending rapidly, though as yet but little money has come in since I left. Boston is the best city I have on my roll. In it a full centre is now almost completed." He praised the Boston members as working systematically, "each sub-centre sending weekly the regular dues," with a "list opened" for contributions by men "who will not be initiated." After referring to his plans for organizing the Pennsylvania railroad men that "will bring overwhelming numbers into our ranks," O'Mahony continues, "Branches of our society have been also started in Vermont, Maine, and Connecticut." Burlington then had the largest concentration of Irish in Vermont. With their long-standing ties to O'Mahony, it is likely that the Lonergans were involved early in organizing the Fenians in the state.

O'Mahony established the headquarters for the Fenian Brotherhood at No. 6 on the appropriately named Centre Street in New York City, the focal point for the Irish nationalist movement. An armory and a drill hall used by militia units for years were conveniently located above the Centre Street Market. The large Irish population in the area provided manpower and funds as a base for the expansion of the Brotherhood throughout North America. Doheny and another organizer of the earlier Emmet Monument Association, James Roche, founded the *Phoenix* newspaper—named after the nationalist groups in Ireland—to spread the Fenian message.

A larger military unit was likewise formed under the aegis of this fabulous

CHAPTER EIGHT - FENIAN BROTHERHOOD

bird when the Irish regiments of the New York State Militia were brought together in the Phoenix Brigade. In March of 1859, the Fenian leaders gave Michael Corcoran command of their military forces. This position was solidified in August when he was elected colonel of the 69th Regiment NYSM by its members. Born in Sligo, Corcoran had served in Donegal as part of the revenue police (acting mainly against smugglers and brewers of "poteen") until he joined the Ribbonmen during the worst of the Famine. Faced with imprisonment, he fled instead to America and became an early member of the Fenians.

STEPHENS' LIEUTENANT THOMAS CLARK LUBY sent O'Mahony letters on August 25 and September 9, 1860, acting as go-between while Stephens remained in Paris. In the first letter, Luby described the tour that he made with O'Mahony's representative, James Butler, in terms of commerce, a completely transparent cover story. Luby cautioned that "some few of our shareholders in the South [of Ireland] are beginning to lose faith in your branch" and leaning toward self-reliance, being disgusted "with the great promises and little performance of some men at the other side."

The second letter is more direct and aimed at contradicting rumors that the movement in Ireland was dead. It took the very risky step of listing the active "centres" in Ireland along with the signatures of persons themselves. Even with the thin disguise of being only "the undersigned local representatives in Ireland of the Irish firm," this would be just the evidence a British prosecutor would find most damning. It names O'Mahony as the "Supreme Director" of the "American branch" and the nature of the Fenian Brotherhood could not be disputed. These "local representatives" expressed confidence in O'Mahony and in "the conduct and devotion of James Stephens, in the general arrangement of the firm," pledging to stand by them. The list of twenty-five "centres" shows a concentration around Dublin and in the southern counties—Cork, Kilkenny, Waterford, and Tipperary.*

Late in 1860, O'Mahony took the bold step of making a personal inspection tour of the revolutionary organization in Ireland, his first visit

---

* Luby was one "centre" in Dublin and Deniffe another. Echoes of O'Mahony's organization of the Confederate Clubs in 1848 resound in the presence of two names for Carrick on Suir. There were as many "centres" in this rural area as in more populous Dublin—not to mention another across the river in Coolnamuck, and two in Clonmel.

since 1848. Now he returned as the head of another group dedicated to the overthrow of British rule. O'Mahony selected a Waterford man, John D. Hearn, to make the trip with him.* Accompanied by Luby, O'Mahony and Hearn moved around Ireland to meet with the local nationalist organizers. They included a trip to Skibbereen for discussions with Rossa and "some of the most active workers" in the area in early 1861.

Stephens could hardly continue to take refuge in Paris with O'Mahony roaming his turf unobstructed, so the head of the IRB arranged to meet with him in Dublin. Heated arguments ensued regarding Stephens' authority over the operations in America. O'Mahony considered himself in control of the Fenians, even with their stated role of supporting the IRB. Despite the deteriorating personal relationship between the leaders, an understanding was reached that the "American branch" would commit to supplying 500 trained men with arms and officers, along with at least 50,000 rifles and ammunition, for an uprising at an unspecified time. These trained men would come from the Fenian units being organized in state militias throughout the United States.

NEARLY HALF A CENTURY had passed since the United States last faced an external threat, and in many states the militia had fallen dormant. Vermont laws requiring able-bodied men in a certain age range to enroll in the militia had remained on the books, modified from time to time, but not enforced. The state's annual training, traditionally held in June, had become a social occasion, rather than serious military preparation. A decade before the outbreak of the Civil War even the laws requiring Vermont's enrolled militia to serve any military duty, such as the annual training, had been repealed "except in cases of insurrection, war, invasion, or to suppress riots." The few uniformed militia companies that existed on paper were disbanded. By 1856 "there was not, and had not been for ten years, even the semblance of a military organization."

That year, however, concerns that a Vermont militia would soon be needed to deal with the domestic threat of insurrection led the state legislature to pass a new militia law "designed to encourage the formation of military companies." The financial incentives from the state were limited; a member who trained at least three days during the year was entitled to three dollars, but would have

---

* Hearn, a sworn Fenian, was a co-founder of the Mitchel Light Guards, made up of Waterford natives.

CHAPTER EIGHT – FENIAN BROTHERHOOD

expended ten times that amount for the privilege of serving. Although arms were to be supplied by the state, militia members had to pay for their own uniforms. Several companies were formed in the 1856-58 period, although each enrolled less than fifty members. These companies, made up of men who had the time and money to participate, were more elite social clubs than military training units. Each company was independent and directly under the control of the Vermont Adjutant and Inspector General (AIG), elected annually by the state legislature. This general officer reported in turn to the governor of Vermont, the commander in chief of the state's forces. No organizational structure existed grouping the companies into higher level units.

Militia companies were governed by their own by-laws, with reference to the Compiled Statutes of Vermont. The Howard Guards of Burlington and the Ransom Guards of St. Albans were each described as a "voluntary association" in the preambles of their respective by-laws. Members pledged themselves as "Gentlemen and Soldiers" to obedience "to all reasonable and lawful commands of our officers." The dues and other expenses of belonging to such units excluded all but the relatively wealthy, as was no doubt the intention.* To ensure that anyone who joined the company met its social criteria, new members of the Howard Guards had to apply in writing and be endorsed by an existing member. Discharge from either company required "furnishing a suitable person who shall be acceptable to the company and shall be duly enrolled in his stead." This strictly controlled process of selecting members would clearly have excluded a working-class Irish immigrant like John Lonergan, had he tried to enlist in the Burlington company.

As specified in the by-laws, officers of the company were elected at the annual meeting "to be holden on the 2nd Tuesday in January." The "regular business meeting of the Company" was likewise held on the second Tuesday of each month and the commander could call special meetings for drill, parade, or other business. The directors of a company were responsible for providing a "suitable Armory for the meetings" and for "safe keeping of the property of the Company and the arms of the State." A directors' bond was required for the state's property held by the company.

---

* The Howard Guards, incorporated in 1856 by leading members of the community, set the cost of the uniform ("except the Plume") at twenty dollars. Fines were established for various offenses in both companies ranging from twenty-five cents for missing a drill to five dollars for unauthorized wearing of the uniform or equipment.

Organizing, or even joining, a uniformed militia company in Vermont was clearly an expensive proposition. Raising a company required support in the community to recruit the members and probably some financial backing from outside the unit to meet the expenses of a meeting place, company equipment not supplied by the state, and the directors' bond. Few towns in Vermont were large enough to supply sufficient men with the money and inclination to form a company. Recruits were usually accepted from the surrounding area, even from some distance away, and the cost of travel to meetings and musters was borne by the individual. No established militia company in the state had reached its authorized strength of eighty-three officers and men before hostilities actually began in the Civil War.

In the summer of 1858, Governor Ryland Fletcher, a former militia officer with a "strong interest in the revival of the militia," invited (it was an invitation and not an order) the uniformed companies in the state "to muster at Brandon for inspection and review."* Nine companies with a total of some 450 men responded to the invitation, an average of fifty men to a company. Those units present included the Allen Grays in the host city of Brandon, the Ransom Guards of St. Albans, Burlington's Howard Guards, the Green Mountain Guards from Bellows Falls, and the Green Mountain Rangers of Granville. The names chosen for the militia companies often reflected the members' identification with Vermont's history and landscape, although some names, such as the Tunbridge Light Infantry, simply referenced the town in which the company was raised.

Public interest in military preparedness had grown as the internal stresses in the country intensified. Many on-lookers, in any case, considered such training good entertainment with military bands, parades, and firing of muskets—even cannon, if any could be found in working order. John Lonergan may well have been one of those visiting this 1858 muster, since the location was easily reached by rail from Burlington. By this time, he likely intended to enroll in the militia and may even have made plans to organize his own militia company of Fenians. His presumed attendance at the Brandon event could account, at least in part, for his enrollment in the militia company in that town the following year.

As more militia companies were formed throughout the state in 1859,

---

* The birthplace of Stephen Douglas, Brandon was perhaps selected for that reason since the small village offered no obvious advantages as the location for a muster, other than being on a rail line.

they were organized for better control into regiments based on location.* An infantry regiment at full strength would consist of ten companies. Since each Vermont regiment comprised only four to six under-strength companies, the militia could be expanded both within the existing companies and by organizing additional companies. As new companies were formed, they would logically be assigned to the nearest regimental headquarters. The four regiments constituted a brigade, which was placed under the command of Brigadier General (Brig. Gen.) Alonzo Jackman, Professor at the Norwich Military Academy.

In July of 1860, Jackman ordered a muster of all companies, this time mandatory. The actual assembly of the troops at the end of August was preceded on July 27 by an "Officers Drill" held at the Fair Grounds in Burlington. Jackman led the training of officers from twelve companies, who were said to "show decided progress and proficiency." The *Free Press* ran articles urging that the muster itself also be held in Burlington, arguing that "a larger number of spectators can be accommodated in Burlington than any other place proposed." Jackman's decision to use a more central location held firm, however, and the troops mustered at Berlin, near Montpelier.

Under the headline "Gineral Trainin'," the *Free Press* announced where and when the muster would take place, advising "All the men and boys who intend to see the trainers, eat gingerbread, and drink spruce beer in the open and under the eaves of a shanty, will make their arrangements accordingly." This article seemed to equate the spirit of the muster with the former June Training, despite a political crisis in the country that now gave a more serious and immediate purpose to the development of military skills.

Through the new regimental chain of command, Jackman ordered that each company should appear, "armed, uniformed and equipped as the law directs" with three days rations and twenty-four blank cartridges, for training in the town of Berlin from August 29 to 31. On August 18, Colonel (Col.) George J. Stannard issued his own order to the four companies of his 4th Regiment. A "Military Warning" was printed in the *Free Press* on August 25 instructing the Howard Guards to report to their armory, armed and equipped in compliance with Stannard's order. The 4th Regiment's three other companies at Swanton, St. Albans, and Fletcher would have received a similar order to rendezvous for the muster.

---

* The 1st Regiment headquarters was centrally located in Northfield, the 2nd in the southeastern part of the state at Bellows Falls, the 3rd in the northeastern town of Coventry, and the 4th in St. Albans, the largest town in the far northwestern area of Vermont.

With fourteen of the seventeen organized companies "which drew pay that year from the state" taking part in the muster,* the brigade assembled close to 900 men on the parade ground, including the "field and staff officers and music." Each company had chosen and supplied its own uniform, so some troops wore blue and others "cadet gray." The strengths of the four regiments varied. Stannard's newly organized 4th Regiment fielded all four of its companies and was said to "have won very general favor and commendation" in its first appearance "as a battalion." The only company attending from the 3rd Regiment was attached to the 2nd Regiment, giving it a total of five companies. The 1st Regiment from Northfield had four companies present, including the Brandon unit. Newly enlisted in the Allen Grays, John Lonergan would have shouldered his musket as one of the "30 guns" carried in the ranks of the Brandon company.

At the end of 1860, the names of only twenty-two organized companies appeared on the "books of the Adjutant General's office" and five of these had "little more than a nominal existence." However, by this time John Lonergan was hard at work organizing a new militia company in Burlington and ensuring that he would be elected its captain.

EVEN AS THE AMERICANS anxiously observed the growing threat to their Union, Canadian loyalty to the British crown was clearly visible on the occasion of a visit by Albert Edward, Prince of Wales, in 1860. The trip may have been intended to demonstrate the monarchy's concern for its subjects and to solidify the ties of British North America with the homeland. The eighteen-year-old heir to the throne arrived in Newfoundland on August 2, traveling on through the major cities of the Canadian provinces as "Baron Renfrew." In Montreal, a crowd of some 50,000 greeted their future king with pealing church bells and roaring cannon. No doubt the former rebel D'Arcy McGee was one of those cheering spectators, but some of the Irish, a quarter of the city's population, must have been disgruntled exiles with a different attitude.

After his tour through Canada, the prince sailed to Boston and became the first member of the British royal family to visit the United States since

---

* Orders were issued at the close of the muster to disband the Marshfield Rifle company of the 1st Regiment and the Topsham Rifle company of the 2nd Regiment, neither of which had participated.

CHAPTER EIGHT – FENIAN BROTHERHOOD

the country had gained independence. He then continued on to New York City, where Mayor Fernando Wood had arranged for elaborate celebrations that included a huge parade on October 11. The local units of the state militia were instructed to present themselves in good marching order for participation in the parade. This included the 69th Regiment NYSM, commanded by Michael Corcoran.

When O'Mahony went to Ireland, Corcoran, the commander of the Fenian forces, was made temporary Chief Officer of the Brotherhood, a position he held when the Prince of Wales came to visit. Upon receiving orders to parade his unit, Corcoran put the question to the members of his regiment—a thoroughly Fenian unit in the Phoenix Brigade—as to whether they should march in honor of the son of the "Famine Queen." The 69th Regiment heartily disapproved of the idea. Corcoran, knowing the consequences of disobeying a lawful order to participate, acted accordingly and did not issue the order for his troops to parade.

He was attacked in the newspapers for his disrespect of the royal guest, some calling for his dismissal from Custom House employment. Public outrage prevailed, so Corcoran was arrested and subjected to a court martial for his refusal of orders. Irish nationalists across the country cheered his action, however, and showered him with gifts.* This gleeful response by the Irish to Corcoran's refusal showed their widespread hostility toward the British crown and at the same time also revealed the weakness of the nationalist movement. Revolution had been reduced to a sad state when a social snub to the prince was hailed as a victory, while no concrete actions were being taken to liberate the homeland.

Corcoran's prolonged court martial, delayed from time to time due to his illness, played out—almost as a farce—against the dark backdrop of crisis developing in the exiles' adopted nation. A successful uprising in Ireland depended largely on assistance from outside the country. Aid had come in the past from France, but now the Fenian Brotherhood was committed to supplying American manpower and funds to support the IRB's efforts at home. Men like John Lonergan were forming companies to meet this need for trained soldiers. Tragically, the American reservoir of both men and money, so essential to a revolution in Ireland, was about to be diverted into a fratricidal civil war.

---

* Including a gold-headed palmetto cane from South Carolina, a one-pound gold medal from San Francisco for the regiment, and a gold-ornamented sword from fellow New Yorkers.

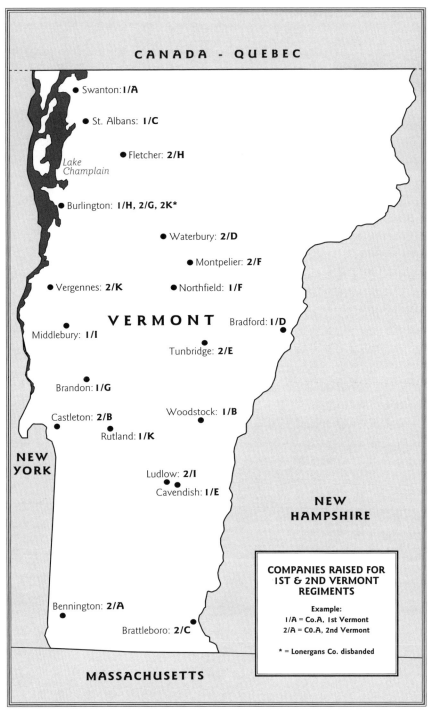

LOCATIONS OF VERMONT MILITIA

CHAPTER NINE

MILITIA MOBILIZED

Hopes for American support of the nationalist movement in Ireland faded because of the crisis facing the United States. The division between free states and those holding slaves, which had festered since the republic was formed, threatened to tear the country apart. In mid-October of 1859, the abolitionist John Brown launched a bloody raid on Harper's Ferry, Virginia, aimed at seizing arms from the federal arsenal there and raising a rebellion of the slaves in the area. Captured and turned over to the state of Virginia for trial, Brown and six others were convicted of treason, murder, and fomenting insurrection. Brown was hanged on December 2.* The deepening conflict between North and South was brought home to Vermont, literally, when Brown's body arrived in the state a few days later, en route to his farm in the hills of eastern New York. Brown was to become the iconic martyr for the abolitionist movement, yet sentiments in the North were still divided on the issue of slavery. The Unitarian minister from Burlington who led Brown's funeral service in North Elba even lost his position for this controversial action.

On the essential question of preserving the Union, the Irish in the United States were generally divided along geographic lines. Most Irish lived in the northern states and basically supported the Union, in part because of its potential for action against Great Britain. In the South, many of them accepted the concept of state's rights that claimed—like the nationalists working for Ireland's freedom—the ultimate prerogative of secession. (The belief that "cotton is king" led many Southerners to expect prompt recognition of their breakaway country by Great Britain because it would appeal to British commercial interests.) Both north and south of the Mason-Dixon

---

* Four more raiders were executed on December 16, and the last two on March 16 of the following year.

Line, however, the working class Irish showed little enthusiasm for ending slavery, because they viewed emancipation as a threat that would increase competition at the lower end of the economic scale.

Irish nationalists in America thus found themselves in a philosophical paradox in regard to the rights of freedom and nationhood. While claiming their own right as a people to be free of British oppression, most Irish turned a blind eye to the institution of slavery, which denied the most basic human right of freedom. Rebellion by the Irish was to be encouraged while rebellion by black slaves, arguably worse off than the Irish, was opposed. The Southern states dissolving their union with the North could be seen as analogous to Irish ambitions of ending the 1801 union with Great Britain. Still, a truncated nation consisting of only those states not holding slaves would have a greatly reduced influence on Great Britain—for example, the decrease in American military power would remove any potential threat to Canada—and subsequently have a negative effect on the Irish struggle for nationhood.

The Irish, including John Lonergan, strongly preferred the Democratic Party—which courted the working class and immigrants—to the newly formed Republicans, but the Democrats were split over slavery and state's rights. The party convention met in April of 1860 in Charleston, South Carolina, a hotbed of secessionist fervor. The leading candidate for the presidential nomination, Stephen Douglas, was rejected despite his condemnation of Brown's raid, and the party split along regional lines. Douglas was then put forward as the candidate of the northern states and John Breckenridge, James Buchanan's vice-president, ran in the South on a pro-slavery platform. This division of the Democratic Party virtually assured the election of the Republican candidate for president.

The Chicago convention of the Republican Party opened in May of 1860 with William H. Seward of New York favored for the nomination, though he faced several other viable contenders. Salmon Chase, a Free Soil advocate from Ohio, seemed his closest rival. Simon Cameron of Pennsylvania and Edward Bates of Missouri, both previously Know Nothing members, had strong support in their own regions. Former Whig Abraham Lincoln of Illinois had crafted a broader base as the general second choice. As a matter of pride, states would also place their "favorite sons," such as Vermont's Senator Jacob Collamer, in nomination. After Seward failed to gain the necessary number of votes on the first ballot, Peter Washburn switched Vermont's ten votes to Lincoln on the second round, helping to secure Lincoln's victory in the next tally. The party approved a platform that remained firmly anti-slavery, though it denounced the Brown raid as the "gravest of crimes" since it sought to foment rebellion.

In the nation-wide elections of November 6, 1860, Lincoln won a clear majority of the electoral votes, but only forty percent of the overall popular vote.* In the ten Deep South states, no Republican slate was on the ballot, and Lincoln received only four percent of the votes in the remaining five slave-holding border states. The North was solidly in favor of Lincoln with sixty percent of the votes; in Vermont he received seventy-five percent. Irishmen like the Lonergans accounted for many of the votes for Douglas in the Green Mountain state.

The split between the free states and the slave-holding states was clear. Still, the reaction of the South to Lincoln's election was startling in its vehemence and speed. Well before his inauguration on March 4, 1861, the country over which he was to preside faced the secession of the Southern states from the Union.

Charleston led the way when it dissolved the union "between South Carolina and other states." on December 20, 1860. Five more Deep South states took the same action in January of 1861, and Texas joined their ranks the following month. The federal government had to decide how to react to these declarations. Was this step a legal recourse by these states or an act of rebellion that must be suppressed? Until Lincoln took the oath of office, President Buchanan held the executive power to deal with the situation. The two men agreed that secession violated the constitution and laws of the United States, yet Buchanan felt that the national government did not have any legal basis "to coerce a State into submission."

Compromise proposals introduced in Congress had no success. On February 4, delegates from the seven seceding states met in Montgomery, Alabama, and in six days organized their new country, the Confederate States of America. Lincoln, in his inaugural address one month later, reaffirmed his determination to preserve the Union, by force if necessary.

LINCOLN'S THREAT OF FORCE may well have rung hollow because the national government had fewer forces available than the swelling ranks of militia in the Confederacy. John Floyd of Virginia, Secretary of War under Buchanan, had

---

* Lincoln placed his competitors for the presidency (and potential critics) in key posts in his cabinet: Seward was appointed Secretary of State, Chase made Secretary of the Treasury, Bates served as Attorney General, and Cameron briefly held the office of Secretary of War.

not only sold off government property to cronies, but had moved arms to the South before he left office in December. The federal arsenals, forts, and other materials of war located in the South had been seized, with a few exceptions, by enthusiastic state militia units. On an island in Charleston Harbor, Fort Sumter remained in federal control, but was under siege by secessionist forces demanding that the facility be turned over to the state.

On entering his presidential office for the first time after his inauguration, Lincoln found a message on his desk from the fort's commander, Major (Maj.) Robert Anderson, advising that only a few weeks of supplies remained. The unfinished fort and its meager garrison were ringed by batteries around the harbor that had been taken over by the South Carolina militia. These batteries had fired on and driven off an unarmed merchant ship trying to bring reinforcements and supplies to the fort on January 9. Anderson had not returned fire from the fort, however, and the uneasy standoff continued.

Still seeking to avoid the outbreak of actual hostilities, Lincoln informed the rebellious governor that ships would bring supplies, but no additional troops, to Fort Sumter in mid-April. The President of the Confederate States, Jefferson Davis, decided to force the issue and ordered that the fort be pounded into submission before any federal ships could re-supply it. Accordingly, firing commenced at 4:30 AM on April 12. Heavy shore batteries at Fort Johnson, located on James Island south of the target and now in the hands of the secessionists, contributed their fire to the 4,000 shot and shell that bombarded the federal stronghold over thirty-three hours.

One of these batteries, seized by the rebels and turned against the fort by men of the 1st South Carolina Artillery, was commanded by Lieutenant (Lt.) John Mitchel, the eldest son of the Irish rebel with the same name. Now another generation of Irishmen had taken up arms in a rebellion, though not to liberate their homeland. Civil war could not be avoided after Anderson surrendered on April 14; in four years of bitter conflict, thousands of Irish patriots on each side would perish or be disabled, lost forever to the cause of Erin's freedom.

To CRUSH THE SOUTHERN REBELLION, Lincoln needed far more troops than were available in the regular military forces. In the spring of 1861, the regular army of some 16,000 men was mostly scattered among seventy-nine outposts west of the Mississippi River, while the 10,000 sailors in the Navy manned forty-two ships, few of them in American waters. An expansion of the federal army and navy was set in progress, but the creation of new units would take time. The President also had to deal with the reality that even these existing forces would be reduced as Southerners withdrew to join the opposing side. About a third of the two thousand army and navy officers decided that their loyalty was to their home state, rather than the Union, and resigned their commissions to bring their valuable experience to the growing Southern forces.

Americans had historically rejected a large national standing army as an unnecessary expense and the potential tool of a military dictator. Instead, each state traditionally enrolled its citizen-soldiers in militia units that could assist the federal military under certain conditions.

By law, state militia units might be called up for federal service to repel a foreign invasion; they could also be mobilized by the president to put down an internal insurrection. The restricted justification for national control of state forces was likewise limited in time; the President could require only ninety days federal service by a state militia unit in any year. Lincoln quickly initiated the procedure to make use of the available state forces, federalizing many of the militia units and placing them under the President's command.

Four days before Lincoln's inauguration, the new breakaway government in the South passed a bill authorizing its president to receive "the arms and munitions of war which have been acquired from the United States." President Jefferson Davis would likewise "receive into Government service" such forces of the seceding states "as may be tendered, in such number as he may require" to serve at least one year, forming the Confederate Army and Navy.

Until the actual hostilities began, the rebels allowed officers and men of the regular army who were still loyal to the Union to leave a state after it seceded, if they chose to do so. Unlike the officers, who had the option of giving up their commissions, the enlisted ranks could be charged with desertion if they went over to the Confederacy. Enlisted men in the regular army also might well be immigrants who felt no overriding loyalty to a particular state.

WORKING AS A COOPER in the family trade, John Lonergan somehow had still found the time and money to join the Vermont militia in 1859. Although the closest uniformed company was the Howard Guards in his hometown of Burlington, he enlisted as a private in the Allen Grays, fifty miles away in Brandon. The young Irish Catholic, who likely would not have been able to obtain the required sponsorship by a member of the elite Howard Guards, would have been more welcome in the Brandon company. The roster of the Brandon company in May of 1861—no earlier roster is available—lists sixteen members from the large Irish community in Rutland, a mere seventeen miles to Brandon's south, and another dozen from area villages with substantial Irish population. Many of these members bore surnames of obviously Irish origin; no doubt this was also the case in 1859. If sponsorship was required at that time, Lonergan could have drawn upon nationalist ties to enroll in the unit.

The direct rail connections from Burlington to Brandon would have made it possible for Lonergan to attend the required monthly meetings and special training events, though at some expense. This travel would also have given him contact with the numerous Irish who had settled along the rail lines. Many of the Irish around Rutland worked for the railroads or in the marble quarries of West Rutland. Some of these quarrymen might well have even been previously employed in the extensive Ahenny slate quarries near Carrick on Suir, briefly seized in 1848 by rebelling workers. Such personal connections would be useful for advancing Lonergan's military agenda, both as an individual and as a budding Fenian leader in Vermont.

Lonergan would have considered joining this company to be the first step in the process of creating his own military unit. As we have already seen, the Fenian Brotherhood had established a circle in Vermont in 1859. The movement encouraged its members to be active in military training and the Fenians likely encouraged Lonergan to join an existing militia unit.

Lonergan served in the Brandon company only a short time, probably resigning from the unit soon after the 1860 muster in Berlin, Vermont, to organize his own company of uniformed militia with Fenian assistance. The muster would have given him an opportunity to solicit support for this plan and it appears that he received encouragement, particularly from Col. Stannard. Certainly within a few months, Stannard, commander of the militia regiment in the northwest region, officially took action to have the Emmet Guards in Burlington entered on Vermont's roll of militia companies. Lonergan's choice of this name was clearly intended to signal that the company was affiliated with the Fenian movement like the Irish militia units elsewhere.*

---

* With its population of only some 300,000, Vermont's contribution of Irish nationalist soldiers would, of course, be on a much smaller scale than that of its neighboring states. Where entire regiments of sworn Fenians were formed in New York and Massachusetts, Vermont could add only a single company to these forces during the Civil War.

CHAPTER NINE – MILITIA MOBILIZED

With the creation of the Emmet Guards, young Lonergan suddenly appears on the scene in official records and newspaper articles, a leader of Irish nationalists in the state. Brash and self-assured, he spared no effort to promote himself and his militia company, attracting support from some influential persons around the state and opposition from others.

Vermont's Irish were still struggling to overcome prejudice and achieve some acceptance in society. Burlington saw no public celebration of St. Patrick's Day in 1860, although the March 16 *Sentinel* printed "To My Wife," a poem written by the prominent Irish nationalist Joseph Brenan.* The author had died of "consumption" in 1857, still hoping for the independence of his homeland. The poem even compared his wife's attributes to Ireland with "Eyes like the skies of poor Erin, our mother" and a smile for "the exile to brighten his dreaming."

THE DEVELOPING NATIONAL CONFLICT made Vermont military authorities anxious to expand the militia and to ensure its loyalty. Erastus Fairbanks, who had failed to win re-election 1853 after the narrow victory of his temperance legislation, returned to the governor's office in Montpelier in 1860. In his inaugural address to the Vermont General Assembly on October 13, Fairbanks included concerns as to whether the present militia laws after "frequent modifications and changes" were now adequate for the existing situation facing the nation. He described the people of Vermont as "warmly attached to the Union of the States" and pledged "to preserve the sacred bond," ready even to "invoke, if necessary, the national arm for its preservation." Although Fairbanks saw Vermonters as "firm and unyielding in their views of human freedom," he came down strongly in favor of state's rights and opposed slavery only where attempts were made to extend the practice "beyond the limits of the States which have legalized it."**

As commander in chief of the state's militia, the governor began to order such actions as he deemed necessary to prepare for a potential conflict. Aware

---

* In 1853, Brenan had hosted Meagher in New Orleans during his speaking tour of the South.

** This fervent supporter of the Temperance League also noted with satisfaction that the "laws prohibiting the traffic in intoxicating liquors have become the settled and approved policy of the State," although local ordnances apparently allowed for the sale and consumption of alcoholic beverages.

that "many towns in this State" had neglected to enroll men in the militia as required by statute, on January 21, 1861, Fairbanks pointed out "the importance of holding the military arm of the State in readiness to respond to any requisition of the President of the United States for aid in suppressing rebellion and executing the laws of the General Government." Town Clerks were put on notice "to require an immediate compliance with the provisions of the statute."

At the governor's instruction, Vermont General Order (GO) No. 10 was issued on January 25, by H. Henry Baxter, the AIG, anticipating such a possible "requisition of the President." The order instructed the "commanding officer of each company of Uniformed Militia" to "ascertain at once whether any men in their commands are unable or indisposed to respond to the orders of the Commander-in-Chief." Such members were to be discharged and replaced "by men ready for any public exigency which may arise." In addition to replacing these unreliable men, the commanders were told to "make proper exertions" to fill the ranks to "the number of men allowed by law." A list of each member, his rank, and place of residence was to be compiled and a copy sent to Baxter's office.

This notice was printed in the *Free Press* on January 30 alongside a personal letter from Maj. Anderson, the commander of Fort Sumter, explaining his inability to return fire on the South Carolina batteries that had driven off the supply ship on January 9. Other news items on the same page documented the rising tension, with rumors of plots to seize the national capital and to assassinate General in Chief Winfield Scott.

ALTHOUGH THE EMMET GUARDS does not appear in any records as an aspiring company of the Vermont militia until early 1861, Lonergan must have begun organization of the new unit in the last half of 1860.* Sometime in 1860, he had started in the grocery and provision business in Winooski, a village in Colchester Town, just across the Winooski River falls from Burlington. Lonergan no doubt chose to form his company in Burlington because of his contacts among the numerous Irishmen in the larger town. The company assembled in Burlington for what may have been its first official meeting, to

---

* Documentation for the period leading up to the Civil War is fragmentary at best. Many of Vermont's official military records were lost in the 1945 fire at the State Arsenal in Montpelier.

include the election of its officers and non-commissioned officers, on January 10, 1861, the second Thursday of the month. Lonergan later insisted that his seniority in rank dated from this election as captain of the Emmet Guards in its initial formation.

The earliest reference to the unit is found in a letter written the next day by Col. Stannard as commander of the 4th Regiment. On January 11, Stannard certified to the Vermont Quartermaster General (QM Gen.) George Davis that "a military company has been organized according to Law in Burlington" and the men are "now anxious to obtain their guns." He asked that the necessary papers be sent to John Lonergan in Winooski, complaining that "there has been so much delay and talk about this" that he would be pleased to have the matter settled. Stannard obviously had supported Lonergan's effort to form another militia company in Burlington, which would add a fifth company to the 4th Regiment.

Lonergan himself followed up promptly with a letter from Winooski dated February 4, 1861, in which he sent the "Directors Bond Signed & Sealed &c." to QM Gen. Davis.* He pressed the man in charge of Vermont's military supplies to provide him with "guns and equipments as soon as possible," saying that he had promised the company that they would have guns at the armory within the week. The new company commander wrote again on February 20 stating, "I have heard nothing from you since I sent our Bond" and asking the quartermaster whether AIG Baxter, "has not reported us entitled to guns and equipment." His postscript warned "if I don't receive guns very soon this company will disband. The men can do nothing without guns to drill with and are waiting 6 months for them." This reference to six months places the creation of the Emmet Guards in August of the previous year and coincides with Stannard's remark about "so much delay." The Berlin muster was held at the end of August and Lonergan evidently set his plans for a new company in motion there.

On March 9, Col. Stannard again pressed Davis in the matter of weapons for the Emmet Guards, writing "Why don't Co. E of this Regiment get their guns?" and offering to take any action necessary. In a postscript he also asked "How about new guns for Co. A Burlington?" saying Baxter had assured

---

* Receipt of the directors' bond was a necessary administrative step before the state would provide any weapons or equipment to a uniformed company. Lonergan must have found sponsors in the community (or the Fenian Brotherhood) to fund the required bond and other expenses of organizing a militia company.

him they were forthcoming. This clearly establishes that, in Stannard's mind at least, Lonergan's Emmet Guards were considered a company of the 4th Regiment and had been assigned the next letter designation, making them Company E.

Providing new arms to the militia was a high priority for the state and the distribution of modern rifled muskets was the subject of much discussion. The Vermont arsenal totaled just under a thousand outdated muskets, mostly smoothbore flintlocks converted to the more modern percussion cap. In a letter dated March 18, Baxter told Davis that Gov. Fairbanks was applying pressure for sixty new guns for the Woodstock company, deferring to the quartermaster as to whether they would be supplied. Regarding guns for the Howard Guards, Baxter claimed to have written them that "they better keep cool." He then went on in the same vein: "The Irish captain in Winooski wrote me several times. I did not reply to his letters, until finally I wrote him to go to the d---l." This comment reveals Baxter's negative, even contemptuous, attitude toward Lonergan and may help to explain the later fate of the Emmet Guards. The support given Lonergan by his regimental commander clearly did not extend to the military authorities at the state level.

THE DAY AFTER FORT SUMTER surrendered, Lincoln issued a call for 75,000 militia troops to serve three months. Telegrams were sent to all states that had not seceded from the Union to supply forces to "repossess the forts, places, and property which have been seized." Both Houses of Congress were convened in special session, but would not meet until July 4; until then Lincoln acted as the sole authority.

Varied responses to Lincoln's call came from the slave-holding states still in the Union; only Delaware and Maryland offered troops to defend the capital of the United States. Virginia rejected the use of its militia "to subjugate the southern states" and its governor told Lincoln flatly "you have chosen to inaugurate civil war." The governors of all the northern states assured Lincoln of their support. In response to the President's question of what to expect from Vermont, Gov. Fairbanks asserted that his state would do its "full duty."

The initial call for 75,000 men was apportioned among the loyal states according to their population. While neighboring New York was asked to

CHAPTER NINE – MILITIA MOBILIZED

supply seventeen regiments with over 13,000 men, Vermont was levied a single infantry regiment of ten companies totaling 780 men. "War meetings" were being held throughout the state to urge enlistment to fill the ranks of the existing militia companies and community leaders promoted the formation of additional companies. Such leaders often envisioned themselves being elected by the members to command the units being raised.

On April 18, a "war meeting" was held in Winooski where the town pledged to furnish a full company of one hundred men. The following evening a rally was held in Burlington to fill the ranks of the Howard Guards. Taking the opportunity to promote his own company, the *Free Press* reported "Captain Lonergan announced that the Emmet Guards were not dead yet, and that those who would attend their meeting to-morrow evening would see how Irishmen would volunteer to sustain the Government of their adopted country." Despite Lonergan's efforts, aided by Col. Stannard and others, the Emmet Guards still had not been enrolled into the ranks of the uniformed militia by the state authorities.

That same evening, the top officers of the Vermont militia gathered in Burlington to select the companies that would constitute the 1st Vermont Regiment. These senior militia officers comprised the brigade commander, Brig. Gen. Jackman, and "the field officers" of the several militia regiments.* Patriotic fervor led most commanders to urge that their militia companies be included, but few units were considered fit for duty based on the number of members and their training. Eight militia companies, including three from Stannard's 4th Regiment, "were reported as substantially full and in efficient condition." There was no single Vermont militia regiment of sufficient strength to fulfill the requirement from the President, so a composite unit had to be formed from companies assigned to the various regiments around the state.

Lonergan may have been present for this process, as he had "at once offered his services to Colonel Stannard, and was ordered by him to attend the first war meeting of the officers of the state militia held in Burlington April 19, 1861." Some other line officers were at the gathering, including the captain of the Calais company and the captain of the Marshfield company that had been ordered disbanded at the end of the 1860 muster. The Irishman's presence among the group, if he did attend, did not produce the result he desired. Lonergan, like the other company commanders, hoped for the honor of having his company

---

* Field-grade officers are those holding the ranks of major, lieutenant colonel, and colonel; line officers are lieutenants and captains.

selected for the first regiment being raised. Stannard wrote to Baxter on April 21 offering four of his five companies in the 4th Regiment, including the Emmet Guards, for immediate service (the colonel did not consider the Fletcher company ready to serve). Stannard must have also made the offer earlier (perhaps verbally at the meeting or by telegraph), as the *Free Press* had reported on April 19 that Stannard had notified Baxter that his regiment was "ready to serve the country on twelve hours' notice."* Based on his statement to Baxter, which one source dates to April 15, Stannard is often credited with being the first Vermonter to volunteer to serve in the Civil War.

After being included in the letter from his regimental commander, Lonergan anticipated that his company would receive its marching orders and therefore published a notice in the *Free Press* on April 22. Under the headline "Attention, Emmet Guard!" the members were "hereby requested to appear at you[r] Armory" that evening "then and there to wait further orders." Their hopes were no doubt raised by Stannard's rating of the company among those ready to serve on twelve hours' notice. The "further orders" the amateur soldiers received after gathering at their armory on College Street, however, were a disappointment. The Emmet Guards were dismissed and could return to their homes, since the company had not been selected for the ninety days of federal service.

The 1st Regiment of Vermont Volunteer Infantry (VVI) was constituted from ten companies of the uniformed militia by order of the Adjutant General on April 27. The commissions received by the regimental field officers and staff from the governor bore the date of April 26. Company officers had their commissions dated from the time of their election to the position in the company. For example, Captain Clark had evidently commanded the Green Mountain Guards in Swanton since July 30, 1859, as this was entered in the records as his date of commission and date of issue. In Stannard's regiment, the St. Albans, Swanton, and Burlington (the Howard Guards) companies were called up for service, leaving the Fletcher company and Lonergan's Emmet Guards for mobilization later. Seven companies, including Lonergan's former unit in Brandon, were supplied by the remaining three Vermont militia regiments.

---

* The article further stated, "The regiment consists of the Burlington, St. Albans, Swanton and Fletcher companies." It is not clear whether this listing intended to include two companies in Burlington (the Howard Guards as Co. A and the Emmet Guards as Co. E) or only the established Howard Guards.

CHAPTER NINE – MILITIA MOBILIZED

The ten companies reported to Rutland, a central location with good rail connections, on May 2. As required by law, the companies were mustered into United States service by a Regular Army officer; Lieutenant Colonel (Lt. Col.) Gabriel J. Rains, who had been detailed to Vermont for this purpose. After the muster and oath of allegiance on May 8 initiated the Vermonters into federal service, the regiment departed the next day by rail for New York City. There they boarded the steamer *Alabama* that carried the unit to Fortress Monroe, still under Union control in rebel Virginia.

THE FENIAN BROTHERHOOD OFFICIALLY supported the Union, but its members in the South generally took up the Confederate cause with equal enthusiasm. Whichever side they chose, throughout the country militia units that had originally been formed for the cause of liberating Ireland eagerly took up arms instead against Americans on the opposing side.

In April of 1861, Col. Michael Corcoran was still under arrest as his trial on charges of disobeying orders dragged on. With the onset of hostilities, the charges against him were dropped and he was released to lead the 69th NYSM Regiment to war. Corcoran, who had been acting as Chief Officer of the Fenians while O'Mahony was in Ireland, now turned over the reins of the Brotherhood to John Murphy. Michael Cavanagh, the secretary, would handle all communications.

On April 21, before departing for the front, Corcoran addressed the Fenians of New York to urge them to "hold aloof from the fratricidal strife and reserve their lives for the cause to which they were already pledged." Stating that there were "ten times as many of their countrymen (who were not yet enrolled Fenians) as he required," he still advised those Fenians who were determined to enlist not to have "their national identity lost among strangers" by joining other than Irish units. An official circular was sent out the next day from the Fenian Headquarters to every circle of the Brotherhood. Corcoran explained that "a sudden emergency" had called him away "from the duty entrusted to me by Mr. O'Mahony." Leaving in "great spirits and hope," his concern was that the "organization be preserved in its strength and efficiency." He optimistically stated, "we will not be the worse for a little practice" that "will be serviceable on other fields."

Cheered by a crowd of "half a million," on April 23, the 69th Regiment marched down Broadway under newly presented national colors. Alongside the Stars and Stripes, the color guard held aloft the green regimental flag with its Fenian symbols. The unit colors also defiantly bore an inscription commemorating the 69th's refusal to parade for the Prince of Wales.

Although Meagher had not yet formally joined the Fenians, he had pointedly made a visit to the organization's headquarters on April 22, 1861. Meagher, a steadfast Democrat and openly sympathetic to the Southern viewpoint, nonetheless strongly condemned the South for firing on his new country's flag.* He cited "duty and patriotism alike" in urging the defense of "the Republic, that gave us an asylum" and declared it "not only our duty to America, but also to Ireland." He recognized the need for "moral and material aid" from America to achieve Irish independence. In a grimmer assessment of the cost of the war than Corcoran's view, Meagher saw it "a moral certainty that many of our countrymen who enlist in this struggle for the maintenance of the Union will fall in the contest." Meagher, who had missed the fighting at Ballingary in 1848 and had yet to hear a shot fired in anger, thought that if only one in ten returned from the war, the survivor would be "of more service in a fight for Ireland's freedom" than the ten inexperienced men.

A company attached to the 69th NYSM Regiment, the Brigade Lancers, did not accompany it south and Meagher was invited to organize a new Company K to fill the slot. Typically, he chose to make it the "Irish Zouaves" decked out in flamboyant red pantaloons and fezzes. Within a few days he had raised the required one hundred recruits eager to serve with "Meagher of the Sword." After drilling for several weeks, the Zouave company caught up with the 69th in Washington on May 23, the day before the regiment crossed the Potomac River into Virginia.

O'Mahony, the absent Head Centre of the Fenian Brotherhood, cut short his work in Ireland when he heard of the hostilities in America and "hastened back to New York." The 69th was already in Virginia by the time he returned and he wrote Corcoran of his intention to enlist with the regiment. Corcoran replied on May 29 to dissuade O'Mahony from this action, stating "our Irish cause and organization in America would grievously, if not fatally,

---

* Meagher had renounced his British citizenship soon after coming to the United States and after the required three year waiting period had become a U.S. citizen in May of 1857. Before the war, he had toured the South extensively giving speeches about Ireland and his experiences and had found the lifestyle there agreeable. With his wealthy background, he felt at home on the plantations and apparently did not see the irony of his rhetoric about Irish freedom in presentations to crowds of slave owners.

suffer" from the loss of his services and supervision. Corcoran thought that "our organization will derive considerable impetus and strength from the military enthusiasm prevailing here," but felt it "most essential that a man like you should remain to enlarge and perfect it." He did invite O'Mahony to visit the camp and the chief promptly traveled to Virginia where he "infused fresh courage into the hearts of his gallant comrades" with his reports on developments in Ireland.

AFTER THE INITIAL LEVY of state militia troops to serve for three months, Lincoln made a more realistic assessment of the situation. On May 3, he then asked the states to provide more troops, this time to serve for three years "or the duration of the war." The loyal states were requested to supply forty regiments—all infantry, except for one regiment of cavalry—plus 18,000 seamen to expand the navy. Simultaneously the regular army would be increased by about 20,000 soldiers—eight regiments of infantry and one each of cavalry and artillery. The Vermont legislature had not waited for the presidential call; on April 26, before its first regiment had even left the state, the legislature had authorized the formation of two more regiments and then an additional four, if required.

After being passed over for the first Vermont regiment, Lonergan did not wait passively for his company to be chosen for one of the next regiments. On April 30, he procured a letter from Lt. Gov. Levi Underwood in Burlington, addressed to Gov. Fairbanks. Underwood told the governor that "the bearer Capt. John Lonergan of this place commanding an organized Co. called the Emmett [sic] Guards desires to be put into the service of the Country." Lonergan had showed him "a memorial signed by our best citizenry" and Underwood described the company as "strong, hardy & patriotic & are willing to fight for the right." However, "they are not armed or equipped," despite their "desire to be put under drill so as to make themselves efficient."

The "memorial"—likewise dated April 30 and addressed to the governor—was signed by sixty-two citizens of Burlington. These prominent townsmen had been "informed that Capt. John Lonergan, of the Emmett [sic] Guards, an organized and enrolled company of the Vermont Militia, is ready with a large portion of his company to volunteer in the service of the State in one of the new regiments recently provided for by the Legislature." The endorsement goes on to "heartily unite in recommending him to your

Excellency as a worthy and patriotic soldier" and trusted that the desires of Lonergan and his company "may be gratified by their immediate enrollment and equipment as a company in one of the two new regiments." In soliciting this support, Lonergan had stretched the facts—his company was not yet "organized and enrolled" in the Uniformed Militia.

With this approach to the governor, Lonergan thus called attention to the availability of his company for service in one of the next Vermont regiments. A newspaper article on the activities of the Volunteers in Burlington on April 30 concluded "The Emmet Guards also drill daily, and will make a formidable company." Whether he was able to meet personally with the governor or not, Lonergan's tactic of combining favorable press reports with endorsements by prominent community leaders succeeded in securing him an appointment as a recruiting officer to raise a company.

Another Irishman, James C. Smith of Hydeville, made his own application to Gov. Fairbanks on May 2 "to raise a Company of Irish Volunteers in this vicinity." The village is about fifteen miles west of Rutland near Fair Haven, only a few miles from the New York state border. Smith wrote again on May 19 asking the governor for "a commission to Raise sd. Company in Hon. of the Greenmountain [sic] State." If Fairbanks refused, Smith was prepared to offer the company to the governor of New York, who had already accepted entire regiments of Irish into his state militia. Given the Vermont governor's generally hostile attitude toward immigrants, it is not surprising that Smith and his offer of a company of Irish volunteers received no encouragement from Fairbanks.

On May 3, Baxter dealt with the flood of applicants for "commissions to enlist Volunteer Militia Companies" from all over the state. The AIG—"as directed by the Commander-in-Chief," the governor—designated recruiting stations and recruiting officers to "enlist and enroll twenty companies only" for the 2nd and 3rd Vermont Volunteer Infantry regiments. Published in the *Free Press*, the announcement listed only nineteen locations and eighteen names of recruiting officers. Four locations were flagged to indicate "At these stations, volunteers from the present Companies of the Uniform[ed] Militia will be first enlisted." John Lonergan was designated as a recruiting officer, but for Winooski—not Burlington, where the Emmet Guards drilled daily—and Winooski was not flagged as having a "present" company. No recruiting officer was designated for Burlington, the only such omission on the published list, despite the presence of two active companies there, including the Emmet Guards. The announcement ended with a cautionary note that companies should not spend any money on uniforms, as the state would furnish them (though Vermont continued to send federalized troops south wearing gray uniforms).

Hardly a week had passed after Lonergan's appointment before a group of irate citizens of Winooski sent Gen. Baxter a letter complaining about Lonergan's conduct. According to the ten men from "Winooski Falls" who signed the May 11 letter, on the second day that Lonergan had manned the recruiting office, he closed it to prevent enlistment by members of the "Ethan Allen Volunteers" that had been formed in Winooski. Instead, he went to Burlington and enlisted men there (probably from his Emmet Guards). The petitioners (all with good "Yankee" surnames) charged Lonergan with giving "preference to all *Irish* citizens" and thus "using unfair means to secure his election as Captain of the Company he is recruiting here." They asked that preference instead be given to "the said Ethan Allen Volunteers" as they believed "it would be impossible to recruit a company in this vicinity" without including some from their ranks. However, they opined that no member of the Ethan Allen company "will enlist with the said John Lonergan thinking he is to serve under him as Captain." This letter was sent the day after the *Free Press* reported that the twenty companies needed for the next two regiments had been selected. Fifty-nine companies had offered their services and "among the disappointed ones we are sorry to learn is the Colchester Company—the Ethan Allen Volunteers, which has accordingly disbanded."

Baxter had his hands full with the mobilization of troops for the next two regiments being raised in Vermont. He wrote a status report to Gov. Fairbanks on May 18 describing how he had dispatched senior officers around the state to inspect companies and hold elections in order to muster the units being organized into state service. He commented that he was not the cause of any delay in organizing the Burlington company (the newly formed Vermont Guards), saying the sooner it was "off my hands, the better I shall like it." He had told the commander, Capt. John T. Drew, to let him know "the moment he had 83 men on his roll," that being the new minimum number required by regulations for units called into service under the May 3, 1861, presidential proclamation.* He went on to explain that Capt. Drew had sent a telegram saying he was ready, so Gen. Hopkins, Assistant AG, would be in Burlington "Monday" (May 20) to inspect his men and hold elections of officers. Then "on Tuesday morning he will do the same thing at Winooski with Lonergan's Co.,"

---

* The maximum for a company of infantry was 101, the difference being only in the number of privates, at least sixty-four and at most eighty-two.

which indicates Lonergan had likewise reported that his company was ready with the required number of members.

Baxter also wrote that the question of payment for boarding men in Burlington had been raised by Carolus Noyes, a lawyer and representative for that town in the Vermont General Assembly. The AIG was eager to muster the men into camp, feeling that it would resolve the matter of paying board and would help as well to prevent desertion, several cases of which had already occurred. Baxter volunteered his opinion that "if any recruiting officer you have appointed has not his roll full at this time and there is not a probability of its being full *at once*, the only way to go is to displace him, disband the few men he may have, and take in his place one of the companies formed outside of recruiting officers, Calais & Montpelier ([William T.]Burnham), for instance."*

Although some residents of Colchester Town did not want to see Lonergan raise a company from Winooski, enough men were assembled there for the unit to pass the inspection by Gen. Hopkins, who traveled from Rutland for this purpose. This company was probably made up mostly of members of the Emmet Guards brought over from Burlington. A handwritten roster, possibly incomplete, of the men in Company K, 2nd Vermont Regiment, shows about half were Irish, a few had French surnames, and the rest appear to be "Yankees." Two dozen names on the roster are lined out, perhaps rejected on medical examination or because they changed their minds about enlisting. This record shows sixty-two privates, just under the minimum number required.

On May 21, the "Company at Winooski" was mustered into the service of the state of Vermont with Lonergan duly elected as its captain. A *Free Press* article reported the event—"General Hopkins addressed the Company after the election, and Captain Lonergan made a patriotic speech."—and listed the officers and non-commissioned officers of the company. The Vermont Guards, whose eighty-six men had been inspected and enrolled in the Uniformed Militia by Gen. Hopkins the previous day, had marched from Burlington across the two-lane covered bridge spanning the Winooski River for a visit in the morning. Both captains, Drew and Lonergan, made speeches "which the companies heartily applauded." No figure was given in the newspaper for the number of men mustered into state service as members of the

---

* This comment mid-May seems ominously prescient in view of what would transpire one month later with Lonergan's company, but it contradicts the process used at the time to augment another company in the same regiment.

CHAPTER NINE — MILITIA MOBILIZED

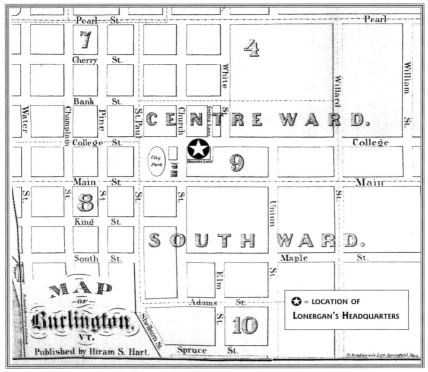

Downtown Burlington, Vermont

Winooski company, though it must have been at least the minimum required.

By the end of the month, the "Winooski Volunteers" were drilling daily at a room in the Leavenworth Block on College Street in downtown Burlington. Taking their meals at the Lake House down on the waterfront, they could easily make use of the nearby open space at Battery Park as well. Lonergan had maneuvered his company into official status and it was now comfortably settled back into its old armory and again answering to the name of "Emmet Guard."* The fiction that Lonergan had recruited a company in Winooski seems to have been a successful navigation around the reluctance on the part of senior state authorities to accept his Emmet Guards in the Vermont Uniformed Militia. After overcoming that obstacle,

---

* The *Free Press* article of June 4 on "The New Regiment" revealed that "the Second Regiment has been ordered to Washington" and would probably depart the next week.
Readers learned that "It will include the Vermont Guard, Capt. Drew, and the Emmet Guard, Capt. Lonergan."

the next step for taking part in the war was to have the company mustered for active duty in federal service.

THE TEN MILITIA COMPANIES considered the best organized had already been selected in April for the 1st Vermont. Now in early May there were some sixty "companies" competing to offer their services for the next regiment. Unlike the Emmet Guards, which had been drilling for some months (even if not recognized by the state), most of the companies had only come into existence at patriotic "war meetings" held in the previous few weeks. Few of the new companies had any claim to being organized or having members with even the rudiments of military skills. From this limited choice, it was up to Baxter to pull together the next two regiments by selecting twenty companies for inspection and muster into the 2nd and 3rd Vermont.

His representatives, such as Gen. Hopkins, fanned out over the state and identified sufficient companies for Baxter to issue General Order (GO) No. 14 on June 3, 1861, which specified that two regiments were to be raised, "each regiment consisting of 10 companies of 83 officers and enlisted men each." The composition of the "Second Regiment of Vermont Volunteers" was listed with the names of those "commissioned as the officers of the several companies." Last on the list was Company K, Winooski, John Lonergan, Captain.

The company letter designations were assigned in general order of seniority based on the date of the captain's commission (the date of his election to the position). Company A was commanded by Capt. James Walbridge, date of commission May 16, the earliest commissioning date given for a line officer in the 2nd Regiment, and the remaining companies follow generally by date of the officers' commissions through Co. I on May 22. Lonergan's election on May 21 should have given him seniority for the Co. I designation instead of Co. K, the last in the regiment. (The letter J is not used to avoid confusion with I in written documents.)

In GO 14, the commanding officers of the companies for the 2nd Regiment were ordered to "report themselves with the men under their command, to Lieutenant Colonel George J. Stannard, Commanding at Camp 'Underwood,' Burlington, on or before Thursday, the 6th inst."*

---

* The camp was named for the lieutenant governor, a resident of Burlington.

Baxter warned that "strict subordination will be inforced [sic] through the camp" and urged the "utmost diligence in the performance of all duties." Stannard was in charge due to the absence of the regimental commander. Henry Whiting, although a native of New York and residing in Michigan, had been chosen by Fairbanks because of his West Point education and was in St. Johnsbury accepting the offer of command of the regiment.

On June 6 Whiting received his commission as colonel; he arrived at Camp Underwood the next day and formally took command of the regiment on June 8. Stannard's commission was also dated June 6, as was that of the English-born Maj. Charles H. Joyce. These two field officers had been the commanders of the 4th and 1st Regiments of the Vermont militia respectively. Stannard and Joyce thus knew each other and at least some, if not all, of the company commanders in the 2nd Vermont.

The regimental camp was located on the northern outskirts of Burlington at the state fairgrounds, easily reached from the railroad station downtown. The "agricultural halls upon the grounds furnish very complete accommodations for the commissariat department" and the soldiers were reportedly well fed. Fine weather made it no hardship to sleep in tents and the officers were provided with cornhusk mattresses, the men making do with blankets and a rubber ground cloth. The published daily schedule called for a full day of military training beginning with reveille at 5:00 AM and ending with tattoo at 9:00 PM. Military discipline was established with the posting of guards, assignments as officer of the day and officer of the guard, and other necessary steps for proper order in a military camp. Despite the guards posted around the unenclosed fairground, a lack of discipline in some young soldiers, many away from home for the first time, tempted them to leave camp without permission. Soldiers from the immediate area, including the members of Lonergan's company, might slip away for a final farewell to friends and family nearby. The illegal sale of alcohol and "running the guard" after lights out gave a number of the recruits an early experience with the guardhouse; some were even court-martialed and fined.

Company commanders were required by GO 14 to report with their troops to Camp Underwood on or before June 6. Lonergan reported to the camp with "about 80 men" on June 4, in compliance with orders he had received the previous day. He was informed in camp that "his commission would be handed to him on the arrival of the Adjutant and Inspector General at Burlington."

The 2nd Regiment received its uniforms and equipment over a period of two weeks, being outfitted with "a frock coat and pantaloons of grey doeskin, with a dark blue cord" on June 10 and 11. Because Lonergan claimed that the Emmet Guards had been in existence since the meeting in January that elected him captain, its members may have already been outfitted with uniforms as a militia company. No doubt Lonergan himself had already purchased his own officer's clothing, sword, and other accoutrements for his role as recruiting officer.

Although busy with the camp routine, Lonergan took time on June 9 to publish a letter of thanks to the ladies of Burlington for their gifts such as sewing items, handkerchiefs, and havelocks.* He included thanks as well to A.O. Hoop, Esq. of Winooski for his "invaluable gift of 100 bottles of his 'Excelsior Liniment'" and signed himself "John Lonergan, Captain, In behalf of the 'Green Mountain Rangers.'" Adding to this confusion about the company's name, a letter from an observer at camp who signed himself *Sigma* informed the readers of the *Rutland Herald* on June 15 that the officer of the day was "Capt. Lonergan, of the Winooski Co. (Green Mountain Guard)." Apparently Lonergan had decided (or been ordered) to downplay the Irish rebel role for his company, and had disguised the Emmet Guards with a name more appropriate to Vermont.

Lt. Col. Rains, a native of North Carolina who was soon to go south to fight for the Confederacy, previously had inspected and mustered in the 1st Vermont. On June 8, he began the same process for the 2nd Vermont. The physical inspections were completed by June 11 after some twenty men, including the commander of Co. H from Fletcher, were rejected for service. (Captain Strait from Fletcher was forty-nine years old and considered beyond the age for active service leading an infantry company.) In Lonergan's unit, the officers and non-commissioned officers (NCOs) were accepted along with "65 or more privates of the company." With the sixteen officers and NCOs, the company strength would have been at least eighty-one men, just under the required eighty-three.**

Strait was replaced by William T. Burnham, who had been mentioned in Baxter's letter to Fairbanks on May 18 in the context of replacing one company with another. Burnham—who ran a hotel in Montpelier and had

---

* Havelocks, a cloth attached to the back of the cap to shield the neck from the sun, were popular additions to the uniforms of the day.

** Each company table of organization also authorized two musicians and one teamster to drive the company wagon, but they were not counted as privates among the combatants.

raised the "Green Mountain Boys" company in the capital—was not a young man either, but he was now elected captain of the Fletcher company with "67 votes to 4." This indicates a company strength of only seventy-one at the time. The main reason for selecting Burnham as a replacement was probably his ability to make up this deficiency in numbers. On June 15, eighteen men from Burnham's Montpelier company arrived to fill up the ranks of the Fletcher company (perhaps in excess of the required minimum). *Sigma* wrote that this "makes the Regiment's complement of men according to 'regulations.'" Obviously the state authorities could take steps to add soldiers to an existing company that lacked a dozen or so men—when they chose to do so.

LONERGAN'S PLAN FOR LEADING his Emmet Guards to war was succeeding, despite local complaints and obstacles at the state level. By employing the ruse of raising a company in Winooski, as authorized, Lonergan had his Fenian unit inspected and accepted as part of the 2nd Vermont. However, several administrative actions remained to complete the process of mobilization. Each company as a group would have to swear allegiance to the Union before a federal civil authority and the regiment would be mustered as a unit by a Regular Army officer. The state would issue commissions to all officers specifying their positions. Lonergan could proudly tell his family and friends in the Irish community—probably including Roseanna Sorrigan, his future bride—that he would soon be marching off to war at the head of his company.

With physical inspection and acceptance of the members of the regiment completed on June 11 and uniforms provided, the unit was ready to be sworn into federal service. After the 7:00 PM dress parade on that Tuesday evening, Judge Bradley B. Smalley of the U.S. District Court for Vermont administered the oath of allegiance that federalized the state unit, transferring command from the governor to the president. Accompanied by Baxter, Smalley inducted each company in turn, which had the effect of enlisting each member of the group in the national army. In the soft summer twilight, a crowd of onlookers no doubt had gathered to cheer on the men of the new regiment as they took the oath that bound them to duty for three years or the duration of the war.

The process went smoothly until Smalley and Baxter reached Co. K, where Lonergan and his two lieutenants stood at attention, swords drawn in salute, in front of less than a company. The exchange between Baxter and

Lonergan is not recorded in detail, but one can imagine the wrath of Baxter descending on this Irish captain as he tried to explain the absence of half of his men. Perhaps the incident the night before, as reported in the *Free Press*, sheds some light on why these local recruits were not assembled for the oath. At 11:00 PM the previous evening, an alarm was raised when a number of men "running guard" left the camp without authority. Every company had to assemble and take roll, reporting those absent. Offenders that were caught "were marched to [the] guard house, which was soon well filled." Coupled with reports of illegal sale of whiskey at the camp, one suspects that men from Lonergan's company were among those who had slipped out of camp and did not returned in time for the next day's parade.

Baxter "declined to swear in a fraction of a Company" and gave the captain until the next morning to have everyone assembled to take the oath. If the ranks were not full, the company would be disbanded. No doubt flushed with embarrassment, Lonergan could only promise to round up the missing soldiers if he was given the chance. The instructions that Lonergan gave his officers and NCOs to retrieve his wayward men probably included cracking heads if necessary. Whatever means were used—and it would not be unusual if a few black eyes and bruises were involved—Lonergan's unit assembled at 10:00 AM the following day with full ranks on the parade ground and was sworn into service.

This incident was the last straw for Gov. Fairbanks and he ordered Co. K disbanded, even though it had already been accepted into federal service on June 12. Clearly Fairbanks held a negative opinion of Lonergan, a brash immigrant who was a Democrat, a drinker, and a Catholic. A letter to Baxter dated June 18 and signed by Fairbanks as "Commander in Chief" contained the following terse instructions:

> Sir,
> Information having been communicated to me that the inspection and acceptance of the 2d Regiment of Vt. Volunteers is delayed in consequence of the fact that Co. K, Capt. Lonergan, has not the requisite number of men fit for service, you are hereby directed to issue your order for the immediate discharge of said company from the service of the State.

CHAPTER NINE – MILITIA MOBILIZED

Fairbanks had obviously made this decision several days before, probably upon hearing from Baxter about Lonergan's failure to have his company ready for swearing in with the rest of the regiment, because actions were already underway to replace Lonergan's company. On June 17, excitement had spread in the 3rd Vermont Regiment camp at St. Johnsbury when Col. William F. Smith ordered the Vergennes Company to report to the 2nd Vermont in Burlington. Certainly the *Free Press* already knew about the fate of Lonergan's company by June 18, because it reported, "We are sorry to learn that Capt. Lonergan's Company has not answered the expectations of its friends, proving the reverse of orderly and attentive to duty, and that the unpleasant duty of disbanding the company has been forced upon the Governor. The Vergennes Company we are informed will take its place in the regiment."

The *Burlington Weekly Times* attributed the situation to the absence of much of the company, rather than a lack of discipline. It reported on June 13 that all members of the regiment took the oath of allegiance "eagerly" except for one man in the Montpelier Company "and the 'Green Mountain Rangers,' Capt. *Lonergan*, who not appearing with full ranks, the oath was not administered." After Baxter's warning "Captain *Lonergan's* company appeared promptly on the ground yesterday at 10 o'clock AM and took the oath of allegiance."

Sigma, in his letter of June 18 reporting the earlier arrival of men to fill out the ranks of the Fletcher company, had added a postscript that "the Winooski Company K, Capt. Lonergan, has been disbanded on account of insubordination. There are various rumors in camp respecting the matter." There was some speculation that "its organization may still be maintained" if some additional men "can be found to join," but the story was already around that the Vergennes company was coming from St. Johnsbury to replace them. Reporting from St. Johnsbury, a soldier wrote on June 23 "the Calais Artillery, Capt. Mooer, is to take the place of the Vergennes company which departed last Tuesday to fill the vacancy in the Second Regiment occasioned by the disbanding of the Winooski Company." The date of that departure "last Tuesday" was June 18, the day that Fairbanks sent Baxter the order, so the move must have been arranged some days before then.

One can choose between the various explanations put forward for disbanding Lonergan's company—insufficient number of men, lack of discipline (actual or anticipated), or both—but there are also hints of a darker motivation, of pure prejudice against the Irish in general reinforced by a dislike for Lonergan as an individual. Only one person had the power to act upon such personal feelings and that was the governor, the commander in chief. He may have been influenced or encouraged in this action by others such as Baxter, but the ultimate decision would have been his. (Despite his English birth, Maj. Joyce apparently did not harbor anti-Irish sentiments, because he later made a statement supportive of Lonergan.) Coming from outside Vermont, Col. Whiting traveled to St. Johnsbury to receive his commission as regimental commander and he could have been cautioned about Lonergan by Fairbanks then.

The captain of the Vergennes company also might have been preferred by both Fairbanks and Baxter, as he was almost the exact opposite of Lonergan: Solon Eaton of Vergennes was a Yankee of many generations standing and, as noted in the *Free Press*, a descendant of the famous Gen. William Eaton, not an upstart immigrant who had connived to cobble together a unit.

Company K was officially disbanded on June 18, upon notification of the governor's order, and Lonergan, under protest, vacated his quarters at camp. His company was paid off for service to June 20.

The regiment was issued arms on June 19, smoothbore muskets for all but Co. A, which received rifles.* Lt. Col. Rains mustered the regiment into federal service at dress parade on June 20 when the replacement of Lonergan's company by Capt. Eaton's Vergennes troops had been completed.

After Lonergan's company was disbanded, most of its members left the camp, but at least six of them, including 2nd Lieutenant (Lt.) Bascom and 1st Corporal (Corp.) Whicher, were absorbed into other 2nd Vermont companies as privates. To add insult to injury, the roster of the new Co. K from Vergennes included three soldiers from Burlington and three more from the immediate area when it was mustered in on June 20. The apparent deficit of two privates in Lonergan's company could easily have been made good, as Burnham had done on a larger scale for the Fletcher company, if the goal of the commander in chief had been to bring Lonergan's company up to strength and so preserve it.

The Burlington *Weekly Times* of June 22 supplies some additional commentary on the matter of disbanding the "Green Mountain Rangers" for "deficiency in the number of men required by law." It stated further:

---

* As the senior company in the regiment, Co. A occupied the right flank in the line of battle, the place of honor, and accordingly they rated the superior arms.

CHAPTER NINE – MILITIA MOBILIZED

We are exceedingly sorry for Capt. Lonergan's sake, as well as a large number of the Company who seemed determined to be soldiers in *earnest*, that this necessity has occurred; but the Governor had no other alternative, and only discharged his imperative duty in disbanding the Company. The officers of Company K, we are informed by Col. Whiting, have been very assiduous in their labors to preserve good order, and enforce discipline in their company, and will leave the regiment with the best wishes of all the field officers. Lieutenant Bascom is determined to be a 'soger' any way, and has enlisted in Company C, Capt. Todd's well-disciplined company.

This endorsement of the "officers of Company K" by the regimental commander is additional evidence that the decision on disbanding the company was made by the governor and not at the instigation of Whiting.

On Monday, June 24, the regiment of 866 men—the exact number listed as a minimum for an infantry regiment under the May 3 proclamation—marched from the Burlington fair grounds to the Rutland and Burlington Railroad depot and boarded the train that would take them south.

Was John Lonergan among the crowds that gathered to line the streets of Burlington and accompany the troops to the depot, waving and cheering them off to war? The refugee from Ireland might have found it emotionally too painful to see them off when he had been part of the unit less than a week before. He may well have avoided watching his recent comrades shoulder their arms and march off to save the Union. Or he may have been there in his uniform to salute his fellow officers and the former members of his wrecked company, scattered through the regiment. Perhaps even then he was weighing a different plan of action.

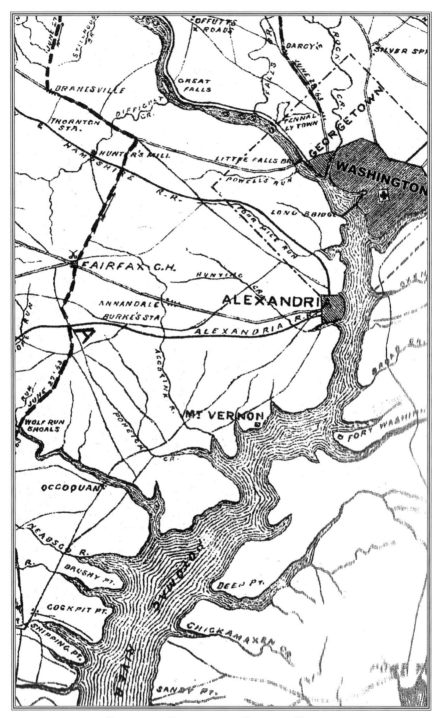

District of Columbia and Northern Virginia

CHAPTER TEN

AWAITING ORDERS

LEAVING A DISAPPOINTED John Lonergan behind, the 2nd Vermont rushed south by rail to join the growing concentration of Union troops in and around Washington. Their immediate task was to guard the nation's capital, surrounded by slave-holding Maryland and vulnerable to attack by secessionist forces. Federal soldiers were being deployed into northern Virginia and put to work building a network of fortifications around the District of Columbia. The President's initial anxiety about protecting the seat of government eased as sufficient troops arrived from the loyal states and fortifications were built to provide an adequate defense of Washington.

As political pressure for offensive action against the rebels mounted, Lincoln's plans then shifted to an aggressive move against Richmond. The strategic objective of "invading" Virginia was to crush the rebellion by seizing the Confederate capital. (Originally the southern Congress had convened in Montgomery, Alabama, but the rebel government accepted newly-seceded Virginia's offer of April 27 to house the permanent capital in Richmond.) The proximity of the two opposing governments dictated much of the subsequent military operations, as each side maneuvered throughout the war to strike a decapitating blow against the other.

In mid-July, needing to act before the ninety-day service of the state militia units expired, Gen. Irvin McDowell led some 30,000 men south. He launched an attack against about 20,000 rebels at Manassas Junction, an important rail connection near a stream called Bull Run.* Amidst confusion

---

* The opposing sides tended to use different conventions in naming battles and armies. The Confederates commonly referred to territories and settlements, while the Union forces usually chose waterways. Thus the Army of Northern Virginia was opposed by the Army of the Potomac and this battle was called Manassas in the South and Bull Run (for the small stream in the area) in the North. Battles where no waterway was significantly involved, e.g. Gettysburg, might bear the same name on both sides.

on the battlefield caused by similar uniforms and flags on both sides, the initial Union success in the morning assault of July 21 was reversed with the arrival of Confederate forces from the Shenandoah Valley in the late afternoon. The losses in killed and wounded were nearly equal in the battle, but the rout of the Union forces left 1,200 prisoners behind.

Among those who surrendered to the rebels were Col. Corcoran, commander of the 69th New York and the Fenian Brotherhood's forces, and Capt. Drew, commander of the Burlington company in the 2nd Vermont. Capt. Meagher fell "senseless on the field" as the 69th was repulsed for the third time in assaulting the enemy lines, but he avoided capture thanks to his rescue by Private (Pvt.) Joseph McCoy, a young Irishman in the 2nd U.S. Cavalry who had recognized him.

THE UNION DEFEAT AT BULL RUN made the need for additional regiments painfully clear. On July 24, the 3rd Vermont departed from St. Johnsbury wearing new gray uniforms of Vermont wool. The regiment had been organized along with the 2nd Vermont by the governor, who had also been authorized by the legislature to raise four additional regiments "at such time as in his discretion it may appear necessary." Using that authority, on July 30 Gov. Fairbanks announced that orders would "be issued immediately" for enlisting the 4th and 5th regiments of volunteers "for three years, or during the war."

While he was on full-time military duty in the summer, Lonergan had no doubt quit the grocery business. After his dismissal, he may have returned to work as a cooper in Burlington. However, he was not content to remain a civilian while the war was in progress. Despite the shame of having his company of the 2nd Vermont disbanded, Lonergan saw an opportunity to regain his status as additional regiments were formed. Swallowing his pride, he offered his services to the governor again.

In a letter from Burlington dated August 7, Lonergan wrote to "His Excellency, E. Fairbanks" in response to his "call for more men to rally around the flagg [sic] of our Country." Even though his original unit had been rejected at the last minute, Lonergan stated with great confidence "I can enlist a company in two weeks." He went on to stipulate his conditions of service: "I will fill any *honourable* place you may think fit to place me. I mean

CHAPTER TEN – AWAITING ORDERS

honourable because of my connections with the military before." Cautioning the governor that he would not join the rank and file, Lonergan explained, "I take it for granted that you would not expect me to again *enlist* as a private. I have already done so twice." He closed "With respect" and a reminder of his recent history, "J. Lonergan, Late of 2nd Vt Regt." No record has been found of any response to this offer from the governor. (Lonergan's reference to having twice enlisted was based on his brief service as a private with the Brandon militia company and also the formality of enlisting in the Emmet Guards before being elected captain of the company.)

The 2nd and 3rd Vermont had been sent off to war at or just above the minimum required strength; the next two regiments would be organized at the maximum authorized strength of 1,046 officers and enlisted men. The state also decided to increase the numbers of the two existing regiments by enlisting additional privates, bringing each company up to the maximum authorized number of 101. At the battle of Bull Run, the 2nd Vermont had, moreover, lost a total of sixty-eight men, including a number captured, and disease took a continuous toll. To fill up the ranks to the new authorization, recruiting officers were detailed from the regiments in the field to return to Vermont and enlist additional members for their companies. Capt. Eaton came home on August 1 to recruit another twenty men for his company (which had replaced Lonergan's unit). He left three weeks later with twenty-five recruits from Vergennes after "more than 50 offered to go."

Several weeks past its ninety-day term of service, the 1st Vermont returned home after seeing some limited combat at Big Bethel and was mustered out August 15. Of the 753 men in its ranks, some 600 reenlisted in other Vermont regiments for three-year terms. In almost four months service, the 1st Vermont had only one man killed in action, while four died of disease and one in an accident. Another four men received discharges for disability and two deserted. Along with the additional category of those taken prisoner, these proportions held generally true for Vermont's losses through most of the war.

Vermont was unusual in sending replacements to maintain the strength of existing regiments throughout the war. Most states preferred to create new regiments (and thus new commanders) while the regiments already in the field were continuously starved of manpower, reduced in some cases to the strength of a battalion or even a company. The rosters of some three-year Vermont regiments show 1,600 to 1,800 members that served in a 1,000-man unit as losses were replaced.

Capt. Burnham—chosen as commander of the Fletcher company when Strait was deemed too old for duty—was, like Eaton, detailed back to his hometown to enlist replacements. Burnham was reported on August 30 to be "dispatched to this State to recruit men to make up the deficiencies caused by the casu[a]lties at Bull's Run and by sickness." Although his company had been raised in Fletcher, Burnham went back to Montpelier to enlist additional men for Co. H.

Lonergan seized this opportunity to act, though how he persuaded Burnham to go along with his scheme is not known. The dismissed Irish captain mingled with the group of recruits gathered by Burnham and traveled with them to the regiment's camp in Virginia. The capture of Capt. Drew, Co. G, at Bull Run had created a vacancy among the company commanders and Lonergan might have seen this as an opening for his assignment to his old regiment. Both captains had raised companies in and around Burlington, so it could have been reasonable to replace Drew with the original Co. K commander. (While in captivity, Drew retained his commission as commander of Co. G; he resigned it only on October 8, 1862, two months after being paroled as a prisoner.)

Burnham left Montpelier by rail with twenty-five recruits for the 2nd Regiment on September 9. A bill sent by the New Jersey Railroad on September 11 charged for thirty-two passengers led by Burnham who had "seated his men at the moment of departure" without the "necessary document." It appears that Burnham had provided transportation to additional and unauthorized persons, including Lonergan, and had disregarded the paperwork required by the railroads.*

Burnham's group reported to Camp Advance in Virginia, just over the Chain Bridge from Washington, where the 2nd Vermont was building fortifications to defend the capital. The Green Mountain Boys had been pleasantly surprised when President Lincoln, Secretary of War Cameron,

---

* In 1910, the 13th Vermont's history told the story somewhat differently, saying Lonergan "followed the regiment to Virginia, taking with him thirty-five men, recruited mostly by Captain Burnham, Company H. Captain Lonergan was welcomed by officers and men of the 2nd Vermont and was under fire with them several times, at Lewinsville, Falls Church and Munson's Hill."

CHAPTER TEN – AWAITING ORDERS

Gen. George B. McClellan, and other notables visited Col. Whiting's unit on September 10. The newly arrived Co. H recruits were mustered into the regiment on September 13, but what to do with Lonergan? Persons not officially on the rolls of a unit might be present in camp as "aides" or "observers" and officers could be attached to a headquarters by orders, but here was a former company commander rejoining the regiment without any military position or status.

An additional man with experience as a line officer could always make himself useful around the regiment. He could even carry a musket when necessary. Lonergan reportedly marched out of camp with the regiment and was under fire with them in several skirmishes. However, his situation clearly could not be maintained indefinitely; some action was required to change his unofficial status with the unit. Perhaps thinking of the recent visit by the President and his entourage to the 2nd Vermont, Lonergan gambled that a bold step could resolve the matter. In late September, "finding himself in the peculiar position of not being recognized by the regimental roll, he secured a pass from 'Baldy' Smith to go to Washington to interview Simon Cameron, Secretary of War."

William F. "Baldy" Smith, the former colonel of the 3rd Vermont, had been promoted to brigadier general on August 13 and appointed the commander of the First Vermont Brigade.* Smith surely knew the details of the disbanding of Co. K, since he had supplied the replacement company from his own regiment. Lonergan claimed to have found sympathy and support in the 2nd Vermont; the brigade commander no doubt also heard Lonergan's version of the affair. Lonergan must have made a very persuasive argument, asking to approach the Secretary of War to plead a personal case during this national mobilization; he secured the general's permission to visit Washington.

The office of the Secretary of War was constantly crowded with soldiers on official business, men seeking contracts to supply the army, and a wide variety of petitioners; Cameron was also notoriously disorganized. Amidst this chaos, Lonergan was insistent enough to receive an audience with Cameron so that he could expound on the unjust treatment of the Emmet Guards and its commander. The history of the 13th Vermont describes the successful outcome:

---

* Made up of the four Vermont regiments in federal service at the time, the 2nd through the 5th, and joined later by the 6th Vermont.

After listening to Captain Lonergan's statement on the disbandment of his first company, Secretary Cameron extended his pass to Vermont, at the same time advising him to report for duty, very often to Adjutant-General Washburn, as also to every U.S. officer he met on the way. Captain Lonergan followed this advice faithfully and as it created quite a stir between Washington and Woodstock, Vermont, the result anticipated was obtained.

(In October of 1861, Peter Washburn—lately Lt. Col. of the 1st Vermont—had been elected by the state legislature to replace Baxter as Vermont's Adjutant and Inspector General. Washburn served in that position for the remainder of the war and he moved the AIG office from Rutland to Woodstock, his hometown.)

Brashly going over the head of Vermont's governor in the military chain of command, Lonergan had evidently convinced the Secretary of War of improper action by Fairbanks. The Emmet Guards had arguably been accepted for federal service and was thus no longer under state control when it was disbanded. Or perhaps Cameron, overwhelmed with organizing the nation's massive military effort, granted Lonergan's request for re-instatement just to get the angry Irishman out of his office.

Greatly pleased with Cameron's endorsement, Lonergan returned to the camp in Virginia, where he no doubt boasted of his achievement to his fellow officers. Based on his "interview" with the Secretary of War, Lonergan wrote Fairbanks from the "Headquarters, 2nd Vt. Regiment, Camp Advance" on October 1. Word might already have reached the governor of Lonergan's presence there, since the dismissed officer had committed a serious breach of military discipline, now compounded by his complaint to Cameron. However, Fairbanks was a "lame duck" at that point, since he had not run for another term, and the Republican candidate, Frederick Holbrook, had easily won the governorship in the state election on September 3. Therefore, Lonergan need not have worried about official retribution by Fairbanks for the following letter, which he provocatively signed as "Capt. Co. K":

To His Excellency Erastus Fairbanks
Governor of Vermont

 Dear Sir, I have the honour to report to your Excellency that the disbanding of my command does not discharge me out of Service. I learn this to be the opinions of the War Department at Washington.

 I am here, Sir, with my Regt. ready to obey any legal command. Col. Whiting desires me to report to him & that you may assign me to the first vacancy and I have the proud satisfaction to know that every commissioned officer in the Regt. desires my restoration to my old 2nd Regt.

 It is a consolation to me to know that I am still in the Service of my country, and that justice will be done to me.

 Should your Excellency condesend to reply, it will reach me at Burlington, as I go there this week for documents, &c.

I have the Honour to remain
Respectfully yours
J. Lonergan
Capt. Co. K, 2nd Vt. Regt.

Satisfied that he had accomplished his goal of reclaiming the right to raise a company, Lonergan again bid farewell to the 2nd Vermont and traveled home to Burlington. While on the trip, he reported frequently to Washburn and any other officer he encountered, as instructed by Cameron, no doubt deliberately creating the maximum possible publicity about his situation. However, further disappointment awaited him in Vermont; another year would pass before he could once more take command of a resurrected Emmet Guards.

A newspaper article on October 7 reported Capt. Burnham under arrest for being discovered asleep on picket duty, an offense for which a private might have been shot. His "nap was so sound that his sword was taken off his person and carried to Gen. Smith without his knowledge. He will probably be court-martialed." He was instead allowed to resign his commission as commander of Co. H on October 18 with a letter that cited no reason for his request to be released. In addition to sleeping on duty, Burnham's health was apparently not good and others had commented about his drinking habits. It is not clear whether his role in bringing Lonergan to Virginia played any part in Burnham's resignation, but the regimental commander may not have been particularly happy that Burnham had delivered the contentious Irishman to his camp.

On the other hand, it is possible that Col. Whiting (or even Brig. Gen. Smith) had approved, either before or after the fact, of Burnham's action in bringing Lonergan to join the 2nd Regiment in Virginia. The colonel may have felt that an injustice had been done (as Stannard said later) and Whiting certainly tolerated Lonergan's presence in the regiment for close to a month. In any event, Burnham's resignation created yet another vacancy among the regiment's company commanders. However, no action was taken to reinstate Lonergan to such a position despite the changes in Vermont's commander in chief and its AIG in October.

Holbrook had been ill with typhus and had not yet taken over the duties of governor when Lonergan defiantly wrote to Fairbanks about his visit with the Secretary of War. The outgoing governor addressed Vermont's General Assembly on October 11, departing "from the usual custom in retiring from the Executive office." Fairbanks had faced an unprecedented situation and wanted to review "the transactions of the past few months, and especially those pertaining to the organization and equipment of the troops for the service of the United States." He pointed out the absence of any "existing military organization, or authorized code" that might have guided him in his efforts, commenting that "not unfrequently responsibilities were assumed for which no specific authority existed."

Reading this passage in the *Free Press*, Lonergan may well have considered the disbanding of his company by Fairbanks as one of those "responsibilities" that the governor had assumed without specific authority. Not long after returning from Virginia to Burlington in early October, Lonergan pursued the matter of the expenses he had incurred in this whole adventure. Never lacking in audacity, he retained Representative Carolus Noyes, the Burlington lawyer who was a member of the Committee on Military Affairs, to present his claim for reimbursement to the Vermont General Assembly. This "memorial" submitted on October 31 was "ordered to lie" on November 16; subsequently the motion for any action on Lonergan's petition for redress was rejected.

Refused any reimbursement by the state and no doubt short of funds at this point, Lonergan took up his cooper's tools again after his return to Burlington. As the long Vermont winter closed in, Lonergan faced an uncertain and gloomy future, reduced to shaving down the staves for a barrel or putting hoops on a

CHAPTER TEN – AWAITING ORDERS

washtub for some housewife at a time when he thought that he would be leading his men on the field of battle. Despite the failure of his first attempt at raising a unit, however, Lonergan was still determined to take his own company to war. Possibly he was also under some pressure from the Fenian leadership to persist in a plan for hardening a group of Vermont's Irishmen in battle, preparing them for a future role in the liberation of their homeland.

Conspicuously Irish military units like Lonergan's Emmet Guards fighting for the Union were favorably received by Lincoln's administration and the general public. Fenian hopes that this would create support for the Irish nationalist cause increased early in the Civil War as relations with Great Britain deteriorated. The secessionist states had turned to England for recognition of their independence and material assistance to their new country. British textile mills relied on a steady supply of cotton from the Southern states, so the Confederate government trusted that this economic relationship would trump the British aversion to slavery. British interests faced competition from the growing strength of the United States and the division of America into two less powerful countries might act as a welcome check on its expansion. British North America, sparsely populated and not yet responsible for its own defense, had been invaded by Americans in the past and annexation by its southern neighbor still appeared possible. From the Fenian viewpoint, hostilities between Great Britain and the United States might create an opportunity for action to liberate Ireland as part of a larger war.

Great Britain in effect granted the Confederate States of America belligerent status on May 13, 1861, when it proclaimed a policy of neutrality in the internal conflict, not long after the breakaway nation was formed and the opening shots were fired. Lincoln's government responded with a threat to break off diplomatic relations if Great Britain had any further dealings with Southern envoys. In November, when two of these representatives, Mason and Slidell, were removed from a British steamer on the high seas by the commander of a U.S. Navy warship, the resulting crisis nearly ruptured Anglo-U.S. relations. Great Britain reinforced its Atlantic squadron and the regular army in the Canadian territories, but Lincoln, anxious to deal with only "one war at a time," released the two captives in December to continue their journey.

Even before this situation strained official diplomatic relations, Irish nationalists on both sides of the Atlantic were organizing a large-scale demonstration against continued British rule of their homeland. The impetus for this action was the death of Terrance Bellew MacManus, who had joined the uprising of the Young Irelanders and shared the same fate as the more renowned leaders—capture, trial, and transportation to Van Dieman's Land—before he escaped to America. MacManus did not prosper in his new homeland and when he died in poverty in San Francisco on January 15, 1861, local Fenians raised the funds to ship his body home to Ireland for burial.

The Fenian Brotherhood exploited the situation to raise awareness of their organization, collecting funds and new members as the body was transported across America. In March, the month when Lincoln took office as president, the coffin escorted by a Fenian honor guard left San Francisco by rail. After a series of stops in cities en route, the remains arrived in New York City in September. Ceremonies in New York were organized by the Fenian leaders—John O'Mahony and Col. Michael Doheny—together with Thomas Francis Meagher, who had not yet joined the Brotherhood. Despite the Roman Catholic Church's generally hostile attitude toward the Fenian movement, Meagher convinced Archbishop Hughes, from the deceased's hometown in Ireland, to hold a Requiem Mass in St. Patrick's Cathedral.

As chairman of the Obsequies Committee, Meagher called a public meeting in the evening of September 5 to discuss the arrangements for the funeral. When the talk turned to the historic valor of the Irish soldier, the public gave three cheers for Meagher's role at Bull Run and another three for the captured Col. Corcoran. Taking the concept of Irish courage beyond the partisanship of the current conflict, Meagher then asked for three cheers for "the two sons of John Mitchel, who are fighting as bravely on the other side." The crowd responded enthusiastically, honoring Mitchel for his service to Ireland's cause, despite his support of the Confederate rebels. (Mitchel and the rest of his family, including his youngest son Willie, were living in Paris at the time.)

Lincoln's government could not have been pleased by the archbishop's praise of MacManus at the Mass on September 14, when he described the rebellious Young Irelanders' actions as justified. The archbishop stated that the Church recognized "that there are cases in which it is lawful to resist and overthrow a tyrannical government." That argument too closely resembled the

CHAPTER TEN – AWAITING ORDERS

rationale of the Southern states now in rebellion against what they considered "a tyrannical government." After the Mass, the coffin was escorted from the packed cathedral by the uniformed Fenian honor guard and placed in a vault in Calvary Cemetery. It remained there for over a month until its shipment to Ireland and reception there was arranged. On October 18, thousands attended the funeral procession as the thirty-two pallbearers, one for each county in Ireland, bore MacManus's coffin to the dockside. There the remains were placed aboard a steamer for Cork, to cross the Atlantic accompanied by an American delegation that included the top Fenian leaders. Returning to Ireland to rekindle the spark of independence seems a bold step for men who had fled their homes just a dozen years before with a price on their heads, and who now publicly advocated the violent overthrow of British rule.

Stephens, head of the illegal Irish Republican Brotherhood, asked O'Donovan Rossa, the revolutionary from Skibbereen in West Cork, to accompany the body from Cork to Dublin. In late October, a solemn throng estimated at 300,000 trailed through Cork city from the chapel where MacManus had lain in state to the railway station. Rossa and a group occupying a compartment on the train next to the coffin were armed with pistols to prevent any action either by the British authorities or by those Irish who were calling for an uprising in hopes that the funeral could rouse the countryside. One nationalist scheme involved carrying off the remains to Slievenamon or some other historic site, but Stephens and the men of Tipperary town had boarded the train to ensure that the orchestrated progress of events was not disrupted.*

Passing through stations filled with mourners, the body arrived in Dublin to be met with the official disapproval of the Church. Archbishop Cullen refused to allow it to lie in state at the cathedral there. MacManus instead spent his last day before interment at the Lecture Hall of the Mechanic's Institute, where thousands came to pay their last respects. On November 10, a priest with Fenian sympathies, Patrick Lavell, officiated over the funeral with support from the Archbishop of Tuam, John McHale. The Dublin Metropolitan Police "abdicated their functions" and left control of the enormous crowd to the nationalist organizations, allowing the ceremonies—

---

* Rossa would later recall that at the Limerick station, the most likely place that an attempt would be made to grab the coffin, Stephens called for the crowd on the platform to "kneel down and say a Pater and Ave for the dead" and the train pulled safely away while all were still on their knees.

sheltering in public behind the "front" of the National Brotherhood of St. Patrick—to proceed without obstruction.

Despite the gloomy, wet cold of the short autumn day, tens of thousands watched the funeral procession, which included a ceremonial harper on an elaborate carriage following the bier. At Glasnevin cemetery in the north of town, further crowds attended the arrival and burial in the early evening. By torchlight, Captain Smith, a Fenian from San Francisco traveling with the corpse, delivered a speech provided by James Stephens to rouse the spirit of Irish independence. While bordering on illegal activity, this was an impressive demonstration of the depth of the people's feelings and the organizational ability of Stephens' movement. The successful staging of this event signaled a rebirth of the nationalist cause, encouraged by the presence of the American delegation from the Fenian Brotherhood. Identification of the overall movement as "Fenian" grew from that point until both the Irish and the American branches soon were commonly, if inaccurately, called by that name.

MEAGHER'S ABSENCE FROM THE FUNERAL in Dublin, seemingly a custom-made occasion for him to showcase his oratory skills for the nationalist cause, might be explained by a reluctance to have his name associated with the new movement led by Stephens and O'Mahony. Or perhaps he was more nervous than the others that a return to Ireland would place him again within the reach of the British authorities (even though he was now a citizen of the United States). However, he probably remained in America because he placed a higher priority at that time on Irish support of the Union war effort. Called "Meagher of the Sword" for his speech in 1848 praising the weapon, he now had earned the title fairly by his action in battle.

After the Mason and Slidell crisis failed to incite hostilities with the British, even the Fenians could see that there was no possibility that the U.S. government would intervene in behalf of the Irish before the fighting between the states ended and the Union was restored. The best tactic for the Irish nationalists during the war appeared to be tangible support of the effort to reunite the country. Military service would gain American sympathy for their cause, provide valuable experience for the armed struggle to win back Irish independence, and perhaps change widespread anti-immigrant attitudes. The "No Irish Need Apply" sign was conspicuously absent from the military recruiting offices. Public awareness of the Irish contribution to the Union increased as entire regiments marched off to war carrying the green Fenian flag alongside the national colors.

After the defeat at Bull Run, the demoralized Federal troops had fled to the shelter of the defenses around Washington. The 69th New York marched back from the battle to Fort Corcoran where, on July 24, it received orders to return home, since its three months service had expired. The regiment was heartily cheered as it passed through Philadelphia, the "foremost part" of the welcome provided by the Fenian Brotherhood "as was natural" in that heavily Irish city. Their homecoming parade in New York City was equally enthusiastic as the troops marched behind Capt. James Kelly, the senior line officer, with Capt. Meagher riding alongside. (The commander, Col. Corcoran, was in prison and the regiment "was then without field officers.") The 69th was mustered out and discharged from service on August 3, satisfied that they had "redeemed the pledges" made to "meet the enemies of the Union." Despite the lost battle, *"they did not feel themselves beaten"* [emphasis in original] and most of the regiment quickly re-enlisted for a longer term of service.

While Lonergan sat frustrated in Burlington, unable to raise another company even after his meeting with the Secretary of War, Meagher rejected a series of proposed command and staff assignments. As recognition of his service in battle (and to encourage Irish enlistments), the War Department offered Meagher a commission as a captain in the Regular Army, but he declined in favor of the more experienced Capt. Kelly as "better entitled to the distinction." Maj. Gen. John C. Fremont, commanding the Department of the West, tried to entice Meagher to join him in Missouri as "Aid de-Camp on my staff, with the rank of Colonel," but this position was also refused. Meagher shrewdly reasoned that the situation would provide him an opportunity for even greater fame as commander of his own unit. The 69th New York was being reorganized for three years' service and needed a new colonel. On August 5, Meager refused command of the 3rd Irish Regiment (of the Phoenix brigade of Fenian units, later mustered in as the 63rd New York) as proposed in a letter of July 31 from the Centre Street headquarters of the Brotherhood, citing his strong ties with the 69th.

Meagher was looking beyond the regimental level; he envisioned bringing Irish units together into a brigade or even a division, as had been done with the regiments of German immigrants. The re-enlisting officers of the original 69th chose him to persuade the War Department to allow the formation of an Irish Brigade. Thomas A. Scott, Assistant Secretary of War, responded to "Colonel Thomas F. Meagher" on August 30 with the acceptance of the 69th New York "for three years or during the war, provided you have it ready for marching orders in thirty days." The Department, while reserving the right to "revoke the Commissions of all officers" it deemed incompetent, authorized Meagher to "arrange with the Colonels-commanding" of another four regiments "to be raised to form a brigade." The "proper authorities of the Government" would designate the brigade commander since confirmation of general officers was reserved to the U.S. Senate, but Meagher expected to be granted the single star of a brigadier general.

Uniquely able to encourage the Irish to enlist in the Union forces, Meagher gave a series of speeches in Boston, Philadelphia, and New York that autumn, calling upon them to volunteer. He was credited with helping to raise the Irish 28th and Yankee 29th Massachusetts regiments, along with the mostly Irish 116th Pennsylvania. His hopes of combining them with New York units into a larger Irish formation were frustrated by the refusal of the governors of the two neighboring states to see their troops included in a brigade with headquarters in New York. The Irish Brigade was therefore initially organized with only New York units. The "First Regiment" of the brigade was designated the 69th New York, while the "Third" and "Fourth" were the 63rd and 88th New York infantry regiments. (The "Second Regiment" of the brigade had been the intended position for a Boston regiment and was therefore left vacant.) The "Fifth" regimental position was occupied by the 10th New York Artillery under the command of Col. Meagher, who was also "the Acting-Chief of the Irish Brigade," although the "regiment" consisted of only two batteries.

Each of these regiments was presented with their colors, both the national flag of the United States and a green regimental flag, before departing New York City. The 63rd received its colors on November 7 and the other three regiments on November 18, the day that the brigade assembled to see off the 69th as it left for the war. The Irish flags displayed the national emblems appropriated by the Fenian cause—the sunburst, uncrowned harp, and shamrock wreath—along with a Gaelic motto on a scroll. The Head Centre of the Brotherhood, John O'Mahony (who was at that time in Ireland for

CHAPTER TEN – AWAITING ORDERS

the funeral of MacManus), had provided the motto "Never retreat from the clash of spears!"*

By mid-December, the three infantry regiments of the Irish Brigade had assembled at their camp on the Fairfax turnpike in northern Virginia; the artillery units were detached to a camp nearer Washington. Command of the brigade was being pressed upon Gen. James Shields, born in County Tyrone, who considered the position lower than he warranted and did not accept. The brigade officers therefore delegated representatives who were "requested to wait on the President of the United States" and present Meagher's name for commander of the unit. On December 19, the delegation met with Lincoln to ask for Meagher's appointment. The next day Lincoln sent Meagher's nomination to the Senate, which confirmed him as brigadier general on February 3, 1862. A few days later, the Irish Brigade was assigned as the Second Brigade of Gen. Edwin B. Sumner's Division, part of the Army of the Potomac. Under a series of army commanders, the Irish Brigade would fight many battles and suffer great losses, but gain undying fame.

RECRUITMENT FOR THE UNION FORCES continued in Vermont through the fall of 1861; the 6th Regiment mustered into service on October 15 to complete the First Vermont Brigade's complement of five three-year regiments. A regiment of cavalry was formed from units throughout Vermont on November 19, the first full cavalry regiment raised in New England. Vermont also provided three companies of sharpshooters and two batteries of light artillery in late 1861. The appointment of Edwin Stanton to replace Cameron as Secretary of War in January of 1862 marked the beginning of significant improvements in the national war effort. Better organization of recruiting came with the assignment of Regular Army officers to stations in each Congressional district. A Regular Army officer released on parole from Texas and prohibited from combat until exchanged, one Lt. Col. Morris, arrived in Burlington in the first days of 1862 as "Superintendent of the Volunteer recruiting services in Vermont."

Imposition of the recruiting office organization was intended to reduce the

---

* "Riamh nar dhruid o sparn lann!" was taken from a passage in the ancient tale of the *fianna* where Oisin describes Finn McCool's bravery to St. Patrick. Over time, these green flags became the instantly recognizable feature of the battle lines of the Irish Brigade during the Civil War.

competition between various elements seeking to enlist men. The governors continued to authorize new regiments in their states, prominent people independently sought to raise units on their own initiative, and officers on detached service from existing regiments, both Regular Army and volunteer, scoured the countryside and cities for recruits. In mid-February, the 7th and 8th Vermont regiments were mustered in for service with Gen. Benjamin Butler's New England division, operating in the coastal states of the Gulf of Mexico. By spring, however, enthusiastic volunteers had produced more manpower than could be usefully absorbed in the Union forces. A senator stated that there were "*one hundred and fifty thousand* more men in our army than could be effectively employed" [emphasis in original] and recruiting was suspended on April 3, 1862, at a time when the Confederates were forced to begin conscription.

A NOTICE ON THE FRONT PAGE of the March 7 Burlington *Sentinel* called attention to an advertisement appearing for the first time. The weekly newspaper announced "the opening of a new Cooper's Shop by J. Lonergan, in the rear of the Leavenworth Block, on College Street and Skinner's Lane" and noted that the location "is a commodious one." The article also pointed out that "housekeepers will find it a convenient place in which to get cooper's jobs and repairs done" near the center of town and commended "Capt. Lonergan's shop to their notice and patronage." An advertisement on a back page offered "Cisterns, Barrels, Tubs and all kinds of work in that line of business done well and promptly" along with "Jobbing and Repairing" as promised by J. Lonergan. The editor of the *Sentinel*, an openly partisan Democratic newspaper sympathetic to the Irish, clearly was steering customers to the new business of this staunch fellow Democrat.

ADVERTISMENT IN THE *SENTINEL*

CHAPTER TEN – AWAITING ORDERS

The "commodious" premises of the enterprise would be explained by its address. Lonergan had set up his shop at the site where the Emmet Guards had trained. Such an armory would have required a large space to accommodate drilling one hundred men. The militia company had been disbanded the previous June, so perhaps the space had been vacant and unused since that time. Lonergan must have received financial backing to cover the costs of organizing a militia company; the only likely source was the Fenian Brotherhood. Possibly the space in the Leavenworth block had been leased for a set period of time and setting up the cooper shop there was preferable to having it sit idle. Although the Brotherhood was an open and legal society in the United States, the Fenians may also have seen some benefit in having a public business run by the organization's state leader, where "customers" could come and go without attracting undue attention. In any case, no Fenian headquarters apparently existed in Burlington or elsewhere in the state and the cooper shop might serve that additional purpose. Since the movement was working to organize the Irish in the Canadian provinces, Burlington offered a convenient location for meeting with those nationalists living north of Vermont.

That winter, Lonergan's prospects of ever getting a command appeared bleak; his offer to raise another company had been ignored by the state. Recruiting for new Vermont regiments had ended by February of 1862. The enlistment of replacements was called to a halt in April. The use of "Captain" in the *Sentinel* article (probably solicited, if not written, by Lonergan) shows his identification by that rank within the Burlington community. Since he never received his commission as commander of Co. K, 2nd Vermont, his claim to this title rested on his election as commanding officer of the Emmet Guards militia company in January, 1861. His insistence on that "date of rank" as captain would bear significant consequences later.

Lonergan's record in the official roster of all Vermonters who served in the Civil War is unique among the listings of hundreds of commissioned officers. His record is the only one with blanks in the columns both for "date of issue" and "date of commission." Indisputably he was elected as captain of the Emmet Guards company (twice, actually, as will be seen), but it appears he was never commissioned as an officer in the state's volunteer regiments.

As the longer days brought welcome signs of the approaching spring, John Lonergan had the opening of his new business to celebrate in mid-

TABLE OF ARMY FIELD UNITS

The regiment was the basic unit of the army, its organization fixed by regulations. Each regiment was uniquely numbered by type of unit and origin. Regiments were either Regular Army or a volunteer regiment raised from a given state, e.g. 1st U.S. Infantry Regiment or 13th Vermont Volunteer Infantry Regiment. Most regiments were combat arms—infantry, artillery, cavalry—though some specialized units like the U.S. Sharpshooters and support elements such as engineers were also formed. Each state numbered its regiments in series by type.

The units above regiment had no fixed organization or designators, being created as required and with the forces available. While the Union Army used Roman numerals for the corps, these designators have been given here as First, Fourth, Tenth, etc. to be more easily recognized by the reader. Divisions, brigades, and even lower units frequently were designated by the commander's name.

UNIT (IN ASCENDING ORDER)	STRENGTH (NOMINAL)	COMMANDER'S RANK
COMPANY	101 MEN	CAPTAIN
REGIMENT	TEN COMPANIES (1,000 MEN)	COLONEL
BRIGADE	USUALLY FIVE REGIMENTS	BRIGADIER GENERAL
DIVISION	USUALLY THREE BRIGADES OF INFANTRY, BUT COULD BE TWO TO FOUR BRIGADES OF INFANTRY, PLUS ONE BRIGADE OF ARTILLERY OR CAVALRY	BRIGADIER GENERAL (OCCASIONALLY MAJOR GENERAL)
CORPS	USUALLY THREE DIVISIONS OF INFANTRY PLUS ARTILLERY, CAVARY AND SUPPORT UNITS	MAJOR GENERAL
ARMY	COMPOSED OF SEVERAL TO HALF A DOZEN CORPS	MAJOR GENERAL (RARELY LIEUTENANT GENERAL)

TABLE OF UNITS, STRENGTHS AND RANKS

March, along with St. Patrick's Day. He might have found strong reasons to put aside his military ambitions along with his obsolete gray officer's uniform from the previous summer. Although he did not cut so dashing a figure in civilian clothes as when he sported a sword at his side, his courtship of a local woman had survived the change in his fortunes and appearance. Roseanna Sorrigan was the daughter of a Plattsburgh, New York, Irish businessman living in Burlington, probably associated with the "Sorragan" hotel on the waterfront. The young couple shared the Roman Catholic faith and likely knew each other from the Irish community and church activities. Perhaps he had already proposed to Roseanna that winter and had set up his own business in March to meet his responsibilities as the future head of a family.

Even in his spacious shop, Lonergan must have fretted to be confined to the Leavenworth Block when the newspapers were reporting the formation of the Irish Brigade and the bravery of Vermont troops in battle. Meagher had just been confirmed to command the Irish Brigade and Lonergan held the new general in high esteem, perhaps bordering on hero-worship. During the Irish uprising of 1848, he likely had seen Meagher at Mass in Carrick, addressing the frantic crowds in the town, and perhaps even sounding the call for rebellion atop Slievenamon. Lonergan would have been eager to emulate Meagher by also leading Irishmen in battle.

Neither his new business nor his romantic attachment to Roseanna would hold Lonergan back when events in the summer of 1862 finally gave him another chance to march to war at the head of his own "Irish Company." The next time that his path crossed that of Meagher no one would doubt Lonergan's courage or his devotion to Ireland's cause.

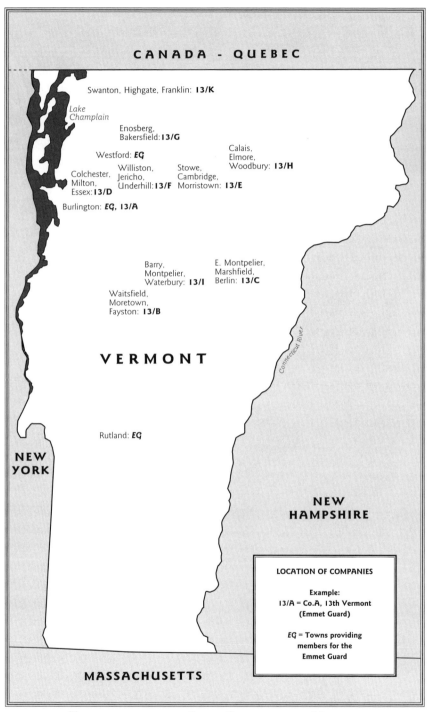

Towns with Members in Emmet Guards and 13th Vermont

CHAPTER ELEVEN

IRISH COMPANY

Lonergan's initial attempt to lead his Emmet Guards off to war had been frustrated by Gov. Fairbanks. In addition, in January of 1862, Lonergan had lost his sponsor at the War Department when Lincoln replaced the incompetent and dishonest Cameron with Edwin M. Stanton. However, the young Irishman had not abandoned his plan. The pressing need for more Union manpower might yet create conditions for him to restore his shattered militia company, even without a sponsor. Working in his new cooper shop in the spring of 1862, Lonergan would have closely followed the war as it was reported daily in the *Free Press,* watching for developments that might give him his opportunity to join in the fight. The weekly *Sentinel* provided its own Democratic-oriented summary of events on a less timely basis.

Lincoln still hoped to strike a fatal blow to the heart of the Confederacy in Richmond, but the war strategy developed by his government also included a slow strangulation of the rebellion through a blockade of Southern coastal ports and control of internal waterways. The winter of 1861–62 brought significant fighting along the Cumberland and Tennessee Rivers, where Gen. Ulysses S. Grant won welcome victories to help secure the border states, whose loyalty was still divided between the Union and the Confederacy.

In the East, Gen. McClellan applied his considerable administrative skills to preparing the Army of the Potomac for a spring offensive, but he remained intimidated by Confederate defenses around Manassas, always overestimating the forces that he faced. Rather than attacking south from Washington against these defenses, McClellan decided on a flanking movement by water. He would move on Richmond over a route that avoided crossing major rivers. Fortress Monroe at the tip of the Virginia Peninsula was still in federal hands and would serve as a base for the offensive channeled between the York and the James Rivers.

Lincoln worried that this could leave Washington open to attack and refused to assign as many forces to the operation as McClellan desired. In early March, the president also showed less than full confidence in McClellan's leadership, reducing him from general in chief to commander of only the Army of the Potomac and appointing that army's four corps commanders without consulting McClellan. The reorganization included "Baldy" Smith, commander of the First Vermont Brigade, who took command of the Second Division of the Fourth Corps, turning the Vermont Brigade over to Brig. Gen. W. T. H. Brooks. The promotion of Smith meant that Lonergan no longer had the ear of a sympathetic commander of the Vermont units, further reducing his prospects of being recalled into service.

THE TWO UNITS OF GREATEST INTEREST to Lonergan were naturally the Vermont Brigade and Meagher's Irish Brigade and he would have eagerly read any reports on their actions. Both brigades were among the more than 100,000 men, along with mountains of equipment and supplies, transported to the Virginia Peninsula that spring by 400 ships and barges in "an awesome demonstration of the North's logistical capacity." Another 50,000 men whom McClellan had requested for the operation were held back in northern Virginia to protect Washington. The units included Gen. Irvin McDowell's corps in which Gen. Shields, once considered for commander of the Irish Brigade, now held command of a division. Further west, Gen. Nathaniel P. Banks led 23,000 Union soldiers facing Gen. Thomas J. "Stonewall" Jackson in the Shenandoah Valley.

A far better administrator than a field commander, McClellan moved against Richmond so slowly that doubts arose as to his loyalties, particularly among Republicans, who questioned the Democratic general's resolve. Hauling massive siege artillery over ground made increasingly soggy by heavy spring rains, McClellan campaigned at a snail's pace against far smaller rebel forces.

Although outnumbered, the secessionist forces contested the progress of the Union troops in a series of delaying actions that allowed Gen. Joseph E. Johnston time to shift his forces from Manassas to the Peninsula. Fortified lines behind the swollen Warwick River comprised the first of the outer defenses of Richmond. On April 16, elements of the Vermont Brigade assaulted part of these rebel positions. Despite heavy losses, Capt. Samuel E. Pingree brought two companies of Col. Breed Hyde's 3rd Vermont through water obstacles at Lee's Mills to take the rifle pits on the opposite bank. Units of the 4th Vermont under Col. Edwin H. Stoughton stormed across a dam while men from Col. Nathan Lord's 6th Vermont crossed downstream. Unable to maintain their bridgeheads when support did not come, the survivors were ordered to retreat.

The loss of over 200 killed and wounded was the first significant bloodletting for the Vermont Brigade, a taste of the casualties to come. This battle also resulted in the first two awards for bravery among the Vermont units. Pingree had led his own Co. F and another company of the 3rd Vermont in the attack and the sixteen-year old drummer boy of Co. E, Julian Scott, repeatedly brought wounded soldiers back across the river. For their actions under fire, each soldier received the Medal of Honor when Congress later authorized the decoration.

Creeping forward despite steady rains and opposition, McClellan forced the rebels first from Yorktown and then out of Williamsburg. By the middle of May, his forces were on the outskirts of Richmond, threatening the capital. As part of Sumner's division, the Irish Brigade marched to the Chickahominy River "on the banks of which they encamped for a fortnight in comparative inactivity." The Irishmen even organized a series of steeple-chase horse races, but just as one of those races ended on the Saturday evening of May 31, the "deep boom of artillery was heard."

This marked the start of the Seven Days' Battles during which Johnston pushed the inactive federal forces away from the rebel capital. Meagher claimed Richmond was but four miles distant from the colors of the 69th New York, the right of the Irish Brigade, when a fierce battle broke out where "the chivalry of Virginia met its match in the chivalry of Tipperary." Sumner urged Meagher's men forward as his last hope. Pointing at his shoulder-straps, the general told them, "I'll go my stars on you. I want to see how Irishmen fight, and when you run, I'll run too!" The battle of Fair Oaks established the aggressive reputation of the Irish Brigade with "an inspiriting opening of a heroic history."

Johnston was wounded at Fair Oaks and replaced by Gen. Robert E. Lee. The new rebel commander recalled Jackson from the Shenandoah Valley and concentrated the Confederate forces against the federal units north of the Chickahominy. Lee's characteristic series of hammer-blow offensives resulted in the "Seven Days' Retreat," (as an officer of the Irish Brigade accurately termed the withdrawal), which involved Meagher's unit in repeated rear guard actions. The Irishmen distinguished themselves particularly at Gaine's Mill, Savage Station, and Malvern Hill where the rebels encountered "the cheers they learned to know so well at Fair Oaks." The war-cry they heard was no doubt the traditional "Faugh a ballagh!" shout, the Gaelic warning to "Clear the way!" used in battle for centuries.* Despite a tactical victory by the Union troops at Malvern Hill, on July 2 McClellan continued backing away to Harrison's Landing to take up defensive positions on the James River.

McCLELLAN'S PAINFULLY SLOW PROGRESS in the Peninsula Campaign, coupled with the perceived threat to Washington, soon forced a recalculation of the manpower needed in the Union army. Only weeks after recruitment had been stopped, Lincoln's War Department hastily resumed mobilization. Telegrams were sent on May 19 to all the governors of the loyal states asking for more infantry. Gov. Holbrook replied the next day that Vermont would raise "one regiment in forty days, and perhaps less, and two regiments in sixty days, or possibly less." The army Adjutant-General instructed him on May 21 to "raise one regiment of infantry immediately, to be armed, clothed, and equipped before it leaves the State. Raise as many thereafter as you can." Stanton warned the governors on May 25 that intelligence "leaves no doubt" of a rebel advance on Washington, asking them to "forward immediately all the volunteer and militia force in your state." Holbrook explained in his telegram of June 19 to Adj. Gen. Thomas that the state was "vigorously recruiting the Ninth Vermont Regiment," but had "no troops except as we recruit them for U.S. service."

On July 2, as McClellan cowered in the face of Lee's aggressive posture, Lincoln levied an additional 300,000 men for three years, offering each a bounty of $100 for their enlistment. To conceal the obvious connection with the disaster on the Peninsula, Lincoln fabricated a request from northern governors that he call for more troops, backdating it to June 28. He followed up the next day with a "Private and Confidential" telegram to the governors explaining his action. The president stated, "I would not want the half of

---

* Several alternative spellings of the battle cry appeared during the time of the American Civil War since standardized spelling of the Irish Gaelic took place only in the 20th century.

CHAPTER ELEVEN – IRISH COMPANY

300,000 new troops if I could have them now. If I had 50,000 additional troops here now I believe I could substantially close the war in two weeks."

The governors' responses included comments indicating that they would make every effort to supply the requested men, but "recruiting for three years is terribly hard" and expressing fear that they were able "to do little to meet immediate necessity." Several suggested that shorter enlistments would produce more volunteers willing to serve three months, six months, or even a year, but to fill three-year terms they would soon "be obliged to resort to drafting." Telegrams to the governors on July 7 informed each of his quota of the twenty-eight regiments of volunteer infantry to serve for three years. Holbrook was "requested to raise as soon as practicable" an additional two regiments in his state.

The War Department's previous request for Vermont troops was met two days after this new levy. Working through recruiting offices in twelve counties in the state and with the enticement of bounties, the 920 officers and men of the 9th Regiment were mustered in on July 9. The new unit was placed under the command of Col. Stannard, called home from his position as lieutenant colonel of the 2nd Vermont, Lonergan's erstwhile regiment. On July 15, Holbrook telegraphed Secretary of War Stanton: "Ninth Vermont Regiment left this morning for Washington by rail. A fine regiment of Green Mountain boys. Much enthusiasm in Vermont about enlistments and furnishing quota promptly. Tenth and Eleventh Regiments both rapidly forming." Holbrook asked that the troops receive "Springfield rifle muskets" to promote recruiting since most Vermonters "are marksmen, and know a good gun."

Elsewhere, however, the initial rush to volunteer had dwindled as the stark realities of the war replaced enthusiasm with caution. A new federal militia law went into effect on July 17 subjecting all able-bodied men aged eighteen to forty-five to mobilization for nine months service in the national forces. This law tripled the term of service of the previous legislation, with conscription authorized if sufficient volunteers did not step forward. Based on this extended obligation, the War Department on August 4 called up 300,000 men to serve nine months. This levy was in addition to the 300,000 three-year men required the previous month. Vermont was assigned a quota of 4,898 men in each category; each three-year volunteer who enlisted in excess of the quota for a state counted as four nine-month men. The total figure levied on Vermont in each category was portioned out by Congressional Districts, then by the state to the towns, based on the town's population and the number of men from the town who had already enlisted.*

Vermont would supply its 10th and 11th Regiments of three-year men on September 1, both mustered in as infantry, although the 11th was converted to heavy artillery to man the Washington fortifications. These were the last Vermont three-year regiments mustered as an entire unit. (After the five nine-month regiments—the 12th through the 16th—were called up, the 17th Vermont was raised piecemeal from January to September, 1864, mostly from veterans mustered in by squads as they reenlisted.) Other recruits for three-year service were sent as replacements to the Vermont regiments raised earlier. It was generally accepted that a man incorporated into a veteran unit was more valuable than two or three inexperienced soldiers in a new unit.

Union forces were being required to maintain an adequate defensive posture to protect the North, particularly its capital, while simultaneously carrying out offensive operations into rebel territory to destroy the Confederate army. These competing missions created the need for a massive increase in the Union army. A large force of new recruits could at least take on the less demanding roles of defense and free up the experienced units for the offensive operations. The nine-month units would thus be used mainly in defensive positions, since their term of service would barely extend through a season's campaigning as part of the mobile field armies.

The pool of eager volunteers, like John Lonergan, upon which the North could draw became smaller with each regiment that marched away and with the growing realization of just what awaited the soldier who did enlist: more hardship, hideous wounds, and chance of death than any recruiting officer would describe and far less glory than a soldier might imagine. At a series of war meetings held throughout the North during the summer, speakers encouraged volunteers to step forward and fill the ranks of the new regiments being raised for three years. While appealing to patriotism, they dangled the carrot of cash bounties and brandished the stick of the draft. Men who were drafted would not receive any of the bounties being offered by the national, state, and local authorities, as well as by wealthy citizens. (The prospect of a draft brought out the bitter comment about "a rich man's war and a poor man's fight" since military service could be avoided by those with enough

---

* Towns, subdivisions of counties best thought of as "townships," are the basic administrative entity in Vermont and should not be confused with its population centers, most of which were and remain villages.

CHAPTER ELEVEN – IRISH COMPANY

cash to hire a substitute or to pay the official "commutation" fee of $300 to the national treasury.)

EVEN AS THE CASUALTIES INCREASED, Irishmen might still be enticed into military service, particularly for the distinctive Irish units. While the Army of the Potomac licked its wounds after the retreat down the Virginia Peninsula, Meagher received a "brief leave of absence" to return to New York for "recruiting the depleted ranks of the brigade." Finding men for his regiments, however, was more difficult than for other units. Within the Irish community, it was thought that "extra risk was to be encountered in his command—it being notorious that the Irish Brigade was assigned more than the average share of the hard fighting."

While seeking replacements, Meagher called at the Fenian Brotherhood headquarters on Centre Street to meet with its secretary. Michael Cavanagh had returned only three months earlier from his trip to Ireland, where the Fenian leadership had voiced support of the Union. Meagher "was peculiarly gratified by the action taken by the Irish Nationalists at the great meeting convened in Dublin to sympathize with the cause of the Union." He praised its effect "on the Irish people at large, and their enemies—the English government and their landlord garrison." At the Fenian office, Meagher encountered a captain from his Irish Brigade, wounded at Fair Oaks and supposedly in the hospital in Philadelphia. Meagher advised him to report back to the hospital as quickly as possible, but offered him the excuse of meeting with his brigade commander in New York City. Meagher then told Cavanagh, "That's all the fault of you Fenians. There's such a mysterious attraction in your Brotherhood that no risk to be incurred, can keep ye apart."

More competition for Irish soldiers developed with the release of Col. Corcoran from his thirteen months of imprisonment in a series of Southern jails. After his capture at Bull Run, Corcoran had been offered parole if he promised no further fighting against the South, but he refused. He became one of the hostages designated to be hanged in reprisal if Lincoln's government carried out the threatened execution of Southern privateers as pirates.* Corcoran was released in a prisoner exchange on August 15,

---

* The Confederates had issued letters of marque authorizing the capture of ships sailing under the American flag. While this was a routine action by a sovereign nation during war, the U.S. considered it an unlawful act for rebels and therefore piracy, punishable by hanging.

returning to a hero's welcome in Washington, where he dined with Lincoln.

Commissioned a brigadier general with the rank dated back to the battle of Bull Run, Corcoran was authorized to raise the regiments for another brigade of Irishmen. Back in New York, he was received with honors and presentations, including a parade up Broadway. Reporting for duty to the governor by telegraph, the new general opened a recruiting drive for his "Irish Legion" in New York City and across the state. He traveled to Poughkeepsie and Albany, even going as far west as Buffalo where he raised a new regiment, the 155th New York, for his brigade. Building on his Fenian connections and his fame as an unyielding prisoner ready to take up the sword again, he was able to find enough men to field five New York regiments within weeks.

In some larger cities with concentrations of Irishmen—notably New York, Boston, and Philadelphia—it was still possible to organize full regiments of nearly 1,000 dedicated Fenians. The idea of drafting men who were not willing to volunteer remained widely unpopular, however, especially among the Irish and particularly in New York City. When John Lonergan raised Vermont's only ethnic-based unit, he was unable to recruit the required one hundred men from the Irish communities scattered around the state and he was forced to bring in some non-Irish soldiers to fill the ranks of his company.

LONERGAN PLIED HIS TRADE as a cooper through the spring and into the summer while the newspapers reported bloody combat involving the Vermont and Irish brigades. The publicity about the Emmet Guards had made Lonergan a highly visible figure in his community. Customers visiting his shop, friends joining him over a "jar," and people he met on the street would know the history of his disbanded militia company and his frustrated ambition to field a company of Irishmen from Vermont. Did he confidently assure those who would listen that he would yet lead his troops into battle? The year before, men had drilled to his orders in what was now his place of business; at times he might have paused in his work at the bench, half-finished barrel stave in hand, in his mind hearing echoes of their marching in the old armory.

That summer Lonergan commanded no company of militia that the state government might call up for service nor did he have any authorization for recruiting such a company (other than the vague encouragement from the former Secretary of War). The members of the Emmet Guards militia company whom the state had accepted for service in May of 1861 had scattered, some transferring to fill up units of the 2nd Vermont when Lonergan's company was disbanded. Others from the Emmet Guards enlisted in regiments both in and outside Vermont.

On June 17, right at the one-year anniversary of his company's dissolution, Lonergan's former first lieutenant came to Burlington on a furlough. Capt. Christopher M. Dolan now commanded Co. E, 4th New York Cavalry (he had enlisted in the neighboring state where Irishmen were welcome to join, even as officers). Dolan's visit might have been more than just a social visit to see friends and relatives in his hometown. Given his Irish surname and leadership role in Lonergan's Emmet Guards, Dolan was most likely also a Fenian. His cavalry company had been raised in New York City, the heart of the Irish nationalist movement. He could have brought Lonergan word of the Brotherhood, perhaps even encouragement to persist in the attempt to raise a company. Lonergan might well have been embarrassed to have his former subordinate, now commissioned a captain, see their old armory filled with the tools of the cooper trade, rather than those of war.

The *Free Press* reported a quiet Fourth of July celebration in Burlington, with only a few fireworks marking the holiday. With temperatures in the 90s, the "boats ran crowded on the Lake, but there was but very little stir in our streets." With the Union still in such peril after McClellan's repulse in Virginia, little enough reason would have been found to celebrate this Independence Day. With Lee commanding the rebel Army of Northern Virginia, the situation would soon become even more serious.

On July 19, the *Free Press* printed the words to a rousing new patriotic song whose chorus promised "we are coming, Father Abraham, three hundred thousand more" even though the men would have to "leave our ploughs and workshops, our wives and children dear." Alongside this text, a notice of "Great Inducements to Volunteers" gave the schedule of bounties; each accepted recruit would receive $7 each month from the State of Vermont, in addition to the regular U.S. Army pay of $13, plus $25 in advance and another $75 upon completion of his enlistment. The "General Recruiting Officer for Chittenden Co." had placed this notice on July 12 seeking recruits for the 10th Vermont, including a two dollar "premium" to be paid to "any citizen or soldier, for each accepted recruit brought by him to the rendezvous."

Not relying solely on volunteers to fill the quotas assigned by the War

Department to each Congressional District of the loyal states, the lottery for a draft began to draw names from the compiled list of eligible men. In the First District of Vermont, the Provost Marshal at Rutland issued orders notifying residents that the district required 1,505 men "as the first proportional part of the quota of troops." To supply this number of soldiers, an additional fifty percent of names would be drawn as a reserve to replace those who might be found exempt or unfit for service. Application forms for exemptions were printed along with this notice. Since drafted men were not allowed the bounties offered to volunteers, those who had their names drawn for the draft in Vermont were usually then given the chance to enlist voluntarily; the state thus officially had only volunteers responding to the nation's call.

The draft for 2, 256 men began in Rutland on July 11, a Saturday, and by Monday the *Rutland Daily Herald* was reporting men leaving town to avoid the army. An editorial castigated "some of the quarrymen in West Rutland" for being quick to fill out naturalization papers (as immigrants, many of them Irish) in order to vote and then failing to do their duty to their new country. Patrols with the authority to arrest anyone suspected of fleeing the draft were established to stop men attempting to "skedaddle" into Canada.*

Chittenden County, containing Vermont's largest population center, was allotted the quota of a company for the 10th Vermont, but found that neither the enticement of bounties nor the prospect of the draft was a sufficient incentive for recruiting 101 men. War meetings were held to encourage enlistments. On July 28, Burlington held such a meeting and "in spite of the rain, the Town Hall was crowded to overflowing." The featured speaker was Chaplain Woodward of the 1st Vermont Cavalry, who brought his moral certitude and war experiences to bear in expressing his surprise at finding "that it was hard enlisting" and there "was even talk of impressing men." This clergyman, coming from the field of battle, was also to address the "Grand War Meeting" scheduled in his home town of Westford on August 1, "which town has already sent so many and such good soldiers to the war," but was "still not weary in well doing."

The Burlington meeting was adjourned after appointing a committee of twenty citizens to "take measures to raise at once the number of recruits

---

* Traffic ran both ways across the border as enterprising Canadian "bounty jumpers" came down to enlist, collect a bounty, and desert at the first opportunity, at times boldly repeating the process under a variety of names. Some specialized in fleecing men who had been drafted and sought to pay a substitute to avoid serving.

CHAPTER ELEVEN – IRISH COMPANY

needed to fill up the Chittenden County Company." It resumed on July 30, again with an overflow crowd in attendance; a heated discussion ensued about whether to authorize a bounty of $25 for each man "enlisting in the town of Burlington in the next six days." The elderly George W. Benedict, opposing the resolution on providing bounties, spoke in favor of allowing the draft to raise the men required as it had when he and many others were conscripted in the War of 1812. At this point, "Capt. Lonergan moved that the first of the two resolutions be laid on the table, which was negatived." Still using his military rank a year after his company had been disbanded, Lonergan probably was a member of the recruitment committee; in any case, he clearly was not shy about speaking up at a crowded public war meeting.

SECRETARY OF WAR STANTON issued his order for a levy of 300,000 militia on August 4, requiring any state that did not furnish its quota of nine-months volunteers by August 15 to make up the deficiency "by the special draft from the militia." The order included provisions for "securing the promotion of officers of the Army and volunteers" to lead the new troops, as well as "ridding the service of such incompetent persons" who were now holding commissions. Vermont would continue with the traditional practice of militia members in each company electing their own officers. These line officers would in turn elect the regimental field officers, other than the commander, who was appointed by the governor, but the War Department reserved the right to remove any officer found "incompetent."

A series of General Orders (GO) signed by "Frederick Holbrook, Governor and Commander-in-Chief," and "Peter T. Washburn, Adjutant and Inspector General," were issued on August 8 to provide Vermont's quota of soldiers.* From his office in Woodstock, in GO No.10, Washburn assigned the "quotas of the several towns in the State" for men to "serve in the army of the United States, for the term of three years." In addition to the new regiments formed in Vermont, another 1,200 men had to be "immediately raised in this State to fill the regiments now in service from the State."

The quotas were established based on the population of the town and the number of men already sent to war as volunteers. Pursuant to GO No. 11, each

---

* A military headquarters, down to the level of company, could issue General Orders applicable to everyone or Special Orders whose effect was restricted, e.g. promotion orders for certain of its members.

town in Vermont was required to compile a list of men who had volunteered for three years, in order to portion out the shares of the current levies. The towns were allowed to deduct from their listed quota the men they had just provided to the 9th, 10th, and 11th Vermont regiments or the Vermont Sharpshooter companies. Some towns, such as willing Westford and sparsely populated Elmore, were not required to furnish any more soldiers. Most towns needed to persuade ten to twenty men to sign up. The larger population centers faced a levy of substantial numbers, with over 800 in total to come from Chittenden County and Rutland County. Burlington had to supply 155 of Chittenden County's allotment of 460, while the town of Rutland was allocated 230 of the eponymous county's quota of 409 men.

Town selectmen throughout the state were appointed recruiting officers and directed to begin a draft on August 18 if there were any "deficiency in the number of men called for in this order." Burlington's three selectmen published a notice alongside the quota list, advising that their recruiting office would be open daily from 8:00 AM to 9:00 PM and urging "prompt and patriotic response to this call of our country." (The response was so poor that by the end of the month Burlington, still short of men, was desperately offering an additional bounty, ranging from $75 to $125 based on the number of dependent children a volunteer was leaving behind.)

The third of the General Orders of August 8 brought the opportunity for which Lonergan had been waiting: GO No. 12 promulgated instructions "to all companies of Uniform[ed] Militia in this State" assigning them to federal service. Although neither the Emmet Guards nor any of the other companies existed as a body of men, Lonergan's unit had been accepted by the state the previous year and was one of a dozen still being carried on the books as a company of Uniformed Militia.

The "commanding officer of each of said companies" was required to report with his company for active duty at a time and place of rendezvous that would be later designated by Washburn's headquarters. Meanwhile, each commander was "hereby directed to hold himself in readiness for active service, with the company under his command in the town in which said company is located, until further orders." The commander was told "to issue his order, thereby directing the company under his command to assemble forthwith at such place as he shall designate." Pursuant to the key section of the order, Lonergan was "hereby authorized and directed forthwith to fill his company, by enlistments, to the number of one hundred and one, including officers."

Anyone enlisting from outside the town where the company had its headquarters would be credited to the town of his residence and counted for fulfilling the quota of his home town, which allowed the company to draw on a wider area to fill its ranks. Each company commander was required to submit "a complete and perfect roll of all able-bodied men of his company" to the Woodstock office by noon on August 25, "whether such company is then filled, or not." This deadline was ten days after the impossibly short schedule imposed by Stanton and recognized the monumental nature of raising almost 5,000 soldiers for nine-months service by enlistments, the draft, or any combination of methods.

Finally, GO 13 laid out the procedure for providing the remainder of the men required for the nine-months regiments.* Specific quotas for the towns could not be established until the enrollment lists required by GO 11 were received by the state. Since the overall number levied against Vermont was known, "the officers of each town can determine with sufficient accuracy" the number that would "probably be required from each town" based on its population. A suggested "contract of enlistment" was contained in the GO stating that the men signing below "hereby voluntarily enlist, and offer ourselves to serve in a company of militia, in the service of the United States." Citizens were urged to enlist for "the lasting honor of Vermont on the page of history" and to avoid the necessity of a draft.

However, as had been the case in Rutland in July, some residents were more concerned about their own safety. Calling them "skedaddle rangers" in the headline, the Burlington *Free Press* on August 9 reported "sixteen men, mostly Frenchmen, left the town of Colchester last night, for Canada, to escape the draft. Numbers are making their way over the line on foot or in wagons." Boats and trains north had been crowded with "sneaks" avoiding the draft, even though many were not American citizens and therefore could not be forced to serve. The newspaper's editorial opinion concluded "there is no reasoning with such cowards, however." The report of "skedaddlers" on August 13 included eleven "stopped in Bellows Falls last night" plus half a dozen at Rutland and

---

* The practical matter of providing uniforms for the five new Vermont regiments concerned the "Quarter Master General Office" located in Brattleboro. A request for bids issued from that office on August 18 solicited sealed proposals to be submitted within the week "for the making of 4,898 Infantry Frock Coats, 4,898 pair of Trowsers, cloth and trimmings to be furnished by the State." The order had to be filled within twenty days of when the contract was awarded "to established manufacturers." The Quartermaster General would also have to furnish the weapons and equipment needed before the regiments left Vermont.

"a number at Island Pond," all seeking asylum in Canada. The writ of *habeas corpus* had been suspended in such cases, but anyone found avoiding the draft could be released by posting a bond to the United States "in the sum of $1,000, conditional for the performance of military duty."

IN SHARP CONTRAST TO MEN fleeing the country to escape the draft, John Lonergan may have been one of the few people in Vermont pleased to see these General Orders published. Now he finally again had the authorization from the state to lead a company into the war. Like the other commanders of Uniformed Militia companies, however, he was faced with the fact that his unit existed only on paper. Of the 101 men who would make up a company, he needed to find 100 volunteers—reserving the position of captain for himself—in a little over two weeks and this at a time when enlistment was generally being avoided. A major factor favoring his call for volunteers was the short term of the enlistment required. A man signing up for nine months might spend the entire time on guard duty and would put himself safely out of reach of the impending draft for three years of service that would surely involve combat.

Facing difficult circumstances and a short deadline, Lonergan threw himself into the mission of filling the ranks of his phantom Emmet Guards. Any unfinished work in his shop would have to be completed by some other cooper or wait until he returned from the war. The College Street premises reverted back to their previous role of armory and headquarters of a militia company. By August 16, a Rutland newspaper report credited Lonergan with having about fifty men enlisted, commenting that "The Irish in Burlington are coming up bravely to the work." On that same day, the required public notice was printed in the *Free Press*:

> ATTENTION!
> EMMET GUARDS!!
> In pursuance of orders received, you are hereby ordered to report in person at my Headquarters on or before Monday, August 18th, 1862 at 2 o'clock P.M., and hereof fail not.
> By order,
> Capt. JOHN LONERGAN

CHAPTER ELEVEN – IRISH COMPANY

Official records for his company show that only two men had enlisted by the date Lonergan ordered its members to report to his "Headquarters." Alvin H. Henry from Westford had signed up on August 10;* five days later James B. Scully enlisted in Burlington. Henry served as First Sergeant of the company until replaced by Scully, suggesting Lonergan had made them some promises about rewards for joining up early. (Perhaps some other men had made verbal commitments to the commander or even signed papers by August 16, but were not mustered in later with the company.) Lonergan had made appeals at war meetings "in Burlington, Winooski, Westford and neighboring towns" and "enrolled the names of those who were willing to enlist." However, it appears certain that any claim of "about fifty enlisted" in mid-August was a bit of the blarney. Probably it was only with Henry's help that Lonergan succeeded in recruiting any men from Westford, a town that had already sent its share of volunteers to the war. An even dozen Westford men, all with "Yankee" surnames, signed the enlistment forms on August 23. Others in the Burlington area joined up by ones and twos as privates, while the company was furnished with a "waggoner" from Essex to act as teamster and a farmer from Westford who served as drummer.

Volunteer companies raised in Vermont were invariably made up of men from the same area, often neighbors and relatives, although Uniformed Militia companies might draw some members from a distance. In no case other than Lonergan's "Irish Company" was the basis an ethnic identity, rather than a geographic proximity. He deliberately assembled his company to maximize its Irish identity, but he could not recruit enough fellow countrymen in the Burlington area to fill the ranks. He had to travel halfway down the state to Rutland where he called upon John Sinnott to help complete the roster of the Emmet Guards.**

Sinnott, from County Wexford, had much in common with John Lonergan. Both were born in the rebellious southeastern part of Ireland, stood 5'11" in height, were of the same age, and were attempting to raise

---

* Henry had served in Co. G, 2nd Vermont, from May 1861 until his discharge for disability in January 1862. He and Lonergan probably knew each other from their service with that regiment. Henry apparently was no longer considered disabled for service in August 1862.

** Various records spell this name differently (Sennott, Sinnot, Sinott). The official Vermont roster uses Sinnott and his tombstone is so inscribed; that spelling is employed here. His military service records in the 13th Vermont muster rolls and the U.S. Archives, however, are under Sennott.

a company of Irishmen in the summer of 1862. As a schoolteacher, Sinnott likely had more education than Lonergan, but in the Fenian Brotherhood hierarchy Sinnott may well have been the subordinate. The concentration of Irish immigrants in the Rutland area, particularly West Rutland, makes it highly likely that a "circle" of Fenians had been organized there by 1862. Sinnott's leadership role in recruiting a company of Irishmen would indicate that he probably was the "centre" for that Fenian organization and therefore reported to the "head centre" for the state, Lonergan.

On August 25, calling for a company of Irish to be raised locally, the *Rutland Herald* wrote, "Much is expected now of our numerous Irish population. They hear the bugle notes sounded by the gallant Corcoran and Meagher, and they can no longer linger away from the field of duty and glory." It reported, "Mr. Sennott has opened a recruiting office, where the flag of Old Erin intermingles its folds with those of the Stars and Stripes." This patriotic rhetoric received practical support the next day when a special train carried passengers free to "a large and spirited meeting" at West Rutland. The audience was "composed in large part of Irishmen" and the "sons of old Erin manifested much enthusiasm" as they responded to a series of speakers, including "Mr. Sennot" and "Capt. Lonergan of Burlington." Several men came forward to enlist during the meeting and it was reported that twenty-five had already enrolled. The concluding call for "Three cheers for the first Irish company from Vermont!" rang hollow, however, as the proposed Rutland company of Irishmen never took the field.

Instead, Lonergan persuaded Sinnott to merge his recruits with the Emmet Guards in Burlington to create a predominately Irish company. This agreement to combine forces soon appeared in the *Rutland Herald* in a notice stating:

> Mr. Sennott, of Rutland, has opened a recruiting office in Merchant's Row, for the Emmet Guards, Capt. Lonergan. Captain Lonergan's Company is to be composed of Irishmen exclusively, and affords an excellent opportunity for our patriotic Irish citizens to enlist. We are requested to ask the farmers in this and surrounding towns to give notice of the fact to the Irishmen in their employ and in their neighborhoods. Mr. Sennott has put out the flag of old Erin with the Stars and Stripes, and his motto is, '*E Pluribus Erin Union go bragh!*' Come on, ye Irish lads, and stand by the flag of your adopted country.

CHAPTER ELEVEN – IRISH COMPANY

Recently scorned, the Irish had become noble "sons of Erin," welcome to enlist. The reporter clearly thought it better to have the quota for Rutland filled by some penniless laborer, likely illiterate and needing to be told the latest news by a farmer, than by a prosperous Vermonter of Yankee stock.

Other militia companies in Vermont had less trouble filling their ranks as men signed up for the nine-months units in preference to taking the chance of being drafted for three years. Both the West Windsor Guards and the Woodstock Light Infantry were organized on August 19. The Howard Guard—still carried on the books as Company A, 4th Regiment of the Vermont Volunteer Militia—reported sufficient men enlisted from Burlington as of August 22 and elections were held the next day. The remaining companies for this next Vermont regiment also found enough volunteers before the deadline. All the Uniformed Militia companies were required to submit a roster of their members to the Woodstock office by August 25.

This report must have concerned Lonergan since the roll of his company enlistments show that only thirty-three men had signed on with him by that date. Another dozen, all from Rutland, joined up the next day, leaving the company still far short of the required 101. This deficiency in numbers, painfully similar to the situation with the original Emmet Guards the previous summer, might explain a letter to the editor printed in the *Free Press* on August 26. It appeared alongside a complete roster of all 110 members of the Howard Guard, the list also showing the company's elected officers and non-commissioned officers.

The letter in support of Lonergan was signed "from one of the Vermont 2nd," indicating that the author probably was Alvin Henry from Westford. To forestall the Emmet Guards again being disbanded due to insufficient numbers and seeking more time to raise the company, Lonergan had likely asked Henry to write. The headline unequivocally declared that the Irishman represented "The Right Man in the Right Place" and the author recommended strongly that he should command a company. The writer explained that "Capt. Lonergan, Commander of the Emmet Guards, a brave man he is and a true one" had "spent some time last fall with the Regiment I had the honor to belong to (the Vt. 2d) in the land of Dixie." Stating that skirmishes at that time "were of almost nightly occurrence," he assured the reader:

Capt. Lonergan was always on hand, one of the first and foremost, with musket in hand on these occasions, he was just *'spiling for a fight,'* and declared he would not return to Vermont until he had one. He is a man of the right metal to command a company; and to those who wish to enlist to fight for the Union and the old flag, I would say he is *the man* to go with–and if there is any chance for glory, he will find it for you.

Whether or not this letter influenced the decision-makers in Vermont government to give Lonergan more time, he was permitted to continue signing up members for another six weeks, right up to the day of mustering in. Whoever penned these praises could not have dreamed how prophetic his claim of Lonergan finding "any chance for glory" would prove to be.

LONERGAN AND LINCOLN FOUND THEMSELVES in exactly opposite situations; the captain without enough followers searched for men to fill the ranks of his company, while the president with adequate forces still had not found the right man to lead them. New three-year regiments were marching off to the war, many units already in the field were being brought up to strength with replacements, and now the 300,000 nine-months men were gathering. Each enlistment added a pebble to the avalanche of manpower rolling down from the North, yet without firm direction this enormous energy might be expended without lasting effect. As commander of the Army of Northern Virginia, Lee soon demonstrated again the crucial value of leadership on the battlefield.

McClellan had permitted Lee to bottle up the Army of the Potomac for a month at Harrison's Landing; Lincoln visited to assess the situation in person on July 8. Upon his return to Washington, the president revived the position of general in chief and filled it with McClellan's recommendation, Maj. Gen. Henry Halleck. Despairing of any renewed Union offensive on the Peninsula, on August 3, Halleck ordered the Army of the Potomac to redeploy by water to northern Virginia, where Gen. John Pope also maintained a defensive posture. These combined Union forces could then again strike south, directly toward Richmond. However, the last troops filed off their boats in Alexandria only on August 28. By then, Lee had exploited the advantage of interior lines of communications to concentrate his own forces.

Stonewall Jackson outflanked Pope on August 26 to capture his main

CHAPTER ELEVEN – IRISH COMPANY

supply base at Manassas Junction, twenty-five miles behind the Union lines. Forced to turn back north to counter this threat, Pope failed to coordinate his attacks against Jackson or his defense against Lee's forces and McClellan did little to support him. As a result, the more numerous Union forces were again defeated by superior generalship in battles on August 29 and 30. The federal troops once more retreated into the outer defensive lines around Washington, where the forces were consolidated under McClellan to counter the serious threat of an invasion of the North.

Lee understood that the South could not win a war of attrition and boldly sought to provide the Confederacy with a political advantage by delivering a punishing blow to the North itself. Maintaining the momentum of his victory at Second Manassas, Lee ordered his Army of Northern Virginia onto Union territory. On September 4, his 55,000 men crossed the Potomac into Maryland, easily taking the town of Frederick on September 6. By this date, thirty-eight new three-year Union regiments had arrived in Washington, with more on the way. (The nine-month regiments in Vermont were still being organized and Lonergan was doggedly searching out men to fill the ranks of his company.)

Upon arriving in Washington in mid-July, the 9th Vermont regiment under Col. Stannard had stayed only a few days before marching into Virginia. They helped build and occupy a fort near Winchester, at the mouth of the strategically important Shenandoah Valley, but were withdrawn along with the other Union troops on September 2. After a forced night march of thirty-four miles, the Vermonters took up defensive positions on the hills around Harper's Ferry.

McClellan reorganized his Army of the Potomac to incorporate Pope's divisions, renumbering the corps and assigning his own commanders. Nearly 100,000 men set out against the rebels, entering Frederick on September 12 while Lee was dealing with the 13,000 men of the garrison at Harper's Ferry. Even though McClellan knew the disposition of the opposing forces, he moved too slowly to relieve the siege of Harper's Ferry. The bungled defense of the garrison, described as "treachery or incompetency," resulted in the surrender of the entire Union force on September 15. Stannard tried to break out with his regiment, but was forced to relinquish his arms and sign a parole not to take them up again until properly exchanged.*

When Harper's Ferry was captured, Lee concentrated his forces on

---

* After being paroled, the 9th Vermont was to spend six months in Chicago, guarding prisoners in Camp Douglas.

good ground for defensive action at Antietam Creek near Sharpsburg, Maryland. On September 17, McClellan launched a poorly-organized series of attacks on the 40,000 rebels. This produced the greatest slaughter of Americans—for both sides were American—on a single day of battle in any war. Outdated tactics resulted in wholesale carnage that accomplished nothing but suffering and death. As part of the Sixth Corps, which was held back until late in the day, the Vermont Brigade was spared the worst of the battle.

The Irish Brigade, however, experienced the full horror of the fighting and confusion. Gen. Sumner, now the Second Corps commander, went off into the battle with Gen. John Sedgwick's division, leaving his other two division commanders, Gen. William French and Gen. Israel Richardson, on their own. Lacking orders, French led his troops against a strong Confederate position in the Sunken Road, feeding each of his three brigades into the fighting piecemeal. Richardson, a native of Fairfax, Vermont, then committed his own troops to French's left, beginning with the Irish Brigade. Shouting "Faugh a ballagh" as they charged, the Irish were stopped by fierce musketry and cannon fire. The 63rd New York lost sixteen color guards in their exposed line of battle. Combined losses for the brigade were 540 men; the 63rd and 69th each suffered almost sixty percent casualties. Meagher was again carried from the field, this time after his horse was shot from under him. Dark rumors after the battle hinted at his incapacity due to drink, though no charges were brought against him. (Richardson himself was mortally wounded in the battle, although it took him seven weeks to die.)

By early afternoon, the Union forces were finally in place for a complete defeat of the Confederates, but they delayed too long. Additional Southern units arrived on the battlefield after capturing Harper's Ferry and saved the day for the rebels. During the night, Lee drew his forces together in a defensive line, in anticipation of a federal attack on the outnumbered Southern troops the next day. McClellan, horrified at the terrific losses suffered by his soldiers and concerned about their combat effectiveness, held back from resuming the battle until September 19. By then, there was no rebel force for him to attack—the Confederates had slipped away during the night, safely crossing the Potomac River without obstruction.

McClellan felt that in repulsing Lee's invasion he had saved the North, while Lincoln could only fume at the lost opportunity to crush Lee and with

CHAPTER ELEVEN – IRISH COMPANY

him the Confederacy. This costly and only partial victory for the Union did at least give the President the opening for which he had been waiting to act on the issue of slavery. On September 23, publication of the Emancipation Proclamation declared that slaves held in those states in rebellion were set free, effective the first day of 1863.*

ENLISTMENTS IN THE EMMET GUARDS were not stimulated by the Emancipation Proclamation, given a generally unfavorable reception of the decree among the Irish. The daily newspaper accounts of Union defeats and casualty figures also discouraged volunteers, but Lonergan persisted in filling the ranks of his company by ones and twos right through September and into October, well after the original deadline of August 25.** Apparently the authorities were willing to allow him the leeway of additional time if he could persuade men to join and help avoid the unpopular draft.

As they enlisted, the men gathered at the rendezvous point of Burlington, where the Westford men stayed in the Howard Hotel downtown and the other recruits from out of town were quartered at the Murphy Hotel on Water Street. The Burlington contingent apparently stayed with their families and enjoyed that comfort as they awaited departure. Their "days were passed in drilling on the Battery or the old Fair Ground, and the nights in telling stories and reading war news from the front." The Battery, built during the War of 1812, provided a suitably martial location for the company's drills. As the soldiers learned the movements of close-order drill, beginning to respond as a unit to the shouted orders, they had the benefit of some military experience in their captain and first sergeant. No weapons had yet been received to remind them constantly of the grim mission awaiting them and the men likely could enjoy the comradeship of marching shoulder to shoulder in the crisp fall air—most of them young and healthy, full of life.

As autumn's brilliant foliage began to mark the passage of another season, the lengthening nights would have been a time for reflection, as many men

---

* This perceived change in the purpose of the war from the preservation of the Union to the abolition of slavery was not universally popular in the North.

** See Appendix A for a roster of Lonergan's company with enlistment dates. The official record shows that the last two men—one actually a boy of sixteen—were recruited from Burlington and Montpelier on October 10, the same day that the company was mustered in with the rest of the regiment.

probably had spent little time away from home. Reading the "war news from the front" must have given them all pause for thought as to their future, especially when the heavy losses at Antietam on September 17 were tallied up. The Irishmen, quartered separately from the Westford Yankees, would no doubt have encouraged each other with stories recounting the bravery of their ancestors. Their view to the west across Lake Champlain looked toward *Tir na nOg*, the Land of Eternal Youth, where Celtic warriors feast forever after death in battle. When a sunburst streamed down through the clouds over the mountains to replicate the symbol of the Fenian Brotherhood, the Irish would be reminded that their service was ultimately for the cause of liberating their homeland*.

Pursuant to orders from the Adjutant General, Lonergan assembled his company at the College Street armory on September 11 to elect their officers. With Lonergan presiding over the meeting, he was not surprisingly the unanimous choice for captain of the unit. Votes for the position of first lieutenant were also unanimous in favor of John Sinnott, who had brought a contingent of some forty men from Rutland into the company. Friction arose in the competition for second lieutenant, however, with Burlington supporting James Scully, Westford backing Alvin Henry, and Rutland pressing for David McDevitt. The last, a 6'2" quarryman from Rutland, "finally won the prize much to the disappointment of a respectable minority." The disgruntled Westford group of twenty-one recruits discussed joining one of the other companies of the county, but "harmony was restored by the distribution of places to non-commissioned officers." Henry was appointed first sergeant and Scully second sergeant, with the remaining positions of two sergeants and eight corporals then judiciously distributed to keep peace within the company.

Lonergan could now report to the Adjutant General that his company of Uniformed Militia was properly organized and up to strength, ready for medical examination. The medical inspector's report of September 17 shows

---

*A note on sources: Many details of the experiences of Lonergan and his company described hereafter are drawn from an extensive, though unofficial, compilation published in 1910 by a committee headed by Ralph O. Sturtevant of Co. K, titled "Pictorial History, Thirteenth Regiment Vermont Volunteers, War of 1861–1865." Although providing the most comprehensive first-hand record of any Vermont regiment in the Civil War, the history was not published until nearly half a century after the events, when some details might have been forgotten or confused.

Another key source is the letters of George G. Benedict, as edited and published with valuable commentary by Eric Ward in *Army Life in Virginia*. They describe events in the Second Vermont Brigade as a whole and particularly in the 12th Vermont.

CHAPTER ELEVEN – IRISH COMPANY

one hundred and two men on the company roster, but he rejected eleven of these as unfit; seventeen others were found to be minors.*

THE SECOND VERMONT BRIGADE was formed in a pattern similar to the initial Vermont regiments mobilized in 1861.** The 12th Vermont, like the 1st Vermont Regiment, was composed entirely of companies of the Uniformed Militia. Seven of the ten companies in the 12th were raised from the same locations as those of the 1st Vermont. However, these were the same companies in name only. The members of these companies were newly enlisted for service in 1862, since the militia companies had been inactive since the original mobilization.

The second regiment of the new brigade that was created in 1862, the 13th Vermont, included the remaining two companies of Uniformed Militia in the state, in this case the Emmet Guards and the Lafayette Artillery of Calais (ordered up as infantry). The other eight companies of the 13th were raised in the towns of northwestern and central Vermont from Montpelier to Highgate. The Colchester company was able to enlist the required number of men from that town and neighboring Milton, while the Richmond company had to draw on eight rural towns in the area to fill its ranks. The first of these ten companies was reported as organized on August 25 and the last not until September 23 (based on the date of commission of their officers).

Once the line officers had been elected, they in turn voted on the field officers for the regiment. The 13th Vermont was constituted by the state along with the 14th, 15th, and 16th Vermont by GO 23, dated September 20. A meeting to organize the regiment was ordered on September 22, to be held in the Pavilion in Montpelier at 11:00 AM on September 24. The governor himself decided who would command Vermont's regiments and brigades and "it was generally understood who would be chosen Colonel." Clearly Francis V. Randall knew that he had already been chosen when he resigned as captain commanding Co. F, 2nd Vermont, on September 9, "to accept promotion."

---

* Recruits below eighteen years of age could enlist if they had their parents' approval. Limerick-born John Hamlin, for example, later described himself as "only 16, but quite large, rugged, and strong" when he signed up for the Emmet Guards at the last minute.

** The existing grouping of the 2nd through 6th Vermont regiments became known as the "Old Brigade" or "First Vermont Brigade." The latter term will be used here to distinguish it clearly from the short-term Second Vermont Brigade.

The Northfield lawyer had acquired considerable experience in the army since he and Lonergan had been equals as company commanders in the 2nd Vermont the previous year. Now Randall would be Lonergan's commanding officer in the 13th Vermont.

Gen. Jackman of Norwich University was authorized to preside over the organization of the regiment. Since Holbrook had in effect dictated the choice of colonel, the only real elections were for lieutenant colonel and major. Both of these field-grade positions were contested among several candidates, among them Capt. William D. Munson, commanding the Colchester Company; Capt. Lawrence D. Clarke of the Highgate Company, who had served with the 1st Vermont; and apparently Lonergan.* Negotiations among the company officers resulted in Capt. Andrew C. Brown, commander of the Montpelier Company, being elected lieutenant colonel on the second ballot and Clarke being promoted to major.

Lonergan might well have helped to elevate Clarke to this higher position in order to advance his own plans to establish seniority among the remaining company commanders. Clarke held a commission as captain of the Green Mountain Guards of Swanton, dated July 30, 1859, which had gained him the senior position of Co. A in the 1st Vermont Regiment in 1861. Based on this seniority, his Highgate company would likely have been assigned the designation Co. A, 13th Vermont. The oldest officer in the 1st Vermont, Clarke was also the oldest field officer (with one possible exception) commissioned in Vermont during the Civil War.

Lonergan had a vested interest in recognizing the validity of an earlier militia commission to support his own claim to seniority among the remaining company commanders. Five companies in the 13th had organized before the reborn Emmet Guards held their election and would all have been given preferential placement in the line of battle based on this seniority. Only by helping Clarke move from the line to a field grade position and insisting that his own captaincy dated from his election by the original Emmet Guards in 1861 could Lonergan claim seniority among the company commanders. It must have been by sheer

---

* One aspirant for lieutenant colonel is given in the 13th Regiment history as Capt. Lewis C. Coburn, commanding the East Montpelier Company, but it appears that the author has confused him with Capt. Lonergan. Stating "his candidacy for the position was well received," the writer goes on to describe "his record as Captain and his valiant conduct" at Gettysburg, attributing to Coburn all of Lonergan's later acts. (One can perhaps substitute Lonergan's name for that of Coburn and agree that "if he had been chosen [it] would have reflected credit to himself and honor to his regiment.")

CHAPTER ELEVEN – IRISH COMPANY

force of personality, rather than the regulations, that the Irishman was able to make that argument successfully. When the letter designations for the 13th Regiment were assigned, the Emmet Guards became the senior company, Company A, to occupy the position of honor on the right of the battle line.

Once the field officers of the regiment had been elected, Gen. Jackman declared the unit to be organized and appointments were made for the regimental staff officers and non-commissioned officers—adjutant, quartermaster, surgeon and assistant, chaplain, sergeant-major, quartermaster sergeant, commissary sergeant, and hospital steward. The announcement of the appointments was followed by speeches, "all of which were appropriate to the occasion and well received." Several orders were then read and notice given as to "future action of the companies, and the regiment." Commanders were informed of the probable time and place for the companies to rendezvous for muster into federal service, when the regiment would likely leave the state, and its probable destination of Washington, D.C. The meeting was adjourned and officers returned to their respective companies to prepare them for the move to Brattleboro on twenty-four hours notice. When the regiment was assembled, the final preparations would take place, with uniforms, arms, and equipment issued before inspection and mustering in.

BRATTLEBORO HAD BEEN CHOSEN as the assembly point for all five nine-month regiments because of its suitable railroad connections, facilities, and proximity to the quartermaster's headquarters. The companies could gather by rail from around the state into regiments, be processed into service, and move swiftly on from the southeast corner of Vermont to the theater of war. Camp Lincoln, on level ground above the village about a mile from the railroad station, had previously been used to assemble the 4th and 8th Vermont regiments and some barracks were available as temporary quarters. The camp commandant was Col. Edwin H. Stoughton, only twenty-three years of age, and the governor's choice to lead the Second Vermont Brigade which was to be formed by the five new regiments.* He had been replaced as commander of

---

* Returning to Vermont in early August to oversee mobilization of the nine-months units, Col. Stoughton had stirred up editorial criticism in the *Free Press* on August 4, for his anti-Lincoln comments at a war meeting in his home town of Bellows Falls. Despite Stoughton's suggestion to clean out Washington as a "nest of abolitionists," he survived the political storm to be confirmed as a brigadier general, but his career was very brief.

the 4th Vermont, part of the First Vermont Brigade in Virginia, by his brother Charles B. (who was even younger, at twenty-one).

The 12th Vermont, made up of ten militia companies of "the best Vermont stock," assembled at Camp Lincoln on September 25. Its members were said to include "many citizens of property and standing and earnest loyalty, whose professional and business engagements forbade their enlisting for a longer term." (After the war, it furnished "more men of prominence in civil life" than any other Vermont regiment, among them two governors and other state officials.) Earlier that same day, the Howard Guard had been escorted through the streets of Burlington to the railroad station by the Emmet Guards. Since the Howard Guard had been inactive for a year, it would not have had its own armory at which to gather, so apparently it assembled at Lonergan's facility. Lonergan led his own company past cheering crowds from the armory on College Street down St. Paul, King, and Water Streets, accompanying the departing unit to the depot. (While the officers of both companies probably had already gone to the expense of outfitting themselves with uniforms, the soldiers would all have been in civilian clothes.) When the 12th Vermont was organized, the Howard Guard was assigned the designation of Co. C—the color company—though Capt. Lemuel W. Page had hoped for the highest honor of being the senior company, Co. A.*

Two days later, notice was published in the *Free Press* that the Emmet Guards themselves had received orders "to take the train for Brattleboro" at 7:15 AM on September 29. Because the "company has rendezvoused here, and to a large extent has been recruited in this town and at Winooski Falls," readers were advised, "It is fitting, and we are sure it will be agreeable, for us to gather, young and old, male and female, as we did when the Howard Guard left us, to give them an escort to the train and a hearty cheer at their departure." Hoping for fair weather and "a general turn-out," the public was informed that the Emmet Guards would leave by the Vermont Central Railroad to ensure that early morning well-wishers showed up at the right station.

The actual departure of the Emmet Guards did not take place until 8:30 AM, probably delayed by the absence of a dozen recruits, who failed to report as ordered. Faced again with the prospect of insufficient men in his company, Lonergan apparently judged that even a unit below the authorized number

---

* While there was more "honor" in the right flank location, more danger arguably attached to carrying the national and state flags at the center of the battle line. As visual markers for the regimental command group, they were obvious targets for enemy fire.

would be accepted in these difficult times. Accordingly, he formed up those men present and "the Guards marched from the Armory on College Street, escorted by a long procession of citizens" who were directed by Louis Follet as marshal. Even though the departure had been delayed, still "the sidewalks were again thronged with men[,] women and children, as when the Howard Guard left on Thursday." The station was "packed full of the relatives and friends of the soldiers, who bade them an affectionate farewell." However, with the train over an hour behind schedule, little time was allowed for sentimental good-byes at the station.

The other companies of the 13th Vermont "took the cars at convenient stations on the Central Vermont Railroad line" that same morning. Franklin County's Highgate company members had boarded before dawn at Swanton, then the Grand Isle County men joined them at St. Albans "in the early morning and so along from place to place until all were on their way down the Connecticut Valley to Brattleboro." As the companies from Richmond, Moretown, and Morristown boarded in turn, the train approached Montpelier to collect its company and another from East Montpelier. Arrival at the Montpelier station may have reminded Lonergan of his unauthorized trip from Vermont's capital the previous September.

His current journey down to Brattleboro stood in welcome contrast to his futile attempt to rejoin his regiment a year earlier. Now he traveled under orders from the state, at the head of his own company of volunteers reporting for duty in the Union forces. He was no doubt firmly determined to avoid a repetition of the disappointment he suffered when his company failed to muster in and was disbanded. The company had spent hardly enough time together in Burlington to establish firm discipline and he would have to rely on his two lieutenants and the non-commissioned officers to keep order. Already there had been desertions from his unit, and men could still be rejected for service, so Lonergan needed to ensure no further gaps appeared in the ranks of the Emmet Guards. This second chance could not be lost because of any deficiency in numbers or discipline that might prevent the company from being mustered in.

On arrival in Brattleboro in the afternoon, a mile of marching from the depot brought the recruits to the rough hospitality of Camp Lincoln, where they were assigned to drafty barracks with plank bunks. The camp did not greet them with the sort of cheering crowds that had accompanied their departure from their home stations, but with the harsh reality of army life. The enlisted men, hungry and tired from their trip, ate a poor meal before a restless night without blankets. At the regimental parade the next day, the "boys did not look much like soldiers, for none but officers appeared in uniforms." The raw recruits began to learn the routine of the military day with formations, drills, inspections, and distribution of equipment. Muskets and bayonets—"dangerous in the hands of a raw recruit"—were issued on October 1, so that drill with weapons could begin under the instructors provided. Many farm boys had done their share of hunting, often with shotguns, but these .58 caliber Springfield rifle muskets were heavier and had a different, deadlier feel.

The 12th Vermont, a week ahead of the 13th in the processing cycle, was reviewed and inspected by Gov. Holbrook, Adj. Gen. Washburn, QM Gen. Davis, and Col. Stoughton on October 4, a Saturday. The men of the 13th received permission to watch the process, in preparation for their own initiation into active duty. The review was "a beautiful and impressive sight, 1,000 men all in uniform, flags fluttering in the breeze" and the camp was full of "distinguished visitors from all over the State" come to see friends and acquaintances before the regiment departed for Washington.

One person who did not attend the review was Lonergan. Saturday morning found him back in Burlington at St. Mary's Cathedral on St. Paul and Cherry Streets, where he married Roseanna O'Reilly Sorrigan. While last minute marriages were not uncommon as soldiers departed from the war, there is no way to know why the young couple, both listed as twenty-four years of age on the marriage certificate, would have postponed the wedding until after Lonergan had reported with his company at Brattleboro. After all his efforts to raise a company for the war, Lonergan surely would not have taken himself away from the hectic activities of Camp Lincoln without permission; travel between Burlington and Brattleboro would have taken the best part of a day each way and his absence from his unit would certainly have been noted. Perhaps the ceremony took place in the morning to allow Lonergan to catch a train back to his duty station that day, or perhaps Lonergan had a pass from his commander that included Sunday. In either case, the couple had little time together before he reported back to Camp Lincoln.

Each day in the Brattleboro camp brought its routine of "company drill in the forenoon, battalion drill and dress parade in the afternoon and guard duty when called." Sunday was a day of inspection in the morning and Protestant divine service in the afternoon. The regiment formed in a hollow square around a chaplain who reminded all present "that life was fleeting" and they

CHAPTER ELEVEN — IRISH COMPANY

should be prepared "for no one could tell the hour that would be our last."

Not until October 8 did each soldier in the 13th Vermont receive "one pair of trousers, one dress coat, a blouse coat, overcoat, cap and shoes if needed, socks, woolen shirts and cotton drawers." Familiarity with their weapons would be more important for survival than their appearance, but the first dress parade with everyone "in blue with glistening brass buttons on cap, sleeve and breast" brought a sense of their collective identity as soldiers. Now that they looked the part, many of the new soldiers had their pictures taken and sent them home to family and sweethearts.

The final issue of "gun straps, knapsacks, haversacks, tin cups and canteens, waist and shoulder belts and straps" came the following day, along with instructions to prepare for inspection and review by Holbrook, Washburn, and their staffs. Clumsy packing and inexperience in drill resulted in "many ludicrous, awkward and amusing incidents" during the review, but neither the governor nor the regimental commander found fault with the new soldiers. Orders were read to prepare for muster into U.S. service the next day, with the promise of receiving state pay immediately afterwards.

Early on October 10, in perfect weather "like an Indian Summer day, warm and still," the regiment formed up to be sworn into the U.S. Army by company. The law required that the oath be administered by a Regular Army officer and the Burlington-based recruiting officer for Vermont, Maj. William Austine, performed this duty with each company in turn. Beginning no doubt with Co. A, Maj. Austine was presented to each company commander by Col. Randall, accompanied by his adjutant. Upon a positive response to Austine's inquiry as to whether all were ready to be sworn into service, the mustering officer then "read the oath of allegiance to serve their Government as soldiers for the full term of nine months." Lonergan and his men would have been first in the regiment to take the oath and "each with his right hand raised heavenward solemnly promised" his loyal service. When all ten companies were mustered in, the "officers of the Field and Staff took the oath at headquarters." At this point, the regiment was transferred to federal control, no longer subject to the orders of the Vermont governor.* Lonergan's first company had been disbanded

---

* Lonergan's long-running argument with the state of Vermont hinged on this point because his original Emmet Guards had been given the oath, but had not yet signed the muster rolls when disbanded by Gov. Fairbanks. In July of 1862, it had "been decided by Judicial authority in Vermont, that a man who has signed the enlistment roll of a regiment, although not sworn in, is bound to service, the same as if he had taken the oath." This ruling clearly makes the administration of the oath the binding act, as Lonergan and his lawyer contended.

after taking the oath, but now he was prepared to take the restored Emmet Guards south to war. No doubt he enjoyed a sense of relief that the process had gone smoothly this time, thinking nothing could go wrong. Or could it?

After mustering in, the company was "marched to a nearby building where, each [man] giving his name and being vouched for by the Captain, was given their State pay then due" unless the soldier had made other arrangements for its disposition. The selectmen from the towns that had promised bounties were also supposed to be present at this time and to pay the sums agreed upon. Postponing this payment until the last minute was a necessary precaution to prevent the too-common practice of "bounty jumping." Apparently the Rutland selectmen were being even more cautious and withheld the $100 bounty due to those of Lonergan's men from their town until the soldiers were actually on the railroad cars.

The regiment was ordered to prepare to leave camp the next day and the men busied themselves with packing their knapsacks, placing two days' rations in their haversacks for the trip south. The remaining three regiments of nine-months service had now arrived and took over the guard and other duties, allowing the 13th to concentrate their efforts on getting ready to leave the now-crowded camp. The regiment rose early on October 11 and had breakfast "served before the usual hour." Although the weather had turned cold and damp, "many citizens from the village and from up the State were in camp through the forenoon." Sad partings took place among the crowd as the troops awaited "the call of bugle and fife and drum" to fall in with the arms and equipment. Last minute marriages had produced some "brides of a day shedding tears of sorrow" that the parting might be forever; perhaps Roseanna was among them.

A letter—unsigned, but from "One of the 13th Regiment"—sent to the Montpelier daily newspaper, the *Walton's Journal,* described the departure of the "Irish Company" that was attended by "many of their wives and sisters and friends." These relatives and friends feared never seeing the soldiers again and "there was consequently a great deal of lamentation, wringing of hands, &c. and the strong feelings of this impulsive people were all excited thereby, making the spectacle appear as though their hearts were all breaking." The published letter described how the disturbance grew out of hand in that company. "Capt. Lonergan and the other company officers did their utmost, but after the battalion line was formed the Colonel and other officers of the staff had to attend to them." This left the rest of the regiment standing exasperated in the ranks, holding their muskets and with knapsacks on, while the Irish clung to each other. One soldier of Co. A "refused to obey the Colonel and got up quite a row about him" until literally kicked back into line by Randall. When Lonergan's men finally fell in with the others, the regiment marched down to the station, "keeping step to the stirring strains of martial music."

Unfortunately, the transportation was delayed and the regiment waited idly until late in the afternoon. Many people had followed the regiment down from the camp and some brought hard drink to share with the departing soldiers. When the train eventually did arrive, another scene occurred at the station, when men in Lonergan's company refused to board until their bounty was paid. A Westford member of the company later commented that withholding the bounty stirred up the Rutland boys and "this fact with a little whiskey, caused what at one time promised to be a small sized riot." This established early on the reputation of the Irish company as fighters.

All patience exhausted in dealing with the rowdy Irish, Lt. Col. Brown gave the order for Capt. Thatcher's company to herd them onto the cars. Surrounding the trouble-makers in two ranks, the men of the Montpelier Company were "ordered to fix bayonets" and "Company A was soon still and in the cars." The writer concluded "I think Capt. Lonergan is a remarkable man. It will be remembered that this is the same company that went into the 2nd regiment and were disbanded on account of their insubordination.* They now behave well, and if ever they go into battle, I pity their foes."

Satisfied that all his regiment was finally on board, Col. Randall saluted the governor and received his handshake before signaling the conductor to start the train. Amidst "cheers loud and long from the assembled multitude," the 13th Vermont departed for New Haven, Connecticut, without further incident. Lonergan was at last on his way to find his chance for glory.

---

* While this company and Co. K, 2nd Vermont were both formed from the Emmet Guards of the Uniformed Militia, Lonergan was the only soldier who had been in both units. The first sergeant of the original Emmet Guards, John L. Yale, now was captain of Co. F of the 13th.

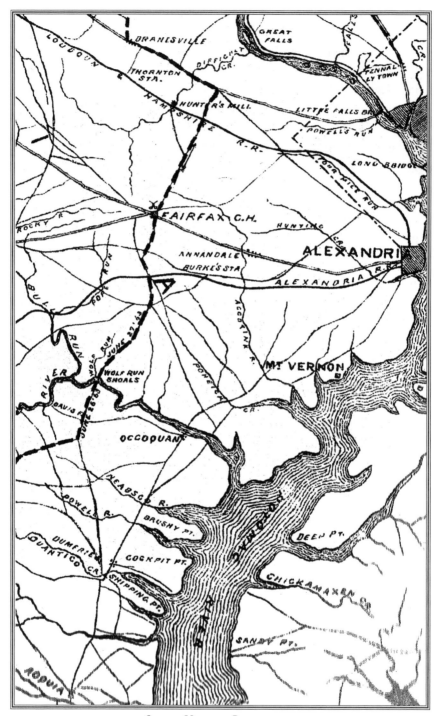

Second Vermont Brigade area

CHAPTER TWELVE

PICKET DUTY

FORCED ON BOARD THE TRAIN BY the bayonets of their fellow soldiers in the 13th Vermont, Lonergan's men then settled down under his watchful eye for the trip to Washington. A somber mood replaced the excitement of departing and Sturtevant commented that the "boys after leaving Brattleboro rode in silence." The train carried the regiment down the Connecticut River Valley into Massachusetts where crowds "thronged to the railroad station to see the Vermonters pass through." Flags and banners waved in time to the patriotic tunes being sung as the train went by, cheering the new soldiers on their way to the war. Good food and pretty girls to serve it greeted the Vermonters on their stop in Springfield, Massachusetts, an episode that the men fondly recalled as a "grand and bounteous welcome."

Arriving at the port of New Haven, Connecticut, near midnight, the "tired and sleepy" soldiers marched on board the steamboat *Continental* for the trip to New York Harbor. While this was the first boat ride on the ocean for most of the men and the rough waters made it an unpleasant experience, the many Irish immigrants in Lonergan's company were surely reminded of the long voyage they had made from their homeland. After landing in Jersey City, the troops were marched through dusty streets on a cold and breezy morning to a promised hot breakfast; it turned out to consist of barrels of unsavory liquid with an offensive look and smell that the men compared to the swill that "filled the troughs of the pig sty at home." With this meal, army life with all its fatigue, deprivation and marching replaced the cheering crowds. The big city impressed the boys from Vermont, but their regiment was just one of the many traveling this route and they received no special treatment from the local population.

Again boarding railroad cars to continue their journey, the regiment that afternoon received much better fare at a stop in Philadelphia, where they also encountered other Vermont units going off to the war. Mostly recruited from Burlington and St. Albans, Companies L and M were headed south to reinforce the 1st Vermont Cavalry. Men in the 13th Vermont greeted relatives and friends, likewise far from home and on the same mission, but facing three years service.

After their meal, the regiment was loaded into freight cars with board seats; the ride from Philadelphia to Baltimore was "cold, slow, hard, dark and dismal." The soldiers knew that slave-holding Maryland was full of rebel sympathizers and that Union troops moving through the city had been attacked by mobs, resulting in casualties on both sides. In the early morning hours, the train pulled into Baltimore and the troops left the railroad cars to be fed; they marched in close order with fixed bayonets, wary of any hostile actions against them. Although not yet in contact with the rebel army, they knew that each step "along the dismal, slippery streets" of Baltimore took them closer to danger. On the final leg of their journey to Washington, the train moved slowly past soldiers guarding the lines against Confederate raids or damage by hostile local residents.

Late in the afternoon of October 13, the regiment arrived in the capital and everyone hung out the windows gawking at the sights, eager to see the landmarks of the republic. One of the few who had been in the city before, Lonergan himself would have noticed the changes since his last visit. While there were more troops in the city and greater military activity, matters were much better organized than under Cameron, in the hectic initial months of the conflict. The new Secretary of War, Stanton, had imposed stricter discipline to preserve order and to channel the new units through to the battlefield. Construction had resumed on the dome of the capitol, a hopeful symbol for the future of the country, even though the building itself housed a military barracks and a 2,000-bed hospital.

The District of Columbia, the physical embodiment of the Union that these Vermonters were now sworn to defend, was probably much less imposing than they had imagined. Livestock still roamed the unpaved streets of the small city with a Southern flavor, and sanitation was primitive at best, particularly with the influx of soldiers. The numerous African-Americans they encountered may well have caused the northern boys to think about the new mission of the war declared three weeks earlier, the emancipation of the slaves held on rebel territory. After a night spent in the Soldier's Rest buildings near the train station with "rubber blankets on the bare floor, knapsacks for pillows, overcoats and woolen blankets for a covering," the 13th marched a mile east to Camp Casey.

Lonergan and his men now became part of the massive war machine being assembled in the capital area. The new troops flooding into Washington were temporarily assigned to Maj. Gen. Silas Casey's division of the Reserve Corps, guarding the capital. Casey had written the army training manual then in use and he was charged with ensuring that the green units were properly equipped and drilled before they were given combat duties. The 12th Vermont had arrived at East Capitol Hill on October 10 and was brigaded with New Jersey regiments. The 13th was assigned to the same brigade at Camp Casey, awaiting the rest of the new regiments from Vermont. The prescribed routine of camp life resumed with drill, work details, and guard duty punctuated by roll calls morning, noon, and evening.

Living in the middle of a bustling city, some men in Lonergan's company were unable to resist its temptations. Each day a few men were given passes to see the sights, but others slipped away without permission, even though the frequent roll calls ensured that absences would be noted. On October 26, a regimental court-martial that included 1st Lt. John Sinnott convened to try Pvt. James Corey, Co. A, for being absent without leave, along with "any other offender that may be brought before the court." Special orders issued that same day reduced Corp. Michael McEnerny, another Irish-born member of Co. A, to the rank of private for "general neglect of duty." While in charge of the line of guards around the camp, the corporal had allowed men like Corey "to pass the line to procure Liquor." McEnerny had also failed to control other guards who let men out of camp and had neglected "to report Soldiers on guard duty for getting intoxicated on their Posts." Clearly Lonergan's company continued to have problems with drink and discipline. (Corey and McEnerny would both later redeem themselves in battle.)

When the 14th and 15th Vermont reported to Washington, they were sent briefly across the Potomac to join two Maine regiments in another brigade of Casey's Division. The last of the state's nine-month units, the 16th Vermont, arrived at the rendezvous on October 27. That same day the Second

Vermont Brigade was formed by GO No. 15 of the division. Back from Virginia marched the 14th and 15th Vermont; the five regiments were then consolidated as the Second Brigade, Casey's Division, to the great pleasure of the Vermonters, who would serve together.*

Col. Edwin Stoughton, who was in charge of the Brattleboro camp while the five regiments mustered in, had been selected by Vermont's governor to lead the new brigade. Although Stoughton was appointed a brigadier general on November 5, he would not take command of the brigade until early December. A handsome West Point graduate with a reputation in the army as a man with an eye for the ladies, the general's absence from his unit is attributed in one source to the death of his sweetheart in New York.

The Second Vermont Brigade was initially led by Col. Asa P. Blunt—a former executive of the Fairbanks Scales company in St. Johnsbury—as the senior regimental commander. When word spread through the camp that Blunt was in command, his 12th Vermont cheered their colonel by companies in front of his tent. Each company received his thanks and a cautionary speech, as he took the occasion to warn his men of what the future might bring. Drawing on his combat experience with the First Vermont Brigade, he told them plainly, "We have hitherto, my boys, seen but the pleasant part of soldier's life. Thus far we have known little of trial and suffering, and nothing of danger. The rough times are yet to come." He charged them to meet the hard times like men, doing their best for the cause of the country and the honor of Vermont.

Short-term regiments did not receive replacements, and the ranks were thinning in the camp, even before any encounter with the enemy. Dozens of soldiers with illnesses and injuries were in hospitals, one private in the 12th had died (apparently from an accident involving mules) and two men in the 13th had succumbed to disease. The bodies of Pvt. Isaac Brooks, Co. F, and 1st Lt. Nathaniel Jones, Co. B, were embalmed and returned home for burial in Vermont. Each company in the brigade had taken up a collection and set aside its own pool of money to cover the cost, about $90, of shipping a member's body back home. Such respectful handling of soldiers' remains depended on the situation and would not always be possible.

---

* As a rule, in order to minimize the impact on any one state of losses in a single battle, brigades were composed of regiments from several different states. Vermont was an exception with both of its brigades made up only of regiments from the Green Mountain state, other than some temporary attachments.

CHAPTER TWELVE – PICKET DUTY

Anticipating a long stay in Camp Casey, the Vermonters began improvements in their rough living conditions by "stockading" the tents (laying a base of log walls to raise the height of the tent) and building stoves for heat. However, the Second Vermont Brigade was ordered into Virginia almost as soon as the unit was formed. Before noon on October 30, the five regiments marched down Pennsylvania Avenue and across Long Bridge. Continuing out through the capital's defenses, past Arlington Heights with a clear view of "General Lee's grand old mansion home," they halted after covering ten miles. Unaccustomed to marching with full gear, the green troops were "all pretty well jaded out" by the hot day on dusty roads.

Pvt. Cornelius Desmond from Burlington took advantage of the situation to move in a different direction and absent himself permanently from Co. A. He was the first of three men to desert Lonergan's company after being mustered in.

ALTHOUGH THE VERMONTERS had entered the territory of the rebel Confederacy, this area of northern Virginia had actually been under the control of Union forces since early in the conflict. The year before, during his unauthorized visit to the 2nd Vermont, Lonergan had seen the massive earthen forts being built just south of the Potomac. Construction of fortifications continued in an unending quest for the security of Washington. Nearly seventy forts were eventually built for the protection of the capital, about half of them in northern Virginia.

A large number of troops occupied these defensive positions, with units spread out across northern Virginia and southern Maryland. The Union forts and garrisons were interconnected with a network of camps and picket lines guarding roads, river crossings, and railroad lines. Sufficient troops for fending off a small group of rebel raiders were maintained at key locations, but the lines remained somewhat porous and susceptible to penetration by stealth or numbers. Maj. Gen. Samuel P. Heintzelman was given command of all the defenses of the capital on October 26, the same day that the last of the Vermont short-term regiments arrived in Washington. For the next eight months, the Second Vermont Brigade was to contribute to extending the defensive network by manning the outermost line as part of Casey's Division of the Reserve Corps. In the overall strategy, such trip-wire outposts represented an expendable force that might be sacrificed, if necessary, to delay a rebel offensive.

On November 1, the 12th and 13th Vermont—both led by Randall as the senior officer, since Blunt was serving as brigade commander—moved ten miles farther into Virginia on another "hot and dusty" day. In their woolen clothing, carrying weapons and heavy knapsacks, the soldiers "were obliged to stop and rest quite often." As Sturtevant observed in his history of the 13th Vermont, this was "new business to most of us," though he reported that none complained.

Only these first two regiments of the brigade had been issued Springfield rifles and thus they were considered the most ready to face the enemy. The other three regiments carried unreliable French and Belgian muskets, which many soldiers thought were as dangerous to them as to the enemy. These outdated weapons were soon replaced by imported muskets of Austrian and English manufacture.

The detached units marched through the important Union supply base of Alexandria during the night. This city on the broad Potomac River provided both a port for water transport and the terminus of the Orange and Alexandria Railroad that connected at Manassas Junction with another rail line to the west. South of Hunting Creek, the two regiments set up camp at the Spring Bank estate, on "quite an elevated plain covered with brush and laurel bushes and timber in abundance, and near a large spring of water." Randall stationed his men at this site on the road to Mount Vernon despite the objections of the estate's owner, George Mason.*

The other three regiments joined the brigade's advance party on November 5 and Sturtevant wrote that the inexperienced Vermonters expected to "settle down for the winter, supposing we were to stay here until the Spring campaign." Larger "A" tents holding six men arrived to replace the two-man shelter tents carried on the march and the soldiers set about making their billets more comfortable. With plenty of timber at hand, stockade walls elevated the tents and "corduroy" floors of small logs, along with shallow outside perimeter drains, kept the footing dry. Bunks filled with pine and cedar boughs were built for beds. Ingenious sheet-metal stoves built into the ground completed the preparations for winter quarters.

The camp itself was situated on the high bank of the Potomac, providing

---

* Mason was a member of a prominent Virginian family and named for his grandfather, who had signed the Declaration of Independence. His brother John was one of the Confederate representatives to Great Britain seized by the U.S. Navy in the *Trent* affair. The estate name is also given as Springbank.

CHAPTER TWELVE – PICKET DUTY

a view of Alexandria a mile away and the nation's capital eight miles farther up the river. An equal distance to the south, the men could see the Mount Vernon estate, though not George Washington's home itself. They watched the many boats on the Potomac passing night and day with military supplies going down the river while human cargo of "soldiers, prisoners of war, the sick from the numerous hospitals" streamed north. The setting reminded the Vermonters of the Champlain Valley, and they "were contented and happy," according to the history written long after the fact. As a token of the soldiers' approval, they named their base "Camp Vermont."

Brigade headquarters was established in one wing of Mason's deteriorating mansion. The owner had declared himself "neutral" and displayed a white flag, hoping to be treated well by whatever forces might occupy his land. Mason eventually accepted Blunt's advice that he should recognize the reality of Union control and took the oath of allegiance to the federal government.

On November 7, the men, who a few days before had experienced the discomfort of woolen uniforms in the Virginia heat, woke to snow falling steadily. It continued throughout the day, with an accumulation of at least five inches by evening. Even in Vermont, this would be an early snow and it was unexpected so far south. However, the effort that the soldiers had put into improving their tents proved worthwhile and they were comfortable in the camp despite the weather.

NOT ONLY THE WEATHER CHANGED that day in northern Virginia—McClellan, commander of the Army of the Potomac, was replaced by Maj. Gen. Ambrose E. Burnside, who led the Ninth Corps. Lincoln, disappointed by the failure to crush Lee's forces after the mid-September bloodbath at Antietam, had urged aggressive pursuit of the rebels. The summer's levies had provided additional forces and McClellan counted twice as many men in his army as did Lee. Not until October 26 did McClellan start the six-day process of moving his army of 135,000 men—which Lincoln had begun to call "General McClellan's body-guard"—across the river into Virginia.

After McClellan squandered his chance for decisive action, Lincoln waited only until the midterm elections ended on November 4. While polling returns gave the Democrats some victories in the state governments and gains in the House of Representatives, the Republicans picked up five Senate seats and retained a majority in the House. The elections had strengthened Lincoln's political position at the national level and the next day he signed the order replacing the popular Democratic commander.

Burnside objected to his own promotion since he did not feel capable of fulfilling the duties of army commander, a self-assessment that would prove tragically accurate. Faced with the alternative of the appointment going to Maj. Gen. Joseph Hooker, however, Burnside reluctantly accepted command. The new commander planned to concentrate his forces across from Fredericksburg on the Rappahannock River, mid-way between Washington and Richmond. Speed was essential to turn Lee's flank and Burnside quickly moved his units to the area. However, he then delayed for weeks before attacking the town, which allowed Lee to move his own troops and to build defenses.

After prolonged deliberation about the attack, on December 9 Burnside held a council of war with his senior commanders to announce his decision. To the amazement and horror of his generals, Burnside revealed his plan to make the main assault right where the Confederates were strongest. One staff officer predicted "there will be a great loss of life and nothing accomplished."

EVEN AS LONERGAN'S COMPANY began to acquire the experience that might help liberate Ireland, newspapers carried articles on the hunger that was ravaging their homeland yet again. The Fenians were reminded of the urgency to free their country from British rule when they read of the general misery, disease, and death once more stalking Ireland—what Meagher called "one of the periodic landlord-engendered, government-fostered famines." Letters from relatives and friends brought personal news that gave faces to the suffering. No doubt Lonergan and his men discussed the situation and what they were prepared to do for Ireland once they had met their military obligation to their adopted country. The immediate goal was to survive. While heroic deeds by the Irish Brigade added to the stories of brave charges led by the Sunburst flag, each battle reduced the ranks of men who could fight for liberation. Duty on the picket line would suffice for Lonergan's "Irish Company" to learn the necessary military skills and still preserve their numbers.

Fenians were also dying in the Confederate army. In the South, the Irish militia companies with nationalistic names reported as eagerly to the rebel forces as their compatriots in the North did to the federal army. Half

CHAPTER TWELVE – PICKET DUTY

a dozen companies of Emmet Guards and Emmet Rifles took the field from Louisiana, Georgia, South Carolina, and Virginia, just as the Vermont unit did for the Union. The 17th Virginia, raised in Alexandria before the Union forces occupied the city, included the Emmet Guards as Co. G, and another militia company by that name became Co. F, 15th Virginia. Clearly, the primary loyalty of many Irishmen in the Confederate forces was to their state, rather than to America or Ireland.

In the fall of 1862, John Mitchel returned from France with his youngest son and became editor of the *Richmond Enquirer* in the Confederate capital. Mitchel accurately reported that a greater proportion of the Irish in the rebel states were serving in the military than in the North (although the larger population in the loyal states meant that a greater number of Irish were in the Union forces). He wrote of these secessionists, "It is true, they flaunt no green banners nor *Sunbursts*, nor shout *Fontenoy!* Nor *Remember Limerick!* They are content to fight simply as Virginians, or as Georgians." All three of Mitchel's sons had enlisted. Willie, now seventeen years old, had joined the Richmond-based 1st Virginia—in which his brother James commanded a company—and was assigned to the color company.

A SMALL PIECE ON THE CHESSBOARD of northern Virginia, where tens of thousands of men moved at a single order, Lonergan's company shifted locations and assignments with the changing role of the Second Vermont Brigade. During their first weeks at Camp Vermont in early November, the regiments each provided daily details of 200–300 men for pick and shovel work on nearby Fort Lyon, unpopular duty that caused much grumbling. Equally demanding, though more what the men considered soldiering, was the brigade's responsibility for a picket line a mile south of the camp. A large detail marched out each day for twenty-four hours of duty on this defense line, which extended "from the Potomac lowlands westward for a number of miles." No tents were taken out on picket and fires were normally forbidden after dark, so the soldiers sheltered as best they could under trees or in brush huts, shivering out their two- or four-hour shift before being relieved. A picket reserve of fifteen or twenty men some distance behind the line posted the fresh guards and provided a resting place for those coming off duty. This reserve could also send reinforcements or serve as a rallying point if the pickets were attacked.

Such assignments were in addition to the usual guard and work details at the camp itself, along with drill at the individual, company, and battalion level. The Green Mountain Boys were kept fully occupied most of their time at Camp Vermont performing the necessary daily duties and learning to operate as a combat force. Proximity to the army supply lines provided the men with good provisions to fuel the hard work and outdoor living, so they "ate and slept well and grew fat and strong." Even so, disease in this camp took its first victim from the 13th on November 18 when a musician with Co. G died. He was soon followed by three more in the same company, including its commander, Capt. Marvin White.

When the Eleventh Corps, part of Maj. Gen. Franz Sigel's Reserve Grand Division, was deployed away from Washington's defenses for a more active role in the field, the Second Vermont Brigade took over some of its positions. Late on November 25, on short notice, Randall ordered the 13th, 14th, and 15th Vermont to assemble at 8:00 PM for a difficult night march in the rain. Led by "the 'bully 13th' as its boys delight to call themselves," the three regiments departed Camp Vermont within an hour. Since it was Co. A of the leading regiment, Lonergan's "Irish Company," likely would have headed up the column of troops. After a few hours sleep in the mud and cold, they arrived at Union Mills, their new post on the Alexandria rail line, around noon the next day. The three regiments assumed the responsibility for picket duty along the Occoquan River and its major tributary, Bull Run. They were now truly on the front line of the defenses.

The nearby Bull Run battlefield, bloodily contested each of the last two years, left no doubt as to the serious nature of their mission. Many of the men visited the scene of the fighting and "found plenty of evidence of deadly struggle, carnage and destruction." Bodies were frequently exposed in their shallow graves "and some had on the blue and some the gray, friend and foe sleeping their last sleep together, and no one knew who they were." Saddened by this neglect of the dead, the green soldiers would later realize that they knew at the time "but a little of the hard and strenuous realities of desperate warfare."

Camp equipment, including their "A" tents, came up from Alexandria by train on November 29 and the three regiments settled in at Union Mills. However, they were soon relieved by several New York regiments and returned to Camp Vermont on December 5, arriving by rail at Alexandria about dusk and marching back to camp "in the face of a blinding snow storm." The

CHAPTER TWELVE – PICKET DUTY

usual Sunday inspection was cancelled by Randall the next day and the 13th celebrated a late Thanksgiving with boxes of food that had arrived from Vermont in their absence.

December 7 brought a visit to the camp by Brig. Gen. Stoughton, the new brigade commander. The weeks with Blunt in charge had raised hopes in the 12th Vermont that their commander might receive the brigadier's star, while the 13th likewise saw their own colonel as "the man for the place." The 13th was disappointed when Randall with his "ability, experience, age and more than ordinary prowess" was not selected.

Along with the change in command, the brigade was also about to be redeployed in connection with Burnside's attack on Fredericksburg. On December 11, Stoughton ordered his units to be ready to march at daylight the next morning. The 12th Vermont was recalled from the picket line and the camp accordingly busied itself to be packed and organized for an early departure. Reveille awoke the troops at 3:00 AM, tents were struck within the hour and the line of march formed at 5:00 AM. In heavy marching order, the men carried all their personal equipment and they took this as a sign they would not return to the camp. An hour later, the entire brigade started off for Fairfax Court House twenty miles to the west, arriving there late in the afternoon, except for some inevitable stragglers who could not keep up the pace.

Uncertain as to their ultimate destination, the rank and file Vermonters confessed themselves alarmed at each rumor of approaching battle. They found "all was confusion, troops moving in [the] direction of Centerville, Manassas and Warrenton in Support of General Burnside" and, not surprisingly, "many believed we were on the way to take part in another Bull Run defeat." Their recent visits to that battlefield had given them a new understanding of just what such a defeat would mean. The impending move up to the front lines appears to have been too much for Co. A's 5th Sgt. Timothy Weeks, born in County Mayo nineteen years before. Regimental orders on December 11 reduced him to private "for absence from his company & Reg't without leave." Canadian-born Pvt. Joshua Fiske also was no longer with Lonergan's company when it arrived in Fairfax; the record shows that he "deserted from Camp Vt. while the regiment was marching" on December 12.

On the morning of December 13, the wind was from the south and the soldiers at Fairfax Court House "distinctly heard…the deep rumbling of cannonading" from Fredericksburg nearly thirty miles away.

John Mitchel and two of his sons were observing that same artillery fire at close hand from Marye's Heights, where the 1st Virginia was stationed. On December 13, Mitchel was visiting Fredericksburg, along with fellow journalist John Dooley. Formerly a major in the regiment, Dooley had a son (also named John) who was the first lieutenant of Co. C, Willie's unit. While eating breakfast together, they could all see the Union forces forming up to attack the heights. As the two fathers said farewell to the soldiers, the cannon on both sides opened fire.

BURNSIDE'S FLAWED PLAN OF ATTACK culminated on December 13, with a futile assault on Marye's Heights.* The attack uphill, against fortified positions where the enemy was strongest, started at 11:00 AM and continued all day, as Burnside sent in brigade after brigade. To reach the rebel line, sheltered in a sunken road behind stone walls, the federal troops had to cross a millrace and several fences before covering five hundred yards of open terrain. The Confederate artillery had so many cannon covering the area that its commander was confident "a chicken could not live on that field" when they opened fire. Each wave was pounded by shelling that littered the field with Union casualties before the attackers were smashed by rifle fire from the sunken road. The thunderous bombardment from cannon on both sides of the river was heard for miles around, carrying all the way to where Lonergan and his men were stationed.

After Maj. Gen. William French's division of the Second Corps was stopped with heavy losses, Maj. Gen. Winfield Scott Hancock's division of "three brigades, seventeen regiments, some of the army's finest soldiers" entered the killing zone. Col. Samuel Zook's brigade quickly suffered the same fate as those from French's division. An aide stated, "the losses were so tremendous that before we knew it, our momentum was gone, and the charge a failure."

Meagher's Irish Brigade moved forward next, taking casualties even as the five regiments formed up for the charge. The three depleted New York regiments that formed the core of the brigade—the 63rd, the 69th, and the 88th—had recently been joined by the 116th Pennsylvania and the 28th

---

* Fighting had actually begun on December 11 when Burnside tried to put his troops across the Rappahannock River at several locations. The First Vermont Brigade—reinforced by the newly assigned 26th New Jersey (a nine-month regiment)—had led the attack at a crossing point downstream. This initial success on the Union left was ultimately repulsed with heavy losses. The Vermont units performed well in the battle, at the cost of twenty-four dead and over a hundred wounded.

CHAPTER TWELVE – PICKET DUTY

Massachusetts. Both Irish regiments, the latter had been specially raised for Meagher's command. Even with these additions, only some 1,400 officers and men were present in the brigade that day.

Even though all five regiments had Fenian connections, only the 28th Massachusetts carried a green flag with the nationalist symbols. The battered banners of the New York regiments had been retired "as souvenirs of Irish loyalty and bravery" and the expected replacements had not yet arrived. Meagher, limping from a boil on his knee that prevented him from leading the charge, ordered each man to place a green sprig in his cap to show that he belonged to the Irish Brigade (hemlock twigs were used in the same way by the Vermont troops).

As the senior regiment, the 69th New York was placed on the right flank and the 28th Massachusetts was assigned the center of the line, apparently because it carried the only Irish flag in the brigade.* Meagher ordered the brigade forward at the double-quick. Survivors of the earlier Union assaults cheered on the charging Irishmen, who shouted their customary "Faugh a ballagh," though this day not even their courage could "clear the way." The Irish Brigade continued forward over the frozen ground until stalled by a wooden fence some fifty yards from the Confederate lines. Firing at close range in ranks three and four deep, the rebel soldiers shattered the lines of Irishmen with a continuous hail of bullets. As casualties rose and their "buck and ball" ammunition ran short, the Irish Brigade was forced to withdraw down the slope.

Despite the obvious failure of any attack under such conditions, Burnside continued to feed still more troops into the battle. In the judgment of a journalist who watched the slaughter, "It was not war, it was madness." Lee watched this unending flow of Union soldiers and asked Lt. Gen. James Longstreet whether he could hold the line against them. His corps commander assured Lee that even if every man in the opposing force crossed the river to approach in the same way, with "plenty of ammunition, I will kill them all before they reach my line."

The attacks halted as daylight faded, but nearly 40,000 men had been thrown into the senseless assault and the Union forces had suffered over 7,000 casualties. None of the hundreds of corpses on the field were closer to the rebel defenses than those left behind by the Irish Brigade, which lost almost

---

* The 28th was also the only regiment in the brigade armed with rifle muskets; the others still carried the smoothbore .69 caliber that was effective only at short distances.

half of the 1,200 men who took part in the charge.* The 116th Pennsylvania had four different leaders in the attack because three were shot down in turn. One of them, Lt. Col. St. Clair Mulholland, declared the bloody repulse to be "the saddest hour that the army of the Potomack [sic] ever knew." Many of the dedicated members of the Fenian Brotherhood who served in Meagher's brigade would never have their chance to fight for Ireland. Brave Irish nationalists were lost in other units as well, both Union and Confederate.

Burnside refused to withdraw on December 14 until persuaded by his generals that a resumption of the battle would only add to the disaster. That night, the northern lights filled the sky and were seen as a good omen by the victorious Confederates. The Irish Brigade, still shivering on frozen ground covered with dead comrades, may rather have perceived the aurora to be a beacon for the souls of the warriors, lighting their passage either to Heaven or to *Tir na nOg*.

Replacement flags for the New York Irish regiments had arrived at the Falmouth camp the day of the battle and were given to their representatives on December 14. The presentation dinner took place as scheduled, despite the horrific losses and the desperate situation of the units still on the battle field. This "Death Feast" in a Fredericksburg theater was attended by twenty-two generals, along with the surviving officers of the Irish Brigade. Meagher, ever one for the dramatic moment, hosted the festivities and led a series of toasts until the Confederate artillery found the range of the gathering and forced them to scatter.

Under cover of darkness during the night of December 15, Burnside retreated in utter defeat back across the Rappahannock. Around a campfire in the Irish Brigade, Capt. Dennis Downing from Cork tried to lift the spirits of his men with the marching song of O'Donovan Rossa's Phoenix clubs in that county, "Ireland Boys, Hurrah." As he sang, the chorus was picked up by countrymen at other campfires around the camp, ringing through the cold winter air until it was finally echoed by Irishmen joining in from the Confederate lines across the river.

The hurried redeployment of the Second Vermont Brigade to Fairfax Court House had been ordered when Sigel's Reserve Corps moved up to join

---

* The 69th New York, after detaching men to defend a knoll on the flank, put sixteen officers and 168 men into the charge. All the officers and 141 enlisted men were killed or wounded.

CHAPTER TWELVE – PICKET DUTY

Burnside's forces. With the bloody failure of the attack on Fredericksburg, the Vermont units were kept at their new location to man a picket line two miles beyond Centerville. Each regiment took its turn on the line, posting its pickets for forty-eight hours of duty plus a day's travel out and another back. The 13th made the eight-mile march to Centerville on December 20, did its two days of picket duty on the outermost defense line for Washington, and returned to camp on December 24.

The regiment spent Christmas Day in camp, excused from duty and with an extra effort made by the cooks who served up a holiday meal. Prepared from army rations of pork and beans baked all night, boiled rice, "old government Java coffee, nice hard tack (worms all shook out)," sweet potatoes, and corned beef, it might not compare with dinner at home in Vermont. This hot food was nonetheless welcomed and enjoyed in far better conditions than on picket duty.

Lonergan had been granted a pass and was in Washington over Christmas Day, presumably on personal business. It is possible that his bride of two months had traveled to the capital and the couple was able to have a delayed honeymoon over the holiday. Roseanna definitely came to visit John at least once while he was stationed in Viriginia; it is not clear when she arrived, but she was present in June of 1863. Some wives spent the winter in camp with their husbands; others traveled down in the spring. With the good train connections available between Vermont and Washington, Roseanna might even have made the trip more than once.

Even though other units such as the Irish Brigade and Sickles' Excelsior Brigade, both from New York, had Catholic priests assigned, Vermont units had only Protestant chaplains.* Attendance at the religious services on Sundays and holidays was mandatory in the 13th Vermont, as with the other regiments of the Second Vermont Brigade, for all personnel not on duty.

To celebrate the holiday in camp, everyone in the 13th was ordered to attend the "public religious service performed by the Protestant chaplain." Until then, Lonergan's company apparently had dutifully formed up with the rest of the regiment to hear, if not necessarily to agree with, the religious message provided by Chaplain Joseph Sargent from Williston. The Catholics

---

* The Vermont legislature on November 1, 1861, had recognized the fact that many of its soldiers were Roman Catholic, particularly the French Canadians and the Irish. They requested the Vermont governor to ask for permission from the War Department to have a Catholic priest named to "visit and remain with the Vermont regiments of volunteers in the service of the United States," but no one was ever appointed.

in the regiment may also have been able to worship on occasion at St. Mary's Roman Catholic Church, a short distance north of the Fairfax Court House camp. This church had been established in 1858 by Irish immigrants and might have allowed co-religionists to attend Mass, even though the Union soldiers were otherwise not welcome in the area.

A request by Company A to be excused from attending the services in camp was denied. The men were ordered to fall in with the rest of the regiment and threatened by Randall with the "Rip Raps," the military prison at Fort Monroe, if they failed to obey. Yielding "with bad grace," the company attended the service, but they greeted Lonergan with their complaints upon his return from Washington.

Apparently Lonergan would not tolerate forcing his men to be subjected to two doses of Protestant preaching only days apart. On the next Sunday, while Randall was absent from the camp and Lt. Col. Brown was left in charge, Lonergan "in his characteristic way" refused to turn out his company. The Sunday services were scheduled for 2:00 PM on December 28, but "neither the Captain nor his men were there." An order to attend was sent, then a second, and finally a third with a threat of arrest by Brown. Lonergan refused all three direct orders, in effect defying the authority of the temporary commander of the regiment. Aware of the consequences of disobeying an order, no one could have been surprised that "for this breach of discipline, Captain Lonergan was placed under arrest and relieved of his sword."

His arrest was reported to the brigade commander along with charges of violating Articles of War 6 and 44, yet the Irishman "was too shrewd a man not to have ready at hand plenty of reasons to justify his action." After examining both sides of the story, Stoughton ordered the regimental commander to "return Capt. Lonergan his sword and release him at once." Although Lonergan was vindicated by the general's decision, it is unclear whether he was released from arrest the same day that his sword was taken from him. Described as "nothing more than a little diversion" in camp, the issue gave Lonergan "much celebrity in camp at the time" and the regimental orders were changed to make attendance at church service voluntary.

LONERGAN'S ARREST ON DECEMBER 28 became a case of bad timing for him when more serious events immediately overshadowed this incident. The

CHAPTER TWELVE – PICKET DUTY

previous night had been marked by the sound of cannon fire to the south of the picket line manned by the Vermonters. Word had come by telegraph from Washington that Maj. Gen. J.E.B. Stuart, commander of Lee's cavalry, had crossed the Rappahanock and headed north. (The previous June, Stuart—respected and feared by the men of the Second Vermont Brigade—had boldly ridden entirely around McClellan's army.)

Three brigades of rebel cavalry with a battery of four guns had attacked pickets of the 66th Ohio and the 77th Pennsylvania on the Occoquan River. In a "sharp engagement" at Dumfries, the Union forces were defeated and sounds of that battle had carried to the Fairfax camp. Stuart had brushed aside the force guarding Wolf Run Shoals and brought most of his troops across the Occoquan River there. Once inside the Union defensive line, two brigades of the swift-moving horsemen with their cannon captured Burke Station, three miles east of Fairfax Station.*

Before his telegraph line was cut late in the afternoon, Stoughton had been informed that Stuart and 4,000 cavalrymen were raiding along the Orange and Alexandria railroad, threatening Fairfax Station. The large supply base at the station had to be defended, along with the nearby village. Drummers sounded the "long roll" in each regiment and the order was given to fall in. The units were "hurriedly marched to the Court House village" where their general and his staff waited, mounted and ready. Only three regiments assembled there, as the 15th was taking its turn on the Centreville picket line and the 16th was stationed at the Fairfax railroad station four miles away. The six guns of the 2nd Connecticut Light Artillery battery attached to the brigade were split up, three sent to the railroad station and three moving with the column. The commanders of the 12th and 13th, Blunt and Randall, were both at a court martial in Alexandria, eighteen miles away. Facing seasoned and highly mobile rebel fighters who outnumbered his inexperienced troops and with his two senior colonels absent, Stoughton clearly was confronted that day with greater problems than Lonergan's contrary views on religious services.

Going into combat for the first time, the Vermonters hurried through the village to take positions "behind a long breastwork, commanding a fine sweep of nearly level plain to the East." Stoughton's West Point training

---

* Installing his own telegraph operator at the station there, Stuart monitored the Federal messages to determine the troop dispositions in the area. The rebels then cut the line serving Fairfax Station, but not before Stuart had scolded Washington about the quality of the mules that he was capturing in great numbers in the raid.

and his experience in the Peninsula campaign earlier that year no doubt eased the men's concerns about proper leadership should there be a battle. The center of the breastwork through which the Alexandria turnpike passed was held by the 12th, with two companies of the 13th and part of the 14th on its right. The remainder of the 13th took up positions on the left, with the rest of the 14th in reserve behind them. The brass howitzer and two rifled cannon were deployed on the turnpike itself. Two companies of the 12th were sent forward as skirmishers and a cavalry picket was stationed in front of them. Hours of tense anticipation followed on this "bright and comparatively mild moonlight night" until about 11:00 PM when a courier brought a message to Stoughton.

The men were then given orders to load their muskets and to hold the position at all cost. Horsemen suddenly dashed down the road toward the Vermonters, but they proved to be the Union cavalry picket "driven in and frightened half to death by the rebels." Riding down the line, Stoughton gave an inspirational speech urging his soldiers to "Keep cool, never flinch, and behave worthy of the good name won for Vermont troops by the 1st Brigade." This steadying talk was reinforced with a more practical reason to hold the line, as the general instructed the sergeants posted behind the line of battle, "File closers, do your duty, and if any man attempts to run, use your bayonets." Searching for movement in the moonlight, men grasped the rifles they had thrust over the top of the earthworks and held themselves ready for battle "with almost perfect self possession." Scattered pistol shots sounded from the woods half a mile to the front. Then came "the shrill cheers of a cavalry squad of perhaps thirty or forty men," suddenly cut off by the "bright flash and sharp rattle of the first hostile volley fired" by men of the Second Vermont Brigade.

Both advance companies of the 12th had "fired at once, and their guns went off like one piece." Then silence fell again and the men at the breastworks could only wait "patiently for whatever should come next." Campfires were noted a mile in front of the line and the artillery was ordered to fire on them, followed by a reconnaissance that found they were only "fires of brush built to deceive us."

A local "free Negro" declared that Stuart, with two brigades of cavalry and some artillery, had pushed on to the north. Fearing this meant an attack on Fairfax Court House from that direction, the 12th was moved at the double-

CHAPTER TWELVE — PICKET DUTY

FAIRFAX COURT HOUSE, JUNE 1863

quick back to take positions "along the brow of a hill, in good position to receive a charge of Cavalry." The 13th was moved to guard the left flank and broke into cheers as Randall galloped back to take command of the regiment, his horse "white with sweat and foam." Well mounted, Randall had passed down the Alexandria turnpike just minutes before Stuart's column had seized two miles of it. Blunt and his adjutant, trailing behind, had been warned by the commander of a squadron of Vermont cavalry operating in the area not to attempt a return until morning or they would likely have been captured by Stuart.

The first action of the brigade ended as "the moon set; the air grew cold; the ground froze under our feet." The men had experienced a rush of excitement tinged with fear, although no shots had been fired by Lonergan's company or by most men in the brigade. Still, this was their first combat as a unit, one that proved to be the only experience with battle for some of its soldiers. The event "added to the confidence of the men in their officers, from Gen. Stoughton down" and Sturtevant believed "the men did not disappoint their commanders."

Sturtevant described the day following the action: "all was quiet, but all sorts of stories were rife throughout our camp, hair breadth escapes and bold and valiant conduct, etc.…some of the boys were prone to magnify their bravery and skill as marksmen." A look around the ambush site on December 29 indicated that the rebels had suffered several casualties, though two prisoners and a few horses were all the tangible evidence. From Sturtevant's viewpoint, this first battle—really only a very minor skirmish—in retrospect "furnished us with knowledge of ourselves and gave us confidence that served us well on the bloody field of Gettysburg."

On December 28, Lonergan had been placed under arrest for three days. Depending on when Stoughton ordered his release, Lonergan might not have been on the battle line with his company. However, it is difficult to imagine him sitting in his tent without his sword while the rest of the regiment went into action for the first time. If he did in fact miss this first chance to lead his company in combat, his mood would predictably have been foul when the regiment returned to camp that Monday morning.

Stuart avoided any serious battle and roamed behind the Union lines until the last day of the year, returning with hundreds of prisoners and a wagon train of captured supplies after losing only a dozen men. (Rumors in Washington at one point had reported the entire Vermont brigade taken prisoner by the rebel cavalry.)

Once released from arrest, Lonergan resumed the usual camp routine with inspection and dress parade on December 30 and 31. The soldiers had not been paid since leaving Vermont and hoped to receive the back pay due them, but this assembly did not include pay call. On New Year's Day, the men were excused from all but essential duties to enjoy packages of food and gifts received for the holidays. The 13th celebrated with "a game of [foot]ball, the old style" with "social equality alike between officers and privates" in a rough and tumble contest. The year in which they would complete the term of their enlistments and return home to Vermont had just begun.

PRESERVATION OF THE UNION by defeating the rebellion appeared a distant and uncertain prospect as 1863 began. Many people thought emancipation to be a desperate action by Lincoln, perhaps intended to spark an uprising by the slaves in the Confederate states. With a decisive military victory still eluding the federal government, freeing the slaves would deprive the South of manpower and discourage support of the rebellion by the European countries,

CHAPTER TWELVE – PICKET DUTY

particularly Great Britain. Reeling from Burnsides' defeat at Fredericksburg and blocked by the fortress of Vicksburg from gaining control of the Mississippi River, the Union found its one bright spot right at the start of 1863, in the hard-won victory at Stone's River in central Tennessee. Lincoln's telegram of congratulations to Maj. Gen. William S. Rosecrans was effusive in its gratitude, despite the loss of almost a third of the Union troops, which left the Army of the Cumberland too crippled to resume the offensive for months.

Although the Confederate casualties at Fredericksburg had been less than half those of the Union forces, Lincoln reckoned an "awful arithmetic" in these figures that none of his generals had yet grasped. He could see that a week of fighting at the same ratio of losses would wipe out the rebel forces and still leave a powerful federal army. What the president needed was a commander able to face the reality of such a strategy of attrition, along with political support from the country despite its terrible cost. When Lincoln signed the Emancipation Proclamation, he also authorized the enlistment of African-Americans into the Union army, a valuable addition of manpower if continued losses were to be sustained.

As the new year began, the Army of the Potomac under Burnside had an aggregate force of over a quarter of a million men assigned, but showed only 185,000 present for duty. Losses in battle, disease, accidents, and desertions—a total of 25,000 had gone "over the hill," at a rate of more than one hundred a day in January—had whittled away the ranks of this army and defeat had dulled its fighting edge. Burnsides' forces were backed up by over 70,000 men commanded by Heintzelman in the "Defenses of Washington" category that included the Second Vermont Brigade. (See Appendix B for the distribution of federal forces.) The greatest concentration of troops in the Union army sat miserable, demoralized, and idle in the cold and mud across from Fredericksburg. Poorly fed and housed, swept by illness in crowded and unsanitary conditions, the soldiers reviled Burnside for squandering their lives both in battle and in camp. When troops being reviewed by Burnside were ordered to give him three cheers, not a man opened his mouth. The army commander realized that he had at best one more chance for a decisive victory to redeem himself in the eyes of the president and the army.

Lured into action by exceptionally dry weather that had lowered the Rappahanock, Burnside ordered the army upstream to cross by ford and pontoon bridge beyond Lee's left flank. In the early afternoon of January 20, the men started their march, accompanied by artillery and supply wagons. That night brought a winter storm with heavy rain that quickly mired the columns in bottomless mud. For two days, men struggled to help the draft animals drag vehicles until dead horses and mules littered the roads and the humans "playing horse" were exhausted. On January 22, Burnside abandoned the hopeless operation and his men slogged wearily back to the inadequate camp from which they had started.

Plagued by what he considered disloyal subordinates, the inept Burnside met with Lincoln on January 24 to demand the president's approval of replacing several mutinous generals, threatening his own resignation as the only alternative. Lincoln the next day removed Burnside from command, substituting his arch-rival Hooker in hopes of restoring the army's morale and confidence in its leader.

LONERGAN AND HIS COMPANY were peripherally drawn into the "mud march" when the 12th and 13th Vermont received orders on January 19 to march south the next morning in support of Burnside's movements. Not pleased with the location of his regiment's camp at Fairfax Court House, Randall had just moved the unit to a better site a mile away. Necessary improvements to this new campground had hardly been finished when the 13th was told to fall in the next day, ready to march, at 7:00 AM. Adjusting to the realities of army life, the men of the 13th by now had no illusions about the permanence of any posting and they were, in fact, pleased to leave the Court House camp. The site was considered "an unhealthy location," flat land with bad drainage and a very poor water supply.

In their six weeks at Fairfax Court House, the regiment had lost two officers and twenty-three enlisted men. The officers had resigned their commissions, ten men had been discharged (usually for disability), two had deserted, and eleven men had succumbed to disease. Typhoid fever and chronic diarrhea had spread through the camp along with measles, colds, and other ailments. Company A recorded one death in the camp when Pvt. Alden Richardson from Westford passed away the second week in January. Another member of the company, Pvt. Joseph Ayers—an Irish-born recruit from the quarries in Rutland—was to die of disease on January 27.*

---

* Sturtevant's regimental history says that Ayers was left at Fairfax Court House when the regiment moved, but the regimental Descriptive Book states that he died at Wolf Run Shoals.

CHAPTER TWELVE – PICKET DUTY

The soldiers in the 13th welcomed the detached duty away from the brigade headquarters, even though the camp rumor predicted that the regiment was off "to join General Burnside and his great army." Discipline in the camp had been strict under Stoughton's direct supervision; a "long list of boys who had been placed under arrest" at his order and "marched off to the guard house, for neglecting to attend brigade drill." Such infractions could cost the soldier time in the guard house, additional duties, or a loss in pay when the paymaster eventually caught up to the regiment.

Company A probably had its share of men who had been the subject of disciplinary actions and its soldiers were likely eager to put distance between themselves and the general. Just the day before the regiment moved, Lonergan had issued his second General Order to his company. It required his men to render the proper military courtesies in camp, saluting all officers or, if on guard duty, presenting arms to anyone above the rank of captain. "Let it be seen that Co. A can be polite as well as fight," Lonergan urged, noting that the order would be enforced. He concluded, "Your Captain feels and hopes that there will be no further necessity than the publishing of this order or his simple request that the Emmet boys will perform whatever may be their duty."

The two regiments marched the fifteen miles to Wolf Run Shoals to take up a position on the north bank in a pine and oak grove on the upper Occoquan River. In a letter to the *Free Press,* Pvt. George G. Benedict compared the Occoquan with a river familiar to local readers, gauging it to be "about as large as the Winooski." At the ford, which Stuart had used during his raid at the end of December, a shallow stretch of the river split by an island provided a good crossing point for north-south movement. Despite the poor roads in the area, the ford "was constantly used by cavalry and other branches of the service." Two Union regiments might slow down a large rebel cavalry force, but without reinforcement would not prevent it from crossing for long. The green Vermont troops would only be expected to give warning of any incursion in force, perhaps delaying it for a while.

The rain had already started when the 13th began its march from the camp at Fairfax Court House, and the mud made it impossible to haul all the camp equipment along with the troops. Only some of the tents were taken and a detail from each company remained in camp to guard the rest of the property, including a supply of rations.

The same heavy rain that bogged down Burnside's forces prevented the regiment's wagons from returning to Fairfax for two days. By the time they got back to camp, the guards had bartered away much of the extra foodstuffs—mostly pork, salt beef, and hard tack that the soldiers avoided—to the locals for fresh produce such as corn meal, apples, sweet potatoes, cider, milk, and butter. The last of the supplies and equipment caught up with the regiment on January 25 and tents were set up just before a storm hit on January 28, "a genuine Vermont blizzard." Six inches of snow came the next day with a frigid northwest wind that "reminded us of our winter homes in Vermont" and made picket duty miserable.

One bright spot in the soldiers' lives was the arrival of the paymaster on January 29, the first pay call since leaving Vermont. The troops had mustered for pay on October 31 and December 31, only to be disappointed. Sturtevant commented that they had "not even received a shin plaster" while on duty and everyone was short of cash. Many had taken advantage of the credit provided by the official sutler, who also circulated sutler's checks, "little pieces of pasteboard, 1 by 2 inches in size, usually red, figures indicating value and signed by the regimental sutler." At pay call, the sutler stood beside the paymaster and collected any debts due him from the soldiers' pay. Men who had "bought Sutler's checks so freely and lavishly" now stood empty handed, pledging to "thereafter subsist on pork and beans, hard tack and coffee," foregoing the treats they had enjoyed on credit.

These first days at Wolf Run Shoals were "the most trying of all our camp life" for the 13th, with "rain, sleet, snow, wind, cold and often down to zero, and disagreeable weather every hour." In addition, they were now "on the front line and were required to be vigilant every hour." Picket duty on the two miles of the Occoquan River that they guarded meant exposure to real danger. Almost nightly, the Vermonters dealt with incidents of guerrilla groups and spies "watching our movements for an opportunity to break through our picket line that they might kill, capture, plunder and destroy." Only three months into their tour of duty, the Vermonters were feeling the stress of rough camp life, bad weather, and the threat of danger. The ranks were shrinking even as the demands on the units were increasing. Still, the "condition of our regiment for an aggressive campaign was as good and strong as ever," even if the men could not avoid grim thoughts of the combat that they would likely face in the spring.

CHAPTER TWELVE – PICKET DUTY

An early ominous sign that the brigade might take the field came on February 2, when Heintzelman's command defending the capital was converted into the Twenty-second Corps. The corps, consisting mainly of three infantry divisions and a cavalry division, paralleled the organizational structure of similar units in the Army of the Potomac. The soldiers understood that this indicated the possibility of a more active role for the Second Vermont Brigade. Stoughton's brigade remained assigned to Casey's division and would presumably do any campaigning as part of that division.

For the first time, daily target practice was instituted in the regiment, "in which all were required to take part." Previously, a crude butt had been set up at which returning pickets would fire, basically as a safety measure to ensure that their muskets had been discharged before they entered camp. Now rewards were given for "hitting the bull's eye on the hill across the valley 300 yards and more away." Those soldiers who showed skill as marksmen were excused all duty for a week.*

The emphasis on weapons training in the 13th even extended to a "school for sword instruction" initiated by Randall. He encouraged non-commissioned officers to learn the skills of handling the sword, since replacement officers would likely be chosen from their ranks. When the school opened on February 18, "nearly every sergeant and some of our more zealous and ambitious corporals also joined the class." The officers, already commissioned, did not take much interest in this preparatory school. As a break from the serious nature of drilling with muskets and "little wooden swords," mock battles with snowballs were organized by groups within the regiment "and all seemed to enjoy this mimic war." With nature supplying plenty of ammunition, such snowball fights "were frequent and much enjoyed. Company was arrayed against company, battalion against battalion, right wing against the left." While some blood flowed on the snow and gave a sense of real conflict, yet "none could tell from conduct in camp who would acquit themselves best in a genuine battle."

Lonergan emphasized this intensified training when he issued one of

---

* This was a common form of reward; for complying with the Co. A order on military courtesy, Pvt. Michael Quilty was "tendered the regards of his Captain and is excused from all Picket, Drill, or Roll Calls for 5 days."

his infrequent General Orders (No. 3 of a total of four) to his company on February 23. It informed all his men that starting the next day everyone would fall in at 10:00 AM for "Company, Squad, and Skirmish Drill, and the bayonet exercise." Each morning "at the Roll of the Drum" a roll call would be taken with a commissioned officer present, in addition to the regular company formations—reveille at the start of the day and tattoo at night. The sergeant calling the roll was charged with reporting as absent any man who did not answer to his name, unless the soldier was on duty. The punishment for missing any roll call would be extra picket and camp duties. The order concluded with praise, saying "Your Captain feels proud of the promptness of Co. A to fall in when called to meet the enemy, which is more important than all, but the minor calls upon you are duties and also require equal promptness." This reference to meeting the enemy suggests that Lonergan might well have been at the head of his company during the Stuart raid of December, even if still under arrest and without his sword.

STUART'S CAVALRY COULD ATTACK Wolf Run Shoals again at any time and likely would come in such strength as to quickly overwhelm the two Vermont regiments spread thinly along the river bank. A more certain threat, however, came daily from roving guerrilla bands, particularly the forces of Capt. John Singleton Mosby. This clever and audacious leader had come to Stuart's attention by helping to scout the route for circling the Union forces on the Peninsula and had performed the same service when the rebel cavalry crossed the Rappahanock right after Christmas. Stuart agreed to Mosby's proposal that he stay behind in the area between the outer defenses of Washington and the Army of the Potomac to do mischief to Union outposts and lines of communication.* With only fifteen men as the core of his group, Mosby drew on local support for information and additional manpower, creating havoc far out of proportion to the size of his unit.

Exploiting his familiarity with the territory and the willingness of local residents to provide aid, the small force selected weak points in the Union defenses, attacking the pickets, keeping them constantly under arms, and

---

* His broad area of operations became known as "Mosby's Confederacy." The practice of removing the planks over the Potomac bridges each night to protect Washington was attributed to Mosby's threat of unexpected raids.

CHAPTER TWELVE – PICKET DUTY

raiding outposts for horses and supplies. Mosby's operations began just as the two regiments of Vermonters were shifted to the Occoquan line, where they became the targets for many of his actions.

The boldest and most successful of Mosby's raids took place on March 9, when, with twenty-nine men, he penetrated the Union lines all the way to the headquarters of the Second Vermont Brigade at Fairfax Court House. Even though the 12th and 13th Vermont were camped fifteen miles away on the Occoquan, Stoughton had positioned his three remaining regiments at Fairfax Station, four miles distant. A "large body of cavalry" from New York commanded by Col. Wyndham, a British soldier of fortune, was camped at the court house headquarters. These troopers were thought to provide sufficient security for the headquarters, even though comments were made about the resulting isolation of the Second Vermont Brigade commander from his own units. Stoughton's mother and sister were spending the winter with him and needed suitable accommodation. The young general stayed in the village with them (consistent with his reputation, some attributed his choice of residence to an interest in a local lady).

Mosby was making "his almost nightly raids with considerable success," to the frustration of the ponderous Union cavalry, which threatened reprisals against anyone assisting the hit-and-run horsemen. After Wyndham offended Mosby's pride by dismissing the rebel leader as a common "horse thief," the Virginian was determined to humiliate the colonel by stealing him from his bed. Aided by a deserter from the cavalry stationed at Fairfax Court House, who knew where the pickets were stationed, Mosby chose a rainy night to pass quietly through the Union lines.

About midnight on March 8, the rebels entered the sleeping village unchallenged and split into three groups to round up prisoners and horses. Wyndham, the intended victim of the raid, was away in Washington that night, but Mosby carried off a more important prize, personally rousing Stoughton from his bed with a slap on his bare backsides, and taking him prisoner. Outnumbered by the prisoners they had taken, and with fifty-nine captured horses, the rebel force assembled in the street to leave as stealthily as they had come.

Evading the inevitable pursuit, the raiders crossed back through the Union picket lines without incident. They reached safety before dawn, although darkness had allowed many of the prisoners to escape. With Mosby riding

Fairfax Station, Virginia

CHAPTER TWELVE – PICKET DUTY

right alongside, however, Stoughton's horse was led by the reins and the high-ranking captive was delivered triumphantly to Stuart's headquarters. The young Vermont general's military career was destroyed by the circumstances of his abduction. Stoughton suffered additional embarrassment after Lincoln commented wryly that he could make another brigadier general in five minutes, but the captured horses had cost the government $125 each.

As the senior regimental commander, Blunt again took command of the Second Vermont Brigade. To avoid a repeat of Mosby's coup, Blunt moved the brigade headquarters down to Fairfax Station, guarded by the 14th, 15th, and 16th Vermont. Randall, now the senior officer at Wolf Run Shoals, was placed in charge of both the 12th and 13th Vermont.

On the day that the brigade lost its general, a grim gift "furnished by the Governor of Vermont, for Vermont troops" was distributed. Both the lieutenants and all thirteen NCOs in Co. A lined up on March 9 to sign a statement that they had "this day received of Captain John Lonergan one Tourniquet each." It was a practical contribution from the Vermont commander in chief, but a grisly reminder that the recipients might have to apply the cord to someone's shattered limb, controlling the bleeding at the risk of inducing gangrene. All the signs pointed to the likelihood that the Vermonters would join in the spring campaign and could expect some bloody combat as part of the Army of the Potomac under its new commander, "Fighting Joe" Hooker. Until then, Lonergan and his men would enjoy life in their new camp as much as possible, counting down the days until their enlistments expired and they could return home.

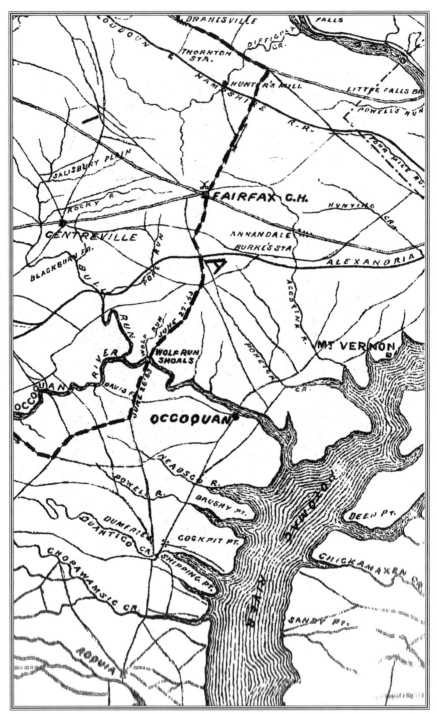

Second Vermont Brigade on the Occoquan

CHAPTER THIRTEEN

CAMP LIFE

GUARDING THE FRONT LINE of the Washington defenses in Virginia, the men of the Second Vermont Brigade settled in to serve out their nine-month enlistments. Mustered in over a period spanning almost three weeks in October, the five regiments would be released in sequence as their tours of duty expired in July of 1863. Still "green" troops with no combat experience—the brush with Stuart's troopers in December barely qualified as even a skirmish—the Vermonters adjusted to the routine of army life as best they could. Some soldiers might still have thoughts of glory to be gained in battle, but most were concerned only with their day-to-day existence and with avoiding the threat of disease that resulted from crowded camps, poor sanitation, and inadequate nutrition. Distractions from the constant cycle of roll calls and picket duty provided welcome breaks from the predictable flow of daily activities. From snowball fights to band concerts, any unusual event helped the time pass more swiftly. Parcels and mail from home would at times brighten the day, and visitors, both official and private, brought excitement to the camp.

Only a few members of the brigade were given furloughs during their nine-months term of service. Even soldiers on longer duty in other units were rarely given the chance to visit home, and there was little expectation that the shorter-term men would return before their enlistments were finished. Benedict, the prolific writer of letters for publication, was granted permission in mid-January to absent himself for twenty days in order to take care of "personal business" in Burlington. As the former postmaster and the son of the *Free Press* owner, Benedict was well-connected to arrange such a privilege.* Several officers in the brigade returned to Vermont after resigning

---

* In February, Benedict was selected by Blunt for promotion from private to Second Lieutenant of Co. C, in conjunction with resignations by officers in the 12th. On March 21, he was assigned by his colonel as an aide-de-camp at brigade headquarters.

their commissions, at times under the threat of being subjected to boards of competency.

The enlisted men, however, usually made it back to Vermont only if discharged for disability or when transferred to the state's military hospitals. Camp hospitals operated by the regimental surgeons provided the first level of treatment for less serious injuries and illnesses. A higher level of medical attention was available at hospitals in Alexandria and Washington, where soldiers were transported by train and ferry after the regimental ambulance delivered them to Fairfax Station.

Concern about the quality of care given sick, injured, or wounded Vermont soldiers eventually led to the establishment of three military hospitals in their home state. In the summer of 1862, Gov. Holbrook convinced the federal government to turn over the unused Marine Hospital in Burlington to his administration. Vermont soldiers were brought there for better care than they would receive elsewhere in the medical system, since convalescent camps were notorious for poor conditions. The governor on occasion even personally searched the federal hospitals to find Green Mountain Boys, bringing them home to be restored to health. The superior care provided by this system was credited with saving the lives of many Vermont soldiers. (Facilities at the Brattleboro camp were refitted for medical use later in 1862, and a 600-bed military hospital was constructed near Montpelier in 1864.)

Twelve men from the 13th Vermont, including three from Co. A, were among the seventy-two Vermonters whom the *Free Press* reported arriving at the Marine Hospital on January 10, 1863. The listing gave each man's company and regiment, along with his residence, but no indication of his condition or the reason for his evacuation from the war zone. For the next two years and more, such notices of hospitalizations would appear along with the casualty lists for battles, as Vermont soldiers continued to do their full duty in the war.

Lonergan lacked Benedict's personal and political connections, but the Irishman somehow managed to wangle a furlough back to Vermont. On March 12, the headquarters of the Department of Washington, the administrative office for the newly organized Twenty-Second Corps, by Special Orders authorized the captain a ten-day absence from the 13th Vermont. The *Free Press* reported Lonergan's arrival in Burlington on March 14 "for a short visit to his friends." Explaining the occasion for his visit home to be the "severe illness of his father,"

CHAPTER THIRTEEN – CAMP LIFE

the brief article in the "PERSONAL" column reassured the readers that the visitor "is himself in fine health." Lonergan also brought "a very favorable account of his 'boys,' (the Emmet Guard) and of his regiment generally."

Probably Lonergan also visited any members of his company still in the Marine Hospital. If time permitted, he might also have conducted Fenian business while passing through Vermont. (Based on his demonstrated willingness to bend the rules, one could even suspect that Lonergan had manufactured the family crisis as a reason to get back home. His father, Thomas Lonergan, survived his "severe illness" to continue working as a cooper for another fifteen years.)

No public celebration of the Irish national holiday in Burlington was reported that March. Although the Irish were welcome to join the ranks of the Union army, they were not yet treated as social equals in Vermont. However, the *Free Press* on March 21 carried a story of how the "birthday of the Patron saint of Ireland" was marked elsewhere. The festivities in the Army of the Potomac were described as the equal of any "in the Emerald Isle itself…the lack of a free fight to wind up with only excepted." Reporting on various dinners held in New York City, Jersey City, and Newark, the article closed with the observation that the holiday "seems to have received more general attention this year than usual."

At Wolf Run Shoals, Lonergan's company no doubt continued its routine of picket, guard, and fatigue duties on March 17 as on any other day. When Randall deployed his regiment to control the ford, Co. A was placed "on a side Hill in support of a Battery of Artillery from Connecticut," some five hundred yards in front of the rest of the regiment. Lonergan's men kept a strict schedule of guard duty there and thus "had little part in the work of building forts, etc." that engaged the other companies. The regimental camp had discovered that life was more "quiet and peaceable with the 'Irish Regulars' away." The Emmet Guards were accustomed to "being wakened occasionally in the night to witness a ruff and tumble scrap in the company street," so their absence from camp was welcomed by the rest of the regiment.

Since his furlough conveniently extended over St. Patrick's Day, Lonergan could gather with friends at home to lift a convivial "jar" or two while his two lieutenants took charge of the Emmet Guards in his absence. Perhaps fellow countrymen scattered in the other units of the Second Vermont Brigade joined with the "Irish Company" on March 17 to recognize their national holiday.

Company A at Wolf Run Shoals on the Occoquan River

An Irish musician in the 12th Vermont, Pvt. Charles Dyer from Rutland, would likely have been a welcome guest at any celebration held.* Lonergan's refusal to attend compulsory religious services the previous December might even have gained the Catholics some privileges. They may have been allowed to attend Catholic services in the area, particularly on an occasion such as St. Patrick's Day.

When his furlough ended, Lonergan may have used the opportunity to bring his bride of the previous October to join him in Virginia, if she was not already there. The wives of many officers and some enlisted men shared their spouses' stay in Virginia for various periods. Mary Blunt, for example, had joined her husband at the 12th Vermont's camp in November of 1862, and stayed with the colonel over the winter; other wives came and went as personal circumstances allowed.

As the days grew longer and the weather improved, the nine-months

---

* Dyer's wife and two babies had joined him in Virginia in December, the family occupying its own tent in the company street with their infant sleeping in a cracker box. The mother did the washing for officers' wives visiting the camp. A letter from Mary Farnham, wife of the lieutenant colonel of the 12th, described her as about twenty years old, "a simple Irish woman, used to all kinds of hardship, and I think the children will be used to the same."

CHAPTER THIRTEEN — CAMP LIFE

soldiers knew that before long they would be back in their own homes. Any earlier dreams of glory had been tempered by the reality of war and few of the Green Mountain Boys would be disappointed if the picket duty continued for the remainder of their time. Rumors persisted, however, that they would be joining Hooker's forces in the spring campaign.

THE ARMY OF THE POTOMAC, as the *Free Press* reported, celebrated St. Patrick's Day in grand style with festivities centering on the Irish Brigade. Meagher—recently returned to the Falmouth, Virginia, camp from convalescent leave—was engaged in a dispute with Hooker over releasing the three battered New York regiments for rest and recruitment. After the debacle at Fredericksburg, the brigade showed an aggregate of only ninety-one officers and 531 men left on the rolls; barely 350 remained actually available for duty, "including pioneers, drummers, etc." Hancock, the division commander, approved the request, but Hooker refused permission. Meagher was threatening to resign his commission as a brigadier general since the current strength of the brigade "hardly exhibits the numerical strength which qualifies it" for even a colonel's command.

Nonetheless, when St. Patrick's Day arrived, Meagher played the genial host in organizing festivities. The drum corps throughout the Army of the Potomac "kept rattling away at one spirit-stirring tune" all evening on March 16 until midnight ushered in the holiday. At daybreak, "crowds of soldiers of every rank and condition" converged on the Irish Brigade where a "spacious chapel had been erected of canvas" and decorated with evergreens. The brigade chaplain, Father William Corby, started the day with a High Mass at 8:00 AM "accompanied by martial music" and attended by hundreds of invited guests. Father Joseph B. O'Hagan, chaplain of Sickles' Excelsior Brigade, preached "an eloquent and patriotic sermon" following the Mass.

Meagher's wife had brought him down the garb of an Irish gentleman for the occasion and she accompanied the general as he made his way around camp in his tall white hat, brown coat, green cravat, and high black boots.* At a large field near Hancock's headquarters, stands had been erected for the spectators to watch the races—horse, mule, and foot—along with contests of Irish music and feats of strength. Men who had gathered under the makeshift stands occupied by Hooker, his corps commanders, and a host of brigadiers

---

* Meagher had married an American girl in New York City after his first wife died in 1854, while living with his family in Waterford, Ireland.

were warned by Meagher of danger. Waving his horsewhip, he humorously commanded them "Stand from under! If that stage gives way, you will be crushed by four tons of Major-Generals." Some ten thousand troops watched three heats of steeplechase run for a prize of $500, which was won by Capt. Jack Gosson, riding Meagher's gray hunter.

Lunch was provided at the headquarters of the Irish Brigade, whose surgeon doubled as its poet-laureate. In a spirited "Poetical Address of Welcome," the doctor castigated "the authors of the Fredericksburg disaster" while praising McClellan and Hooker "most fervently." Dr. Lawrence Reynolds—born in Meagher's hometown of Waterford—also served as the treasurer of the Fenian "Officers' Circle" in the Army of the Potomac and "no man was more enthusiastic or zealous" in the cause of Irish independence. After lunch, the sporting contests were resumed, only to be interrupted by the sound of heavy firing in the distance. In ten minutes the grounds were deserted, as officers and men rushed back to their camps.

The St. Patrick's Day celebrations had been disrupted by the attack of 2,000 Yankee horsemen on the Confederate forces across the Rappahannock at Kelly's Ford, upstream from the Union camp. Although the federal troopers did not press their tactical victory over the rebel cavalry and rode back across the river, the aggressive action showed a new confidence among the soldiers in the Army of the Potomac.

HOOKER HAD TAKEN COMMAND of a defeated and demoralized army after its bloody repulse at Fredericksburg and the farcical "mud march." His first task was to restore the spirit of his soldiers and instill confidence in their leaders. A reorganization of the command structure abolished Burnside's Grand Divisions and the corps again became the largest unit in an army. For the first time the Union horsemen were consolidated into a corps. Hooker now had available seven infantry, one artillery, and one cavalry corps, but he continued to agitate for additional manpower.

Hooker understandably wanted to build up his army as much as possible. He had his eye on the units in the Twenty-Second Corps and the garrison at Harper's Ferry in particular. After the Reserve Grand Division was disbanded and Heintzelman's command was converted into the Twenty-Second Corps, the Second Vermont Brigade anticipated taking the field as part of the

CHAPTER THIRTEEN – CAMP LIFE

Army of the Potomac. As spring approached, a thorough shake-up of corps commanders weeded out some of the less competent generals who had been promoted through seniority in the Regular Army or by political favoritism.

The creation of a cavalry corps, probably the most important of the organizational changes, concentrated the mounted units previously assigned in smaller units for patrolling and scouting. Now the Union had an offensive arm that could match Stuart and counter his embarrassing raids, like the one the Vermonters had faced when he crossed through the lines in December. George Stoneman was promoted to major general in March to command three divisions of volunteers and a reserve brigade of Regular Army, twenty-six cavalry regiments with attached horse artillery. Equipped with better arms and replacement mounts, the cavalry was ordered to operate more aggressively and began to take the fight to the rebels, as it had on St. Patrick's Day.

Hooker not only reorganized his forces, but also improved the situation of his men with healthier food and living conditions. Thousands of men were in the hospitals with a variety of contagious diseases and as the result of a bad diet that led to scurvy and other ailments. Desertion had become so common and widely accepted as "no disgrace" that the army was bleeding a stream of able-bodied soldiers, despite the occasional execution by firing squad.* In March, Lincoln issued a policy of amnesty for deserters intended to encourage men to return to their units for the spring campaign.

Lincoln's comment about being able to create a new brigadier general with the stroke of his pen was confirmed when the captured Stoughton was replaced. Col. George J. Stannard had received his appointment as brigadier on March 11, two days after the young general had been spirited away by Mosby. Citing Stannard's bravery at Harper's Ferry, the U.S. Senate quickly confirmed his appointment. Although Stannard did not arrive in Virginia to take command of the Second Vermont Brigade for over a month, clearly the intention was for him to fill Stoughton's vacant position.**

---

* Originally intended to identify stragglers in battle and deserters for delivery back to their divisions, Hooker introduced what became a permanent practice in the military. Every soldier was required to wear a badge on his cap, initially cloth and later metal, identifying the unit to which he was assigned. Each corps in the army was given a distinctive outline (circle, cross, etc.) with divisions indicated by color. Over time, these became badges of pride for the men.

** Stannard and his 9th Vermont, paroled after the surrender of Harper's Ferry, had been guarding Confederate prisoners at Camp Douglas near Chicago. An exchange on January 10, 1863, allowed them to resume duty in the field.

Casey's division headquarters and a large portion of his command displaced forward from Washington to Centreville in late March. On March 23, the division commander redeployed the three Vermont regiments guarding Fairfax Station, sending the 14th to join the 12th and 13th in picket duty on the Occoquan. Blunt's brigade headquarters also moved to Wolf Run Shoals, safely protected by his three regiments stationed there. The 15th and 16th were placed at Union Mills Station, about ten miles south of Fairfax Station on the Orange and Alexandria Railroad, where units of the brigade had been posted the previous November. Col. Redfield Proctor was in charge of this detachment. In addition to protecting the railroad bridge over Bull Run, the two regiments manned a section of the picket line along the river that continued to the north. On March 29, extra ammunition and ten days' marching rations were issued throughout the Second Vermont Brigade in expectation that it would take the field. Although they remained on the picket line, the brigade was "under marching orders about half the time" as the weather improved.

Regulations had clearly established that the term of an enlistment began when a unit was mustered in (or an individual was added to the muster roll) and not when the soldier signed his enlistment papers. Even so, some soldiers considered it unfair to serve longer than the stated term and protested the situation. Volunteer regiments even organized appeals to their state governors for release from duty based on the date of enrollment in the state militia. Politics played a role in such agitation; many Democrats had lost enthusiasm for the war, particularly for the new mission of emancipation. In late March, a petition addressed to Gov. Holbrook was being circulated in the Second Vermont Brigade asking that the nine-months service be calculated from the time "when they were enrolled, and not from the time of their muster into the United States service." A description of this petition to return home in May, rather than July, was sent to the editor of the Democratic-leaning Burlington *Sentinel*, along with comments as to the reception that the petition received in the "Irish Company." In a letter from Wolf Run Shoals, dated April 2, "One of Co. A" wrote to assure the public that Lonergan's men had unanimously rejected the proposal.

According to the anonymous reporter, at the end of March "a mighty long string of *foolscap* paper with a great profusion of 'Therefore's' and 'Whereas's' was sent to Company A, Captain Lonergan, in the 13th Regt. with the request that Company A would sign it." The petition was then to be passed on alphabetically by company through the regiment. This "*foolscap* didn't fool Capt. Lonergan, nor Company A. The Captain looked it over, scanned it with his steady quick eye, and decided that Company A would not sign the document." At evening tattoo, Lonergan advised his men to let the regiment know that "Company A are in no hurry to go home" and would support the government as long as anyone. Their captain urged them "Let it be seen, boys, that the *Emmet Guards* are not the first to sign the paper." His company shouted back "Bully for the Captain" and "We will sign no such paper!"

The letter had been written to the editor so that "it be known that Captain Lonergan and his gallant Irish Emmets sent the project reeling." The petition was, however, signed by one or two hundred men in the regiment. When Randall examined it and found no names from Lonergan's company, he reportedly stated "Bully for Co. A" since he "would not have such a paper as that leave my regiment for the world." The author of the letter asked that credit be given for refusing to sign and that the editor should "say that Capt. Lonergan and his Irish Company of *Democrats* did not beg to go home," as other companies (of mostly Republican soldiers) had. With growing numbers of Democrats throughout the country opposed to the war, Lonergan was anxious to demonstrate that he and his men were committed to achieving victory for the Union.

As the 13th braced itself for imminent action, Randall was deprived of one of his two field grade subordinates. A former steamboat captain on Lake Champlain and the oldest officer in the brigade, Maj. Clark had for months been making arrangements to transfer to more suitable service with the navy. He resigned his commission on March 31 and reported for his board of examination, but was "mortified" to find that he was a few days beyond the navy's age limit of fifty. The ex-major, "now much grieved and disappointed," returned home to Vermont and resumed farming. Although the *Rutland Daily Herald* reported that Clark "contemplates going into the privateering business if letters of marque and reprisal are issued," he took no further part in the war.

When his Co. K from Highgate mustered in, Clark had included his foster son, Martin Clark, on the rolls as being eighteen when he was actually less than sixteen. A sickly lad and not of much use as a soldier, the boy had been transferred to Lonergan's company at Brattleboro. Upon the major's resignation, Martin was reassigned back to Co. K and discharged for disability.* (Randall's eighteen-year-old son Charles was also carried on the original roll of Lonergan's company until becoming regimental sergeant major and then, on January 22, 1863, second lieutenant of Co. G.)

ON THE FIRST OF APRIL, the 13th was ordered to move about five miles downriver to guard the ferry crossing at Occoquan village and man a picket line extending to Davis's Ford, three miles below Wolf Run Shoals. The regiment replaced a cavalry force that had been sent to Fairfax Court House to join other mounted regiments concentrated there in Maj. Gen. Julius H. Stahel's cavalry division.

Everyone in the 13th was "anxious to leave" the Wolf Run Shoals camp where they had experienced much sickness, but some found the news too good to believe and feared it "was an April fool."

On April 2, a beautiful spring day, the regiment marched to a new camp considered "an earthly paradise" in comparison with the one they were leaving. Setting up their tents "in a broad open field of meadow and pasture land surrounded with groves of pine and oak on an elevated plateau overlooking the Occoquan less than a mile south," Randall's unit found this place on the farm owned by "Widow Violet" to be an ideal camp site. Provided with good water from "great springs and flowing streams" and ample timber for the camp needs, the attractive landscape opened to vistas of the wide Potomac.

The regiment occupied good defensive ground because the ferry crossing was dominated by Mount Vision, rising steeply nearly two hundred feet above the river. The Rutland quarrymen in particular would have explored the granite pit in this rocky hill. Men from the Burlington area no doubt remarked on the neighboring village of Colchester, since the town across the Winooski River at home shared that name.

Earlier in the war, the Confederate army had stationed 16,000 men on the south bank of the Occoquan, but now the area was abandoned, subject only to the infrequent raiding of irregular rebel cavalry. Threatened by "no particular danger here," the men of the 13th Vermont took pleasure in their situation and Sturtevant reported "some of the more timid among us said [they] would

---

* The following November, Martin Clark enlisted in the 11th Vermont. He was captured on June 23, 1864, and at the end of August died at Andersonville prison, where he was buried in an unmarked grave.

CHAPTER THIRTEEN – CAMP LIFE

ARMY BEEF SWIMMING THE OCCOQUAN RIVER

willingly remain here until the war was over." With this extension of their area of responsibility, the Vermont brigade thinly covered a total of "some twenty odd miles of line, as the river runs." Confederate deserters were now more frequently being captured crossing the Union line, a good indication that the rebel forces were about to begin field operations.

Although the weather remained unreliable, with a foot of snow falling on April 5 "like a genuine March blizzard in Vermont," the men set about creating a tidy and attractive camp. One incentive was the arrival of "fair ladies…in camp," which brought the opportunity for more social interaction, at least for the officers. Whether Roseanna Lonergan had indeed traveled south with her husband in March or had joined him at some other time, she apparently was among the wives staying on the Occoquan that spring. Randall was described as "a very courteous gentleman and extremely partial to the ladies," making them welcome and as comfortable as possible in camp. He succeeded to such a degree that "some were so much taken up with camp life they remained until June and departed with regret." A "fast day" was celebrated on April 9 when Randall, "accompanied by officers and ladies, with the drum corps for music, went for a sail down the Occoquan as far as the Potomac." Sturtevant paints an almost idyllic scene of such diversions amidst the general hardships of the war and the demands of camp life for the soldiers.

During April, even in this appealing location, the 13th suffered considerable sickness and many men were sent to the hospitals in Alexandria. The regimental chaplain, Rev. Sargent, died on April 20, probably from disease contracted when ministering to the sick. Although Lonergan had protested against mandatory attendance at Sargent's religious services, no doubt the Irishman joined in mourning the death of the popular clergyman. (The Rev. Edward H. Randall, the colonel's brother, received an appointment as chaplain on May 5, but never accepted the commission.)

A more auspicious event for the Green Mountain Boys also took place on April 20, when Stannard arrived at Wolf Run Shoals to take command of the Second Vermont Brigade. The new commander was personally known to many of the officers and men and "had the hearty approval of every soldier in the 13th regiment and the brigade."

The physical appearance of the "Widow Violet" camp and the soldiers of the 13th received special attention on April 25, in preparation for a visit by Stannard. Small pine and cedar trees were set out around the camp, the tents properly aligned, weapons and equipment cleaned, clothes brushed and army shoes blackened. When the new commander arrived the following morning, he was accompanied by a large bodyguard of Michigan cavalry. Stannard was taking no chances of a repeat of Stoughton's misadventure. After the regiment demonstrated their mastery of drill, going "through the various evolutions for an hour or more," they formed a hollow square on the parade ground into which Stannard rode. He praised the unit for its "soldiery [sic] appearance, fine drilling and good looks," telling them "I have no fear if ever it should be my privilege to lead you into battle, but what you will be brave and fearless and acquit yourselves with credit and honor to Vermont." Three hearty cheers for the general rang out over the Virginia countryside, where the Vermonters expected to face any test of battle.

This visit could possibly have given Lonergan a chance to renew his connection with Stannard. Before the war, the general had commanded the 4th Regiment of Vermont militia, which had included the original Emmet Guards. Stannard also had held the position of lieutenant colonel in the 2nd Vermont when Lonergan's company was disbanded by the governor. The presence of a revived Emmet Guards in the 13th Vermont, probably noted by Stannard, testified to Lonergan's commitment and persistence. However, the general and his bodyguard rode off down the highway to Fairfax Station immediately after the welcoming ceremonies; on this occasion Lonergan would have had little opportunity for personal contact with Stannard.

A visit by the paymaster on April 27 was a welcome surprise, coming as it did before the end of the month, and each private received his $52.00 for four months service. As required by regulations, a muster to verify the rolls of each company took place at the end of each month, but the men were paid

CHAPTER THIRTEEN – CAMP LIFE

irregularly. On May 1, the regiment was excused from duty to enjoy May Day, and the men were allowed to leave the camp as long as they avoided Mosby's bushwhackers. The "ladies in camp from Vermont, wives of officers," no doubt including Roseanna Lonergan, joined in the social activities led by Randall.

The holiday was an altogether relaxing and enjoyable interlude, but the following day the Vermonters "could distinctly hear the heavy, deep rumbling of cannonading in the direction of Fredericksburg." With the wind from the south on May 3, the sounds of battle carried clearly to the camp on the Occoquan. Marching orders were received the next day and the rumor spread through camp that Stannard had received orders "to advance his command as fast as possible to the front." For three days, the entire brigade stood ready to march, hoping for assignment to Maj. Gen. John Sedgwick's Sixth Corp, along with the First Vermont Brigade.

Even as Lonergan moved camp with the 13th Vermont on April 2, a renewed emphasis that spring on drill had begun to sharpen the blunted edge of the Army of the Potomac. Reviews were held to remind the men of the powerful force they comprised, culminating early in April with a grand assembly attended by President Lincoln, who visited the army for three days. The commander in chief urged Hooker to press the rebels and to hold nothing back in the next battle. Although the Union forces had twice the number of men in the area as the Confederates did, over fifty federal regiments were approaching the end of their two-year or nine-month enlistments. With nearly a third of the soldiers in the army scheduled to be released from service by June, operations were planned to resume in April, before the men left. However, the spring campaign was repeatedly delayed by bad weather.

Even so, the Irish Brigade's commander nearly missed the action; Meagher returned from another medical leave in New York City only on April 26. Meagher had been a featured speaker, along with prominent figures like Archbishop Hughes and McClellan, at a meeting in the city on April 11 to raise funds for relief of the latest famine in Ireland.* Meagher had praised

---

* In thanking him for helping to raise funds, Meagher suggested that the Democrat McClellan—"should events legitimately give him the chance"—would "render Ireland, after another fashion, a more lasting and nobler relief." Clearly Meagher was hinting that a President McClellan might act in support of Irish independence, given the opportunity. This was not the first such political meddling by Meagher and it further reduced his popularity with Lincoln's Republican administration.

McClellan as "the best beloved and foremost" of the country's generals, the "young and gifted organizer of the Army of the Potomac."

Confident of his coming victory over Lee, Hooker finally put his army into motion on April 27. Three corps crossed the Rappahanock upstream, while two corps prepared to assault Fredericksburg again and two corps were held in reserve. Hooker's plan to outflank the rebel defenses succeeded, but he then proved unable to manage his extended forces. Caught in the tangles of The Wilderness, the Union superiority of numbers was negated. Lee responded with his usual audacity; dividing and shifting his forces to achieve local advantage, the rebel commander sent Jackson to outflank the federal concentration around Chancellorsville, driving Hooker into a defensive posture.

Hooker planned an attack on May 3 to regain the initiative, but was preempted by a rebel assault at daybreak that was heard by the Vermonters on the banks of the Occoquan. Sedgwick's Sixth Corps, including the First Vermont Brigade, overwhelmed the weakly-manned Confederate lines at Marye's Heights. Cautiously moving west to join the main Union effort until blocked by rebel forces, Sedgwick abandoned the heights above Fredericksburg, which were then reoccupied by Confederate troops. Stunned on May 3 by the concussion of a cannonball, as well as by Lee's bold actions, on May 6 Hooker withdrew his forces back across the Rappahanock, to the widespread dismay of his officers and men. Despite his president's instructions, Hooker had failed to put in all his men at the crucial point when he might have achieved victory.

At Chancellorsville, Meagher's Irishmen did some hard fighting as part of Hancock's Division, suffering another fifty casualties in their diminishing regiments. Hancock had ordered Meagher to command the division's retreat and the Irish Brigade units had been among the last to cross back over the river on May 6.

After three days of standing ready to march in support of Hooker's forces, the Second Vermont Brigade learned of the Union defeat and the unit returned to its established routine of picket duty. With only two months left to serve on their enlistments, it appeared possible that the 13th Vermont would return home without seeing any real combat. Unless the Vermonters' situation changed dramatically, Lonergan might never prove the courage of his Emmet Guards on the battlefield.

Back again in the Falmouth camp, Meagher wrote the division adjutant-

CHAPTER THIRTEEN – CAMP LIFE

general on May 8 to "beg most respectfully to tender you, and through you to the proper authorities, my resignation as Brigadier-General, commanding what was once known as the Irish Brigade. That Brigade no longer exists." Referring back to his "memorial to the Secretary of War" in February asking for relief of his three regiments, to which no response had been received, Meagher stated that he could not "be a party to this wrong." He framed his decision as an act of conscience and went on to "offer my own life to sustain this good Government."

Within the week, his resignation had been accepted by the War Department. Meagher bid farewell to his brigade, less than 400 strong, on May 20. Command passed to the senior regimental commander, Col. Patrick Kelly of the 88th New York. (Kelly was succeeded by other field grade officers during the war as the brigade continued to shrink; Meagher was the only general to command it.)

RANDALL LOST HIS OTHER field grade officer in the 13th—the major's position had been vacant since Clark left at the end of March—right at the time of the Chancellorsville battle. Lt. Col Brown resigned on May 5 to become, at Holbrook's request, the Provost Marshal in charge of raising additional troops in the First Congressional District in Vermont. The regiment felt "a general disappointment" at Brown's departure since he was well respected as an officer.

Promotions from within the regiment filled both vacancies on May 5. The commander of Co. D, William D. Munson, was made lieutenant colonel and the "whole regiment was pleased with the promotion." Perhaps Lonergan was the exception to this general approval, since he claimed seniority over Munson. However, the captain from Colchester was a graduate of Norwich University, where he had received military training, and he must have been considered better qualified than Lonergan. Captain Boyton of Co. E was promoted to major and "entered at once upon the discharge of his duties as such." Lonergan was no doubt doubly disappointed as he had been twice passed over, despite his established (though questionable) seniority among the line officers.

Stannard visited the 13th again on the afternoon of May 9; in anticipation, Randall had ordered a thorough policing of the camp and house-cleaning of the tents that morning. The general—along with his entourage of staff, orderlies, and a mounted guard—rode in about 2:00 PM to inspect the regiment on parade.

SWORD PRESENTED TO LONERGAN ON OCCOQUAN RIVER

With the camp in particularly good order for the general's visit, the men in Lonergan's company apparently deemed it a suitable occasion to present him with a sword and belt as a token of their esteem. This practice of giving such a gift to a commander was widespread, the cost being covered by contributions proportional to rank. A general like Meagher might consider an inscribed gold medal no more than his just reward from his officers. As a captain, Lonergan would have been quite content with an engraved sword and accompanying belt, presented with a statement of admiration and respect bearing the names of the men in his company.*

AS SECOND IN COMMAND, responsibility for the presentation fell to Sinnott. In his prepared speech, the first lieutenant assured Lonergan that this duty was performed "with pleasure and with pride." The Rutland schoolteacher represented all members of the company in expressing "the high opinion they have of your gallantry and courage as a Soldier—the great respect they entertain for you as a man of upright integrity, and faithful and fearless attachment and devotion to what is *right and just*." [emphasis in the original] (Lonergan championing what is "right and just" may have referred to his work to free Ireland from British rule, perhaps reinforced by the recent dispute over mandatory attendance of religious services.) Everyone appreciated Lonergan's "endeavor to soften and mitigate the hardships of the camp, the march, and the bivouac," but above all his lieutenant praised him for having done "all in your power to make us good soldiers." When the new sword "flashes and gleams on the battlefield," Sinnott said, they would be secure in knowing that

---

* The Rutland newspaper in a brief article on May 19 described the gift of the Emmet Guards as "a splendid sword and belt...an evidence of their respect and esteem" for Lonergan. This presentation sword with engraved inscription remains in the possession of his descendants today.

the "trusted steel cannot be propelled by stouter arm, nerved by braver heart" than Lonergan's. The lieutenant concluded with a wish for his captain, "Long may you live to wear it."

The memorial document, which testified to the respect and affection of the Emmet Guards for their leader, includes the names of fifty-one men, and provides an overview of the company roster in early May of 1863. Both lieutenants, four of the five sergeants, all eight corporals, and thirty-four privates—plus the wagoner and the two musicians—are listed, probably everyone present in the Occoquan camp. The original first sergeant of the company, Alvin Henry, does not appear on the list; he may well have been in the hospital at the time, as his health had again declined during his service. On April 30, James B. Scully had taken over from Henry the duties of "orderly sergeant," whose position in the battle line is the right of the front rank.

Lonergan likely was wearing his new sword on May 11 when he attempted to take command of the 13th Vermont, an action that Sturtevant described as "quite an amusing episode at dress parade." When Randall temporarily left the camp, he put the new major, Boyton, in charge because the recently promoted lieutenant colonel, Munson, was absent on provost marshal duties. Lonergan announced that since Boyton had not yet received his commission as major of the regiment, the senior captain would, according to regulations, be in charge of the unit and the camp. The assertive Irishman's claim was supported by the commander of Co. C, Capt. Lewis L. Coburn, who "seemed quite willing to stand by Captain Lonergan in his contention."

At the regimental formation, both Boyton and Lonergan tried to take the commander's position on the parade ground and both began giving orders to Adjutant James S. Peck. When the adjutant refused to obey Lonergan's commands, the Irishman ordered him arrested and demanded his sword. Peck refused to surrender his symbol of authority and "after considerable sharp talk, and without proceeding further," Boyton resolved the "awkward situation" by dismissing the regiment. The companies, according to Sturtevant, "returned to their respective quarters considerably excited and disgusted with the foolish and boyish exhibition of Captain Lonergan, who sullenly returned to his tent loudly proclaiming his right to command."

When Randall returned to camp late in the evening, he ordered both

Lonergan and Coburn to be placed under arrest. The incident "made considerable excitement in camp and furnished food for talk and wise opinions for a number of days" until the whole matter was dropped after "some explanations and apologies." Put down as a difference of opinion on the interpretation of military regulation, everyone involved was "exonerated and restored to good standing" with harmony restored in the camp.

The long roll of the drum summoned the soldiers to assemble on May 14, when word came that Mosby's men had captured the regimental supply wagons on their way to Fairfax Station. Several companies were sent out to block the crossings on the Occoquan, but they arrived too late to take action against the rebels. As in the previous December, Lonergan had managed to get himself placed under arrest just at a time of contact with the enemy. Half a dozen men of the 13th Vermont were taken prisoner and treated by the rebels to a bareback ride of over thirty miles to Gainesville before being paroled and allowed to return to camp.

As the spring weather brought greater military activity, the 13th had crossed the river at times to probe the area south of the Occoquan in search of irregulars who might be supporting Mosby. The soldiers had a free hand to confiscate any war materials that they found and often extended the definition to include horses (and any other livestock that appeared to be rebel sympathizers). Randall sent Capt. Orcas B. Wilder and his Co. B over on the ferry to forage in rebel territory on May 15. Angry at the capture of his supply wagons the day before, the colonel told them to "take every dam[n] thing you can lay your hands on." Wilder returned with five work horses to replace those lost in the raid, plus a gray mare and a three-year old colt. Keeping the young horse for himself, Wilder diplomatically presented the mare to his colonel, who was quite pleased with the horse. Other officers, including Lonergan, had also supplied themselves with mounts while at the Occoquan camp, probably by the same method.

Bloodless raids like the capture of the supply wagons did not spoil the holiday mood that seemed to accompany the regiment's stay at the camp.* Fine weather prompted "quite a number of social gatherings, principally on account of the Vermont ladies in camp, and they were of course accorded due attention

---

* Regimental morning reports from this period are marked "Camp Carusi," rather than the bucolic "Widow Violet" name. The large tract of land where the 13th was camped was owned at the time by Augustus Carusi, but apparently that section was locally called "Widow Violet's farm."

CHAPTER THIRTEEN – CAMP LIFE

by our Colonel and his associate officers." A visit by Stannard on May 21 created the occasion for an evening dance given by the officers for their guest.

The report of a more serious raid on May 30—Mosby had used his mountain howitzer to attack a train at Catlett's Station that was guarded by men from the 15th Vermont—hardly dampened spirits down on the Occoquan. Upon learning that Mosby had pulled out of the brigade's area and back to the mountains, an even more relaxed atmosphere prevailed in the 13th. Basking in the warm June weather, the men counted down the few days remaining on their enlistments and sent packages of excess personal belongings home to Vermont. However, an unimaginable whirlwind of events was about to propel the regiment into mortal danger and finally give Lonergan his chance for glory.

LEE'S DECISION TO INVADE the north came after his careful consideration of the military and political situation facing the rebels. Vicksburg, the key to control of the Mississippi River, was under siege by Grant; its loss would sever the Confederacy in two. Rosecrans was operating in force against central Tennessee and Hooker threatened Richmond itself with his huge army. Union assaults on the coastal states and an increasingly effective blockade were tightening the federal stranglehold and no diplomatic support of the secessionists was forthcoming from the European countries. The North was, however, becoming weary with the war and its heavy losses. Perhaps another stunning victory, this time on Union territory, could persuade Washington to negotiate with the rebels.

Starved for manpower on every front, the Confederacy was falling victim to the terrible arithmetic that Lincoln had noted after Fredericksburg. Repulsing Hooker at Chancellorsville had cost the Army of Northern Virginia more men killed in action than it had the Army of the Potomac. Moreover, Jackson had been mortally wounded by his own pickets at a time when superior generalship was the South's greatest advantage. On May 15, Lee presented his plan in Richmond, insisting that the Union could not be allowed to seize the initiative. Lee's concept of a strategic offensive was quickly approved and he developed his plan for another thrust into Union territory. The goal was both to threaten Washington and to inflict another bloody defeat on the Army of the Potomac. If the Confederates selected a strong defensive position on Northern territory, Hooker might be forced into an attack similar to the disaster at Fredericksburg.

Lee restructured the army from two massive infantry corps into three less cumbersome units, each made up of three divisions. The First Corps would still be led by Longstreet, with Richard Ewell taking command of the Second Corps and A. P. Hill the Third Corps. Both new corps commanders were also promoted to lieutenant general. Stuart's cavalry division was reinforced to 12,400 troopers; Lee would march north on June 3 with a total of some 80,000 men.

Lee tried to concentrate his forces without alerting Hooker as to his intentions. He ordered Longstreet and Ewell to assemble their corps at Culpepper Court House while leaving Hill's Third Corps occupying the defenses of Fredericksburg. On June 4, however, Hooker became aware of the rebel movement up the Rappahannock. A probe of the Fredericksburg positions by the Sixth Corps sent the First Vermont Brigade over the river again.* The federal troops were repulsed and Lee's remaining corps also started on the march north.

HOOKER MET WITH HIS OWN national leadership in mid-May to discuss plans for the spring. Lincoln had summoned him to Washington on May 13 to discourage any resumption of offensive operations on the Rappahannock. Hooker had by now lost the President's confidence in his leadership. The crisis in the high command was further aggravated by an impending reduction in forces. Expiring enlistments would soon reduce the army by a third. Every day a thousand men were leaving camp for home, their loss marked by the departing soldiers' joyous shouts.

Hooker wanted to replace these losses by the reassignment of units such as the 8,600 men in the "movable force" of the Washington defenses that included the Second Vermont Brigade. Halleck insisted that no men could be spared from the capital area and blocked Hooker's request for the Harper's Ferry garrison as well. Lincoln continued to explore candidates for a new army commander, working his way through interviews with various corps commanders without finding a willing replacement.

---

* Some of the men in the attached 26th New Jersey Regiment reportedly refused to cross with the unit because their nine-month term of enlistment was too near expiration for them to risk their lives.

CHAPTER THIRTEEN – CAMP LIFE

STUART GATHERED HIS FIVE BRIGADES of cavalry and six batteries of horse artillery—the largest cavalry force ever seen in the Confederacy—around Brandy Station on the Orange and Alexandria Railroad.* His mission of screening the northward march of Lee's columns was to begin on June 9 and his cavalry units spread out to cross the Rappahannock at various fords simultaneously.

However, Pleasanton struck first with his 8,000 horsemen, reinforced with 3,000 infantry and four artillery batteries, catching the rebels by surprise at first light. Stuart beat back the uncoordinated Union attacks, but his move north had been delayed.

On June 10, Ewell's Second Corps led off the march as scheduled, through the Blue Ridge Mountains into the Shenandoah Valley. The First Corps under Longstreet was to stay east of those mountains to conceal the ultimate objective of the operation from Hooker. The Union general would be forced to move north as well, keeping his army between the rebels and Washington. Lee's Third Corps would march to the Shenandoah Valley once it had disengaged from contact with the Army of the Potomac. Within a week, Ewell had cleared the Shenandoah Valley of its Union garrisons and opened the way to the Potomac and beyond. His attached brigade of cavalry penetrated through Maryland and raided Chambersburg, Pennsylvania.

Pleasanton's cavalry probes were unable to determine the location of Lee's army, effectively screened by Stuart's horsemen, who held key passes into the Loudon Valley. However, enough information was gathered on the rebel deployments to give Hooker the confidence to issue orders on June 13 to pursue Lee, even though neither Longstreet at Culpepper nor Hill at Fredericksburg marched north until June 15.

The Army of the Potomac was split into two major columns, its headquarters traveling with the eastern wing made up of the Second, Sixth, and Twelfth Corps, along with the reserve artillery. The wing nearer the rebel forces—the First, Third, Fifth, and Eleventh Corps—initially followed the Orange and Alexandria Railroad. After first considering Maj. Gen. George G. Meade to command this wing, Hooker placed Maj. Gen. John F. Reynolds, commander of the First Corps, in charge of the column. Hard marching in the summer heat spread Union forces across northern Virginia until a halt was called on June

---

* The Second Vermont Brigade was guarding stations on the same rail line north of the river.

17 to sort out Lee's intentions. A series of cavalry clashes followed as each side attempted to determine the disposition of the other's forces.

With Lee on the offensive and his own army shrinking as enlistments expired, Hooker renewed his demands for reinforcements. His relations with Halleck, already troubled, turned poisonous as the general in chief repeatedly denied the requests for additional manpower. Warning Hooker on June 16 to respect his subordinate relationship to Halleck, the president finally intervened to order 15,000 men transferred from two departments. Two infantry brigades and the cavalry division from the Twenty-second Corps defending Washington were shifted to the field army. Stannard's Second Vermont Brigade, one of the two infantry units, received orders on June 23 to report to Reynolds' First Corps for assignment to his Third Division.

SOUNDS OF THE CAVALRY BATTLE at Brandy Station on June 9 had been plainly heard by the 15th Vermont stationed at Bristoe's and Catlett's Stations. Rumors of an impending move spread through the Second Vermont Brigade, reaching the 13th Vermont on June 10 where everyone expected to "be ready to fall in at the sound of the bugle." Even so, their regimental commander was among a group of about twenty-five brigade members who toured the Bull Run battlefield on June 13, with Randall providing commentary on his experiences there as a company commander.

By this time, the visitors to the Occoquan camp had likely been asked to leave in anticipation of the regiment's return to Vermont. Lonergan's wife took lodging in Washington, no doubt with other ladies from the camp who planned to meet their husbands there and travel north when the regiment was sent home. The ladies would suffer anxious days of worry about the fate of their loved ones before they were reunited.

Elements of Hooker's army were already appearing at the picket line manned by the Second Vermont Brigade; the Eleventh Corps bivouacked that night at Catlett's Station. A large number of escaping slaves also halted at the camp, thinking themselves safely within the Union lines. However, the four companies of the 15th at that post were advised by Brig. Gen. John Buford, whose cavalry division made up the rear guard of the Union column, to move north immediately to avoid capture. All federal forces in the area were giving up their positions to pursue Lee, so the Vermonters retreated to

CHAPTER THIRTEEN – CAMP LIFE

join the rest of their regiment at Bristoe's Station that night. The headquarters of the cavalry corps was at Union Mills Station on June 15, where Pleasanton accepted Stannard's invitation to dinner that night.

At the same time, the eastern wing of the Army of the Potomac was also crossing the line guarded by the Second Vermont Brigade. All the roads from Fredericksburg between the Potomac River and Manassas Junction were crowded with troops raising clouds of dust by day and lighting the night sky with their campfires. The 13th Vermont helped to construct a pontoon bridge over the broad stretch of the Occoquan at the village near their camp on June 14. The Twelfth Corps took several days to cross this bridge while the Sixth Corps passed over the river at Wolf Run Shoals. After fording the Occoquan, the First Vermont Brigade bivouacked at Fairfax Station on June 15, giving some members of the newer Vermont brigade a chance to visit with friends. The 13th was busy breaking down their camp at this time, sending the big "A" tents to Alexandria and preparing to march north. Hooker established his headquarters at Fairfax Station on June 16 (where he was visited by Secretary of the Treasury Chase, his sole proponent in the Lincoln cabinet).

LEE HAD TO DECIDE HOW to employ Stuart's remaining three brigades of cavalry; two brigades were already guarding key mountain passes and raiding to the north. He could bring the horsemen along with the main Confederate columns or allow them to roam more widely in another ride around the Union forces. Mosby assured Stuart that the gaps between the Union corps would make it easy to cross their line of march and swing north to guard Ewell's right flank in Pennsylvania. Lee therefore was satisfied to issue Stuart a vague directive on June 23 giving him the discretion of crossing the Potomac with the main body at Shepardstown or passing in the rear of Hooker's forces to enter Maryland east of them.

In the saddle by 1:00 AM on June 25, Stuart found that Mosby had been too optimistic about taking a large force of cavalry across the Union line of movement because infantry columns blocked the way. Even swinging his route further south, Stuart encountered units of the Second Corps and he failed to blast a way through them with his horse artillery. Although it put even more distance between his 5,000 troopers and Lee's columns, Stuart had to continue probing to the south and east, where he found the roads full of marching federal soldiers. In frustration, he spent the night in the Bull Run Mountains until finally making his way around Hooker's rear guard in the afternoon of June 26.

THE ASSIGNMENT OF STANNARD's brigade to the field army involved a demanding mission: the Vermonters were required to maintain their picket line until after the passage of Hooker's great army and then fall in with the cavalry screen as the rear guard. Moreover, their inclusion in Reynolds' First Corps, now in the vanguard of the western column, required that the brigade make up two days' marching to join his Third Division.* A final Sunday inspection of the 13th was held in their camp on June 19 and four days later, when the Army of the Potomac had moved through the Occoquan crossing points, the regiment received orders to prepare to march on June 25.

The last "Consolidated Morning Report" form submitted by the Adjutant of the "13th Vermont Volunteer Militia" Regiment was filled out at Camp Carusi, Virginia, on June 25. It shows thirty-two commissioned officers and 726 enlisted men present for duty, out of a total of 843 on the muster roll. Although the regiment had yet to lose anyone in combat, deaths from disease and accident, men in hospital, desertions, discharges for disability, and those on detached service had thinned the ranks. The average company formed up with a total of about seventy men. Lonergan's Emmet Guards reported three officers and sixty-eight enlisted men present, with one non-commissioned officer (probably the ailing former first sergeant Henry) carried absent as "Sick." The 13th was representative of the number of men on duty in Stannard's five regiments; the brigade would add over 3,500 men to Hooker's force. Compared with the few hundred still serving with the Irish Brigade, this was a huge unit and Stannard's troops would later be mistaken for an entire division, the Vermont regiments thought to be brigades.

The men were told to carry six days' rations, even though the haversacks could hold only enough for four days and the extra food had to be stuffed into their knapsacks. Knowing that hard marching lay ahead, most men got rid of anything not essential. Inspections ensured that they took the road with knapsack and haversack, canteen and cup, musket and forty rounds of ammunition, fly tent and blankets (rubber and woolen), along with the

---

* Until the Second Vermont Brigade was added, Brig. Gen. Thomas A. Rowley had only two brigades in his division, both made up of Pennsylvania regiments.

CHAPTER THIRTEEN – CAMP LIFE

bayonet, cartridge box, and cap box on their belts. Individuals might also choose to carry an extra shirt and pair of socks, needle and thread, letter paper, testament, and photos.

Some men, "the homesick and anxious," persisted in believing that the march would take them only to Washington and loaded themselves down with overcoats, woolen blankets, and other items that would be useful back in Vermont. The line of march all the way to Edwards Ferry over the Potomac would be strewn with clothing, bedding, and cooking utensils, as men rid themselves of everything except what they needed to survive and to fight.

Union Mills had been designated by the brigade commander as the assembly point for the five regiments. On June 25, the 12th and the 14th stepped out at 7:00 AM from Wolf Run Shoals and reached the station in two hours, joining the 15th and 16th already camped there. The 13th also made an early start from camp, heading a few miles up the road toward Fairfax Station and then turning onto a road parallel to the Occoquan River that led directly to Union Mills. With twenty miles to travel from their camp on the Occoquan, the 13th did not catch up to the rest of the brigade until 2:00 PM. Given an hour to rest while the company commanders made a final check of the men and equipment, the entire brigade marched away from the station at 3:00 PM, the last federal infantry to leave the area. Soon after the 13th marched westward along the river, Stuart discovered that the Union foot soldiers had abandoned the line and within a few hours brought his entire cavalry force splashing across Wolf Run Shoals. Finally headed north to join Lee's forces in Pennsylvania, he swept on through Fairfax Court House, scooping up small detachments of Union troops on his way to cross the Potomac near Rockville, Maryland.

It had been a close call for Lonergan and the rest of the 13th Vermont. Any later start for Union Mills might well have seen the regiment cut off and captured by Stuart. The Vermonters' continued presence on the Occoquan had helped delay his cavalry, who would be out of contact with the other rebel forces during the next crucial week. Stuart's absence would deprive Lee of urgently needed intelligence on the Union forces as the two armies moved north.

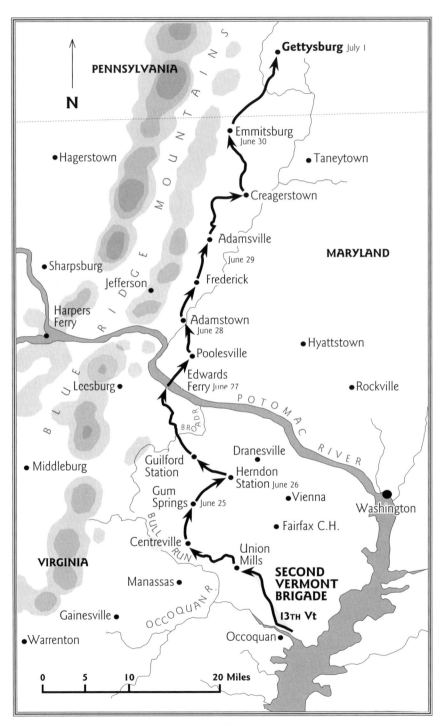

March to Gettysburg

CHAPTER FOURTEEN

FORCED MARCH

THE 13TH VERMONT REGIMENT was the last unit to abandon the Union lines on the outer defenses of Washington. With the other regiments of the Second Vermont Brigade, they now found themselves in the rear of the Army of the Potomac as it moved north to stay between Lee's army and the capital. The five Vermont infantry regiments had been placed in an isolated and vulnerable position in hostile territory. Behind them, only a screen of federal cavalry units followed the army's supply trains to ward off Confederate raiders and to collect stragglers in the area.

Late on June 25, the brigade finished a march of eight miles in steady rain from Union Mills and bivouacked just beyond Centreville, finally camping in safety alongside units of the Sixth Corps. Starting from the Occoquan camp, Lonergan's "Irish Company" and the rest of the 13th Vermont had covered nearly thirty miles that day. The evening meal from their haversacks was a choice between "boiled pork and hard tack, or hard tack and boiled pork." The exhausted soldiers stretched out on the muddy ground in pairs with a rubber blanket below them and another above, too tired to erect the shelter tents they carried.

In the final weeks of their enlistments, after months of defensive picket duty, these Vermonters were finally taking a more active military role. The veteran First Vermont Brigade had earned a reputation for bravery in a number of battles, but the short-term regiments could not expect to add much to their state's laurels in the little time they had left to serve.

However, their immediate challenge was to report as assigned to the First Corps, far in advance at the head of the Army of the Potomac. On June 25, the vanguard of the First Corps was already crossing the Potomac River at Edwards Ferry, fifty miles to the north. Reynolds' units were a full two days' march ahead of the Second Vermont Brigade, yet Stannard was determined to catch up with them as ordered.

After a wet night and a cold morning meal that offered the same choices as that of the night before, the troops fell in at the bugle call and were ready to resume the march at 6:00 AM. The heavy rain had affected the condition of the roads causing widespread delays in movement. An impatient Stannard was forced to wait while the Sixth Corps, the largest corps in the Army of the Potomac, preceded his brigade. Sedgwick's infantry marched out by regiment and brigade—including the First Vermont Brigade—along with artillery, ambulances, supply wagons, and other traffic, churning the muddy roads into a morass that grabbed at the soldiers' feet.

Stannard would have to drive his troops hard to close the distance to the First Corps and the marching was made even more difficult by their position at the rear of the long federal columns. The Second Vermont Brigade was essentially orphaned on the march, separated from their parent corps and apparently not given any priority in the detailed staff work of the higher headquarters that assigned march routes and supply points.

A number of men in the brigade, eager to travel home with their comrades, had left the regimental hospitals to join their units on the march. The extreme demands of the next six days would see many of them fall out along the way, unable to keep up the rapid pace. A widespread lack of serviceable footgear also plagued a number of the Vermonters. The nine months of picket duty, camp life, and frequent marching had worn out the shoes of most of the Second Vermont Brigade, but the quartermaster had failed to provide replacement shoes for troops so close to mustering out. By the end of the forced march, many of the footsore men were almost barefoot.

Each company had its own wagon to carry supplies of food and ammunition, along with some essential equipment. Otherwise, every man carried his own belongings and the basic necessities of soldiering. Men faltering along the way might be assisted by their messmates or even carried for a while on the supply wagons or the regimental ambulances. At the brigade level, even more supply wagons and ambulances accompanied the columns; these could also be pressed into service to carry stragglers.

Many officers had supplied themselves with horses, a benefit for mobility and effective command in the field, and the march was thus less demanding on their physical stamina. Their responsibilities during the movements and

CHAPTER FOURTEEN – FORCED MARCH

in camp, however, reduced their opportunities for rest. While a private might trudge along resenting the captain on his horse, the officers with their myriad duties had less chance for unbroken sleep at night.

On the second day of the brigade's march, the pace of these units in the rear was slowed by the need to guard against any raids on the vulnerable wagon trains by Stuart's cavalry, reportedly operating off the right flank of the columns. The route passed Aldie, Virginia, where Confederate and Union forces had clashed in "a sharp cavalry fight only a few days before." Rebel horsemen did scout out the moving troops, but made no attacks on the watchful units. The Vermonters reached Herndon Station near the Alexandria-Leesburg pike without incident and camped there for the night, posting guards for security as always.

Pushing hard to join up with their new superior unit, the brigade was on the march at daylight on June 27 to reach the double pontoon bridges that spanned the Potomac at Edwards Ferry. Moving along the Alexandria and Loudon railroad line, at Guilford Station the brigade first "struck the line of march of the First Corps," which had been there two days previously and "was now a day's march into Maryland." That afternoon, Stannard's men crossed the Potomac and found a suitable campground one mile beyond the bridge.

They again were bivouacked near Sixth Corps units, among them the First Vermont Brigade, but after the hard day's marching few men had the energy left for visiting with the other Vermonters. In three days, Stannard's brigade had covered fifty miles—and Randall's regiment closer to sixty—in both driving rain and summer heat. By now the soldiers had thrown away everything that they could and were carrying "only what was strictly necessary" under what they called "light marching orders," when non-essentials were normally left in camp. Benedict reported that the hard marching caused men to discard "knapsacks and blankets by hundreds" on this part of the route.

Some of Stannard's men had been doubtful that they would be sent off to battle so close to discharge, thinking they would instead be ordered "to Washington to do guard duty for a few days and then go home to Vermont." Headed north with the Army of the Potomac, even the most optimistic soldiers now realized that their final days of service would be spent in the field.

Although June 28 was a Sunday, there was no change in the routine. Sturtevant observed "if not a sin to shoot and kill our fellowmen on Sunday, it could not be a sin to march and overtake if possible the enemy." The brigade

LONERGAN'S CANTEEN WITH NAME AND UNIT SCRATCHED ON THE SURFACE

continued north, just east of the Potomac River, passing through Poolesville in the early morning and then crossing the Monocacy River at Greenfield Mills.

In fording the "turbulent and now muddy waters of the Monocacy," Lonergan fell off his horse into the river. He received no serious injury, "simply a needed bath and nothing more," and dealt with the incident in good humor. The Irishman remarked on reaching the far shore, "Too much liquid on the outside, and not enough on the inside, or it would not have happened." His expressed preference for liquid "on the inside" was no doubt a desire for something stronger than water.

After crossing the Monocacy, the brigade stopped for its meager noon meal before proceeding on. The break gave Lonergan at least a chance to pour the water out of his boots, if not dry out completely from his soaking. Lonergan and other line officers who had been able to secure mounts for the campaign shared them as circumstances allowed, marching with their soldiers while an enlisted man rode. This gave "many a tired soldier a ride and rest for a few miles," men who otherwise might have dropped out and been left behind on the forced march north. Arriving in the late afternoon of June 28 at Adamstown, located on the Baltimore and Ohio rail line, the Vermonters camped two miles beyond the village.

The contrast between prosperous Maryland and the war-torn territory of northern Virginia had been immediately apparent. Availability of local food

CHAPTER FOURTEEN — FORCED MARCH

brought a welcome change to the unvaried menu of hardtack and pork, staples that were running low as the fast-marching troops outpaced their wagon train. Maryland was a slave-holding state of divided loyalties and had supplied men to both sides of the war. The enterprising local residents were likewise willing to sell their wares to each side in turn as they passed through. Reduced to short rations—some of their cracker boxes were dated 1860 and contained "marching hard tack" crawling with weevils—the hungry soldiers of the 13th Vermont did not object to the inflated prices. Paid off with greenbacks before leaving the Occoquan, the men happily exchanged them for bread, cheese, milk, and pies, commenting with hard Yankee logic "no use to save our money; may be killed to-morrow."

WHEN THE REBEL SOLDIERS in Lee's army passed through the state a few days before, they had behaved well toward the residents of Maryland, not wishing to alienate those who sympathized with their cause. After they crossed the Mason-Dixon Line into Pennsylvania, however, they entered unambiguously hostile territory. Lee issued orders forbidding his army from simply plundering the rich towns and farms, offering instead worthless payment in Confederate money. In addition, tribute was levied from communities under threat of destruction and any black person might be seized and sent south as an escaped slave, regardless of individual history.

Far-ranging cavalry, including irregulars like Mosby's troopers, and columns of rebel infantry sowed widespread panic from the time the Confederates entered the northern state. While the countryside was being stripped of anything useful to the rebel army, the major towns of eastern Pennsylvania, particularly the capital city of Harrisburg, also felt threatened. The War Department ordered the Army of the Potomac to protect these towns, in addition to Baltimore and Washington.

Lee's strategy had succeeded in drawing the Army of the Potomac away from Richmond. His deployments in Pennsylvania did not reveal any specific geographic objective for his campaign. The main intention was not to seize a city, especially one as well defended as the nation's capital. Instead, by forcing Hooker to pursue the Army of Northern Virginia, Lee sought a resounding victory in the North that would have political consequences. Another bloody defeat like Fredericksburg might result in war-weary Yankees demanding that Lincoln seek terms with the South.

On June 28—the Sunday when Lonergan tumbled off his horse into the Monocacy—two of Lee's three large corps occupied the Chambersburg area of southwestern Pennsylvania behind South Mountain. Ewell's corps, the advance element of the army, had continued to the northeast to move on Harrisburg, with one of his divisions sent to York to sever transportation lines. Lee planned to deploy his army east, with Longstreet's corps supporting the attack on the state capital and Hill's corps directed toward York. Stuart's cavalry should have been supplying information on the disposition of the federal forces, but he had not been in touch for almost a week. Lee assumed that the Army of the Potomac remained south of its namesake river, the last position reported to him, and that he had a free hand in Pennsylvania.

That evening, a spy working for Longstreet was brought to the Chambersburg headquarters by the provost guard. Lee was startled to learn that Hooker had all his forces well up into Maryland and concentrated in the Frederick area. Striking north from there, they could sever Confederate columns strung out from west to east across Pennsylvania. The rebel commander immediately recalled Ewell's corps and cancelled the planned march east by the other two corps. Lee was anxious to bring his forces back together under his control at a location offering good defensive ground. The point of rendezvous would be the small town where a number of roads connected—Gettysburg.

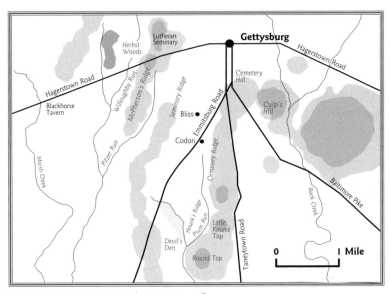

APPROACH TO GETTYSBURG

CHAPTER FOURTEEN – FORCED MARCH

An important change also took place in the Army of the Potomac that Sunday. Hooker was replaced by Meade, the Fifth Corps commander. Disputes with Halleck over control of the garrison at Harper's Ferry, which Hooker wanted to block Lee's return to the south, had culminated in Hooker's resignation. Lincoln was doubtful of Hooker's performance after the defeat at Chancellorsville and accepted the resignation, promptly appointing a successor. Meade was thrust into command of the army on the brink of its engagement with the rebel forces. Before June 28 ended, the new commander issued orders: His forces were to start northward at 4:00 AM the next day, moving toward the Emmitsburg-Taneytown line just below the Pennsylvania border, on routes that would converge at Gettysburg.

Steady rain lasting all of June 29 soaked the Second Vermont Brigade as they made their way up muddy roads to Frederick, where they halted at noon for three hours to get supplies. There were rebel sympathizers in the city, so officers of the line were held accountable for the conduct of their men to avoid any incidents. As the brigade took its well-earned rest, word spread through the ranks that Meade, a figure not well known to them, was now in command of the army.

Lonergan and the other company commanders would have been less concerned about the head of the army than about the feet of their men. The worn-out shoes had resulted in most of the soldiers marching with blistered and bleeding feet. An inspection of their condition removed the worst cases from the ranks. The brigade left some ninety disabled soldiers behind at Frederick and moved on to bivouac at Creagerstown. Just outside Frederick, Hooker and his entourage rode past the brigade, the dismissed general looking "downcast and sad."

The footsore men left behind at Frederick would not have been able to complete the difficult trek over muddy roads that the brigade undertook on June 30, in order to reach Emmitsburg, two miles south of the Pennsylvania border. By forced marches, they had effectively caught up with the First Corps and Stannard sent Benedict—appointed as the general's aide in March, soon after receiving his commission—ahead to announce the brigade's approach. The lieutenant found Reynolds resting in the corps headquarters at Moritz

Tavern, near his divisions, which were camped half a dozen miles south of Gettysburg. Benedict carried back Reynolds' instructions for Stannard to join the corps as soon as possible, "for he was likely to need all the men he could get."

Reynolds also sent along his compliments to the Vermonters for having marched well.* Reynolds had driven his First Corps hard, at one point marching them thirty-six miles through Maryland in just over twenty-two hours, with a two-hour stop in Frederick. (Hancock had pushed his Second Corps thirty-two miles in eighteen hours on June 29, but Maj. Gen. Daniel E. Sickles was chastised by Meade for moving his Third Corps only twelve miles on the same day.)

Despite the summer heat, orders had been issued that no one was to break ranks on the march to stop for water. Units were to be held together with no stragglers, even though the wool-clad soldiers were tormented by thirst. Regiments rotated in the order of march within the brigade and on June 30 the 16th Vermont led the way with the 13th in the rear. From the viewpoint of the trailing regiment, it seemed that the pace was unusually fast and the inevitable contractions of the column forced the 13th to move frequently at the "double-quick" to keep the ranks closed up. Lonergan and the other line officers could see up close that their men were suffering from the pace and a lack of water to relieve their parched throats.

After repeatedly seeking and being denied permission to provide his men with water, 1st Lt. Stephen F. Brown of Co. K, 13th Vermont, took a private from his unit with all the empty canteens that they could carry and started for a nearby spring. The "mounted safe guard" there refused him access, citing the standing order against his action. Providing them with his name and unit, Brown and his helper then filled all the canteens as the guard rode off to report him. Upon returning to Co. K, the two men were hailed with thanks by the thirsty soldiers, but Brown was placed under arrest for his insubordination and relieved of his sword. However, he continued to march with his company.

Unlike the two previous occasions when the Second Vermont Brigade had prepared for battle with the rebels, this time Lonergan managed to avoid being put under arrest on the eve of action. Perhaps he and his men were on their best behavior given the serious situation at hand, or possibly they had become more skillful at not being caught when infractions were

---

* The hard marching during their brief assignment to the army was a source of justifiable pride for Stannard's Vermonters. The Pennsylvania Reserves had been transferred from the Twenty-second Corps to the Army of the Potomac at the same time as the Second Vermont Brigade, but were reported by Meade as not able to keep up with the army. (In the end, however, these veteran Pennsylvania units would arrive in time for the battle.)

CHAPTER FOURTEEN – FORCED MARCH

committed. With less than two weeks remaining in their term of service, everyone in the 13th Vermont, part of the huge army streaming north, must have sensed an impending battle.

For Lonergan, there may have been a particular sense of his personal destiny approaching. After all his efforts to form an Irish company and have his Fenians tempered by battle, the time was at hand. Marching into Emmitsburg past Mount St. Mary's—the Roman Catholic college with its church on the hillside of Carrick's Knob—and then by St. Joseph's Church in town, his eyes would have been drawn to the symbols of his faith, built by his fellow countrymen. A chance to make confession and attend Mass before battle would have been a great comfort, yet no time could be spared. His marching soldiers would have to be content with the blessings being given by the priests who had stationed themselves at the side of the road.

Perhaps Lonergan could take it as a good omen that the last night before the Emmet Guards went into battle would be spent at Emmitsburg.* For him, the slanting rays of the sun setting behind the hill called Carrick's Knob might have evoked the Fenian sunburst, the Slievenamon mountain of his boyhood, and *Tir na nOg*. Irishmen under Lonergan's command might soon discover whether there was, in fact, a Land of Eternal Youth as the legends said or the Heaven promised by the church. Their captain would do everything in his power to keep his Fenians alive to fight for Ireland's freedom, but they could not shirk their duty now.

BEFORE HE WAS REMOVED from command, Hooker had sent cavalry north into Pennsylvania looking for Lee's forces. About 11:00 AM on June 30, Buford passed through the town of Gettysburg with two brigades of his division to scout for rebel units reported to the west. A brigade of Confederate infantry was discovered moving on the town, perhaps in hopes of collecting the stock of badly-needed shoes reported to be there. Upon spotting the federal cavalry, the rebels withdrew, in accordance with their orders not to precipitate a general battle. Lee wanted to avoid a fight until his forces were concentrated and he could pick good defensive ground.

---

* Founded in 1785 by Samuel Emmit, who was of Irish origin, and settled primarily by Irish, German, Scots, and English. (Both "Emmit" and "Emmet" spellings of the surname are common.) The mountain land above the town had been purchased by Daniel Carrick, who gave it his name.

At his headquarters in Taneytown, Maryland, Meade was also looking to gain the tactical advantage; he had distributed a circular to his corps describing his plan to establish a line of defense at nearby Pipe Creek. However, the commanders of both armies were now overtaken by events. Meade's instructions regarding the defensive line were immediately superseded by his orders on June 30, which moved his forces toward Gettysburg.

Late in the evening, Meade's headquarters received Buford's report of contact with the Confederate forces and that night the army commander sent orders for Reynolds to move his forces forward to support the cavalry. When a much stronger rebel force marched down the Cashtown road early on July 1, the Union cavalry fought a dismounted delaying action until Reynolds could bring up his units. Expanding conflict northwest of the town forced Lee to accept battle at Gettysburg.

Reynolds' First Corps divisions were led by Brig. Gen. James S. Wadsworth, Brig. Gen. John C. Robinson, and Maj. Gen. Abner Doubleday, each division containing only two brigades until Stannard's brigade was assigned.* The inclusion of Stannard's men would constitute a significant increase in the firepower of the Third Division and a welcome addition in battle. As well as his own First Corps—the leading element of the Army of the Potomac—Reynolds was also in command of the army's left wing, which included Sickles's Third Corps and Maj. Gen. Oliver O. Howard's Eleventh Corps.

Reynolds had received his instructions at 4:00 AM on July 1 and acted swiftly to implement them. Forgoing the usual daily rotation of units in the order of march, he kept Wadsworth's division, camped at the most advanced position, in the lead of the corps. As left wing commander, Reynolds now turned direct command of the First Corps over to Doubleday, who was the senior division commander in the corps. Brig. Gen Thomas A. Rowley took command of the Third Division, to which Stannard's brigade would report. Reynolds ordered the Eleventh Corps to follow the First, and the Third Corps was also directed to move up through Emmitsburg.

Just when Stannard had caught up with Reynolds, the entire First Corps rushed forward before the Second Vermont Brigade could join its designated division. Reynolds accompanied Wadsworth's division toward Gettysburg

---

* The recent departure of nine-months and two-year regiments had greatly reduced the numbers in the Army of the Potomac. In the First and Second Divisions of the First Corps, five regiments made up each brigade. The Third Division had only four regiments in its First Brigade and in the Second Brigade just three regiments (though each of the three had more men than average for the depleted regiments of the corps).

CHAPTER FOURTEEN – FORCED MARCH

and then rode ahead to confer with Buford. To assist the hard-pressed cavalry troopers, the leading brigade of Wadsworth's division was deployed into action straight from the march. Reynolds was directing the next unit in the column, the famous Iron Brigade, forward on McPherson's Ridge when he was killed instantly by a rifle ball in the neck.

Command passed to Doubleday, the senior officer on the field, as the rebels were stalled in their assault. In a mid-day lull in the bloody fighting, the other two divisions of the First Corps arrived on the ridge, followed by the Eleventh Corps. The Second Vermont Brigade was not able to join the First Corps before Reynolds moved it forward that morning, and so was not among the units that suffered heavy losses when thrown against the overwhelming rebel forces. The Vermonters had been delayed in Emmitsburg and, after so much hard marching, were frustrated in closing the final gap with the First Corps.

Stannard had made every effort to deliver his brigade to the First Corps as ordered and had it ready to march from Emmitsburg early on July 1, but he was unable to find space on the crowded roads. As the "cloudy and gloomy" morning progressed, the Vermonters were forced to watch as every "road was filled with a moving mass of soldiers occupying every available avenue, path and field over which an army could march." Separated from their parent First Corps, the brigade anxiously waited for Sickle's Third Corps to pass by and give them the opportunity to move. Stannard had made known his instructions from Reynolds to join the First Corps as soon as possible, but it was not until mid-morning that the brigade found an opening to begin their march. The 13th Vermont was placed in the lead of the brigade that day and "with spirited and elastic step moved rapidly [and] courageously forward with ranks all well closed up and every soldier in his place," according to Sturtevant.

Based on Benedict's report the previous evening, Stannard expected to meet up with the First Corps at their Marsh Creek camp about eight miles away. The brigade "hastened along for two hours and about noon arrived where the First corps [sic] had camped for the night." Although the fires were still smoldering in the camp, it was empty except for the corps wagon trains and the rear area personnel left behind that morning.

The brigade was ordered to leave two regiments to guard these wagon trains and to bring the remaining three to Gettysburg as quickly as they could march. Stannard selected his two smallest regiments, the 12th and the 15th, to stay behind on guard duty. As instructed, he put the 13th, 14th, and 16th on the route to the northwest followed earlier by the Third Division. This roundabout path avoided entanglement with other units on the march, but covered more distance.

The Second Vermont Brigade was on the left flank of the army, still hurrying to close up with the elusive First Corps. As the column "reached the crest of a considerable hill" early in the afternoon, Stannard halted it when a courier appeared on a foam-flecked and weary horse. Doubleday's aide, seeking out the brigade commander, delivered the message that Reynolds had been killed, Doubleday was now in command, and there was "a big fight in progress at Gettysburg." The aide directed Stannard to make haste to join the battle and returned to report the approach of the Vermonters. The general passed the word down through the three regiments to move forward as fast as possible, keeping the ranks well closed up, and he rode conspicuously up and down the column to urge the men on.

The 13th led the column even faster than before "over hill and through valley," often in mud over their worn-out shoes, until they reached an elevated plain about four miles from Gettysburg. Panting from the exertion, the brigade stopped involuntarily as "the sound of cannon rolled down the valley" and they could see clouds of smoke rising in the distance. Lonergan and his company, probably setting the pace for the column at the head of the 13th, would have had the clearest view of the crucible of fire that awaited them.

Approaching Gettysburg from the southwest, Stannard moved his men across Marsh Creek and Willoughby Run to reach the Emmitsburg Road, where they came upon Buford's cavalry. These horsemen were now protecting the left flank of the retreating Union forces, which had made their way back through Gettysburg to rally on Cemetery Hill south of the town. The Vermonters crossed the valley of Plum Run and ascended Cemetery Ridge, passing hundreds of wounded men streaming back from the battlefield. From the ridge, the men had a clear view of the valley and Seminary Ridge to the west, as well as of the hills and plains to the north and northwest.

Benedict was dispatched to find Doubleday and report the arrival of the brigade. He soon returned with orders to join the corps in the defensive lines being established and the exhausted men took up a "position on the southwest front of Cemetery Hill just west of the Taneytown road." The federal forces on the hill, most of them badly battered in the day's fighting, occupied a horseshoe curving around Culp's Hill and Cemetery Hill with Howard's Eleventh Corps in the middle and First Corps divisions on each flank. Various commanders competed in their claims on the Second Vermont Brigade and the three regiments were shifted back and forth on the hillsides. In reaction to this additional marching about, Sturtevant recorded that "General Stannard swore like a piper and Colonel Randall filled the air with his accustomed and peculiar dialect."

The Vermonters, "completely worn out with seven long days of marching, especially the hurried march to reach the battlefield," were finally allowed to stretch out in a wheat field, but told to rest "with straps and belts all on and gun in hand." Although himself fatigued, Stannard had no opportunity for rest; he was appointed "General Field Officer of the Day" and made responsible for overseeing the placement of pickets, including some 200 men from the 16th Vermont.

Deprived of water for most of the day, as frequently happened on the march north, half a dozen men from each company were detailed to search for a spring or stream. Finding a small brook in the woods, the men returned with full canteens for their comrades. Few had any food left in their haversacks and no wagon train of supplies was anywhere to be found. Despite the lack of rations, "the opportunity to lay down gun and knapsack even on a battlefield in sight of the dead and hearing of the wounded" offered a welcome respite. A rubber blanket spread on the ground and the shelter half as a covering against the dew were sufficient under the conditions.

The night was "perfect, a gentle breeze from the south, clear and warm," with enough light from moon and stars to guide the placement of cannon for the certain renewal of the fighting when daylight returned. Writing decades later, Sturtevant remembered that many men, although bone-tired, "could not sleep, but thought intensely concerning the consequences of the coming day." After seeing to the needs of the men as best they could, the three officers of the "Irish Company" would also have been left to their thoughts on the eve of battle. Lonergan might well have gazed off into the darkness, full of looming danger, wondering how the Emmet Guards would perform in combat and whether he would ever see Roseanna again.

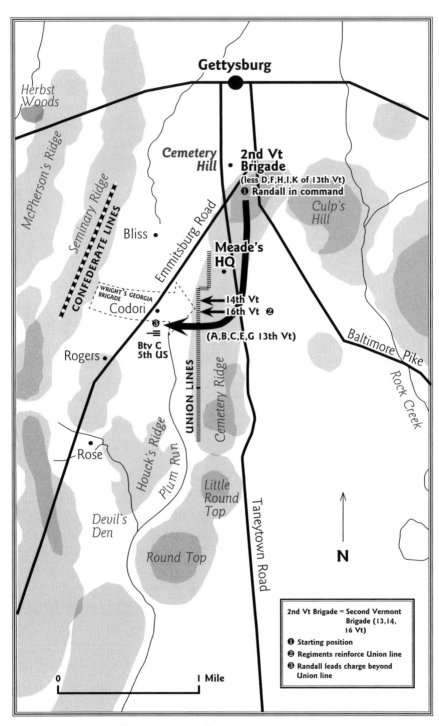

Deployments on July 2nd, late afternoon

CHAPTER FIFTEEN

INTO BATTLE

DAYBREAK ON CEMETERY HILL showed John Lonergan that his ambition to lead men in battle would likely be fulfilled that day. At first light, Sturtevant would recall, the "whole army was astir," while the entire 13th Vermont "seemed to have taken a standing position simultaneously as if by military orders." After the night of uneasy rest in the wheat field, the men found "no drum or bugle necessary" to rouse them. Everyone was anxious to examine the situation, half expecting to see "lines of gray with fluttering banners and glistening bayonets charging across the valley." Instead, the Vermonters were reassured to find Union soldiers occupying not only Cemetery Hill itself, but also Cemetery Ridge, which extended southward. The horseshoe of Union positions was now shaped more like a fishhook, with Cemetery Ridge as its shaft. From the Union position, a "solid line of cannon more than a mile in length" pointed across the valley at Seminary Ridge and the rebel forces hidden there.

Reports of the fighting on July 1 had convinced Meade to concentrate the Army of the Potomac at Gettysburg and more of his units had arrived throughout the night. Too late for the first day's fighting, the Second Vermont Brigade instead helped reinforce the surviving First and Eleventh Corps forces on Cemetery Hill, where the Union troops had rallied. Meade shifted his headquarters from Taneytown to the battlefield, coming on the scene with his staff about midnight. Stannard spent a sleepless night watching over the front lines as general officer of the day. Around 3:00 AM on July 2, he encountered Meade on horseback, personally reviewing the disposition of his army.

After conflicting orders sent them marching and counter-marching for an hour on Cemetery Hill, most of Stannard's brigade had finally been allowed to rest for the night. However, 200 men of the 16th Vermont had been detailed as skirmishers to relieve Buford's cavalrymen in front of the left wing. At first light, the detached Vermonters were in turn replaced by troops from Sickle's Third Corps, which occupied Cemetery Ridge.

That morning the quartermaster of the 14th Vermont, on his own initiative, brought four wagons of rations forward for the hungry men. He was halted by pickets on the Emmitsburg Road, who prevented him from blundering into the Confederate lines with the badly needed food and redirected him to the brigade's position on Cemetery Hill. As welcome as the food was, it was not adequate to supply the Vermont contingent and many of the men remained unfed.

When the 15th Vermont rejoined the brigade early on July 2, Stannard was surprised to find that four of his five regiments were on the battlefield. Sickles had come upon the two Vermont regiments guarding the First Corps wagon train some five miles from Gettysburg. He later described this as "a duty those splendid soldiers did not much relish" and he took the responsibility of ordering the larger of the regiments to join his Third Corps column. A head count of each regiment, whose accuracy was disputed by the disappointed 12th Vermont, determined that the 15th was slightly larger. The 15th accordingly fell in to march with Birney's Division and spent the night alongside it on Cemetery Ridge.

When Col. Redfield Proctor, commander of the 15th, reported his presence to brigade headquarters on July 2, Stannard requested permission for his errant regiment to remain on the battlefield, but the request was denied. Sickles' interference, resented at the First Corps headquarters, was countermanded by orders from the Third Division sending the 15th back to the rear.* Both the 12th and 15th Vermont remained on guard duty with the corps trains during the ensuing battle.

During the morning, the Second Vermont Brigade finally joined up with their designated division, taking their place among soldiers wearing the round blue identification patch of the Third Division, First Corps. At that time, the division was being held in reserve on the back slope of Cemetery Hill, a little east of the Taneytown Road. The men kept busy drying out cartridges dampened by rain and picking lice from their clothes, as they stretched out in the sun "awaiting events."

---

* Proctor attempted to return by the same route covered the night before, but he was also warned away from Emmitsburg Road by pickets. Sickles had decided to move his corps forward from the battle line to occupy ground about to be attacked by Longstreet's corps. Guided by a local civilian, the 15th was passing over the ridge between the Round Tops as a fierce cannonade marked the opening of a bloody day on the federal left.

CHAPTER FIFTEEN - INTO BATTLE

DURING THIS LULL IN ACTIVITY, Lonergan may have found a moment to muse about the similarity of his situation to that of another July day, fifteen years before, on a mountain in Ireland. Likewise dedicated to a higher purpose, a crowd in the tens of thousands had come together atop Slievenamon at a crucial time in their struggle, willing to fight for a just cause, surrounded below by men of property seeking to keep a people in virtual slavery. While the Young Irelanders, lacking any military skills, had failed utterly in their uprising of 1848, a new generation of Irish nationalists such as himself had been organized by the best of the earlier leaders—including Meagher, O'Mahony, and Doheny—and were taking up the sword to preserve the Union in America. At a terrible cost, Fenian forces like the Irish Brigade were learning the art of war; afterwards they would not shrink from spilling blood for Irish freedom.

Inside Lonergan's stained and dirty blue uniform frock coat, tidy stitching outlined the Fenian symbols of uncrowned harp and sunburst. The needlework most probably had been done by his wife, Roseanna, presently waiting for him in Washington. Although Lonergan no doubt prayed to survive and be rejoined with her, he could not regret now the choice that had brought him to this place, at this time. He was determined to lead his men with courage in the coming battle and to set an example that would inspire other Irishmen in a future struggle under the Fenian banner.

Hancock's Second Corps, including the Irish Brigade of just over 500 men led by Col. Patrick Kelly, had joined the growing Union forces early on July 2. The corps had been deployed along Cemetery Ridge, extending southward from the Eleventh Corps positions on Cemetery Hill. Vermont's "Irish Company" thus found itself on the battlefield not far from the legendary unit of Fenians, first commanded by Meagher. In the presence of this heroic brigade, Lonergan could have felt a particular need for his own company to uphold the reputation of Irish units for bravery in combat.

AFTER BEING DRIVEN THROUGH the town of Gettysburg in full retreat the previous day, Union troops knew that the rebels would continue to press them hard, seeking complete victory in the coming battle. Despite the arrival of additional federal troops and their good defensive positions, Lee's forces might attack from different directions, converging to sweep over Cemetery Hill and inflict a disastrous defeat on Meade. The Union lines first had to beat back attacks on their left flank and center; later the right flank anchored on Culp's Hill came under assault. Units were hastily shifted within the Union positions to counter each attack in turn. The Union positions were subjected to artillery bombardments preceding each rebel operation, answered in kind by the federal cannon.

Stannard was placed "in charge of the infantry supports of the batteries on the left brow of Cemetery Hill" about 2:00 PM on July 2, leaving Randall in command of the Second Vermont Brigade. Within an hour, rebel artillery fire caused the first combat casualties in the 13th Vermont, when a shell passed over the crest of the hill and badly wounded Capt. Merritt B. Williams, the commander of Co. G, as well as injuring several others.* The Confederate gunners often overshot their intended target, the Union battle lines on the perimeter, and the Second Vermont Brigade was shifted nearer to the base of the hill to provide them better shelter. Lonergan and his men watched as the infantry supports stationed with the cannon on the crest fled "to escape the deadly shower of shot and shell that hailed down among them." The retreating men—what appeared to be the remnants of a regiment—were persuaded to return to their positions after being rallied by their officers and Randall, who shamed the shaken troops with the example of his own green regiment holding steady.

Half of the 13th Vermont—the second battalion, consisting of the five companies that made up the left of the battle line—was ordered up by Stannard to support a battery on the western front of the hill. Under the command of Lt. Col. Munson, companies D, F, H, I, and K moved up to the crest of hill and were ordered to lie down for safety. These Vermonters soon learned "why there had been a break and scamper down the hill." The veteran troops had known when to run for cover after the heavy converging fire of solid shot and exploding shell began pounding the federal artillery positions. Casualties in the gun crews had silenced some of the cannon placed among the grave stones of the cemetery. Helping to put the guns back into action, 1st Lt. Brown of Co. K took several volunteers to handle the ammunition.**

While Lonergan and the rest of the Second Vermont Brigade could only

---

* Williams, a schoolmate of Sturtevant at Bakersfield Academy, was carried from the field and eventually returned home, only to succumb to his wounds in late September.

** Brown had just been released from arrest for the incident of stopping for water on the march. His sword was in a wagon back with the supply train, so he had armed himself with a camp hatchet as a makeshift symbol of authority.

CHAPTER FIFTEEN – INTO BATTLE

follow the progress of events by the sounds of the battle, Munson and his battalion could see the movement of troops and the signs of fighting along the battle line to the south. Sickles had pushed his Third Corps forward from its assigned place on Cemetery Ridge to create a salient right at the point of Longstreet's assault. In the late afternoon, attacks on its front and flanks smashed the Third Corps and drove the survivors back toward the Union lines. A desperate defense of Little Round Top barely held the left flank of Meade's line against the rebels. Fifth Corps reserves were sent in to rescue the situation.

Hancock also stripped his Second Corps positions and rushed Caldwell's division, including the Irish Brigade, to plug the gap in the line. Before the Fenians went into battle, the chaplain of the 88th New York, Father Corby, gave the Irishmen absolution as they knelt with cap in one hand and musket in the other. Within a few hours, the brigade lost over two hundred men in heavy fighting in a hotly contested wheat field, suffering forty percent casualties, including many dead.

Meade then ordered Hancock to send yet another of his brigades into the fight at the salient and to take command of what remained of the Third Corps after Sickles was wounded. The dispatch of troops to the left flank dangerously thinned out the forces holding the center section of the left side of the Union lines. These hasty reinforcements late in the day stalled Longstreet's assault on the Union left, but a gap was thus created in the line of the Second Corps. The second phase of Lee's offensive was aimed at the weakened center of the Union positions on Cemetery Ridge.

Two Union regiments, supported by the six cannon of Lt. Gulian V. Weir's battery, had been pushed forward from this sector on Cemetery Ridge to the Emmitsburg Road near the Codori farm. Isolated in this advanced position, they faced Wright's brigade of Georgia soldiers, part of Anderson's Division of Hill's Corps. The division on Longstreet's left had already committed two of its five brigades in support of his assault, but Wilcox's Alabama regiments and Lang's Floridians had both been repulsed in heavy fighting after crossing the Emmitsburg Road.

Around 6:45 PM, Wright advanced his brigade in turn, with one regiment detached as skirmishers. Posey tried to move his brigade of Mississippians forward to cover Wright's left flank, but was unable to keep pace and Anderson's northernmost brigade, Mahone's Virginians, remained in position. About 1,000 of Wright's men pushed through the Union skirmish line, knocking down fences as they came. The outnumbered federal infantry on the Emmitsburg Road was forced to retreat in disorder and the gunners were not able to bring away all of Weir's cannon. The Georgians, unsupported on either flank, pressed forward up the slope toward a part of the Union line that was essentially bare of infantry.

STANNARD HAD PLACED HALF of the 13th in the dangerous position of support duty, although late in the afternoon Munson moved the battalion up to the protection of a stone fence on the Taneytown road. The rest of the brigade was held in reserve at the base of Cemetery Hill, sheltering as best they could from the rebel bombardment. Anticipating combat at any moment, Randall sent his orderly, Pvt. Ziba McAllister, back to the rear with the extra horses and his son, Francis V. Randall, Jr., who served as drummer. The colonel retained the gray mare that he had acquired on the Occoquan, although any man on horseback—commander, aide, or courier—might especially draw fire from the enemy.

When Meade observed Wright's brigade approaching the Union lines, he cast about for any available infantry to fill the gap for which the Georgians were headed. The unsupported artillery in that sector could slow the rebel advance, but was in danger of being overrun. An account by Lt. Col. George Meade, the army commander's son who served on his staff, said that the chief of artillery of the cavalry corps drew Meade's attention to a brigade being held in reserve. Noting that "the enemy have pierced our centre," the cavalryman told Meade, "If you need troops, I saw a fine body of Vermonters a short distance from there, belonging to the First Corps, who are available." Meade then sent orders for the Second Vermont Brigade to plug the hole on the left of Brig. Gen. John Gibbon's division "at once."

Doubleday himself, according to some sources, delivered the order to his newly-assigned Third Brigade, riding hard to where the Vermonters were being held in reserve. Lying close to the base of the hill, the main body of Vermonters had been unable to see what was happening on the front lines, but they could hear the volleys of musket fire rippling down the ridge. Clearly a tremendous battle was taking place, and they were about to enter the fight. Doubleday reportedly identified himself as the division commander and asked Randall to introduce him to the troops, whereupon the general gave a brief speech and received three cheers before the brigade was sent forward into action.

Upon receiving his instructions, Randall led the brigade about a quarter of a mile down Taneytown Road, past Meade's headquarters, and up over the

CHAPTER FIFTEEN – INTO BATTLE

WEIR'S BATTERY

ridge to the front line. Sturtevant, part of the battalion supporting the artillery, recognized Randall's familiar gray mare as the Vermont brigade passed their immediate rear and he set the time of the movement at 7:00 PM.

Even with only half of its units in the column, the brigade was still as large as many of the depleted divisions on the battlefield. When Randall led the column of infantry over the crest "at a sharp double-quick, flags flying, arms at right shoulder," the younger Meade first thought that it was two divisions of the First Corps. His father greeted the Vermonters with a wave of his hat and rode with them to close the gap in the line.

When the column reached the front line on Cemetery Ridge, the 14th Vermont, the first regiment in the formation, was posted behind a threatened battery and prepared to engage the enemy by "fronting into line of battle." The 16th Vermont next performed the same movement to turn back a line of rebels about to overrun another battery left without supports. By then, Wright's unsupported charge had spent its force and his men had begun to

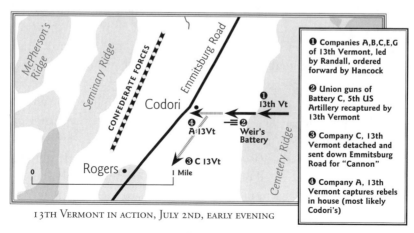

13TH VERMONT IN ACTION, JULY 2ND, EARLY EVENING

retreat, even though some rebels had reached the Union positions along a stone wall, just south of a copse.

After the 14th and the 16th dropped out of the column, only Randall with his demi-regiment remained available to rescue the other Union cannon in peril. The five companies of the 13th moved forward along the crest of the ridge until Randall encountered Hancock, who was anxious to save the artillery that he had personally advanced to the Emmitsburg Road. Battery C, 5th U.S. Artillery, had been left behind as its infantry support retreated and Weir had brought off only four of his brass Napoleons; the remaining two had fallen into the hands of Wright's men. Pointing to rebels swarming over the artillery pieces one hundred yards away, Hancock asked, "Can't you save that battery, Colonel?" Randall replied without hesitation, "I can, and damn quick too, if you will let me." Led by Lonergan's "Irish Company," the first battalion of the 13th then raced down the slope toward the road, tracing in reverse the path of their previous day's arrival.

As the Vermonters charged down into the twilight of the valley, Wright's Georgians fought back. Randall's gray horse from the Occoquan soon fell, shot through the shoulder, and he was pinned beneath it. The colonel urged his men forward, "Go on, boys, I'll be at your head as soon as I get out of this damned saddle." Several soldiers quickly rolled the regimental commander's mount off him. The colonel's sixteen-year-old son, a lieutenant in Co. G, asked permission to help his father, but soon returned to his place in the column as the elder Randall limped to its front, hatless and waving his sword.

Deploying into a line of battle, the Vermonters quickly unleashed a volley from their muskets to drive the enemy back. As their "wild Irish yell" warned the rebels to "clear the way," Lonergan's company charged with fixed bayonets to recapture the cannon. Rebels who lost heart threw themselves to the ground in surrender and the 13th passed over them, as Hancock shouted that he would himself take charge of the prisoners. Not a man was lost in the headlong rush against the withdrawing Confederates.

Randall and Lonergan reached the battery at the same time and Co. A was told to put down their muskets in order to retrieve the Napoleons by hand. The cannon were moved back manually until gunners arrived to hook up their teams of horses. Varying versions of these events, understandable in the confusion of battle, tell of recapturing four cannon and also taking two additional artillery pieces from the rebels. (Lonergan's Medal of Honor citation would include these figures, even though he made no claim of capturing any

CHAPTER FIFTEEN – INTO BATTLE

Capture of Rebels at the Codori house

enemy cannon.) At this point, the soldiers of the 13th Vermont were isolated on the battlefield and exposed to enemy attack, far in front of the Union lines, but still in view of their comrades on Cemetery Ridge.

On receiving rifle fire from a nearby farmhouse,* Randall ordered Lonergan's company (and perhaps one other) to clear out the rebel marksmen. Surrounding the house as best he could with his company, at this point numbering perhaps sixty men, Lonergan brashly addressed the occupants. He claimed later to have knocked down the door and demanded, "Surrender! Fall out here, every damned one of you!" Relieving a Confederate officer of his sword and pistol, Lonergan then had his men disarm the rebel soldiers as they filed out of the house, stacking their muskets in a pile. When the last prisoner had given up his weapon, the "Irish Company" found they had a picket reserve of three officers and eighty men in their grasp, exceeding their own numbers by nearly half.

In the gathering darkness, Randall sent his adjutant back for further orders and received permission to return to the lines. As the 13th approached with its prisoners, cheering broke out among the troops on the ridge above,

---

* Most sources identify this as the Rogers house, but both Lonergan and Randall—directly involved participants—place the action at the Codori house. See Appendix D for details on the identification of the farmhouse and the cannon retrieved or captured.

who had watched the regiment's first action in combat. Word reportedly even reached the veteran First Vermont Brigade on the far left flank of the Union position and they joined in the praise of what they termed the "Infant Brigade" of nine-month soldiers. Other veterans were less impressed by the reckless behavior of Randall and his men. As the Vermonters entered the Union lines, one old hand asked, "What troops be you fellers?" Many of the men proudly identified themselves as Green Mountain Boys. The more experienced soldier observed dryly, "Well, I thought you must be green, or you'd never have gone in there."

Randall had been sent to Hancock by Doubleday, the division commander, but on returning he had to face the ire of his brigade commander. Stannard had been "looking all over the field" for the 13th, according to one of the general's aides. Rebuked by Stannard for "wandering off without his orders," Randall explained that he had been following directions from his superiors and was soon vindicated by aides from Doubleday, Hancock, and others, who arrived to congratulate the colonel.* The half of Randall's regiment under Munson had been released from its support of the battery soon after the brigade passed and was also sent to reinforce the line under assault. The second battalion had followed the same route to the battle line as the first, perhaps thirty minutes later, and the rebel bombardment in support of Wright had caused a number of casualties in the column during the movement. Munson arrived on the front line "between sundown and dark," just as the colonel and the first battalion brought in their prisoners, and his men welcomed the other half of the 13th back "with hearty cheers."

DARKNESS BROUGHT AN END to action on the left side of the Union position, although fighting on the right raged around Culp's Hill through the evening and into the night. Twelfth Corps units had been rushed to the left to reinforce the beaten Third Corps; they now hurried back to their positions on the right flank as Ewell's troops attacked. Lee and Meade, at their respective headquarters, reviewed the situation that night and made plans

---

* Lonergan later told how Stannard had also scolded him at the end of the day for "violating all military laws in capturing those prisoners" from the farmhouse. Asking what the general meant, the captain was told with a smile that the command for forming a company line is "Fall in!" and yet Lonergan had ordered the rebels to "Fall out!" Going along with the joke, Lonergan explained, "Yes, General, but they were already in, and so had to 'fall out.'"

CHAPTER FIFTEEN – INTO BATTLE

for the following day. Meade had received information on the Confederate deployments that correctly reported the arrival of Lee's last major unit, Pickett's division, on the battlefield.

Pickett's three brigades had been in Cashtown, securing the lines of communication for the Army of Northern Virginia. On the road headed east before dawn on July 2, the division had crossed over Cashtown Gap by noon, making good time on firm roads despite the heat and dust. The rear guard responsible for preventing stragglers from dropping out of the column was commanded by 1st Lt. John Dooley, Co. C of the 1st Virginia, whose ranks included Pvt. Willie Mitchel, youngest son of the famous Irish nationalist, John Mitchel. Dooley noted, "It is a hard thing to keep these men on the move" and even the long day of marching brought them to the battlefield too late to join in the fighting. Pickett was instructed to let his men rest overnight when they reached Marsh Creek. Because his troops had not been involved in the previous two days of fighting, they were therefore in the best condition of any of Lee's divisions for an attack on July 3.

A poll of the Union corps commanders, crowded into the small house that served as Meade's headquarters, supported a decision to remain in position and on the defensive for another day. The commander of the Army of the Potomac predicted that Lee, after failing to turn either Union flank, would next strike the center again, where Wright's men had briefly penetrated the lines that day.

STANNARD'S THREE REGIMENTS took up their positions for the night with empty stomachs; any supply of food in their haversacks was long gone and they had no hope for replenishment. The top priority for wagons moving to the front would be to carry ammunition, rather than rations. The Vermonters were fortunate that a "large flowing spring" that fed Plum Run was close by, in front of the battle line. The men of the 13th quenched their thirst during the evening and filled their canteens for the following day. Lonergan's company occupied the right of the brigade's line of battle as the regiment laid down to rest with their weapons at hand. As they sought what sleep they could find in their second night "on the field of awful carnage and great slaughter surrounded by thousands of the dead and wounded," everyone realized that the next day would likely bring a renewal of the battle.

The 14th had initially been positioned in support of artillery in the lines of Gibbon's Second Corps division late in the afternoon. In the evening, the 14th was shifted to the south, moving alongside the 13th on the battle line. The 16th was again called upon to perform picket duty beyond the main line and its commander, Col. Veazey, was detailed as division field officer of the day. Three companies of his regiment were deployed along the Emmitsburg Road and backed up by a strong reserve to connect to the picket line of the Fifth Corps. The remainder of the 16th also spent the night forward of Stannard's other two regiments. Veazey's picket line ran across the field where heavy fighting had "thickly strewed the ground [with] the dead and wounded of the two armies, lying side by side." The colonel understandably found it the saddest night he had ever passed on picket. As the wounded begged for help, the stretcher-bearers from both sides were allowed to pass freely through the picket lines to gather their own casualties, but Veazey reported that "scores of wounded men died around us in the gloom" before anyone could reach them.

Benedict described the same horrific scene on the battlefield and he also saw first-hand the "absolutely appalling" extent of the fighting up to that point. After only an hour or two of rest, Stannard's aide was detailed to search for an ammunition train to replenish the Vermonters supply of cartridges for the expected continuation of the battle. He rode through the rear of the army the rest of the night without success, encountering streams of wounded men looking for hospitals to treat them. The hospitals themselves seemed to occupy every barn in the region. Their lamp-lit floors were filled with "mutilated soldiers, piles of amputated arms and legs lying outside." Trains of ambulances were delivering more groaning victims and he realized that he was only seeing a fraction of the casualties. It seemed to him "that every square yard on a stretch of many miles must have its blood stain." The brigade hospital had been set up in a barn near the Taneytown Road, "about a mile and a half south of General Meade's headquarters," and the surgeons there worked through the night. Despite serious injuries, some of which later proved fatal, nobody in the 13th had been killed outright that day.

Harrow's brigade of Gibbon's division made up the core of the units immediately north of Stannard's brigade on the battle line. Various regiments and even detached companies had been thrown into the line to repulse Wright's attack. Much of the firepower in the sector came from Battery B,

CHAPTER FIFTEEN – INTO BATTLE

1st New York Light Artillery, commanded by Capt. James McKay Rorty, a dedicated Fenian.*

Lonergan's company rested that night behind a low stone wall alongside Rorty's battery and the two Fenian captains might well have been in contact. Rorty had been born in Donegal in 1837, so he and Lonergan were the same age and rank. Although their homes had been at opposite ends of Ireland, they shared the common dream of independence for the land of their birth. Rorty had corresponded with John O'Mahony and had written essays that were published by the Fenian Brotherhood, so Lonergan might have known of Rorty even before they stood side by side on the battle line. Lonergan's exploits on the battlefield that day had distinguished his "Irish Company" to the watching Union troops; his nature suggests that he might well have boasted of their exploits upon his return to the lines, particularly to any nearby fellow countryman. Hearing the Irish spoken among members of the Emmet Guards, Rorty could have made a point of congratulating his fellow Fenians for their bold action.

After two years of fighting, Rorty would have had few illusions about the brutal nature of combat and perhaps he would have counseled more caution in the future. Lonergan had just experienced his first day of battle without losing a man, but his ideas of glory would have been tempered by the reality of war. Facing the likelihood of renewed bloody fighting the next day, both Irishmen may well have offered up prayers that the Fenians involved would survive to help in the struggle for Ireland's liberation.

---

* Rorty had enlisted with the original 69th New York regiment and was captured with Col. Corcoran at the first battle of Bull Run, but later escaped from a Confederate prison in Richmond. He had been commissioned lieutenant in the 14th New York Independent Battery, part of the Irish Brigade, and was serving as the secretary for the Fenian circles in the Army of the Potomac.

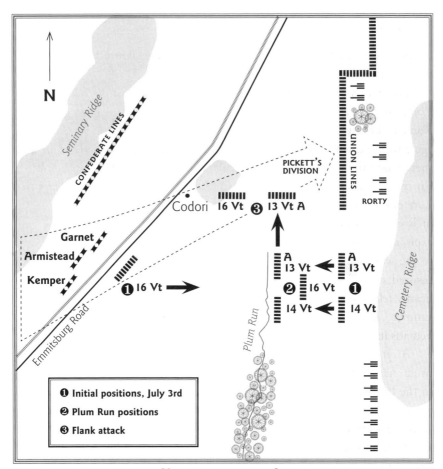

13TH VERMONT DEPLOYMENT, JULY 3RD
A - LONERGAN'S COMPANY

CEMETERY RIDGE AND CODORI FARMHOUSE FROM REBEL LINES

CHAPTER SIXTEEN

FLANK ATTACK

LONERGAN'S MEN AWOKE ON the morning of July 3 to the roar of cannon from across the valley, instead of the familiar bugle call of reveille. The rebels began the third day of the battle early with intense bombardment of the Union lines on Cemetery Ridge. Union guns along the ridge replied with their own morning salute for the Confederates. The rebel cannonade of this sector was intended only as a distraction, to divert attention away from their attack on Culp's Hill by Ewell's Corps, but the shelling could still have deadly effect. Firing had also commenced at first light on the Union right, as cannon opened up in support of a federal assault to regain ground lost there the previous day.

During the enemy shelling, the men of the 13th Vermont huddled behind a "tumbled down stone wall" and "even the most tidy of the boys" hugged the ground without regard of further dirtying his uniform. The rank and file were ordered not to move about unless told to do so, yet the officers stood erect and exposed when their duties required. Sturtevant reported lying behind the low wall, watching "with wonder and pride the cool and deliberate conduct of officers" during the cannonade and having no wish to exchange positions with them. The bombardment of Cemetery Ridge ceased after about an hour, as the true Confederate target of the morning became evident from the "distant thunder of cannon and roar of musketry" on the Union right.

Lonergan had spent another night on the bare ground with an empty belly and woke to a field strewn with corpses, turning black and swollen in the summer heat. Unlike the tales of Finn McCool that he had heard in childhood, no feast celebrated the heroic exploits of the previous day, no harper sang the warriors' praise; instead he saw only hideous wounds and death, sudden or lingering. Yet he and all his men were still alive and prepared to do their duty, whatever the cost. Proud of the bravery of his unit in action the day before, the captain must have known that his "Irish Company" would fight again that day.

Soldiers of all ranks were conscious that they might not survive the coming battle and many made preparations in case they were killed. While high-ranking officers could be assured of someone noting their death or capture, less prominent soldiers might simply disappear unnoticed on the battlefield. Since the army did not provide soldiers with any kind of identity tag, sutlers produced metal identification discs for men willing to spend the money. Most soldiers simply wrote their name and unit, perhaps including their home town, on a slip of paper which they pinned to their uniform or stuffed in a pocket.

Soldiers might also write letters to be passed on if they were killed; Lonergan and his second lieutenant, McDevitt, probably prepared such testaments. Sinnott left instructions for the disposition of his property in a letter which he wrote "after the first day's battle" and placed in a pocket of his uniform. He included "a kind farewell to his future wife" (he was engaged to be married and had already purchased a suit for the wedding once he returned home). Given their close friendship, it seems likely that before the impending battle Sinnott would have asked Lonergan to deliver his final letter if he fell in the fight.

Sinnott had just been promoted to be captain of Co. F, replacing its commander, who had resigned on June 3. However, he had not yet received his commission when the Vermonters marched north and he remained with the Emmet Guards. Lonergan considered him "a good disciplinarian, an excellent executive officer." Though he would have been sorry to see his schoolteacher friend leave Co. A, Lonergan surely would have given his strong endorsement and hearty congratulations at the promotion.

Everyone in the Second Vermont Brigade faced danger early that morning. The skirmishers of the 16th near the Emmitsburg Road were deployed well forward of the target zone during the bombardment, but were engaged early on the front lines. Fighting between individual soldiers began before 4:00 AM in the dim pre-dawn light. Pressure from the Confederate picket line made it too dangerous to relieve the soldiers of the 16th in full daylight and they were forced to remain down in the valley. The men of Veazey's regiment, "hungry, thirsty and exhausted by want of sleep," sheltered in small groups as best they could. On the main Union line, the 14th was spread out along the low

CHAPTER SIXTEEN – FLANK ATTACK

stone wall to the left of the 13th, both regiments only poorly protected by the rubble. The thin soil on the rocky ridge offered little opportunity to dig trenches and the only tools available were the soldiers' bayonets, along with their tin cups and plates.

The other two brigades of Doubleday's division had taken heavy losses on July 1 and were now mostly held in reserve behind the main battle line. Two regiments of his First Brigade, however, had been shifted into the gap south of Gibbon's division on July 2; the veteran 80th New York and the nine-month 151st Pennsylvania held a position behind Stannard's Third Brigade.* This placed the larger, but inexperienced, Vermont regiments on the front line and established a defense in depth. If the Vermonters broke during the Confederate attack, Col. Theodore B. Gates would try to hold the main line with the 235 men left in these two regiments. Both Stannard and Gates were isolated from command by the First Corps to which they belonged. Rushed to the Second Corps area to help repulse Wright's attack, these units now fell under direct control by Hancock.

As the senior company of the 13th, Co. A held the position of honor on the right of the regiment's battle line, closest to the nearby artillery. Most likely it was Lonergan's men who responded to a call from the adjacent battery when "several men from the 13th" volunteered to give up their shelter behind the wall to help serve the guns. Rorty's gun crews had suffered heavy casualties and only three of his original sixty-five men remained in action. With two of his guns still serviceable, Rorty asked for assistance from the infantrymen, since even an untrained soldier could help pass ammunition up to the cannon from the metal-lined boxes of the caissons kept to the rear of the guns. Rorty himself stripped to the waist and took on the duties of Number One gunner. Lonergan's "Irish Company" might well have learned how to serve field artillery pieces while they were at Wolf Run Shoals, sharing their camp on the bank of the Occoquan River with a section of a Connecticut battery. The men of Co. A would have observed the drill of the cannon crews and probably learned the basic duties involved.

---

* The schoolteacher Sinnott would have found some kindred souls among the one hundred teachers serving in the 151st Pennsylvania, nicknamed the "Schoolteachers Regiment." Due to muster out the end of July, the 151st was badly shot up on July 1, a fate that the Vermonters might well have shared if they had arrived a day earlier at the battlefield. The 151st suffered seventy-two percent losses at Gettysburg (337 men out of 467). The 80th had Irish connections; mostly raised in Ulster County, New York, it bore the name "Ulster Guard," and used the Red Hand of that province as its symbol.

The early morning shelling caused some casualties among the Vermonters. Several men in the 14th were killed when the ammunition in the caisson of a battery close to them exploded. The commander of the 14th, Col. William T. Nichols, requested and received permission to move his regiment forward about fifty yards to a position where the Plum Run swale and "some scattered trees and bushes" would provide better shelter for his men. With the 16th stranded between the lines on picket duty, two-thirds of Stannard's men were thus well out in front of the main battle line. They occupied a forward position similar to what Sickles had created with his decision to advance his Third Corps on July 2. This salient extending out from the line made the Second Vermont Brigade vulnerable to assault on three sides and it would likely be overwhelmed if a strong Confederate force should attack that section.

Elsewhere along the Union lines, men strengthened their defenses where they could. Muskets scattered around the battlefield were collected and loaded, placed handy along the wall to provide a steady stream of fire without the need to reload (the Vermont units apparently did not employ this tactic). Wright's Georgian units carried smoothbore weapons, a large number of which had been left on the field the day before. Some Union soldiers removed the .69 caliber ball from the "buck and ball," cartridges and filled many of these muskets with only the buckshot, lethal when the attackers came within range. The gun crews brought up more close-range canister rounds for the cannon, making them in effect massive shotguns that would devastate the enemy ranks.

Poorly sheltered behind the loose stones of the derelict wall, the 13th also became the target of Confederate sharpshooters when the soldiers exposed themselves. All morning they were essentially pinned down, with nothing to do but consider their situation. Although the men "gave but little heed to the many dead scattered over the field in every direction as far as we could see," they did use blankets to cover the closest "bloated, mangled corpses with open eyes constantly crossing our vision."

As the sun rose, some of the men placed their shelter tents on inverted muskets to provide shade and Sturtevant noted, "the burning heat demanded water to quench our thirst." Volunteers risked crawling down to a spring to the left, taking as many canteens as they could manage, to elbow their way

CHAPTER SIXTEEN – FLANK ATTACK

between others seeking the trickle of water. Men used their cups to bail water out of the wooden box built into the spring, but the demand exceeded the flow and each dip brought up only about a teacup of water. Again 1st Lt. Brown of Co. K took action to provide his men with water, walking upright to the spring to return with filled canteens, but only once. He warned others not to attempt the trip. A number of men were killed at the spring that morning, after the activity attracted the attention of snipers with telescopic sights. Union sharpshooters, hidden in buildings and treetops, countered when they could spot the source of the deadly fire.

The rebels targeted officers and cannon crews in particular. Stannard, revealed to be a general officer by the movement of staff officers to and fro around him, drew fire from the enemy sharpshooters. A bullet through his coat and another that took a piece from his hat riled the brigade commander, who sent a squad of federal sharpshooters to suppress the more persistent snipers.

Except for this long-range rifle fire, around 11:00 AM—as the fighting on the right finally ceased after six hours of continuous musketry—the battlefield sank into a mid-day torpor; Benedict called the silence "oppressive." While the 13th "patiently waited for the expected charge," 1st Lt. Albert Clarke, now in command of Co. G, approached Randall to propose building a breastwork of fence rails for protection. Receiving the colonel's permission, Clarke called for ten volunteers from each company for the work. Led by the fleet-footed Sgt. Scott of Clarke's unit, the men "charged the rail fence" that divided the fields. Although harassed by rifle fire from the sharpshooters in the valley, they carried the wooden rails about one hundred yards forward to build a low breastwork alongside the position of the 14th. The hasty fortification rose only two feet above the rocky soil, but could provide some protection against musket balls and shell fragments for men lying flat behind it. Stannard observed this preparation and "approved it with a nod and smile," while cheers greeted the volunteers on their return to the line of the 13th.*

Soon after the breastwork was built, Sturtevant saw his "cousin and playmate from birth to early manhood" approach. Corp. Wesley C. Sturtevant of Co. E, 14th Vermont, wanted to tell his relative of a sure premonition of death. Saying "I shall never see home and dear friends again, something tells me I shall be slain in this battle, and I cannot drive away the awful thought," Wesley asked Ralph to tell his family at home good-bye for him. Giving Ralph letters of

---

* Sturtevant later commented, "For this brave deed medals of honor should have been awarded by our government and no doubt would have been long ago had applications been made."

farewell, the corporal explained that when he was "awakened this morning by the roar of cannon," he knew that he would not survive. His hope was to be buried in his hometown of Weybridge, but he could not speak of these matters to his comrades in the 14th and so he had sought out his cousin. Wesley "with deep emotion" shook Ralph's hand and walked deliberately back to his unit "not two hundred yards away." Before Wesley reached his company, two signal guns in Longstreet's artillery "broke the awful silence."

OVER ONE HUNDRED AND FIFTY rebel cannon opened fire in response to the signal guns, concentrating on the Union lines just to the right of the 13th. Some one hundred Union guns replied and just after 1:00 PM a "deafening roar" began to fill the air with "deadly missiles that went screeching across the valley on errands of death and destruction."

Randall ordered his men forward out of the target zone to take shelter behind the newly built breastworks. The men crawled out from behind the stone wall to rush westward down the upper slope of the ridge. The regiment did not move forward "according to strict military rule," but rather in "a helter skelter zig zag croutching [sic], crawl and run each taking his own way" to reconstitute the battle line by companies. Some men were slightly wounded, but none killed, as they worked their way to the new position, "full one hundred yards in advance of the battle lines in support." The 13th flattened out behind the stacked rails to the right of the 14th, which was hidden "on the low flat ground of Plum Run behind [a] thick copse that lined its banks." Lonergan again claimed the right flank of the line as the senior company of the senior regiment. Those of his men who had been detached to help with the cannon would of necessity have abandoned Rorty's battery and rejoined Co. A when it moved forward. (Rorty recruited replacement volunteers from the 19th Massachusetts and other adjacent units to keep his two remaining cannon in action.)

All three regiments of the Second Vermont Brigade were now well forward beyond the Union lines. Stannard positioned his command group on a nearby knoll and observed the battlefield from there with his staff and orderlies.

Not only did this new advanced position provide better cover from enemy fire, but Lonergan and his men now occupied a point that also gave them a panoramic view of the battlefield. Lying in advance of and somewhat below

CHAPTER SIXTEEN – FLANK ATTACK

the smoke belching from the Union cannon, the "whole battlefield could be plainly viewed from Round Top to Cemetery Hill" and out across the valley to the Confederate lines. While it was safe enough to look back over their shoulders and survey the reassuring long lines of infantry and cannon behind them, the men were ordered to keep down below the breastwork and to rely on their officers to alert them to any movement by the rebels in front.

This was likely the time when Lonergan offered words of encouragement to his men. The company clerk, Pvt. Heman Allen,* described the captain's speech, "before the hottest part of the battle," as saying: "Boys, you have been quite anxious for a fight ever since you enlisted; now you have got a chance to fight and show what kind of stuff you are made of." A straightforward talk, brief and to the point, it reminded the "Irish Company" that here, near the end of their service, was another chance to prove their bravery and bring honor to the unit.

A steady cannonade of both solid shot and exploding shell pounded the Union lines; Sturtevant calculated that it lasted almost two hours. Its concentration on the Second Corps divisions of Gibbon and Hays clearly indicated the point on which any rebel attack would be focused. The exposed artillery units along that part of the line were the particular target of the shelling and they suffered continuous losses in the duel with their counterparts on Seminary ridge. One such casualty was Rorty, mortally wounded when a spark exploded an ammunition chest.** Several devastated batteries were replaced by fresh artillery units as men, horses, and equipment fell victim to rebel cannon fire.

Survivors of the battle agreed in their later writings that words could not give an adequate description of this bombardment, though some tried. Sturtevant remembered the "tremendous roar of cannon, the crack and crash of shell, the exploding caissons here and there, the horrid whiz of shrapnel, the consternation and anxiety, all this held us prostrate and fast to the ground." Perhaps five hundred explosions a minute, muzzle blasts combined with shell bursts, occurred at the height of the exchange; the thunder was reportedly heard over one hundred miles away.

---

* Although he bore the same name as one member of Vermont's founding Allen family, no direct relationship has been determined.

** Capt. Gleason of the Irish Brigade described Rorty's death as a severe loss to the Irish nationalist movement.

Even so, many men, exhausted by a week and more of marching and battle, now fell asleep. Veazey reported that probably a majority of his 16th Vermont picket line were observed asleep, stretched out in the July sun in "a stunned and weary drowse," despite the hellish noise. The colonel himself stayed awake only "with the greatest effort" as he anticipated "the more fearful scenes [that] would speedily follow." Closer to the impact area of the shelling, the 13th and 14th regiments were less likely to fall asleep, although some fatigued soldiers probably could not keep their eyes open.

Everyone was aware that the bombardment by the rebels was intended to clear a path for an infantry assault on Cemetery Ridge. Once the artillery preparation ended, the attack would soon follow. Meade's chief of artillery wanted to lure the Confederates forward while his defending cannon were still effective. After about an hour of responding to the rebel cannons, he therefore ordered the Union artillery to cease firing, tapering off to mislead the rebels. Longstreet had planned the timing of the attack based on the effect of the bombardment in suppressing the opposing artillery. The infantry would advance when the rebel cannonade had produced its maximum impact on the enemy.

Most of the Union artillery went silent as planned. Hancock took it upon himself to order some cannon, the closest support to the left of the Vermont brigade, to keep firing. The Second Corps commander worried that the Union soldiers would be discouraged by a one-sided artillery bombardment with no response by their supporting cannon. Despite Hancock's interference, the silence on the Union side served its purpose. The rebel cannon, in any case running out of long-range ammunition, began to cease firing within half an hour. Many of the shots during the bombardment had been long, passing over the crest and doing their damage on the reverse slope. Others exploded prematurely, due to the persistent problems that the Confederate artillery had with faulty shell fuses.

When the rebel cannon fire slackened, curious soldiers in Lonergan's company had stood to peer over the breastwork, watching for the infantry that were sure to attack. Perhaps the rebel artillerymen deliberately fired at the two Vermont regiments taking cover forward of the Union lines, but Stannard's troops were probably not visible from Seminary Ridge. More likely a fuse burned too fast and exploded a shell directly over the right flank of the 13th. As Sinnott rose up from behind the rails to caution the men of the "Irish Company" to stay down, a fragment of the bursting shell struck him in

CHAPTER SIXTEEN – FLANK ATTACK

the forehead. Passing through Sinnott's hat, the jagged piece of iron shattered his skull and dropped him to the ground at Lonergan's side, gravely injured. Lonergan tied his handkerchief around Sinnott's head, looking at his next in command "pale, wounded, bleeding, and dying." Sinnott took his captain by the hand, "pressed it as he could not speak," and lapsed into unconsciousness. Randall must have been told of the casualty in Co. A immediately because the regimental sergeant major, Henry Smith, was quickly assigned to fill the gap in the company command structure.

Lonergan could spare neither the men to remove his wounded lieutenant for medical attention nor the time to grieve over the loss of his comrade. The ominous silence on the battlefield told him that the anticipated assault was fast approaching. As a breeze came in from the south and the smoke from the bombardment began to clear, some of the Vermonters raised their heads cautiously above the breastworks. They could see the ranks of gray-clad rebels gathered atop the ridge on the other side of the valley. On the knoll behind the Vermont battle line, Stannard and his staff watched through field-glasses as the Confederate infantry passed through the rebel artillery positions. With their units formed up by regiment, brigade, and division, the line of battle stretched for over a mile along Seminary Ridge.

DIRECTLY ACROSS THE VALLEY from the Vermont units, the greatest concentration of rebel forces seemed aimed straight at Stannard's three regiments. Pickett's division—three brigades with fifteen regiments, all Virginia units totaling nearly six thousand men—looked ready to march forward right over the exposed Vermonters. This thrust was directed toward the section of the Union line where Wright's brigade had briefly succeeded in reaching the stone wall the previous day. Pickett's division made up only about half of the troops involved. Another rebel force on Pickett's left would assault the Union line just north of Gibbon's sector, while a third component was to come forward on Pickett's right. This southern prong of the attack would consist of two brigades from Anderson's division, Wilcox with five Alabama regiments and Lang leading three Florida regiments.

Descriptions of the formations of the rebel units involved in the assault vary—a member of Gibbon's staff, Lt. Frank A. Haskell, called it simply "an ocean of armed men." Other Union observers thought their opponents were moving in a column "by divisions" with some units marching forward in a battle line of two ranks by brigade. The extremely wide front at the line of departure would benefit from a common reference point as an objective. The prominent copse on the ridgeline was broadly designated as the target. Commanders were also given instructions on how to adjust the lines to maintain the formation. Pickett's units were told to guide on the unit in the center of the overall line, aligning themselves with Fry's brigade under Pettigrew in the northern wing of the assault. The Virginians would "dress left" as they moved forward, closing up to their left to fill in the gaps in the lines resulting from losses and concentrating the attack at the chosen point.

Pickett placed two brigades forward—Kemper on the right and Garnett on the left—while Armistead's brigade followed in a second echelon about eighty yards behind the first two. The men in each brigade were deployed in a single line of battle, two ranks deep. Officers had been ordered to make the charge on foot, but both Kemper and Garnett went into the fight on horseback. Kemper's five regiments marched forward with the 24th, 11th, 1st, 7th, and 3rd Virginia lined up from right to left. In the center of the middle regiment, Lt. Dooley led the color company of the "Old First" from Richmond with Pvt. Willie Mitchel as part of the color guard.*

Pickett's men, who had been lying in a swale between Spangler's Woods and the Confederate artillery positions, rose and fell into formation upon command. Around 3:00 PM, as they moved forward and passed through the line of cannon, the rebel forces became visible to the Vermonters opposite. The gray-clad soldiers in turn could see the open fields to be crossed to reach the enemy lines and clearly understood the danger they faced. Pickett even warned Garnett to "make the best kind of time in crossing the valley; it's a hell of an ugly looking place over yonder." Lt. Dooley later described his feelings on beginning the assault, saying, "Instead of burning to avenge the insults of our country, families and altars and firesides, the thought is most frequently, *Oh, if I could just come out of this charge safely how thankful would I be!*" [emphasis in original]

The Union artillery resumed firing on the rebel infantry soon after they appeared in view, causing serious casualties in the assaulting forces as they moved over the open terrain. The goal of Pickett's division lay to the left of its starting point and even the continuous dressing to the left was not sufficient

---

* Some sources claim that Mitchel was actually carrying the regiment's flag; he was certainly one of the group designated to protect the colors.

CHAPTER SIXTEEN ‒ FLANK ATTACK

to close the gap to Fry's brigade, which had lagged behind and was not even in sight. In Kemper's brigade, the steady shifting to the left caused the 11th Virginia to overlap the adjacent 1st and arguments broke out between officers of the two regiments as they crowded together. As Pickett's two leading brigades came over the Emmitsburg Road, the order was given to change direction by making a march to the left oblique. This separated his division from the forces on his right, which had also not kept pace with his advance, and thus exposed his flank. When they "faced to charge up Cemetery Hill," the Virginians "passed directly in review" before the 13th Vermont.

SKIRMISHERS FROM THE 16TH VERMONT were recalled by the brigade commander to rejoin their regiment as the Confederates advanced. Stannard placed the 16th "in close column by division" in the immediate rear of the positions occupied by the 13th and 14th. Lying behind their flimsy breastwork of fence rails, Lonergan's men clutched their rifles in sweaty hands as they watched the powerful rebel assault approach. The word was passed down the line of the 13th from company to company, "steady boys, hold your position don't fire until the word is given, keep cool, lie low till [the] order is given to fire, make ready, take good aim, fire low." As the rebel forces came "about half way from the Emmitsburg Road," Randall finally gave the order to fire, "quickly repeated by every officer in the line." His regiment rose up, as did the 14th, took deliberate aim at the rebels, and "poured in a volley that seemed to level their front rank," according to Randall's official report.

Continuing to "fire as best we could," Randall saw that "very soon the charging column seemed to slacken and nearly halt" before beginning "to move by their left flank." The change in direction was perceived by many of the defenders as a reaction to their unexpected musketry, rather than a necessary movement to the left as described by Confederate sources. Stannard's official report credits his men with driving off the rebels: "The charge was aimed directly upon my command, but owing apparently to the firm front shown them, the enemy diverged midway, and came upon the line on my right." This maneuver exposed in particular the 24th and 11th Virginia, the right-hand regiments of Kemper's brigade, to fire from the Vermonters. At about three hundred yards range, the rifles of Lonergan's men and the others took a deadly toll; casualties marked each step on the Confederates' route.

If Pickett's division had continued straight ahead, rather than veering to its left, Stannard and his men would no doubt have been either overrun or forced to retreat to the main Union battle line. The Vermont brigade was outnumbered four to one by Pickett's veterans, despite the Virginians' losses from the federal artillery fire. The Vermonters' exposed salient would have been impossible to hold if the direction of the charge had not been changed.

Randall reported that he had shifted his regiment to the right when the rebels veered off because shrubbery was masking some of his companies from firing. Lonergan's men would have had the longest opportunity to engage the enemy since they had a continuously clear field of fire and were the closest as the rebels moved to the Vermonters' right. After the initial volley, each Vermonter would have reloaded and fired as fast as his individual skills allowed before Pickett's men moved out of his field of fire. (Sturtevant stated that "a dozen or more volleys had been discharged with deadly effect," but it is more likely that the men fired "at will," rather than by volley.) The target practice in Virginia had trained the 13th to shoot accurately, but even the poorest marksman was likely to hit someone in the mass of rebels marching past.

When Pickett's division moved to its left and up the slope, the change in direction placed Stannard's battle line perpendicular to the enemy force. The only men with a clear field of fire were those on the extreme right of the Vermont line—Lonergan's 1st Sgt. James Scully, along with Corp. John Patten in the front rank and Pvt. Heman Allen in the rear rank. Most of the 13th and 14th had their own soldiers between themselves and the enemy and were therefore unable to bring their weapons to bear. They needed to be in a different position in order to keep up the pressure on the attacking force, so Stannard ordered the 13th to follow the enemy to the right. Unable to make himself heard by his regiment over the terrific din of the battlefield, Randall "sent word to the captains of the left wing" and moved down the right wing telling each company, "By the right flank, follow me." Lonergan faced his men to the right, formed them into a column of fours on the meadow in front of their position, and, sword in hand, led the 13th forward in pursuit of the enemy.

Randall later wrote that Doubleday rode up to him to approve the movement by the 13th and ordered his regiments on the main battle line to Randall's right, the demi-brigade under Gates, to cease firing so that the Vermonters could pass in front of them. (This incident was later disputed by

CHAPTER SIXTEEN – FLANK ATTACK

Second Lieutenant David McDevitt

the general, although one of Doubleday's aides might have been involved.) The "Irish Company" moved some one hundred yards over the rolling field at the double-quick, loading as they ran. The rest of the regiment followed their lead, trailing in a column. Stannard then also ordered the 16th to move by the right flank, passing them behind the 14th, which remained in place.

LONERGAN RUSHED HIS COMPANY forward until they were about seventy-five yards from the rebel flank. Stannard was concerned that they had advanced too far and might be captured. He sent Benedict to stop the Irishman, but before the aide arrived, Randall had halted Co. A and ordered Lonergan to "change front forward." Lonergan posted Scully, rifle at "present arms" as if on parade, to provide the pivot point for the maneuver. With the help of 2nd Lt. McDevitt and Sgt. Maj. Smith, acting as a replacement for Sinnott, Lonergan formed his company in two ranks to the left of Scully; the Emmet Guards faced the enemy with a clear field of fire at "half pistol shot" distance.

Randall then passed the order "change front forward on first company" down the regiment to bring the other companies in line with Co. A. As each company passed from column into a double rank, they formed to the left, pivoting ninety degrees in the process to face north. This brought them parallel to the rebel line of assault and at a right angle to the main Union line, perfectly placed to attack Pickett's flank.

When Hancock saw the opportunity developing for this flank attack, the 13th apparently had already been ordered forward by Stannard. (There was also some dispute and confusion about this point after the fact.) An aide of Hancock, Capt. Henry H. Bingham, supposedly had been sent to alert Stannard to the possibility. He may also have been the reported "drunken aide" who "gave orders to Company 'A' to move back upon the line" as the flank attack was being developed, demanding of Randall "what in Hell he was forming a new line for." Lonergan did not allow this interference to disrupt the formation of the new battle line. The Irishman continued to follow Randall's orders and the colonel in turn referred the aide back to Stannard. Under the circumstances, any discussion on the battlefield would have been brief, to the point, and profane.

Hancock himself then rode down to the knoll to question Stannard about the tactic employed, fearing it exposed the Vermonters by moving them too close to the rebels. Stannard recalled Hancock's remark that the brigade commander "was gone to Hell" and his own response of "to Hell it was then," in order to save the day. Moments later, Hancock reeled and was eased to the ground by aides, including Benedict. A bullet had passed through the pommel of the corps commander's saddle, carrying a saddle nail and splinters into a serious wound in the upper thigh.

The 16th quickly came up on the same line as the 13th and changed front forward on its own first company, extending the flanking formation to the west almost to the Emmitsburg Road. As each unit in the two regiments reached its designated position and formed to the left, it opened fire on the Confederate

CHAPTER SIXTEEN – FLANK ATTACK

units. Since Longergan's company led the entire maneuver up to the rebel forces, his was the first to begin "a deadly fire on their flank which surprised and disconcerted officers and rank and file alike." Although the main thrust of Pickett's division continued up the slope, individual rebels began reacting to the galling musketry from the right by shooting back at the Vermonters.

As the rebel forces approached the main Union line, they understandably began rushing forward, abandoning the "common step" of the march for a headlong charge. The two-rank battle formation became compressed into a mass of men aimed like a spear at the area of the copse. Only the rebels on the edges of the charge could bring their weapons to bear; the rest were essentially defenseless targets for the artillery and increasing musket fire. In front, Union soldiers crowded the stone wall up to four men deep and their many extra muskets were now discharged in rapid succession with deadly effect. Although the bombardment had crippled several of the Federal batteries in the area, some (not including Rorty's battery, which had been reduced to a single cannon) had been replaced during the lull in firing that had enticed the rebels to attack. One of these replacement units sent up to the crucial point in the line was Weir's battery, repaired and replenished after its rescue by Lonergan's soldiers.

When the rest of the 13th dressed on Co. A and the 16th fell in to the left, a double line of Green Mountain Boys leveled perhaps a thousand muskets at the charging rebels. The 13th reportedly sent ten or fifteen rounds into Pickett's troops, with Lonergan's men having the most time to load and fire. The other Vermont companies down the line had progressively less time. Arriving later, the 16th had the opportunity for only about half as many shots in the flank attack as the 13th. The line officers of both regiments, no doubt including Lonergan, were even firing their pistols with effect at this range. At a minimum, the two units would have sent several thousand bullets smashing into the enemy ranks, causing devastating casualties.

Stannard's brigade had been recently assigned to Doubleday's division, but it had been operating at Hancock's direction through most of the battle. Even so, when Doubleday saw the charge of the 13th and 16th, with Lonergan's company in the lead, the division commander was reported to have waved his hat and shouted, "Glory to God, glory to God! See the Vermonters go it!" Doubleday was willing to praise the bravery of the daring action regardless of who might have ordered it.

A threat of this magnitude on Pickett's flank could not be ignored. To counter it, the 24th and 11th Virginia on the right began to refuse their line, turning to face Stannard's units and return their fire. A sizable number of rebel soldiers were thus diverted from the assault; an officer in Garnett's neighboring brigade believed "a few hundred men" turned south to protect their flank. Kemper personally ordered his center unit, the 1st Virginia, to "move by the right flank" against the Vermonters, but the lieutenant now commanding the regiment—probably the only officer in the regiment still on his feet—was unable to comply. Later he explained that "the few men left were shot down as fast as I placed them in position," saying "it was too late and there was no 1st Virginia left to execute the movement." The entire color guard of the regiment had been shot down before they reached the Union lines. Lt. Dooley was shot through both thighs thirty yards from the stone wall (but survived his wounds and subsequent capture). Pvt. Willie Mitchel, born eighteen years earlier in Ireland, lay dead and anonymous among the members of the color guard. Considering their location on the battlefield, it is quite possible that both these Irishmen were struck by bullets fired by Lonergan's men.

As Kemper's brigade withered under fire from the front and flank, even Garnett's brigade felt the impact of the Vermont regiments. Some of his men turned their rifles to the south, even crossing muskets with those still shooting to the front, to push the 13th back from the flank. While they continued to devastate the rebel forces on the right of the charge, men in the 13th also fell in the exchange of bullets. Lonergan saw his ranks begin to thin as four of the Rutland Irishmen were killed in his battle line. Sgt. Thomas Blake died in the fight, along with Pvts. Michael Moylan, Michael McEnery, and James Corey.* Half a dozen other men in his company were wounded, but some of them—like seventeen-year-old John Hamlin from Burlington, shot through the jaw and spitting out blood and teeth—continued to fight. Scully later reported that he was injured when, just as he fired his musket, a rebel ball entered its muzzle and exploded his weapon.

After briefly penetrating the Union lines in front of them, the rebel charge stalled in the face of the determined defenders. Some veterans on the other side of the stone wall shouted derisively, "Fredericksburg! Fredericksburg!" as they took their revenge for Burnside's similar repulse in December. Too late

---

* These last two named had been court-martialed in Washington the previous October for offenses while on guard duty. They now had washed their record of service clean, at least in the eyes of their comrades, with this sacrifice.

CHAPTER SIXTEEN - FLANK ATTACK

to affect the outcome, the tardy Confederate units that should have protected Pickett's right now crossed the Emmitsburg Road. Wilcox and Lang plunged ahead and passed south of the 14th, which was still guarding the approach to the Union lines. The two rebel brigades marched forward in clear view of Stannard, who sent word to recall the 16th.

Sturtevant wrote that the men in the 13th "as they turned half way around to load their guns discovered the passing Rebel column in the rear and without orders faced square to the rear and opened fire" on the new assault several hundred yards south of their line. His is the only account that depicts the front rank of the regiment continuing to attack Pickett's units while the rear rank faced in the opposite direction and "with steady aim firing as rapidly into the charging left flank of the belated columns that had come in support of General Pickett's right flank with equal effect."

At this point, Pickett's men had begun to retreat or throw down their arms in surrender; only a few continued to fight in desperation. When "the dead and wounded covered the ground so as to make progress almost impossible," the rebels seemed "to realize their awful situation, and then they waved handkerchiefs, and threw up their hands as evidence of surrender." The 13th did not cease firing until Randall risked his life by stepping in front of his regiment. Exposed to danger both from those rebels still resisting and the rifles of his own troops, he "passed rapidly down the line and shouted 'Stop firing.'" His regiment advanced to take the rebels prisoner and "rushed up against them with bayonets pushed forward." Some Confederates continued fighting and "many fell wounded and bleeding pierced with bayonet, sword and pistol and musket balls." As the fighting finally stopped in "the great slaughter pen on the field of Gettysburg," covered with the "dead, dying and horribly wounded," the 13th began gathering in hundreds of prisoners. Companies G and I were detailed to escort the large number of rebels to the rear.

Sturtevant remarked that "Quite a number of the boys brought from the field pistols, sabers and guns" and other souvenirs of the battle from the field. After going through the fight waving a camp hatchet, 1st Lt. Brown replaced his missing symbol of authority with the belt, sword, and pistol of a captured rebel officer.*

The eight companies of the 13th not guarding prisoners fell into a

---

* The Gettysburg monument to the 13th Vermont depicts Brown with his famous hatchet on the ground by his feet.

column to return to their Plum Run position. They watched as the 16th, reinforced with several companies of the 14th, charged into the flank of the rebel assault force to the south. These Vermonters quickly drove back the two weak brigades, capturing several flags and many prisoners, to the cheers of Union soldiers on the line above. A few Confederate cannon that still had some long-range ammunition opened fire to cover the retreat of Pickett's shattered division, as well as Anderson's troops to the south, who had just been repulsed. Several men in the 13th were killed, including Sgt. Maj. Smith, and a number wounded when a shell exploded in the ranks of Co. K, Sturtevant's company. He wrote, "The shelling that the 13th received when returning to position was accurate and destructive, and it was miraculous almost that more were not killed and wounded."

Around 6:00 PM, "some little time before the sun disappeared," Lonergan and his surviving men reached the position from which they had led the charge. Sinnott's crumpled body would have still been there at the breastworks, since there had been no time to carry him to the rear for medical attention. Seeing him unconscious from the ghastly head wound, Lonergan could have had little hope that his friend would survive; perhaps he removed the letter of farewell from Sinnott's pocket to safeguard it until it could be delivered, keeping the promise he would have made earlier.

The "battle of the day was evidently over, nothing to indicate its renewal," yet Lonergan's men were still subjected to sporadic artillery fire. They thought that the cannon were aimed mainly at Stannard's brigade, in revenge for its role in driving back both prongs of the rebel assault. The Vermonters again lay flat on the ground behind whatever cover they could find, waiting for darkness to bring a halt to the cannon fire still threatening them. One battery which they could plainly see across the valley continued to fire occasionally; Sturtevant was of the opinion that this was the "same Washington battery that fired the signal guns that opened the artillery duel in the afternoon."

The Vermont unit remained in their advanced position until about 10:00 PM, when "it was dark enough so there was no danger from sharp shooters" before searching out the casualties of the battle. It was still too risky to collect the dead, but survivors were moved off the battlefield for medical attention whenever possible. Stannard had been wounded in the leg by shrapnel from the artillery fire covering the rebel retreat, but he had refused to leave the field until his units were relieved and the other injured removed. A surgeon

CHAPTER SIXTEEN – FLANK ATTACK

removed the ball in his thigh an hour after he was hit. The general remained on the field after the operation and continued to perform his duties until his three regiments were ordered back to the lines. He then "sank fainting to the ground." Randall, the senior colonel present, assumed command of the brigade and turned the 13th over to Munson. Sturtevant reported, "It was long after dark when orders came to move back to the reserve lines for refreshment and sleep."

The weary brigade, deafened by the hours of battle and shocked by the carnage they themselves had helped to fashion, marched to "a position directly back and over the crest near the Taneytown pike in an apple orchard." Although rations were still not available, the men were "told we could lie down and sleep." The soldiers were now "very hungry and thirsty," but "every one laid down where he was and soon were sleeping the sleep of the victorious." A storm rolled in with flashes of lightning and thunder roaring like the deadly cannon they had faced that day. Despite heavy rains that drenched the men on the open ground, the weather did not prevent them from getting "the first night's sound sleep we had had since we broke camp on the banks of the Occoquan nine days before."

The officers were the last to bed down, seeing to their own needs only after ensuring that their men were cared for. Rest and a merciful cessation to the horrors of the day were the immediate requirements of everyone who had survived the battle unscathed. No one could be sure that the fighting would not resume the next day, either with renewed Confederate attacks or with an effort by Meade to finish off Lee's army.

Perhaps Lonergan was able to muster the energy to visit his wounded lieutenant, searching out Sinnott in one of the temporary hospitals that filled every structure in the area. If Lonergan did not retrieve the letter from Sinnott's pocket before his lieutenant was carried unconscious from the field, then he may have taken it later at a crowded medical station. Any doctor tending Sinnott would have given little hope that he could survive such a serious wound and Lonergan must have known that he was parting forever with his friend. The two Fenian leaders would never again share their dreams of liberating Ireland, but Lonergan would continue their work for the cause.

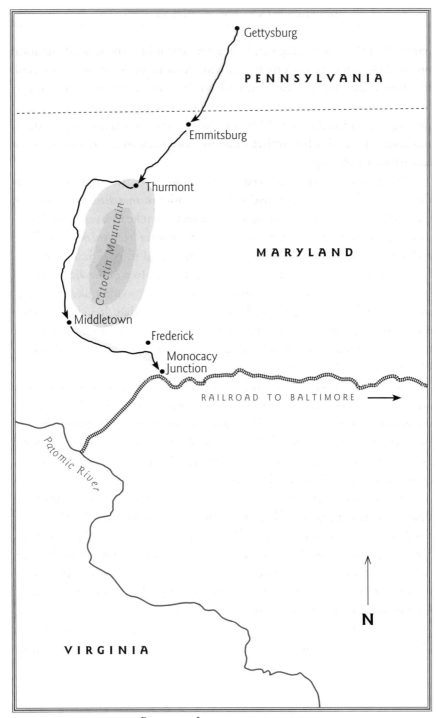

Pursuit of Lee and return march

CHAPTER SEVENTEEN

RETURNING HOME

EAVY RAIN CONTINUED through the night, washing the blood-soaked battlefield and soaking Lonergan's men as they slept. Parched from battle in the summer heat, the soldiers welcomed the water that appeared in every "little hole, rivulet and brook" and let each man quench his thirst and fill his canteen. At daybreak, ignoring the occasional "bursting shell or the sharpshooters' deadly bullets," everyone was "soon up and astir to learn the news and look for the promised hard tack and coffee." Bugle calls "from Round Top to Culp's Hill resounded in the morning air," as aides rushed between headquarters and officers with "their quite numerous staff were passing to and fro." The two wounded armies, both savaged to a similar extent, still lay opposite each other. No one could be sure whether the fighting was really over or if this was only a pause that would be broken by renewed battle. Sturtevant wrote that "not a murmur or any grumbling was heard" as the men in the 13th Vermont "stoically and patiently waited for the commissariat to appear."

Independence Day was celebrated by the survivors in Lonergan's "Irish Company" on the battlefield at Gettysburg only with thankful awareness that they were still alive and had done their part to preserve the Union. Arrival of the commissary wagons on Taneytown Road around 9:00 AM brought the first food that most of the Vermonters had seen in two days. Loud cheers for the assistant quartermaster who pulled up in front of the brigade were quickly followed by distribution of the rations and a "royal feast of hard tack and rain water."

Knowing that they had helped to win an important victory, the Vermonters took pride in their performance on the battlefield. Well-deserved approval came from their leaders, as "officers praised their commands and the rank and file heartily cheered in response." Lonergan, never shy about speaking, no doubt was one of those who lavished commendations on his company, while at the same time recognizing the losses that had been the cost of their bravery.

Once the bodily and emotional needs of the living had been met with food and speeches, the sad task of collecting the dead began. Ambulances were still "rapidly moving out on the field and slowly and carefully returning" with those men so seriously wounded that they had been unable to make their own way to the many field hospitals. Squads detailed from each of the companies reporting men likely killed in action—Co. A knew that several had been shot down in their ranks—were sent to search for their fallen comrades. Recovery of the dead was "a sad and solemn duty, but none hesitated to respond." Armed now with mattock and spade, the men "slowly and silently marched out on the field" strewn with the dead to recover the remains. Each detail retraced its positions in the battle looking for the soldiers who failed to answer the morning roll call, hoping to be able to identify their bodies. Now the wisdom of the pinned scrap of paper with name and unit became apparent. The distinctive cap badges of the 13th may also have helped to identify the unit, if not the individual. The corpses, even if not mangled beyond recognition by their wounds, were rapidly becoming so bloated and blackened that even the closest friend might not be sure who lay at his feet.

Each of the three Vermont regiments had lost over a hundred men in the battle—killed, wounded, or missing—with the 123 total casualties of the 13th somewhat greater than the other two. The number killed was lower in the 13th, though, with an aggregate for the two days of eleven (several more died later of their wounds). On the day of the great charge, eight men were killed in the 13th, half of them Irishmen in Lonergan's company. This high percentage of the regimental deaths reflects a longer exposure to rebel fire in the open; Co. A had arrived first on the flank of Pickett's division.

The bodies that the burial details found were carried back to the current position of the 13th on a slight elevation, "near a stone wall at the south end of an apple orchard" where the living had rested that night. They were buried "as they were, without removing their clothing, covering them over with their blankets, for shrouds and coffins." Only shallow graves were dug, as it was expected that all would soon be removed and taken back to their home towns in Vermont. For the burials, "the solemn rites of the battlefield were observed" and each grave was "rudely marked" with the name of the deceased, his company

CHAPTER SEVENTEEN – RETURNING HOME

and regiment, and the date of death.* All this was "carved on a cartridge box cover or pieces of board from hard tack boxes" so that the remains could be found and identified. This was considered a suitable temporary monument for a soldier who had made the final sacrifice for his country.

Sturtevant had sought out his cousin Wesley in the 14th after Randall brought his regiment back from its flank attack, but was met instead by his relative's tent mates. They showed Ralph the mangled body, "shot through the breast by a solid shot or a shell," the violent death Wesley had divined beforehand. With his jackknife, Ralph carved identifying information on a cartridge box cover before his cousin was given a temporary burial.

CAUTIOUS RECONNAISSANCE OF the Confederate lines on July 4 revealed that the Army of Northern Virginia was still in place and dangerous. The Union army spent the day replenishing supplies and dealing with the aftermath of their victory. Rations were brought up and distributed based on the strengths of the units reported before the battle; due to the heavy losses, this now provided a surplus.

The huge number of rebel prisoners had to be transported from the area of operations. Many were marched to Westminster, Maryland, and put on trains for Baltimore. The 12th Vermont, still protecting the corps wagon train in the Westminster area, was assigned guard duty for one such prisoner transport. The unit's term of service expired on July 4: the first of Vermont's nine-months regiments began its long journey home by escorting prisoners.

Stannard, accompanied by his aide Benedict, had been taken to a hospital in Baltimore, where he received the special attention due a general officer. With the departure of Blunt, the commander of the 12th Vermont, Randall was now the senior colonel in the brigade, not just on the battlefield, and thus he remained in command. Munson, although wounded in the battle on July 3, continued to perform the duties of regimental commander. One account mentions that Lonergan was offered a promotion to field grade officer of the 13th, but refused—probably in reaction to being passed over for such a position earlier—and chose to stay with his "Irish Company" for the duration of their service.

---

* Sturtevant claimed that "no one was removed until fully identified," yet this clearly was not the case as the graves of over a dozen "unknown" soldiers are scattered among the rows of Vermont dead at the Gettysburg National Cemetery.

The afternoon and night of July 4 were marked by a severe storm with heavy rain and high winds. Sturtevant noted that the soldiers of the 13th had "fixed up our cotton tents as best we could," but they provided little protection from the storm and everyone awoke the next morning "drenched to the skin." In the morning, sunshine and a cool breeze from the west quickly dried their uniforms, as rumors flew around the camp that the army would soon be on the move. The Federal cavalry had probed the Confederate lines and found that Lee had slipped his army away during the night, under cover of the storm. The Sixth Corps, including the First Vermont Brigade, pushed forward on the Hagerstown Road only to find Fairfield Pass strongly held by a rebel rear guard.

MEADE ORDERED HIS ARMY to march on July 6, taking even those units whose terms were nearly expired in pursuit of the retreating rebels. Sturtevant described how Randall led the Second Vermont Brigade by a route that took them "across the field where we had our most desperate fighting" and past the places where the "Irish Company" had distinguished itself on July 2. They retraced their steps into Maryland over "the same road that had brought us to Gettysburg on the 1st of July" and reached Emmitsburg about mid-day. After an easy day's march of only twelve miles, the 13th was "in very good condition for we were rested and now had plenty of hard tack and coffee." Spirits were high "in pursuit of the vanquished" and with the knowledge that their term of service would expire on July 10.

Most of the men who had been listed as "missing" after the battle caught up with the 13th when the fighting was over and while the regiment was still at Gettysburg. Many of them had fallen out on the last day's march "overcome with heat and fatigue and faint because of thirst and hunger," though some had been "suddenly stricken with symptoms of cannon fever" when they heard the sounds of the battle. A few had wandered away from the battle lines in search of water and sat out the fighting "behind trees, fences and walls and the banks of the brooks." Sturtevant wrote that there were "no native born cowards" in the 13th and singled out only a few French-Canadians—out of a number in the regiment—who did not stand up to the demands of battle. (This may have been a reflection of the author's own prejudice or of the stereotypes of that era.)

CHAPTER SEVENTEEN – RETURNING HOME

After the easy march that Monday and with the availability of Catholic religious facilities in Emmitsburg, perhaps Lonergan was able to provide his men with some spiritual support during their bivouac in the town. Doubtless every Catholic in his company would have welcomed the chance to give thanks for his survival and to make a suitable gesture for the souls of their departed comrades. Even if Lonergan was not able to arrange for his men to attend any services, he surely would have sought an opportunity to offer up his own prayers for the life of his friend Sinnott, who had been left behind in a field hospital.

Early on July 7, the Vermonters left Emmitsburg "in good marching condition," with hopes that they might yet intercept the retreating rebels and bring the war to a victorious conclusion. Word had spread that the heavy rain in the area had swollen the Potomac River so that it was impossible for Lee to cross at the fords. The brigade's line of march took them back down the Monocacy Valley on the same roads they had used to travel north the week before. Then they turned west over new territory to cross Catoctin Mountain on the route to Middletown, Maryland. Muddy roads and large numbers of infantry, cavalry, and artillery made "progress very slow and tiresome." A hard march of six miles over the mountain was part of the day's total of more than thirty miles, some of them in the rain. This was the longest day's march on the Vermonters' campaign and they arrived at a bivouac on the west slope of the mountain well after dark during a heavy downpour.

During the march over the mountain in "Egyptian darkness" where only the flashes of lightning showed where it was safe to step, both Lonergan and Capt. Orcas C. Wilder, commander of Co. B, were "separated from their companies in the confusion." They rode together in an ambulance for a while, which Wilder thought to be "not much easier than walking." Before resuming the search for their units, the two officers commandeered a bed in a small house and fell into it with their boots still on. (Wilder stated that "it would have been a query which was the cleaner [,] the bed or the boots.") They were roused around 11:00 PM by someone looking for Wilder, saying that there was a very sick man outside.

Together with Lonergan, Wilder helped bring Lt. Albert Clarke of Co. G into the house and sought out a surgeon to treat him. Clarke had been hit in the right ankle by the same shell that severely wounded Capt. Williams on July 2, but he had stayed in the fight through July 3 and led his company with vigor despite his injury. Only after the battle ended did the lieutenant spend two days in a field hospital for medical attention. On hearing that Lee was retreating and the Army of the Potomac following in pursuit, however, Clarke found an abandoned horse on the battlefield and set out to rejoin the 13th. He fell off the horse unconscious from the pain of his wound before reaching the summit and "might have died if he had not been found by Captains Lonergan and Wilder." Clarke received medical attention that night from his twin brother Almon, an assistant surgeon with the 10th Vermont, who had "turned back from the march over South Mountain to find him."* The next morning, Clarke limped down the mountain to find his regiment and overtook the 13th before nightfall.

A sunny morning dawned on July 8, but spirits in the 13th were dampened by orders to start for Boonsboro with the rest of the infantry who were in the vicinity of Middletown, a march that would take them over South Mountain through Turner's Gap. With their enlistments running out in two days, the men still were generally willing to stay on duty to finish off Lee's army.

With the retreat blocked by high water in the Potomac, the rebel forces had lost no time in creating a formidable defensive position on the Maryland side of the river. Two parallel lines of trenches created an arc of defense in depth, with both flanks resting on the swollen river, fortifications that could be overcome only at the cost of many lives. After the slaughter Union forces had suffered at Fredericksburg and the more recent failure of the rebel assault on Cemetery Ridge, Meade would have had to consider carefully whether to attack such a defense.

With a short march ahead for the Vermonters, they started "down the steep mountain road" only at 9:00 AM and soon reached the tidy village of Middletown "in the lovely and fertile valley between the Catoctin and South Mountain." Passing through the village, the four regiments remaining in the brigade marched a mile or so beyond and halted in the forenoon. This was a welcome respite after the previous day's hardships, and the news spread rapidly that the Sixth Corps had also just arrived and the First Vermont Brigade was encamped nearby. "Many hastened for permission to go and see them" and men from the First Vermont Brigade also visited their sister unit in the afternoon. Members of each brigade had friends and relatives in the other and seized upon the opportunity to greet them. (Sturtevant was "one of quite a large delegation

---

* The 10th had been stationed at Harper's Ferry on June 22 and then reassigned to the Third Corps soon thereafter.

CHAPTER SEVENTEEN – RETURNING HOME

that visited the camp of the old brigade," as he was particularly anxious to see his brother in the 5th Vermont.) The veterans of a number of battles—"yet many were boys under twenty"—gave the "Infant Brigade" its just dues and "heartily congratulated us on the record we had made at Gettysburg."

A rumor spread through camp during the day that the 13th was to be detached from the brigade to return home. This was confirmed by Randall "riding in among his regiment" to spread the welcome word. He had just turned the brigade over to the commander of the 16th. (Although Veazey was in fact the junior of the three remaining colonels, this would avoid having to pass the brigade command through the 14th and 15th in a matter of a few days.) Late in the afternoon, orders came to be ready to march early the next morning, heading through Frederick City to Monocacy Junction where the 13th would "take cars for Baltimore." The news was greeted with joy that "the next day's march would find us on our way home." Men from the other three regiments in the brigade came to bid their comrades goodbye and to wish them good luck, sharing "the hope they would soon follow." The evening of their last night in camp, the happy soldiers sat around the campfires, as "the army songs rang out with unusual spirit and emotion." Outside their camp, they heard "much moving of troops and commotion about during the night indicating a general advance of the army."

LONERGAN AND HIS MEN rose with the rest of the 13th "before the morning sun began to light up the eastern sky," marking the direction they would take on their trip homeward. The orders for their last day in the field set "the hour for breaking camp" at 7:00 AM and everyone was busy preparing breakfast and getting ready for the march. "Knapsacks were carefully looked over, arranged and packed for the homeward march, haversacks were filled with rations, our uniforms, straps and guns cleaned and brushed up as best we could under the circumstances." Sturtevant considered his outfit "at this time a pretty seedy, dirty, hard looking set of soldiers." This was hardly surprising as they had been fifteen days on the march and in battle in the same clothes, and their uniforms and shoes were falling apart. Only now that they were leaving the war zone could they take time to be concerned about their appearance.

Well before the designated hour, everyone had finished his morning meal and stood ready to shoulder knapsacks and muskets, anxious to start the march home. On the "lovely morning" that ended their active role in the war, the men of the 13th knew that thousands of other Vermonters were moving westward to confront Lee, "held at bay by the high waters of the Potomac." The regiment fell in and formed a column to retrace its steps near Middletown and gain the national road leading east. They soon encountered the First Vermont Brigade marching in the opposite direction as part of the Union forces gathering against the rebel army. Despite hopes that the Army of Virginia might yet be crushed and the war ended, Vermonters would in fact face more years of sacrifice and battle.

As the 13th waited for the "Old Brigade" to pass, Lonergan must have felt some sense of vindication as he stood at the head of his "Irish Company." The 2nd Vermont was the unit to which he had first reported with his Emmet Guards, only to see it disbanded by Erastus Fairbanks. Now Lonergan, taking great pride in the performance of his reincarnated Irish nationalist company, could return the salutes of his former comrades with satisfaction. Knowing his role in the recent battle had proved that he was indeed a commander of men and worthy of his rank, he must have relished the moment when the 2nd marched by. Watching the three-year men head west to continue the war, however, Lonergan no doubt was content to be returning home with the laurels he had won at Gettysburg.

Stepping out along the national road—built with a gentle grade that ascended gradually along the mountainside for a number of miles—the regiment had "a grand panoramic view" of the valley below when they reached the top around noon and rested for an hour, lunching from rations in their haversacks. Spread below them was "a great army in camp and moving[:] cavalry, infantry and artillery and white cotton covered wagons loaded with supplies" with the hills around Harper's Ferry in the background. An inspiring and awesome spectacle, but one that no longer included the 13th—they had done their full duty and were now released to return home. When the order was given to fall in, "the boys all along the line involuntarily commenced to sing." The well-known lines of "John Brown's Body" rang out with great fervor and emotion as they turned for home.

THE COLUMN MARCHED ACROSS the mountain and on a zigzag road down to the valley below, arriving in Frederick late in the afternoon, where Randall granted the men half an hour to receive the adulation of the citizens. Flowers

CHAPTER SEVENTEEN – RETURNING HOME

and food were pressed on the combatants from Gettysburg. Even though not all the residents were pleased at the outcome of the battle, Sturtevant thought that more people were now displaying loyalty to the Union than had been observed on their visit ten days before. Moving on through the city, the 13th arrived at the railroad station of Monocacy Junction and "indifferently lunched from the contents of our haversacks, realizing that likely it was the last supper on army rations."

Unfortunately, no passenger cars awaited them for the trip to Baltimore. The offer of boarding the soldiers on "a few old dirty cattle cars" sparked the profane wrath of Randall. The colonel had been assured of proper transportation and had hurried his regiment on to reach the station at the designated time. According to Sturtevant, Randall "never lacked adjectives" when he vented his disgust and displeasure at the idea of placing his heroic troops in cars filthy from the delivery of cattle to the army. His regiment would not be "obliged to stand up or wallow in the dirt and offal that covered not only the floor[,] but [the] sides of the cars, besmeared with manure, hair, mud, etc." He would sooner march his men all the way to Baltimore—or even all the way to Vermont, the colonel raged—rather than allow them to be treated with such disrespect. The cars were moreover dangerous and Randall did not propose to allow men who had fought at Gettysburg to now be killed by the railroad.

Within an hour, clean box cars in good repair were brought in from the east and the men loaded into them, fifty or more to a car. There were no seats, but the men "sat our guns up in the corners and made seats of our knapsacks, those that had any." Soon after dark, the train started for Baltimore. The ride was so rough a soldier could not stand up without holding on or bracing on the side of the car. Yet the men were quite content, "for it was better than marching in the mud and hot sun… and carrying your own baggage" and the car was "a palace" compared to the sleeping quarters of the past fifteen days. The time was passed "telling stories and cracking jokes and relating experiences of march and battle," along with talk of the future.

The travel was slow, so they did not reach Ellicott City until after midnight. Delays there brought the train into Baltimore just before daylight. Stacking arms on the platform of the depot, the soldiers spent the day in the city getting cleaned up. Those with any money visited bath houses and barber shops, and purchased food to supplement the provided rations of coffee and soft bread.

In Baltimore, Lonergan temporarily turned over command of his company to 2nd Lt. McDevitt so that he could travel to Washington and collect his wife, Roseanna. She had evidently gone there from the camp on the Occoquan when the brigade had taken to the field and had waited in the capital to rejoin her husband for the return trip to Vermont. Since other ladies had also been at the camp, arrangements may have been made for them to stay as a group in Washington. (If Sinnott's fiancé had also made the trip south—properly chaperoned, of course—she would have been waiting with Lonergan's wife.) The published lists of casualties in the recent battle would have been anxiously scanned to determine who had survived the conflict uninjured. At least friends from Vermont would have been on hand to comfort a new widow or the wife or sweetheart of a wounded soldier when she learned of his fate.

As when he left Camp Lincoln in Brattleboro for his wedding in Burlington, Lonergan would have secured his colonel's permission to travel to Washington to collect Roseanna. Probably the husbands made the train trip to the capital and returned with their wives as a group. The regiment was in any case delayed overnight in Baltimore, waiting for the unit's surgeon to deliver those men from the hospitals in Washington and Alexandria whom he deemed able to travel to Vermont. Randall appears to have been determined to bring the members of his regiment back home together, as far as possible. (It is not clear whether the ladies were able to travel with the regiment, but it seems likely that Randall included them in the arrangements for transportation.)

Departing Baltimore on the evening of July 11, the train arrived in Philadelphia early the next morning. As on their trip south nine months before, the Vermonters were again treated to a generous meal. This was the first time the men had "sat down to a table to eat" since the previous visit to the city on October 12. The 13th received a particularly "warm and hearty reception" since they were the first regiment that had fought at Gettysburg to pass through Philadelphia. The population knew of their exploits on the battlefield and pressed fruit and bouquets on the men, cheering them as they marched through the city. Randall and his troops basked in "their manifestation of joy and satisfaction for victory and the driving of General Lee and his great marauding army from their state."

CHAPTER SEVENTEEN – RETURNING HOME

In sharp contrast, Sturtevant dismissed the arrival in Jersey City, at a little past noon on July 12, with distasteful memories of the foul food they had received in that port city on the trip south. Well-fed in Philadelphia, "there was not a soldier in the regiment that had any desire for Jersey Soup or Jersey food of any kind." Just before sundown the men embarked on a steamboat, but it remained tied up for the night and departed only the next morning. Disappointed that they did not wake up already in Connecticut, the Vermonters were in part compensated by the view of the busy New York harbor that included passing near the enormous steamship *Great Eastern*, at the time the "largest leviathan that had ever rode the sea." The men "had heard and read of it and to see it was an unexpected privilege." The daylight "journey up the sound was delightful, and all were thankful for the delay," despite their eagerness to get back home.

Docking in New Haven around noon, the 13th only had a short wait before being loaded onto passenger cars for the train ride to Brattleboro. Sturtevant wrote that the homecoming of the 13th, now known as heroes in the battle at Gettysburg, "had been announced in the newspapers" and "every hamlet, village and city we passed through were out in great numbers waving handkerchiefs and flags" as the train made its way through Massachusetts. No sooner had it pulled to a stop in Springfield about 8:00 PM than "the cars were filled with loyal citizens, lovely girls with baskets of ham sandwiches, pies and cakes, and pails with hot coffee." They "freely gave" to the men and "the boys cheered and thanked them for their kindness and generosity." The exploits of Stannard's brigade were "even now a familiar story in every patriotic home of New England," and accounted for the "unusual demonstrations" as they returned home. Sturtevant claimed that it "was a continuous ovation from New Haven to Brattleboro," with every town and city striving to outdo the others in their appreciation.*

The three regiments of the Second Vermont Brigade still in the field continued their service until Lee had crossed back into Virginia the night of July 13-14. With only days left to serve on their enlistments, "it was not considered worth while longer to retain the brigade, and the regiments were relieved" on July 18. (See End Note.)

---

*The 12th Vermont had preceded them to Brattleboro, arriving on July 9, but received no such tumultuous welcomes since it had not taken a direct part in the fighting at Gettysburg. Although that regiment lost two officers and sixty-two men to disease, it suffered no casualties from combat during its service.

JUST BEFORE MIDNIGHT, the train carrying the 13th reached Brattleboro and the regiment was back in Vermont, even if not yet home. Despite the late hour, to the "great surprise" of the soldiers "the whole town seemed to be at the depot waiting and as we rolled into the station cheer upon cheer expressed the hearty welcome to their own Green Mountain Boys now fresh from the battlefield of Gettysburg." Governor Holbrook, Adjutant General Washburn, and Colonel Blunt with his 12th Vermont were all at the station "with torches and music and banners" to give the 13th "a royal welcome." The arriving heroes were escorted to Camp Lincoln to the strains of "Home, Sweet Home," along with "Yankee Doodle Dandy" and other tunes. The regiment was housed in the same barracks where they had spent their first days of service and some men even took the same bunks as before. No one complained now about "only bare boards for beds." These were luxuries after what the men of the 13th had experienced—"neither woodticks nor black snakes could crawl in during the night." With "no vigilance required on the picket line," the men could sleep soundly, well satisfied with their welcome home.

ALTHOUGH EVERYONE WAS EAGER to complete the necessary administrative process and muster out, a full week was consumed in the paperwork and inspections required. While in the camp, "flattering inducements of honor and money were made to the boys of the 13th to re-enlist, [and] accept commissions to recruit for the 17th Vermont Regiment which was soon to take the field as a veteran regiment." Many of the men considered re-enlisting to continue the fight to suppress the rebellion, but generally took the approach "will go home first before deciding." After their service, "experience begot wisdom, and wisdom conservative thought and action." Meanwhile, everyone was busy as "officers were preparing pay rolls and accounts for final settlement and the boys were looking up to see if guns, straps, etc. charged up in their account were in hand to be turned over to the government."

Some men "had foolishly left their guns behind," but others had collected an extra rifle on the battlefield and "placed them in the hands of the boys who lost their guns." Despite having to pay for weapons and equipment not

CHAPTER SEVENTEEN – RETURNING HOME

returned, "a few of the boys retained their guns, straps, etc. to take home as mementoes of service in the Civil War." While waiting in camp for the paperwork to be completed, "time began to hang heavy," as "friends and relatives from up the state were arriving on every train" and "the boys were anxious to leave for home." Urged to tell of their exploits on the battlefield, some soldiers perhaps exaggerated their personal roles in the victory. Yet Sturtevant granted each man who was actually on the battlefield the right "to fairly tell the numerous instances of imminent peril from shot and shell on that great field of slaughter."

The 12th was mustered out on July 14, the day after the 13th arrived, and so Randall was placed in charge of the camp. He allowed the numerous visitors to make use of the spare barracks for accommodations and there was a relaxed atmosphere in the camp with "plenty of room and abundance to eat." Rumor flew through the camp that "the accounts had been figured up, pay rolls made out, discharge certificates filled out and signed and the paymaster would commence to pay off on Saturday." This meant that mustering out might take place that day, when "all would be ready to leave for home." A few of the men had been able to spruce up their appearance with new clothes, but until payday most were still forced to wear their worn-out shoes and to disregard the "holes and rents" in their coats and trousers.

Friday came, July 17, and all weapons and equipment had been turned in or accounted for, pay rolls adjusted and verified, but Randall found that some of the line officers had not made their companies ready for mustering out. As a consequence, Maj. Austine, the Regular Army officer who had mustered them in nine months before, could not proceed. Sturtevant diplomatically does not name the company commanders who were delinquent in preparing their reports.

It takes no stretch of the imagination to picture Lonergan as being the captain least "diligent and faithful and prompt and accurate in all matters pertaining to his position." Sturtevant claims that his own commander, Capt. Blake, had his paperwork done first.

It would give a tidy symmetry to Lonergan's military career if he were responsible for delays in both mustering in the 2nd Vermont and mustering out the 13th. Whoever was responsible for this "needless neglect" of the paperwork, Randall corrected the situation when he "manifested his feelings in his usual forceful language," and mustering out was rescheduled for Monday.

WHILE THE 13TH VERMONT processed out of Camp Lincoln, the other three regiments of the brigade were headed home. Traveling by train through Baltimore, they arrived in New York City on July 20 to find that draft riots had been raging for four days. The Irish were particularly opposed to the draft and had been largely responsible for the bloody disturbances. The police had been unable to control the situation and the military had been called in to suppress the riots. The general commanding in the city asked that the Vermont regiments remain to keep order until other forces could arrive.

The men of the 14th listened to "an earnest speech" by Nichols asking them to volunteer to stay a few more days, but they voted to return home and their commander honored their wishes. The 15th and 16th still had a short time left to serve and were not given any option. They stayed on for two more days to assist in quelling the riots until they were relieved by other units and continued their journey to Vermont.*

As in New York City, Boston, and elsewhere, the Rutland Irish had reacted violently against the instigation of the draft and had attacked the agents sent to enforce the conscription of the unwilling soldiers. Marshals entering the West Rutland quarries were driven off by the "stonepeggers" hurling chunks of rock with painful effect. Editorials in Vermont newspapers railed against those immigrants who would enjoy the benefits of citizenship, only to refuse to do their duty to protect their adopted country. The only non-citizens who were subject to being drawn in the draft lottery were those who had exercised their voting rights, as this was seen as tantamount to claiming citizenship. The draft lottery was supposedly random, but many Irish felt that the selection of the names was in fact rigged to send a disproportional number of them to the war.

ON MONDAY, JULY 20, each of the companies of the 13th Vermont fell into line near their quarters in Camp Lincoln and the roll was called to determine if all the men were present or accounted for. The company commanders

---

* Each of the regiments processed through Camp Lincoln in turn: the 14th mustered out on July 30, the 15th followed on August 5, and the 16th on August 10, closing the books on the Second Vermont Brigade.

CHAPTER SEVENTEEN – RETURNING HOME

reported the status of their units when Austine and Randall, along with some of the regimental staff, appeared before them. Austine gave a quick look at the final written report and made a personal inspection of the line before telling the men with a smile, "You are released from further service." Discharge papers had been prepared for each man and were delivered to them before they left camp. Pay call took longer, as each soldier had to sign for the amount received. This was a small sum since they had last been paid on the Occoquan—many miles away, yet only five weeks before. Much of the pay was quickly spent by the soldiers treating themselves and their comrades to lemonade, ice cream, and cake—a welcome change from hardtack and coffee.

The first half of July 21 was spent in packing the few personal belongings left to the men, along with bidding farewell to comrades whom they might not see again. A bugle call at mid-day assembled the companies for a final roll call, each man answering to his name in turn. When the orderly sergeant reported "All present or accounted for," the company was marched to the parade ground where the regiment was formed up in a hollow square.

Randall, the other field-grade officers, and the regimental staff entered the square for a parting ceremony. The colonel thanked his men for their loyalty and bravery, expressing his pride in their performance of duty "and especially your dash and courage in battle." He acknowledged that his heart was saddened by the loss of so many fine comrades from their ranks. Stating "I do not enjoy fighting," he nonetheless planned on offering his services again "unless the war is soon over." Nothing would please him more than to lead these same men if they were to re-enlist and he was made their colonel. Wishing everyone well, he invited each man to "come forward that I might take you by the hand before we start for home."

Breaking ranks, the men surged forward "helter skelter" to shake their commander's hand and then returned to their barracks before marching to the depot around 2:00 PM. Rail transportation to the station nearest their home had been arranged at no cost to the soldiers. Most still wore their uniforms "and were proud that we had earned the right to do so," but now they were mustered out and "free to go wherever it pleased us best." Boarding the waiting trains at the depots, the companies scattered across the state and the short, but glorious, history of the 13th Vermont Volunteer Infantry Regiment came to an end.

Each company was delivered by rail to the place where it had boarded the trains some nine months previously. Word of their homecoming would have spread and suitable arrangements made for them to be welcomed back, whatever the hour of arrival might be. The disbanding of the 13th meant that most of these former soldiers were now no more than individuals from the same area who had been members of a company and shared that common bond.

Lonergan's group of men, however, retained its identity as the militia company that had been designated as Co. A, 13th Vermont. They were hailed as the Emmet Guards in the headline to an article in the *Rutland Herald* of July 23. It reported "This company arrived here from Brattleboro Tuesday night at midnight, and were welcomed at the depot by a large number of friends. Yesterday morning those not belonging in this vicinity left for Burlington. This company distinguished itself in the recent battles and merits a warm welcome from all."

The scene on arrival at the Rutland depot probably resembled the departure from Brattleboro the previous autumn. There no doubt was some "drink taken" among the crowd of friends waiting to greet the returning soldiers and the alcohol—whether "bootleg" liquor or home-brewed "poteen"—was surely shared with the boys in uniform at the station and later. Joy at greeting the survivors would have been tempered by mourning for the loss of the men who had died while in the service. Tears would have been shed in both cases, accompanied no doubt by keening for the departed and Gaelic words of affection for the living. In addition to the four members of the "Irish Company" killed in the battle, word of Sinnott's death at a Gettysburg hospital had only recently arrived.* Two more Rutland Irishmen had died of disease while on duty; the only other deaths in the company had been two men from Westford, both from illness. Several additional Rutland soldiers were also absent from the ranks of the Emmet Guards that night, still in hospitals recovering from wounds or illness.

During the overnight stay in Rutland, the recent exploits of the returning veterans and the general situation with the Civil War would naturally have been the main topic of conversation. Lonergan likely also discussed the status of the Fenian movement with his fellow Irish. The death of half a dozen

---

*After some optimistic reports in the Rutland newspapers of his likely recovery, Sinnott died from his head wound, probably on July 10.

CHAPTER SEVENTEEN – RETURNING HOME

Irishmen in Lonergan's company, probably all Fenians, was an indication of the losses that the movement was suffering in the war. A free and independent Ireland remained the goal of the Fenian Brotherhood and glasses were no doubt raised to toast the day when the crown would be removed from the harp. Combat experience gained by dedicated Fenians, even at the cost of many members, could provide the skills and leadership to make this dream a reality, once the Union was restored.

Did the Westford soldiers now feel they were "honorary Irish" and join in the celebrating? These solid Yankees had spent enough time in the "Irish Company" to have learned the ways of their comrades and perhaps a bit of the language, including the battle cry and useful curse words. Even if excluded from the Fenian discussions, the Westford men may have taken part in the welcoming festivities for the local boys, their comrades in battle. Certainly the Burlington contingent of Irishmen, headed up by Lonergan, would have had no reason to hold back from fully joining in the celebration. Some men may have been less than sober when they boarded the train again the next morning, but at least they would have a few hours to sleep in the cars before arriving in Burlington.

While a larger and equally enthusiastic crowd in Burlington welcomed Lonergan and the thirty or so men remaining in his group, the greetings and praise were clearly for "Company A of the 13th Regiment." In contrast to the Rutland paper, which consistently used the name of the militia company, underscoring its Fenian ties, the *Free Press* gave full coverage to the arrival of the heroes of Gettysburg without making any reference to the Emmet Guards. The emphasis among the Yankees was on the Vermont connection, not the Irish nationalist character of the unit. On July 22, nonetheless, Lonergan and his men were the focus of attention throughout the area as their train pulled into Burlington about 9:00 AM. The sunny day promised to be warm later, even with the trees in full leaf and a breeze off the lake, but the men could change their wool uniforms for cooler civilian clothes after the ceremonies were finished.

A reception line of dignitaries was drawn up at the depot to meet the train, accompanied by a large number of spectators who no doubt included friends and relatives of the Emmet Guards. (One hopes that Lonergan's family was given a prominent place in the reception line.) Lonergan formed up the remaining men of his company to take their place in a procession. A "military escort" was provided by Co. C of the 12th Regiment—they had arrived a week before to greetings "alike in extent and enthusiasm" by the community—and the parade included the area fire companies, while a large number of citizens brought up the rear. The Jericho Coronet Band joined forces with the Westford Drum Corps to furnish suitable martial and patriotic music. As Lonergan led his men past the receiving line, a thirteen-gun salute, the number presumably reflecting the regimental designation, boomed from cannon on the battery overlooking the lake.

Lonergan's company was "greeted with constant and repeated cheers" from the crowd at the depot and on the streets "thronged with the citizens of the place, male and female, on foot, in carriages and on horse-back, all hearty in welcoming and honoring the men who had served their country well." The procession moved uphill from the lake along Main Street to the park in the center of the town and formed a circle around the speaker's stand. Sullivan Adams, Esq., presented "a pertinent and eloquent speech" in which he praised Lonergan and his men for their good service, especially "the gallantry they had displayed in the recent battle." He pointed out that they were volunteers, not drafted men, who had responded bravely when "asked for by the government." Credit was also given to their willingness when almost safely home "to again turn back and aid in crushing treason in New York City," a clear reference to the draft riots and a warning to disaffected Irish protesting conscription. These men honored here, said Mr. Adams, were "true patriots and loyal men—an honor to the State of Vermont, deserving of distinguished honor from their fellow citizens." Sketching out the career of the Second Vermont Brigade, the speaker praised it highly before introducing the man of the hour, Capt. John Lonergan.

Lonergan responded with "a very soldierlike [sic] and appropriate speech, thanking the citizens of Burlington for their hearty and gratifying welcome." He "spoke with justifiable pride of the achievements of his own men, and of the 13th regiment," his remarks being "frequently interrupted by cheers." Calling the battle of Gettysburg the "proudest day of his life," Lonergan was glad to have "helped secure a triumph for the flag whose inspiration cheered him on the field." With "the national flag streaming in the sunshine on all sides, with the stirring notes of Yankee Doodle" blaring from the coronet band, people naturally would assume that the flag that inspired Lonergan was the Stars and Stripes, carried into battle by the 13th. Still, some of the Irish in the applauding crowd would have been aware that he was implying

CHAPTER SEVENTEEN – RETURNING HOME

13TH VERMONT GETTYSBURG BATTLEFIELD MARKER AND MONUMENT

something different. Although he was loyal to the Union cause and respected the American flag, the Fenian banner, whose sunburst and uncrowned harp he wore inside his uniform, inspired the Irishman as well.

After describing the successes of his troops—the *Free Press* declared they had "won so much honor for the Union cause and for Vermont," again avoiding any mention of the company's Irish identity—Lonergan called for three cheers for the wounded Stannard, the brigade commander. These were followed in turn by cheers "given for Captain Lonergan and for Company A." Standing on the speaker's platform, he acknowledged the accolades for him as a Vermonter, but he probably also noted the studied avoidance of any recognition of the "Irish Company" as such. The persisting anti-Irish bias in the state had been recently reinforced by the draft riots, but Lonergan and his men had set an example of bravery and loyalty to the Union that could not be ignored.

From the elevated platform, Lonergan could see the roof of his Emmet Guard armory, beyond the courthouse located on the park's edge. The Skinner's Lane building had served him as a drill hall for the militia company and as his personal cooper's shop. Soon it would be transformed into the state headquarters of the Fenian Brotherhood, where the struggle for Ireland's freedom would be organized in Vermont. Lonergan's fame as a war hero would be a valuable asset in promoting the cause; his military skills and leadership experience would be put to a new use.

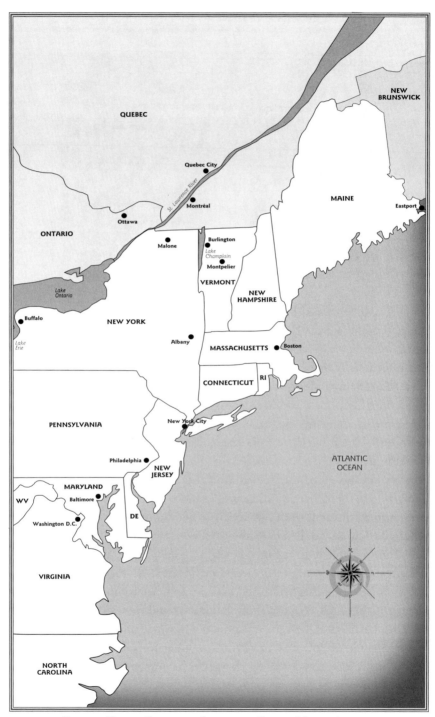

Eastern United States and Southwest British North America

PART THREE

CANADA

CANADIAN HOME GUARD AND DEAD FENIAN

"And we'll go and capture Canada for we've nothing else to do."

— FENIAN MARCHING SONG, 1870

John Lonergan (probably circa 1880)

CHAPTER EIGHTEEN

FOSTERING IRISH NATIONALISM

After mustering out of the army, Lonergan no longer drew his pay as a captain. Even though everyone recognized him as a war hero, he needed to earn a living for himself and his wife of less than a year. Reunited after the Gettysburg campaign, a time that Roseanna had spent waiting anxiously in Washington, they could finally set up housekeeping back home in Burlington. Steady work for John and a roof over their heads were needed to provide for the children likely to come. From the sketchy information available, Lonergan seems to have devoted the first year after he mustered out mainly to local politics and the promotion of Irish nationalism. Like other men in his family, John was an accomplished cooper; he also had experience in the grocery business. But neither of these two options apparently had any immediate appeal for him. The expanding Fenian Brotherhood was paying local organizers at this time and the movement may have provided him some financial help in return for his work in Vermont.

With his combat experience, Lonergan might have resumed service in the army. Despite the Union victories at Gettysburg and Vicksburg, Lee's successful retreat across the Potomac ensured that the Civil War would continue. However, volunteers, including Lonergan, were increasingly reluctant to enlist in the Union military. The draft, necessary under the circumstances, proved widely and sometimes violently unpopular, particularly among the Irish working class.

Those men who could be raised in Vermont through the inducements of bounties or the enforcement of conscription were needed just to keep the existing regiments up to strength. However, Governor Holbrook on August 3, 1863, authorized a special effort to recruit veteran soldiers from the disbanded nine-month regiments of the Second Vermont Brigade into a new unit, the 17th Vermont Volunteer Infantry Regiment. Some officers from the disbanded regiments volunteered to serve with the 17th, and Randall, former commander of the 13th, was appointed to lead the new regiment.

Stannard, the Second Brigade commander, remained on active duty while recuperating in Vermont from the wound he received at Gettysburg.* (An intense public interest in the battle and the key role played by Stannard's troops prompted the general's aide, Benedict, to present lectures on the subject in Burlington.) Hancock, who had commanded the Second Corps at Gettysburg, similarly spent time at home in Pennsylvania being treated for his own severe wound. A dispute arose between the accounts of Stannard and Hancock as to who had ordered the flank attack that helped shatter the rebel assault on July 3. The official reports of both generals claimed the initiative in exploiting the situation. One established fact never brought into question was the leading role of Lonergan and his "Irish Company" in the crucial maneuver. In each general's version of events, Lonergan's unit was clearly acknowledged as the first to take up a position on the rebels' right flank. Stannard's official report of the battle, written at Gettysburg on July 4, stated unequivocally that firing into the rebels' right flank started when "the Thirteenth changed front forward on first company" as ordered.

SAFELY HOME FROM THE WAR, Lonergan appears to have been content to rest his military career on the fame earned at Gettysburg and turned his attention again to the Irish struggle for liberation. Any successful uprising in Ireland would depend on American support in arms and manpower, especially proven commanders. The plan for effective action in the homeland was based on an end to the Civil War in America and the experienced Irish soldiers who would be mustered out.

The British government's continued assistance of the Confederacy helped to prolong the conflict. In particular, the sale of purpose-built and well-equipped ships to the rebels allowed these "commerce raiders" to effectively attack American merchant vessels. But any hopes the Irish nationalists held that the United States might either declare war outright or support them

---

* Stannard was not yet able to ride a horse and so could not take the field. As a result, on September 1, he was assigned to New York City. He was subsequently placed in charge of the defenses of the city and harbor on November 11, reporting to Maj. Gen. John A. Dix, commander of the Department of the East.

CHAPTER EIGHTEEN – FOSTERING IRISH NATIONALISM

in an uprising against the British went unfulfilled. Lincoln was too canny a politician to be dragged into war with Great Britain while he was entangled in putting down his own rebellion.

However, even as the war continued between the states, steps could be taken to organize the forces of Irish nationalism in Ireland and abroad, preparing to strike when conditions were favorable. From the viewpoint of the nationalists, neither the political situation in Ireland nor the economic plight of its common people had improved significantly through the early 1860s and the country was still ripe for revolution. Given Lonergan's position in the movement, he probably was kept informed of nationalist developments in Ireland through Fenian channels. He surely was aware of public reports such as the article that appeared in the *Rutland Courier* on September 4. Copied from the Dublin *Daily Express*, it described a "Monster Meeting to Protest Against Public Wrongs" held the previous Saturday, August 29, "on the heights of Slievenamon Mountain" near Lonergan's birthplace.

Despite bad weather, about seven hundred people, "principally of the laboring class," reportedly made the climb to where "a flag of red [sic], white, and green," displaying an Irish harp without any crown, flew over Finn McCool's cairn. The massive stone, "Finn's Chair,"—renamed Meagher's Rock after the Young Irelander who had spoken so movingly from there in 1848—provided a natural platform for Charles Kickham of nearby Mullinahone to preside over the meeting held to "renew their vows never to cease until they had achieved the independence of Ireland." As the crowd shouted "Down with the landlords!" and other revolutionary slogans, each speaker in turn urged them to prepare for the time when forces abroad would come to their aid. They announced their intention to hold a series of nationalist meetings on the mountains of Tipperary, although admitting that speeches would not achieve their goal. Independence could only be won "by the pike" and nationalists should "rally round the green flag till they planted it forever above the red on the highest parapets of Dublin."

The reference to Slievenamon would have recalled for Lonergan that familiar landmark of his boyhood, along with memories of the chaos and failure of 1848. He had personally experienced the destructive power of modern firearms at Gettysburg and must have shuddered at the thought of his rebel countrymen taking the field still armed with pikes. Clearly, any successful rebellion would require proper arms, leadership, and organization.

Ireland depended in large part on the nationalists in America to provide the necessary weapons and commanders.

Organization of the revolutionary movement was progressing on both sides of the Atlantic as Stephens expanded his clandestine efforts in the British Isles, while open recruiting for the Fenian Brotherhood brought in thousands of new members in America. Lonergan remained committed to striking a blow for Irish freedom and the Fenians were obviously the group that would give him an opportunity. With his release from military service to the United States, the time to act for Ireland had now come.

Growth in the American branch of the movement had reached the point where the chief, John O'Mahony, decided to call a national convention to build the foundation for the next phase. Chicago was chosen as the location, probably reflecting the strong support for the Fenian Brotherhood in the surrounding states, even though the headquarters of the organization remained in New York City and the bulk of the members were still from the Northeast.

The meeting convened on November 3, 1863, and was likely timed to coincide with the usual cessation of military operations in the autumn. Representatives attending the convention included soldiers from the Army of the Potomac, the Army of the Cumberland, and the Army of the Tennessee, as the forces went into winter quarters. Despite British objections, Lincoln allowed serving Union army officers to be released from duty and permitted to travel to the Fenian congress, an action that Her Majesty's servants considered to be tacit support by the American government of Irish revolutionary designs. This was no doubt Lincoln's intention. The Fenians were a useful tool with which British interests could be threatened, perhaps discouraging their aid to the Confederacy.

A dozen northern states sent delegates to the gathering. However, Vermont is not listed among the participants and no record of Lonergan making the trip to Chicago has been found. In addition to the American delegations, representatives from the neighboring British dominion were present. Members of the Irish nationalist circles in Montreal, Quebec City, Hamilton, and probably Toronto attended the meeting (although some of them may well have been serving the British by reporting on the activities to the governor of Canada).

Stephens sent Kickham, organizer of the Slievenamon gathering, to the American convention as his own representative, to observe the

CHAPTER EIGHTEEN – FOSTERING IRISH NATIONALISM

proceedings first-hand. At the meeting, the structure of the Fenian Brotherhood was modified from a strictly military force into essentially a government in exile for Ireland. O'Mahony was confirmed as the national head centre, subject to annual elections, with the power to appoint state head centres. New circles were to be formed as the minimum sixty members were initiated, each man to be proposed by a trusted Fenian. State agents were designated to visit likely communities to recruit new members and help organize circles; in areas with multiple circles, districts were established. The initiation fee was set at one dollar and membership dues were to be at least ten cents a week. When a candidate was accepted, he took an oath to "labor with zeal for the liberation of Ireland from the yoke of England" and to obey the commands of his superior officers in the Brotherhood. The previous military oath was superseded and men were no longer required to be able-bodied.

In addition to the publicly approved resolutions, the convention adopted three secret statements to be carried back to Stephens by Kickham. One of these declared "the Republic of Ireland to be virtually established" and another acknowledged Stephens' role as the "Supreme Organizer of the Irish race." Nonetheless, O'Mahony continued to act as his equal in developing the Fenian Brotherhood on the western side of the Atlantic.

Despite its expansion and reorganization, the movement faced enormous challenges, both internal and external. Within the American branch, a group called "the men of action" was agitating for an operation against British interests in North America and they hoped to unseat O'Mahony as chief of the Brotherhood. Stephens perpetually complained about lack of financial support from America and his relations with O'Mahony steadily deteriorated. On both sides of the ocean, the Catholic Church generally disapproved of the revolutionary movement; much of the religious hierarchy condemned both the Fenian Brotherhood and Stephens' IRB because of their secrecy and the oath required. Moreover, the British government had succeeded in placing its agents and informers within the ranks of the movement and was consequently well-informed about the Fenians' situation and plans.

To promote nationalism and to raise funds for the cause, Stephens followed the example of earlier political leaders by publishing his own weekly newspaper, the *Irish People,* beginning November 28, 1864. It became the focal point of IRB operations, with the key jobs in Dublin held by stalwart revolutionaries. Kickham and Thomas Clarke Luby were the chief writers, while John O'Leary served as editor and O'Donovan Rossa as the business manager. High Catholic officials such as Cardinal Cullen denounced the newspaper for its revolutionary tone. Anti-clerical responses were provided by Kickham; as a Catholic he could challenge the Church's attitude with more credibility than Luby, who was a Protestant.

ALTHOUGH LONERGAN HAD TAKEN a leading role in the Irish nationalist movement in Vermont for some time, his formal appointment as "head centre" of Vermont appears to date from the fall of 1863. Apparently resulting from decisions made at the first Fenian convention, this position was created only when a state had sufficient active circles of Fenians. His former neighbor in Ireland, O'Mahony, may himself have put Lonergan forward to be the state chief of the Brotherhood. As the Irishman in Vermont most widely considered a war hero, Lonergan would have been an obvious choice to promote the nationalist organization; he is described in various sources as personable and humorous, a good public speaker and a fervent nationalist. In the year following the convention, the number of circles in Vermont increased dramatically, presumably as a result of organizational efforts. Lonergan likely was the driving force in this recruiting, although he also had assistance from outside the state, especially Boston. Paid organizers (who received $70 per month by 1866) were sent out by the Brotherhood to recruit members and help with the paperwork in forming new circles.

The Irish nationalist movement suffered the loss of an important leader just before Christmas of 1863. Corcoran, now a division commander, had been playing host to Meagher, who had been in Virginia visiting the Irish Legion at Fairfax Court House—familiar ground to the Second Vermont Brigade. Meagher departed on December 22; in the holiday spirit, Corcoran insisted on riding with him to the Fairfax railroad station. On his way back to camp, Corcoran tumbled from his horse onto an icy road. He was dying when found by his staff; he had survived combat and captivity only to take a fatal fall in connection with a social visit. Meagher marked the death of the original colonel of the 69th New York as "a black Christmas with us." Word came the day after the accident that the army had reinstated Meagher to active service, although no command assignment had been

CHAPTER EIGHTEEN – FOSTERING IRISH NATIONALISM

made. (The Irish Legion would have been an appropriate choice, but this strongly Fenian brigade might have had reservations about Meagher, since he had only taken the Fenian oath the previous July. At Meagher's request, O'Mahony himself had initiated him into the Brotherhood at the general's country home in New Jersey.)

Partly to deflect the criticism of the Catholic Church, the Fenian Brotherhood found it useful to organize more open and less revolutionary Irish associations as well.* Lonergan fulfilled this public role when he formed the Hibernian Society in Burlington in February of 1864, ostensibly for celebrating St. Patrick's Day the following month. He was elected president of the society by the members, which numbered over one hundred at the founding meeting and were expected to increase. The ladies of St. Mary's Church intended to present the group with "a handsome Irish banner" as part of the festivities.

The key feature of Burlington's first official St. Patrick's Day celebration, however, was the announcement that Meagher had been invited to speak on the occasion. With remarkable brashness, Lonergan had asked the most famous Irishman in the country to spend the most significant Irish holiday in a small town in Vermont. Surprisingly, Meagher accepted the invitation, although events delayed his visit. The orator was much in demand as a speaker and Lonergan must have pulled some strings (perhaps through his Fenian connections) to persuade Meagher to make the journey, especially on that holiday. A proud announcement appeared on February 27 that "Gen. Meagher has accepted the invitation of the Hibernian Society to deliver an address here on the 17th of March," but with the caveat that he would "be present unless prevented by some call of the military service not now anticipated." The general was described as "an eloquent and truly patriotic son of the Green Isle" whose appeal extended beyond the Irish community.

---

* In Canada West, Michael Murphy (also a cooper by trade) had taken over the secret Toronto circle of Fenians in 1860 and similarly used it as a base to control the larger Hibernian Benevolent Society in the city. Organized after a riot between Catholics and Orangemen on St. Patrick's Day of 1858, the Hibernians could justify arming themselves and holding military drills as necessary for the protection of the Irish Catholic community.

A Montreal branch of the Hibernians likewise surfaced in 1864 to arrange for St. Patrick's Day celebrations. Not as large as the official St. Patrick's Day Society, they compensated for their numbers with greater revolutionary fervor in songs and speeches. The former revolutionary D'Arcy McGee denounced this group for their disloyalty to the British monarchy.

According to the article in the *Free Press*, "all of our citizens will be glad to greet and hear him."

The schedule for the Burlington celebration that was published on March 14 still listed an evening "address by Gen. Thomas F. Meagher before the Hibernian Society," but warned that his "presence is not absolutely certain." The railroads offered to carry passengers round trip for the cost of a one-way fare and many visitors from other towns were expected at the festivities. At the last minute, apparently some "sudden call of military service" prevented Meagher from making his promised visit, much to the disappointment of Lonergan and other admirers.

The rest of the day's activities took place as planned, beginning at 9:00 AM with the presentation of a banner to the Hibernians at the Town Hall. Deliberately, no Fenian involvement surfaced in this first St. Patrick's Day celebration. The Hibernians, fully acceptable to the Church, stood in as the organization in charge even though their president, Lonergan, doubled as the head Fenian in Vermont.

The procession down Church Street in the bright morning sunshine was led by a detachment of "bould soger boys" from the 17th Vermont, whose camp was in Burlington. The contingent from the St. Patrick's Benevolent Society of Winooski followed them to the Town Hall, where the Hibernians and a large crowd had already gathered. The ladies of St. Mary's delivered "an elegant green silk flag, bearing on one side the Harp and Shamrock, and on the other the Eagle and Shield, with the inscription 'Ireland and America,' all beautifully painted and very handsomely mounted." This product of Annan & Co. of New York "was received by Capt. Lonergan, who responded in befitting terms." In expressing his appreciation, Lonergan referred to the glorious past of the green flag and the daring patriotism of those who had fought beneath it. He connected this green flag with the current conflict, saying, "Here, in America, where we are permitted to unfurl it, while we are ready to fight under the starry flag of our adoption, as we should do, no American will object to us fighting for it [i.e. America] under the flag of our native land."

The procession, headed by the Jericho Cornet Band, then marched to St. Mary's where Bishop DeGoesbriand celebrated a High Mass and Father Dennis Ryan preached a sermon. Father Ryan chose John 15:16, as his text: "I have chosen you, and have appointed you, that you should go and bring forth

CHAPTER EIGHTEEN – FOSTERING IRISH NATIONALISM

fruit, and your fruit should remain." While the *Free Press* reported that the sermon "related mainly to the life and example of the patron Saint of Ireland," many in the audience may well have exchanged meaningful glances. The nationalists listening to Ryan's sermon could easily interpret the admonition as extending to the fruit of their revolutionary movement, a free Ireland.

After the church services, the procession formed up and "marched through the principal streets, led by Capt. John Lonergan, Chief Marshal, who was handsomely mounted." (One spectator commented to the reporter that he "looked beautiful.") The ten Assistant Marshals included Lonergan's former first sergeant, James Scully. The parade was among the longest ever seen in Burlington up to that time and included delegations from Rutland and a number of other Irish communities. The Jericho Cornet Band marched immediately behind Lonergan in the procession, followed by 250 Hibernians, one hundred representatives from the St. Patrick's Society, the drum corps of the 17th Vermont, seventy members of that regiment, and a multitude of citizens. Stopping in front of the bishop's residence to receive his blessing, the crowd then assembled at the Town Hall "where some eloquent speeches were made by John J. Monahan and Capt. Lonergan," which were received with tremendous applause. These orations completed the daytime festivities and the "great gathering then dispersed."

A banquet for 250 guests at the American Hotel "fitly crowned and closed the ceremonies of the day." The Irish trooped into the hall at 10:00 PM, together with a number of invited guests. When the "bountiful supper, served in Mr. Drew's best style" had been consumed, Lonergan called for order and the toastmaster read the regular toasts, each toast followed by appropriate music from the Cornet Band. At the direction of J. E. FitzGerald, the glasses were first raised to "The Day we celebrate" to the tune of "St. Patrick's day." As president of the Hibernians, Lonergan responded to the toast. Speaking of the purposes of the society and the members' duties to each other as Irishmen, he closed with a quotation from "one of Erin's bards."

After a toast to "Our Native Land," the music of "Hail, Columbia" accompanied the toast in honor of "The President of the United States." Benedict, one of the invited guests, was called upon to respond. Stannard's former aide saw this respect for the leader of the country as yet another indicator of the patriotism of the Irish in America. He highly praised this loyalty and commented that one effect of the war was the removal of prejudices, allowing the creation of harmony between the native-born and the adopted citizen. His own experience convinced him that "certainly the men of the Green Isle, and of the Green Mountains, having fought side by side for the country; could never be aught but friends." Benedict's view of this military comradeship must have been based largely on serving with Lonergan and his "Irish Company," although there were Irishmen scattered throughout the Second Vermont Brigade. A dozen other toasts singled out the priesthood, Vermont, the adopted country, the army and navy, the American flag, and the Irish Brigade, trailing off into recognition of the Burlington press, the town's Young Men's Association, and the ladies.

These obligatory "regular toasts" then gave way to "volunteer toasts" with Provost Marshal Rollo Gleason calling for "our Irish soldiers" and "to your dinner," citing Irish hospitality with "Cead mille failthe." Glasses were then raised to "our worthy president," accompanied by the couplet:

> The gallant John Lonergan,
> He's with us to-night, faith, we're glad he's not gone again.

Lonergan recognized the invited guests and then gave the memories of Robert Emmet, Archbishop Hughes, and Lt. John Sinnott in succession, the honors to the dead received in silence. This somber moment passed and was replaced with "abundant hilarity" as singing changed the mood. Although the banquet continued into the "small hours" of the morning, the *Free Press* paid the respect due to the celebration for its "good order and propriety" and the patriotic tone of "Erin go Unum E pluribus bragh" expressed by the Irish.

Just below the lengthy article on the celebration (probably written by Benedict), the paper published a sobering notice from the Office of the Assistant Provost Marshal General in Brattleboro, dated March 16. This was addressed to the editor of the *Free Press* informing him that Lincoln had just issued a call for 200,000 men, in addition to the 500,000 requisitioned on February 1. In the notice, Brig. Gen. T. G. Pitcher advised the editor to urge the towns to avoid a draft and to take advantage of the "very liberal bounties" offered until April 1 to fill the ranks of the 17th Vermont. The editor appended his comment that the towns should consider themselves urged accordingly, though it had little effect in producing volunteers after nearly three years of bloodshed.

CHAPTER EIGHTEEN – FOSTERING IRISH NATIONALISM

Around this same time, Stephens had grown dissatisfied with the American support of the joint nationalist movement and decided to leave Ireland for a personal visit to solicit funds and to reinforce his own role as leader. The trip was timed so that he could participate in a second Fenian gathering in Chicago, a fair organized by "the men of action" to raise money for the Brotherhood and at the same time to promote their own agenda. Their emphasis on attacking British interests "by the shortest route" was at odds with the commitment of Stephens to an uprising in Ireland itself. However, he recognized that "the men in the gap" who took the field in Ireland might be helped by drawing British forces across the Atlantic to deal with troubles in Canada. Before departing Dublin, Stephens wrote a letter on March 9 that turned over executive power in Ireland to a committee made up of his *Irish Nation* staff—Kickham, Luby, and O'Leary.

The Fenian Fair opened on March 29 with the support and participation of the mayor and city council of Chicago. Although Bishop Dugan had threatened to withhold the sacraments from Catholics who were involved, the opening ceremonies and subsequent activities were well attended. Many gifts had been shipped over from Ireland as prizes for the various lotteries that were part of the fundraising.* The week-long fair reportedly took in $50,000 through the sale of tickets and donated articles, as well as the lotteries. O'Mahony had agreed to the fair on the condition that the funds would pass through the American organization, but Stephens had consented to his trip only with the understanding that the money would be channeled directly to him. Squabbles arose within the movement about the handling of these and other funds.

After the fair, Stephens procured a pass to travel the area under the alias of Daly. He visited Fenian circles in the Army of the Cumberland and the Department of the Mississippi, some of the nearly 15,000 Fenians serving in the military at that time. To bolster enthusiasm for the cause, Stephens

---

* Along with many items of Irish life like blackthorn walking sticks, numerous nationalist mementos were donated, such as an oak model of O'Connell's monument and a piece of wood supposedly from the coffin of Lord Edward Fitzgerald. Other artifacts from the risings of 1798 and 1848—including pikes, swords, and the spike from Mullinahone castle on which Norton's head had been placed in 1798—served the nationalist cause once more, this time to stimulate contributions.

pledged that either an Irish revolution would take place by 1865 or the IRB would be dissolved. O'Mahony opposed such a deadline since the support of the American wing was crucial and the Civil War could still be dragging on, preventing the release of the experienced Irish soldiers to support a rising.

On the day that the Chicago Fair opened, all the Hibernians in the Burlington society were notified by Lonergan to meet at their hall to conduct "business of importance." Consistently a loyal supporter of O'Mahony, Lonergan may have instructed his covert circle of Fenians, meeting as Hibernians, as to developments in the Brotherhood concerning the growing internal rifts. Such factional dissents had persistently plagued the Irish nationalist movements and must have been distressing to those men more interested in the cause than in personalities.

ON A POSITIVE NOTE, Lonergan also posted a notice in the newspaper that the Hibernian Society would soon host Meagher on a rescheduled visit to Burlington. Meagher had promised to present a lecture at the Town Hall on April 7 to compensate for his absence on St. Patrick's Day.

Meagher was booked to speak in Boston on April 6 and the *Free Press* carried an article on that date reassuring readers that the general would arrive the next day for his talk in Burlington. Accordingly, a reception was prepared at the train station on the following afternoon. The 17th Vermont and the Hibernian Society, together "with a large number of citizens," waited in vain for the first train from Boston. Supposing that he might have been delayed, the two evening trains were similarly greeted without success. The *Free Press* reported on April 8 that the large audience that had assembled in the Tremont Temple in Boston to hear Meagher on April 6 was "in a like manner disappointed by his non-arrival." Lonergan must have been embarrassed by his arrangements falling through without word from Meagher. Only on April 16 did the *Free Press* publish a note that Meagher had explained his absence as being due to military orders and had again rescheduled his visit to include two lectures the following week.

An advertisement offered the opportunity to hear Meagher speak at the Town Hall on April 21 and 22, admission each evening costing 25 cents and trains again offering round trip travel at one-way fares. Lonergan had received a letter from Meagher in New York City, dated April 13, which the

CHAPTER EIGHTEEN – FOSTERING IRISH NATIONALISM

Free Press printed in full on April 18. Meagher wrote to "My Dear Captain Lonergan" expressing his "mortification and vexation" at the failure of his aide to telegraph a cancellation of the lecture as instructed when the speaker was suddenly ordered to Washington. To make amends, Meagher offered to present two lectures, rather than just the one previously scheduled, and included his travel plans that would bring him by boat across Lake Champlain on April 21. Meagher begged Lonergan to pass on his regrets to all the general's friends in Burlington and to assure them that he would make the "long promised visit" before returning to the battlefield.

When Meagher did arrive by the steamer *Canada* on April 21, he was greeted almost as a head of state. The Hibernian Society, led by Lonergan, had assembled on the dock. A cannon salute was fired from the battery on the bluff as Meagher came ashore, accompanied by two civilians from New York City and Capt. Gosson, detailed from the 69th New York to Meagher's staff. Meagher entered a barouche drawn by four white horses and was escorted to the American Hotel. Lonergan had managed to bring the best-known Irishman in the United States to Burlington and had to be quite proud of this accomplishment, despite the earlier false starts.

That evening, Meagher's first lecture at the town hall attracted a large audience. He was introduced to the crowd by Capt. Lonergan with "some fitting remarks," and took the stage along with his entourage, Father Ryan, and W. H. Hoyt, editor of the *Sentinel*. Drawing on his considerable skills as an orator, Meagher compared the plight of Ireland to that of a wounded man, leaving a trail of blood and suffering that awakes a passion in all true sons of the country. He gave full credit to the late Corcoran for his love of their common native land, describing in details the exploits of the first commander of the 69th New York. Corcoran combined the best characteristics of "the loyal citizen, the brave soldier, the true Irishman" ready to fight for his adopted country and eager to strike a blow for Irish freedom. When he died in command of a division and his body lay in his quarters, Meagher drew a poignant picture of the Irish Legion marching in tears past his bier. Meagher was rated in the newspaper account as "a pleasing and effective speaker" and "passages in his lecture were received with frequent and hearty applause."

The following evening the town hall was "well filled" for Meagher's second lecture before the Hibernian Society, "Personal Recollections of the Irish Brigade and the Army of the Potomac." The audience was reportedly in a roar of laughter for half an hour as he recounted humorous incidents of camp life, before taking a more serious tone in reciting the sacrifices the Irish Brigade made in battle. He appealed to the audience to ensure that "the loss of so much blood and treasure" would not be in vain and that the Union would be preserved. Following this speech, about fifty local citizens joined the general and his group for dinner at the American Hotel. Meagher held forth at some length during the banquet, railing against the "Copperhead" Democrats who were undermining the war effort. Several others also spoke at the dinner, including Capt. Gosson and Mr. Clark of the general's entourage. Lonergan did not neglect this opportunity to express his personal gratitude toward Meagher for the visit, along with his own strong opinions about the Irish nationalist cause.

Meagher and his group left for New York the next morning. Although Meagher had been reinstated to service at the end of 1863, he was still waiting for an assignment. (See End Note.)

While Meagher soon accepted a position on the fringe of the war in Tennessee, the surviving sons of his former comrade in Ireland, John Mitchel, continued to serve in the thick of the battles. James had survived Gettysburg to fight in the trenches at Petersburg before the 1st Virginia moved into the Shenandoah Valley with Early's division. In June of 1864, the eldest son, Maj. John Mitchel, took command of Fort Sumter, where the first shots of the conflict had been fired. Union cannon had pounded the fort with over 40,000 shells in eleven months of bombardment without breaking its resistance. On July 20, Mitchel was atop a parapet when an exploding mortar shell drove a fragment into his chest, a fatal wound. Echoing Sarsfield when he died in Flanders in 1693, Mitchel expired with the words, "I willingly give my life for South Carolina; Oh! That I could have died for Ireland."*

Casualties among the Irish nationalists fighting for the Union also continued. When the 69th New York marched off to the war at its very beginning, John O'Mahony had been prepared to enlist as a private in order to join this Fenian regiment. Now, after three years of bloody fighting in which most members of that unit had been killed or disabled, O'Mahony raised his

---

* His dying words can be read on his tombstone in Charleston, where the grave lies surrounded by a representation of the parapet on which he perished.

CHAPTER EIGHTEEN – FOSTERING IRISH NATIONALISM

own regiment, with himself as colonel. At age forty-eight, the Fenian chief was beyond the limit for conscription, but he could still volunteer to lead a unit as a commissioned officer. The continuing need for new Union troops had drained the reservoir of volunteers and conscription was an unwelcome last resort. Various incentives such as bounties and short-term service were put forth, often with disappointing results. New York was accepting units for varying periods and that summer O'Mahony organized a regiment for only one hundred days service, recruiting men from the ranks of the Fenian Brotherhood in the city.

This action carried several related advantages. A primary benefit was to remove hundreds of sworn Fenians from the threat of conscription that would likely have taken them onto the battlefield, where the Brotherhood had already lost a large number of members. While their sacrifice helped the Irish to integrate into American society, preservation of fighting men was essential for the liberation of Ireland from British rule. A regiment serving only three months usually would not be sent into the field; instead, such units were routinely restricted to postings in the rear, particularly guard duties. Even the brief term of service would, however, provide valuable training in military skills and further validate the patriotism of the Irish toward their adopted country.

O'Mahony was unable to recruit a full regiment despite the enticements of short-term duty in a non-combat environment and only nine companies were mustered in on August 2, 1864, as the 99th New York. The newly-formed unit was shipped to Elmira, a small town in south-central New York just north of the Pennsylvania border, where part of an army post had just been converted into a prisoner of war camp. The 99th New York served out its three months before the conditions at the camp deteriorated too badly, but there was no glory in guarding miserable prisoners and even more danger of disease than in the average Union army camp. The regiment was mustered out on November 9, returning home in time to avoid the harsh winter.

THAT SUMMER, LONERGAN EXPLOITED his new-found fame to involve himself in local politics. When the Chittenden County Democrats met in Richmond, Vermont, at the end of July to nominate candidates for the upcoming elections, Lonergan was one of the three men chosen for the Burlington town committee. This committee organized the Democrats in Burlington, renting a room in Payne's block and holding weekly meetings. The first such meeting chose Morillo Noyes as president and Lonergan as one of the four vice-presidents. W. H. Hoyt, editor of the *Sentinel* and supporter of the Irish nationalist movement, also served as a vice-president.

In an on-going feud, Hoyt was singled out by the *Free Press* for scorn in accepting the platform of the Vermont Democrats. Benedict's newspaper—overtly partisan in favor of the Union Party that incorporated the Republicans—reported the Rutland and White River Junction Democratic conventions as being "Copperhead" in nature. In White River, they were said to have nominated a "fossil silver-gray whig" who was a "bitter sympathizer with the rebels" as the candidate for their Congressional district. The editor continued this diatribe against the Copperheads the next day. He pointed out that Meagher, who was currently expressing his support for McClellan as the Democratic candidate for president, had not manifested this approval of the former commander of the Army of the Potomac during his recent visit to Burlington.

The Union was having difficulties in raising the troops recently levied by Lincoln.* Towns around Burlington offered generous bounties to volunteers, often supplemented by amounts added by their wealthier citizens. The Town of Bolton dangled an incentive of $500 for a one-year enlistment and $700 for three years' service, substantial amounts of cash for the time. Official recruiting agents were even sent into the areas of the Southern states under federal control to seek volunteers; one such recruiter for the Vermont quota was Munson, who retained his 13th Vermont rank of lieutenant colonel for his duties in Nashville. He returned home in mid-August after penetrating as far south as Marietta, Georgia, without a single volunteer to his credit.

A major Union victory was celebrated when Sherman forced Hood to evacuate Atlanta on September 1. One hundred gun salutes were ordered to mark the capture of this important city. Apparently Lonergan was in charge of one of the cannon firing the salute in Burlington on September 3, probably some of the same guns in Battery Park that had welcomed Meagher in the spring. The *Free Press* reported that the salute had reached "the last round or two" when a premature discharge took place.

The cannon had likely not been properly sponged to remove burning residue after rounds had been fired in quick succession. Claude Amblow, who

---

*The *Free* Press reported on August 19 that three boys from Brandon, the oldest of whom was only sixteen, had been kidnapped by brokers supplying substitutes for drafted men. They were taken to Poughkeepsie, NY, and sold as substitutes after being plied with liquor.

CHAPTER EIGHTEEN – FOSTERING IRISH NATIONALISM

was ramming the blank load, lost his right hand in the accident. Lonergan had his thumb badly injured and his face burned by flame from the vent. Clearly he was in charge of the piece and responsible for stopping the hole with his thumb, protected by a leather guard, to prevent oxygen from entering the barrel while loading. Perhaps the captain had been negligent in this duty and could be held responsible for the incident. After a local doctor promptly amputated Amblow's arm, a "liberal subscription for his relief" was made among the citizens of the town, with Lonergan no doubt contributing what he could afford.

Lonergan was perhaps also involved in raising public support for his homeland a month later. The Brougham Amateur Dramatic Club of Burlington presented a drama entitled "Ireland As It Is" at the Town Hall on October 6. This play would provide not only entertainment, but might also persuade a broader circle in Vermont that the cry for Irish independence was justified. Even though neither the Hibernians nor the Fenians were openly sponsoring the show, its theme would be good promotion for their cause. Unlike most of the stock plays of the era, which depicted the Irish in a comic or dismissive manner, this Irish national drama was sympathetic to the peasantry and their suffering under the landlords. To provide emotional relief from this grim description of hard times in Ireland, the 25 cents admission included a "side-splitting farce" called "Box and Cox."

Any distraction from the war would have been welcomed, as the state's losses continued to grow through the summer of 1864 and on into the autumn. Vermont troops suffered numerous casualties in the battles at The Wilderness, Spotsylvania, and Cold Harbor. These losses continued during the siege of Petersburg and included hundreds of Vermonters sent to a slow death as prisoners at Andersonville after their capture in the badly organized assault on the Weldon Railroad. By autumn, most of the Vermont infantry units had been transferred to operations in the Shenandoah Valley under Sheridan. The three-year enlistments of the surviving early volunteers were coming to a close and most men gratefully started for home, rather than re-enlist. Happy to leave war-ravaged Virginia, they anticipated relief from both the summer heat and the destruction of the war when they reached Vermont again.

Instead, the war unexpectedly descended on Vermont itself when a group of rebels entered the state in mid-October. They were not part of a column attacking from the south like Lee, but rather came as a stealthy infiltration over the period of a week by twos and threes from the north. British North America had, as part of the Empire's policy of favoring the Confederate cause, provided sanctuary for rebel representatives and escaped prisoners of war. Various schemes had been developed in Canada for raids on the United States to free rebels from the northern prison camps and to visit destruction on northern cities.

One such raiding party attacked St. Albans on October 19 under the command of Bennett H. Young, a cavalry lieutenant who had been captured, but then escaped from Camp Douglas to Canada. The twenty-two raiders considered their operation a legitimate act of war as approved by the Confederate government. Seizing what arms and horses they could from the townspeople, the rebels robbed the banks and attempted to burn the town before fleeing back to Canada. Several townsmen were shot and a brickwork contractor from New Hampshire fatally wounded. Pursued by a posse of angry Vermonters, the raiders made it across the international boundary, only to be captured by the Americans—who ignored the border and rode on north—or arrested by Canadian authorities.

This bold action struck panic in towns near the Canadian border and along the rail and steamboat routes. Arms were issued to various units of home guards and detachments of veterans back from the war; these groups were then rushed to points thought to be threatened. General Jackman even boarded the cadets from Norwich University on a train for Newport to seal off that possible entry point. Angry editorials called for the immediate passage of an effective militia law that would provide for security in the state against any future such depredations. The former commander of the 15th Vermont, Col. Redfield Proctor, was placed in charge of a provisional force that was to be provided with 2,000 muskets and 80,000 rounds of ammunition, a full combat load for each rifle. One thousand guns were to be sent to St. Albans, 800 to Burlington, and the remaining 200 to Montpelier to protect the capital. Guards were posted at all bridges and a rifled six-pounder cannon emplaced on the steamboat wharf in Burlington. When the *Canada* arrived from Rouses Point, New York, at 10:00 PM, there was concern that it might be carrying "another party of robbers." The steamer, which had delivered Meagher in the spring, proved to be free of any hostile elements and landed its passengers without incident.

Other familiar names from the Second Vermont Brigade appeared in

CHAPTER EIGHTEEN – FOSTERING IRISH NATIONALISM

newspaper accounts of the reaction to the St. Albans raid. Benedict resumed his role as an aide to the commander, in this case to Proctor.

LONERGAN IS NOT MENTIONED among the eager participants defending Vermont's territory. He may have still been recovering from the accident with the cannon the previous month and thus not fit for active duty. Perhaps his services were not sought for other reasons or he was otherwise engaged in his own affairs.

He had resumed his efforts to be reimbursed by the state for the dismissal of his original company in 1861 and he was gathering affidavits in support of his claim. Roseanna was carrying their first child and ready cash would be welcome. Lonergan evidently thought that his new status as a war hero might sway the Vermont government to reverse their earlier rejection of his request and so he asked top officers from the 2nd Vermont regiment to help him in the matter.

Lonergan began assembling his supporting affidavits in September with a statement from B. Walter Carpenter of Burlington, former assistant surgeon of the 2nd Vermont and surgeon of the 9th. Carpenter affirmed that he and Lt. Col. Rains had inspected and accepted Lonergan with all his company in the same procedure as the other companies of the regiment. On October 21, Charles H. Joyce said on oath that he served with Lonergan while Joyce was major of the 2nd. In his opinion, "Lonergan was a good officer and he had a good company, and I suppose[d] it was to constitute a part of my Regt. until I heard, to my surprise, it had been disbanded." Joyce never found out why the company had been disbanded, "but always supposed it was to gratify some personal feeling of somebody." Joyce concluded, "Capt. Lonergan did his duty well while he was with me, and I hope the State will pay him as he deserves."

The most persuasive argument in Lonergan's favor came from Stannard, former lieutenant colonel of the 2nd Vermont and now a brevet major general. Stannard had resumed field duty in May as a brigade commander in "Baldy" Smith's Eighteenth Corps. Further wounded twice in his left leg (and accidentally shot in the hand by one of his own officers), Stannard survived to take command of the First Division of the corps. At the end of September, an attack on the outer defenses of Richmond saw over one-fifth of his division's men fall as casualties, but Stannard succeeded in capturing Fort Harrison. While repulsing a determined rebel counter-attack, the general's right arm was struck by a musket ball, a wound that necessitated amputation above the elbow. Sent home to recuperate, Stannard was in Burlington and St. Albans from October 2 to December 12. This presented an opportunity for Lonergan to approach his mentor from the militia days and seek his support for his claim.

On November 7 at St. Albans, the brevet major general provided a ringing endorsement of Lonergan, that read in part:

> Captain Lonergan performed *all* his duties *well* and his company was considered a good one. His company was disbanded, *the cause of which I never knew*. I considered the act at the time, a piece of injustice to Capt. Lonergan and was sorry to loose [sic] him and his company, and especially after their having been *inspected, accepted and sworn into the United States service.*
>
> Capt. Lonergan spent considerable time and money, and in my opinion, was dealt with unjustly and ought to receive a compensation for same. [emphasis in the original]

In his telling comment, Joyce had surmised that the disbanding of the Emmet Guards in 1861 had been ordered to gratify someone's personal feeling. Given that the governor himself gave the order, Lonergan's chances for approval of his renewed claim no doubt improved when that governor, Erastus Fairbanks, passed away on November 20 and no longer could influence the decision.

Fairbanks had taken Vermont into the war with his firm declaration that the state would do its full duty. Although he did not live to see the end of the conflict, the former governor survived until after the national election that kept Lincoln in office to prosecute the restoration of the union. Vermont went solidly for the Union Party and celebrations of the president's re-election were held in the major towns. On November 14 a grand torchlight parade and illumination lit up Burlington with lights in the windows of homes and downtown office buildings. An exception was pointed out by the gleeful

CHAPTER EIGHTEEN – FOSTERING IRISH NATIONALISM

account in the *Free Press*, which noted that the office of the rival *Sentinel* was dark because the Democrats had nothing to celebrate.

THE REUNION SOCIETY OF VERMONT OFFICERS originated from a conversation between Proctor and his aide, Benedict, at the American Hotel in Burlington the first week of November. They decided to organize a dinner to honor Stannard while he was home in Vermont recovering from the loss of his right arm. Since some former officers were now members of the state legislature, which was in session at the capital, the meeting would be held in Montpelier. Railroad connections to the capital were good and participants from throughout the state could attend. Invitations were quickly sent out to the highest ranking officers and state dignitaries, while a notice was published in the newspapers five days before the November 17 meeting. About seventy officers assembled at the Pavilion Hotel mid-afternoon before moving to larger accommodations in the Military Committee Room of the adjacent capitol building. Ten former members of the 13th Vermont attended, including Lonergan.

The head table at the banquet included the guest of honor, Gov. John G. Smith, Adj. Gen. Washburn, and Col. Ripley, commander of the sharpshooters. Dillingham, the lieutenant governor, was at the head of another table with other political officials and the officers, seated by regiment, filled the long tables "to the last chair." The first toast after the dinner was to Stannard, who rose with "his pale face and empty sleeve pinned across his breast" to thank the group for this honor. A series of toasts followed with Benedict acting as toastmaster. Drinks were raised to the governor and to various Vermont units, the sixth toast being to the Second Vermont Brigade, so well represented at the dinner. The response was jointly from Col. Veazy of the 16th Vermont, who spoke of the brigade's actions at Gettysburg, and Col. Nichols of the 14th. The latter, after some serious remarks, continued in a humorous vein about "peculiarities of the regiments" and "standing jokes of the campaign" that brought "constant laughter and applause." His comments included a recounting of Lonergan's fall from his horse while crossing the Monocacy River on the march to Gettysburg.

The eleventh toast was to "The Irish soldiers," with a reference to the role of Meagher's Irish Brigade in the Peninsula campaign, stating, "At Savage's Station and Gettysburg, the Shamrock of Ireland and the Evergreen of

Vermont were entwined around the staff of our victorious flag." Lonergan, the man most identified with Vermont's Irish soldiers, was called upon to respond and he did so in fine style. He "kept all convulsed with laughter" with his description of discovering the Monocacy and returned his compliments to Veazy and Nichols for alluding to events in his personal history. Some hard drinking must have been involved in carrying the toasts on through the thirteenth in the series to "The Commanders of the Provisional Army of the Frontier" because the fourteenth to honor "The Press" was cut short and the gathering dispersed at 1:00 AM.

THE SMALL RAID ON ST. ALBANS had given Vermont a scare that more such incursions would be made from Canada, despite official British statements that such cross-border actions would not be tolerated. The legislature passed a new militia law that was promulgated as General Order No. 1 at the end of November. This plan organized Vermont into twelve geographic districts, each of which was required to raise a regiment of ten companies with fifty-one officers and men apiece. Appointments were made to raise the companies and recruiting was to begin in December, when Stannard would assume command of the forces on the northern frontier. On the national level, General Order No. 100, issued in mid-December, modified earlier instructions from the Department of the East that authorized the pursuit back across the border of any raiders from Canada. Under the new order, specific permission was required from Gen. John A. Dix's headquarters in New York before any federal troops entered the neighboring country.

As the long northern winter closed in and the birth of his first child approached, Lonergan cast about for opportunities to provide for his growing family. He had not been listed among those authorized to organize the new militia units, either because he had been excluded from the revived system of part-time soldiers or because he chose not to get involved again with the militia. He had already exploited the Vermont militia system twice with his Emmet Guards, a ploy that would probably not work a third time, and his energies were centered on promoting the Fenian Brotherhood.

Instead, Lonergan made overtures to Hancock for a commission in the corps that the general was forming. Facing a bleak Christmas on limited financial resources, Lonergan on December 2 wrote "Major General Hancock,

CHAPTER EIGHTEEN – FOSTERING IRISH NATIONALISM

U.S.A., Washington, D.C." to ask for a position. The correspondence to Hancock claimed that Stannard had suggested this direct communication and would be sending his own letter of endorsement. Lonergan had been in contact with Stannard to obtain his affidavit in early November and then had also attended the dinner of the Reunion Society. The recuperating Vermont general apparently wanted to help his former subordinate.

LONERGAN'S LETTER TO HANCOCK

The audacious young Irishman hopefully assumed that Hancock had been so impressed with his performance on the battlefield of Gettysburg that he would remember a particular line officer among the thousands of soldiers in the fight. Modestly leaving it to Stannard to describe his qualifications, Lonergan asked for "at least a major's commission." He claimed that he could recruit for the corps in Vermont "as much as any man" and closed by reminding Hancock of his service as captain of Co. A, 13th Vermont. No doubt he trusted Hancock to recall that this was the unit that led the charge against the flank of the assaulting rebels at the climax of the crucial battle. (No record has been found of any response from Hancock in this matter, even though Lonergan also forwarded his application for a commission to the U.S. Adjutant General.)

Opportunities were dwindling for Lonergan to resume any participation in the war as the situation of the rebels grew steadily worse. Sherman jauntily presented Savannah, Georgia, to Lincoln as a Christmas present after his successful March to the Sea, which split the Confederacy and foreshadowed its defeat. Hancock's First Corps began recruiting in January of 1865 without calling upon Lonergan for his services; some one hundred Vermonters enlisted in the corps for a term of one year.

Still pursuing the goals of the Irish nationalist movement as well, Lonergan was likely responsible for arranging a visit by the principal New England Agent of the Fenian Brotherhood. On December 29, a Mr. Hynes made a presentation at the Old Baptist Church in Burlington, where he expounded on the principles of the Brotherhood, "an organization of Irishmen in this Country and Canada, having for its object the delivery of Ireland from British rule." The newspaper reported a large audience of Irishmen present, many of whom signed the membership roll at the end of the meeting.

THE SAME DECEMBER 30 ISSUE of the *Free Press* that reported on the Fenian meeting also published a general order from the Woodstock headquarters calling for two companies of cavalry to be raised in Vermont. In reaction to the St. Albans raid, Dix had been authorized to organize a full regiment of cavalry for one year's federal service to guard the northern boundary of the Department of the East. Volunteers would receive the same bonuses and pay as for other units and would be credited toward the quotas of men

CHAPTER EIGHTEEN – FOSTERING IRISH NATIONALISM

for the town in which they enlisted. Lonergan had received no offer of a commission from Hancock and joining the militia did not provide a living wage. The only military option open to Lonergan seemed to be enlistment in this new cavalry, with the advantage of serving close to home. Lonergan was soon to be a father, and full pay as a soldier, even as an enlisted man, had to be attractive.

Lonergan's enlistment in Frontier Cavalry

It appears that Lonergan convinced the Burlington selectmen to permit him to recruit a contingent from that town for the Frontier Cavalry being formed. In a big step down from the major's commission he had sought from Hancock, Lonergan settled for the rank of sergeant in Company M of the new cavalry regiment. The regiment drew most of its men from New York, was headquartered in that state, and bore the designation 26th New York Cavalry. Two companies were supplied by Vermont, both raised in Burlington by the Provost Marshall there, Capt. Gleason, since his district covered the northern border. (Company F drew more men from the south of the state and Company M was largely recruited in the northern part.) On January 3, 1865, Gleason squeezed the names of nine Burlington men, including Lonergan, onto a single Certificate of Muster stating that they had been duly examined and accepted for federal service for one year, unless sooner discharged.

Lonergan organized this group enlistment, which included his former first sergeant, James Scully, along with three Murphys, three other Irishmen, and his own younger brother. Thomas Lonergan, the last of the family born in Ireland, is listed on the rolls as a cooper and aged eighteen years, even though he was only a few months past his sixteenth birthday. Starting life in the depths of the famine and carried across the Atlantic as an infant, Thomas apparently was not robust and it is surprising that he was able to pass the medical examination. He may have been eager to follow his older brother, the war hero, and willing to try his own hand at military service. The bounties and pay made enlistment enticing, while the danger of enemy action on the border was minimal, particularly during the winter. Probably all the men signing up along with Lonergan were involved in the Fenian movement and were persuaded that this would be useful military training, as well as profitable.

Both cavalry companies were initially quartered in barracks on the old fair ground in Burlington and kept occupied with dismounted drill and the routine of army camp life. Later in the winter, they were transferred to new barracks at St. Albans and provided with horses. The men soon became proficient troopers and took up regular picket duty as weather conditions allowed. Patrolling the northern border against incursions from Canada could prove equally useful as familiarization with the area for any invasion of that country from the south, as Fenian members of the two companies learned the roads and terrain for future reference.

CHAPTER EIGHTEEN – FOSTERING IRISH NATIONALISM

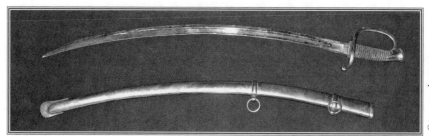

LONERGAN'S CAVALRY SABER

An announcement was published in the *Free Press* of March 10 that the Hibernian Society of Burlington would celebrate St. Patrick's Day of 1865 in grand style the following week. Spirits might have been somewhat dampened by the notice placed just above this announcement; the notice advised that the War Department had ordered the draft to commence in Vermont on March 15. The Hibernians had a new president, Edward Murphy, who was organizing a parade with delegations of Irishmen from throughout the state and distinguished speakers for the festivities.* Lonergan, stationed in St. Albans, also relinquished his role as Chief Marshal to Murphy, but he did show up in Burlington for the celebrations. Despite unfavorable weather that left the streets in poor condition, the usual contingents such as the Bethel band and a drum corps participated in the parade after the church services, the procession led by Murphy on horseback.

The "highly imposing" parade ended at the City Hall, where Mr. James McClaughin spoke to the assembled crowd. His speech was followed by Lonergan "in an eloquent address depicting the misfortunes, wrongs and glories of Old Ireland." The public exercises concluded with the presentation of a "green flag with appropriate emblems" to the Society of Juvenile Hibernians. Thus another generation of nationalists was being organized and encouraged to take up the cause. A grand banquet at the American Hotel was the final event in the day's activities.

Dinner and dancing preceded the call to order at 11:00 PM by the new president, Mr. Murphy, who turned to his vice-president, Mr. John Michaud, to read the regular toasts. The usual toasts were given to Ireland, America,

---

* An Edward Murphy had enlisted in the Frontier Cavalry along with Lonergan and was serving on active duty. It was more likely another man by that name, possibly a relative, who was now leading the Hibernians.

Vermont, and the priesthood before Lonergan was called upon to respond to a glass raised jointly to "Ireland and America," using the image of the Shamrock and the Eagle entwined together. The next toast was to "The Army and Navy," but G. H. Bigelow centered his remarks on the Irish soldier in particular, praising their patriotism and expressing regret that no member of the Irish Brigade was present to respond in his place. He then "brought down the house by an allusion at the close, in praise of the Fenian Brotherhood." Even though the celebration was under the auspices of the Hibernian Society, the participants clearly supported the Fenians and most were likely members of the revolutionary movement. After thirteen toasts, letters read from dignitaries unable to attend, and songs by the ladies, the festivities ended "with the good order and decorum which characterized all the proceedings of the day."

Two weeks later, Lonergan's first child was born, a son he named Thomas Francis. He was following the traditional Irish pattern in giving his first son the name of the paternal grandfather. However, he broke with his family's practice by adding a middle name, no doubt to show his respect for Thomas Francis Meagher, who had visited Burlington less than a year before. The baby was baptized on March 31 with the grandfather Thomas and a maternal relative, Jane Sorragan, acting as sponsors. Presumably Lonergan was able to secure leave from his duties as a cavalryman in St. Albans to attend the important event. With threats on the border unlikely at that time of the year, he possibly had been given permission to stretch out his St. Patrick's Day visit to await the birth of his child. In any case, the good rail connections between St. Albans and Burlington ensured that Lonergan could travel rapidly between the two towns.

A SECOND FENIAN CONVENTION should have been held by O'Mahony in November of 1864, but it was delayed until the following January in order to gather information about the true situation in Ireland. When the meeting did convene in Cincinnati, delegates arrived from most of the Fenian circles, now numbering 237. All the key meetings were held in secret in an effort to conceal the bitter factional infighting that resulted when the "men of action" attempted to oust O'Mahony from the leadership. He managed to stave off the coup and was re-elected head centre, but the split in the movement had deepened.

CHAPTER EIGHTEEN – FOSTERING IRISH NATIONALISM

Stephens had committed the IRB, and by extension the Fenian Brotherhood, to either act in 1865 or disband the organization. The Fenian council in New York authorized O'Mahony to select a special representative to inspect the state of preparations in Ireland. He chose Thomas J. Kelly, a former officer in the 10th Ohio, a largely Fenian regiment.* Kelly left for Ireland early in March, as events were swiftly leading to a final victory for the Union. A month later, Gen. F. B. Millen also made the journey across the Atlantic on a similar mission to determine the true military situation of the IRB. Upon Millen's arrival, Stephens made him head of an Irish Military Council formed mainly from American officers.

With the Civil War finally drawing to a close after four costly years of conflict, experienced American officers from both Union and Confederate forces were becoming available to lead an Irish rebellion. Richmond was taken and Lee surrendered the Army of Northern Virginia at Appomattox Court House on April 12. Two days later Lincoln was shot, dying just as his long struggle to restore the Union was successful.

Other rebel forces remained in the field after Lee's surrender, but the South had essentially lost the war. The Sixth Corps was detached from the Army of the Potomac and ordered to North Carolina, where Joe Johnston still had significant rebel forces in the field. The veteran Vermont Brigade did some hard marching, but Johnston agreed on terms with Sherman on April 26 and no more fighting took place. The Green Mountain Boys began their journey homeward in stages. A grand parade took place in the capital on May 23 and 24 in which 200,000 men of the Army of the Potomac and Sherman's Army of Georgia were honored. They passed in review before Grant and the new president, Andrew Johnson, but the only Vermont troops saluting their leaders were the cavalry regiment and the 17th Vermont, the last infantry regiment mustered from the state.

The first week in June, the five senior Vermont regiments, the "Old" Brigade, were joined in their Washington area camp by the 8th and 10th Vermont Infantry and the 1st Vermont Cavalry. On June 7, Gov. John

---

* Kelly had served mostly as a signal officer on the staff of the Fourteenth Corps in the Army of the Cumberland. His highest grade in federal service was that of captain, but he is most frequently referred to as colonel, his Fenian rank. Millen likewise held his general's commission from the Brotherhood, which freely handed out such high ranks. The wording of the Fenian commissions was closely pattered after that of the U.S. Army and signed by equivalent officers.

G. Smith and other Vermont dignitaries held their own review at Bailey's Cross Roads in northern Virginia. Nearly 5,000 men were under the overall command of Brevet Maj. Gen. Lewis A. Grant, formed into two brigades under Brevet Brig. Gen. George P. Foster and Col. John B. Mead. Foster had commanded the 4th Vermont since February 2, 1864, and several times had been placed in charge of the Vermont Brigade, earning him his brevet general rank "for gallant and meritorious service." A large and imposing man, Foster was a no-nonsense commander, a favorite with his men and known as a fighter. (The next day the Vermonters passed in review in Washington as part of a separate parade given the Sixth Corps, which had been absent from the earlier honors rendered the Army of the Potomac by President Johnson.)

Gov. Smith was credited with expediting the return of the Vermont units, which began arriving back in their home state soon thereafter to be mustered out. From mid-June until nearly the end of July, regiments and batteries of Green Mountain Boys returned to joyous welcome.* The 206 members of the two Vermont companies of Frontier Cavalry, including Lonergan and his contingent, were mustered out of service on June 27. These units had suffered no casualties in their brief tour of duty on the northern border, although one officer had been discharged and the wagoner of Company M had deserted in the spring.

Figures for the first regiment in which Lonergan served, the 2nd Vermont, told a far different story. The 2nd had mustered in with 866 men and almost a thousand additional soldiers served in the regiment during the war. Losses during slightly more than four years of service included 139 killed in action; another eighty-four died of wounds, 136 died from disease, nearly two dozen perished in Confederate prisons, three were killed in accidents, and one man was executed. These casualties place the 2nd Vermont among the top one percent of over 2,000 Union regiments in terms of men lost, and the totals do not include others who died from their wounds or illness after they had been discharged.

For all the disappointment and embarrassment that Lonergan suffered when his Co. K was disbanded, he was likely better off as a result. He might not have survived the many encounters fought by the 2nd, especially

---

*The exception was the hard-luck 7th Vermont, which had served on the Gulf Coast in some miserable conditions and was posted to south Texas when the fighting was over. It did not reach home until April 5, 1866, almost a year after Appomattox.

CHAPTER EIGHTEEN – FOSTERING IRISH NATIONALISM

considering the hard-charging temperament he displayed when leading his Emmet Guards into combat. It is remarkable that he came through his one battle at Gettysburg unscathed.

Now the time had come for which Stephens, O'Mahony, and others in the Irish nationalist movement had waited. The end of the American Civil War released great numbers of battle-hardened Irishmen eager to apply their military skills to the liberation of their homeland from British rule. The United States government, now led by Andrew Johnson, harbored deep resentment toward Great Britain for supporting the Confederacy. If these two factors could be effectively combined to ensure American support of a military uprising, perhaps the long-cherished image of Ireland "a nation once again" would become reality. Lonergan was ready to play his part in achieving this goal.

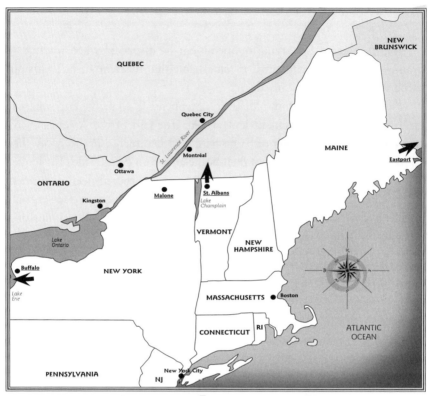

Border areas of Fenian activity in 1866

Battle of Eccle's Hill

CHAPTER NINETEEN

FENIANS ARGUE STRATEGY

WHEN THE AMERICAN CIVIL WAR ended, Irish nationalist leaders agreed that the opportunity had finally come to strike for freedom from British rule. Even the recent hostility that resulted from the four-year conflict between the states was quickly resolved among many Irishmen in America. Whether they had supported the Union or the Confederacy, they now joined in common cause to liberate their homeland. Unfortunately, sharp disagreement as to the strategy and timing of military action divided the movement into factions, one insisting on direct support of an uprising in Ireland and the other favoring an attack on Canada. Dissatisfaction increased among many Fenians over both the style and the substance of O'Mahony's direction. A growing element sought to depose him and to aim the coming military operation at Canada.

Lonergan's loyalty lay with John O'Mahony, the national leader and founder of the Fenian Brotherhood, at least in part because of their common Tipperary heritage. He may also have been indebted to O'Mahony's influence and patronage for his own position as head centre of Vermont. Such fealty to the chief, as much as to the cause, was deeply rooted in an Irish clan tradition that retained its influence even in America.

After mustering out of the army, Lonergan worked hard in Vermont both to expand the membership of the Brotherhood and to ensure that the circles in the state adhered to O'Mahony's policies. Assisted on occasion by paid organizers sent up from Boston or New York, Lonergan's meetings and recruiting events emphasized the need for unity under O'Mahony's leadership. O'Mahony needed all the loyal supporters that he could muster while he faced continuing trans-Atlantic disputes with Stephens, in addition to increasing opposition within the Fenian Brotherhood itself.

The United States government appeared to favor Irish aspirations of independence, partly due to the importance of courting the Irish vote and partly due to disagreements with Great Britain. Resentment of British support of the Confederacy had festered in the North throughout the Civil War. The Johnson administration put forth reparations claims for the damage caused by the previously mentioned commerce raiders Britain had sold to the rebels, as well as for actions like the St. Albans raid mounted from Canadian territory.

The Irish nationalists persisted in unrealistic hopes that a war between Great Britain and the United States might provide the chance to achieve their goal of nationhood. Even if no such direct conflict occurred, an expectation remained that the American government would not interfere with Fenian actions aimed at independence. Both factions of the Brotherhood claimed that they had been given such assurances by the Johnson administration. Their delegations had visited Washington separately to ask directly what the official response would be to an incursion into Canada and the proclamation of an Irish Republic.

The Neutrality Act of 1794 made it illegal for any American to wage war against another country at peace with the United States, and included a provision banning any preparations carried out on American soil for such a war. Despite this clear legal prohibition, both Fenian groups reported that the President and the Secretary of State had given them an ambiguous response by indicating that the government would "acknowledge accomplished facts." However, the Irish were overly optimistic in believing that this statement gave tacit approval for any nationalist action that they might undertake.

Once the Union was restored, the U.S. government as a practical matter began disposing of the vast amounts of war material accumulated by both sides during the Civil War. The Johnson administration raised no objection to the acquisition of sizable numbers of small arms, ammunition, and other equipment by agents known to be acting on behalf of the Fenian Brotherhood. The nationalists' goal of liberating Ireland from British rule was no secret and the government had to know that these weapons were intended for use against the British. The cheap prices for this surplus equipment made it possible to establish stockpiles at Fenian headquarters in various locations.

Continuous solicitation of money by the Brotherhood emphasized the need to supply the men in the field with such necessary means to achieve victory. Contributors were at times shown rooms where the weapons bought

CHAPTER NINETEEN – FENIANS ARGUE STRATEGY

with their donations were being packed for shipment to Ireland. After the donors left, however, the muskets would then be removed from the crates and stored until the next performance by the Fenian fundraisers. The management of the large amounts of cash received became a contentious issue, particularly with Stephens demanding that increasing funds be sent to him in Ireland.

The British government, on the other hand, accused the American administration of complicity in fomenting rebellion in Ireland. Secretary of State Seward rejected this assertion, stating that no laws were being broken by the Fenians.

The U.S. Ambassador to Great Britain, Charles F. Adams, toured Ireland and reported that the Fenian movement in that country, though poorly armed, was spreading in the south and west. Stories were being circulated there about the extent to which Irish regiments in the British Army had been subverted to the nationalist cause. Exaggerated numbers of Fenians were said to be organizing in Canada, ready to support any operations from the United States.

The plans to strike against the British that were rapidly developing in the summer of 1865 did not involve two of the leading Irish nationalists in America. After the defeat of the Confederacy, the firebrand John Mitchel had moved to New York City to run the *Daily News*. Although repeatedly warned by Gen. Dix of his pending arrest for alleged maltreatment of Union soldiers held prisoner in Richmond, Mitchel refused to flee and was taken into custody at his newspaper office on June 14. He was sent under guard to Fortress Monroe and imprisoned there with Jefferson Davis and other Confederates. Mitchel remarked wryly:

> I suppose that I am the only person who has ever been a prisoner-of-state to the British and the American government one after the other. It is true, the English government took care to have a special Act of Parliament passed for my incarceration; but our Yankees disdain in these days to make any pretence of law at all—they simply seize upon those who are inconvenient and suppress the delinquents.

As required by General Order 79 on the demobilization of the wartime army in 1865, Thomas Francis Meagher resigned his commission as general of volunteers on May 12. However, in a letter of June 20 he then applied for a brevet grade of major general. Meagher hoped that the government would see that awarding him the requested rank might balance out the imprisonment of Mitchel in the eyes of the American Irish.* Meagher further asked that he be appointed to the post of governor of Idaho. Instead, he was offered the position of military secretary of Montana, which he accepted in July. (The governor found this a convenient excuse to leave the territory and the Irishman assumed the duties of acting governor on his arrival in October.) After making his career as the grand orator for Irish independence, this famous Young Irelander bowed out of the movement just at the crucial point when he might well have served it best.

Other Irishmen did not fail to seize the moment. At the June meeting, the Fenian Brotherhood's council received information from its representatives sent to assess the situation in Ireland. Col. Thomas Kelly and Gen. F. B. Millen had both sent back reports in which they judged the time was favorable for action. O'Mahony's personal representative, Gen. William G. Halpine, after being dispatched to Ireland with the warning that he should "swear fealty to no man in Ireland," also confirmed their view.

Stephens resented this inspection of conditions by the American council and continued his complaints of insufficient financial support. Two additional members of the council, Peter Dunne and James Meehan, were sent from New York to verify the accounts of men and arms available in Ireland. When they were searched on arrival, the $2,500 that they were supposed to deliver to Stephens was confiscated by British authorities. In July, the two wrote O'Mahony optimistically that only military commanders and money were needed for a revolution to succeed in Ireland.

Accordingly, the "final call" was issued by the Fenians on August 5 and bonds redeemable from an independent Irish Republic went on sale. By the middle of the month, an enthusiastic response had produced a sizable war chest at the Fenian treasury in New York City. The problem lay in moving the funds to where they were needed for the purchase of arms or political support. In August, some $30,000—worth close to half a million dollars in today's currency—was carried to Ireland, only to be lost when the authorities discovered it on the couriers. Soon thereafter, however, Capt. Lawrence O'Brian, the head centre for Connecticut, succeeded in bringing $50,000 to Stephens.

The revolution would have a better chance if it began after the fall harvest was gathered, when the manpower of the countryside could join the

---

* One record indicates that Meagher was commissioned as a major general, but when he led the remnants of the Irish Brigade in the Fourth of July parade, he wore civilian clothes instead of a uniform with the coveted two stars.

CHAPTER NINETEEN – FENIANS ARGUE STRATEGY

ranks. Stephens therefore selected the significant date of September 20, the anniversary of Robert Emmet's execution in 1803, for the uprising.

In addition to financial support, the uprising required experienced military leadership. The state head centres were informed that recruiting was under way to provide 300 officers. A fitness board was convened at Fenian headquarters in New York to examine officers volunteering for service in Ireland in order to certify their physical qualification and competency for duty. The Chicago *Tribune* wrote that many officers from the Irish Brigade and Corcoran's Legion stepped forward, along with some former members of the Confederate army. Once the officers were approved by the board, they were then sent to Ireland individually or in small groups. Often they carried sums of cash for the IRB, in addition to personal weapons, and some bore incriminating documents associating them with the revolutionary movement.

British police were aware of this influx of Irish-Americans recently released from military service, conspicuous in their felt hats and square-toed boots. The Fenian volunteers sent to organize and train the Irish were cautious about their behavior, avoiding any actions that would cause their arrest. Most were United States citizens, either native-born or naturalized, and this status afforded some protection, despite the position held by the Queen's government that British citizenship could not be renounced.

These American advisors, however, commonly visited the offices of the *Irish People* in Dublin soon after they arrived, drawing even more attention to Stephens and his group there. Because an employee named Nagle had been selling information to the authorities for the past eighteen months, the government was already aware of the nature of the operations in the newspaper offices. On September 8, Stephens wrote a letter concerning the uprising, to be carried secretly to the revolutionary cell in Clonmel.* Instead, it fell into the hands of Nagle, the informer.

On September 15, five days before the planned uprising, the police raided the newspaper offices and arrested those rebels present. The registered owner, O'Donovan Rossa, was taken into custody, along with the staff and reporters, but Stephens, Kickham, and other key revolutionaries avoided arrest. (After the raid on the Dublin offices, publication of the *Irish People* was moved to New York City.)

---

* In Lonergan's home town of Carrick, another informer for the police had passed himself off as a fervent nationalist so successfully that he was widely thought to be the head centre for the South of Ireland.

Despite the considerable reward offered for his capture, Stephens continued living on the outskirts of Dublin under an assumed name, and he provided shelter to Kickham and others on the run. One of the Fenian council representatives sent to Ireland, Meehan, had lost a letter linking the American organization with the IRB and Stephens blamed him for precipitating the raids and arrests. Meehan was held for several weeks by the IRB and his life threatened, but he was eventually cleared of any intentional betrayal and released.

Dunne, the other council member, returned to the United States on September 18 to urge continuation of the planned uprising. An average of $7,000 a day was being received at Fenian headquarters in response to the "final call," but no effective channel existed for funneling the money abroad to support the cause. An urgent meeting of the council was called by O'Mahony to decide on matters related to the uprising. Over his objections, however, a faction of the council insisted that a new constitution be adopted for the Fenian Brotherhood and a general convention called to approve it. The revolution in Ireland had to be deferred until the internal power struggle in America could be settled.

Delegates from thirty states assembled in Philadelphia on October 16, representing a membership estimated at the time to be 300,000 followers in the Brotherhood's 613 circles. (Earlier in 1865, a supporting Fenian Sisterhood had been founded by Miss Ellen O'Mahony, principal of the Chicago Normal School. By the time of the convention, the ladies' organization numbered 300 circles.) A financial report for the seven weeks preceding the convention showed the number of circles within each district and their geographic distribution. Most of circles were concentrated in the northeast, particularly around New York City and Boston; in Pennsylvania; and in the mid-west—especially Indiana, Illinois, and Ohio. Many states in the south listed a single circle. The number of circles attributed to the "British Provinces" was understandably not disclosed. The district of Vermont, head centre "Capt. John Lonergan," was credited with six circles in the fall of 1865.

After much bitter argument in secret sessions, the "Senate" group led by William F. Roberts prevailed over O'Mahony's supporters, such as Lonergan, in pushing through the new constitution. It established a legislative branch as part of the Irish government in exile, more closely paralleling the model of the American republic. The leader's position of head centre became that of president; a senate of fifteen members replaced the ten-man council. The

CHAPTER NINETEEN – FENIANS ARGUE STRATEGY

senate would be elected by a lower house whose members were to be selected by vote in the circles. As the founder of the Brotherhood and the leader who had raised it to a national organization of such importance, O'Mahony survived the change in title and was unanimously elected president by the two houses in joint session. His powers were greatly reduced, however, and continual rivalry ensued between his presidential faction and the Senate led by Roberts.

Stephens had sent a representative to Philadelphia to urge that money be provided for a rescheduled revolution. The senators blocked the release of money to the IRB representative, intending to use the funds for their own purposes, in an operation against Canada. At the time, the Fenian treasury held $70,000 of the $120,000 received in response to the final call. The district contributions ranged from the $13,000 sent by Chicago, through the $10,000 from California, to lesser amounts from smaller organizations. At least $500 came in from each of thirty-four cities "in every part of the United States and Canadas;" the latter referred to Canada East and Canada West, indicating support for the movement in British North America. O'Mahony proposed to the council that John Mitchel would be a suitable agent to handle the funds abroad. Mitchel was still being held in Federal prison, but Bernard Doran Killian of St. Louis reported that arrangements were being made for his release once the convention had ended.

As hoped, Mitchel was released from confinement following the convention and he agreed to accept the position of financial agent offered by O'Mahony. He sailed for Paris on November 10 with the funds that Stephens sought for the revolution, now rescheduled for December 5. Mindful of his promise to rise up or disband before the year was out, Stephens gambled that he could put the necessary arrangements in place with only a few weeks to prepare and winter coming on. Hardly had Mitchel left America, however, when Stephens, Kickham, and two companions were arrested on November 12. Thrown in Dublin's Richmond prison, they awaited trial before a special commission that was to be convened on November 28.

As HEAD CENTRE FOR VERMONT, Lonergan would have been entitled to represent the state at the Philadelphia conference and he evidently attended the contentious assembly of Fenians there. He no doubt loyally took the side of O'Mahony in the disputes about strategy, finances, organizational structure, and leadership that were shaking the unity of the Brotherhood.

In the fall of 1865, Lonergan was juggling the demands of providing for his wife and infant son with the requirements of his Fenians duties. In partnership with another Irishman, he had opened Lonergan & Munnigan Grocers at a choice location on the west side of Burlington's main square, opposite the court house and the customs building. Benefiting from his war hero status and the patronage system then in effect, he had also obtained an appointment as an Inspector of Customs for the port city. This seasonal position was filled only during the warmer months of the year when Lake Champlain was open to navigation.

Only indirect evidence shows that Lonergan added his voice to the heated debates at the Philadelphia conference. He was absent from the second meeting of the Vermont Reunion Society of Civil War officers, held in Montpelier on October 25, 1865, to make the organization permanent. Some 140 officers gathered to approve a constitution and subsequently elected Stannard president. The nine representatives of the 13th Vermont who signed the constitution did not include Lonergan.

Stannard presided over the evening banquet, with the governor and the speaker of the house at the head of the other two long tables. An attitude favoring the militant expansion of the United States was displayed that would have not have discouraged Fenian aspirations of attacking Canada. A belligerent toast proposed expanding the scope of the Union as glasses were lifted to "The Western Continent – One Constitution – one People – one Flag – the opinions of a world in arms to the contrary notwithstanding." With no objection from the state government leaders present, Randall "expressed his hearty approbation of this sentiment." Lonergan's former commander proposed that the American flag "must eventually float over the length and breadth of this continent." Randall went on to make "a capital speech in advocacy of the Monroe Doctrine" that in effect urged the annexation of neighboring Mexico and Canada and that "was loudly cheered on all hands."

After the interjection of this expansionist proposal, the usual order of honors was resumed. President Johnson was toasted, followed by "The Governor of Vermont – The representative of true democracy." Paul Dillingham rose to "a tornado of applause" as he remarked that Vermont had never been a colony of England or France, never held in bondage by a man or a kingdom. He implied that the status of Canada would be greatly improved by liberation from British rule and incorporation in the United States. Clearly, the Fenian plans afoot for attacking Canada might serve this goal, along with that of freedom for Ireland.

Further rounds of toasts continued, with one to "The Second Brigade – It graduated with honor at Gettysburg." Proctor responded with anecdotes and then introduced Maj. Nathaniel B. Hall, 14th Vermont, to sing the popular Irish ballad "Pat Malloy."* In his introduction, Proctor made some "faceshus" remarks about "Captain Lonergan and the Fenian Congress, of which body that gallant and popular officer was reputed to be member." It seems certain that Lonergan's absence from the gathering was due to his participation in the Philadelphia conference taking place around the same time.

THE NEW ORGANIZATION THAT the Fenian Brotherhood approved at the Philadelphia convention institutionalized the split between the Senate faction led by Roberts and the former head centre, now president, O'Mahony. The Senate rented offices in New York City and sought cabinet appointments for its members in the government of Ireland being formed in exile. When O'Mahony insisted on his supporter Killian as treasurer, the incumbent treasurer, who backed the Senate wing, refused to hand over the books. The result was in an impasse in the handling of Fenian funds.

O'Mahony had also nominated Gen. Thomas W. Sweeney as Secretary of War for the new Irish Republic, despite that officer favoring the Senate faction and an attack on Canada. Sweeney, an actual general in the Union army who had lost an arm in the Mexican War, had even placed an option on military supplies, intending them to be used for the Canadian operation.** This initiative was rebuffed when Killian ignored Sweeney's requisition of the funds needed for the purchase.

When Millen had arrived in Ireland from America, Stephens had placed him at the head of the military council of the IRB. Millen sent word to

---

* The "Pat Malloy" song tells of a lad of sixteen sent away from Ireland by his mother, because: "I've fourteen children, Pat, says she, which Heav'n to me has sent; / But childer ain't like pigs, you know – they can't pay the rent." The lyrics refer to the common practice of raising a pig in the family home to give to the landlord as rent.

** Sweeney was removed from U.S. Army service on December 25, 1865, for absenting himself without leave to attend to Fenian matters.

New York that the December uprising would go forward even with Stephens in prison. O'Mahony thus found himself desperately short of funds at this critical time and issued bonds of the Irish Republic (in denominations from $10 to $1,000) over his own signature. When the opposing Senate faction objected to this, a final split in the movement was precipitated, with a bill of impeachment initiated against the president on December 13.

O'Mahony's troubles were compounded by his trust in James "Red" McDermot. Many Fenians were suspicious of McDermot, who was in fact selling the secrets of the Brotherhood to the British Consul in New York City, but the president rejected all accusations of his friend.

Overall control of the IRB had passed to Kelly when Stephens was arrested on November 12. British authorities had also begun to round up the military advisors sent over from America and to remove Fenian supporters from the regiments in Ireland. With the cooperation of two Fenian warders in the Richmond prison, Kelly organized a successful escape by Stephens on November 23. Despite a reward of £1,000 offered for Stevens' recapture, he remained at liberty. Once freed, Stephens reluctantly decided that the December uprising would have to be called off, even though the military council still pressed for immediate action.

The Roberts faction spoke openly of their intention to launch military operations against the nearest British territory, Canada. After the indefinite postponement of any rising in Ireland, this plan became even more appealing to those Irish nationalists demanding action. Canadian authorities gathered intelligence on the Fenian plans from agents controlled by Gilbert McMicken, police magistrate of the border town of Sarnia, and his counterpart in Montreal, Charles Coursol. The British government was seriously concerned about the possibility of an invasion and pressured the United States to prevent any such incursion.

In the face of this increasing threat, London increased its efforts to consolidate the various provinces of British North America into a unified Confederation that could defend itself, rather than relying on the Empire.* British military supplies were shipped to Canada, but increasing reliance would be placed on militia units, instead of regular British units, to repulse any eventual Fenian incursion. In the Irish communities of British North

---

* Canada East (Quebec) and Canada West (Ontario)—also called Lower and Upper Canada—were to be joined in Confederation by the Maritime Provinces of Nova Scotia, New Brunswick, Prince Edward Island, and Newfoundland.

CHAPTER NINETEEN – FENIANS ARGUE STRATEGY

America, the authorities gave preference to creating militia companies composed of Protestant Orangemen, considered more loyal to the crown than the potentially revolutionary Catholics.

Hugely exaggerated claims were made by Fenian organizers like Michael Murphy in Toronto that 70,000 Irishmen in Canada stood ready to support military operations from the United States. Still, there were some disgruntled Irish north of the border prepared to cheer on the Fenian actions, though hardly enough to represent any credible internal force to assist the invaders. One former Irish nationalist, now part of the Canadian government, the Honorable D'Arcy McGee, recognized this threat when he addressed a workingmen's festival in Montreal on December 28. McGee warned of the danger that the public in the United States did not understand attitudes among their northern neighbors and might wrongly think that the Fenians would be greeted as liberators. He claimed that his latest adopted country had "passed at a bound, with the tocsin of the great civil war ringing in our ears, from one stage of colonial existence to another, a more advanced and more important one." He cautioned that "there is a new republican America, born in blood and baptised in fire, within these five years last past; there must soon be a new British America, or British America must shortly cease to exist."

A SPELL OF MILD WEATHER opened 1866 in Burlington, but the warm break in the harsh winter cold disappeared on January 4 when "a snow squall… came across the lake like a solid wall, and made things hum when it struck shore."* The interlude of peace enjoyed by America after four years of war also threatened to vanish as swiftly; persistent tales of an impending invasion of Canada circulated in the newspapers.

Trials of the arrested revolutionaries continued in Ireland and were reported in the Burlington papers. The editor of the *Irish People,* John O'Leary, was "sentenced to 20 years penal servitude" and others such as O'Donovan Rossa received long terms in prison. Some defendants like Captain John McCafferty, a native-born American and former Confederate cavalry officer, were acquitted as aliens because of their citizenship. Anticipating further unrest connected with the trials and concerned about Fenian subversion of

---

* The Arctic blast from Canada dropped the temperature 50 degrees in eighteen hours; it stood at twenty-one degrees below zero the next morning.

some units, two reliable British regiments had been hastily sent from England to Dublin in early January.

Meanwhile, the rift in the Brotherhood continued to deepen. O'Mahony held a congress in New York on January 10 that expelled from the movement those senators who disagreed with him. The senate itself was abolished and O'Mahony was reappointed as head centre. A newspaper report from New York City commented, "The Senators pay no attention to the Congress." O'Mahony immediately followed the congress with a military convention that issued an appeal for every Fenian to buy at least a $20 bond. Aother news item from New York City reported on January 22 that O'Mahony was "about to visit Paris to confer with Mitchell in relation to an immediate movement on Ireland."

While these preparations continued for Fenian action in Ireland, Lonergan could read frequent reports about the opposing faction in the Burlington newspapers. President Roberts held a meeting in which he called for giving Canada—along with the Irish there who supported the British government, such as D'Arcy McGee—"a taste of the treatment meted to Clarke, Luby, and O'Donovan Rossa." The audience rose up to cheer the notion, ready to be led by Sweeney with "his armless sleeve." Roberts warned that they must avoid letting "the great strength now available fritter away uselessly or in a Quixote manner." If the Brotherhood would "sustain the soldier, give him the muskets," he promised them hostages for their helpless brothers thrown into Dartmoor Prison.

The *New York Citizen* quoted Halpine's statement that an Irish Republic would be set up somewhere within ten weeks "with a flag, an army, a port of entry and exit, a navy of privateers, and the tacit encouragement both of France and the United States" in these acts of war against Great Britain. He could not specify where this republic would be located, but it would provide "an immediate basis of operations for the transfer of active hostilities to the Canadian and Irish soils."

Printed alongside this prediction was the report of twenty-one fully armed Fenians who had landed in Sligo, on the west coast of Ireland, and were immediately arrested. Police had also seized a store of over 800 pikes, a suicidal weapon for use against modern arms in an uprising. Even though a substantial reward was offered for his capture, Stephens continued to remain at large and was believed to still be in Ireland.

CHAPTER NINETEEN – FENIANS ARGUE STRATEGY

At the end of January, Lonergan was also active in promoting the Fenian cause. He and J. J. Crowley, an organizer sent up from Boston, addressed the Montpelier circle of the Brotherhood. Both men spoke against any premature raid on Canada, insisting that the proper course was "to strike England first on Irish soil, and take Canada afterwards." The *Free Press* reported on February 5 that the "Fenian scare is said to be increasing on the border." (The article also facetiously announced that "Gen. Sweeney and Pres. Roberts have actually invaded Canada" when their train was routinely routed over the border and the two men passed through the city of Hamilton in a sleeping car on February 2. Hamilton's mayor "viewed the sleepers" in their berths, but "made no arrest for fear of disturbance.")

As Lonergan and Crowley continued their circuit through Vermont, the *Free Press* gave notice on February 10 of a "mass meeting" of the Fenian Brotherhood to be held at their hall in Strong's Block in downtown Burlington that evening.* The gathering at 7:00 PM on a Saturday was predicted to provide "some spirited speaking and doubtless a lively time."

The Hibernian Society met at their own hall in Bank Block the first Thursday of each month, thus avoiding scheduling conflicts for the overlapping membership of the two organizations.

On Monday, the newspaper described the "rousing meeting" in a hall "crowded with the Fenians and their friends." The Vermont head centre and the Boston organizer gave "very earnest and eloquent speeches urging the Brotherhood to fresh efforts to sustain the cause of Irish independence, now approaching its crisis." The next day the *Free Press* reprinted an item from the Montreal *Gazette* headlined "Fenian Scare" that reported "a Fenian raid is contemplated into Canada via Rouse's Point and Missisquoi Bay, to converge at Chambly, and then march on Montreal."

Alongside this warning of a forthcoming invasion, notice was provided of the plans for celebrating St. Patrick's Day in Burlington and Winooski. The Irish holiday festivities were to include "a State Mass Convention" of Fenians with "a Grand Fenian Ball" at the Lake House in the evening. Description of an invasion plan printed next to the article on the gathering of Fenians in

---

*Headquarters of the Brotherhood was first listed in the Burlington Directory in 1865, when it was located in Union Block, where meetings of the Sarsfield Circle were held each Friday evening. The directory listed Lonergan as Centre, John McNamara as Secretary, and John McGrath as Treasurer. A three-man "Committee of Safety" was included in the officers of the Brotherhood.

Burlington seemed to justify the Canadian alarm at the approaching Irish holiday.

On February 18, in an unusual Saturday session, the British Parliament suspended *habeas corpus* in Ireland for six months. This was aimed at dealing with the 500 men from America and several hundred from Scotland and England thought to have come to Ireland in connection with the intended uprising. The eighty-five men arrested in the first week of suspension included forty-five Irish-Americans. Some of the expedition evaded arrest by returning to the United States and others, who stayed in the area, by going to England, where *habeas corpus* had not been suspended.

The special commission established for the Fenian trials at Dublin was closed down on February 20, but detentions continued. Three soldiers and seven civilians were reported arrested on that same date at Carrick; Lonergan's hometown remained a hotbed of revolution. Questions were raised in the House of Commons regarding the involvement of American officers and "the issue of bonds by the so-called Irish Republic" on American soil.* In the debate, charges were raised that the conspiracy was of American origin and that Secretary Seward was the real head centre of the movement.

The Senate faction of the Brotherhood meanwhile held a congress in Pittsburgh with over 400 delegates, where "the fighting element from the west is largely represented." On February 19, a military procession escorted Sweeney and the Senators to the hall through streets thronged with cheering supporters. Widespread Fenian demonstrations of this nature fed into British fears of military operations against Canada.

Although Lonergan supported the O'Mahony policy of attacking British rule by an uprising in Ireland, he also had reportedly added to the threat of Fenian action closer to home. On February 24, a letter was sent from the Office of the Warden, County of Missisquoi, at Philipsburg, Quebec, just across the Vermont border on the northern end of Lake Champlain, complaining about Lonergan's activities. In the correspondence addressed to John A. Macdonald as head of the militia (and soon to become the Confederation's first Prime Minister), the warden was responding to a request from local residents that he pass on information about a pending Fenian invasion. He cited "satisfactory evidence" of large meetings recently held in Burlington, St. Albans, Brattleboro, Windsor, and other places in Vermont that advocated "a demonstration to be made all along the Canadian frontier."

---

*Although the cattle plague then raging in the British Isles was "the leading topic in both Houses."

CHAPTER NINETEEN – FENIANS ARGUE STRATEGY

Captain Lonergan of Burlington was singled out as the "most conspicuous and virulent in his avowal of hostile designs against British Rule everywhere." The "Seventeenth Proximo," (St. Patrick's Day), had been fixed at these meetings as the date for a widespread assault upon "a certain exposed and weak point of the British Empire." Validation of this threat had come from the warden's sources of "respectable and reliable parties in the State of Vermont" who were neither alarmists nor at all sympathetic with the Fenian movement.

Rumors of immediate action included another "Fenian scare" reported in the *Free Press* on February 26; supposedly St. Jean, not far up the Richelieu River on the traditional invasion route, was about to be attacked by 1,800 Fenians coming up the rail line in thirty-two cars.* In reaction, "the military was out and patrolled the streets, and much excitement prevailed." Fenians were reportedly gathering at many locations in preparation for movement against Canada. In Louisville, Kentucky, "an imposing torchlight procession" of some 4,000 Fenians, was followed by "an enthusiastic meeting at the Court House," on February 27.

IN RESPONSE TO THE SITUATION in Ireland, O'Mahony issued an appeal on March 1 from the "Headq'rs Fenian Brotherhood," which was printed the next day in the *Free Press*:

> *Brothers*: The hour for action has arrived. The *habeas corpus* is suspended in Ireland.
> Our brothers are being arrested by hundreds and thrown into prison.
> Call your circles together immediately. Send us all the aid in your power at once, and in God's name, let us start for our destination.
> Aid, brothers, help, for God and Ireland.
> (Signed) JOHN O'MAHONEY [sic]
> "God save the Green"

---

*Even though frozen lakes and rivers might be crossed on the ice during the winter, the railroad presented the only means of moving troops rapidly in this region at that time of the year. The rail system was undergoing improvements on both sides of the border, including the development of the important rail center at St. Albans.

The Fenian military department was to "take charge of military contributions and mobilize them" while the financial department would "strain every nerve to supply the brave men in the gap." The *Irish People* encouraged the movement with assurances that as soon as the revolution took place against English rule, the new Irish Republic would be recognized as a belligerent by France. Widespread meetings of the Brotherhood's circles were reported with "large sums of money and quantities of arms and ammunition collected."

The Brotherhood's heart-felt reaction to events in Ireland defied the efforts of Archbishop McCloskey in New York City to apply the authority of the church against the Fenians. He had directed that a circular be read to the congregations of his subordinate churches in the city at the Sunday services on March 4 instructing all Catholics to "withdraw" from the movement. Some pastors added their own remarks approving of the ban on the Fenians, but in St. Bridget's Church a man rose up and "vehemently protested against it." Although the priest told several persons to eject the protestor, they declined to do so.

Lonergan summoned the centres of the Vermont circles to an evening meeting in Burlington's Fenian Hall on Monday, March 5, "to act on the recent news." He likely repeated the policy of moving first on Ireland, as was expressed elsewhere that same evening by a representative of the O'Mahony group. Mr. Collins of New York claimed at the Lawrence, Massachusetts meeting of Fenians that the nationalist movement had "300,000 good and true men in Ireland, and the officers are men who have seen service in the American war." From his own headquarters in New York, Roberts, "the other president of the Fenian Brotherhood," made a competing urgent appeal for assistance that he claimed would "enable us to take the field within a few days. Let men who will fight report to General Sweeney." Contributors to the headquarters of the Senate faction would receive "Irish national bonds" in return for their money.

An impassioned plea for unified action to counter the situation came from two centres in Boston, John M. Tobin and Patrick A. Sinnott. Without expressing any preference between the options of Ireland or Canada, they called upon their "Brother Fenians of New England" to close ranks now that "time lifts the curtain on the drama of Irish revolution."

Given the penchant of the Irish nationalists for selecting significant dates to signal the start of action, as St. Patrick's Day approached, the increasing

CHAPTER NINETEEN – FENIANS ARGUE STRATEGY

nervousness of the Canadians was understandable. Moreover, the Reciprocity Treaty governing trade with the British North American provinces by the United States was to terminate on March 17. Its renewal depended in part on a resolution of American claims for reparations from Britain for damages caused during the Civil War. Washington no doubt found the Fenians useful to increase the pressure for a settlement, despite Secretary Seward's assurances at several meetings with the British minister in Washington that "no violation of the neutrality laws" would be permitted. Canadian preparations to repel an invasion were termed "only time and labor thrown away" in a *Free Press* article on March 9 that detailed Fenian plans for celebrating St. Patrick's Day in Burlington. After "a grand procession through the principal streets," orations at City Hall would follow and a banquet would be held at the Lake House in the evening. All the railroads in the state would provide transportation to and from the event at half fare. Tickets good for three days could be "had from Capt. Lonergan," the Grand Marshal for the celebration. Lonergan's wife had just taken on the duties of secretary in the circle of Fenian Sisters organized in Burlington on March 3 with "between 20 and 30 members."

The harmless nature of the publicized Fenian gathering was brought into question by reports that all the cannon in Burlington had disappeared, along with the two brass 12-pounders taken to St. Albans after the Confederate raid. The presumption prevailed that the Fenians had stolen them, though the possibility was also considered that the state had removed them to prevent just such a theft.

Adding to the fears of an imminent invasion of Canada, an "immense Fenian meeting" at the Cooper Institute in New York City on March 9 featured "inflammatory speeches" by leaders of the Brotherhood. That same day, rumors of approaching Fenian forces under Sweeney caused a "lively" scare in Toronto and Montreal. Canadian militia units were mobilized to counter three imaginary columns invading from New York via Niagara and Ogdensburg, as well as from Detroit, Michigan. Regular troops were ordered to the frontier and soldiers patrolled the cities of Montreal, Toronto, and Ottawa nightly.

A "sensational story" soon circulated in Baltimore, Maryland, that 800 Fenians were about to depart "for Canada or somewhere else," adding to the uncertainty of the situation. The "somewhere else" could as well be Ireland, where Stephens insisted that he had 25,000 men ready to move at his signal, but the logistical difficulties of moving men across the Atlantic dictated that any immediate action would be directed against Canada.

The "greatest enthusiasm prevailed" at a meeting in Boston on March 12 where Roberts, Sweeney, and others made speeches that brought in $10,000 in cash for Fenian bonds. In New York, the demand for the bonds had exhausted the supply and "throngs that beset the treasurer's office" were pacified only by the promise of more being printed as fast as the engravers could work.

Further movement of Canadian troops brought militia on a special train from Montreal to towns in the border region of Quebec. Companies arrived at Stanbridge and St. Armand, while a total of six companies were under arms in St. Jean, a key point on the route to Montreal. The Governor General of Canada called up some 8,000 men in the volunteer militia, placing the force under the command of Lt. Gen. Sir John Michel together with his 10,000 British regulars. Forces were moved up to the American border, earthwork defenses were begun at key locations, and cannon were mounted to cover possible lines of attack. These were described by the Governor General as defensive actions "against the threatened piratical attacks of lawless men" and not the result of "a condition of war between our sovereign and any foreign State." Militia companies were said to be organizing in all towns of any size along the border.

Newspapers in Montreal and Toronto railed against President Johnson's failure to act against the Fenians. The editor of the *Free Press* dismissed their complaints, citing the St. Albans raid, the British-built commerce raiders, and supplies funneled through Canada for the Confederacy as ample justification for allowing the Irish their own rebellion. Speculation even appeared that the Fenian threat was being greatly exaggerated by Canadian politicians in order to frighten the reluctant Maritime Provinces into agreement with the proposed Confederation.

An open letter from "Erin" addressed to his "Beloved Countrymen" was printed in the *Free Press* on March 15 in which the writer, identifying himself only as "one of the eldest Irishmen now amongst you," appealed to the Fenians to abandon their plans for rebellion in Ireland. The editor vouched for the origin of the message as being from "an honest and true-hearted Irishman" well-known to him. The author admitted that the hatred of the Catholics of Ireland would not be softened towards British occupation, but warned that any uprising would only create "a greatly increased stringency of Irish

CHAPTER NINETEEN – FENIANS ARGUE STRATEGY

misrule." He feared that any revolt would only lead to great destruction of property, the senseless slaughter of the Catholic people, and an excuse for the Orangemen to crush them further. Under the circumstances, the anonymous local writer probably did well to conceal his identity in advocating such an unpopular position.

Amid increasing concerns that some Fenian action violating the Neutrality Act might in fact take place on St. Patrick's Day, the U.S. government took the precaution of sending a full company of regulars to Burlington. Drawn from the 3rd U.S. Heavy Artillery Regiment stationed at Fort Warren in Boston Harbor, the troops entrained on the afternoon of March 16. Not only these soldiers were en route to Burlington from Massachusetts; it was reported that many Fenians were also leaving the state for that same destination.

The one hundred regulars were a small force and likely to be greatly outnumbered by the Fenians gathering in Vermont, but a company would be sufficient to demonstrate the government's resolve that any border violation would not be tolerated. Occupation of the key railroad facilities would prevent the movement of any sizable expedition to the north. Fear of any movement across the border by road was reduced by a period of heavy rain with thick fog in the mornings, producing "unfathomable" mud as the frost came out of the ground.

The excitement had nearly disappeared in the major Canadian cities by March 16, but British troops were still standing ready on the border with the United States. Arrests for treason were reported in Lower Canada and citizens in Montreal were enrolling in the militia. The Governor General received telegrams from the governors of the reluctant provinces of New Brunswick and Nova Scotia that the legislatures were hastily passing resolutions in favor of Confederation.

As THE FENIAN SCARE reached its peak, Lonergan ensured that the 1866 St. Patrick's Day festivities in Burlington both demonstrated the determination of the Irish to achieve independence and deflected any ideas of attacking Canada. The extensive report on the holiday activities that was published in the March 17 evening edition of the *Free Press* ridiculed the expectation that the Burlington circle of the Brotherhood would supply thousands of arriving Fenians with arms and uniforms from hidden stores of equipment. Those hoping to see "a young forest of Fenian pikes" start from the city "with wild hurroos and banners flying for the conquest of Montreal" had been disappointed.

Instead, Lonergan organized "a quiet and orderly assemblage of some three hundred well-behaved Irishmen, with the banners of their circles and societies." A preliminary meeting was held in City Hall the evening before the event, serenaded by the Jericho Band, and "addressed by Captain John Lonergan and Mr. Monahan." Lonergan explained that the Fenian plans did not include any invasion of Canada—clearly speaking only for the O'Mahony branch of the movement—and called for purchases of bonds the next day to support the cause of the Irish Republic.

Even though St. Patrick's Day was favored with sunshine, the turnout of about 300 marchers must have been disappointing. Few participants showed up from outside the immediate area. Rutland had been expected to send a hundred men, yet less than a dozen appeared. Delegations from other towns in Vermont were smaller than anticipated and no mention was made of the supposed contingent from Massachusetts reported on the way to Burlington. The dissention in the ranks of the Brotherhood no doubt caused the absence of many men who disagreed with Lonergan and instead supported the Roberts faction.

A summary of the Brotherhood's organization in Vermont, titled "FENIAN INTELLIGENCE," accompanied the story on the celebration. The figures for the state, no doubt supplied by Lonergan, gave a total of over 1,000 members organized in thirteen circles. The largest of these was, not surprisingly, found in Rutland, where the most populous Irish community in Vermont listed 115 men in their circle. The smallest was Montpelier, with only thirty-five. Between these two extremes, circles were also active in West Rutland, St. Albans, Bennington, Brattleboro, Windsor, Wells River, St. Johnsbury, Northfield, Waterbury, Moretown, and, of course, Burlington. Clearly the Fenian circles in Vermont tended to be organized in railroad towns, reflecting both the concentration of Irish along the lines that they helped build and the fact that it was easier to reach these population centers to recruit for the movement. (In 1866, Vermont was home to perhaps 10,000 adult male Irishmen, including the first-generation Irish born in North America. Lonergan had thus done a creditable job of recruiting about one in ten into the Fenians.)

Mid-morning on March 17, Grand Marshal Lonergan on horseback led the parade down the main thoroughfare of Church Street, aided by two

CHAPTER NINETEEN – FENIANS ARGUE STRATEGY

mounted assistant marshals and twenty foot marshals to ensure good order. The St. Patrick's Society of Winooski headed up the groups, followed by Lonergan's Sarsfield Circle of the Fenian Brotherhood. His circle carried a "handsome green banner" from the Tara Circle of Brooklyn, New York—presumably brought for the occasion by one of the invited speakers from that city—and the American colors. The Hibernian Society then preceded a string of open barouches carrying "thirty beautiful young ladies representing the counties of Ireland" dressed in green and white. Their flag showed the motto "God save the Green," while the Fenians of the Stephens Circle from St. Albans following them bore an elegant banner with "Our cause is just."

Passing store windows on Church Street decorated with the colors of Ireland, the parade wound through the principal streets of the town. They received a warm welcome and approval from the spectators, who turned out in numbers despite occasional snow flakes on a "rather raw March day." At 2:30 PM, the procession returned to City Hall, which was soon jammed "well nigh to suffocation by Hibernians of both sexes, with a large sprinkling of the native Yankee element curious to see and hear." Lonergan had again brought in notable men to address his community. Lawrence D. Kiernan of New York, "a finished and elegant speaker," held forth with classical allusions to describe the deplorable conditions in Ireland. He declared that another twelve months would see an Irish Republic take its place with other free nations of the world, saying that the Fenians "had gone too far not to go further." He emphasized that the "fight must take place on the soil of Ireland," not elsewhere as proposed by the Roberts faction.

Another New York resident, Capt. William H. Stephens, was introduced by Lonergan as a relative of "the great Head Centre," James Stephens. He too called upon the gathering to support direct efforts to free their homeland, where he claimed 350,000 Fenians, "organized but not yet fully armed," only needed a loan to sustain them another three months. Despite his claim that there were also 80,000 Fenians on British territory just to the north who should not be denied the right to cooperate with their countrymen in Ireland, Stephens "desired no filibustering raid against Canada." He closed his speech by flourishing a handful of the bonds on sale to support the cause. Subscription to the bonds started with Mr. Reilly, centre of the St. Albans circle, who put down $100, followed by the Fenian Sisters of Burlington for the same amount and $50 from Montpelier's Ethan Allen Circle. Then

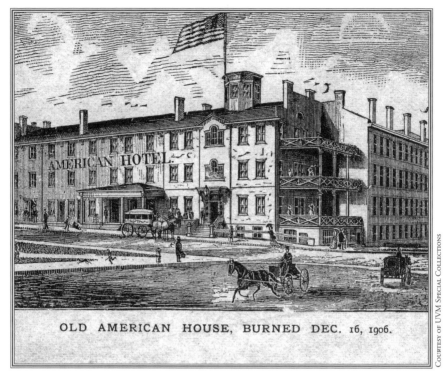

OLD AMERICAN HOUSE, BURNED DEC. 16, 1906.

AMERICAN HOTEL, FREQUENTLY THE SCENE OF BANQUETS IN BURLINGTON, AS WAS THE LAKE HOUSE

the donations dried up, even with further urging from Stephens, and he wisely concluded by calling for cheers for the American Constitution, the Irish Republic, Capt. Lonergan, the Fenian Sisterhood, and others as the meeting dispersed.

At the Lake House that evening, Lonergan presided over both the dance in the ball room, where some eighty couples took the floor, and the three long tables filled for the banquet in the dining hall. The Fenian Sisterhood had decorated the hall for an excellent supper, followed by spirited speeches and songs. The toastmaster, J. J. Monahan, led off with "The Fenian Brotherhood—May it increase in strength and numbers until Ireland is free and Republican Governments rise from the ruins of all monarchies." After the accompanying tune of "St. Patrick's Day," Lonergan gave the response to this toast. The

CHAPTER NINETEEN – FENIANS ARGUE STRATEGY

President of the United States then received his due respect before glasses were raised to "The Men in the Gap" honoring those on the front line in Ireland. Capt. Stephens responded as the Jericho Band played the "Wearing of the Green." More toasts and music recognized, among others, the state of Vermont, the local Fenian Sisterhood, the press of Burlington, and the *habeas corpus* act. The banquet concluded in the small hours of Sunday morning with a closing speech by Lonergan.

The reporter attending the celebration commended the good behavior of the participants, noting that the city authorities had closed the saloons and beer shops as a precaution. He further observed that the event failed "as a demonstration of Fenian numbers, or as a means of filling the Fenian treasury." This surely must have been a disappointment to Lonergan after his concerted effort to mark the day with a show of strength and a unified position as to where the Fenians would strike their military blow. The reduced number of participants and the lack of enthusiasm for purchasing bonds could undoubtedly be attributed, at least in part, to the split in the Brotherhood.

Lonergan would face a further disappointment the next day. Although he had taken pains to ensure that the St. Patrick's Day event loyally promoted the O'Mahony strategy of rejecting any move on Canada, the national head centre had just reversed his policy.

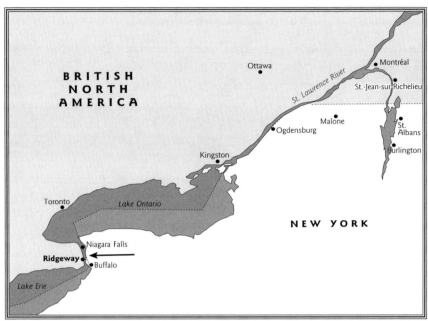

Fenian attack on Ridgeway, 1866

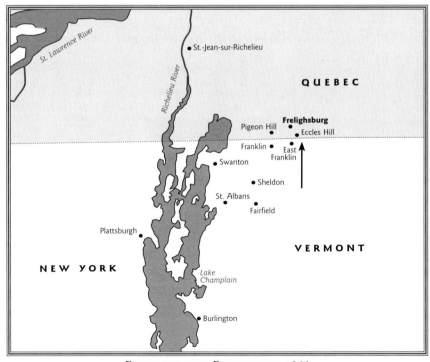

Fenian attack on Frelighsburg, 1866

CHAPTER TWENTY

FENIANS INVADE CANADA

O'MAHONY HAD BECOME PERSUADED that a preemptive strike by the Fenians still under his command would restore the Brotherhood's faith in his leadership and undercut the appeal of his opponents. Most press reports on Fenian activities at the time centered on the threat of an assault on Canada by the Roberts wing of the movement. Purchases of bond issues to support this action were diverting funds into the coffers of the competing Senate faction, rather than O'Mahony's treasury.

Killian, O'Mahony's treasurer, proposed an expedition to seize Campobello Island, a sparsely-inhabited piece of New Brunswick at the mouth of Passamquoddy Bay, just off Eastport, Maine. The province had a large Irish population, though many of them were Orangemen loyal to the British crown. The Fenians were keen on seizing a seaport from which they could send out privateers authorized by letters of marque from the Irish Republic; to avoid being treated as pirates, the privateers needed recognition as belligerents (like that received by the Confederate commerce raiders). Confederation of the British North American territories had not yet been effected, so the Fenians assumed that New Brunswick would have no assistance from other provinces. Though Patrick A. Sinnott of Massachusetts was strongly in favor, the majority of O'Mahony's council was opposed to the plan and thought that no action should be taken until Stephens arrived in the United States.

After several months in hiding, Stephens and Kelly had slipped out of Dublin early in March and the head of the IRB had made his way to Paris. There Stephens met Gustave Cluseret, a soldier of fortune who had served as a brigadier general with the Union Army early in the Civil War. The two struck a deal: Cluseret would take command of rebel forces in Ireland; the general demanded a well-equipped army of at least 10,000 men, wisely refusing to place himself at the head of a disorganized mob brandishing pikes. Stephens was expected to leave France for New York in the spring to mediate the serious split in the Fenian movement and to preclude any movement against Canada.

Even as the Burlington Fenians celebrated St. Patrick's Day of 1866, great excitement about a Fenian invasion reached as far as Nova Scotia. The militia was called up and both Royal and Provincial Artillery manned all the forts in Halifax, though the day passed without incident. Such fears of Fenian action in the Maritime Provinces were not without foundation—on March 18 O'Mahony approved Killian's plan to seize Campobello Island.*

The schooner *E. H. Pray* was immediately purchased to transport arms and equipment to Eastport. (Misnamed the *Ocean Spray* in various accounts of this Fenian operation and even called the *Troy* in some newspaper stories, official U.S. Army reports and shipping records provide the correct name of the vessel.) Sinnott, captain of the Sarsfield Guards in the Massachusetts militia, would be in command of the military forces. Men taking part in the expedition would travel by rail and on other ships when the operation began.

The Senate faction meanwhile continued its own, separate military preparations. An article in the New York *World* on March 20 credited Sweeney's army with a strength of 53,000 men—including 1,200 from Vermont—and expected it to move on Canada at any time. With both sides of the Brotherhood issuing bonds to finance their own operations, readers of the *Free Press* were warned that the bonds were being extensively counterfeited and sold by unauthorized agents. The head centre in Canada, Michael Murphy, claimed that $85,000 in Fenian bonds had been purchased by the Irish there.

Operational security of the Fenians was so poor that the entire Campobello escapade was known to the British consul in New York both through "Red" McDermot's treachery, and through newspaper accounts. On March 22, the *Free Press* published a report from New York of a meeting of the Central Council at O'Mahony's headquarters the previous day. Discussions had concerned "an immediate movement against the British Government." A

---

* Warnings about plots to attack New Brunswick had come to the attention of British authorities as early as December of 1864. Late in 1865 D'Arcy McGee again pointed to the province as a likely target, when Killian's scheme became known to him. McGee was also rumored to be using the Fenian threat for his own political purposes, to help achieve the goal of Confederation.

rumor that Stephens had landed in New York "created considerable excitement" the following week, but it proved unfounded. His movements were more accurately reported in the *Free Press* on April 2 in an account from Paris stating that Stephens had arrived in that city on March 20, "having been in Scotland." A week later, O'Mahony announced in the press that Stephens would soon be leaving France for the United States to heal the split in the movement.

The New York *Herald* reported on April 5 that a Fenian ship had sailed for Campobello to seize the island. Within days, the boarding houses and hotels in Eastport were full of Fenians and further detachments were based in towns to the west along the St. Croix River. No evidence has been found that Lonergan took part in this expedition, but his loyalty to O'Mahony—no doubt surviving the leader's reversal about attacking Canada—indicates that he would have participated, if ordered to do so. Killian himself, along with other men from the headquarters and two printing presses, went by rail to Eastport, where he hired a hall and put out the implausible story that the Fenians were gathering for a convention. Protests from the British ambassador in Washington pressed the Johnson administration into action to preserve American neutrality.

A U.S. Navy warship, the *Winooski*, had steamed up to Eastport and was waiting there when the *E. H. Pray* entered the port on April 17 bringing the vital arms and equipment from New York City.* The commander of the *Winooski*, Capt. Cooper, telegraphed for orders on how to deal with the situation. He received only ambiguous instructions from the Navy Department about preventing any violation of neutrality. In addition to the navy bringing its guns to bear on the Fenian ship, customs agents under the Treasury and U.S. Marshals controlled by the Attorney General were present.

Bureaucratic overlap allowed members of Johnson's cabinet to shift responsibility between the Navy and War Departments in Washington. Cooper held back from any action, awaiting the arrival of Maj. Gen. Meade, who had been sent by Grant to take charge of the situation for the War Department. (In June of 1865, an administrative reorganization of the department had placed Meade in charge of the District of the Atlantic, a

---

* Following the guidelines for a steamship of the second-class (one carrying between twenty and forty guns), the *Winooski* had been named for an American river, the same Vermont waterway that separates the village of that name (where Lonergan once had his grocery shop) from Burlington. (If Lonergan had gone to Eastport, he curiously would have been the second captain from a Winooski—and another cooper—involved in the affair.)

major territorial command. The district included the Department of the East in Philadelphia, whose authority extended to Maine.) The personal presence of the district commander on the scene was a clear indication of how seriously the government considered the threat to international relations. Meade, accompanied by some regular troops, arrived on April 18 and seized the contents of the *E. H. Pray*, except for a few cases of arms that had been slipped over the rails to Fenian boats during the night.

Michael Murphy in Toronto had been ordered to bring Canadian Fenians to the coast in support of the Killian forces that intended to cross the border, and to choose twenty "drilled and temperate men" if he could find them. He gathered only half a dozen men, who were kept under close surveillance by the police as they traveled east. The group was pulled off the train by troops in Cornwall, Ontario, and placed under arrest, even though they had not yet committed any crime. Cornwall and other towns on the St. Lawrence River had been garrisoned with both militia and regular units to deal with the threat of an invasion. The overzealous troops exceeded their authority by confining Murphy and his men.

British warships were at anchor in the bay off Campobello, one of them carrying 800 regular soldiers to reinforce the militia on duty at the frontier. Faced with well-alerted Canadian forces prepared to repel any incursion, and hampered by the interference of the U.S. government, the Fenians in Maine had to be content with some minor acts of vandalism before they abandoned the idea of crossing the border. By April 27, Fenians were in full retreat from Eastport by steamer and train. However, on May 3, one group of sixty under a Col. Kelly tried their luck as privateers, using a fishing vessel to sail out of Eastport. They captured the British schooner *Wentworth* off the Manan Islands, transferring their arms and provisions to that ship. Pursued by the *Winooski*, the Fenians soon landed back on shore and returned the prize ship to its captain.

The attempt to steal the thunder from the Roberts wing turned out instead to be a total embarrassment. Valuable weapons and accoutrements worth thousands of dollars had been seized by the government. The transportation of men and material had been expensive and there were large bills for accommodations. Not only had the operation cost the treasury of the O'Mahony headquarters $20,000, but many participants in the expedition complained of having paid their own expenses. Reportedly, one group

CHAPTER TWENTY – FENIANS INVADE CANADA

stormed into the New York office after their return claiming thirty dollars apiece in lost wages and personal costs for the ill-fated adventure. The leaders supposedly held their pistols on O'Mahony until they were all reimbursed.

Even more damaging to the cause, however, was the fact that the Fenians had now become the target of jibes and scorn for their military incompetence and timidity. Disruption of the annual Town Meeting in Rutland was attributed to a rowdy group repeatedly called the "Finnegans" in an April 30 report in that town's *Herald*. A satirical column on the Fenians by Artemus Ward in the *Philadelphia Home Weekly* was reprinted in the *Free Press* on May 2. In the broadest of brogues, Ward explained about the "Finians" and their dueling head centres as being two parties, the O'McMahonys and the McO'Roberts. One side wanted to establish an Irish Republic in Canada and the other insisted on sailing direct for Dublin, but the two agreed on the one point of needing funds: "You send a puss [i.e. purse] to-night to Mahony, and another puss to Roberts. Both will receive 'em. You bet."

Lonergan most likely avoided any entanglement in the Eastport fiasco, remaining in Vermont to pursue several concerns. As state head centre, he continued to organize the Fenian circles and to recruit new members, although the possibility of engaging the veterans of the Civil War in actions in Ireland or elsewhere was fading, as the demobilized soldiers resumed civilian life. Lonergan's partnership with Munnigan in the grocery store had ended and John had been joined in that business by his father, Thomas. Regular steamship navigation opened up on Lake Champlain on April 16, so John's seasonal appointment to the customs office presumably then provided him full-time employment. In addition, Roseanna was several months pregnant with the couple's second child. However, even if Lonergan was not personally involved in Killian's expedition, its consequences still affected his relationships in the Fenian Brotherhood.

THE DISCOURAGING FAILURE of the Eastport operation sparked an angry reaction within the O'Mahony organization. On April 30, delegates from the seventy circles in the Manhattan district subjected the head centre to a two-hour interrogation, during which he admitted that his decision had been a mistake. O'Mahony fended off the demands for his resignation on the spot by showing a letter from Stephens. The recognized overall leader stated that he was coming to the United States to sort out the disputes among the Fenians. Killian was also blamed for the Maine fiasco; a committee took charge of the Union Square headquarters and its treasury books until Stephens arrived.

Despite his status as a founder of the movement and his skills as an organizer, Stephens was ill-suited to mediate the quarrel between the two factions of the Brotherhood. His irascible nature had so alienated John Mitchel in Paris that the financial agent, crucial to channeling funds to Europe, warned of his resignation if Stephens took over the American branch. A comment on the likelihood of Stephens uniting the feuding sections of the Fenians appeared in the *Free Press* on May 8: "The Kilkenny cats have devoured each other, except the tails, and Mr. S. proposes to join the tails." The article went on to report that the "Fenian fury in New York city" had turned upon both leaders, as Stephens was accused of complicity with O'Mahony's mismanagement. There were cries for Stephens to be arrested once he reached America and to be tried on suspicion of being a British agent.

Upon arrival in New York on the evening of May 10, Stephens—traveling with Kelly and his staff, the military council of the IRB—was greeted by thousands of Irishmen who escorted him to the Metropolitan hotel. At midnight, he was serenaded there by the 99th New York, O'Mahony's regiment, and he announced his intention of uniting all the Irish people, taking no sides between parties. Stephens soon appointed a committee to investigate matters in the O'Mahony wing, particularly the finances. When the committee reported back, Stephens declared himself to be astonished and indignant that only $500 was found in the treasury of "the hundreds of thousands of dollars that have been contributed." Faced with the result of the investigation and the disorganization in the Brotherhood, O'Mahony resigned his position, but not before dismissing Killian as treasurer. John O'Leary summed up this tragic end to the head centre's command of the Brotherhood, saying "O'Mahony was not, indeed, an ideal leader, but he was an ideal Irishman."

On May 15, some 6,000 Fenians gathered at Jones Wood in New York to give Stephens "an enthusiastic ovation," although it was noted that none of the Roberts men attended. The only speaker at the rally, Stephens called upon Roberts to follow O'Mahony's example and resign in the interests of unity within the movement. Roberts declined to step down from leadership of the Senate wing. Unable to reconcile the schism in the movement, Stephens

CHAPTER TWENTY – FENIANS INVADE CANADA

himself replaced O'Mahony as head centre of the Brotherhood. On May 21, he set off on a tour intended to establish his authority outside the New York City region, but not before insisting, as the newly self-appointed leader, that no thought should be given to invading Canada.

When John Mitchel learned that Stephens had taken charge in America, he resigned his role as financial agent in Paris in disgust and returned home to Richmond, Virginia. Since Stephens and his military council had fled to America, the near future held little possibility for an armed uprising in Ireland. The loss of the movement's agent in France, moreover, disrupted the flow of any funds to finance the rebellion. Impatient to strike a blow, many Fenians—Lonergan apparently among them—switched their allegiance to Roberts and his plan for action closer to home. With O'Mahony gone from power, Lonergan no longer owed his support to the chief personally, nor to his policies, and could turn Vermont toward the more aggressive Senate wing.

Even as Stephens assumed power from O'Mahony, Roberts was already setting his operation in motion. The Fenian senators had issued bonds on May 10 and each of the fifteen senators further pledged $5,000 to fund Sweeney's ambitious plan for a multi-pronged attack on Canada. The usual celebrations would be held throughout the British Empire on May 24 to mark Queen Victoria's birthday. British troops would presumably be distracted by participation in the ceremonial event. The symbolism of a blow struck for Irish freedom on this date increased apprehensions in Canada, even though the birthday of the "Famine Queen" passed without incident. The veteran Sweeny clearly intended to base the timing of his action as the Fenian military commander on operational, rather than symbolic, considerations. In the broader sense, however, the entire venture was symbolic.

A popular song among the Fenians at the time included the lines:

> We are the Fenian Brotherhood, skilled in the arts of war.
> And we're going to fight for Ireland, the land that we adore.
> Many battles we have won, along with the boys in blue.
> And we'll go and capture Canada, for we've nothing else to do.

The Fenians had no hopes of conquering and defending any portion of British North America. The disaffected Irish of Canada—clearly a minority in the Irish community, given the large proportion of loyal Orangemen—were unlikely to rise up in support of an invasion. Even if they were joined by the French population in rebellion against British rule, the power of the Empire would still prevail. The goal of Roberts and his followers was rather to revive the nationalist movement by actually taking the field with an organized Irish military force. Seen in contrast to the farce in Maine, this would also help to consolidate his leadership of the fractured organization. The declaration of a *de facto* Irish Republic–in–exile by Fenian forces on Canadian soil would be a powerful statement of their resolve for independence. Some wishful thinking might have persisted that the United States would thus be dragged into a war with Great Britain to the advantage of the Irish cause, but this was hardly a realistic possibility.

Sweeney's strategy envisioned three lines of advance threatening Canada in sequence, although this attack in echelon proved difficult to coordinate. The left wing and center of the Army of Ireland would aim for objectives in southwestern Ontario, to draw off British forces protecting Toronto and Ottawa. The larger right wing would cross from New York at Buffalo and other points along that state's northern border, while a force from Vermont would move on Montreal. Sufficient quantities of arms and ammunition had been purchased from the U.S. government and secreted at depots in major cities or in towns near the invasion routes. This material was then shipped forward at the proper time, mostly by rail in crates misleadingly labeled "hardware," to smaller caches nearer the border. Well-founded complaints to Seward by the British ambassador in Washington gave details of the number of boxes shipped and the intended recipients, particulars no doubt provided by informants within the Fenian movement.

In late May, Sweeney began to move the men toward assembly points where they would receive their weapons. Fewer men reported for action than had been promised by the circles supporting him; even so, difficulties arose in moving and arming those who did respond. Railroads in some cases refused to provide transportation, boats to cross the Great Lakes were not available, and cases of weapons were seized by the U.S. marshals, who had been alerted to block any violation of neutrality. However, contingents numbering hundreds of men departed from distant states like Kentucky and Maryland to converge with groups from the Midwest, New York, and New England. Rumors of large gatherings at many locations along the border appeared in newspaper reports, perhaps spread deliberately by Fenians attempting to mislead the British as

CHAPTER TWENTY – FENIANS INVADE CANADA

to the actual points of action. By the end of May, growing concentrations of Fenians were confirmed around Buffalo, Malone, and Ogdensburg in New York and St. Albans, Vermont.

Because of transportation problems and a lack of manpower, operations of the left wing under Gen. Charles Tevis in Chicago never developed. Similar reasons caused the headquarters of Gen. William Lynch, commanding the center of the Fenian offensive, to be shifted from Cleveland to Buffalo. On the right, Gen. Samuel Spear had more success in the preparatory phase of moving men and material to the staging area at St. Albans. The scope of the overall action meant that it could not be concealed and newspapers on both sides of the border were filled with stories of the pending assault on Canada.

ON MAY 31, 1866, THE FENIANS launched the first organized military operation for their country's independence since the United Irishmen uprising of 1798. Surplus blue uniforms from the Union army, modified with green stripes and buttons marked "IRA," were used to outfit this new Irish Republican Army. A mass meeting at Buffalo was followed later that night by Fenian troops crossing the Niagara River on barges, landing on the Canadian side at daybreak on June 1. About 800 men under the command of Col. John O'Neill were successfully transported over the water before the U.S.S. *Michigan* intervened to block any reinforcements. O'Neill brought with him a proclamation from Sweeney assuring that the army of liberation had no quarrel with the people of the provinces, but was only seeking to strike a blow against British rule in Ireland. It called upon the Irishmen in Canada "in the name of seven centuries of British iniquity and Irish misery" to offer the hand of brotherhood to the Fenians and help revenge "our desolate homes…our millions of famine graves, our insulted name and race."

The Canadian authorities had already moved both regular troops and militia into the area. At Ridgeway on June 2, O'Neill ambushed a column of volunteers in the green uniforms of the Toronto-based Queen's Own Rifles and the red coats of the 13th militia regiment from Hamilton.* The more experienced Fenian soldiers drove the Canadian forces from the battlefield in a skirmish that cost the British ten dead and thirty-seven wounded. O'Neill

---

* Rifle regiments in the British Army at the time traditionally wore green. The "QOR" nickname of the unit was later mocked as "Quick Out of Ridgeway" for their disorganized flight from the scene of the conflict.

lost three dead (including a Lt. Edward Lonergan of Buffalo) and sixteen wounded in the firefight; scattered detachments of Fenians were taken prisoner in the area by the superior British forces. Cut off from supplies and reinforcements, the Fenians retreated back across the river on the night of June 3. As their vessels arrived on the American side, they were detained by the captain of the *Michigan*.

Reaction by the U.S. authorities followed the same pattern as in April, with involvement by elements under the control of the Departments of War, Navy, and Treasury, and the Attorney General. Coordination between the members of Johnson's cabinet was delayed due to the funeral for Gen. Winfred Scott, which closed down all government activities in Washington on June 1. The detention of the Fenians at Buffalo by the navy was a matter for which no politician was eager to claim responsibility. Meade arrived in Buffalo on June 3 and in consultation with the district attorney arranged for the prisoners to be released on parole, except for O'Neill and a dozen other leaders who had to post bail.

Clearly Meade had chosen to be personally engaged in dealing with the Fenians, taking to the field like an old war horse hearing the bugle call. As the commander of a large administrative element of the army, his presence at the scene was not required and he might in fact have managed the situation better from his headquarters in Philadelphia. However, the Irish had given him one more chance to be in the thick of a conflict, so he shuttled along the border with Canada by train, giving orders on the spot and by telegraph.

News of the action on Canadian soil had rekindled the enthusiasm of many Fenians and hundreds more reported for duty. Sweeney shifted the focus to the frontier of northern New York and Vermont, east of the St. Lawrence River, where the border could be crossed on dry land. On June 4 the Fenian commander left New York City for Malone with 200 additional men.

At one point, when both Fenians and the U.S. military converged on Malone, Meade and his staff traveled on the same train as Sweeney and his contingent. Finding a sizable force of Fenians at Ogdensburg, Meade recommended that martial law be declared and the militia called out to deal with the situation.

At a meeting in Montreal to organize a home guard in reaction to the Fenian threat, D'Arcy McGee, Member of Parliament, spoke about "turbulent characters" who bore watching and who were lurking in the city. He cited "skeddadlers" who had fled from the draft during the Civil War, "blackguards

CHAPTER TWENTY – FENIANS INVADE CANADA

and burglars from New York" ready to commit arson, and other villains who might take advantage of the absence of loyal volunteers serving on the border. Anyone from the American South, he pointed out, who was participating in the trouble on the frontier failed to recognize the help that Canada had given the Confederacy. McGee reminded the crowd that he had cautioned them from the same platform a few months ago not to flirt with the Fenians "who were bent on disturbing the peace along our border." Amid cries from the audience that they remembered his admonishments, the former revolutionary somberly repeated, "I warned you that trouble might come of it."

FENIAN OPERATIONS IN VERMONT during this offensive hinged on the important rail center of St. Albans, some fifteen miles south of the border with Canada. In late May, Deputy U.S. Marshal J. A. Arthur had seized arms and equipment belonging to Sweeney's Fenians at the express office in St. Albans. The property was brought to Burlington and stored in the Custom House— where Lonergan was employed—and in the vestibule of the post office, for safe keeping. As O'Neill landed his force opposite Buffalo on June 1, the *Free Press* reported the arrival of 300 Fenians in St. Albans. A company of U.S. Army regulars was once again coming to the town from Boston, with orders from Gen. Hooker, now commander of the Department of the East, to guard against any violation of the neutrality laws. Just across Lake Champlain, the presence of two companies of regular troops at the garrison in Plattsburgh had not prevented a body of local Fenians from moving north under the command of a Capt. Dolan. (This New York officer was no doubt Lonergan's old comrade and the first lieutenant in his original Emmet Guards militia.) The strategic objective in the Quebec sector was two-fold—an advance threatening Montreal that would draw off Canadian forces, and the seizure of Sherbrooke, where an Irish government in exile would be proclaimed. Columns of Fenians would move north on both sides of the Richelieu River, the historical invasion route for the area, to converge at St. Jean. Command of the men concentrated in Vermont had been entrusted to Gen. Samuel B. Spear, formerly a major in the regular army.* The operations plan had assigned him seventeen regiments of infantry and five of cavalry, which would total over 10,000 men.

---

* He was credited with being a graduate of the U.S. Military Academy at West Point in some accounts, but was not found among those listed as commissioned from that institution. His name was also given as "Spears" in various reports.

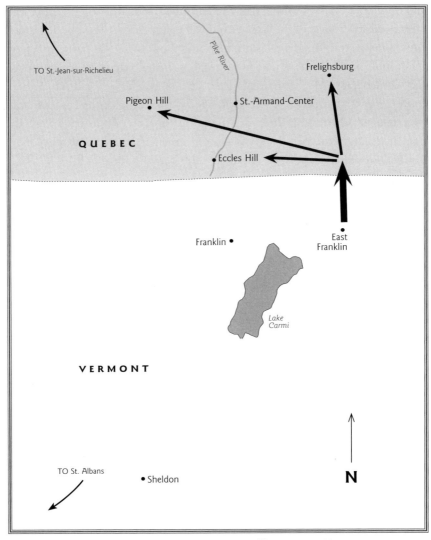

FENIANS CROSS THE BORDER FROM VERMONT, 1866

On June 2, the *Free Press* reported that a total of about 1,400 men had arrived in St. Albans; 800 of them from New York, Massachusetts, and Connecticut had gotten off the trains in the last two days. Overall, perhaps 2,000 Fenians reported for duty at the rendezvous point (although some additional forces were delayed and arrived after the operation ended).

CHAPTER TWENTY – FENIANS INVADE CANADA

As soon as the men assembled at the railroad station, they were marched off in good order under the control of the officers. Most were carrying three days rations in their haversacks, but few displayed weapons or much in the way of military equipment. They moved on foot to the camp set up on the hill behind St. Albans or to other encampments near Swanton Falls, Fairfax, and Fairfield. The arms and ammunition stored in caches along the border, mainly under the care of Irish farmers and shopkeepers sympathetic to the cause, would be distributed away from the observation of U.S. authorities.

Both civil and military officials were engaged in foiling an operation that threatened to become an international incident. Regular army troops had been ordered to St. Albans and Swanton to control the railroads at those points. On June 1, the U.S. Marshal, Hugh H. Henry, and the District Attorney, Dudley C. Denison, had both relocated from Burlington to St. Albans, where they would remain "until all is again quiet." The Secretary of War (acting "in the temporary absence of Mr. Seward," the Secretary of State) had that same day assured the Collector of Customs in Washington of the President's approval for seizing any shipments of Fenian weapons.

On May 31, as O'Neill's men were crossing into Canada, the Sarsfield Circle began meeting behind closed doors at Fenian Hall in Burlington for three nights running. Until the hall was jammed with people on Saturday night, June 2, no public indication had been given that Lonergan's group would get involved with Sweeney's operation. The excited crowd heard from Maj. Burke of Sweeney's staff, just arrived from New York City. The audience was further addressed by Lonergan and Monahan, his second in command of the Sarsfield Circle. Despite Lonergan's earlier adherence to O'Mahony's policy of rejecting any action against Canada, circumstances had now changed and he was throwing his support to the operation by the Roberts wing. A collection of funds was made for the Fenian cause, while a more direct contribution of sixty stand of arms and 5,000 ball cartridges were to be shipped that night to St. Albans from supplies in Burlington.

With the trains being closely watched, the Irish were employing alternate means of transport; reportedly "a large quantity of arms and ammunition was landed at St. Albans Bay" by boat on June 2 and carried from there to the Fenian camp in wagons. A correspondent for the Boston *Journal* observing the Fenians in Fairfield wrote that arms and equipment arrived from Burlington on wagons that same night. These were "said to be the arms seized at St. Albans" and it suggests that Lonergan may have helped retrieve them from the Custom House for delivery back to the Fenians. Rather than risk transporting the weapons on the trains again, teamsters were organized to take them directly to the camps. This would necessarily have required the connections of a local Fenian leader like Lonergan.

Even as the newspapers reported in detail the repulse of O'Neill's sortie from Buffalo, other stories described groups gathering at Ogdensburg and Malone in northern New York, as well as St. Albans and Newport in Vermont. The movement of Sweeney and his staff to St. Albans, and the continuing influx of men there, plainly indicated that any additional movements against Canada would be directed from Vermont. On June 4, the Fenian leaders held a council of war in St. Albans and decided to move on Canada immediately, though hindered by the lack of ammunition and supplies. At Malone, Gen. Michael Murphy agreed to take his 1,000 men over the border in coordination with Spear, who would have overall command of the right wing of the IRA. Spear's forces were to rendezvous about five miles south of the frontier, east of St. Armand in Quebec, from camps outside St. Albans and in Fairfield. The numerous Irish in Fairfield had welcomed the Fenians, saying that they would board them for a week if necessary. Some houses and barns sheltered thirty men apiece and the *Free Press* claimed "one priest boards ten Fenians." A prominent surgeon in Fairfield had reportedly offered to accompany the troops.

The St. Albans *Messenger* commented favorably on the "admirable conduct of the Fenians," stating that their orderly behavior was "still the wonder of our citizens." The men occupied themselves in the camps with military drill and there were no complaints of "rowdyism." Many U.S. Army units passed through the rail center and continued on their way to Malone and Ogdensburg, leaving only two companies at Swanton and a single company of seventy-five men in St. Albans on June 4. The regulars were under orders to seize all suspicious baggage in order to deprive the Fenians of their supplies. The total number of U.S. soldiers posted in Franklin County was only 225, clearly insufficient to prevent the Irish from moving to the border.

The Burlington Fenian Hall was the scene of "another crowded meeting" on the evening of June 4 when Lonergan urged active cooperation with Sweeney's effort. He announced his intention to join Spear and said that he "would be glad to take 300 Vermont Fenians with him." Although sympathetic to the situation and donating some forty dollars to the war treasury, most of the Brotherhood present at the meeting proved reluctant to join the ranks of the men in the field.

Gov. Dillingham spent a few hours in St. Albans on June 5 and was expected to return with Adj. Gen. Washburn, presumably to command the Vermont militia if it was decided that they were needed. The annual June training of the militia companies was going on at this time, but these units were not called up to assist the federal troops. The regulars had been increased to detachments of almost 300 men at each of the two important railroad centers, Swanton and St. Albans. On June 5 Hooker ordered them to arrest all armed men moving toward Canada and any others thought to be Fenians. Alongside this report, the *Free Press* published a warning that anyone involved in military preparations to violate U.S. neutrality would be subject to $3,000 fine and three years' imprisonment.

Likewise, U.S. Attorney General James Speed on June 5 issued an order to the district attorneys and marshals under his jurisdiction to "cause the arrest of all the prominent leaders or conspirators, persons called 'Fenians'" that might be guilty of violating the neutrality laws. Despite concerns by the administration that these steps might jeopardize its support by Irish voters, President Johnson followed up these instructions with a proclamation of neutrality on June 6. Somewhat after the fact, it specifically empowered Meade "to employ the land and naval forces of the United States and the militia to arrest" those involved in the Fenian operation. The military was authorized under this proclamation to stop the movement of Fenians and their war materiel, as well as to cut them off from any communication by telegraph.

An editorial titled "What will it Amount to?" decrying the folly of "this Fenian business" was featured in the *Free Press* on the day of the proclamation. Absent the only possible condition for its success, "viz, a general uprising of the Canadian people against their government," in the author's opinion there was no chance for the Irish incursion. The anonymous commentator—probably Lonergan's former comrade in arms, Benedict—called on every sensible man to "utterly refuse aid, comfort, or sympathy to the Fenian movement," since it could not help Ireland or Irishmen in any possible way, but only cause "incalculable harm to all concerned."

During the night of June 5, "a large number of arms and a considerable quantity of ammunition" were secured by the Fenians "through strategy." As reported in the *Free Press* on June 6, an expedition of "trusty officers and faithful men" had been sent to where a large quantity of goods was known to be stored. The weapons were sorely needed by the Fenians, but taking possession potentially involved conflict with the U.S. authorities. The officers detailed for the mission, which clearly involved the retrieval of seized arms and ammunition now under government control, were "well informed about the whereabouts of the goods, how they are guarded and the like." Every precaution had been taken to ensure the success of this inside job; the most likely target for this raid was the Burlington Custom House across the square from Lonergan's grocery store. If this location was the source for the weapons that had been seized on June 2, then this would have been the second such escapade. As a customs official himself, Lonergan would have had access to the building and he obviously had the local connections to move the weapons for the Fenians.

Another 600 Fenians reportedly arrived at St. Albans on June 6. A group of 200 stopped the morning train about a mile south of the town by pulling the bell cord and applying the brakes. A hundred who were carrying weapons then leaped from the cars. Other Fenians attempted to throw off five cases of arms and a box of ammunition, but these were seized by U.S. Marshal Henry as the train pulled into the station. A brief item titled "Personal," and stating only "Capt. John Lonergan reported to Gen. Sweeney yesterday," appeared alongside the account of this incident, printed the next day. The timing suggests that the armed group that halted the train might well have been led by Lonergan. The Burlington men would have had access to muskets from their armory and could likely have boarded in that town with their weapons. Only a local group would have had the requisite familiarity with the route to know when to stop the train and avoid the troops and marshals at the station. Such a flamboyant arrival in the field would not have been out of character for Lonergan and, given the situation, it was in fact an effective tactic.

On June 6 the Fenian troops had moved to East Franklin, just below the Canadian border, where they received a large amount of supplies. Cases of weapons, probably those taken from the Burlington Custom House during the night, were opened and placed by the side of the road. The men marched up and, according to an eyewitness, received their rifles and ammunition "joyfully." The reporter who described the scene observed that the weapons

CHAPTER TWENTY – FENIANS INVADE CANADA

were pulled from distinctive crates, ones which he had previously seen at St. Albans, where they had been seized, adding further evidence to the hypothesis that Lonergan played a key role in arranging for the theft and transportation of the arms.

Locally purchased horses provided the Fenian cavalry with mounts and the troopers carried small arms, including sabers. Although the Irishmen were short of provisions and lacked equipment such as tents, the morale of most of the Fenians remained high despite heavy rains that had muddied the roads. Spear cheerfully boasted that he had arrived with no horses and now had a dozen, putting the best face on his shortages.

Back in St. Albans, the commander of the regulars there, Maj. Augustus Gibson, arrested Sweeney around midnight on June 6, acting on the authority of the President's proclamation. The Fenian general was comfortably asleep in his bed at the Tremont House and offered no resistance to the soldiers as he was led away to their headquarters on the Common. Spear was at the same hotel, but he got word of the raid and hid from the troops in a closet. He slipped out an hour later, leaving town around 3:00 AM to join his troops in the field.

As THE RANKING FENIAN OFFICER still at liberty in the area, Spear decided on his own to continue with the invasion plan. Seizure of quantities of arms and the arrest of the Secretary of War had significantly reduced the scope of action possible. Of four Fenian generals assigned to lead brigades under Spear, only Mahan from Boston had reported to St. Albans. The regiments of the force at hand were far below strength and not fully armed. Nonetheless, Spear appeared before them at 8:30 AM in uniform, booted and spurred, to face men who were chafing at the delay. He roused them with a speech that declared his determination to lead them into Canada even if they carried only "pebble stones," (perhaps a comparison with David and Goliath).

The arrival of wagons with ammunition and provisions put the men in better humor for the march to the border. There Spear reminded them that, although they were entering the "territory of the mortal enemies of Ireland," they must conduct themselves as soldiers; no maltreatment of women and children would be tolerated. He then led them cheering across the border onto British soil at 10:00 AM on June 7. The columns moved in good order through an abandoned countryside to a point three miles east and a little beyond Pigeon Hill. The plan was to entrench a position for defense while awaiting reinforcements. The cavalry under Col. Contri (who had formerly served with Mosby in Virginia) put out pickets at Cook's Corners, Pigeon Hill, and Frelighsburg (also called Slab City), about four miles into Canada.

At Frelighsburg that evening, Capt. O'Hara led fifteen Fenian horsemen in a minor skirmish with some fifty mounted Canadian volunteers, who retreated after slightly wounding one Fenian. The British flag from the Custom House at Frelighsburg was carried as a trophy to Spear's headquarters, the home of a farmer named Eccles, who had fled the area. The Union Jack was triumphantly displayed below the green flag of Ireland with its uncrowned harp. A few shots were also exchanged with Canadian volunteers on June 8 as they probed the Pigeon Hill position, but they were quickly driven off after wounding three Fenians. (One of those injured may have died, as a funeral was held in New York City a few days later for Eugene Corcoran, aged nineteen, reportedly killed at Frelighsburg.)

Another flag displayed in front of the headquarters had been presented to Gen. Mahan by the ladies of Watertown, New York, and bore the motto "In one short hour comes death or victory." Mahan, in a show of Irish bravado, had given a reporter a copy of President Johnson's proclamation, which the general had endorsed with his comments. He was sending the proclamation back from the "Headquarters, 2nd Brigade, 1st Division of the Army of Fenians at Camp Sweeney, Canada East," telling the president that he should report to that headquarters on British soil. Mahan wanted Johnson to explain why he had not consulted with the invading force before prohibiting their action. Mahan considered this a breach of military rules and declared "Andy must give a clear account of himself."

Lonergan's name does not appear in any accounts as a participant in the incursion. However, given his announced intention of joining Sweeney's forces and the item in the *Free Press* stating that he had gone to St. Albans, it is quite possible that he crossed the border with the men under Spear's command. Lonergan's knowledge of the area from his role as head centre in Vermont and his service with the Frontier Cavalry the year before would have made him a valuable addition to the expedition. While his actual combat experience was limited to the battle at Gettysburg, this was more than sufficient to establish both his personal bravery and his ability to lead men.

CHAPTER TWENTY – FENIANS INVADE CANADA

THE CANADIAN PARLIAMENT CONVENED on June 8 and passed a bill to suspend *habeas corpus* to deal with the situation, even as the Governor General delivered a speech congratulating the country on repelling the Fenian invasion. Johnson's proclamation of neutrality had been well received in Canada, as an appropriate action to remove the threat of further incursions from American soil. In New York, however, it was reported that June 9 was the day that had been "fixed for the rising of the Canadian Fenians" and stories were still circulating of additional attacks being prepared by way of Detroit, Malone, and other cities.

The day after their arrest, Sweeney and his chief of staff, Col. Meehan, were transferred from military custody into that of the civil authority in the person of U.S. Marshal Henry. A hearing took place on June 8 before U.S. Commissioner William H. Hoyt, up from Burlington to assist in the process of reining in the Fenians. Sweeney waived any examination and his bail was set at $20,000 while he awaited trial at the U.S. District Court in Windsor, meeting next on the fourth Tuesday in July. Meehan remained in custody with his commander, even though his bail was $5,000. Other Fenian leaders were being arrested throughout the country, including Roberts in New York. Stephens reportedly left Washington in secret on June 8 to avoid arrest, although he had just declared in a speech at Baltimore on June 5 that he "would have nothing to do with the leadership of either faction" of the Brotherhood. The new head centre felt that he had been "deceived, if not betrayed," by both wings of the Fenians through their escapades of attacking Canada. Henceforth, he would "address himself directly to the rank and file of Irishmen inside and outside of the Fenian Brotherhood."

A detachment of twenty-five men of the 3rd U.S. Artillery commanded by Lt. Arthur arrived in Burlington June 8 and were quartered in the vestibule of City Hall. The troops had been sent down from St. Albans to guard the large quantity of Fenian arms that had been seized and stored in the nearby Custom House. This step was likely taken in reaction to the recent disappearance of weapons from that location.

Meade issued a proclamation at Malone on June 9 ordering "All persons assembled at this place in connection with, and in aid of, the Fenian organization for the purpose of invading Canada" to comply with President Johnson's earlier proclamation to desist and disband. He offered to pay transportation costs for the enlisted men and all line officers who signed a parole, though field and general grade officers would be required to post bonds. If there was not prompt obedience to his orders, Meade promised to compel it by whatever force required. That same day, Sweeney's chief of staff sent out an order over the general's name from the "Headquarters Army of Ireland" at St. Albans instructing "the senior officer with troops of the Army of Ireland at Malone, Potsdam, and elsewhere" to take advantage of the offer of transportation home. Citing the "stringent measures adopted by the United States authorities" that prevented men and war supplies from reaching the forces on the frontier, the general had decided "the object of the expedition cannot be accomplished at present." Being jailed must have strongly influenced Sweeney's appreciation of the situation.

Even with the overwhelming force of British regulars and mobilized Canadian militia in the field, their commander, Sir John Michel, focused more on the protection of towns and lines of communication than in repulsing the intruders. He correctly understood that no pitched battle would be necessary and that the "invasion" would collapse on its own without any logistical base. Some newspaper accounts credited Michel with a strategy of luring the Fenians far enough into Canada that a pincer movement could cut off their retreat, making the entire force prisoner. The British commander appears rather to have been satisfied to let the Irish make their own way back to the United States without bloodshed. Michel had delayed his advance partly because there had been no cavalry to scout ahead and he paused at St. Jean until a troop of the Royal Guides from Montreal joined him. On June 9, the British commander moved a strong force of regulars and volunteers—infantry, cavalry, and artillery—toward Pigeon Hill.

Spear had halted the main body of his forces less than a mile into Canada to await reinforcements. News that Sweeney had called off the operation came as mounted scouts brought Spear reports of approaching Canadian forces greatly outnumbering the Irish. Discouraged by the lack of manpower and equipment, as well as by the news of the arrest of Sweeney and his staff, some Fenians had already abandoned the expedition from St. Albans in disgust, to return home. Spear decided that the demonstration made by the Army of Ireland in crossing the border under arms would have to suffice, choosing not

CHAPTER TWENTY – FENIANS INVADE CANADA

to doom his men to death or capture in a pointless battle. The troops fell in at his order around 9:30 AM on June 9 and marched back to the frontier. Some men fired off their ammunition in frustration, while others simply threw away their muskets.

A rear guard of about 200 men took up a defensive position behind an improvised barricade and faced the British regulars and Canadian militia arriving from St. Jean. As the infantry formed up for an assault, the Irish could see half a battery of artillery unlimbering on nearby Pigeon Hill. With no possible response to a long-range bombardment, the Fenians rightly judged their position to be hopeless and quickly pulled out of their hasty fortifications.

When the Irish rear guard began its retreat to the border, the forty troopers of the Royal Guides charged with drawn sabers to rush them on their way.* The captain had instructed his men to use only the flat of their swords, tumbling the Fenians as they ran. Wild shots from some Irish failed to cause any casualties to the horsemen. Over a dozen of the invaders were taken prisoner.

SAFELY BACK ACROSS THE BORDER, the defeated Fenians who had escaped capture straggled their way back to St Albans "without any attempt at military order." A company of U.S. regulars had taken up position outside the town to receive the Fenians. Any weapons still in the possession of the retreating Irish were collected as they filed past and any officers identified were placed under arrest. An extra train was arranged, scheduled to leave for Boston in the afternoon "loaded with despondent Fenians." Before being allowed to return home, each man had to sign a parole recognizing himself as a prisoner of the U.S. government and "promising to abandon Fenianism." After stating on June 9 that "the Green Flag waves defiantly" over Pigeon Hill and declaring "victory or death," later that day Mahan turned himself in to the authorities in St. Albans, by one account weeping bitterly.

An editorial in the *Free Press* again cited the penalties for anyone enlisting in an expedition violating the neutrality laws, but called on the American

---

* The Royal Guides, chosen as the Governor General's Body Guard in 1863, were essentially the Montreal Hunt Club in a military role. The image of these aristocratic men of property riding down the fleeing Irish seems a particularly appropriate symbol of British oppression.

authorities to treat the rank and file involved "with great forbearance and leniency." Ignorance of the law should be assumed for "the misguided men who have rushed into this reckless scheme without thought of the consequences." The editor also asked that the English authorities avoid "precipitate and passionate action" in dealing with the Fenian prisoners captured in Canada. Newspapers had printed baseless tales of Fenian bodies lying unburied around the countryside near Pigeon Hill and of Fenians hanged on the spot when captured. The only confirmed fatality in the Quebec operation occurred after the Fenians had retreated: Margaret Vincent, an elderly and deaf maiden lady living with her sister near Eccles Hill, was shot by a nervous picket of the Royal Fusiliers when she went to fetch water in the dark.

These reports on June 9 were accompanied in the *Free Press* by an item stating tersely, "The current rumor of a change in the Custom House is only a little premature." Perhaps as a consequence of the theft of seized arms from the Custom House, word had gotten around that the Burlington Collector of Customs was soon to be replaced. Lonergan appears to have escaped arrest by U.S. authorities for his involvement in the entire Fenian escapade, including any role he had in "liberating" weapons from the Custom House. His Vermont contingent may well have been part of the rear guard of Spear's force, since they had the least distance to return home when the expedition collapsed. The prisoners taken by the Canadians were mostly from Massachusetts, suggesting that the Vermonters, particularly those led by Lonergan, would have used their familiarity with the area to reach the border without capture.

Once back in the United States, Lonergan and his men could have found a route home that dodged the American soldiers rounding up the Fenians. Lonergan likely remained in the St. Albans area for a while because of his responsibilities as Vermont's chief in the Brotherhood. Given his connections in the surrounding Irish communities, he was uniquely suited to handle matters locally after the operation failed. War materials, especially arms and ammunition, which had not been confiscated by the authorities, needed to be stored safely for future action. Lonergan could also have arranged for Fenian officers to be hidden with friendly residents to avoid arrest.

That same day, Meade arrived in St. Albans from Malone and was welcomed at the train station by a large group. The band of the 3rd U.S. Artillery played a serenade at the gathering that Saturday evening. After an introduction by U.S. Marshal Henry, Meade spoke to a cheering crowd to

CHAPTER TWENTY – FENIANS INVADE CANADA

thank them for their display of good will on the occasion of his first visit to Vermont. He praised the glorious deeds of Vermont's sons in the recent war, calling them excellent soldiers and "as fine a body of men as any in the army." The victor of Gettysburg singled out Stannard's troops for their role in that "decisive battle of the war." Meade stated that no group had rendered greater service at a critical moment than the comparatively raw Vermont units. It is not known whether Lonergan stood in the audience that June evening to hear this praise of his actions in 1863, coming from the man now committed to thwarting the Irish nationalist invasion.

Speaking at St. Albans, Meade expressed sympathy for the "sincere, but misguided" Fenians, explaining that he could not allow this sympathy to interfere with his duty as a soldier. In Malone, Meade had been mistaken for a Fenian leader when he stepped off the train; he accepted the cheers of the Irish in good humor before ordering them to disperse. On June 9, he declared that "the cloud that has hung over us is drifting away and all difficulties will be satisfactorily settled." Meade was being overly optimistic, however, as the hundreds of Fenians at Malone still hoped to march on Canada. Meade and his staff returned there by train on June 12 and finally cleared the town of its unwelcome visitors.

Other spots along the border were still flaring up with Fenian activity, real or rumored. Arms seized by the authorities at Ogdensburg were retaken by force in a Fenian raid and the regulars had to capture them for a second time. O'Neill claimed that 62,000 Fenians were still mobilized on the Canadian border and 10,000 armed men in Michigan stood ready to move at a signal. The Canadians remained tense about the situation, first recalling units from the border and then rushing them back in reaction to actual or imagined threats.

The last of the Fenians from outside Vermont left St. Albans for Boston on June 10. Among the one hundred men who boarded the train that Sunday was Mahan, who had somehow avoided arrest despite his conspicuous role in the failed expedition. The regular U.S. Army troops were initially scheduled to depart St. Albans on June 14, but did not leave for their home garrisons until June 19, when the affair had definitely come to a conclusion. Before leaving, Maj. Gibson issued a special order from the headquarters of the District of Champlain that included his thanks to the locals for their "prompt and courteous aid." Along with the citizens of St. Albans, the railway officials, and the civil authorities in general, he specifically expressed his gratitude to U.S. Marshal Henry. Henry reportedly carried out his "delicate duties" with prudence and tact, earning the respect of even the Fenians for his fairness.

ONE OFFICIAL IN BURLINGTON apparently lost his position with the federal government as a result of the Fenian escapades. The earlier hint in the *Free Press* of the replacement of the Collector of Customs for the District of Vermont, William Clapp, was verified in the newspaper on June 13 by a short notice of the appointment of Gen. Stannard to the position. The change would supposedly "give universal satisfaction, outside of the Custom House." The following day an editorial was printed with the opinion that this "proper and popular appointment" would suit everyone except the incumbent being removed. Clapp had held the office, "a very important and lucrative one" and the best one for earnings in New England, for the past five years, but was now being removed "somewhat suddenly." No cause for the change was offered, suggesting that it might have been common knowledge as to why Clapp was being suddenly replaced. The theft of the seized Fenian arms in his custody seems the obvious reason.

Stannard was praised in the editorial as a brave and worthy soldier and, perhaps as importantly in the era of winner-takes-all political patronage, a staunch Republican of "the truest Vermont stamp." Stannard had been considered as a candidate for the U.S. House of Representatives, but the customs position would pay more than he would have received in Congress. The one-armed general was confirmed by the U.S. Senate on June 15, but at that time was still on active duty in the army. In mid-March of 1866, he had been placed in charge of the Freedman's Affairs for the state of Maryland, a difficult position dealing with emancipated slaves entering a free society. Stannard visited Burlington on June 22 on his way back to Baltimore from his home outside St. Albans, and on June 28 he resigned his commission to take the position with Customs.

Lonergan could not have asked for a better person to be in charge of the Vermont district than his former mentor in the militia and the commander of the Second Vermont Brigade at Gettysburg. Although Clapp almost certainly lost his position because of his failure to safeguard the Fenian weapons in his custody, Lonergan appears to have avoided any unpleasant repercussions

CHAPTER TWENTY – FENIANS INVADE CANADA

from the incident. His seasonal customs job continued under Stannard. Perhaps the young Irishman had been clever enough to have organized the raid without personal involvement. Well-known in the community and, obviously, recognizable to fellow customs employees, Lonergan may have provided the necessary information to retrieve the weapons and stayed out of the action itself. If suspicion did fall on him as an accomplice, he apparently talked his way out of any guilt in the affair.

FENIAN LEADERS BLAMED FAILURE of their military operations on the betrayal of their movement by the Johnson administration. Sweeney wrote from his cell in St. Albans that the Brotherhood had acquired 60,000 stand of arms, mostly from the U.S. government, and Meade had robbed them of 40,000. Others insisted that the movement had been misled by the Johnson administration with hints that it would not intervene, and the Fenians clearly felt that the Irish had been used by Seward to press American claims against the British. Not only had the U.S. Army prevented implementation of the war plan, but now the weapons purchased with contributions by Irish patriots were locked up in federal arsenals. As president, Johnson had been required to enforce the Neutrality Act despite any sympathies he might have had for the Irish cause. (When O'Neill visited him some two years later, Johnson remarked that he had given the Fenians five full days before issuing his proclamation. He asked O'Neill, "What more did you want? If you could not get there in five days, you could never get there.")

The issue of the Neutrality Act itself came up for debate in Congress as a result of the Fenian operation. One representative proposed a bill to repeal the act and another put forward a resolution of censure for the Johnson administration's actions; neither one succeeded. The Irish had now achieved a larger measure of acceptance in American society, in part due to their well-publicized exploits in the Civil War. Some politicians were no doubt sincerely supportive of the nationalist aspirations, while others were simply calculating how to attract the Irish vote in next election.

The collapse of the Fenian incursions into Canada was, of course, due mainly to the unrealistic nature of the operation itself and the organizational problems inherent in such a grandiose plan. Expectations of an uprising among the Irish in Canada or even any useful support for a military expedition were totally unfounded, despite the presence of a few Fenian circles in larger cities such as Montreal and Toronto.

The number of men promised by Fenian circles for the operation was also greatly exaggerated and it proved logistically impossible to gather the forces effectively. Even as the invading troops retreated from British territory, groups of Fenians were still boarding trains as far away as Kansas, days too late to participate in the action. Spear expected to have 17,000 men on the right wing itself, yet he only saw about one thousand concentrated under his command at any given time. Meade provided transportation home for some 7,000 men scattered from Buffalo through Ogdensburg and Malone to St. Albans. The total number available was obviously much fewer than the 30,000 Sweeney had required for his plan.

After casting his lot with the Roberts wing of the Brotherhood to assist with the Fenian operation based out of St. Albans, Lonergan was no doubt disappointed with the results achieved. He took steps to bolster the spirits of the Vermont Irish, even though no real battle had taken place in their sector. On July 2, he convened a meeting in Burlington sponsored by, but not restricted to, the Fenian supporters. At the gathering, a set of resolutions was approved "by the Irish citizens of Burlington" and published in the *Free Press* over the signatures of Lonergan and his deputy McNamara. They defiantly declared first of all that "The Irish people are desperately in earnest and pledged to redeem the land of their birth from the tyranny of England" and that the Irish-American citizens intended to give aid and assistance to any enemy of England. Trusting that the wrongs of centuries might be righted in a day of victory, they resolved that "the sympathies of the American people are with the people of Ireland in struggling for independence."

Lonergan's commentary then expounded on the idea that the people were correct in their sympathies, while the government was at fault for having deceived the Fenians and prevented them from freeing Ireland. Making his own declaration of independence just before the Fourth of July, Lonergan withdrew his support from any man, Democrat or Republican, who "deceives a confiding people and receives English money." He declared the Fenian Brotherhood and the Irishmen of Burlington—though he certainly was not authorized to speak for all Hibernians of the town—independent of the Democratic or Republican parties. They would henceforth support and vote for the people serving the "best interests of the land of our adoption and for the friends who stand boldly for the independence of Ireland and true liberty everywhere." Not content to speak only for the local Irish, Lonergan concluded with a recommendation that these resolutions be adopted by all Irishmen in the state. Despite the setback just suffered by the nationalists, Lonergan clearly had no intention of abandoning the cause. The liberation of Ireland from British rule continued to be the central focus of his life.

CITIES of BURLINGTON AND SOUTH BURLINGTON

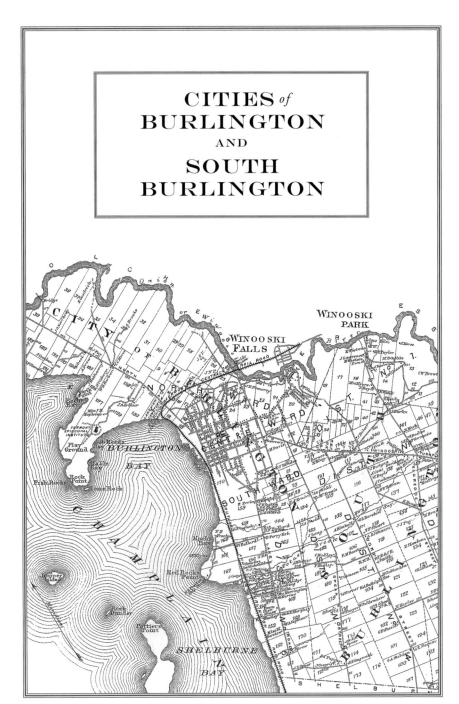

Burlington and South Burlington, circa 1866

CHAPTER TWENTY-ONE

FRACTURED FENIAN EFFORTS

LONERGAN'S DEDICATION TO Ireland never wavered and he supported each action aimed at restoring its independence. Like many other Fenians, Lonergan no doubt welcomed a chance for an armed attack on any part of the British Empire. Once the movement against Canada had collapsed, the focus of the Irish nationalists shifted back again to Ireland itself.

Stephens and other leaders like O'Mahony had always insisted that freedom from British rule could ultimately be gained only by revolution in the homeland. A raid on Canada might help an uprising in Ireland by diverting British troops elsewhere, but it could not be the only, or even the main, effort. With Stephens as the new head centre in America, Fenian efforts to revitalize the revolutionary movement in Ireland resumed. They faced great difficulties in reviving the organization there, which had been badly disrupted by the arrest and imprisonment of so many nationalists during the crackdown in 1865-6. The IRB operated an ocean away from its main source of support in America. Transportation of men and money, as well as the maintenance of clandestine communications between the IRB and the Fenian Brotherhood, presented enormous challenges.

The incursions by the Roberts wing of the Brotherhood into Canada brought serious consequences on several levels. More than a hundred Fenians had been taken prisoner in Canada; their uncertain fate depended in large part on relations between Great Britain and the United States. Meade had offered a soldier's opinion at Malone, when he said that Britain had the right to shoot the invaders. International relations, however, called for more subtle considerations. A resolution was passed in the U.S. Congress requesting that the prisoners be released, but in October trials began in Canada for those accused of waging war on the British sovereign.

Twenty-two prisoners had already been freed for lack of evidence when Robert B. Lynch, Galway-born and now a U.S. citizen, went before the court in Toronto. Despite his claim of only being present on the battlefield as a reporter, the jury found him guilty after an hour of deliberation. He was sentenced to be hanged on December 13. A priest from Andersonville, Indiana, Father John McMahon, was next to be brought before the court and he too was swiftly sentenced to death. Five more Fenians were condemned to death in November, causing a great outcry of protest in America.

Appealing for clemency and "a judicious amnesty" from the British government, President Johnson informed the U.S. Congress on December 3 that he had employed counsel to defend the American citizens on trial in Canada. Setting the example by "enlightened and human judgment" of those prominent Fenians arrested on the American side of the border, Johnson had already directed that prosecutions instituted against them be discontinued.

Relations between Great Britain and the United States remained strained because of unsettled claims from the Civil War. The Johnson administration had been using the Fenians as a threat in the abstract, but real costs had been incurred when the Irishmen actually moved against Canada. The British were now asking for reparations to pay for the expenses incurred in repelling the Fenian incursions launched from American soil. The case for Canadian Confederation also benefited from the Fenian actions, as a new national identity was forged in common action against the invaders.

The Catholic Church, ever hostile to the Fenians, even found the Irish nationalists of use as a divine instrument of retribution. In mid-July, the bishop of "Three Rivers, in Lower Canada" (present day Trois Rivières, Quebec) sent out a pastoral letter lecturing the men in his flock for intemperance and the women for extravagance. In this missive, the bishop considered "the current incessant rains and the Fenian invasion as chastisements from Heaven for these and like sins." The Irish quest for independence was thus reduced to the level of a punishment appropriate for excessive drinking and spending too much on fashion.

Repercussions rocked the Fenian Brotherhood throughout America in the aftermath of the failed invasion. On July 19, the leaders of the expedition were brought to Burlington from St. Albans, where they had been confined only loosely and were free to move within the town limits. At the U.S. District Court, they were released on bail provided by Daniel P. Barnard of Brooklyn,

CHAPTER TWENTY-ONE – FRACTURED FENIAN EFFORTS

New York. The bond for Generals Sweeney and Spear was $5,000 each, while Col. Meehan was set free for $3,000. Roberts himself stayed in jail in New York City "just long enough to rattle his fetters and to issue a proclamation" before making bail.

The Roberts faction held a convention in Troy, New York, in September of 1866 where Sweeney made his official report on the operation. He castigated the colonels of the regiments involved for their delays in reporting for duty and for their inaccurate accounts of available manpower. However, Sweeney put the immediate blame for the collapse of his plan on the American government's seizure of his weapons and supplies. Roberts urged support of the Republican Party in the upcoming off-year elections to retaliate for Johnson's interference with the assault on Canada.*

The convention voted to appoint Sweeney commander in chief of the Irish army, but the general resigned and severed his connections with the Fenians. Even though Gen. Phillip H. Sheridan was the first choice to replace Sweeney, the newly re-elected Roberts settled for moving Spear up to the position of Secretary of War. O'Neill received an appointment as the inspector general of the Fenian army. Spear issued an ambitious General Order calling for the organization of twenty-one regiments of infantry. The 1st Fenian Regiment was to be formed of men from Maine, New Hampshire, and Vermont.

Stephens toured the country seeking money in support of his renewed promise of action in the Ireland by the end of the year. He asked that all Fenians unite behind this effort. Further, in opposition to Roberts (who favored the Republicans), the new leader of the O'Mahony wing advised the Irish in America to vote for the Democrats nationally.

Reports were brought from Ireland that fall claiming that conditions for an uprising were even better than the previous year and that action would take place whether or not aid came from America. The British had extended the suspension of *habeas corpus* beyond its original expiration in August and continued to arrest any suspicious persons arriving in Ireland.

Late in October, Stephens announced at a meeting in New York City that this would be his last public appearance before leaving to lead an uprising in Ireland in December. Cluseret, the commander selected in 1865, sailed

---

* Johnson was a southern Democrat, who had been chosen by Lincoln as his vice-presidential running mate in the 1864 elections to demonstrate that the new Union Party extended beyond its Republican base.

for the United States to confer with Stephens,* but the American military group of Fenians headed by Col. Thomas Kelly demanded to be included in the planning for the uprising. When Stephens refused to share his plans, he was deposed as head centre and temporarily replaced by a directorate headed by Col. John H. Gleason. (A Tipperary man, Gleason had served three years with Meagher's Irish Brigade, rising to command the 63rd New York.)

IN HIS JULY 2 DECLARATION, Lonergan had already withdrawn his own political support from both the Democratic and the Republican parties, regardless of the competing endorsements of the two Fenian factions. It is not clear which branch of the Brotherhood claimed his loyalty in the fall of 1866, but his continued dedication to the Fenian cause itself was obvious from statements he made at the Vermont Reunion Society meeting held at Montpelier on October 29.

Although no toast was offered to the Irish soldiers from Vermont at this third reunion, after all the speeches and formal toasting concluded, Lonergan nonetheless amused his "Comrades and Fellow Fenians" at the banquet with his tales of army life. He made special reference to his "Fenian friends" who supposedly included Gov. Dillingham and closed his performance "with an enthusiastic announcement in his faith in the future success of Fenianism." Major Hall repeated his rendition of "Pat Malloy," the condescending popular song about the Irish that he had sung the previous year (when Lonergan had not been present).

Soon after this meeting of the Reunion Society, where Lonergan basked in the fellowship of influential politicians—including the governor—and former comrades, he received welcome news from the state government. His renewed claim for reimbursement for expenses related to raising the first Emmet Guards had finally been approved.

After the rejection of his initial claim in 1861, another suit had been filed by Carolus Noyes on January 18, 1862. The state adjutant general had replied to Lonergan in a letter dated May 14, 1862, stating that the roster of the 2nd Vermont did not show that he had mustered into federal service. In the fall of 1864, Lonergan had acquired sworn letters from Stannard, Charles H. Joyce (former major of the 2nd), and B. Walter Carpenter, the

---

* Cluseret brought along his immediate subordinates, an Italian and another Frenchman.

CHAPTER TWENTY-ONE – FRACTURED FENIAN EFFORTS

regimental surgeon. All three attested that Lonergan and his company had been inspected, accepted, and sworn into the U.S. Army by Lt. Col. Rains. Noyes argued that even though the muster rolls did not show this unit as Company K, the governor of Vermont had acted beyond his authority in disbanding a federalized unit that was no longer under his command.

Apparently the affidavits secured from officers knowledgeable of the facts were persuasive enough for Noyes to make the case for Lonergan in his third attempt. Perhaps sharing drinks with the governor and other politicians at the Reunion Society helped influence the legislature after five years of inaction.

In any case, the General Assembly of the State of Vermont on November 10, 1866, approved "An Act to Pay John Lonergan the Sum Therein Mentioned." Section 1 of the act instructed the Auditor of Accounts to draw an order for the Treasurer to pay $704 to John Lonergan for "military services and expenses in the service of this State." The final Section 2 specified that this amount was the full settlement of "said Lonergan's claim" and directed the Auditor to have Lonergan sign a receipt to that effect on accepting the money. The amount authorized was about the equivalent of six months pay as a captain at the time of Lonergan's service and was possibly calculated on that basis, plus some reimbursement for expenses.

This settlement would have come at a particularly good time; the season for employment at Customs was ending as navigation on the lake closed down for the winter. The grocery store on the west side of City Hall Park, T. Lonergan & Son, ensured food on the Lonergan table, but there soon was another mouth to feed. A second child, Sarah Ellen, was born to John and Roseanna on November 19.

ALARMED BY THE RUMORS in early December that Stephens had sailed for France or Ireland to begin the uprising in 1866 as he had promised, the British government offered the substantial sum of £2,000 for his arrest. However, the deposed head centre had instead gone to ground, living in disguise in New York City at an address known only to his closest supporters. Repeated accusations had been made among the nationalists that Stephens himself was an informer, based in part on his daring escape from Richmond prison in 1865. The bitter factional fights within the Fenian Brotherhood now caused Stephens to fear his fellow Irishmen as well as the British authorities. At a meeting with the military leaders of the movement in mid-December, John McCafferty reportedly tried to kill Stephens in a rage and was only prevented from doing so by Kelly's intervention.

Stephens passed from the scene of Irish nationalism, as the other original founder of the movement had before him. He and O'Mahony had played the crucial role in organizing the IRB and the Fenian Brotherhood into a creditable force to liberate Ireland. In the end, however, both were pushed aside by less visionary men who fractured the nationalist effort into competing groups.

Kelly, Cluseret, and the other military leaders sailed for France in early January of 1867 and from there slipped into Ireland. Kelly took charge of the Dublin directorate and McCafferty set himself up as head of the group that had gathered in London. An uprising in Ireland was scheduled for the spring, coordinated with action in England to capture arms. The plan to attack the British government arsenal at Chester Castle on February 11 was betrayed by Joseph Corydon, a member of the London directorate. Several hundred men had arrived by rail in Chester, a town on the Welsh border, to storm the arsenal there—a newspaper report claimed 1,400 tickets had been purchased for the late night train—but they did not move swiftly enough to overcome the single company guarding it. By the time the Irish had retrieved the weapons they had secreted in the area for the mission, it was too late to seize the arsenal's stores.

As a result of the failure of this raid, the rising was postponed for several weeks. However, word of the delay did not reach everyone and some operations were initiated on the original schedule with a predictable lack of success. Rebel action that began on March 5 was greatly hampered by an unusual period of cold weather and snow that made movements difficult, particularly in the hills.

The revolutionary movement was by now fully identified with the name of its American branch and the events were labeled on both sides of the ocean as a "Fenian Uprising," not one led by the IRB. Headlines in the *Free Press* like "Tipperary Threatened" and "Proclamation of the Irish Republic" must have leaped off the page as Lonergan read them. (Newspaper reports of widespread risings in Ireland were published on a timely basis in the *Free Press* until the British Ambassador in Washington recommended that the new trans-Atlantic cable no longer be allowed to carry such information.)

CHAPTER TWENTY-ONE – FRACTURED FENIAN EFFORTS

The Fenians achieved scattered successes in attacking isolated police and coast guard stations around the country. Urban areas were menaced by flying columns and 1,600 men reportedly threatened Tipperary town from the Galtee Mountains. The disaffected residents of the "capital of the famous county of that name" were said to be "strongly disposed" to help the rebels.* Just upriver from Lonergan's birthplace in Carrick, 300 rebels attacked Clonmel, losing several men killed and two dozen captured.

The Roberts wing of the Brotherhood offered support to those in the field in Ireland—"the men in the gap"—by announcing on March 7 that another raid into Canada was being prepared. This time a force of 20,000 men was to collect arms and ammunition from secret caches in Canada after crossing the boundary.

A news item in the March 9 *Free Press* might have given pause to Irishmen considering participation in a second incursion across the border. Eighteen convicts, participants in the 1866 attempt, had arrived at the penitentiary in Kingston, Canada West. Originally condemned to death for treason against the crown, their sentences had been commuted to avoid antagonizing the United States government and much of the Irish public. Still, serving out twenty years' imprisonment might mean that they would end their lives behind bars.

A London dispatch of March 14 cited in the *Free Press* admitted that the "Fenian troubles are not altogether ended" and the government stationed four gunboats on the River Liffey in Dublin as a precaution. The rebels had retreated into the traditional refuge of the Wicklow Mountains just south of the capital, but were "perishing there from the extremely cold weather."

Widespread arrests followed the attempted uprising in Ireland and particular attention was paid to rooting out Fenians among the Irish soldiers in British regiments. Cluseret withdrew as commander of the disorganized rebellion when he discovered there were virtually no arms available.

The uprising in Ireland, abortive though it was, sparked renewed enthusiasm for the nationalist cause in the United States, but the American factions remained unable to overcome their differences and unite. Even so, a report on March 14 of Fenian movements near St. Albans caused the Canadian government to transfer a company of regulars "with full supply of

---

* The Fenian leader in Tipperary, Col. Thomas P. Bourke, fell into British hands after a skirmish at Ballyhurst outside Tipperary town on March 6. Placed in irons, he occupied the same jail in Clonmel where the leaders of 1848 had been held awaiting trial.

ammunition" from Montreal to the border area. The approach of St. Patrick's Day and news of the rising in Ireland had sparked this action since "last year there was great fear of a Fenian invasion on that day." Roberts further fueled this anxiety with a statement that the Fenian Senate would move 15,000 to 18,000 men armed with breech-loading rifles into Canada as soon as transportation could be arranged. The ambitious objective was to be Montreal, with attacks as well against Toronto and Kingston (where the Fenian prisoners were jailed). Additional Canadian forces were rushed to the border in response to this threat.

St. Patrick's day of 1867 fell on a Sunday. In accordance with Roman Catholic practices governing saints' days and the Easter season, the celebration in Burlington was postponed until Monday. However, on Saturday morning, March 16, the "Fenian Guards of this city" paraded through Burlington "bearing their green banner and headed by martial music." Lonergan had mustered his men to make a public appearance, probably hoping to increase the Canadians' nervousness about the possibility of an incursion north. Moreover, his Fenians had not been invited to march in the St. Patrick's Day procession that year. By showing their flag two days before the official celebration, Lonergan could remind the Irish community of his presence and his continuing ability to bring a segment of that group together under his command.

Lonergan no longer took the leading role in organizing the event, but was relegated instead to acting as one of two aides to John Dullahan, the new president of the town's Hibernian Society. Joined by the St. Patrick's Society of Winooski, the Hibernians formed up at City Hall at 9:30 AM on March 18 to make their way to St. Mary's for a High Mass and sermon. The parade then wound its way through the main streets to return to City Hall.

In a spirit of unity with the Irish in Canada, the Honorable Henry J. Clark of Montreal had been invited to present the day's oration.* Clark spoke to a packed hall on the significance of the traditional holiday of Ireland's patron saint, raising memories of home and friends in the hearts of Irishmen. He reviewed the history of wrongs done to the country, particularly referencing the time of the Great Hunger and the rising of '48. His listeners should

---

* Clark was not further identified, but apparently was a prominent Irishman in Montreal who supported the British system of government.

CHAPTER TWENTY-ONE – FRACTURED FENIAN EFFORTS

always be thankful, he claimed, for the refuge from such troubles provided by the lands of free institutions opened up to them in the United States and the Canadian provinces. Every Irishman owed undying gratitude to the land of his adoption, Clark urged, as he appealed for tolerance to avoid political and religious bigotry that might cause conflict within and between these countries.

Later, over a hundred members of the Hibernian Society and invited guests assembled at the American Hotel for a banquet. Dullahan presided at the head table under both Irish and American flags, assisted by the toastmaster for the evening, Edward Lonergan. John's younger brother read the usual series of toasts to the saint being celebrated, the President of the United States, the priesthood of Ireland, Vermont, "our adopted country," and other patriotic subjects. Clark was called upon to respond to the sentiment of "Ireland and America" and spoke at some length on relations between the two countries. He cited the pressure on the British government from Ireland's many sons in the United States and Canada that resulted in the recent "opening of the highest offices in Ireland to Roman Catholics." This showed that the "Irish and Yankees together could work revolutions not of war, but of peace."

John Lonergan forcefully rejected this reliance on peaceful means to improve the situation in Ireland. When he responded to the next toast proposed by his brother—"The men in the Gap"—John offered up "a spirited speech." These brave men on the front line of the cause, "perhaps even now striking for the country's liberty," should receive the sympathy and aid of every true Irishman in America. Despite his involvement in the raid on Canada the previous year, Lonergan now emphasized that it would be "on Irish soil that the struggle must come" and "no invasion of Canada was prudent or right." Yet, "if the movement across the water failed, he could say, God help Canada, for the Irish would have their revenge." He hoped "to see the union of all Irishmen and the independence of Ireland consummated before next St. Patrick's Day." Lonergan's further remarks on the role of D'Arcy McGee, portrayed as misleading the Irish in Canada to support the British monarchy, offended the keynote speaker from Montreal.

The next toast was to "Our invited guest," giving Clark the opportunity "to defend Mr. McGee to whom allusion had been made by the previous speaker." A personal friendship with McGee required Clark to point out that the former rebel remained "one able and desirous to do more for the cause of Ireland by his present course than by any other." Clark thanked the Hibernian Society for their kindness and courtesy toward himself and closed with the wish that all unpleasantness between Canada and the United States might disappear forever.

Lonergan rose to disclaim any "intention of discourtesy or wounding the feelings of Mr. Clark," as he had been entirely ignorant of the guest's relationship to McGee. Still, he reiterated that the opinion of McGee he had expressed was shared by "many an Irishman this side of the line." No offense had been meant and Lonergan excused himself by explaining that "we talk free in the United States," but abstain from "ungentlemanly conduct."

His brother Edward then added his own commentary on the situation in a response to the final toast. Noting that the homeland was in ruins and her people in chains, but still celebrating St. Patrick's Day, Edward closed with a speech "of some length and considerable poetic fervor." The banquet ended at half past one in the morning in "the utmost good humor," despite the exchange between Clark and John Lonergan.

An account dated March 18 described the Burlington event in terms flattering to Clark, as published in the *Quebec Mercury* (reprinted on March 27 in the *Free Press*). The unidentified reporter stated, "The anti-Fenian Irishmen celebrated St. Patrick's Day by a grand procession" followed by Clark's oration to a crowd at City Hall that included a number of ladies. When the speaker from Montreal "declared the Irishmen of Canada were perfectly happy and contented with their government," he was supposedly "loudly cheered—the ladies waving their handkerchiefs." Noting that several clergymen were on the platform for the speech, the reporter flatly assured his readers "Fenianism may be said to be dead here as far as Canada is concerned." Praising Clark as "in every respect unmistakably a gentleman," the writer went on to approve the "public sentiment of the people of Burlington" whose "solid, steady New England character" led them to reject the revolutionary Fenian cause.

Events proved the declaration of the death of Fenianism in Burlington premature, because Lonergan continued to direct the movement in Vermont from the "Queen City." Lonergan most probably supplied the brief item of Fenian news that appeared in the "Personal" column of the *Free Press* on March 21 along with such notices as appointment of Regular Army officers to assignments connected with Reconstruction in the South. It may have slipped past an unwary editor used to seeing reports of promotions in the U.S. Army.

CHAPTER TWENTY-ONE – FRACTURED FENIAN EFFORTS

Looking very official, it announced, "Brig. Gen. John H. Gleason has been confirmed as Major General by brevet" before explaining, almost as an aside, that Gleason "is the present Head Centre of the Fenians in this country." The Fenians had handed out so many commissions to general officer that the new head centre had to be promoted to two-star rank, even if temporarily by brevet, to give him authority over the brigadiers.

THE CANADIANS REMAINED very much on edge about the prospect of another assault by Irish nationalists. Rumors circulated of an Irish plot to destroy Victoria Bridge in Montreal and to blow up the powder magazine near the city. The St. Patrick's Day parade in Toronto was "given up for fear of provoking trouble" and Buffalo, New York, was reportedly "full of Canadian spies" keeping an eye on Fenian military units parading through the streets during the celebrations there. Sailors off Her Majesty's steamer *Aurora* had been sent from Quebec to equip gun boats on the Great Lakes for early service, contrary to the restrictions of the treaty with the United States. In a county bordering on Vermont, all the farmers had supposedly armed themselves with repeating rifles and "could muster 2,000 on the Line at a few hours notice."

Nine carloads of U.S. Army regulars and their equipment were posted to Oswego, New York, on March 19 as a precaution, "undoubtedly intended to operate against any movement of the Fenians" on the border. Even at the end of March, as the ice went out early on the St. Lawrence River, there was excitement at Ogdensburg. The garrison across the river at Prescott had been "materially strengthened" and night crossings of the ferryboat between the two countries had been cancelled. The Fenians in the Ogdensburg area were said to be "very numerous and daily increasing," although the assumption was that they would join a concentration of forces at Malone to cross the border on dry land.

A resident of Malone said that there were more Fenians in town than before the attack in 1866. A correspondent from the New York *Herald* posted to Malone wrote, "The great number of pianos that come boxed up here via rail is astonishing." Marked "Pianoforte—handle with care," such crates had appeared with increasing frequency over the past month and were always claimed by Irishmen who did not look like they played the piano.

THAT SPRING, THE FENIANS purchased an 81-foot brigantine to carry arms directly to the rebels in Ireland. The *Jacmel* sailed from New York City on April 12 loaded with over 5,000 stand of arms, 5,000,000 rounds of ammunition, three batteries of artillery, and other war supplies. While in transit, the vessel was renamed *Erin's Hope* and a green flag was hoisted. After slipping past the patrols of the vaunted British navy, the ship arrived at the west coast of Ireland on May 18. However, the expedition could find no one to receive their arms at Sligo and so made its way to Dungarvan in the southeast. Unmolested during almost a month of exploring the coast as he tried to deliver the weapons, the Fenian commander on board decided to put the military advisors ashore and bring the weapons back to the United States. All but a few of these men were arrested upon landing, but the ship returned safely to New York, having demonstrated that supplies for a revolution could be successfully moved over such a distance.

Following the collapse of the planned uprising, many of the Irish-American revolutionaries in Ireland took refuge in England where *habeas corpus* was still in effect. Kelly and his aide, Capt. Timothy Deasy, were arrested on September 11 in Manchester, England. A week later they were being transported in a locked police van when the local Irish nationalists rescued them.* A pistol shot through the keyhole of the van unintentionally killed one policeman. Three men out of the twenty-six tried for the crime were publicly hanged before a large crowd on November 23. These Manchester Martyrs—Allen, Larkin, and O'Brien—took a prominent place on the list of those who had died for the revolution. Their cry of "God save Ireland!" from the dock during their trials was immortalized in a song that became the unofficial anthem of the cause.

THE DOMINION OF CANADA was officially established on July 1, 1867, by the confederation of the Province of Canada—separated into Ontario and Quebec—with Nova Scotia and New Brunswick. The Fenian actions of the previous year no doubt helped stimulate the formation of the federalized

---

* Both men avoided recapture and later escaped back to the United States.

CHAPTER TWENTY-ONE – FRACTURED FENIAN EFFORTS

state, an arrangement better suited to joint defense of the British territory.

The same day Canada was created also marked the mysterious death of Thomas Francis Meagher, the acting governor of the territory of Montana, not far south of the new dominion's border. During the night, he fell (or was pitched) overboard into the Missouri River from a paddle-wheeled steamer docked at Fort Benton and was never seen again.

CUSTOMS INSPECTIONS KEPT LONERGAN employed through the navigation season on Lake Champlain and he continued to operate the grocery store with his father during 1867. On October 30, he attended the Reunion Society's fourth meeting. Held in Montpelier, it occasioned the largest gathering of Vermont officers ever assembled in the state. The guest of honor was Gen. Sheridan, the son of immigrants from County Cavan and a West Point graduate, who had distinguished himself as a Union cavalry commander during the Civil War. Sheridan had been invited by the governor and the legislature; he was welcomed by a crowd of 10,000, including some 400 officers and "thousands of the rank and file of the Vermont regiments." Toasts at the dinner included a salute to Gen. Michael T. Donahue—born in Lowell, Massachusetts, to Irish parents—who had formerly commanded the 10th New Hampshire.

As usual, Maj. Hall gave his rendition of "Pat Malloy" and Lonergan was called upon to respond. Referring to the guest of honor, Lonergan claimed rather than dwelling on the unfortunate lad Pat Malloy, his spirit was with another Irishman, Gen. Sheridan. His oft-repeated story of discovering the Monocacy River on the way to Gettysburg rounded out Lonergan's response. Keeping with the Irish theme, the former drum major of the 12th Vermont read a letter purporting to be from "Judy Holligan, late of the town of Tulley McGurttey, near the Parish of Ballyraggit, in the county of Killarney, Ireland." Gen. Donahue's rendition by request of "Ye Sons of Hibernia" brought loud applause. In memory of the officers and soldiers who had fallen in action, the entire group at the suggestion of Gen. Foster sang "Auld Lang Syne," as the reunion ended at 2:00 AM.

BURLINGTON'S IRISH COMMUNITY celebrated a significant milestone with the consecration of its Roman Catholic Cathedral of the Immaculate Conception on December 8, 1867. Construction of St. Mary's had started on St. Paul's Street at the beginning of the Civil War and continued even during that conflict. The chapel housed a school and St. Mary's Hall, which became the gathering place for meetings of the Irish in the city. Bishop DeGoesbriand remarked in his diary that, due to the winter consecration, "I had to use ice in place of holy water" to bless the outer walls of the stone building.*

That same month, Lonergan embarked on the new enterprise of publishing a weekly newspaper, the *Irish Watchman*. Like a number of nationalists before him, he sought a platform for expressing his views on current Irish matters, while hoping to make a profit. No copies of the short-lived weekly have been found, but contemporary comments reveal the editorial thrust of Lonergan's newspaper. He had approached the publisher of the Democratic-leaning *Sentinel*, William H. Hoyt, on December 11 to propose "a new Irish Catholic paper." Hoyt's diary records two more meetings at his office that week before a visit was made to Father Cloarec about the paper. Despite the church's misgivings about the Fenians, the priest apparently gave his blessing to the venture since Hoyt published the first copy on December 28.

Even before the initial *Irish Watchman* had been printed, the Burlington *Times* questioned whether such a paper, "devoted exclusively to guarding and fostering the interests of our Irish fellow citizens," was necessary. Although it could be independent in politics, as it claimed, and support anyone who advanced the cause of Ireland, Lonergan's publication might not benefit "the actual interests of the Irish people." Rating it a "good reliable Democratic paper, with just enough Fenian flavor" to attract some Irish citizens, the *Times* noted that it would be issued from the office of the *Sentinel* and that the names of the two papers were virtually synonyms. The *Times* suggested that they be united into "The Burlington *Watchman* and *Irish Sentinel*" with the motto: "United we Stand, Divided we Fall—E Pluribus Erin, Buncombe Go Bragh."

On reading the second issue of the *Irish Watchman*, the editor of the *Free Press* took his counterpart Lonergan to task for proposing a quota system for local officials to give the "*common* people, Irish-Americans and Canadians" guaranteed representation. Two of the six school commissioners would be from this group, one a Catholic priest and the other a layman. Citing the absence of such demands from other denominations, the *Free Press* dismissed this idea

---

* The building was destroyed by fire in 1972.

CHAPTER TWENTY-ONE – FRACTURED FENIAN EFFORTS

as a poor one that would be "stirring up class and sectarian distinctions."

The day before the first issue of the *Irish Watchman* was published the Lonergans suffered the loss of John's brother Thomas, the last of the family to have been born in Ireland. Just over eighteen years of age, Thomas died of "lung fever" on December 27. Probably never robust, Thomas' health may have deteriorated as the result of following his older brother on military adventures. He had enlisted underage in mid-winter in the Frontier Cavalry in 1865 and probably joined in the Fenian expedition into Canada the following year. The death notice of young Thomas listed his occupation as "cooper;" now one less pair of skilled hands plied the Lonergan family trade.

THE NEXT ST. PATRICK'S DAY marked not only the anniversary of the death of Ireland's patron saint, but also the birth of Lonergan's second son, John Patrick. The choice of names reflected the practice of bestowing the father's first name on the second son, just as the recently deceased Thomas had been named for his father. The infant John received the less common feature of a second name with the addition of Patrick because he came on March 17, 1868.

Lonergan no longer had any responsibility for organizing the celebration in Burlington. His replacement, Dullahan, clearly lacked the nationalist fervor that had characterized control of the event by the Fenians. Mud season arrived in mid-March that year, making the unpaved streets of the town almost impassable for the smaller and less militant parade. The usual oration at City Hall to recount the grievances of Ireland under British rule was not part of this year's event. Instead, the main feature of the day was a performance of songs and stories by the pupils of the Catholic schools to benefit the orphan asylum. Even this modest presentation was interrupted by the fire alarm; men rushed out to help fight the nearby blaze, as children cried and women fainted.

The barn behind the H. H. Reynolds building on Church Street had erupted in flames that quickly spread to a neighboring structure and threatened the entire center of the town. Fortunately, the two rival fire companies, the Boxers and the Ethan Allens, were assembled at their stations holding the election of officers at the time. The engines were swiftly pushed into place and water drawn from nearby cisterns, though that supply was soon exhausted. The newly installed water mains, a subject of much controversy because of the expense of the waterworks, saved the day when hoses were connected to the hydrants.

The excitement of the dangerous conflagration delayed the evening banquet at St. Mary's Hall on St. Paul Street. Although places had been set for 200, only 125 attended, including the new mayor-elect and other invited guests. Dullahan presided from the head table, again calling on Edward Lonergan to serve as toastmaster when the dining was finished. For the response to the first toast, "The Day We Celebrate," the toastmaster called upon Dullahan as president of the sponsoring society. Instead, Dullahan deferred to "someone more competent to speak," saying that he "desired to hear Capt. John Lonergan" give the response. Lonergan offered his appreciation for the celebration under the difficult conditions and declared himself satisfied with the event.

His brother Edward led the group through the series of toasts that included one to "Our Adopted Country." The response by George H. Bigelow, honored even though he had been "born the other side of Erin," cited the patriotism of the Irish soldiers in the Civil War.* He noted the exploits at Gettysburg by "his friends Capt. Lonergan and James Scully" as sufficient proof of this. Bigelow closed his remarks by presenting the regrets of Gen. Stannard, who could not be present at the celebration.

The death of Thomas Francis Meagher the previous July received solemn recognition with a toast and a poem proclaiming in part:

> That tongue, that magic tongue is mute
> Is Ireland's unhappy wail.
> Brave Meagher of the sword is dead,
> Lost, lost to Inishfail!

The response came from J. J. Monahan, Lonergan's Fenian compatriot, who sketched briefly the life of the Young Irelander and his services to Ireland's cause.

Reaching even further back into the history of Irish rebellions, glasses were lifted to "The Men of '98" with a cautionary ode asking "Who fears to speak of Ninety-eight/ Who blushes at the name/ When cowards mock the

---

* Evidently born in England, but considering himself Irish, Bigelow closed the evening with the popular drinking song "The Cruiskeen Lawn" about a "full little jar." A Burlington resident, Bigelow had enlisted as Quartermaster Sergeant in the 12th Vermont and was then commissioned a lieutenant in its Co. F in May of 1863.

CHAPTER TWENTY-ONE – FRACTURED FENIAN EFFORTS

patriot's fate/ Who hangs his head in shame?" Appropriately, John Lonergan rose to state that the spirit of '98 still existed, along with their determination to give Ireland her independence. He assured the audience, "Should the men of '68 fall, the spirit will yet exist and the cause be as just as ever." Before another St. Patrick's Day arrived, he hoped "to see such a change in public affairs as shall promise speedy freedom for Ireland."

Edward Lonergan steered the group through toasts to the American flag, President Washington, Daniel O'Connell, and others. Before concluding with glasses raised to "The Ladies," a toast was given to "The *Habeas Corpus* Act," which Fenian heroes would defend even though British tyrants might suspend the writ. John Lonergan remained until the gathering broke up at 2:00 AM, when he proposed a toast to the Hinesburgh band, which had provided the music for the event.

WITH THE FAILURE OF the attempted uprising in Ireland in 1867, the focus for nationalist military operations returned to Canada the following year. After a futile effort to close the divide in the Fenian Brotherhood by reuniting with the O'Mahony wing, now led by John Savage, Roberts resigned as president of the Senate faction in December of 1867.* O'Neill, who had just moved up to vice-president, suddenly found himself in charge of the "men of action" and he again turned his eyes to the north.

During the Civil War, O'Neill had served with and fought alongside Maj. Henri Le Caron. They renewed their friendship after the war when both settled in Nashville, Tennessee, and O'Neill introduced Le Caron to influential Fenian leaders, including Gen. Sweeney. Although he joined the U.S. Army in 1861 as an immigrant from France, Le Caron actually had been born in England as Thomas M. Beach. (Beach had lived in France and apparently took on this new persona as a lark when he enlisted.) When Beach realized the importance of his access to the inner circles of the Fenians plotting against his mother country, he volunteered to serve as a secret agent for the crown. On instruction from the British government, he joined the Fenians and at the same time set up contact with Gilbert McMicken in Canada as his conduit for passing information.

---

* Roberts, a wealthy merchant, successfully ran for the U.S. Congress in 1870 and 1872. Under the Cleveland administration, he served as ambassador to Chile.

In the spring of 1868, Le Caron met with McMicken to provide the latest on Fenian plans. At the time, another rash of reports circulated that Canada would again be attacked and preparations were definitely under way for another attempt by the Senate wing. Weapons and equipment were reportedly being moved up to the border and stored in caches, as they had been two years before.

The British government no longer courted the support of the Irish in Canada as actively once the Dominion was established in 1867. D'Arcy McGee, the subject of Lonergan's disagreement with Clark at the 1867 banquet in Burlington, had lost his cabinet position in the shuffle following Confederation. Still, McGee succeeded in winning the Montreal West seat in Parliament in 1868, despite strong opposition, including occasional violence, from the pro-Fenian Irish in the Griffintown area of Montreal. McGee's statements supportive of the new Canadian government, particularly those approving of its suspension of *habeas corpus*, had triggered threats against him. Lonergan had spoken darkly of revenge on Canada if the 1867 uprising in Ireland was crushed, citing the low opinion that many Irish held of McGee and his political alliance with the British government.

In the early hours of April 7, 1868, after a late night session of the legislature, McGee was felled by a single pistol shot to the head as he approached his lodgings on Sparks Street in Ottawa. In a controversial trial that lasted less than a week, Galway-born Patrick Whelan, thought to have Fenian sympathies, was convicted of the murder on scanty evidence and sentenced to death. (Whelan was hanged at the Ottawa jail on February 11, 1869, and buried there in an unmarked grave.) No connection has been demonstrated between Le Caron informing on the Fenians, the aborted invasion of 1868, and McGee's assassination, yet the timing and contacts involved suggest such a possibility. Lonergan's threats of revenge and contempt for McGee might even hint at some involvement on his part in a decision to make an example of those Irishmen collaborating with the British government.

IN MAY, LONERGAN "SUSPENDED" PUBLICATION of the *Irish Watchman* until he could sign up 1,000 subscribers who had paid in advance. A meager 300 subscriptions had been sold by spring and only one hundred of them had been paid up when the newspaper went inactive. Each issue was coming out

CHAPTER TWENTY-ONE – FRACTURED FENIAN EFFORTS

at a loss of $24 a week. As gratifying as it must have been to Lonergan to have a platform for his opinions, the cost was too great to sustain. Printing was never resumed after the initial run of five months. Enthusiasm for the Fenian cause was clearly dwindling and contributions for dues and subscriptions, including Lonergan's newspaper, were dropping off.

With the decline in income for the Brotherhood, the Fenian Hall may also have become too expensive to rent. After its 1865 edition, the Burlington City Directory no longer listed the Union Block meeting place of Lonergan's Sarsfield Circle. Perhaps the Fenians were meeting elsewhere or perhaps Lonergan chose to avoid a charge, if one was levied, for listing that headquarters in the directory. In a town the size of Burlington, directions to the Brotherhood's meeting place could no doubt be easily obtained.

THE FENIAN SCARE THAT DEVELOPED in the spring of 1868 sparked a rash of reports, some of them accurate, that men and weapons were being moved up to the border. Activity was supposedly taking place at the familiar gathering points of Ogdensburg, Malone, and Buffalo in New York, along with St. Albans in Vermont. In late May, the Hamilton (Ontario) *Evening Times* predicted a "Fenian invasion upon a gigantic scale" in which 30,000 men "abundantly supplied with arms and war material, including artillery of the best description" would be led by battle-hardened officers. Although the new Dominion was expected to defend itself, the 17th and 60th regiments of British regulars, which had already departed by ship for England, were hastily intercepted and recalled to Canada. The Canadian militia in June received new instructions on their reaction to Fenian threats that authorized the district militia officers of the newly formed country to call up their units as required.

The Canadian government was kept well informed of Fenian plans by their new source of information. Le Caron had risen swiftly in the organization because of his friendship with O'Neill and his eagerness to take on work. On June 8, McMicken sent Macdonald a letter making the prime minister aware of his well-placed agent. Arrangements were made for the Canadian government to pay Le Caron $150 a month. (When the pseudo-Frenchman became the Military Organizer of the IRA in August of 1868, he also received $60 per month and $7 per day expenses from the Fenians.)

Based at least in part on reports from Le Caron, mobilization of the Canadian militia was in fact ordered in mid-June, after O'Neill appeared to be touring the border areas in preparation for action. The new president of the Senate wing passed through St. Albans on June 6 and Maj. Gibson of the U.S. Army, who had been in charge of the area in 1866, returned to that town on June 8. The major was part of the increased surveillance of the key points of the border undertaken in response to the latest invasion scare. Even the new commander of the District of the Atlantic, Gen. Hancock,* relocated his headquarters to New York City on June 6, spending a week there monitoring the situation.

A shipment of Fenian artillery and three boxcars of muskets was reported to be coming out of Rouse's Point, New York, by rail on June 10. The rifles were part of the weapons seized in 1866, which were being returned to the Fenians after they had posted bond not to use them for any illegal purpose. Over 1,200 stand of arms (there was no artillery) were released from Fort Montgomery at Rouse's Point and passed through St. Albans and Burlington on June 19 on their way to New York City. Maj. Gibson in St. Albans had required guarantees from the Fenians to ensure that the weapons were in fact shipped south.

The next afternoon, a Fenian convention met behind closed doors at an undisclosed location in Burlington. This secretive meeting was called to order by J. J. Monahan, not by Lonergan as might have been expected. The evening of June 20 the Fenians gathered openly in City Hall for an address by O'Neill himself, who declared that the invasion of Canada by the Brotherhood, now numbering 100,000 men, "would inevitably result in the liberation of Ireland." He vowed never to give up the struggle against English rule until the Fenians "gain the liberty of their country or are exterminated." Since taking charge of the Senate wing, O'Neill had spent four months inspecting the various circles and had "found them well organized and nearly ready for action." At the close of the speeches, Monahan and a Maj. Rafferty, who accompanied O'Neill, "called for men and money to aid the cause and got some of both."

Where was Lonergan during the closed meeting and when O'Neill spoke at City Hall? His absence is puzzling. Considering his involvement with the

---

* Meade had been replaced at the end of 1867 when he was assigned to duties in Atlanta, Georgia.

CHAPTER TWENTY-ONE – FRACTURED FENIAN EFFORTS

Senate wing of the Brotherhood during the 1866 incursion into Canada, it seems unlikely that Lonergan boycotted the visit of such an important figure as the new president of that faction. While Monahan was actively involved in Fenian affairs in the Burlington area—including Plattsburgh, New York, across the lake—there is no indication that he ever replaced Lonergan as the leader of the Brotherhood or any faction of it in Vermont.

In Burlington on the following Monday evening, Lonergan attended the Fourth Annual Reunion of the 2nd Vermont, the regiment in which he had served so briefly at the outbreak of the Civil War. The intended public meeting with an address by Col. Joyce was disrupted by a violent rainstorm that reduced participation in the event. Instead, the reunion was held as a private affair in the American Hotel. About fifty members of the regiment were present, with Gen. Stannard presiding over the group. The business portion of the assembly included submission of a constitution for the society and a vote to meet in Burlington again the following year. Responses to the toasts given at the dinner consisted of speeches presented by former members of the unit, including Lonergan.*

Although O'Neill left the Canadian border area for a series of additional fund-raising speeches elsewhere, reports of the movement of arms in preparation of an invasion persisted. The commander of the Plattsburgh Barracks, Capt. James W. Powell, 4th U.S. Infantry, was sent to St. Albans at the end of June to investigate the story that numerous wagons loaded with weapons had passed through the town during successive nights, headed toward Fairfield. Supposedly these were additional Fenian arms that had recently been released from the Plattsburgh Barracks and transported by steamer across Lake Champlain. The captain was unable to discover any caches of weapons and concluded on July 3, "if arms have been sent to Fairfield, they were distributed in the farmers' houses—the residents there are chiefly Irishmen."

Newspapers published rumors that 20,000 muskets and 60,000 rations had been transported to the boundary area. Claims were made that stores of weapons, ammunition, and supplies had been secreted at various points along the Canadian border. The British consul at Buffalo, New York, informed the commander of Fort Porter in that city on August 20 that he had received information that Fenians armed with "many thousands of breech-loaders"

---

* Lonergan clearly enjoyed attending the state-wide Reunion Society meetings and the 2nd Vermont reunions whenever he could. Later he expanded this circuit to include reunions of the 13th Vermont when a society was formed for that unit in 1888.

would attack Canada before the end of the first week in September. Yet the only marching that the Fenians under O'Neill did that fall was to parade, armed and in uniform, at their convention in Philadelphia on November 24. Despite a continued shortage of funds, the convention resolved to move on Canada the following year, still hoping to take advantage of tensions between the United States and Great Britain.

The long-standing issue of naturalization was being settled by a treaty between the two countries. The British government had maintained the position that citizenship and allegiance to the crown were inalienable. This view, now being relinquished, had meant that naturalization as an American citizen did not release someone born in Ireland from loyalty to the monarchy. The concept had complicated the legal situation of prisoners taken both in Ireland and in the raid on Canada.

Still unresolved was the question of reparations for damages suffered by the United States and its citizens between 1861 and 1865, when Great Britain recognized the Confederacy as a belligerent. After the election of Ulysses S. Grant in the fall of 1868, President Johnson hoped to also settle the matter of reparations before leaving office. The chairman of the Committee on Foreign Relations in the U.S. Senate, pricing the liability of Great Britain at two and a half billion dollars, suggested that Canada should be ceded to the United States as part of the settlement.

After taking charge of the British Liberal Party in 1867, William Ewart Gladstone led it to victory in national elections in December of 1868. The new Prime Minister's policies gave a top priority to improving the situation in Ireland and normalization of relations with the United States. Although he had spoken in support of the Confederate States of America in 1862, Gladstone had later revised his stance. As head of the British government, he stressed the avoidance of foreign conflicts. Accordingly, he opened up new channels for resolving the long-standing Irish objections to the nature of British rule and the disputes with the United States. Correcting the worst of British abuses in Ireland and crushing the Irish nationalists' hope of a war between Great Britain and America would spell a serious setback to the Fenian cause.

CHAPTER TWENTY-ONE – FRACTURED FENIAN EFFORTS

As a life-long Democrat—despite his angry repudiation of both parties in 1866—Lonergan fell victim to the unbridled political patronage of the era when the Republican Grant took office as President on March 4, 1869. After rising to Deputy Collector of Customs in 1868, Lonergan lost his seasonal employment to a Republican appointee. Even his military connection with Stannard, a staunch Republican who kept his position through the change of administrations, did not help Lonergan to avoid dismissal.

In 1869, the Burlington Directory shows that Lonergan was running a grocery store on his own at Champlain and Maple Streets. This location near the waterfront was far less prestigious than his shop on the city square. Thomas Lonergan, his father, had resumed his work as a cooper and had a shop also located on Champlain Street. Likely the two businesses and the family residences were all grouped together.

Not only was Lonergan having economic difficulties, but also his influence in the Irish community apparently continued to decline. The man who had organized the first St. Patrick's Day celebration in Burlington, leading the parade as the mounted Grand Marshal, played no role in 1869. Instead, the largest event of this nature to date was led by Chief Marshal Dullahan, with Capt. J. J. Bain riding alongside. The captain was in charge of the military units marching at the head of the procession. These comprised two infantry companies, one a flashy Zouave unit, and an artillery section, all from the Vermont militia. Again no Fenian detachment participated. The Hibernian and St. Patrick Societies from the area swelled the ranks of the marchers, including a group of children, as green flags were carried along with the American colors through most of the downtown streets.

City Hall was filled to overflowing for a two-hour talk on the woes of Ireland under British rule presented by Professor J. P. Brophy of New York. He called upon all Irishmen to unite in the cause of the liberation of the homeland without advocating any particular means of achieving this goal. In this long speech, no reference to the Fenians was made—or at least not reported—even though this was almost certainly the Professor Brophy who was acting as treasurer for O'Neill at the time.

Nearly 200 sat down to dinner at the American Hotel that evening where Lawrence Riche served as toastmaster. As in past St. Patrick's Day dinners, a series of predictable toasts were made with the toastmaster calling on someone to respond. The response to "Ireland – The land of our birth, may we yet see her as free from oppression as the land of our adoption – where Britons rule no more" was given by Edward Lonergan, John's younger brother. Was the selection of Edward a nod to the absent captain?

Three months later, John Lonergan conspicuously appeared in the newspaper coverage of the fifth annual reunion of the 2nd Vermont, held at the G.A.R. hall in Burlington on June 18.* The Friday evening meeting was well attended. Business connected with the regimental society was quickly concluded under the able chairmanship of Stannard. The members then adjourned to City Hall where a large audience had gathered to listen to an "oration" by Col. Charles Joyce of Rutland. The speaker recalled the way Vermonters rallied to the flag to form the state's first three-year regiment and described the unit's history of bravery in battle over the course of those three years.

Listening to Joyce recount the extensive battle honors of the 2nd Vermont, Lonergan must have recalled how the governor had dismissed his services by disbanding his company before they could go off to the war. At least he could face his former comrades of the 2nd Vermont with his head held high, knowing that his actions at Gettysburg had redeemed his military reputation.

Following the oration, about thirty members of the Society and a few invited guests moved to the American Hotel where they "partook of a collation." After the tables were cleared, the usual round of toasts offered respects to the Old Vermont Brigade, the Second Vermont Brigade that "turned the key that saved the day at Gettysburg," the First Vermont Cavalry, the commissary and quartermaster departments, and the Union soldier in general. When they raised their glasses for the seventh time, Lonergan was singled out for recognition. He was asked to respond to the toast to "The Irish Brigade and Co. A of the 13th Vermont regiment—as American citizens they are entitled to protection at home and abroad." He commented in "his

---

*The Grand Army of the Republic (G.A.R.) was a Union veterans' organization first formed in Illinois a year after the war ended. Structured in departments and posts that mimicked the army's administrative hierarchy, it quickly grew to become a potent political force for many years. Many mid-sized and larger towns in Vermont had their G.A.R. posts named for historic or important military figures. Post 2 in Burlington was the Stannard Post, while Post 3 in Vergennes honored Ethan Allen. Post 12 in West Rutland bore the name of John T. Sennott [sic], Lonergan's lieutenant who was mortally wounded at Gettysburg, and the St. Albans post was named for "Baldy" Smith.

CHAPTER TWENTY-ONE – FRACTURED FENIAN EFFORTS

usual forcible manner, taking strong grounds in favor of the protection of Irishmen who had become our adopted citizens in every part of the world and enforcing their protection, if necessary." Clearly his declaration was aimed at encouraging the intervention of the U.S. government on behalf of captured Fenians, many of whom were naturalized American citizens.

CONDITIONAL PARDONS HAD BEEN GRANTED in May to forty-nine of the Fenian prisoners arrested in Ireland during the crackdown of 1865-67. This limited clemency, part of Gladstone's concessions to mitigate Irish dissatisfaction with British rule, did not extend to thirty-two leaders being held in British prisons. Those rank-and-file Fenian convicts who were pardoned in 1869 had earlier been transported to Australia to serve out their sentences. A number of them had become acclimated to life "down under" and remained there, but when released most either returned to Ireland or took ship for the United States. In both these countries, the freed felons were greeted by large and enthusiastic crowds.

When the pardons were granted, however, John Boyle O'Reilly from County Meath had already escaped from the Australian penal settlements. O'Reilly had been sentenced to twenty years imprisonment in 1866 for subverting men in his regiment, the 10th Hussars, to the Fenian cause and, as a British soldier, had little hope of a pardon. Slipping away from Western Australia in February of 1869, he embarked on a series of adventures. Avoiding recapture despite stops in British ports on various vessels, O'Reilly finally arrived in Philadelphia on November 23 to be welcomed as a fellow revolutionary by the American Fenians.*

Gladstone also addressed the widespread grievances of the Irish people on two key issues, religion and land. An act passed on July 26 disestablished the Church of Ireland as the official religion of the country and released all the inhabitants from supporting it with mandatory contributions. The census of 1861 had showed that this state religion had only about 700,000 members out of a population of 5.7 million. Four and a half million Catholics were to be unburdened from the despised tax effective January 1, 1871.

Efforts to relieve the plight of the Irish tenant farmer were less effective,

---

* O'Reilly settled in Boston and found work as a reporter for the *Pilot*, rising to become editor of the paper in 1876. The oldest Catholic newspaper in the country, the *Pilot* regularly offered guidance to immigrants and helped them to contact relatives through its "Missing Friends" column.

even though a well-intentioned Irish Land Act was passed in 1870. Evictions had peaked in the early 1860's before declining sharply as a decade of good harvests reduced the constant hardships on living on the land. Rural employment also reduced the availability of willing recruits to the nationalist cause. The IRB—now more commonly known simply by the title of the American branch, the Fenians—had failed to establish itself strongly outside the urban environment. The reluctance of men in the countryside to join an armed uprising was reinforced by their church's condemnation of the movement. Although a body of Catholic clergy in January 1868 had announced their support for repeal of the legislative union, the staunchly conservative Archbishop Cullen had soon thereafter issued a pastoral letter banning his flock from involvement in any armed challenge to authority, including specifically "Fenianism."

The collapse of the 1867 uprising and subsequent smashing of the Fenian organization in Ireland by the imprisonment of its leaders left the nationalists with only legal options by which to achieve change. A widespread amnesty campaign pressed for release of the jailed rebels; its mass rallies drew up to 200,000 people. The campaign made the obstinate revolutionary O'Donovan Rossa a symbol for the severe conditions under which they suffered.*

Other political movements were organized around tenant farmers' rights and the developing Home Rule solution that sought to restore the Irish Parliament. These three competing issues—amnesty, land reform, and Home Rule—were combined by a remarkable lawyer, Isaac Butt, who served as president of the Amnesty Movement and lent it respectability. A Protestant and conservative by nature, Butt was proud of his Irish heritage and had been appalled by the destruction of the famine years. He had defended both O'Brien and Meagher in 1848; from 1865 onward he represented many Fenians in court. This demonstrated commitment to the nationalist cause gave him the authority to unite various factions, including a number of Fenians, under the Home Rule banner. The prospects of any attempt at an armed uprising in Ireland faded as these political avenues gained popular approval. Even though the country seethed with anger and unrest in 1869, these feelings were being expressed through legal channels that undercut the Fenian commitment to achieving a sovereign and republican nation through revolution.

---

* For pitching the contents of his toilet pail at the prison warden, Rossa spent thirty-five days with his hands manacled behind him, except during meals. He brazenly put himself forward as a candidate for the 1870 by-election in Tipperary and won the seat from his prison cell.

CHAPTER TWENTY-ONE – FRACTURED FENIAN EFFORTS

BOTH FACTIONS OF THE FENIAN BROTHERHOOD in America persisted in their single-minded dedication to the liberation of Ireland by force of arms. Neither the original O'Mahony organization, led since 1868 by John Savage, nor the Senate wing controlled loosely by O'Neill proposed any political solution to the plight of their homeland. Nothing less than a revolution that restored Ireland to nationhood under a republican form of government would satisfy them. Intrigue and politics abounded within each of the two Fenian groups, along with ample involvement by them in American national politics. The leaders of both factions continued to place unfounded hopes on a conflict between Great Britain and the United States, even as Gladstone worked to resolve disputes such as naturalization and reparations for Confederate commerce raiders' damage to Union shipping.

The proximity of the new Dominion of Canada continued to lure the American Fenians toward action against the northern neighbor, despite the failure in 1866 and their inability even to mount an operation in 1868. The sale in 1869 of the vast holdings of the Hudson Bay Company in the west, to be incorporated into the territory of Canada, created unrest in the sparsely-populated Red River Valley. Some Fenians saw this as an opportunity to be exploited if the meager regular military forces of the Canadian government were to be deployed far from the border. A group of American settlers in the Red River area was even urging that the region be annexed to the United States, rather than become part of Canada.

Despite a decline in support for the Fenian Brotherhood and its militant strategy among the general Irish population in America, the two opposing wings each could still draw on dedicated circles of dues-paying members. Cynical commentaries were published in the press accusing the leaders of continuing to feed false hopes of liberating Ireland only in order to keep their salaries. Savage and O'Neill were each being paid over $2,000 a year in their positions, quite a respectable wage for the time.

Lonergan at this point probably did not realize any significant financial benefit from his role as head centre of Vermont. Even though he served as the state's chief of the Brotherhood, the position was too low in the Fenian organization to warrant a salary that would provide for his growing family. Vermont's Irish population was small and scattered as compared with concentrations of their countrymen in areas such as New York City and Boston, as well as growing cities like Chicago.

Yet Lonergan apparently remained loyal to the cause of Ireland's freedom and the Fenian fixation with armed revolution. Living in northern Vermont, he probably did not view Canada as a merely abstract target of opportunity for military action against the British Empire. No doubt Lonergan knew many people who had come to the state from Canada, he likely had traveled there himself, and he might well have had friends among the numerous Irish in places like Montreal. Many of the Irish in northern Vermont towns such as Fairfield had business and family connections across the border. With such ties of blood and commerce, they did not view the residents of Canada as enemies.

Any Fenian invasion of the Dominion would have to negotiate the tricky path of attacking the British government and its misrule in Ireland while avoiding harm to the Canadian people and their property. By now it should have been obvious to even the most unrealistic Fenian planners that there would be no popular uprising by the Irish, or the French, in response to an assault on Canada. On the contrary, the events of 1866 had helped consolidate a sense of national identity and the new Confederation had taken effective steps to expand its militia. Particularly along the border, an upwelling of Canadian patriotism had combined with a practical concern for defending home and property. Many men joined the officially sanctioned companies of militia; others formed privately organized local groups of home guards.

AFTER HE LOST HIS POSITION with the Custom House, the navigation season no longer added to Lonergan's income. In addition to operating his grocery store, he probably helped his father out with the cooper work that came their way. The waterfront location of their businesses would have been convenient for handling goods and containers transported by boat on the lake.

Personal tragedy struck John and Rosanna on August 24 when John Patrick, aged one year and five months, succumbed to diarrhea. The grieving mother, well along in yet another pregnancy, had lost two of her three children in infancy (Sarah had passed away in March of 1865). Their first-born, Thomas Francis, then died of complications from croup on November 24 at just under five years of age. The family's mourning might have been

CHAPTER TWENTY-ONE – FRACTURED FENIAN EFFORTS

U.S. Custom House and Post Office, Burlington

relieved somewhat as the year drew to a close; Roseanna gave birth to another boy the day before Christmas.

The father's dedication to the cause of Irish freedom and his hero-worship of the late Thomas Francis Meagher were both apparent as the family gathered at church on December 26, 1869. His new son was christened Thomas Francis Lonergan, just a month after the first child of that name had died. Looking down on this two-day-old American, bundled against the cold of winter, Lonergan must have wondered whether his third son would survive. If Thomas Francis grew into manhood, would he still be called upon to carry on the fight to liberate Ireland like his father and his namesake? Perhaps one more effort by John and his generation would finally achieve success and spare his son that burden. As events unfolded, this newly baptized member of the Lonergan family would, unlike his father, live to see Ireland "a nation once again."

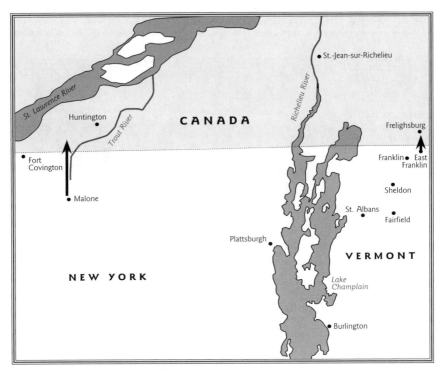

Fenian operations, 1870

Canadian medal for repulsing
the Fenian Raid, 1870

CHAPTER TWENTY-TWO

FINAL FENIAN FOLLY

Riding the Fenian wave throughout the 1860s, Lonergan had transformed himself from an unknown youth into a war hero and the leading Irish nationalist in Vermont. The wave had crested with the 1866 incursion into Canada and the failed uprising of 1867 in Ireland. As the decade ended, the tide was clearly turning against popular support for the Fenian movement, particularly as Catholic leaders took action against the Brotherhood. Not only the cause of Irish independence faced bleak prospects; Lonergan's personal situation had suffered setbacks, including the loss of three children and his job with Customs. His status in the Irish community of Burlington had deteriorated with the rejection of Fenian revolutionary policies by a growing segment of the population. Despite these difficulties, Lonergan remained an active supporter of the Brotherhood and its militant republican program.

The Fenians received a severe blow on January 12, 1870, when the pope expanded the provisions of previous edicts that allowed the expulsion of Freemasons and Carbonari to include the Fenian Brotherhood among the "associations prohibited because of their evil or dangerous object." Pius IX, no doubt influenced by the hostility of Cardinal Cullen toward the republican nationalists, had decided that the Fenians were one of the "sects that plot either openly or secretly against the Church or legitimate authorities." The category of banned organizations was described in Article 4 on the list of offenses reserved for action by the pope himself. No distinction was now made between secret or open organizations, previously a serious consideration for the church. Political parties were specifically excluded from the provisions of the article. By expelling the advocates of armed revolution and simultaneously approving political parties, this sanction gave further impetus to a reliance on legal opposition as the means to improve Ireland's situation.

In addition to banning the Fenians, Pius IX—who was to become the longest-serving pope in history—also convened a council to decree that the pope was infallible, thus closing down any discussion as to whether such an action as the ban could be a mistake. Catholics would have to accept and comply with any decision by the pope without questioning. A practicing Catholic throughout his life, the ban on Fenianism must have caused Lonergan distress, yet he remained an active member of the Brotherhood.

ALTHOUGH LONERGAN STILL LOUDLY advocated force as the only means of restoring Irish independence, he also ventured into politics at this time. Vermont's strongly democratic political process that continues even today— its citizen legislature meets only for the first part of each year—begins when each party holds its organizing meeting prior to Town Meeting Day on the first Tuesday in March.*

In 1864 the state legislature had approved the incorporation of Burlington as a city, to be governed by a mayor and board of aldermen. Three wards titled North, Centre, and South were responsible for certain administrative functions within the city. The Burlington Democrats met in caucus by ward on February 25, 1870, to nominate their candidates for the upcoming election. In the North Ward, the vocal Fenian J. J. Monahan called the meeting to order as secretary and made a rousing speech, "shouting the battle cry of freedom" for change in the local politics.

In the heavily Irish South Ward, the caucus at the American House was so poorly attended that no slate of nominees was approved. Too many people were participating in meetings of "the Hibernian and other societies the same evening." The Democrats in the South Ward had to reschedule their caucus to take place after the city-wide gathering on February 26 at City Hall. At the overall Burlington meeting, it was agreed that Daniel C. Lindsey would be the Democratic candidate for mayor and all other business was quickly concluded. The South Ward representatives then moved into the courtroom to select a chairman and secretary for their caucus. Lonergan was named to keep the minutes. After a slate of ward candidates was approved, the ward meeting then adjourned.

---

* The town's business for the year is conducted at Town Meeting, when all residents of the township are free to speak their minds before the votes are cast on each issue.

CHAPTER TWENTY-TWO – FINAL FENIAN FOLLY

In 1870, town meetings were held on the first day of March (a Tuesday). The results of the elections in Burlington were printed the next day in the *Free Press*. In what the newspaper termed the "most closely contested fight in Burlington for many a year," the Democrat Lindsey was elected mayor by a margin of just 29 votes in over a thousand cast. His victory came from support in the North Ward, while the other two wards narrowly preferred the Republican candidate. In the South Ward, Lonergan won the race for Clerk by 151 votes to 119 over one F. H. Wilkins. James Scully—formerly the first sergeant of Lonergan's company and now a prosperous merchant—was elected to the office of Inspector in the Centre Ward; Scully ran as a Republican, an exception in the strongly Democratic Irish community.

IMMEDIATELY BELOW THE FEBRUARY 28 newspaper report about postponement of the South Ward caucus, an announcement had appeared that the Hibernian Benevolent Society of Burlington was making preparations to celebrate St. Patrick's Day "as in years past." (Planning for the holiday celebration had caused the poor attendance at the originally scheduled South Ward Democratic organizing meeting on February 25.) The Hibernians were said to have "already secured the City Hall" for an oration in the morning. Invitations had been sent to Irish groups in Rutland, Winooski, and Charlotte, as well as to some "Americans." An offer to participate in the event had even been extended to the French organizations of St. Joseph and St. John the Baptist in Burlington. (The French declined in favor of a separate celebration the following day.)

A handbill was circulated the following week announcing a mass meeting of Irishmen at the City Hall on March 7 to elect a Grand Marshal for the coming St. Patrick's Day celebration. This gathering was intended to resolve the dispute between the Hibernian Society and "the other wing," which called itself the "Independent Irishmen," as to who should be in charge of the event. Lonergan was clearly involved in the growing controversy between Irish factions over the nature of the St. Patrick's Day event. The militant Fenians were being pushed aside in favor of a more moderate approach to the holiday.

John McNamara acted as chairman for the March 7 assembly and nominations for marshal were made. John McInnerny, secretary of the

Grand Rally! Come one, Come all!

There will be a grand rally of the Democrats and Conservative men of Burlington, at their Headquarters in **Commercial Block**, Church Street, **Monday Evening, Sept. 5th, at 7 1-2 o'clock.**

EDWARD J. PHELPS, Esq.,

and other gentlemen will address the gathering. We earnestly invite the laboring, the working men and mechanics, who constitute the bone and muscle of society and the nation, to be present this evening. Irish   ho having felt the hand of oppression that rules ov   ld Isl come to America by instinct and principle, lovers of free government, we ask you esp around the old flag of Democracy in opposition dard of that other party which is always ready to raw seek your votes and having used you, will scoff and sneer at you, because you are Irish and foreign born citizens. Experience has taught you this in the past. Do not forget its lessons now.

We shall have interesting speeches, music, &c., at the Hall this evening, and we hope to see you all THERE.

    F. J. HENDEE, } Democratic
    C. A. HOYT,   } Town
    JOHN LONERGAN, } Committee.

DEMOCRATIC RALLY HANDBILL 1870

CHAPTER TWENTY-TWO – FINAL FENIAN FOLLY

Hibernian Society, stated that he did not regard the meeting as authoritative and withdrew the society from the proceedings. When the vote was taken without the Hibernians, Edward Murphy was elected marshal with all but two of the ninety-six ballots cast. (Murphy was most likely the same man who had been recruited by Lonergan for the Frontier Cavalry in January of 1865. He apparently represented the "Independent Irishmen" led by Lonergan.)

The *Free Press* commented that "there seems to be considerable feeling on both sides of the controversy, among our Irish American citizens, and there is a possibility that two different programmes will be issued for the same occasion." The hope was expressed that "all differences may be adjusted" and St. Patrick's Day "may be marred by no discord among those who celebrate it."

The following day, the mayor convened a meeting of the city's Board of Aldermen, asking them to "advise and instruct him" on how to resolve the use of City Hall on St. Patrick's Day since two competing groups were claiming their right to organize the celebrations. On February 21, the Hibernian Society had been granted use of the City Hall "for a *general* celebration of St. Patrick's day, as in years past." A reconsideration of that vote by the aldermen came the following week in response to "a petition numerously signed by the Irishmen of Burlington."

The mayor did not "find that harmony existing among the Irishmen of Burlington and the Hibernian Society" that would make him confident that the event would be peaceful. After a thorough discussion of the subject, a resolution was unanimously adopted by the Board reviewing the situation and directing action by the mayor. The mayor was instructed to communicate with the "respective parties among the Irishmen," telling them that if they would unite and harmoniously celebrate the occasion, the City Hall would be opened to them without charge. If such assurances were not given, the building would be closed for the event and not opened to either party.

St. Mary's Hall was filled with "quite a large number of Irishmen" on March 10, meeting in an attempt to resolve the standoff between the two factions. After "a number of speeches" calling for conciliation were made, it was finally moved and carried that the Grand Marshal would be appointed by the Rev. Father Lynch. His choice was to be unrestricted, going outside either the Hibernians or the Independent Irishmen as he saw fit. The *Free Press* was of the opinion that this action "will bring about the desired harmony" so that the celebration "will not be distinguished by faction broils."

The day before the event was to take place, the *Free Press* could report that, "all differences having been happily adjusted," the St. Patrick's Day procession would be under the direction of Marshal F. McWilliams. After services in the cathedral, the various groups would form into a parade led by the military, returning to City Hall for an oration by the Hon. John Kiernan of New York; the day would close with a banquet at the American House. Arrangements for the speaker were disrupted, however, as a heavy snow delayed all trains into Burlington the night before the holiday. Moreover, Kiernan had suddenly announced that he could not "meet his engagement" to speak at City Hall. Instead, P. W. Cronan, Esq., of Lawrence, Massachusetts, would address "the Hibernian Society and other Irish Brotherhoods." This formulation gave a nod to both the Hibernians and Lonergan's group without using the name of the organization that had recently been banned by the church and that was also subject to the growing disapproval of the *Free Press* editor, Benedict, Lonergan's former comrade in arms.

Despite the threat of continuing snow, the skies cleared mid-morning on St. Patrick's Day in time for the Hibernian Society and "other Irish citizens of Burlington" to meet passengers off the nine o'clock train, welcoming those who had traveled from West Rutland to join in the event. At St. Mary's Cathedral, a Grand Mass was celebrated. Father Lynch, who had mediated the conflict between the opposing local groups of Irish, spoke on the life of the saint and "the great work he did for Ireland and Catholicism." The visitors from out of town were given lunch at St. Mary's Hall before the "grand procession formed on St. Paul Street."

The military contingent led the parade, right behind the local cornet band. Four companies of Vermont state militia marched under the command of Col. Theodore S. Peck. Capt. J. J. Monahan, the staunch Fenian from Burlington's North Ward, was in charge of Company A, apparently repeating Lonergan's ploy of organizing volunteers in the state system to train them for Irish nationalist goals.* The long procession "made a very fine appearance," with the reporter making special note of the flags displayed. The Rutland

---

* A revitalization of the Vermont militia after the Civil War had replaced the largely social antebellum units, raised on private initiative, with a state-wide military organization. The fanciful names for the companies, such the Emmet Guards, disappeared in most cases and only the standard letter designations were used.

CHAPTER TWENTY-TWO – FINAL FENIAN FOLLY

Hibernian Society carried a banner with the hopeful inscription "Ireland and Unity," an appropriate appeal given the divisive attitudes among the Irish. Apparently the choice of Chief Marshal McWilliams, appointed by Father Lynch, was an acceptable compromise that defused the explosive situation; the parade was held without any open conflicts.

AT CITY HALL, WHERE THE PROCESSION ENDED, Dullahan announced that the substitute orator, Mr. Cronan, had been delayed by the weather and would not give his presentation until the evening. McInnerney stepped forward as secretary of the Hibernians to present the society's president, Dullahan, with a silver water service as an expression of appreciation "for the manner in which you have conducted their affairs." Dullahan accepted with profuse thanks, but then calls came from the crowd for Lonergan to speak. Obviously the Hibernians were not to be allowed exclusive use of the opportunity to address the gathering.

Lonergan's remarks were quoted at length in the newspaper report. He spoke in conciliatory tones about the benefit of all the Irish coming together on the day honoring their patron saint, while not ignoring the unresolved issues among them. Lonergan commented, "To be here in peace and harmony was surely better than to fight, as some had threatened. This was no day for contention. Let Irishmen differ as they may, this day is for Ireland and the disputes can be settled tomorrow." Trusting that no one had failed to "drown the Shamrock" to honor St. Patrick, he took a lesson from "their Yankee friends" of settling problems "indoors out of sight" on an occasion such as this.

The policy of bringing in an outside speaker was questioned by Lonergan, who wondered why it was necessary to go "abroad" when there were orators available at home. He asked, "Did New York ever send to Burlington for a speaker for St. Patrick's Day?" and hoped that the community in the future would appreciate the men that lived in town with them.

He concluded his impromptu speech with consideration of the dual loyalty of the Irish in America: "On a day like this, we should all be proud. We are all from Ireland and we should regard her with love and pride." He noted that some might ask how an Irishman could love two countries at once, but an Irishman's heart was large and had room for both Ireland and America. "When an Irishman takes a wife, as he is sometimes liable to, does he therefore forget his mother? America is the Irishman's wife, but he does not forget his mother Ireland." With this appeal to keep faith with their homeland, Lonergan ended his remarks, "which were received with approval and three cheers."

St. Mary's Hall was completely filled that evening for the presentation of a drama about Robert Emmet, the revolutionary executed so brutally in 1803. McInnerney, the secretary of the Hibernians, took the leading role in the play and the performance occasioned "hearty applause" for the recitation of Ireland's woes and its martyred hero. At 35 cents per ticket, a considerable sum was raised for the St. Mary's Brass Band. The nationalists in the crowd could also be satisfied that the audience had thus been reminded of the history of justifiable rebellion for the cause of Irish freedom.

An hour of dancing and socializing followed the drama, so those participating would have been in a less somber mood when they "repaired to the American" for the banquet. The "bountiful and excellent supper" was not served until 11:00 PM as the "long tables were filled with substantial and well dressed Irishmen and bright-eyed Irish women." Dullahan presided, flanked by the new mayor-elect Lindsey and Cronan, the orator who had finally arrived. After the meal, Dullahan introduced John Lonergan as toastmaster for the evening, to give the regular toasts and call upon speakers to respond. Since Dullahan presided as the head of the Hibernians, this balancing of conspicuous roles in the festivities was likely part of the compromise arrangement between the feuding factions. Lonergan took full advantage of the platform to promote his Fenian views to the assembled Irish.

Compilation of the list of toasts and the people to be called upon to respond would surely have been a contentious matter, given the different views of the Hibernians and the "Independent Irishmen" on suitable subjects for the toasts. A bit of doggerel served for the usual first toast to "The Day we Celebrate"

> Is there a heart of Irish mould
> That does not own the magic sway
> That tempts the generous Irish soul
> To celebrate St. Patrick's Day.

Following the band's rendition of "St. Patrick's Day in the Morning," Dullahan rose to extend thanks to all present who had aided them in ensuring a "successful and pleasant celebration." Perhaps he spoke too soon, as responses to other toasts plainly showed the differences of opinion in the audience.

CHAPTER TWENTY-TWO – FINAL FENIAN FOLLY

The Catholic Church and its local clergy had been recognized by toasts at such banquets in the past, but a break with precedence came when the glasses were next raised to the current Pope, Pius IX. McInnerney responded to the toast, since Father Lynch was not present to do so, offering his view that "if the council in Rome should decree the infallibility of the Pope, as he trusted it would," all good Catholics everywhere would accept the dogma that the church cannot err. Apparently McInnerney, fresh from portraying the martyred Emmet, executed for rebelling against authority, saw no contradiction in the fact that the pope now had banned similar actions by the Fenians.

Lonergan called on Capt. Bain of the militia to respond to "The President of the United States—Our President, the Nation's choice and chief; good, when the Nation calls, for the first and last relief." Bain had enlisted as a private in Co. A, 1st Vermont Cavalry, in September 1861 and was captured by the rebels in fighting the next spring. He had recognized the wisdom of surrendering when placed in an untenable position. On this occasion, Bain could see that he was being placed between two opposing groups of Irishmen—one supportive of Grant and the other hostile to the Republican president—so he declared himself unwilling to make a speech. Instead, he called upon Lonergan to come to his "relief."

The toastmaster obviously had no such reservations, saying that he was "satisfied that the President could take care of himself." Grant had been elected even "if we didn't vote for him, as some of us did, and would perhaps be re-elected, unless we should take hold and re-organize this Society once more." Lonergan stated his belief that "Gen. Grant *was* good for the first and last relief, whether it was for the Alabama Claims or the next thing." Lonergan did not let the opportunity pass to remind the assembled Irish of the still unresolved dispute over the Confederate commerce raiders, of which the *Alabama* had been the most notorious. The issue remained a faint hope for the Fenians that they might profit from a war between England and the United States.

A backhanded compliment came with the next toast to "Our Adopted Country—If not quite as good as the land we left, every Irishman should make the most of it." Finding his own name down for the response to this, Lonergan constructed an "Irish bull" in expressing his wish that "we had speakers enough, so that we could all listen, instead of talking." Passing on from this logical contradiction, he considered Ireland a good country "to emigrate from; good to be born in and to live in, till one is old enough to come to this country." All nations, in his opinion, owed a debt to Ireland and Irishmen who have "furnished the bone and muscle" to build the roads that brought prosperity and power to other countries. He hoped that a time was coming when the Irish people, "a people older than the Gospel," would add another anniversary to celebrate, that of the freedom of Ireland. Before they would meet again, Lonergan had faith that something would be done so that "her green flag would soon float free, over a free people." Anxious to keep the cause of Irish liberation alive, he was preparing his listeners to expect military action within the year.

The reporter observed that "Captain Lonergan spoke with earnestness, as well as with his characteristic humor, and his remarks both to this and the previous toast were heartily applauded."

In response to the rather lukewarm toast "Vermont—Not a bad place to live in, and too good for us to go from," John Quinlan praised his neighbors in Charlotte, south of Burlington. They had treated him well for the past twenty years, even though he had never denied being an Irishman, a Catholic, and a Democrat.

A drink was taken to honor the press, noting the demise of three newspapers in the city, the *Sentinel*, the *Watchman* (presumably Lonergan's short-lived *Irish Watchman*), and the *Times*, leaving the field to the *Free Press*. Its editor, Benedict, expressed his pleasure at being among the Irish and his hope that questions concerning Ireland were being resolved by the English Parliament. After this endorsement of legislative remedies over armed rebellion, he called in turn upon Capt. Albert Clarke, editor of the St. Albans *Messenger*.

Clarke commented that he did not feel a stranger in the group as he had some Irish blood in his veins. He had "never been prouder of it than when he stood at Gettysburgh [sic] by the side of Capt. Lonergan and the brave Irishmen of his company." Clarke had commanded Co. G, 13th Vermont when the Vermonters made their flank attack on the rebel assault of July 3.* His company had taken its place in the line of battle next to Lonergan's Co. A. This direct observation of the Irish Company in the fierce combat left no doubt in Clarke's mind as to the courage and steadiness of the company under Lonergan's command. Even seven years after the battle, this was an image fresh enough in minds of the audience to stir respect for Lonergan and his men.

---

* The captain of Co. G had been wounded in the fighting on July 3 and command then passed to Lt. Clarke.

CHAPTER TWENTY-TWO – FINAL FENIAN FOLLY

Not failing to address the political question of Ireland's situation within the British Empire, Clarke offered his hope that "the day was soon coming when Ireland would be free" and "the tenants could own their homes." As a resident of St. Albans, he would have seen the events of 1866 at close range and been aware of the serious intent of the Fenians. He urged the Irish not to go back to their homeland since they "were needed here." Of course, he realized "they could never forget in the language of the song that 'Ireland was their country and their name was Pat Molloy.'" This was received as "a pleasant speech, and was duly applauded."

Even the following toast, the obligatory to "The Ladies," took on political tones. The response by George Bigelow, who was "organizing and running the women suffrage movement in this county," reached back in history to claim "Who but the women lit up, in 1789, the watch-fires to guide the peasantry of Ireland?" Speaking to current events, he asked "From whose pockets but those of the Irish girls of America, was the Fenian treasury replenished?" He hoped that the old bell at Philadelphia would soon ring out liberty for all, Ireland as well as America, and that the new declaration of independence would declare all men and women to be free and equal.

When Lonergan called on "The Orator of Day" for a response as glasses were raised to him, Cronan at first declined, claiming fatigue. He had spent the night before shoveling snow on the New Hampshire railroads when the storm had stopped the trains. However, he revived to present a "spirited speech" in which he declared "the one thing to be accomplished for Irishmen everywhere, is the freedom of Ireland, and that can only be done by minie balls and flashing sabers." There could be no question as to where Cronan stood regarding parliamentary measures for the liberation of their homeland and his remarks "were received with enthusiastic applause."

Lonergan, who had kept up "a running fire of humor" through the evening, guided the assembled Irish through the rest of the formal toasts with responses by honored guests, including Gen. William W. Henry, Col. Peck, and the new mayor-elect Lindsey. The final glass was lifted to honor "Old Ireland," a reminder of their land of origin.

The following evening Cronan presented his own version of Robert Emmet's history at St. Mary's Hall, in which he emphasized the revolutionary nature of the martyr's actions. His lecture probably was heavily attended by the more radical faction of Irishmen since "Three rousing cheers were given to

Mr. Cronan at the close of the oration." The celebration of St. Patrick's Day—extended through Saturday, March 18, by Cronan's presentation—had passed peacefully enough, but the fault lines splitting the Irish community were clear. (The local population of French heritage celebrated St. Joseph's Day on the 18th without any of the public controversy displayed by the Irish.)

The *Free Press* commented on March 18, "This is almost sugar weather." Maple syrup production, or "sugaring," requires nights below freezing and days above that temperature for the sap to run. Spring was approaching and, once "mud season" had passed, conditions for travel would improve enough to make a military operation possible, should the Fenians choose to act.

A FUND-RAISING LECTURE by George Francis Train in Burlington gave Lonergan a brief exposure on the national political scene on April 8. This speaker from New York had declared himself a candidate for the Democratic nomination for President of the United States and was touring to raise money for the 1872 election. Train was rabidly anti-British and an outspoken advocate of Ireland's liberation. During the 1867 Fenian uprising, Train had been arrested when his ship docked at Queenstown (now Cobh), Ireland, on the way to France. In announcing the lecture at City Hall, the *Free Press* described Train as a "fiery, versatile, and erratic orator" and predicted that a large crowd would attend, particularly the Irish.

In the spring of 1870, the situation in Ireland remained unsettled and a new coercion bill was put into effect. Aimed at "preserving the peace in Ireland," the law gave the police sweeping new powers to close down the press, to "search any man's house for arms at all hours of the day or night," and to imprison suspects without trial. These measures ran counter to the liberal reforms being proposed by Gladstone; they were considered likely to "aggravate the sufferings of the Irish people, and render the ancient differences between England and Ireland hopeless of adjustment."*

Against this backdrop of unrest in both Ireland and North America, Train was greeted at the railroad station on April 8 by "a number of our [Burlington] citizens and the Queen City Coronet Band." A four-horse team

---

* Lonergan might take pride in his Tipperary roots in this situation. More police were needed to patrol the population of 250,000 in that southern county—"such is the spirit of the 'Tipperary boys'"—than were required for a million residents (many of them loyal supporters of the monarchy) in three northern counties.

CHAPTER TWENTY-TWO – FINAL FENIAN FOLLY

conveyed him to his hotel to rest up for his energetic lecture. That evening the City Hall was filled with those eager to hear Train and to "see him walk about on his presidential platform for 1872." Train "was handsomely introduced by Capt. Lonergan," although it is not known whether Lonergan had invited Train to present the lecture or whether his status as a Fenian leader made him the most appropriate local personality to introduce the speaker.

The newspaper report on the performance mocked Train's bombast and claims, saying the "lecturer's object was to astonish." Foregoing any description of the content—"his subject is all creation, with George Francis Train in the foreground, every time"—the reporter dismissed Train's pretensions to be a viable candidate for President. Despite this bad press, Train must have been satisfied with the packed house, which provided him with funds, and with his introduction by a fellow opponent of British rule in Ireland. (Upon his return to New York City, Train was soon invited by a Fenian organization to speak at the Old Bowery Theatre. In his reply, Train urged not only an attack on Canada, but that the Fenians in the city should "hang the British consul on a lamp-post.")

EVEN AS TRAIN SPOKE in Burlington, the government of Canada was receiving information "of the time appointed for the Fenian raid" through several channels. No doubt Lonergan was alluding to this plan when he assured the St. Patrick's Day celebrants in Burlington that the cause of Ireland's freedom would soon be advanced.

Archibald, that British consul in New York City whom Train wanted to lynch, effectively collected information at the heart of the Fenian movement. Consuls in Buffalo and Boston also were alert to developments in those regions. The American Secretary of State shared with the British Ambassador in Washington a letter on Fenian activities that his office had received from the U.S. Marshal in northern New York State. From within Canada, McMicken had established a network of observers reporting on movements in the border area.

On April 7, the Governor-General of Canada "received a confidential note from the Secret Police stating that the raid was positively arranged for April 15 and containing the plans for the attack." Such insider information probably had been supplied by Le Caron, apparently earning his salary as a spy, but the general outline of the intended operation was being confirmed by other sources.

In reaction, Canadian volunteers were called up all along "the frontier," mobilized and under arms by April 9. The decision was made on April 12 to "call out 4,000 men of the active militia in the province of Quebec" and to concentrate them at Montreal. Considerable excitement was reported in the counties of Chateuguay and Missisquoi since it was expected that the raid would take place "at the same points at which the one occurred in 1866, between St. Armand and Frelighsburgh."

Both houses of the Canadian Parliament voted on April 14 to suspend *habeas corpus*, as requested by Prime Minister Macdonald and with the assent of the Queen's representative, the Governor General. Macdonald had cited reliable information "that the peace of the country was again in danger from the invasion of lawless men from the United States belonging to the Fenian organization." However, the government "could not place their information before Parliament without danger to their informants," including no doubt McMicken's agents and Le Caron. O'Neill not only had to contend with spies within his wing of the movement, but also with political opposition to his plans by his own Fenian Senate. Hoping to avoid any action by the senators that would prevent the mid-April operation, O'Neill scheduled a Fenian Congress to meet in New York City on April 19, four days after the intended launch of his incursion into Canada. Suspicions were aroused, however, and the Senate issued its own call for a congress for April 11, to be held in Chicago where O'Neill had less influence. O'Neill refused to attend the meeting, where the unpaid senators accused him in absentia of initiating military operations without their approval and of the misappropriation of funds. (O'Neill had even borrowed several hundred dollars from Le Caron the previous December to cover some dubious expenses. Le Caron was receiving money from both the Canadian government and the Fenian Brotherhood, so he could probably afford the loan, which O'Neill never repaid.)

Even though the Chicago congress reorganized the executive of the Brotherhood to abolish the presidency and thus get rid of O'Neill, a competing New York congress re-elected him president and voted in a new senate. The movement had now splintered even further. O'Neill, frustrated in mid-April by Canadian knowledge of his plans, rescheduled his invasion of Canada to commence symbolically on May 24, the Queen's Birthday.

Newspapers continued to report the transport of arms to the northern border and the possibility of a Fenian operation at a later date. On April 21,

CHAPTER TWENTY-TWO – FINAL FENIAN FOLLY

the *Free Press* wrote of "loaded teams, supposed to have some connection with Fenian movement" passing through the city between one and two o'clock in the morning. Five such teams were said to have been seen in Fairfax, headed for the largely Irish farming community of Fairfield. Public awareness of the plight of Ireland and its revolutionary history was further heightened by a repeat performance of the play "Robert Emmet" at Burlington City Hall. Before a large and appreciative audience, the drama again presented its connections "that do not fail to deeply interest the Irish heart." The reviewer commented that "Emmet, whatever may have been his failings, was intensely enthusiastic over the subject of Ireland's liberty."

The Montreal *Witness* speculated in a mid-April editorial that the alarms about a raid by the Irish were being generated by the Canadian government to "distract public attention from the Red River" military expedition being prepared to deal with unrest in the newly acquired territory. Some American papers were equally ready to condemn the Fenian leaders for creating the situation only to motivate further contributions to the cause.

A correspondent for the New York *Herald* filed a detailed report from St. Albans on April 18, although many of its facts were challenged by the editor of *Free Press* when he reprinted the letter. Dismissing first of all the claim that "the State Militia of Vermont is composed almost wholly of Irishmen," the editor thought many other specifics in the report "no nearer the truth." Perhaps some local Fenians were deliberately spreading such misleading information through a gullible or complicit newspaperman.

According to the *Herald* report, great amounts of cannon ammunition were supposedly being produced right in Vermont. Artillery had allegedly been smuggled into Canada under a load of wheat, "consigned to a Fenian confederate on the line of the Grand Trunk Railway, about midway between Montreal and the American frontier" to be collected by the advancing Irish forces. More plausibly, "a considerable quantity of arms and ammunition at Malone, N.Y." had been taken to "Fort Covington and other points nearer the frontier." The men to take up these arms were standing ready for orders in "nearly all the cities in the Eastern and Middle States, and in some of the Western."

O'Neill was reported to have visited St. Albans in secret while touring "all along the frontier." While inspecting Fairfield, "where a large number of arms are stored," he made the statement "in conversation with one of his prominent aides" that arms and ammunition for 75,000 men were available between Portland, Maine, and Ogdensburg, New York. (Lonergan would have been the appropriate local escort for O'Neill on a visit to Fairfield, so perhaps he was the "prominent aide." Although the reporter appears to be quoting from direct contact with O'Neill, Lonergan could also have been the journalist's source of this information.)

Admitting that "a great many stupid blunders" had been made in the invasion four years earlier, O'Neill claimed that the experience gained would serve them now, particularly in the transportation of men "without the aid of railroads." Arrangements were said to be in place to maintain large bodies of men at different points along the border for several days around the first of May. He expressed "every confidence that the movement now on foot [sic] would prove sufficiently disastrous to Canada to force the British government to allow Irishmen to rule Ireland." The "opinion commonly entertained in this section of Vermont" was that Grant might not be as "officious in putting down an actual invasion" as his predecessor Johnson had been. The author of the article considered this to be wishful thinking on the part of the Fenians.

A lengthy editorial titled "The Fenian Bubble" was printed in the *Free Press* on May 4, pointing out that the first of May had passed without "the predicted Fenian invasion of Canada." It had proved to be "only a bubble, which burst even before it was touched." All the "large promises" by which the leaders could extract "the gifts of patriotic Irish men and Irish women in humble circumstances" for their own personal use proved to be "words and nothing more." As their schemes had collapsed, now "the Head centres, the nine central high functionaries, the generals, &c." were wracking their brains to produce new plans and larger promises by which they could "replenish their exhausted treasury." The writer (probably Benedict) found the continuing attempt to embroil Canada and the United States in a quarrel that the Fenians could exploit to be "a very great nuisance" that should be ended. The Canadian militia and Home Guards were still securing the border against "the locust swarm of Fenians" threatening to "sweep over the country with the besom of destruction." This threat should be permanently lifted, allowing the men to return to their homes and "go quietly about their summer's work."

NO FURTHER FENIAN SCARES were reported for the next three weeks and it appeared that the immediate threat to Canada had disappeared. The Canadian militia units had been released from active duty at the end of April, although the Dominion's agents continued to keep a close eye on the border, even as life along that boundary returned to its normal routine.

Instead of Fenian developments, the Burlington news in late May concerned such local matters as whether Gen. Stannard would be reappointed as Collector of Customs for the District of Vermont or be replaced by Gen. William Wells.* The U.S. Marshal in Burlington, George P. Foster, was busy organizing the ten-year census to be carried out by his Assistant Marshals. A long list of questions, some of them (like place of birth) asked for the first time in this census, was published on May 23, 1870. Foster "respectfully requested" the citizens of Vermont to examine the questions and be prepared to give accurate information when the Assistant Marshals called upon them.

The Burlington Board of Aldermen, which had been embroiled in the Irish dispute on St. Patrick's Day, met on May 23 to consider the usual business of running the expanding city: an ordinance regulating privies, permission to store building materials on downtown streets, and procurement of a set of six-ton hay scales for the City Market were on their agenda. The application for a saloon in Skinner's Lane, site of Lonergan's old armory and cooper shop, was rejected. (The supposed prohibition on trafficking in liquor in Vermont had obviously been relaxed and the open sale of alcoholic beverages permitted, at least on a local basis.) Everything appeared quiet and in order as the board adjourned until the first Monday in June.

The *Free Press* also reported on a celebration of the 15th Amendment to the Constitution by the "colored people of Rutland," set for June 2. This amendment, which granted men (but not women) the right to vote without restriction by race, had been ratified by the requisite number of states on October 20, 1869.

The Grand Army of the Republic, representing that force by which the slaves had been freed, had first proclaimed the new holiday, Decoration Day (now Memorial Day), in 1868. Ceremonies were to be held each May 30 to decorate the graves "of the martyred dead of the late war for the Union." An invitation was extended to "all the soldiers, military and Fire companies, civic societies and organizations, and the citizens generally" to participate under the direction of the Chief Marshal for the event, Gen. Henry.

---

* Despite strong support by Republican leaders in Vermont and Washington, Wells did not secure the position until 1872 when Stannard resigned because a large deficit was discovered in his funds.

In St. Albans, the G.A.R. Post named for "Baldy" Smith, first commander of the Vermont Brigade, was making similar plans, inviting various organizations such as the Fire Department and all "returned soldiers" to join in the procession. Upon request, carriages would be provided for the disabled and all friends of deceased soldiers were asked to report the location of their graves to the organizers. Capt. Albert Clarke "accepted the position of orator for the occasion."

The seven members of the Burlington "committee of arrangements" for Decoration Day included Scully and Benedict, along with Gen. William Wells and four other prominent veterans. The arrangements by this committee emphasized the preservation of the Union as the goal of the war and left any celebration of Emancipation and voting rights up to the "colored people." The event in Burlington was clearly being organized by local Republican leaders. It is therefore not surprising that the Democrat Lonergan, despite his general recognition as a war hero, was given no role in the ceremony.

However, Lonergan may have been unconcerned at being left out of the Decoration Day events, since he was busy elsewhere with his own arrangements. While his former comrades from the federal army peacefully planned to honor the dead who had fought to preserve the American Union, Lonergan was deeply involved in another attempt to free Ireland from its union with Great Britain.

THE FENIANS BURST BACK into the headlines on May 24, as the region's newspapers suddenly filled with reports of men moving to rallying points near the Canadian border. Apparently O'Neill had learned a lesson from the previous month and improved his operational security, this time keeping his plans secret from the public. However, the Canadian government had again been supplied with the proposed date by Le Caron. If not for this warning, the celebration of Queen Victoria's birthday on May 24 might have distracted the government's attention from the border. O'Neill's choice of this meaningful date for the incursion also meant that the Dominion's volunteer units could be mustered for the event without revealing Canadian knowledge of the Fenian intentions.

The objective of the raid—it did not rise to the level of an invasion attempting to seize and hold ground—was far more psychological than

CHAPTER TWENTY-TWO – FINAL FENIAN FOLLY

military. Growing rejection of armed revolution by the Irish on both sides of the Atlantic required a victory, or at least a heroic defeat, on British soil to revive support for the Fenians.

The straightforward operational plan envisioned in essence a repeat of the 1866 effort, this time aimed generally at St. Jean, Quebec. Feints would be made at Buffalo and other points while two columns would be sent forward, one on each side of the Richelieu River. From the St. Albans base, a force of 1,200 men would cross the border and occupy Eccles Hill, not far from the 1866 headquarters on Pigeon Hill. The western wing would concentrate at Malone, New York, and invade through Holbrook Corners, where the Trout River flows into Quebec. (The plan also considered seizing a train on the Montreal line to carry a detachment of 500 men directly into St. Jean, a high-risk effort that was never attempted.)

Supplies for the aborted April operation had been kept stored at many points along the border. The Canadian Governor General claimed to know where the arms were hidden, "some buried, some in garrets, some in groceries and whiskey houses." Le Caron had been responsible for many of the arrangements to pre-position the war materiel and no doubt reported its location to the Canadian government. However, the British dominion could take no action in a foreign country. Even if supplied with this information by the Canadians, the American authorities had no legal basis on which to seize the weapons until they were used to violate the neutrality laws.

The main problem that O'Neill faced in mounting the raid was the need for rapid concentration of his forces at the border, which required the movement of a large number of men over considerable distances just prior to the attack. Despite his earlier claim to the contrary, the railroads were still the only means to accomplish this. Steamboats and wagons were used locally, but long distance travel depended on moving men swiftly by rail.

Coordination of the effort was further complicated by the need to hide the operation not only from the Canadian and American governments, but also from opposition factions within the Fenians. Because only selected leaders would know the details beforehand, public appeals could not be made for volunteers until the campaign was launched. Inevitably, this resulted in the piecemeal arrival of contingents from distant cities to the area of operations, so that the commanders had neither the promised number of men nor any chance to organize them into an effective fighting force.

Hindsight gave significance to movements noticed over several days prior to the Queen's Birthday, such as the teams of horses that pulled heavily loaded wagons through Burlington "at a late hour Friday and Saturday nights." Local farm workers had "taken unceremonious leave of their employers without assigning any reason," while parties sympathetic to the Fenian cause had been approached on Sunday, May 22, to contribute money. Reported as reliable fact by the *Free Press* was the absence of "thirty or forty Irishmen, employed on the city water works and in the lumber yards" who left their work on Monday morning.

Specific movements of men on May 23 included a carload-and-a-half of young men from Burlington on the 6:20 PM train to the north. The lake steamer *Adirondack*, coming up from the south, brought word of 300 men waiting for passage at Port Henry, New York. That evening, the little *Curlew* began ferrying these men across Lake Champlain, with the first voyage bringing Capt. Monahan and seventy-five men. The ship continued its crossings, bringing as many Fenians as it could to Burlington for the morning train at four o'clock.

Residents of St. Albans expected "a renewal of the scenes of the great Fenian raid of four years ago," although the Irish were keeping their own counsel about their intentions. The secret depots of arms and ammunition at Fairfield and nearby points were estimated "by a party in a position to have accurate information as high as 20,000 stand of muskets and carbines, together with at least one battery of light artillery." The number of men observed gathering in St. Albans on May 23 could easily be armed with a fraction of the weapons said to be available in the vicinity.

Hundreds of strangers were arriving in St. Albans, along with local Irishmen, all reporting for duty. A company from Burlington had marched from the St. Albans station toward Fairfield on the evening of May 23, observed by a deputy U.S. marshal who had not yet received any orders to intervene. A number of men were traveling from Rutland by steamer up Lake Champlain to St. Albans Bay and another company was en route from Rutland by rail. They were all urged on by the presence of "Capt. Lanagan of the Fenian General Staff," according to an article published in the New York *Times*.* Lonergan was "hurrying men to the front" from Rutland and was quoted in the article as being "himself confident of the success of the movement."

---

* A phonetic spelling of the common pronunciation of Lonergan; such variants often appeared in transcriptions of oral statements, including official records such as census reports.

CHAPTER TWENTY-TWO – FINAL FENIAN FOLLY

The Tuesday, May 24, morning edition of the *Free Press* shouted half a dozen headlines over its story of an impending Fenian raid on Canada, including "A Real Fenian Movement, Burlington Fenians for the Front, Recruits Pouring in from all Sections, Great Excitement in St. Albans." Steamboats and railroad cars were said to be arriving in St. Albans loaded with "live Fenians." Contingents coming from other parts of the country were being reported by telegraph and a general move on Montreal was rumored. Mosby, the Confederate guerrilla who had threatened the Vermonters in Virginia seven years before, was said to command the Fenian cavalry. Wild tales circulated of 5,000 Fenians concealed in Montreal and ready to seize the city, of 40,000 men to strike north across the border, of another 75,000 ready to attack west into Ontario from Buffalo, and even of nine iron-clad ships steaming up the St. Lawrence.

In 1866, President Johnson had delayed two full days before issuing his directives for action against the Fenian violation of the Neutrality Act. In 1870, Grant gave O'Neill no such leeway and published a proclamation signed in Washington on May 24. On May 25, the New York *Times* carried the full text of the proclamation, accompanied by numerous items received by telegraph telling of Fenian movements in Buffalo, Boston, Chicago, and elsewhere.

In his proclamation, the President tersely described his knowledge that "sundry military enterprises and expeditions are being set on foot" within the United States, directed against the Dominion of Canada ruled by "Her Majesty the Queen of the United Kingdom of Great Britain and Ireland, with whom the United States is at peace." Grant admonished "all good citizens" of his country not to aid, abet, or take part in such actions, warning that they would "forfeit all right to the protection of this Government." All officers in government service were instructed to employ "their lawful authority and power to prevent and defeat" the operations and to arrest all persons involved in them. The U.S. Marshals in particular were now empowered to seize the Fenian weapons and to take the leaders into custody.

TIME WAS RUNNING OUT for O'Neill after the publication of Grant's proclamation. The Fenians faced preemptive action by the American government to forestall any movement over the border. Once regular Army troops arrived on the scene to support the U.S. Marshals, O'Neill's forces would be disarmed. It was unthinkable that he would order his men, many of whom had served in the Union army during the Civil War, to fire on federal soldiers. His only choice was to act swiftly, even before most of the promised 2,000 Fenian troops had arrived.

The first of O'Neill's units to report to the field were two companies of the 1st Fenian Cavalry Regiment, men from Vermont and just across Lake Champlain in New York. (The sound tactical decision had been made to supply the invading force with cavalry that could scout ahead, move rapidly to strike lines of communication, and protect the flanks of an advancing column of infantry. For over a year, Col. E. C. Lewis had been in Vermont organizing the cavalry units in the area.) These advance units—Company A from Burlington, about fifty men under Capt. William Cronan, and Co. C from the Plattsburgh area, commanded by Capt. Carey—wore cavalry-style green jackets with blue pants. Supplies of saddles, sabers, revolvers, and carbines had been stored along the border, but one essential item was missing—horses. The two companies would have to lead the invasion on foot. Perhaps Le Caron, now adjutant of the Fenian forces under O'Neill, had deliberately failed to provide the cavalry with mounts. In fact, only O'Neill himself and Lonergan were reliably reported to have been on horseback during the operation.

At much effort and expenses, stores of arms, ammunition, and other supplies had been moved right up to the border and even across it. Teamsters were being given the attractive sum of $10 for a night's work and one man claimed that he had been offered $25. Reportedly "in Fairfield everything that could draw a load, and that money could hire, was engaged." Scores of wagons were passing through to the north and east at night. As early as May 23, seventeen loaded wagons left from the east side of Fairfield Pond after dark. The supply dumps required guarding and the password "Winooski" was given to the teamsters to ensure their safe passage through the sentries on the roads.

As each detachment arrived in St. Albans, it marched out of the town to Fairfield to be armed and partially outfitted with uniforms. On May 24, only 300 men representing four different regiments had concentrated in the area, spending the night in barns and houses of the Irish community. The next morning an early start covered the fifteen miles to the rallying point at Hubbard's Corner, just beyond the village of Franklin and a mile south of the border.

CHAPTER TWENTY-TWO — FINAL FENIAN FOLLY

At 9:00 AM, O'Neill's available forces were gathered among the ammunition boxes waiting alongside the road. A guard post was set up to stop all travel along the road while the boxes were opened and cartridges distributed to the men. News that a company of Canadian militia was guarding the road at the boundary did little to dampen the spirits of the soldiers. The men were "anxious to press on, confident of their ability to brush any such opposition from their path."

O'Neill was accompanied by his chief of staff, Gen. John J. Donnelly; the regimental commanders; his traitorous friend Le Caron; and Lonergan as aide-de-camp. (With Col. Lewis in charge of the Vermont troops, Lonergan later explained that he had "no special command, but occupied a volunteer position on Gen. O'Neill's staff.") A group of reporters was also present, including Boyle O'Reilly from the Boston *Pilot* and correspondents from Troy, New York, and Burlington. The Fenian leaders likely had invited newspapers to cover the heroic deeds of their hometown boys, hoping to promote the cause with favorable publicity that would increase the Brotherhood's membership and treasury.

At 11:00 AM, Foster arrived on the scene in a closed carriage with his deputy, Thomas Falley of St. Albans. The marshal immediately informed the officer in charge of the guard post that they had no right to block the public highway. Foster clearly still retained an authoritative presence from the days when he commanded the First Vermont Brigade because the officer meekly withdrew the guards from the road. Foster then sought out O'Neill to cite the President's proclamation and the authority that it gave the marshal to prevent any violation of the neutrality laws. The erstwhile general then "formally ordered [O'Neill] to desist from his unlawful proceeding," but the "order was received by O'Neill very coolly and with apparent unconcern." Having done his duty to the extent possible, the marshal then continued northward past the Fenian position.

The warning by a U.S. official resolved any question O'Neill had about whether to move forward with his few hundred troops or to wait for reinforcements. The demonstration of legal authority was not sufficient in itself to stop the Fenian operation, but troops were certainly being sent to enforce the marshal's order. Any delay in launching the raid could result in the U.S. government preventing the attack altogether. O'Neill accordingly gave the order for his men to advance. The column proceeded half a mile down the road before halting to load their rifles and then continued northward.

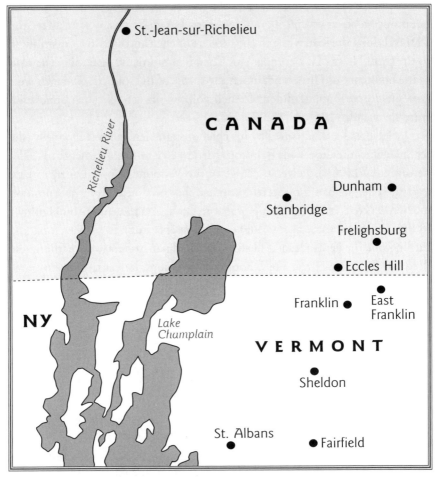

AREA OF OPERATIONS ON VERMONT BORDER, 1870

PREPARATIONS UNDERWAY IN CANADA to repulse the Fenians were said to be "unquestionably much more formidable than on the occasion of the former raid." Key locations such as St. Jean were reinforced by selected units of regulars and militia from Montreal. In the border area where the attacks were expected, the militia received orders on May 24 to be ready for immediate service. The 52nd Battalion concentrated its companies at Dunham and marched toward Eccles Hill. The border with the United States runs close to the foot of this prominent hill which overlooks the only road north in the area. The Fenians under Gen. Spear had occupied this commanding feature of the terrain in 1866 and the Canadians knew they would likely attempt to seize it again.

Mustering and moving the militia companies required time, however. That day, a small detachment of Home Guards was the only force of armed Canadians actually present at the point under an immediate threat from the Fenians. However, many of the settlers in the border area were descendants of the United Empire Loyalists who had opposed the American Revolution. These Loyalists had been rewarded with land grants when they relocated to the north. Now prosperous farmers, men such as Asa Westover had been disappointed by the failure of the British government to protect their property from the Fenians in 1866. Still skeptical of the capacity of the new Dominion to repulse any repeated assault across the frontier, they had formed themselves into local defense groups under the guise of "shooting clubs."

At their own expense, these civilians had purchased arms and ammunition for their members. Westover captained a group known as the "Red Sashes" for the identifying symbol they wore in lieu of any other uniform. After the 1866 experience, Westover had gone to the United States to acquire a sufficient quantity of Ballard sporting rifles to arm the dozens of Red Sash members. A breech-loading weapon with a heavy 30-inch barrel, the Ballard had a good reputation for accuracy and reliable rapid fire.*

Westover even had his own informal intelligence network, relying on S. N. Hunter—previously a resident of Fairfield, Vermont—to stay in contact with his former neighbors. During the 1866 incursion, Hunter had kept the Canadians informed of events in that hotbed of Fenian supporters. (He subsequently moved to Lagrange, Quebec, perhaps due to hostility generated by his actions in the first Fenian raid.)

Westover had not waited for the Canadian militia. When it became evident that the Irish planned to cross the border again, Westover mustered his few dozen men to occupy Eccles Hill, a natural choice for defense against an invading force. Its rocky outcroppings on a partially wooded forward slope

---

* By 1870, regular military forces in both Canada and the U.S. were commonly armed with muskets converted from standard issue Springfield and Enfield rifles into breech-loading weapons. Even though they were still single-shot rifles, the metallic cartridges could be fed into the chamber while the user remained prone and protected, in contrast to the exposed process of loading a musket from the muzzle. The Fenians had also set up their own workshops to modernize their arms into breech-loading rifles.

would give good cover with a clear field of view. Their Ballard rifles could sweep the open area of the road and close off the border with accurate and sustained fire.

Early the next morning, Hunter crossed the line to Franklin to scout out the situation. He reported back at noon that wagonloads of arms and ammunition had been unloaded at Hubbard's farm close to the border. The teamsters were returning to bring up more arms from Fairfield, as well as the men who would use the weapons. From nearby Frelighsburg, Westover sent a telegram with this information to the militia officers and in the evening hours of May 24 received a reply from Lt. Col. Brown Chamberlin, commander of the 60th Missisquoi Battalion.* Westover was instructed to occupy Eccles Hill, which he had already done. At dinner time, however, most of the Red Sash men returned to their homes, leaving a dozen posted on the hillside.

Around 3:00 AM on May 25, this Home Guard picket stopped a wagon on the road north of the border. When challenged, the teamsters responded with "Winooski," the password used by the Fenians, and said that they were looking for O'Neill. Westover's men seized Thomas Murphy from St. Albans and his brother Lewis, along with the supplies that they were transporting for the Fenians. On delivery of the two prisoners to Cook's Corners, the Home Guard received orders to fire on any invaders and then fall back across the Pike River on the road to Stanbridge.**

Chamberlin was by this time already in Stanbridge, five miles from Cook's Corners, mustering the volunteers. Because of the false alarm the previous month, the 60th Battalion had been slower in assembling and only forty men reported for duty on the morning of May 25. The small company from Dunham—only twenty-one men—marched in to reinforce the detachment on the hill at 4:00 AM and by mid-morning Chamberlin, with two other officers, brought the Missisquoi Volunteers from Stanbridge. Both the 52nd and the 60th Battalions were under the command of Lt. Col. Osborne Smith, a former regular officer and now deputy adjutant-general for the militia.

---

* Chamberlin represented Missisquoi County in Parliament and was editor of the Montreal *Gazette*, the newspaper where Lonergan's son later worked as the literary editor.

** Appearing on modern maps by its French name, Rivière aux Brochets, the Pike River rises just outside Frelighsburg to flow in a horseshoe north, then west, and finally south into the Missisquoi Bay of Lake Champlain. The river got its name from the fish, but there is an ironic coincidence that the battle took place in a valley whose name recalled the traditional primitive weapon of the Irish rebel, the pike.

CHAPTER TWENTY-TWO – FINAL FENIAN FOLLY

In the late morning, this mixed force of armed Canadians was approached by U.S. Marshal Foster, who drove his carriage across the border to warn them of imminent attack by the Fenians. Foster had just been in the Fenian camp where O'Neill had asked Foster to deliver a message to the Canadians that the invading forces would observe the rules of warfare. Chamberlin, as the British commander on the spot, rejected any message from people he considered pirates and marauders. The marshal explained to the Canadians that, although President Grant had issued a proclamation that allowed him to enforce the neutrality law, he was unable to prevent the Irish from attacking until U.S. troops arrived.

Foster turned his horse and started his carriage back to Franklin near noon on May 25. On the road just south of the boundary line, he passed a column of soldiers in Fenian uniforms headed north. The former general watched several hundred Irishmen march by fours toward the border, carrying loaded rifles on their shoulders and hope for Erin's freedom in their hearts.

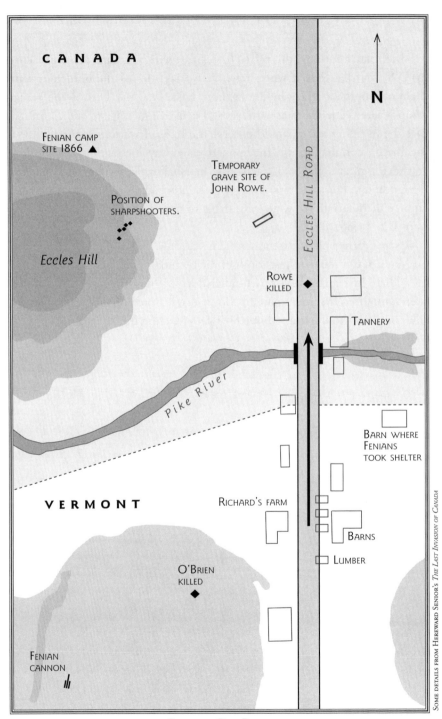

BATTLE OF PIKE RIVER

CHAPTER TWENTY-THREE

GREEN FLAGS FURLED

THE VAST EXPANSE OF CANADA came into view as the Fenians reached the brow of a hill. As O'Neill's aide, Lonergan would have ridden in front of the column with the commander. A few hundred Irishmen were about to challenge the immense power of the Queen and her empire on which "the sun never set." O'Neill halted his meager forces and the men looked down into a narrow valley where a small stream ran parallel to the boundary between the two countries. Eccles Hill, occupied by the Fenians in their last raid and the objective of the current operation, was plainly visible across the valley about a quarter of a mile north of the border and west of the road. Armed men, some in red-coated uniforms, could be seen moving along the crest of the hill and onto the forward slope flanking the road.

O'Neill spoke to the Fenians at this point, "in substance" declaring:

> Soldiers—this is the advance guard of the Irish Republican Army for the liberation of Ireland from the yoke of the oppressor. For your own country you now enter that of the enemy. The eyes of your countrymen are upon you.
>
> *Forward,* MARCH!

Burlington's Company A, 1st Fenian Cavalry (dismounted), would be the tip of the pike about to be thrust into the territory of the hated monarchy. The commander, Capt. William Cronan, lifted his hat to O'Neill, saying "General, I am proud that Vermont has the honor of leading this advance. Ireland may depend upon us to do our duty." After these obligatory pronouncements, the main body of troops deployed in line of battle facing north, still on the American side of the border. Cronan's company was sent ahead to form a skirmish line on the Canadian side, taking its orders from Col. John H. Brown of Lawrence, Massachusetts, who would accompany them into position.

The road from Franklin passed through a cluster of buildings on each side of the border. The substantial brick house of Alvah Richards dominated the scattered dwellings, outbuildings, barns, and stacks of lumber on the American side. Across the bridge spanning the small stream (locally called Chick-a-biddy Creek), a tannery and several farmhouses faced the road where it headed north to St. Armand, Quebec. The Vermonters moved at double-time down the hill and over the bridge, still in a column of fours, followed by a company from New York.

Thinking that they remained safely out of range of Canadian rifle fire, the lead element moved to deploy as skirmishers on the north side of the creek before the main battle line advanced. Just as they crossed the bridge, however, these Fenians were shocked by an accurate volley of bullets from the rocks on the forward slope of Eccles Hill to their left. John Rowe of Burlington fell dead on the spot with a bullet through his throat.* He lay in the road, clutching his converted Springfield rifle beneath his body, not thirty yards into Canada. His corpse, still wearing the belt of a sergeant in the Burlington Boxer Fire Company, marked the deepest penetration into the British Empire in this sector of the Fenian operation. As the Irish halted their advance to return fire, several of Rowe's comrades were also wounded. The Home Guards, protected in their positions, suffered no casualties as they continued to unleash a hail of bullets on the exposed invaders.

An aide to O'Neill, Maj. Charles Carleton of Burlington, toppled from the bridge and was initially thought to have been killed. Many of the Fenians who had crossed the bridge were young men with no combat experience, and panic soon replaced any order in the ranks. A few scrambled beneath the bridge for the shelter of the creek banks while most fled back across the stream, some flinging away their weapons. The main body of Fenians, still on the American side of the boundary, opened fire at the Canadians on Eccles Hill, also without effect. In the exchange, the Fenians took half a dozen more casualties. William O'Brien from Moriah, New York, was killed outright and several soldiers were severely wounded. O'Neill ordered his men back up the

---

* Rowe was reportedly shot by a Mr. Pell of the Home Guard, who fired just before the others and saw his target fall. Fenians had entered Pell's house near the border in 1866, causing much damage and smashing his piano.

CHAPTER TWENTY-THREE – GREEN FLAGS FURLED

CORPSE OF JOHN ROWE

hillside and behind the trees. Most of the men from the two companies out in front took cover inside the Richards barn.

O'Neill observed the fighting from an upstairs window of the Richards home, safely behind stout brick walls, until his command group—no doubt prominently displaying the green flag carried by the Fenians—drew fire from the Canadians. Finding the Irish leader in one of the bedrooms, the owner of the house "peremptorily ordered him to leave the premises." O'Neill was reluctant to abandon his observation post, but exited the dwelling when threatened with physical ejection by the muscular farmer.

The Fenians fired several volleys from the woods to the west of the road with no visible results. Meanwhile, bullets were whistling across the international boundary in their direction and men began to fall back in disorder. They were rallied by O'Neill and his staff, no doubt including Lonergan. O'Neill berated his soldiers for acting as cowards:

> Men of Ireland, I'm ashamed of you. You have acted disgracefully. But you will have another chance of showing whether you are cravens or not. Comrades, I will lead you on again, and if you will not follow me, I, with my officers, will go and die in your front.

Shamed into following O'Neill's orders, the men returned to their positions. Their compliance spared him the gesture of a pointless sacrifice of his life, perhaps taking Lonergan and other officers to the grave with him.

When the Fenian main body returned to the fight, "a scattered fire was kept up across the line for an hour and a half, with no particular effect on either side." Several more Irishmen—mostly members of the Meagher Rifles from Bridgeport, Connecticut—were wounded in the exchanges. Seeing his forces again drifting to the rear and out of the fight, O'Neill determined to break the stalemate by maneuvering his troops. Another frontal assault would have no chance of success, so he decided to detach a company from his right to outflank the Canadian positions. Curiously, O'Neill did not send a staff officer such as Lonergan to carry the orders, but instead went himself to the rear.

Even stranger was O'Neill's final act: handing command over to Boyle O'Reilly, who ostensibly was present only as a newspaper correspondent. Before leaving the scene of the battle mid-afternoon, O'Neill asked the ex-soldier and escaped felon to accompany him to deploy the Fenian forces. (Perhaps O'Reilly was really present as part of the military operation since he reportedly did become involved later in the day, using the alias of "General Dwyer." O'Reilly's own account claimed that he was on the scene only as a journalist.)

O'Neill withdrew from the battle line and walked with O'Reilly down the road toward Franklin. Foster, who had been watching the fighting at a distance, now saw his opportunity approaching. The marshal turned to a dozen nearby civilian spectators and announced his intention of taking the Irish leader into custody. Saying "Gentlemen, I propose to arrest Gen O'Neill," he asked whether they would support him in the discharge of his duty and received an affirmative response.

As O'Neill stopped to speak to a wounded Fenian in the road, Foster approached him and laid the hand of the law upon him, declaring, "I arrest you in the name of the United States government." O'Neill protested that he would not allow himself to be arrested, but in fact offered no physical resistance as Assistant Marshal Falley pulled the carriage up beside them. Calling upon O'Reilly to witness that he was taken against his will, O'Neill appointed the Boston journalist commander of the Irish forces in his place.

Warned by Foster than any outcry could cost him his life, O'Neill sat quietly in the closed carriage as it passed the Fenians guarding the supplies in the rear area. Once safely beyond the Irish lines, the two marshals conveyed their prisoner on to St. Albans. Their carriage likely passed groups of Fenians marching toward the battlefield, because several hundred more men had

CHAPTER TWENTY-THREE – GREEN FLAGS FURLED

arrived at St. Albans and set out for Franklin. They arrived too late to influence the outcome of events.

After observing O'Neill's arrest, O'Reilly spread the word among the Fenians that their leader was taken. When O'Reilly made his way back to the border, he in turn relinquished command to Gen. Donnelly, pinned down with the forward element in the Richards barn. Upon learning of O'Neill's capture by the authorities, Donnelly reportedly wept.

As the day wore on with occasional exchanges of gunfire causing additional Fenian casualties, reinforcements arrived on both sides of the border. The number of Fenians engaged probably remained about the same since the forces marching in were balanced out by men straggling away from the battle. Individuals and groups of Irish were headed back toward St. Albans, many discarding their weapons and green uniform jackets. The Canadians, however, were augmented by ninety men of the Victoria Rifles, a small detachment of additional militia, and a troop of cavalry.

TWO DEAD AND SEVERAL WOUNDED Fenians lay exposed to the bright sunlight of the afternoon as the accurate musketry of the alert Canadians prevented the Irish from retrieving them. Around 3:00 PM, Gen. Donnelly and several other Fenian officers met with Canadian representatives from the Home Guard under a flag of truce to negotiate removal of these casualties. (A correspondent from the Boston *Advertiser*, C. H. Tuttle, formerly on the editorial staff of the *Free Press*, accompanied Donnelly and reported that the Canadians had sent the truce flag down. Another account claimed that the Fenians had come forward first.) Dealing with only the Home Guard was not acceptable to the Fenians and "General Lonergan" requested to speak to an officer. Word was sent to the British commander, Col. Smith, who "refused to hold any communication with General Lonergan" and the negotiations failed, both parties returning to their respective lines.

Although Lonergan had never even officially received his commission as a captain in the Vermont militia, he apparently had been awarded the rank of general in the Fenian forces. Boyle O'Reilly commented with disdain on the inflated rank structure of the Fenian army, "We use the word general as a mean—there might have been a colonel, and there probably *was* a field-marshal." [emphasis in the original]

Most of the reporters present took advantage of the flag of truce and left the scene in their carriage at 4:00 PM, carrying word of the debacle back to St. Albans. Three dwindling companies of Fenians still occupied the woods west of the Richards house, but the men had already lost their taste for the fight by the time that they learned their leader had been arrested. The companies led by Captains Cronan and Carey, around seventy-five men, were pinned down with Gen. Donnelly in the outbuildings, unable to move without drawing fire. Another contingent of New York Fenians, numbering about 150 soldiers, arrived in the late afternoon, bringing the total Fenian force back up to some 350 men. A council of war was called to decide what course of action to take. Lonergan agreed with the consensus that the operation had failed and he supported the consequent decision to withdraw.

Benedict—the editor of the *Free Press*, who identified himself only as "your humble servant" in his first-person reporting on the event—had arrived in St. Albans by train on the morning of May 25. The livery stable had already hired out all available conveyances, but the newspaperman was able to "secure a seat in a carriage" with Sheriff L. A. Drew, leaving at noon with dispatches for Foster. On the road from Highgate to Franklin Center, they met a horse and buggy bearing Albert Clarke of the St. Albans *Messenger*, the first man back from the "front."

Clarke informed them that he had accompanied the Fenian column until it came "under sharp fire from a body of Dominion Militia" and the non-combatants scattered to the rear. A British bullet had knocked the hat off his head, encouraging the veteran of Gettysburg to leave the area. He reported one killed and several wounded among the Fenians before he left, with the conflict still under way.

The sheriff and his companions pushed on, passing small groups of stragglers headed away from the battle—"boys, all under twenty, without uniforms or arms, who were making good time to the south." Arriving in Franklin, they found the small village crowded with wagons and people. Some of those present wore the Fenian uniform, though less than a third of the Irish were outfitted with the green jacket. While visiting wounded Irishmen in the hotel, the group learned of O'Neill's arrest, and they then continued on to the Fenian lines through a rear guard that did not prevent their passage. Men and supplies were scattered along the roadside, including crates of breech-loading rifles and a six-pound rifled field piece with its caisson. Some cavalry saddles lay on the ground, but the one horse in sight belonged to O'Neill, "a good looking bay, with army saddle" hitched to a fence nearby.

The only mounted Fenian seen as the reporter moved up toward the border was Lonergan, leading a column of forty men, their muskets at right shoulder shift, behind a green silk battle flag. Ever ready to express his opinions, Lonergan described the situation to Benedict as hopeless. Too few men had reported to Franklin, he said, and many of them came twelve hours late. With O'Neill under arrest and Donnelly cut off in the barn, there was no effective command. Any further attempt to dislodge the Canadians from Eccles Hill would no doubt be a waste of lives. Lonergan "evidently considered the thing over" and said that he would return to St. Albans that night. Benedict and his party then hitched a ride to the Richards house on a double wagon driven by a tanner from Fairfield, who had been going to pick up a load of hides in Canada. On learning of the Fenian casualties, the tanner was instead offering to transport the wounded Irish to Franklin.

In the late afternoon, the entire Fenian artillery—the single breech-loader mounted on a field carriage—was wheeled by hand up to the brow of the hill. As dusk approached, the lone cannon lobbed a few shells in the general direction of the Canadians without causing any casualties. This feeble bombardment distracted attention for the moment, as intended, and Donnelly led his detachment in a dash across the fields into the woods east of the house. The Canadian forces hurried them on the way; one company of their 60th Battalion and some of the Home Guard advanced toward the border. Several more Fenians, including Donnelly, were wounded as they retreated. The British forces continued unscathed even though "for about ten minutes the firing was kept up with great spirit, and for the time sounded like the commencing of a battle."

A general retreat by the Fenians ensued as stragglers threw away their equipment, offering to sell their muskets to local inhabitants for a few dollars. Rifles were free for the taking along the road and from the abandoned supply dump, until Deputy Marshal Flanagan confiscated what remained of the arms and ammunition. Footsore Fenians arriving in St. Albans found the town occupied by the 5th U.S. Artillery. A company from Plattsburgh had been rushed across the lake on May 25 to make camp in the park. Three companies of the same regiment led by Lt. Col. George Kenall arrived by train the next day from Boston. Two of them joined the company already bivouacked on the square, while the other remained at the railroad depot. On May 26, 200 more U.S. regulars also passed through St. Albans in the evening on their way to Malone. An equal number of Fenians who were determined to continue the fight took the same train west into New York.

The U.S. Army units in the St. Albans area were under the command of Gen. Richard Arnold, but Gen. McDonnell, head of the Department of East, was on the way to the center of action in Vermont. He would be joined by Gen. Meade, reinstated as commander of the Division of the Atlantic in March of the previous year and reprising his role of 1866, when he quelled the earlier Fenian attempt at an "invasion."*

The raid on Canada not only faced opposition by the U.S. government, but was also denounced at the highest level of the Fenian organization. In a statement issued from Philadelphia, James Gibbon, President of the Executive Council of the Fenian Brotherhood, declared on May 25 that the operation was not authorized by the Fenian leadership and was "merely a personal enterprise by irresponsible parties."

The lead of the main article in the *Free Press* on May 26 read, "Captain Lonergan came to St. Albans from the front about midnight last night." Upon arriving in the town, Lonergan let people know that a council had been held by the Fenian leaders still in the field and "the decision made to go no further with the invasion, in this section." After sharing information on the situation in Vermont, Lonergan "inquired anxiously for news from the West." He clearly hoped to learn of better results by the Fenian forces operating out of New York, but "seemed disappointed at hearing of no specially active operations there."

DESPITE WHAT LONERGAN HEARD in St. Albans, hundreds of Fenians were actually concentrating at the railroad hub of Malone in northern New York. During the night of May 24, a camp had been established at the farm of Patrick Leahy near the Canadian border at Trout River. Supplies were being distributed there as the men arrived by train. Contingents from circles in Buffalo, Troy, Albany, and New York City were joined by groups from other states to the west and south. Canadian militia units had been called up to

---

* This would be Meade's last campaign; he died November 6, 1872, in Philadelphia, his home town and headquarters.

CHAPTER TWENTY-THREE – GREEN FLAGS FURLED

assemble in towns across the border from Malone, while regular British units were on the way from Quebec City and Montreal.

In Vermont, scores of defeated Fenians were scattered along the country roads between Franklin and St. Albans on May 26, "seeking to get back as best they may, most of them bitterly accusing others for failing to do their duty." Enough arms and ammunition had been available in Franklin and Fairfield for 5,000 men, but far fewer than that had answered the call for action. The last to leave the scene of battle was Capt. Cronan's company, which held its position as rear guard long after the rest had gone. In the afternoon of May 26, they marched into St. Albans in good order, though presumably without their weapons. To avoid being disarmed by the U.S. troops, the Fenians apparently cached their rifles for future use as they passed through friendly communities such as Fairfield.

Other key figures of the 1866 incursion had gathered in St. Albans. Fenian Gen. Spear, who had successfully taken Eccles Hill in the previous effort, arrived in town at noon on May 26. He claimed to be a private citizen with no involvement in this new adventure, but was careful to steer clear of U.S. Marshal Foster. The skeptical reporter (probably Benedict) who interviewed Spear felt "satisfied that he is now the leader of the whole matter." The Fenians reportedly held a council of war in Spear's rooms at the Tremont House that evening, no doubt with Lonergan attending before he caught the evening train for Burlington. John H. Gleason—once colonel of the 63rd New York of the Irish Brigade and now one of the many Fenian generals—had accompanied Spear and probably also took part in the meeting. The crucial question was whether to abandon the operation entirely or take the remaining forces to support the western wing at Malone. Spear accepted the role of commander offered him and urged that the remaining men be rushed to Malone.

The evening train from St. Albans on May 26 was greeted by a large crowd at the Central Railroad Depot in Burlington. On board were Captains Lonergan and Cronan, along with several dozen Fenian soldiers from the city. The group went straight from the train station to the hall of the Boxer Hook and Ladder Company—the firefighters must have included other Fenians among their Irish members besides the slain Rowe. The leaders addressed an overflow crowd. From inside the hall, "frequent and loud cheering was heard and was responded to by a crowd in the street." The *Free Press* reported that the same Fenian company that had just returned from the battlefield would leave the next morning for Malone. Far from giving up, the Burlington Fenians meant to continue the fight, avenging Rowe's death if they could. Efforts were under way to retrieve his body from the Canadians and to bring it, along with that of O'Brien, to Burlington for a proper funeral.

While the Fenians made the Fremont House their headquarters in St. Albans, the nearby Weldon House was likewise profiting from visitors connected with the Irish adventure. O'Neill was being held at the Weldon, where accommodations were also provided to the government officials opposing the Fenian action. Vermont's governor, attorney general, quartermaster, and adjutant general had taken up temporary residence there, along with various U.S. Army officers, Foster, Stannard, and the district attorney from Montpelier.

With the town full of disgruntled Fenians, the saloons in St. Albans were wisely ordered closed and army patrols ensured that order was kept. Local citizens were nervous about the Irish hanging around and began a collection to pay their train fare back home. (Meade had arranged transportation back to their starting points for some 8,000 Fenians in 1866, but Grant refused Meade's proposal to authorize such an expenditure in 1870.) Most of the defeated soldiers wanted only to return home, although a hard core was determined to reach Malone and participate in further military action.

The authorities in St. Albans tactfully gave the lesser Fenian leaders an opportunity to leave with their troops, waiting to take action until the afternoon of May 27. Rather than allowing the commanders of the invasion to continue "hanging about here and plotting fresh violations of the law," Foster—assisted by the sheriff and U.S. troops—arrested Colonels Brown and Sullivan, along with Majors McGinnis and Murphy. Captain Monahan of Burlington was also held until he could post a $1,000 bond.

After remaining in the field for a day to secure the arms left behind, Col. Sullivan had returned to St. Albans just in time to be rounded up with the other officers. Sullivan had managed to collect and hide many of the abandoned weapons. He had failed to retrieve the Fenian cannon, however, and some enterprising Vermont boys hauled it across the border to sell to the Canadians.*

On the Quebec side of the border, photos were taken of the cannon surrounded by triumphant Home Guard, as well as of the Red Sash men after

---

* The cannon was removed from its wheeled carriage and placed on Eccles Hill as a monument to the action by the Canadian forces in repelling the Fenians, where it remains today.

CHAPTER TWENTY-THREE – GREEN FLAGS FURLED

CAPTURED FENIAN CANNON WITH RED SASH HOME GUARD

the battle. Another poignant image shows several uniformed Canadian militia volunteers posed standing over the body of Rowe, crumpled in the dust of the road still clutching his rifle. His corpse was afterward carried to the side of the hill and buried in the thin soil under a cairn of stones. O'Brien's remains had also been hastily interred on the American side where he fell, a necessary step in the warm weather of late May.

SPARED DURING THE 1866 attacks by the Fenians, the communities across the border from Malone had not formed any Home Guard as had those in the Pike River area. Militia battalions at Huntingdon and Hemmingford each had several hundred men on their rosters. However, mobilization of the part-time soldiers would take about as long as the transportation of regulars and volunteers from Montreal. From those men available to him, the mayor of Huntingdon cobbled together an improvised Home Guard to provide some patrols and scouting of the situation. On May 26, the Fenians still had no organized opposition to face when they made a probe several miles into Canada, but the invaders contented themselves with cutting the telegraph wires at Holbrook Corners.

The operation at Malone suffered from the same problem of coordinated arrivals that had plagued O'Neill at St. Albans. By May 26, perhaps a thousand

Fenians had arrived at the rendezvous point and more were on the way. As word of O'Neill's arrest and of the total defeat of the eastern prong of the attack reached the camp, however, many men lost heart and deserted for home. New arrivals perhaps balanced out the losses, but the ensuing chaos made any effective organization of an attack impossible. At this point, no U.S. Army troops had appeared on the scene, though they certainly could be expected at any time. The pressure was on the Fenian leaders to act before the American authorities could prevent them.

Dawn the next day revealed movement on both sides of the border. The 50th battalion of Canadian militia in Huntingdon had been joined at midnight by the 69th Regiment of regulars brought down from Quebec.* At 3:00 AM on May 27, the combined forces assembled under Col. Bagot for the move to Trout River, followed by cavalry and artillery units. The regulars passed the time on the ten-mile march singing "rousing songs and choruses" that included the familiar "Pat Malloy."

On the American side, the Fenians also formed up early after a council of war decided to attack. The leaders disagreed on the timing, however, with some wanting to wait for the arrival of additional forces. About 200 men rallied to the orders of Col. Owen Starr (who had fought alongside O'Neill in 1866) and moved across the border around 7:00 AM. A good defensive position was selected about half a mile into Canada, on a slight rise with three hundred yards of mostly open fields on level land before it. A hasty fortification of fence rails was anchored on the right by the Trout River, while skirmishers were sent forward to await the British reaction.

A mounted patrol of local scouts led by Lt. Butler, intelligence officer of the British 69th Regiment, was on reconnaissance in the area when the Fenians crossed the border. After being fired upon without effect, Butler rode hard to inform the column that the invasion had started. Around 9:00 AM, almost 1,000 British troops began to deploy opposite the Fenian position with the Huntingdon Borderers out as skirmishers. The Fenian skirmishers were pressed back to their main line and the outnumbered defenders opened fire on the redcoats. However, they aimed too high and

---

* The 69th was an iconic designator for the Irish, based on historical connections, and a number of the Fenians awaiting them had served with the 69th New York in the Irish Brigade. However, this British regiment—nicknamed the "Ups and Downs" from the numerical image—had been formed as the South Lincolnshire regiment in 1758. Like most British regiments of the era, it probably included some Irishmen.

CHAPTER TWENTY-THREE – GREEN FLAGS FURLED

the British were unharmed by several volleys that passed overhead. Unable to face the steady approach of the regulars any longer, the Irishmen turned and fled the battlefield for the safety of American soil.

TRUE TO THEIR PROMISE at the fire hall the night before, on the morning of May 27 a contingent of Fenians left Burlington for Malone. The *Free Press* article reporting their departure, however, commented that not all those returning from the Pike River fiasco decided to join in this further expedition and "the majority remain" in Burlington. Considering the degree of his involvement in the Fenian operations and his adventurous nature, Lonergan was likely among those who boarded the morning train. Two carloads of Fenians from New York City were also on the same early train. The veterans of the Pike River battle would have had an eager audience for their first-hand news of events that marked the end of militant Fenian activities in Vermont. Long before their train arrived at the new scene of conflict, however, the brief clash at Trout River had already ended.

General Gleason left St. Albans that same day on the noon train, stepping down in Malone at 6:00 PM with "a good deal of flourish about the streets during the evening." Described as "a stout man, nearly seven feet tall, with a face distorted with excess," Gleason assembled the Fenians in Malone—numbering between one and two thousand as men continuously arrived and departed—at the fairgrounds on May 28. Despite his appeal for another attempt at invasion and even with backing by Father McMahon (who had been captured by the British in 1866), only some thirty men formed up behind the Fenian banner and Gleason gave up the effort to renew the attack.

By this time, Generals Meade and McDowell, after stopping off in St. Albans, had set up headquarters in Malone for the command of the hundreds of U.S. Army troops pouring into the town. The Canadian forces had also been augmented, standing ready to repel any further crossing of the border. The U.S. marshal, assisted by soldiers, began seizing the Fenian war materials, and on May 29 Meade helped him arrest Gleason and a dozen other Irish leaders. The remaining Fenians, disarmed and discouraged, boarded trains for home with their green flags furled.

Apparently Lonergan made some public statements about the whole situation afterward, stirring up feelings in Vermont against the role of the

U.S. government in suppressing the Fenian military action and making uncomplimentary remarks about the Canadians. A telegraphic exchange that took place on May 31 in response to his statements was published in the *Free Press* on June 2. The U.S. Consul in St. Jean, L. E. Smith, sent the following message addressed to Capt. John Lonergan, Burlington, tersely advising him to "Dry up." Not content to let Smith have the last word, Lonergan replied the same day: "Yes Sir. Take something. Call and see us about the 4th of July." The "Volunteers from Montreal" also weighed in on June 2 with expressions of "appreciation of courtesies extended them" by Consul Smith.

In the United Kingdom of Great Britain and Ireland, the Irish Land Bill passed out of committee on May 27 and was reported to the House of Commons for action. Gladstone, against considerable opposition and after accepting some amendments, had succeeded in his major legislative effort to relieve the plight of the common Irish. Along with the military defeats in Canada, this concession to the Irish tenant farmer sounded a death knell for the militant nationalist movement both in Ireland and America. Decades would pass before another generation of Irishmen again took up arms to fight for Ireland's liberation.

THE FUNERAL FOR THE TWO Fenians killed in the clash at Pike River provided a sad footnote to the matter. After some negotiations, the Canadians agreed to allow Rowe's decomposing body to be retrieved from its shallow grave on Eccles Hill. An undertaker from St. Albans went there on May 31 and disinterred the remains, placing them in a coffin that was transported to the railroad station for shipment home to Burlington. Rowe's uniform reportedly had been stripped from his corpse and presented as a trophy to Prince Arthur, third son of Queen Victoria, who served on the staff of Gen. Lindsay during this latest Fenian scare.

Rowe's commander, Cronan, escorted his body back to Burlington on the June 1 evening train from the north. Cronan and Dullahan had also arranged to transport the corpse of the other Fenian killed in the fighting to Burlington for a joint funeral. Since O'Brien was an immigrant with no relatives in the United States, the decision was made to bury O'Brien in Burlington as well. O'Brien's remains, exhumed from its burial in a rude coffin near Franklin, arrived on the morning train at 8:00 AM the next day.

CHAPTER TWENTY-THREE – GREEN FLAGS FURLED

Because the city was in the midst of a hot spell that peaked at ninety-nine degrees, the funeral and interment took place immediately. Services were held at 9:00 AM in St. Mary's Cathedral, but the caskets were kept in state in St. Mary's Hall due to the extreme decomposition of the bodies. After the funeral services, both men were buried in the Catholic cemetery, a sobering reminder of the consequences of nationalist rhetoric calling for the use of force.

From their vantage points as editors of the leading newspapers in the region, two of Lonergan's former comrades in the Second Vermont Brigade decried the recent Fenian actions. Clarke wrote in the *Messenger* as one who had seen the Fenians up close during both raids and as one who, trailing after their more recent expedition, had nearly lost his own life. Reprinted in the *Free Press* on May 31, the same day the unfortunate Rowe was disinterred, Clarke's editorial condemned that faction of the Fenians seeking to make war on Canada as having been "conceived in sin and born in corruption." He was sure that the experienced soldiers who concocted this wild scheme must have known that they "have undertaken the most unmilitary fizzle …since Quixote's famous encounter with the wind mills." After collecting "the money of poor laborers and servant girls who loved their country," they marched patriotic men into "the jaws of certain death and defeat" and deserved "the severest retribution."

Benedict, who also had viewed the operation first-hand, asked in a lengthy editorial on June 6, "What was the object?" He dismissed the notion that "any intelligent Fenian" could answer since "the merest child in years and experience" could not credit the idea of taking possession of Canada as feasible. The only purpose, in Benedict's opinion, might have been to precipitate a conflict between the Great Britain and the United States so that Americans would make the Fenian cause their own. He could find no "sane and plausible reason for the raid" that would advance the cause of Irish independence. Benedict wrote that "all this stir, trouble, expense, and loss of life has been incurred in order that some corrupt and thievish leaders may put money in their purses from the Fenian treasury." With this recent failure, he thought that "game must now be about 'played out'" and could not be repeated.

O'Neill, the focus of this criticism, was arraigned the next day for his "offence against the neutrality laws" which Judge Smalley condemned in decided terms. The judge did, upon request, agree to a reduction in O'Neill's bail from the original $15,000 to the same $10,000 required of other Fenian generals arrested. (Upon conviction, O'Neill was sentenced to two years in prison and was actually incarcerated in Windsor, Vermont, until October when Grant pardoned all the imprisoned Fenians. The Irish vote was important to his Republican administration in the fall elections.) A New York City newspaper summed up O'Neill's "late glorious campaign" by suggesting that the inscription for his banners in the future read "Erin go brag."

Despite the generally negative reaction of the public and the specific criticism of the Fenians by Benedict, Lonergan sat down with him at the fourth annual reunion of the 2nd Vermont on June 17. Only twenty members of the regiment attended the banquet at the G.A.R. Hall in Burlington. Stannard, "who wears more stars than arms," presided, and the address was presented by Col. Randall, former commander of the 13th Vermont. Randall and Lonergan had both been company commanders in the 2nd Vermont until the original "Irish company" was disbanded by the governor.

Remarkably, one of the guests was Col. Donnelly, "formerly of the army of the Cumberland and lately of the Fenian army," apparently enough recovered from his serious wound of the previous month to attend. Donnelly had no connection with the Vermont regiment and was out on bail at the time; perhaps Lonergan was responsible for the presence of his Fenian brother-in-arms. The usual rounds of toasts were offered and Lonergan "told once more the story of the Monocacy," along with some "fresher recollections of the battle of Pike River." He offered his opinion that the Fenian defeat had been "like Bull Run, one of those things that will happen sometimes." The old songs were sung, drink was taken, and the camaraderie of the shared experiences of campground and battlefield appears to have overcome current disputes, as the reunion was "admitted to have been one of the pleasantest" held.

AFTER THE 1870 RAIDS on Canada, the fortunes of both the Fenian Brotherhood and its Vermont leader declined. Lonergan no longer could inspire the Irish community to support the militant nationalist cause. To avoid conflicts such had marred the celebrations of 1870, no St. Patrick's Day parade was held in Burlington the following year. Instead, the Irish gathered for the holiday in Rutland, where matters were more easily controlled by conservative elements under the guidance of the church.

CHAPTER TWENTY-THREE – GREEN FLAGS FURLED

On the national scene, the newly formed Clan na Gael took up the banner of independence in competition with the Fenians, who had fragmented into squabbling factions. Another attempt was made to reconcile the differences within the Brotherhood when the ninth convention of the original organization, now headed by John Savage, appointed a committee to bring O'Neill back into the fold. In September of 1870, O'Mahony and two other prominent members of the inner circle traveled to Windsor, Vermont, and were allowed to visit O'Neill in his prison cell. He signed an agreement of union with the Savage organization "with the earnest hope that it will tend to the union of all Irish nationalists in the common cause."*

The fault lines between Irish groups in America took deadly form on July 12, 1871, when Orangemen parading in New York City to celebrate King William's victory on the Boyne were attacked by armed Fenians and Hibernians. The police, backed by militia units, fought pitched battles in the streets with the Catholic protestors. Initial reports were of forty deaths, though this was greatly exaggerated. More Irish died fighting each other in this incident, however, than were killed in both the Fenian raids into Canada, making this riot an ominous portent of Ireland's future.

Remnants of the Fenian Brotherhood survived in reduced form beyond the 19th century. In the early 1900s, circles at remote army posts in Texas still sent dues to the headquarters. However, after 1870, leadership in the Brotherhood was no longer a focal point in Lonergan's life. By siding with O'Neill during both his incursions into Canada, Lonergan had cut his ties with the O'Mahony wing. He now found himself adrift in the nationalist tides. While no doubt still committed to the cause of Irish independence, Lonergan seems to have withdrawn from an active role and largely dropped out of public view. He was absent from the Reunion Society meetings until 1878 when the list of attendees included him again.** In subsequent years, Lonergan repeated his tale of "discovering the Monocacy" at reunions up through 1894.

---

* Ignoring this pledge, a year later O'Neill was off on a final adventure. On October 5, 1871, he crossed the Canadian border into Manitoba with a few dozen men and a wagonload of arms, intending to support Riel and his Metis in their actions against the Canadian government. O'Neill was quickly arrested again by the U.S. Army, but was released without a trial.

** Foster, still U.S. marshal, gave the first toast of the evening, to the President of the United States, at the 1878 reunion.

An association of former members of the 13th Vermont was formed in 1888 and brought many of Lonergan's old comrades to the Custer House in Underhill on June 15. Lonergan had no role in the organization until 1891, when he was elected president, for the prescribed one-year term, at a meeting in Waterbury. Despite his misadventures after the Civil War, his reputation among the men with whom he served seems to have remained sound.

Times were hard for Lonergan in the decade and a half after the collapse of the Fenian movement. Any income he might have derived as an organizer disappeared, his family grew, and the grocery business failed—due in part, no doubt, to his distraction with the Irish nationalist movement. Each month Lonergan did receive five dollars disability pension for piles and chronic diarrhea contracted during his military service. This was his only reliable income, as other physical problems (for which he later submitted disability claims) prevented him from any strenuous labor. A second daughter, Jane (called Jennie), was born in November of 1871 in Burlington and baptized at the cathedral. In November of 1873, Roseanna bore their next child, Mary Catherine, while the family was living in Boscawn, New Hampshire. A personal item in the *Free Press* in 1874 informed the public that the Lonergans resided at that time in Brookline, New Hampshire, and were "doing well."

By 1875, the family had returned to Burlington and John again had a cooper shop listed at Maple and Battery Streets in the city directory. Mary Lonergan, John's mother, died of "dropsy" on April 4 of that year, aged fifty-four. The following year another daughter, John's last child, arrived on April 8. For some reason Roseanna (also shown as Rose Ann in some documents) was not baptized until May 24, perhaps because the family had already moved to southern Addison County. Despite their deep roots in the Burlington community, John took his family to the tiny village of Lincoln sometime in the mid-1870s. Living in the hills some thirty miles south of Burlington, Lonergan would have been isolated from his previous life, cut off from friends and relatives.

Lonergan's reason for moving to Lincoln is unknown. The small community held no significant Irish population and the closest Catholic church was five miles away in Bristol, (a walkable distance in that era). However, John Hanlin, the underage soldier in the "Irish Company" who fought on despite his wound at Gettysburg, was likewise a cooper and lived

CHAPTER TWENTY-THREE – GREEN FLAGS FURLED

GENERAL AFFIDAVIT.

State of _Vermont_, County of _Addison_ {ss

In the matter of _John Lonergan – late Capt Co F 13 Regt Vt Vols_

ON THIS _24th_ day of _July_ A. D. 188_2_, personally appeared before me, a _Justice of the Peace_ in and for the aforesaid county, duly authorized to administer oaths, _John Lonergan_ aged _43_ years, a resident of _Lincoln_ in the County of _Addison_ and State of _Vermont_ whose Post Office address is _Lincoln Addison Co_ and

aged _43_ years, a resident of

in the County of _____ and State of _____ and whose Post Office address is _____

well known to me to be reputable and entitled to credit, and who being duly sworn declare in relation to the aforesaid case as follows:— I was injured by being thrown from my horse at the Monocacy — injuring my back and right testicle producing Hydrocele on the right Side. The pain in my left Side I don't know whether it is caused by Hydrocele of right Side or not — I only State the fact — I was at the time of accident very weak being under treatment for Chronic Diarrhea and rode bad back — and presume Hydrocele was caused by my effort to Sit on my horse —

I further State that the loss of my trade to me exposed my whole prospects in life — that I tried to work and was obliged to Stop — that in the later part of 1865 — I received an appointment as Inspector of Customs in Burlington — and also in 1866 — and also in 1867 — and a Deputy Collector in 1868 — these commissions gave me a living Salary for 6 Months in each year — during navigation — the rest of the year I earned nothing whatever. In 1868 I was out of Custom house employ — not being able to work at the paying part of my trade I left Burlington finally came to this Town — and about half the time I have labored at a great disadvantage at the lightest part of the trade hooping butter tubs — a third class position for me — and further, that under medical advice I must quit that all together. The nature of the work requiring wrenching of the body and causing me severe pain, and of much loss of time and money.

And I further declares that I have interest in said case and am not concerned in its prosecution.

John Lonergan
[Signature of Affiant]

[If Affiants sign by mark, two persons who can write sign here.]

LONERGAN'S APPLICATION FOR DISABILITY

in Bristol at the turn of the century.* A prospering lumber yard in Lincoln produced quantities of products made by coopers, particularly butter tubs, and Hanlin might have helped his former company commander find work there.

In 1880 and again the following year, Lonergan wrote from Lincoln applying for an increase in his disability pension, claiming that injuries he suffered in the war precluded well-paid work at his trade. After years of humorous retelling of the fall from his horse when crossing the Monocacy River on the way to Gettysburg, he now blamed the incident for his ailments. Now "compelled to do what I could at my trade as a last resort and a means to live," he was reduced to working "at the tightest part of the trade—hooping butter tubs." The initial request in 1880 must have been denied since he repeated his claim, citing witnesses to his injury and deceased physicians who had treated him.

Considering the circumstances of his service and the conditions under which he claimed he was injured, the response from the War Department is a model of bureaucratic apathy toward his claim. In a fine hand, a captain from the 16th Infantry, acting as an assistant adjutant general, notes dryly that the company muster-roll for May and June of 1863 and the regimental roll for June are missing from the files. Therefore, the "Regimental records furnish no evidence of disability as alleged." The consolidated morning reports show Lonergan present for duty from June 1-25, 1863.

There seems to have been no consideration given to the reason that the administrative paperwork was missing. The regiment, along with the rest of the Second Vermont Brigade, in that period was straining in a heroic effort to catch up with the corps to which it had been assigned, arriving at Gettysburg by forced marches in time to help turn the tide of the bloody battle. When the regiment returned to Vermont, the medical staff remained at Gettysburg dealing with the huge number of wounded soldiers. The surgeon therefore had been not available to examine an injury such as Lonergan suffered in his fall from the horse that he was riding bareback. No corroborating records found; therefore, request denied.

Lonergan apparently stayed in Lincoln for about a decade, raising his four children as best he could with his loyal wife, Roseanna. The tranquil beauty of the area in all seasons might have compensated to a degree for the

---

* The Hanlin family of coopers may have been established in the area well before then. John Hanlin had married May Slattery from Montpelier; Lonergan's youngest daughter later married a Slattery in Canada, so there may have been some connection among the three families.

CHAPTER TWENTY-THREE – GREEN FLAGS FURLED

long winters in a hillside village, probably snowbound at times. Financially, life was no doubt hard, yet the children seem to have received education and care that prepared them well for later life.

The election of Grover Cleveland in 1884 signaled a welcome opportunity for Lonergan, exiled from government service during the twelve years of Republican administrations. With a Democratic president in the White House again, Lonergan must have actively campaigned for an appointment as part of the political spoils that routinely fell to the victor because, in 1886, he was given a position with the U.S. Customs Office in Montreal, acting as inspector on the Grand Trunk Railroad line. He moved his family to Point St. Charles and resided there for the remainder of his life.

Did Lonergan find it uncomfortable to resume living under the Union Jack, even though he was an American citizen? Lonergan's family had fled Ireland nearly forty years before and he had dedicated much of his adult life to the liberation of Ireland from British rule, yet he made his home among those who gave their loyalty to the ruler who was still called the "Famine Queen" by resentful Irishmen. As an official representative of the U.S. government and a family man seeking good relations with his neighbors, Lonergan clearly had to suppress his Fenian sympathies.

In addition to finding steady work with the government, Lonergan also benefited from a new pension law signed by President Benjamin Harrison on June 27, 1890, which qualified him for benefits without having to prove that his disability was the result of injury while on active service. Any veteran of the Union Army who served at least ninety days "in the late war of the rebellion" and whose disability was "not the result of their own vicious habits" could receive up to twelve dollars a month. Lonergan wasted no time in reapplying for a disability pension, sending a completed form sworn before the U.S. Consul in Montreal on July 31 to George E. Lemon, an attorney in Washington, D.C. Under the new provisions, Lonergan was granted a pension that apparently continued until his death. He sent an update on his marriage and the dependent status of his children to the Department of Interior's Bureau of Pensions in response to their inquiry in 1898.

ONE FINAL REQUEST LONERGAN made was also granted by the U.S. government. He asked for a medal recognizing his actions at Gettysburg.

In the 1890s, a spate of ageing veterans of the Civil War received the sole decoration authorized at that time, the Medal of Honor. During this period, before the requirements were made more stringent, forty men from Vermont were awarded the medal for bravery during the Civil War. Only eight Vermonters had been so honored during the conflict itself.

Urged by a friend and former commander from Burlington, on October 11, 1893, Lonergan wrote to Redfield Proctor, colonel of the 15th Vermont during the war and now a U.S. Senator from Vermont. Lonergan reminded Proctor—who was only briefly on the battlefield since his regiment and the 12th had been detailed to guard the army wagon train—that he had been the first man at the guns when the 13th recaptured the Union cannon. He also staked his claim to having opened the door to the Codori house alone and ordered the eighty-three Confederate soldiers out as prisoners. Asking for recognition "for the sake of the boy and my family hereafter," he stated bluntly, "I won a Medal—I deserve a Medal." (He was likely aware that Maj. Gen. Wells, 1st Vermont Cavalry, and Col. Wheelock, 16th Vermont, on the same day in September of 1891 had both been awarded the Medal of Honor for action at Gettysburg. The following year, Benedict also was given the medal for having "delivered orders and reformed the crowded lines" under fire in the battle. Lonergan's claim rested on more tangible acts of bravery than those cited for Benedict.)

The Irishman sent the letter to Proctor from 77 St. Etienne Street, Montreal, on letterhead for the Office of the U.S. Customs at the Grand Trunk Railway Company of Canada and closed with apologies for troubling the busy senator. Lonergan ended with his stock reference at all gatherings, "[I] now beg to call your attention to the fact that I did a lot of things besides discovering the Monocacy!"

Lonergan backed up his account with a letter from Col. Randall dated July 13, 1869, which substantially confirmed his claims. Randall praised the bravery of Lonergan and the company that the colonel called "my Irish Regulars" for their outstanding military conduct. The leader of the battalion that made the headlong charge on July 2 also calls the farmhouse where the prisoners were taken the Codori house (not the Rogers house, as it is commonly identified). The colonel assured Lonergan that he had not "laid up anything against you personally on account of the *ranking* officer affair," referring to Lonergan's attempt to command the regiment as the senior captain. Lonergan requested that Proctor return the prized letter from his colonel.

CHAPTER TWENTY-THREE – GREEN FLAGS FURLED

Lonergan's Medal of Honor

Senator Proctor sent the application for a medal forward promptly on October 11 with his endorsement of "Capt. Lonergan, who was a gallant Irish Captain of the 13th." He went on to say, "I heard at the time and have always heard Lonergan's conduct highly praised," and that it gave "good reason for the award of a medal."

No bureaucratic delay slowed the processing of this request from a senator. The reply on October 21 was signed by L. A. Grant, who had been colonel of the 5th Vermont and held brigade and division commands during the war, rising to Brevet Major General. He was appointed an Assistant Secretary of War on April 5, 1890, and was probably sympathetic to awards being given Vermonters. Grant assured Proctor "the matter having taken the regular course has been sustained by the records, and the issue of a medal in accordance therewith has been directed." He also returned the original of Col. Randall's letter after making a copy.

A memorandum was issued from the Record and Pension Office of the War Department on October 23 stating that the Acting Secretary of War had directed the issue of a medal of honor to Captain John Lonergan, 13th Vermont Volunteers, to be engraved as follows: "The Congress to Captain John Lonergan, Co. A, 13th Vermont Vols. for distinguished gallantry in action at Gettysburgh, [sic] Pa., July 2, 1863."

Official notification of the award was sent to "The Adjutant General, State of Vermont, Burlington, Vt." who at that time was Theodore S. Peck, compiler of the 1892 Roster of Vermonters in the Civil War with the help of State Military Historian, George G. Benedict. Lonergan's award, like many others, came too late for inclusion in that roster's listing of Vermonters who received the medal. Only twenty-one names are given, along with their ranks, units, and basis for the medal. An item under "Vermont Personals" was also published in the *Free Press* announcing the award. It noted that Lonergan was "at present an officer in the United States customs house at Montreal and his many friends in Vermont will congratulate him upon receiving at the hands of the government this recognition of his valor."

LONERGAN DID NOT LIVE to see Ireland become "a nation once again," yet he did survive beyond the reign of Queen Victoria. The monarch, who had taken the throne the year that Lonergan was born, died of natural causes at nearly 82 on January 22, 1901. She was followed on the throne by her first son, Albert Edward, who would be crowned after a suitable period of ceremonial delay.

A period of ill health forced Lonergan to resign his position with the customs office. At age sixty-five, Lonergan succumbed at his home on St. Etienne Street to edema of the lungs brought on by cardiac disease. The death certificate, issued on August 6, 1902, stated that he had been deputy collector of customs for about fifteen years, during which period the certifying physician had attended him. Lonergan apparently had requested that he be buried in Vermont, since arrangements were made to transport the body to Burlington where it would lie among those of his relatives.

CHAPTER TWENTY-THREE – GREEN FLAGS FURLED

Lonergan's grave, St. Joseph's Cemetery, Burlington, Vt.

Notice of his death was published in the *Free Press* the next day and was followed on August 8 with an announcement that his remains would arrive from Montreal at 12:15 PM, to lie in state in St. Patrick's Chapel from 2:00 to 3:00 PM when the funeral would take place at St. Mary's Cathedral. The casket, draped in the American flag, was "viewed by many old friends and acquaintances" before the funeral service. A wreath was sent by the editorial staff of the Montreal *Gazette*, where his son Thomas was employed. Burial was in St. Joseph's Cemetery; the pall bearers included J. J. Monahan, J. B. Scully, and Thomas Murphy, all former comrades who had served in uniform—Union, Fenian, or both—with Lonergan.

The newspaper coverage of Lonergan's death and funeral was relegated to a back page of the *Free Press* because it coincided with the coronation of the new king, Edward VII, which was described in detail on the front page. With all the pomp and ceremony that could be mustered by the Empire, the Archbishop of Canterbury on August 9 crowned the new monarch. Edward was proclaimed ruler "by the grace of God, of the United Kingdom of Great Britain and Ireland and the British Dominions beyond the seas, King, defender of the faith, Emperor of India."

Under the freshly turned Vermont soil, the man from Tipperary was laid to rest. Others would have to take up the cause for which he had fought so bravely.

Maid of Eireann, Kilrush, Co. Clare

EPILOGUE

IN THE LAST YEARS OF HIS LIFE, John Lonergan must have thought the cause of Irish independence lost, perhaps forever. The goal of seeing Ireland "a nation once again" seemed to have faded into the mists after the failure of the Fenians. From time to time, the continued oppression of British rule that exploited the common people still sparked acts of violence, but political movements restricted themselves to achieving reform within the law.

When Lonergan went to his grave in 1902, the glacial progress toward equality through parliamentary channels had relieved some of the worst abuses. A compromise solution of "Home Rule" that would keep Ireland within the Empire seemed to be the most that the Irish could expect. Even this was unacceptable to Protestants in Ulster, who believed "Home Rule is Rome Rule" and stood ready to fight against severing ties to the United Kingdom.

A generation passed after Lonergan had joined O'Neill for the 1870 assault on Canada. Despite the military failures of the Fenians, they had planted seeds of revolutionary nationalism that put down deep roots. Slowly, support for the cause began to grow again. Pride in an Irish heritage was fostered by the creation of organizations like the Gaelic Athletic Association that promoted Irish games, especially the ancient sport of hurling. (The GAA first met in Thurles, County Tipperary, in 1894. Maurice Davin, born and raised in Lonergan's still fiercely nationalistic home town of Carrick, presided over the gathering.) The Gaelic League began to revive a respect for the Irish language and to promote its teaching. The writings of W. B. Yeats and Lady Gregory recounted in English the tales of Cuchulain and Finn McCool, which were still being recited in Irish at the turf fires in remote cottages.

In August of 1903, one year after Lonergan's death, the foundation stone for a monument was laid on the square at Kilrush, in the center of this market town in County Clare on the banks of the Shannon River. Why Kilrush? Clare had the highest percentage of evictions of any county in Ireland during the famine years of 1849-54 and Kilrush the most in Clare. The £350 cost for the monument had been raised mostly by the Claremen's Association of New York with some local contributions. The figure of a young woman with a faithful Irish wolfhound crouched at her feet was carved from County Galway limestone. She became known as the "Maid of Éireann," a public symbol of defiance toward British rule.

The dedication carved on three sides of the monument in Irish, French, and English is not to any hero of legend or to rebels of times long past. Instead, the remarkable inscription is to the memory of the Manchester martyrs: Allen, Larkin, and O'Brien, hanged just thirty-six years before. The words chiseled in stone declare bluntly that these men "were judicially murdered by a tyrannical government" in 1867 for their "gallant rescue of Kelly and Deasy, the Fenian chiefs, from the prison van." Bold, even treasonous, such words clearly were aimed at moving the hearts of the Irish against their British rulers. The inscription even ended with "God save Ireland," the cry of these martyrs that was set to the music of a Union army marching song of the American Civil War and became the unofficial national anthem for Ireland. The Maid of Éireann would remind all Irish that the Fenians had fought against such outrages.

Over half a century after the ordeal of Irish emigrants who came to Canada during the Famine years, the Ancient Order of Hibernians in America solemnized their plight with the erection of huge Celtic cross near the mass graves on Gross Île. The somber granite symbol, nearly fifty feet tall, stands atop a high bluff on the western end of the island, visible at a distance as the tour boat approaches the Parks Canada site. The monument was placed there in 1909 and commemorated by a gathering of thousands that included survivors of the quarantine experience in 1847. Three sides of the base show carved inscriptions, two of them similar in tone. In English there is a religious slant to the epitaph: "Sacred to the memory of thousands of Irish immigrants who, to preserve the faith, suffered hunger and exile in 1847-48, and stricken with fever ended here their sorrowful pilgrimage." The French text echoes this sentiment, adding that the victims were "comforted and strengthened

EPILOGUE

CELTIC CROSS AT GROSS ÎLE

by the Canadian priests" and ending with the hope that "Those who sow in tears will reap in joy." Neither of these inscriptions contains the bitterness and accusations of the Gaelic version.

The old Irish script on the eastern side of the base, facing Ireland, spells out in Gaelic the Hibernians' true feelings, preserved in their hearts decade after decade:

> Children of the Gael died in their thousands on this island
> Having fled from the laws of the foreign tyrants and an artificial
> Famine in the years 1847-48. God's loyal blessing on them.
> Let this monument be a token to their name and honor from the
> Gaels of America.
>   God save Ireland

Seven years after the erection of this monument, Ireland rose up yet again to free itself from English rule.

———•———

IN APRIL OF 1914, PARLIAMENT passed a bill granting Home Rule for Ireland, though implementation was postponed in the face of a growing threat of war with Imperial Germany. The Ulster Volunteers that same month received weapons from Germany, arming themselves to fight against Home Rule if necessary.

Formed to counter the militant Orangemen, by May the nationalist Irish Volunteers had in turn enrolled 100,000 members. Within this group, the Irish Republican Brotherhood had control of the three-man Military Committee and received financial support for its revolutionary goal from the Clan na Gael, the successor to the Fenian Brotherhood in America. Padraic Pearse, the leader of this Military Committee, was a visionary nationalist who had founded St. Enda's school outside Dublin in 1908. Instruction at the school was in Irish and the walls were covered with images of Irish heroes.

When O'Donovan Rossa died in New York City, the IRB arranged for his burial in Dublin among other nationalist dead. Although the Fenian Brotherhood had virtually disappeared from the scene, the descriptor "Fenian" had been appropriated to identify the militant attitude of the Irish intent on overthrowing British rule. On August 1, 1915, tens of thousands attended the funeral at Glasnevin Cemetery. Pearse, wearing the uniform of an Irish Volunteer, spoke at the graveside of this "unrepentant Fenian."

His stirring speech "on behalf of a new generation that has been re-baptised in the Fenian faith" called for union to achieve the freedom of Ireland. He scorned the "Defenders of this Realm" who had worked "in secret and in the open," thinking they "have purchased half of us and intimidated the other half." Mistakenly, they thought to have foreseen everything and provided against everything. Pearse ended with a prophesy that declared "but the fools, the fools, the fools!—they have left us our Fenian dead, and, while Ireland holds these graves, Ireland unfree shall never be at peace."

On Easter Sunday the following year, the Irish Volunteers led an uprising—originally intended to be nationwide, but confined mostly to Dublin. On April 23, 1916, Pearse as the commander proclaimed the Irish Republic from the steps of Dublin's General Post Office. The rebels held out for five days before Pearse surrendered to the British forces. Within the month, Ireland had a new set of martyrs; he and fourteen others, after facing perfunctory military courts-martial, were shot by ones and twos over a period of days in the courtyard of Kilmainham gaol.

The party advocating Irish independence swept the general election of mid-December of 1918, right after the end of World War I. Sinn Fein—the Irish for "we ourselves" that indicated both a desire for self-government and a reliance on achieving it without depending on outside help—took three-quarters of the seats, even though nearly half of its candidates were in British prisons. In the six counties of Ulster where Unionists prevailed, the nationalist program was rejected.

On January 21, 1919, as the international Peace Conference opened in Paris, the Irish convened their first parliament since 1800 when the Dáil Éireann met in Dublin to declare both independence for Ireland and that a state of war existed with Great Britain. The first attack on British rule came that same day when two constables were killed in Tipperary and the explosives they were guarding were stolen by the rebels.

For the next two years, the country was torn by a hit and run war of small-scale assaults. The Irish had finally learned that they could not defeat the British in a conventional conflict. Using guerrilla tactics inspired in part by the Boer War, Michael Collins waged a campaign of assassinations and bombings that in 1921 brought about a treaty partitioning the country. (Knowing of the opposition within the Irish Republican Army to any partition, Collins remarked that by signing the treaty he had signed his own death warrant.) Ulster remained within the United Kingdom under the provisions of the agreement, a stipulation which split the Irish nationalists into pro-treaty and anti-treaty factions.

A bitter civil war ensued between the nationalist wings as the Republicans who insisted on a united Ireland fought the Free State forces led by Collins, commander in chief of the new national army. Collins was also president of the secretive IRB that descended in a direct line from the movement founded by Stephens and O'Mahony and supported over the years by dedicated Irishmen like Lonergan. The tragedy of factionalism that had plagued the Fenian Brotherhood repeated itself as Irish prisoners were again shot in Kilmainham gaol, this time by the Irish Free State government.

Collins himself entered the near-mythical realm of Irish hero-martyrs when he was killed in an ambush in his native County Cork on August 22, 1922, close to the end of the civil war. Although accompanied by an armored car—named "Slievenamon"—for protection, his small column of vehicles was attacked by Republican diehards at Béal na mBláth. Despite urging by his comrades to take shelter from the rifle fire inside "Slievenamon" (as Finn McCool had once found refuge within the mountain itself), Collins chose instead to fight in the open and paid with his life.

An outpouring of national mourning marked the funeral of the young warrior in Dublin's Pro-Cathedral and his burial at Glasnevin might well be considered the end of the Fenian movement. Although death in battle could be seen as fitting for the head of the IRB, his loss was marked by the sad irony that he was slain by a fellow countryman who was fighting for a united and independent Ireland.

AFTER JOHN LONERGAN DIED, his American-born family stayed on in Montreal. Roseanna applied for a widow's pension on September 6, 1902, and payments from the United States government were sent to her monthly until her death. (The last monthly check was for $30.00.) She lived until February 19, 1923, long enough to see John's dream of a free Ireland fulfilled, at least in part. Residing in the Dominion of Canada, any celebration by Lonergan's family of Erin's liberation from British rule must surely have been muted.

Thomas Francis Lonergan, John's only surviving son, lived to age 86, but never married. With his passing, this branch of the Lonergan family name died out in 1956. After studying for the priesthood in Montreal and France, Thomas had a career as a newspaperman that spanned almost forty years with the editorial staff of the *Gazette*. His obituary noted that he was "an enthusiastic collector of books with an extensive library" and "also a student of American and church history." Thomas provided the information for the biographical sketch of his father that was included in the history of the 13th Vermont, consulting John's papers in doing so. His father's personal papers that could provide details of John's life and the library amassed by Thomas have since unfortunately disappeared.

Although the uniform that Capt. John Lonergan wore at the battle of Gettysburg has been advertised for sale by a collector of Civil War memorabilia, some of the artifacts from John's military service remain in the hands of his descendants. Along with his canteen (at times no doubt filled with something stronger than water) and two swords, the family has proudly retained his Medal of Honor.

This award brought the story of Lonergan's life full circle in 1962. The Civil War Centennial Commission was established in 1957 to commemorate the passage of one hundred years since the conflict. (The chairman was Gen. Ulysses S. Grant III and one member was Senator Joseph O'Mahony from Wyoming.) At the time, the country was beginning to deal more directly with unresolved issues of racial equality that extended long before the Civil War. A growing civil rights movement made any national recognition of this anniversary politically explosive and the commission mostly left the organization of events up to the individual states.

However, Washington was the appropriate venue for some national aspects of the Centennial that reached beyond any state or region. One such gathering was held at the White House on April 28, 1962, only six months shy of one hundred years since Lonergan's "Irish company" had mustered into the 13th Vermont. President John F. Kennedy invited the immediate descendants of Union servicemen who had received the Medal of Honor for action in the Civil War to be his guests for a special tour of the White House.

Over 1,500 Medals of Honor had been granted to members of the Union forces during the rebellion. These men were all long since dead at the time of Kennedy's ceremony. A search for the children of these veterans found only three surviving offspring. One of these three was John Lonergan's daughter Roseanna.

Still spry at age 86, Mrs. Timothy Francis Slattery flew down from Montreal to take part in the White House tour and other special events. Roseanna attributed her health and good spirits at this age to her love of the outdoors as a young girl in Vermont. Lonergan's long exile to the village of Lincoln thus may have counted as a positive factor in bringing up his son and three daughters.

Her father's Medal of Honor was placed on display in a glass case with others in the Washington Cathedral. Kennedy told Roseanna and the rest of the group of about 300 descendants gathered on the lawn, "your credentials to come into the White House are second to none." British Prime Minister Harold Macmillan, who was also visiting at the time, added his remarks about

Monument to Captain John Lonergan
in Carrick on Suir, dedicated May 8, 2010

"the courage which your forebears showed" in earning their decorations. (Macmillan would have been unaware of Lonergan's courage in trying to overthrow British rule of Ireland.)

As she listened to the President of the United States welcoming her visit, perhaps Roseanna thought of her father's quest to improve the lot of the Irish people. As a lad, John had come to an America where prejudice warned that "No Irish Need Apply." Now his daughter was the honored guest of an Irish Catholic who had achieved the highest office in the land. The heroism of Irishmen during the Civil War had contributed to the acceptance of the immigrants as Americans. Moreover, despite all the disappointments and failures suffered by the Fenian Brotherhood, John Lonergan, to his credit, had helped make it possible for Ireland to take its place among the nations of the world once again.

AUTHOR'S NOTE

A DECADE AGO, JOHN LONERGAN reached out from his final resting place in Burlington, Vermont, some thirty miles (as the spirit flies) from where I live, and challenged me to tell his story.

Here in northern Vermont, two transitional periods are generally added to the usual four seasons. In the spring, our "mud season" turns dirt roads into bottomless mire as the frost comes out of the ground. Then, from late October until the snow inevitably arrives, we deal with "stick season," when the vivid foliage of autumn blows into sodden piles under the bare-branched hardwood trees.

In the fall, the ancient Celts celebrated Samhain—the mid-point between the harvest festival of Lughnasa and the winter solstice, Imbolc—as the time when portals open from the underworld into the realm of the living. We call it Halloween now, but its spiritual attributes remain the same. At this time of year in particular, then, it may be possible to receive a message from beyond the grave.

At the end of October ten years ago, I was spending the evenings comfortably reading next to my woodstove. Ignoring the blustery cold outside, I studied the history of Vermont's units in the American Civil War. Howard Coffin's popular book on the short-term Vermont regiments, *Nine Months to Gettysburg*, had sparked my interest in Captain John Lonergan with its several references to the exploits of his "Irish Company." My own Irish heritage motivated me to learn more about the man and his times.

After pondering the subject for some weeks, I realized that at some point I had decided—or perhaps had been ordered by Lonergan's spirit—to write this book. The mission of discovering and sharing what I could of the Fenian's life has literally haunted me since that time.

Although I am not related to Lonergan, I feel a certain kinship with him. We were born almost exactly one hundred years apart, but in quite different surroundings. Lonergan first saw the soft light of Ireland among the green hills of Tipperary on the Suir River boundary with County Waterford in April of 1837. Harsh rays of Texas sun greeted me in the flat, dusty town of Laredo in May of 1937 on the Rio Grande River, our border with Mexico. Starting from very different and distant places, our paths have converged in the Green Mountains of Vermont. Lonergan started his life in the shadow of Slievenamon; mine is finishing at the foot of Mount Mansfield—which in the Irish would be Slieve na Mansfield.

The Lonergan family and the McKeons (as my surname was once spelled) both left Ireland around the same time and for the same reasons, bad potatoes and worse politics. The head of my branch of the McKeon family was a blacksmith in the village of Killucan, near Mullingar in County Westmeath. He thus was of the same artisan class as the Lonergans, who were coopers. Our family's oral history claims that this ancestor was a rebel and escaped Ireland with a price on his head.

Both emigrating families had sons named John who were born in Ireland and fought for the Union in the Civil War, volunteering in 1862. My great-grandfather served three years with the 86th Illinois Infantry Regiment, marched with Sherman to the sea, and paraded through Washington as part of that army at the end of the war. John McKeon saw his share of fighting, but he receives no mention in any history book. His regiment comprised a mix of ethnic groups, mainly Yankee and German with a scattering of Irish and other nationalities. Though I have found no record of his membership, he probably belonged to the Fenian Brotherhood like so many other Irish soldiers.

In 2002, I organized a graveside ceremony to pay respects to Lonergan on the 100th anniversary of his death. The Burlington *Free Press* and WCAX, the local television station, covered the event, which was attended by a small group of spectators in addition to the invited participants. An honor guard of Veterans of Foreign Wars was joined by a bugler and a rifle squad from the Vermont Air Guard, modern-day Green Mountain Boys.

After my brief introductory remarks, Father John McSweeney, a relative of the Lonergan family, offered a prayer. Howard Coffin spoke about the importance of the Civil War and Lonergan's role in the conflict. Irish-

AUTHOR'S NOTE

ST. JOSEPH'S CEMETERY, 100TH ANNIVERSARY OF LONERGAN'S DEATH

born Colonel Michael Gately of the Vermont Air Guard shared a personal perspective on patriotism to both Ireland and the United States. Auburn-haired Kathleen Knight, wearing a traditional long green Irish cloak, then stepped forward with a wreath that she had fashioned from wild grapevine and hemlock sprigs, decorated with an emerald-green ribbon.

Assisted by the colonel, she placed the wreath between the Irish and American flags set at the foot of Lonergan's tombstone. Three volleys of rifle fire crashed out at solemn intervals and the bugler rendered "Taps" while the military saluted and the civilians bowed their heads.

The last plaintive note was fading when I imagined a voice coming into my head from Lonergan's grave. "A grand show this, for sure," he seemed to growl, "but where is the book about me life?"

So, Captain, here 'tis, at last—may we both rest more quietly now that it is done.

Samhain 2009

Terry Flynn and the author on the old bridge in Carrick on Suir

The author and Wattie Dumphy on Slievenamon

ACKNOWLEDGMENTS

MY DECISION TO SELF-PUBLISH this book has succeeded only through the dedicated efforts of what I call "Team Fenian," the talented group of professionals who agreed to apply their skills to the project. More experienced in publication than I, they knew even at the start how long the process can take. Without their encouragement and support, no doubt I would have despaired of ever finishing the book. Fortunately, we all live in the same area of northern Vermont and were able to meet frequently in person during production.

As editor, Katherine Quimby Johnson effectively pared my rambling narrative into a tighter and more compelling story, often testing passages on her husband, Greg. In addition to guiding me as a writer, she also compiled the index and recruited a student from her copy editing class at Champlain College to proofread the manuscript. Jennifer Lunney carefully noted the corrections necessary before publication, helping to avoid a number of embarrassing errors of style and punctuation.

Until naively embarking on this book, I was ignorant of the role of the designer in the production. My good luck held, however, when I chanced to meet Carrie Cook, who has applied her artistic skills to ensure that the story is presented in a visually attractive manner. Carrie worked her magic on old photos and documents, produced maps, and designed the cover, as well as developing the overall look of the product. Peter Cook, her husband, helped considerably with the production, drawing on his many years of experience as a printer. Kathleen Knight provided photos and art work for the project, while also encouraging my efforts over the past ten years. Sadly, an original member of our team, Ronnie Little, passed away before the manuscript was completed; his input to the process has been sorely missed.

The impetus for telling Lonergan's story began when I read Howard Coffin's books on Vermont's role in the Civil War. The tantalizing bits about Lonergan sparked my interest to a degree not anticipated when I first started to search out further information on the man and his times. Although this project has occupied the better part of a decade, I am grateful for being introduced to Lonergan and for Howard's continuing activities to bring history alive for so many people.

Portions of the manuscript were read by people I asked to steer me through complex subjects. I particularly appreciate the time spent by Andrew Ward, registered Gettysburg guide, to provide his comments on the battle there, and by Paul Zeller, who wrote the authoritative history on Vermont's 2nd Regiment and reviewed my account of Lonergan's experience with that unit. It was reassuring to have Michael Ruddy cast his expert eye on my treatment of the Fenian Brotherhood's history. Vince Feeney not only wrote the foreword to this book, but also checked my information on the Irish in Vermont. Other historians, authors, and members of the Civil War community—too many to name individually without risking the omission of some—have likewise been without exception helpful, generous, and encouraging. Researching and writing this book has given me access to this multifaceted group and I trust that the product merits their collective approval. Any and all errors of fact or interpretation are, of course, mine.

A grant from the Chittenden County Historical Society provided me much-appreciated resources that were applied to seeking out relevant local history. The League of Vermont Writers has repeatedly revived my enthusiasm as an author with useful workshops and inspiring speakers.

A number of librarians and archivists patiently assisted me in collecting information on Lonergan and his era. Most of my exploration naturally took place in Vermont, where I was helped by many people in addition to those singled out here; I thank all of you for your support.

I would like to express my appreciation to the following individuals and organizations specifically;

Here in Vermont, I want to thank librarian Paul Carnahan and his staff at the Vermont Historical Society Library in Barre; the University of Vermont's Baily Howe Library, where I extensively studied the microfilm of Civil War-era newspapers, aided by helpful work-study students, and spent many hours in its Special Collections, now headed by Jeffery Marshal; the Vermont Military Records archives at Middlesex; the Secretary of State Archives in Montpelier—Gregory Sanford, the State Archivist, and his experienced colleagues guided me to valuable information available nowhere else; and State Curator David Schutz, who provided the image of the Middleton painting for the cover and frontispiece.

Elsewhere in North America, the National Archives and Records Administration in Washington, DC; the U.S. Army Military History Institute, Carlisle, Pennsylvania; Dolores Elder at the Occoquan Historical Society and

ACKNOWLEDGMENTS

Susan Gray at the Fairfax Museum and Visitor Center, both in Virginia; and the Gettysburg National Military Park records all were valuable sources of information. In Canada, the National Archives in Ottawa gave me access to the perspective of British North America and the Dominion. At the Eastern Townships Research Center of Bishop's University, Sherbrooke, Québec, archivist Chloe Southam provided photos of the Fenian raid of 1870.

In Lonergan's home town of Carrick on Suir, the local branch of the Tipperary Libraries and the Heritage Center assisted me for days on end as I combed through local records for any information on the family before it left Ireland. The late Patrick Power, who wrote the authoritative study of Carrick's history, kindly met with me to share his knowledge of the area. On my several visits to Carrick, many doors were opened and hospitality extended. In particular, I would like to thank Dolores and John Lonergan—namesake of the man whose story is told here—for my time at their bed and breakfast, which included many trips around the region together.

Other folks in the area who have become good friends include Walter "Wattie" Dunphy, who in 2008 led the members of "Team Fenian" up Slievenamon to Finn's cairn on a clear day when we could see for miles and centuries in all directions. Terry Flynn and Maria Madden helped make our stay a most memorable one during the Clancy Brothers Festival, and Maria's brother, Martin, reliably bused us to various historical sites. Jean Morris lives in England, but her father is from Carrick; she has long been a fan of Captain John Lonergan and, as an author herself, has encouraged my work to document his life. Michael Coady, noted Carrick poet, has supported both my book and the erection of a monument to Lonergan in Carrick in May of 2010.

Lonergan's descendants in Canada and Australia graciously shared what information they have about Captain John, including photos of the man and of those artifacts that they retain. Although I want to express my thanks for their cooperation, at their request their names are not included here, out of respect for their privacy.

Finally, my thanks to Tim Dilli of United Book Press in Baltimore, Maryland, for his extensive tour of the print shop there and his patience with my elusive deadline for sending the book to him.

Gur a mile maith agaibh go leir—many thanks to all of you.

APPENDICES

Appendix A

Roster of Company A, 13th Vermont Volunteer Infantry Regiment

(From the *Revised Roster of Vermont Volunteers*
by Theodore S. Peck, Adjutant General, 1892)

Abbreviations:
Des. – deserted, **Disab.** – disability, **Disch.** – discharged,
Prom. – promoted, **Red.** – reduced, **Tr.** – transferred,
Wd. – wounded, **wds. recd.** – wounds received

Note the absence of any entries for Lonergan's
"Date of Commis'n" [date of commission] and **"Date of Issue."**
No other record for an officer in Peck's roster omits both these entries.

THIRTEENTH REGIMENT.

COMPANY A.

Name and Rank.	Residence.	Date of Commis'n.	Date of Issue.	Remarks.
Captain. John Lonergan,	Burlington,			Must. out July 21, '63.
1st Lieutenant. John T. Sinnott,	Rutland,	Sept. 11,'62	Oct. 4,'62	Died July 6, '63, of wds. recd. July 3, '63.
2d Lieutenant. David McDevitt,	Rutland.	Sept. 11,'62	Oct. 4,'62	Must. out July 21, '63.

Name and Rank.	Residence.	Date of Enlistment	Date of Muster.	Remarks.
Sergeants. Alvin H. Henry,	Westford,	Aug. 10,'62	Oct. 10,'62	Red. to Sergt. Apr. 30, '63; Must. out July 21, '63.
James B. Scully,	Burlington,	Aug. 15,'62	Oct. 10,'62	Prom. 1st Sergt. Apr. 30, '63; Must. out July 21, '63.
Thomas Blake,	Rutland,	Aug. 26,'62	Oct. 10,'62	Killed in action July 3, '63.
Fayette W. Burtch,	Westford,	Aug. 23,'62	Oct. 10,'62	Must. out July 21, '63.
Corporals. John Patten,	Rutland,	Aug. 25,'62	Oct. 10,'62	Must. out July 21, '63.
Thomas Traynor,	Rutland,	Aug. 30,'62	Oct. 10,'62	Prom. Sergt. July 3, '63 ; Must. out July 21, '63.
Thomas J. Culligan,	Williston,	Sept. 22,'62	Oct. 10,'62	Must. out July 21, '63.
Timothy Cummings,	Rutland,	Aug. 22,'62	Oct. 10,'62	Must. out July 21, '63.
Torrey W. Sibley,	Westford,	Aug. 23,'62	Oct. 10,'62	Wd. July 3, '63; Must. out Aug. — '63.
Jacob S. Drew,	Westford,	Aug. 19,'62	Oct. 10,'62	Died July 12, '63, of disease.
Allen G. Frisbie,	Westford,	Aug. 22,'62	Oct. 10,'62	Must. out July 21, '63.
Michael McEnery,	Rutland,	Aug. 25,'62	Oct. 10,'62	Red. ; killed in action July 3, '63.

VERMONT'S IRISH REBEL

Name and Rank.	Residence.	Date of Commis'n.	Date of Issue.	Remarks.
Musicians.				
Otis N. Rublee,	Middlesex,	Aug. 25, '62	Oct. 10, '62	Must. out July 21, '63.
Julius F. Goodrich,	Westford,	Aug. 22, '62	Oct. 10, 62	Must. out July 21, '63.
Wagoner				
David T. Hard,	Essex,	Aug. 19, '62	Oct. 10, '62	Must. out July 21, '63.
Privates.				
Allen, Heman W.	Westford,	Aug. 23, '62	Oct. 10, '62	Must. out July 21, '63.
Ashey, John	Westford,	Aug. 23, '62	Oct. 10, '62	Must. out July 21, '63.
Ayers, Joseph	Rutland,	Aug. 23, '62	Oct. 10, '62	Died Jan. 27, '63, of disease.
Bixby, Freeman	Montpelier,	Aug. 25, '62	Oct. 10, '62	See Hospital Steward.
Breslin, Barney	Rutland,	Aug. 26, '62	Oct. 10, '62	Disch. Jan. 24, '63, for disab.
Brewin, John	Burlington,	Sept. 8, '62	Oct. 10, '62	Must. out July 21, '63.
Cain, John	Burlington,	Oct. 3, '62	Oct. 10, '62	Must. out July 21, '63.
Cannon, Feargus	Montpelier,	Oct. 10, '62	Oct. 10, '62	Tr to Co. H. Oct. 10, '62.
Cannon, Michael	Burlington,	Sept. 13, '62	Oct. 10, '62	Must. out July 21, '63.
Clark, Martin L.	Highgate,	Sept. 11, '62	Oct. 10, '62	Tr. to Co. K. Mch. 15, '63.
Collins, John	Rutland,	Sept. 19, '62	Oct. 10, '62	Must. out July 21, '63.
Corey, James	Rutland,	Sept. 2, '62	Oct. 10, '62	Must. out July 21, '63.
Corey, Patrick	Rutland,	Sept. 1, '62	Oct. 10, '62	Killed in action July 3, '63.
Crowley, John	Rutland,	Aug. 26, '62	Oct. 10, '62	Prom. Corp. Dec. 12, '62; Must. out July 21, '63.
Crawford, Stephen O	Westford,	Aug. 23, '62	Oct. 10, '62	Must. out July 21, '63.
Cusack, James	Burlington,	Sept. 2, '62	Oct. 10, '62	Must. out July 21, '63.
Daniels, Charles	Westford,	Aug. 23, '62	Oct. 10, '62	Must. out July 21, '63.
Desmond, Cornelius	Burlington,	Sept. 1, '62	Oct. 10, '62	Des Oct. 30, '62.
Donnelly, Anthony	Rutland,	Sept. 19, '62	Oct. 10, '62	Must. out July 21, '63.
English, John	Rutland,	Aug. 26, '62	Oct. 10, '62	Must. out July 21, '63.
Farrell, Thomas	Rutland,	Aug. 26, '62	Oct. 10, '62	Must. out July 21, '63.
Fisk, Joshua	Burlington,	Sept. 13, '62	Oct. 10, '62	Des. Dec. 12, '62.
Garrity, Peter	Rutland,	Aug. 27, '62	Oct. 10, '62	Must. out July 21, '63.
Gleason, Timothy	Wallingford,	Sept. 1, '62	Oct. 10, '62	Must. out July 21, '63.
Guinnetts, Adolphus	Rutland,	Aug. 26, '62	Oct. 10, '62	Wd. July 3, '63; Must. out July 21, '63.
Hamlin, John	Burlington,	Oct. 10, '62	Oct. 10, '62	Wd July 3, '63; Must. out July 21, '63.
Horrigan, John	Burlington,	Sept. 1, '62	Oct. 10, '62	Must. out July 21, '63.
Joyce, Patrick	Rutland,	Sept. 27, '62	Oct. 10, '62	Must. out July 21, '63.
Knowles, James	Rutland,	Aug. 26, '62	Oct. 10, '62	Must. out July 21, '63.
Lamb, Nicholas	Rutland,	Sept. 15, '62	Oct. 10, '62	Died July 4, '63.
Lang, John	Burlington,	Sept. 26, '62	Oct. 10, '62	Must. out July 21, '63.
Lynch, Thomas	Rutland,	Aug. 26, '62	Oct. 10, '62	Must. out July 21, '63.
Lyons, Edward	Rutland,	Aug. 25, '62	Oct. 10, '62	Must. out July 21, '63.
Maloy, Martin	Burlington,	Oct. 3, '62	Oct. 10, '62	Wd. July 3, '63; Disch. July 31, '63.
Mangan, Patrick	Rutland,	Aug. 29, '62	Oct. 10, '62	Must. out July 21, '63.
Martin, Lewis	Westford,	Aug. 23, '62	Oct. 10, '62	Must. out July 21, '63.
McEnerny, Patrick	Rutland,	Aug. 26, '62	Oct. 10, '62	Must. out July 21, '63.
McLaughlin, Joseph	Rutland,	Aug. 25, '62	Oct. 10, '62	Must. out July 21, '62.
McMahon, Patrick	Rutland,	Aug. 26, '62	Oct. 10, '62	Must. out July 21, '63.
McNellis, Edward	Burlington,	Aug. 19, '62	Oct. 10, '62	Must. out July 21, '63.
Miller, Robert H.	Burlington,	Aug. 23, '62	Oct. 10, '62	Must. out July 21, '63.
Moylan, Michael	Rutland,	Sept. 2, '62	Oct. 10, '62	Killed in action July 3, '63
Newgint, John	Burlington,	Sept. 1, '62	Oct. 10, '62	Must. out July 21, '63.
O'Laughlin, Michael	Rutland,	Sept. 4, '62	Oct. 10, '62	Must. out July 21, '63.
O'Neil, Michael	Burlington,	Aug. 20, '62	Oct. 10, '62	Must. out July 21, '63.
Quilty, Michael	Rutland,	Aug. 28, '62	Oct. 10, '62	Must. out July 21, '63.
Ransom, Samuel H.	Burlington,	Aug. 25, '62	Oct. 10, '62	Disch. July 21, '63.
Ready, Patrick	Burlington,	Sept. 17, '62	Oct. 10, '62	Must. out July 21, '63.
Reed, Isaac	Rutland,	Sept. 13, '62	Oct. 10, '62	Must. out July 21, '63.
Richardson, Alden	Westford,	Aug. 23, '62	Oct. 10, '62	Died Jan. 11, '63, of disease.
Ryan, William	Georgia,	Aug. 28, '62	Oct. 10, '62	Must. out July 21, '63.
Salmon, William	Rutland,	Aug. 26, '62	Oct. 10, '62	Must. out July 21, '63.
Segar, Paul	Burlington,	Sept. 10, '62	Oct. 10, '62	Must. out July 21, '63.
Shanahan, John	Burlington,	Aug. 31, '62	Oct. 10, '62	Wd. July 3, '63; Must. out July 21, '63.
Sheridan, Barthol'mew	Rutland,	Aug. 26, '62	Oct. 10, '62	Must. out July 21, '63.
Shiatt, Peter	Burlington,	Aug. 31, '62	Oct. 10, '62	Must. out July 21, '63.
Stapleton, Patrick	Rutland,	Aug. 22, '62	Oct. 10, '62	Must. out July 21, '63.
Sullivan, John	Rutland,	Aug. 28, '62	Oct. 10, '62	Must. out July 21, '63.
Swan, Albert	Westford,	Aug. 23, '62	Oct. 10, '62	Must. out July 21, '63.
Tisdelle, Albert	Westford,	Aug. 23, '62	Oct. 10, '62	Must. out July 21, '63.
Tully, Terence	Rutland,	Aug. 22, '62	Oct. 10, '62	Prom. Corp July 3, '63; Must. out July 21, '63.
Vedelle, Israel	Burlington,	Aug. 23, '62	Oct. 10, '62	Must. out July 21, '63
Wallace, Joseph	Milton,	Sept. 13, '62	Oct. 10, '62	Wd. July 3, '63; Must. out July 21, '63.
Weeks, Joseph	Burlington,	Sept. 19, '62	Oct. 10, '62	Prom. Sergt. Dec. 12, '62; Must. out July 21, '63.
Woodruff, Edgar	Westford,	Aug. 23, '62	Oct. 10, '62	Must. out July 21, '63.
Woodruff, William	Westford,	Aug. 23, '62	Oct. 10, '62	Wd. July 3, '63; Must. out July 21, '63.

Appendix B

Status of manpower in Union Army at the end of 1862

UNION AUTHORITIES.

Consolidated abstract from returns of the U. S. Army on or about December 31, 1862.

Command.	Present for duty. Officers.	Present for duty. Men.	Aggregate present.	Aggregate present and absent.	Date of return.
Department of the Cumberland a (Rosecrans).	3,342	61,621	74,555	119,175	Dec. 31, 1862
Department of the East (Wool)	127	2,548	3,473	4,019	Jan. 31, 1863
Department of the Gulf (Banks)	1,471	29,782	36,508	42,074	Dec. 31, 1862
Middle Department (Schenck)	528	11,656	13,332	15,391	Do.
Department of the Missouri (Curtis)	2,264	43,602	59,162	75,082	Do.
Department of New Mexico (Carleton)	111	2,275	3,011	3,638	Do.
Department of North Carolina (Foster)	821	17,642	21,917	27,385	Do.
Department of the Northwest (Pope)	241	5,286	6,182	8,934	Do.
Department of the Ohio (H. G. Wright)	2,784	57,045	70,183	86,652	Do.
Department of the Pacific (George Wright)	239	4,138	5,721	6,082	Do.
Department (or Army) of the Potomac (Burnside).	7,984	148,787	185,386	267,379	Do.
Department of the South (Brannan)	447	10,428	13,370	14,464	Do.
Department of the Tennessee (Grant)	2,330	44,262	53,540	67,479	Do.
Department of Virginia (Dix)	945	18,759	22,787	25,898	Do.
Defenses of Washington (Heintzelman)	2,153	46,911	66,603	71,865	Do.
District of West Virginia b (Cox)	1,061	24,368	28,433	33,074	Do.
Total	26,848	529,110	664,163	868,591	

a Less post forces at Bowling Green, Ky., also reported in the Department of the Ohio. These troops had 111 officers and 1,721 men for duty; 2,170 aggregate present, and 4,227 aggregate present and absent.

b Ewing's brigade (about 2,600 strong) left this district December 28, 1862, en route to the Department of the Tennessee (Grant). It is not borne on any returns for December, 1862.

OR, Series III, Volume II, page 957

Appendix C

Selected order of battle, Gettysburg

UNION ARMY OF THE POTOMAC

Maj. Gen. George G. Meade

<u>First Army Corps</u> – Maj. Gen. John F. Reynolds,
Maj. Gen. Abner Doubleday

First Division – Brig. Gen. James S. Wadsworth

Second Division – Brig. Gen. John C. Robinson
Maj. Gen. John Newton

<u>Third Division</u> – Brig. Gen. Thomas A. Rowley
Maj. Gen. Abner Doubleday

First Brigade – Col. Chapman Biddle
Brig. Gen. Thomas A. Rowley

Second Brigade – Col. Roy Stone
Col. Langhorne Wister
Col. Edmund I. Dana

<u>Third Brigade</u> – Brig. Gen. George J. Stannard
Col. Francis. V. Randall

12th Vermont – Col. Asa P. Blunt
<u>13th Vermont</u> – Col. Francis V. Randall
Lt. Col. William D. Munson
Maj. Joseph J. Boynton
14th Vermont – Col. William T. Nichols
15th Vermont – Col. Redfield Proctor
16th Vermont – Col. Wheelock G. Veazey

UNION ARMY OF THE POTOMAC

Second Army Corps – Maj. Gen. Winfield S. Hancock

Third Army Corps – Maj. Gen. Daniel E. Sickles

Fifth Army Corps – Maj. Gen. George Sykes

Sixth Army Corps – Maj. Gen. John Sedgwick

Eleventh Army Corps – Maj. Gen. Oliver O. Howard

Twelfth Army Corps – Maj. Gen. Henry W. Slocum

Cavalry Corps – Maj. Gen. Alfred Pleasanton

CONFEDERATE ARMY OF NORTHERN VIRGINIA

Gen. Robert E. Lee

First Army Corps – Lt. Gen. James Longstreet
    McLaw's Division – Maj. Gen. Lafayette McLaws
    Pickett's Division – Maj. Gen. George E. Pickett
        Garnett's Brigade – Brig. Gen. Robert B. Garnett
        Kemper's Brigade – Brig. Gen. James L. Kemper
            1st VA – Col. Lewis B. Williams
            3rd VA – Col. Joseph Mayo, Jr.
            7th VA – Col. Waller T. Patton
            11th VA – Maj. Kirkwood Otey
            24th VA – Col. William R. Terry
        Armistead's Brigade – Brig. Gen. Lewis A. Armistead
    Hood's Division – Maj. Gen. John B. Hood

Second Army Corps – Lt. Gen. Richard S. Ewell
    Early's Division – Maj. Gen. Jubal A. Early
        Gordon's Brigade – Brig. Gen. John B. Gordon
    Rodes Division – Maj. Gen. Robert E. Rodes
    Johnson's Division – Maj. Gen. Edward Johnson

Third Army Corps – Lt. Gen. Ambrose P. Hill

Cavalry Division – Maj. Gen. James E. B. Stuart

Appendix D

Lonergan's July 2 combat at Gettysburg

Not surprisingly, the details of Col. Randall's wild charge down to Emmitsburg Road on July 2 vary among the sources describing the bold recovery of the Union cannon. While most reports agree on the basic facts, two aspects of the isolated action in the twilight deserve some clarification, where possible.

First, there is the question of whether the cannon retrieved by the Vermonters were restricted to Weir's weapons just taken by the rebels and who reached them first. Probably only the four Union guns were recaptured by the five companies of the 13th led by Randall, although the citation for Lonergan's Medal of Honor credits him with participating in "the capture of two additional guns from the enemy." Maj. Gen. Doubleday uses these figures in his report on action by the Third Division, First Corps, which he commanded in the battle, probably taking them from Stannard's report dated July 4. Randall wrote his account of the action on July 10 while camped at Middletown, Maryland, and he repeated in a letter in 1869 his claim of "the retaking of Hancock's guns and the capture of two guns from the rebels". Randall insisted "the rebels had advanced two pieces of artillery into the road about 100 rods to the south of us, and commenced to shell us down the road, whereupon I detached one company and advanced them...."

As ordered by Randall, Co. C moved down the Emmitsburg Road to seize the supposed cannon to the south. Two enlisted members of that unit later stated that the company found only caissons which had been destroyed. In the fading light, the wheeled remains of the caissons could easily have been taken for guns from a distance, although this does not explain Randall's belief that he had seen cannon fire from that direction. This confusion may be the origin of the idea that two Confederate cannon had been captured along with the Union guns recovered. In 1867, Benedict even published an account detailing that Randall had captured "two 12 lb. brass guns, brought down by the enemy while following up the 3rd corps."

Lonergan was satisfied with his role in retrieving the Union cannon and he did not offer any information on the capture of rebel guns. Rebel accounts apparently do not record the loss of any cannon to Union soldiers in this fight (or elsewhere in the battle).

In Sturtevant's history of the 13th, he cautions that he cannot say with any confidence how many cannon had been retaken or if any Confederate guns had been captured since he was not present in the action. He does credit 1st Sgt. Scott of Co. G with being the first man to lay hands on the Union cannon, although Lonergan also claims that distinction in his application for the Medal of Honor and Randall corroborates the fact. In a speech on Gettysburg that Scott gave in 1870, he had Randall being "one of the first to reach the battery with Capt. Lonergan by his side." Scott went on to state that two guns were withdrawn by the artillerymen and "four were passed to the rear by hand by men of the Thirteenth."

Even more problematic is the identification of the farm house where Lonergan captured a group of rebel soldiers. The Vermonters involved could not have known the name of the house during the action itself and must have identified it later, presumably from detailed maps of the battle. Some accounts have Co. A operating alone in clearing the Confederates from the house, while others state that Co. C helped in the capture.

Sturtevant's history long after the fact, apparently influenced by letters from Lt. Clarke, states in the section about Co. G that Clarke's company was in front of the Rogers house and returned fire coming from it. Lonergan then supposedly took Co. A to the rear of the house and the regimental adjutant, James Peck, demanded and received the surrender of the rebels at the front door. However, in the section on Co. A, Sturtevant lets stand the narrative that Randall ordered Lonergan to capture the rebels and "there was no hesitation to comply." Scott in his 1870 speech reverses the process and describes how Lonergan reported "a house" (not further identified) full of rebels to Randall, who then personally captured the group.

Not only were there disputes later as to what unit or units took the Confederates prison, the location and identification of the house itself is questionable. The sequence of events, drawing on a composite of the various sources, appears mostly likely to have involved the five companies returning to the Emmitsburg Road in a rough line of battle, after returning the four re-captured Union cannon to the artillerymen. Coming straight down the slope to the road, Company A, on the right of the line, would probably have been approaching the Codori House. The left of the formation, containing perhaps 200 men in two ranks, might have stretched 100 yards to the south of that structure, but certainly not all the way to the Rogers house, some 500 yards away. This distance is roughly the same as the "100 rods" to the supposed rebel cannon, as estimated by Randall when he detached Co. C to deal with them.

When Co. C was detailed to move south on the road, this would have left the other four under Randall's command much closer to the Codori house than to the Rogers dwelling. A source of confusion may be the wording of Randall's report since he describes Co. C "most gallantly" seizing the reputed Confederate cannon a quarter of a mile down the road and follows immediately with: "We also captured the rebel picket reserve, consisting of 3 officers and 80 men, who had concealed themselves in a house near by." Use of the phrase "near by" so close to the movement of Co. C to the area of the Rogers house has probably misled some writers to identify that as the location of the rebels who were captured. It seems more likely that Randall meant "near by" the main body of Vermonters, not the detached company, and they were no doubt closer to the Codori house.

Both Randall and Lonergan several times refer to the structure as the Codori (or "Codories") house and never as the Rogers house. Sturtevant edited Randall's letter that is cited in the section on Co. A (p. 432) to conform with what had become the conventional identification of the building. Randall's original letter of July 13, 1869, plainly states "to you & your company belongs the immediate honor of capturing the eighty three prisoners from Codoris house on the Emitsburgh [sic] road. I remember distinctly all the circumstances." Lonergan specifies that he took a group of rebels prisoner at "Codories house" in his application for a medal on October 11, 1893. Surely he would have had ample time by then to correct the name of the house where he had boldly captured the Confederates if he had earlier misidentified it. Since Randall and Lonergan were the two commanders most directly involved, their identification of the building as the Codori farmhouse seems to the author more reliable than that supplied by others who were not involved, such as Benedict.

The number of prisoners taken has usually been cited in the low eighties, though Scott in 1870 quotes Randall as sending back word that he had "taken a hundred prisoners." Benedict, on the other hand, reduces the number in his 1867 publication to forty men captured with their captain; this account may also be the first that identifies the location as "in and about Rogers' house, on the Emmetsburgh [sic] road." Scott stated in his speech that the men were from "an Alabama regiment" without providing any attribution for this information. If the men in fact were taken at the Codori farm, it seems more likely that they would have been Georgians from Wright's brigade that had just been repulsed. Scott may have based an assumption that the prisoners were from Alabama on the presence of Wilcox's brigade of Alabama regiments in the area of the Rogers house.

APPENDICES

NOTES

Part I

Chapter 1

4 – Carraig MacGriffin around 1247: Patrick C. Power, *Carrick-on-Suir and its People,* Dun Laoghaire, Anna Livia Books, 1976, p. 12.

4 – present county boundaries: Damien Enright, *Ireland, County by County,* London, Salamander Books, 1997, p. 7.

5 – only 235 Protestant: *Parliamentary Gazetteer of Ireland 1844-45,* Dublin, A. Fullarton, 1846, Vol. 1, p. 332.

5 – St. Nicholas Church: Isaac Slater, *Commercial Directory of Ireland,* Manchester, 1846, p. 160.

5 – different parish, barony, and county: ibid, p. 161.

5 – Upwards of £7,000: ibid, p. 160.

6 – a most beneficial effect: ibid.

8 – could later be reimbursed: Power, p. 70.

9 – principal trade now: Slater, p. 160.

10 – the poorer, the earlier: Power, p. 109.

11 – returned to Cashel: Eoghan Ó Néill, *The Golden Vale of Ivowen: Between Slievenamon and Suir,* Dublin, Geography Publications, 2001, pp. 506-511.

11 – roughs and toughs: Power, pp. 106-108.

11 – in a delightful situation: Slater, p. 160.

11 – trades and situations provided: ibid, p. 161.

12 – further educating himself: Ralph Orson Sturtevant, *History of the 13th Regiment Vermont Volunteers,* [no publisher given], 1910, p. 427.

13 – a special graveyard: Power, p. 110.

14n – singing the Fianna: Ó Néill, pp. 236, 276.

16 – remembered only as fairies: Peter Berresford Ellis, *Celtic Myths and Legends,* New York, Carroll & Graf, 2002, p. 57.

16 – stringent tests ensured: Seumas MacManus, *The Story of the Irish Race,* The Devin-Adair Company, New York, 1921, p. 65.

18 – Land of Eternal Youth: ibid, p. 70.

Chapter 2

22 – invent noble ancestors: Carmel McCaffrey and Leo Eaton, *In Search of Ancient Ireland,* Chicago, Ivan R. Dee, 2003, p. 230.

24 – declared null and void: MacManus, p. 65.

25 – required to submit: ibid.

28 – His last words: Robert Kee, *The Green Flag: A History of Irish Nationalism,* New York, Penguin Books, 1972, p. 18.

28 – See Kee, p. 19, for the Penal Law provisions.

Chapter 3

33 – Lord Cornwallis had been: Kee, p. 105.

33 – appearance of insurrection: ibid, p. 128.

34 – See, Erin's song: ibid, p. 145.

Chapter 4

53 – sheer brute force: Michael Cavanagh, *Memoirs of Gen. Thomas Francis Meagher*, Worcester, Massachusetts, The Messenger Press, 1892, p. 119. This book is the source of much detail about the 1848 uprising and the Irish role in the American Civil War.

54 – crime of high treason: Cavanagh, p. 120.

54 – smiths and cutlers: ibid, p. 136.

54n – place of honor: ibid, p. 141.

55 – He warned the House: ibid, p. 157.

56 – would join hands: ibid, p. 164.

56 – than ever Sunburst flashed: ibid.

57 – reported upon by government spies: ibid, p.167.

59 – returned to Dublin: ibid, p. 173.

60 – issued a proclamation: ibid, p. 186.

60 – a guilty verdict was achieved: ibid, p. 199.

61 – Mitchel might usefully serve: ibid, p. 205.

61 – The priest shortly thereafter: ibid, p. 212n.

61 – be given enough information: ibid, p. 212.

62 – suppressed in conjunction: Kee, p. 273.

63 – ten years transportation: Cavanagh, p. 219.

63 – where he posted bail: ibid, p. 228.

64 – marched past him: Kee, p. 272.

64 – Cork looks to Dublin: ibid, p. 273.

64 – No more appropriate spot: Cavanagh, p. 273.

65 – Carrick was the centre: ibid, p. 266.

66 – the Rev. Mr. Byrne: Michael Doheny, *The Felon's Track*, Dublin, M.H. Gill & Son, 1914, p 155.

67 – the determined muster: Cavanagh, p. 267.

67 – the making of pikes: Power, p. 115.

68 – the case in County Tipperary: Cavanagh, p. 258.

69 – This left the initiative: Kee, p. 275.

Chapter 5

72 – James Dobbyn was also employed: Kee, p. 274n.

72 – suspension of *habeas corpus:* Thomas Keneally, *The Great Shame,* New York, Anchor Books, 2000, p. 154.

72 – tribe-lands of his ancestral clan: Cavanagh, p. 244.

72 – An emissary was also sent: ibid, p. 245.

73 – able to board a train: ibid, p. 247.

73 – The site of the major battle: ibid, p. 250.

74 – give the signal of insurrection: ibid, p. 251.

74 – prepared to take the field: ibid, p. 251.

74 – three best fighting counties: ibid, p. 252.

74 – urged to be ready: Kee, p. 278.

75 – only one in four had weapons: ibid.

75 – a couple of Earls: Cavanagh, p. 253.

76 – follow Dillon to Tipperary: ibid, p. 255.

76 – In a symbolic gesture: ibid, p. 258.

76 – Not a townland in Tipperary: ibid, p. 257.

76 – if they hadn't guns: Arthur Griffith, *Meagher of the Sword*, Dublin, M.H. Gill & Son, 1916, p. 216.

77 – After dining at the public house: ibid, p. 220.

77 – impressed with Mahony: ibid, p. 224.

77 – He offered the Young Irelanders: ibid, p. 227.

82 – He attributed it: Cavanagh, p. 273.

86 – A vicious man with the talents: Keneally, p. 164.

Chapter 6

89 – In contrast to the consequences: Kee, p. 286.

90 – Recognized and given hospitality: ibid.

91 – At O'Mahony's call: Cavanagh, p. 288.

92 – This attempt at organizing: John O'Leary, *Recollections of Fenians and Feniansim*, London, Downey & Co., 1896, p. 22.

94 – The Sentence is that: Cavanagh, p. 290.

94 – Earlier in Queen Victoria's reign: Kee, p. 287.

95 – My lords, you may deem: Cavanagh, pp. 292-294.

96 – The condemned men were returned: ibid, p. 294.

96 – He eventually reached sanctuary: Power, p. 117.

100 – Of the estimated 100,000 Irish: Edward Laxton, *The Famine Ships: The Irish Exodus to America*, New York, Henry Holt and Company, 1996, p. 40.

Part II

Chapter 7

107 – Most Irish who came: Lawrence J. McCaffrey, *The Irish Diaspora in America*, Bloomington, London, Indiana University Press, 1976, p. 63.

107 – Their route to Vermont: Vincent E. Feeney, *Finnigans, Slaters, and Stonepeggers: A History of the Irish in Vermont*, Bennington, Vermont, Images from the Past, 2009, p. 24.

108 – Often facing a hostile: ibid, p. 43.

109 – A fort built in 1666: Michael Sherman, Gene Sessions, and P. Jeffery Potash, *Freedom and Unity – A History of Vermont*, Barre, Vermont, Vermont Historical Society, 2004, p. 45.

110 – In 1770, Ethan Allen: ibid, p. 84.

110 – On May 10, 1775: ibid, p. 96.

111 – Burgoyne wrote that: ibid, p. 109.

111 – Allen met with: ibid, p. 114.

113 – Chittenden appointed Ira Allen: ibid, p. 131.

114 – Legislation had been passed: ibid, p. 145.

114 – Resentment of British rule: ibid, p. 192.

116 – In Vermont, the earlier Irish: Feeney, pp. 27-33.

118 – One of the largest ports: Sherman, p. 196.

118 – The busy waterfront Irish: Feeney, p. 28.

118 – The Irish were clearly arriving: J. Kevin Graffagnino, Samuel B. Hand, and Gene Sessions, *Vermont Voices, 1609 Through the 1990s: A Documentary History of the Green Mountain State,* Montpelier, Vermont, Vermont Historical Society, 1999, pp. 159-160.

119 – In 1843, Vermont's General Assembly: Sherman, p. 215.

120 – George P. Marsh: Graffagnino, p. 182.

121 – Fairbanks, a staunch advocate: Sherman, p. 205.

122 – As his son would write: Sturtevant, pp. 426-427.

Chapter 8

127 – The "generalized simultaneous" rising: Cavanagh, p. 283.

127 – Lalor, in chronic bad health: Kee, p. 291.

127 – By 1852, the League: ibid, p. 294.

127 – Any hopes for a radical: ibid, p. 295.

128 – Some members proposed: Jeremiah O'Donovan Rossa, *Rossa's Recollections, 1838 to 1898: Memoirs of an Irish Revolutionary,* Guilford, Connecticut, The Lyons Press, 2004, p. 149.

129 – In August of 1850: Keneally, p. 221.

129 – MacManus had better luck: ibid, pp. 223, 236.

129 – Meagher, despite his recent marriage: ibid, pp. 242, 246.

130 – To the tune of "Garryowen": Cavanagh, p. 314.

131 – Despairing sometimes at the lack: Kee, p. 304.

131 – O'Brien, who had returned: ibid, p. 305.

132n – Rossa claimed it was there: Rossa, p. 9.

133 - Stephens was able to persuade: Kee, p. 307.

134 – On St. Patrick's Day: ibid, pp. 308-309.

134 - This worked to Stephens' advantage: ibid, p. 310.

135 - In theory, this would isolate: ibid, p. 309.

136 – Though he accepted it: Rossa, p. 235.

136 – Mitchel contributed $50: Kee, p. 307.

137n – Stephens signed this letter: Rossa, p. 269.

138 – Closer to home, O'Mahony: ibid, pp. 300-304.

139 – In the first letter, Luby: ibid, pp. 291-296.

139n – Echoes of O'Mahony's: ibid, pp. 296-299.

140 – Accompanied by Luby: Kee, p. 312.

140 – They included a trip: Rossa, p. 295.

140 – Despite the deteriorating personal relations: Kee, p. 312.

140 – Vermont laws requiring able-bodied: George G. Benedict, *Vermont in the Civil War*, 2 vols. Burlington, Vermont, The Free Press Association, 1886, Vol. 1, p. 9.

140 – By 1856, "there was not": ibid, pp. 9, 10.

141 – Militia companies were governed: *By-Laws of the HOWARD GUARDS*, Burlington, Vermont, D.A. Danforth, 1858, pp. 1, 7-11; *By-Laws of the Ransom guards, V.V. M.*, Burlington, Vermont, Sentinel Print, 1860, pp. 1, 4, 11.

142 – In the summer of 1858: Benedict, p. 10.

142 – As more militia companies: ibid, p. 11.

143 – In July of 1860: *Daily Free Press*, hereafter cited as *Free Press*, Burlington, Vermont, June 27, 1860.

143 – Through the new regimental: *Free Press*, August 25, 1860.

144 – With fourteen of the seventeen: *Free Press*, August 25, 1860.

144 – At the end of 1860: Benedict, p. 11.

145 – This included the 69th Regiment: Pia Seija Seagrave, editor, *The History of the Irish Brigade*, Fredericksburg, Virginia, Sergeant Kirkland's Museum and Historical Society, 1997, pp. 13-14, 18-19, 21.

Chapter 9

148 – The Chicago convention: for the overall political aspect of this narrative on Lonergan's life, see Doris Kearns Goodwin, *Team of Rivals: The Political Genius of Abraham Lincoln*, Simon & Schuster, New York, 2005.

150 – One of these batteries: Keneally, p. 320.

150 – To crush the southern rebellion: for a single volume on the overall military aspects of the Civil War, set in political context, see James M. McPherson, *The Illustrated Battle Cry of Freedom*, Oxford University Press, New York, 2003.

151 – Although the closest: Sturtevant, p. 427.

152 – The roster of the Brandon company: Theodore S. Peck, *Revised Roster of Vermont Volunteers and Lists of Vermonters Who Served in the Army and Navy of the United States During the War of the Rebellion, 1861-66*, Montpelier, Vermont, Watchman Publishing Company, 1892, pp. 20-21.

152 – Certainly within a few months: letter from Stannard to Davis, January 11, 1961, Vermont Secretary of State Archives, which is the source of all official correspondence cited here.

153 – In his inaugural address: www.Vermontarchives.org/govhistory/gov/govinaug/inaugurals/PDF/FairbanksE1860/.pdf.

154 – Sometime in 1860: Sturtevant, p. 427.

157 – Lonergan may have been present: ibid.

158 – The 1st Regiment of Vermont: Peck, pp. 5-25.

159 – In April of 1861: Seagrave, p. 21.

160 – A company attached: Cavanagh, pp. 369-370.

164 – A handwritten roster: Vermont State Military Archives, 2nd Vermont Regiment file.

166 – The company letter designations: Peck, pp. 30-63.

167 – Lonergan reported to camp: Sturtevant, p. 427.

168 – Rains, a native of North Carolina: Paul G. Zeller, *The Second Vermont Volunteer Infantry Regiment, 1861-1865*, Jefferson, North Carolina, McFarland & Company, 2002, p. 12

171 – In the official history, Benedict states in a footnote on the formation of the 2nd Vermont, "A company of Irish Americans, recruited in Burlington and Colchester, was among those originally accepted, but being found deficient in number and discipline was disbanded by order of the Governor, and the Vergennes company took its place."

Chapter 10

176 – Capt. Meagher fell: Cavanagh, p. 37.

177 – At the Battle of Bull Run: Zeller, p. 35.

177 – Several weeks past: Peck, pp. 9, 27.

178 – A bill sent by: Vermont Secretary of State Archives.

179 – The newly arrived Co. H: Peck, pp. 57-58.

179 – In late September: Sturtevant, p. 428.

181 – A newspaper article: *Free Press*, October 7, 1861.

184 – The Fenian Brotherhood exploited: Kee, p. 313.

184 – As chairman of the Obsequies: Cavanagh, p. 416.

184 – Lincoln's government could not: Cavanagh, p. 419.

185n – Rossa would later recall: Rossa, pp. 236-238.

186 – At Glasnevin cemetery: Kee, pp. 314-315.

187 – After the defeat at Bull Run: Cavanagh, pp. 406-407.

187 – Meagher was looking beyond: ibid, pp. 411-412.

188 – Uniquely able to encourage: Keneally, p. 337.

189 – The Head Centre of the Brotherhood: Cavanagh, pp. 426-427.

189 – For recruitment of units in Vermont, see Peck.

190 – A senator stated that: *Free Press*, April 4, 1862.

191 – Lonergan's record in the official roster: Peck, p. 484.

Chapter 11

196 – The two units of greatest interest: McPherson, p. 358.

197 – The Irishmen even organized: Cavanagh, p. 443.

197 – Sumner urged Meagher's men: ibid, pp. 444-447.

198 – The Irishmen distinguished themselves: ibid, p. 450.

199 – Working through recruiting offices: Peck, p. 338.

201 – While seeking replacements: Cavanagh, pp. 253-257.

203 – Lonergan's former first lieutenant: *Free Press*, June 17, 1862.

204 – On July 28, Burlington held: ibid, July 29, 1862.

205 – Capt. Lonergan moved that: ibid, July 31, 1862.

206 – Burlington's three selectmen: ibid, August 11, 1862.

207n – The practical matter of providing: ibid, August 27, 1862.

209 – Official records for his company: Peck, pp. 484-485.

209 – Lonergan had made appeals: Sturtevant, p. 428.

211 – Other militia companies in Vermont: Peck, pp. 484-501.

213 – Stannard tried to break out: George S. Maharay, *Vermont Hero: Major General George J. Stannard*, Shippenburg, Pennsylvania, White Mane Books, 2001, p. 89.

214 – Combined losses for the brigade: Cavanagh, pp. 460-462.

215 – As they enlisted, the men gathered: Sturtevant, p. 425.

216 – With Lonergan presiding over: ibid.

216n – Benedict enlisted in the 12th Vermont as a private, even though he was the postmaster for Burlington and thus exempt from service. His father owned the Burlington *Daily Free Press* and Benedict wrote thirty-one letters for publication in the newspaper during his service. Benedict was commissioned as a replacement second lieutenant in Co. C in January of 1863.

217 – The governor himself decided: Peck, p. 50.

220 – After the war, it furnished: ibid, p. 456.

220 – Lonergan led his own company: *Free Press*, September 25, 1862.

220 – the Howard Guard was assigned: ibid, September 30, 1862.

221 – Accordingly, he formed up: ibid, September 29, 1862.

222 – One person who did not attend: ibid, October 4, 1862.

223 – Not until October 8: Sturtevant, pp. 45-57.

223 – Orders were read to prepare: ibid, pp. 59-61.

223n – Lonergan's long-running argument: *Free Press*, July 19, 1862.

225 – A Westford member of the company [Heman Allen]: Sturtevant, p. 425.

Chapter 12

227 – A somber mood replaced: Sturtevant, pp. 69-71.

227 – With this meal, army life: ibid, pp. 71-73.

228 – In the early morning hours: ibid, p. 73.

229 – After a night spent: ibid, p. 75.

229 – On October 26, a regimental: 13th Vermont Special Orders 29 and 30, Washington, DC, National Archives and Records Administration, [hereafter NARA], Record Group [RG] 94, E112-115, Vol. 3 of 5.

230 – Dozens of soldiers with illnesses: Eric Ward, *Army Life in Virginia: The Civil War Letters of George G. Benedict*, Mechanicsburg, Pennsylvania, Stackpole Books, 2002, pp. 111-112.

231 – Unaccustomed to marching: Sturtevant, p. 81.

232 – Only these first two regiments: Ward, pp. 68, 73.

232 – South of Hunting Creek: Sturtevant, pp. 81-83.

232n – Mason was a member: Ward, p. 76.

233 – Brigade headquarters was established: Sturtevant, p. 85.

234 – The Fenians were reminded: Cavanagh, p. 480.

235 – Mitchel accurately reported: Kee, p. 377.

235 – During their first weeks: Sturtevant, p. 87.

236 – Proximity to the army supply lines: ibid, p. 89.

236 – Late on November 25: ibid, p. 91.

236 – The nearby Bull Run battlefield: ibid, p. 93.

237 – The usual Sunday inspection: ibid, p. 94.

237 – December 7 brought a visit: ibid.

237 – On December 11, Stoughton: ibid, p. 97.

238 – John Mitchel and two of his sons: Keneally, p. 373.

238 – After Maj. Gen. William French's division: Jeffry D. Wert, *The Sword of Lincoln: The Army of the Potomac*, New York, Simon & Schuster, 2005, p. 200.

239 – As the senior regiment: Seagrave, p. 64.

239 – His corps commander assured: Wert, p. 201.

240 – The 116th Pennsylvania had: ibid, p. 204.

240 – Replacement flags for the New York: Keneally, p. 371.

240 – Around a campfire in the Irish Brigade: ibid, p. 375.

241 – To celebrate the holiday: Sturtevant, p. 103; *Sentinel*, February 6, 1863.

243 – Before his telegraph line was cut: ibid, pp. 103-107; Ward, pp. 114-118.

246 – Once released from arrest, Lonergan: Sturtevant, p. 111.

248 – Lonergan and his company: ibid.

249 – Just the day before: Order Book, Companies A, I, and K of 13the Vermont,

NARA, RG 94, E-112-115, Vol. 4, pp. 1-17.

249 – The two regiments marched: Ward, p. 131.

250 – One bright spot in the soldiers' lives: Sturtevant, p. 121.

250 – These first days at Wolf Run Shoals: ibid, p. 123.

251 – For the first time: ibid, p. 125.

251n – for complying with the Co. A order: NARA, Company A Order Book.

252 – It informed all his men: ibid.

253 – The boldest and most successful: Ward, pp. 145-149.

255 – On the day that the brigade: NARA, Company A Order Book.

Chapter 13

259 – At Wolf Run Shoals, Lonergan's company: Sturtevant, pp. 425-426.

260n – Dyer's wife and two babies: Howard Coffin, *Nine Months to Gettysburg*, Woodstock, Vermont, The Countryman Press, 1997, p. 137.

261 – After the debacle at Fredericksburg: Cavanagh, Appendix, p. 23.

261 – Nevertheless, when St. Patrick's Day arrived: ibid, pp. 478-480.

264 – On March 23, the division commander: Ward, p. 153.

265 – As the 13th braced itself: Sturtevant, pp. 141-143.

265 and 266n – When his Co. K from Highgate: ibid, p. 718.

267 – With this extension of their area: ibid, pp. 141-147.

268 – The new commander was personally known: ibid, p. 151.

268 – This visit might have given Lonergan: ibid, pp. 151-158.

269 – Even so, the Irish Brigade's commander: Cavanagh, p. 482.

270 – Back again in the Falmouth camp: ibid, Appendix, pp. 26-27.

271 – Within the week, his resignation: ibid, pp. 482-485.

271 – Randall had lost his other: Sturtevant, p. 163.

271- Stannard visited the 13th again: ibid, p. 165.

272 – As second in command: ibid, p. 429.

273 – Lonergan likely was wearing: ibid, pp. 165-166.

274 – The long roll of the drum: ibid, p. 167.

274 – As the spring weather brought: ibid.

275 – The report of a more serious raid: ibid, p. 169.

276n – Some of the men in the attached: Zeller, p. 143.

278 – Rumors of an impending move: Sturtevant, p. 171.

279 – The 13th Vermont helped to construct: ibid, p. 173.

280 – A final Sunday inspection: ibid, p. 175.

280 – The men were told to carry: ibid, p. 189.

281 – Union Mills had been designated: ibid.

Chapter 14

283 – Late on June 25: Sturtevant, p. 191.

284 – After a wet night: ibid.

284 – An impatient Stannard was forced: Ward, p. 184.

285 – Pushing hard to join: Sturtevant, p. 193.

286 – Lonergan fell off his horse: ibid, p. 197.

287 – the hungry soldiers of the 13th Vermont: ibid, pp. 197, 207.

289 – Lonergan and the other company commanders: ibid, p. 205.

289 – The brigade left some ninety disabled soldiers: Benedict, p. 440.

290 – Benedict carried back Reynolds' instructions: ibid.

290 – Regiments rotated in the order of march: Sturtevant, p. 209.

290 – After repeatedly seeking: ibid, p. 229.

293 – Stannard had made every effort: ibid, p. 215.

293 – The brigade was ordered: Ward, pp. 188-189.

294 – The 13th led the column even faster: Sturtevant, pp. 217-219.

295 – Deprived of water for most of the day: ibid, pp. 227, 240.

Chapter 15

297 – Daybreak on Cemetery Hill: Sturtevant, pp. 240-241.

298 – During the morning, the Second Vermont Brigade: ibid, p. 245.

299 – Inside Lonergan's stained and dirty blue uniform: May, 2004, Sale Catalog 126, Item 5, Gary Hendershott collection.

300 – Stannard was placed "in charge...": Sturtevant, pp. 259-263.

302 – Anticipating combat at any moment: ibid, p. 473.

302 – An account by Lt. Col. George Meade: Benedict, pp. 453-454.

303 – When the column reached: ibid, pp. 455-456.

304-306 – The five companies of the 13th: ibid, pp. 269-271, 431-432.

306 – Other veterans were less impressed: ibid, p. 810.

306n – Lonergan later told how Stannard: Marius B. Peladeau, *Burnished Rows of Steel: Vermont's Role in the Battle of Gettysburg*, Newport, Vermont, Vermont Civil War Enterprises, 2002, p. 329. This useful compilation pulls together information from official reports and other documents into a single volume. Peladeu provided the image of Sinnott's hat, which was in his possession.

307 – On the road east before dawn: Noah

Andre Trudeau, *Gettysburg: A Testing of Courage*, New York, HarperCollins, 2002, p. 333.

307 – Lonergan's company occupied the right: Sturtevant, p. 283.

308 – The 16th was again called upon: Benedict, p. 459.

309 – Much of the firepower in the area: Trudeau, p. 479.

Chapter 16

311 – During the enemy shelling: Sturvevant, p. 283.

312 – Sinnott left instructions: ibid, p. 437.

312 – The men of Veazy's regiment: Benedict, p. 161.

313 – Most likely it was Lonergan's men: see Earl J. Hess, *Pickett's Charge—The Last Attack at Gettysburg*, Chapel Hill, North Carolina, The University of North Carolina Press, 2001, p. 141.

314 – The commander of the 14th: Peladeau, p. 140.

314 – All morning they were essentially: Sturtevant, pp. 288-289.

315-316 – Receiving the colonel's permission: ibid, pp. 289-293.

316 – Randall ordered his men forward: ibid, p. 295.

317 – This was likely the time: ibid, p. 425.

318 – Even so, many men, exhausted: Benedict, p. 466.

318 – As Sinnott rose up from behind: Sturtevant, p. 437.

320 – Lt. Dooley later described his feelings: Hess, p. 167.

321 – The word was passed down the line: Sturtevant, p. 303.

322 – Randall reported that he had shifted: Peladeau, p. 165. [the pages of Randall's report are out of sequence in book]

322 – Unable to make himself heard: Sturtevant, p. 305.

324 – When Hancock saw the opportunity: Trudeau, p. 499.

324 – Hancock himself then rode down: Peladeu, p. 215.

325 – Since Lonergan's company led: Sturtevant, p. 305.

325 – Even so, when Doubleday saw: Benedict, p. 478.

326 – The entire color guard of the regiment: Hess, pp. 225-229.

327 – Sturtevant wrote that the men: Sturtevant, p. 311.

327 – The 13th did not cease firing: ibid, p. 305.

327 – Sturtevant remarked that: ibid, p. 309.

328 – A few Confederate cannon: ibid, pp. 313-315.

329 – The weary brigade, deafened: ibid, pp. 319-321.

Chapter 17

331 – Parched from battle: Sturtevant, p. 321.

331 – Well-deserved approval came: ibid.

332 – The bodies that the burial details: ibid, p. 323.

333 – They showed Ralph the mangled body: ibid, p. 317.

333n – Sturtevant claimed that: ibid, p. 323.

334 – Sturtevant described how Randall led: ibid, p. 327.

335 – The brigade's line of march: ibid, pp. 329-330.

335 – Together with Lonergan, Wilder: ibid, pp. 450, 593.

336 – With a short march ahead: ibid, p. 331.

337 – A rumor spread through camp: ibid, pp. 333-335.

338 – The regiment fell in and formed: ibid, pp. 337-339.

339 – Unfortunately, no passenger cars awaited: ibid, pp. 349-351.

340 – In Baltimore, Lonergan temporarily: NARA, Lonergan affidavit to McDevitt's disability pension request.

340 – Departing Baltimore on the evening: Sturtevant, p. 353.

341 – In sharp contrast, Sturtevant dismissed: ibid, pp. 353-357.

342 – Despite the late hour: ibid, p. 357.

343-343 – Some men "had foolishly…": ibid, pp. 369-375.

343 – The 12th was mustered out: ibid, p. 383.

343 – Friday came, July 17: ibid, pp. 387, 391.

344 – The men of the 14th: Benedict, pp. 492-493.

344 – On Monday, July 20: Sturtevant, p. 391.

345 – The first half of July 21: ibid, pp. 399, 407-411.

Part III

Chapter 18

354 – Stannard, the Second Brigade commander: Maharay, p. 186.

354 – The 17th Vermont failed to enlist a full complement for its ranks for mustering in as a regiment. Instead, companies or even squads of the regiment were mustered in separately as sufficient soldiers volunteered to re-enlist or were drafted for the unit. A greater percentage of substitutes, paid to replace men drafted, appeared in this regiment than in units formed earlier; this was also reflected in the higher rate of desertions. Peck, pp. 568-597.

356-357 – Growth in the American branch: Mabel Gregory Walker, *The Fenian Movement*, Colorado Springs, Colorado, Ralph Myles Publisher, 1969, pp. 22-25.

357 – To promote nationalism and to raise funds: Kee, p. 315; Keneally, p. 408.

358 – Lonergan likely was the driving force: Walker, p. 66.

358 – Meagher marked the death: Keneally, p. 389.

359 – Lonergan fulfilled this public role: *Free Press*, February 8, 1864.

360 – The schedule for the Burlington: ibid, March 14, 1864.

360-362 – The rest of the day's activities: ibid, March 18 and 19, 1864.

362 – Just below the lengthy article: ibid, March 19, 1864.

363 – The trip was timed: Walker, pp. 29-32.

365 – When Meagher did arrive: *Free Press*, April 22, 1864.

366 – Meagher was offered the command of a Veterans' Corps to be part of Sherman's march to the sea. This punitive campaign intended to lay waste to a great swath through Georgia, destroying civilian resources supporting the war. Meagher was repulsed by the nature of this plan and refused the command. In February of 1865, he again resigned his commission and returned to New York. Cavanagh, pp. 492-493.

366 – In June of 1864, the eldest son: www.scocr.org/Chapters/03.

366-367 – Casualties among the Irish nationalists: www.civilwarhistory.com/ElmiraPrison/.

367 – Lonergan was one of the three men: *Free Press*, August 2, 1864.

368 – In an on-going feud: ibid, August 16, 1864.

368 – "a fossil silver-gray whig": ibid, August 18, 1864.

368 – one such recruiter for the Vermont quota: ibid.

368-369 – Apparently Lonergan was in charge: ibid, September 5, 1864.

370 – One such raiding party: ibid, October 19-22, 1864.

371 – He had resumed his efforts: Suit originally filed by Carolus Noyes, *In the Matter of Capt. John Lonergan, Co. K, 2d Regiment vs. The State of Vermont*, on January 18, 1862, was resubmitted with affidavits procured in 1864, Vermont Secretary of State Archives.

373 – The Reunion Society of Vermont Officers: collective of authors, *Proceedings of the Reunion Society of Vermont Officers*, Burlington, Free Press Association, 1885, two volumes, Vol. 1, pp. 1-14; *Free Press*, November 19, 1864.

374 – Instead, Lonergan made overtures to Hancock: NARA, Lonergan files.

376 – Still pursuing the goals of the Irish nationalist: *Free Press*, December 30, 1864.

378 – In a big step down: Peck, p. 657.

378 – Gleason squeezed the names of nine: University of Vermont, Special Collections.

378 – Both cavalry companies were initially: Peck, p. 656.

379 – Despite unfavorable weather: *Free Press*, March 17, 1865.

379 – Dinner and dancing preceded the call: ibid, March 18, 1865.

380 – Two weeks later, Lonergan's first child: Burlington Cathedral baptismal register, Vol. 2, March 31, 1865.

380 – When the meeting did convene: Walker, p. 36.

381 – Kelly left for Ireland early in March: ibid, pp. 39-40.

387 – A grand parade took place: Howard Coffin, *Full Duty: Vermonters in the Civil War*, Woodstock, Vermont, The Countryman Press, 1993, pp. 352-353.

382 – Foster had commanded the 4th Vermont: Peck, p. 371.

382 – The 206 members of the two Vermont companies: ibid, pp. 657-658.

382 – Figures for the first regiment: ibid, p. 66.

Chapter 19

386 – Both factions of the Brotehood: Walker, p. 53.

386 – Contributors were at times shown rooms: ibid, p. 63.

387 – Mitchel remarked wryly: William Dillon, *Life of John Mitchel*, London, K. Paul, Trench & Co. 1888, Vol. 1, p. 218.

387 – Meagher resigned his commission as general: Paul R. Wylie, *The Irish General: Thomas Francis Meagher*, Norman, Oklahoma, University of Oklahoma Press, 2007, p. 219.

388 – offered the position of military secretary: ibid, p. 226.

388 – Other Irishmen did not fail to seize: Walker, pp. 39-41.

389 – Because an employee named Nagle: Kee, pp. 319-321.

389 – After the raid on the Dublin offices: Walker, p. 45.

390 – Many states in the south listed: *New York Times*, December 15, 1865.

391 – At least $500 came in from each: ibid.

391 – Mitchel was still being held: Walker, p. 52.

391 – Thrown in Richmond prison: Walker, p. 61.

392 – Stannard presided over the evening: *Reunion Society*, pp. 20-23.

393 – Further rounds of toasts continued: ibid, p. 28.

393 – O'Mahony had also nominated: Walker, pp. 60-61.

394 – O'Mahony thus found himself: ibid, p. 62.

394 – Canadian authorities gathered intelligence: Hereward Senior, *The Last Invasion of Canada: The Fenian Raids, 1866-1870*, Toronto, Dundurn Press, 1991, p. 43.

394n – Sweeney was removed from U.S. Army: Jack Morgan, *Through American and Irish Wars: The Life and Times of General Thomas W. Sweeney, 1820-1892*, Irish Academic Press, Dublin and Portland, Oregon, p. 205.

395 – Hugely exaggerated claims were made: Senior, pp. 37-38.

395 – One former Irish nationalist: *Free Press*, January 2, 1866.

395 – A spell of mild weather: ibid, January 5, 1866.

395 – Trials of arrested revolutionaries: ibid, January 8, 1866.

395 – The senate itself was abolished: ibid, January 11, 1866.

396 – Police had also seized: ibid, January 29, 1866.

398 – The Senate faction of the Brotherhood: ibid, February 20, 1866.

398 – Although Lonergan supported the O'Mahony: Michael Crawford and Kenneth Armstrong, *Canadian Jackdaw Learning Kits: No. C21, Fenian Kit*, Toronto, Clarke, Irwin, and Company, no date.

399 – In reaction, "the military: *Free Press*, February 28, 1866.

400 – The military department was to: ibid, March 2, 1866.

400 – Widespread meetings of the Brothehood: ibid, March 6, 1866.

400 – The Brotherhood's heart-felt: ibid, March 5, 1866.

401 – Washington no doubt found: ibid, March 13, 1866.

401 – The harmless nature of the publicized: ibid, March 13 and 17, 1866.

401 – A "sensational story" soon: ibid, March 12, 1866.

402 – The "greatest enthusiasm prevailed" at: ibid, March 14, 1866.

402 – The Governor General of Canada: ibid.

403 – Amid increasing concerns that: ibid, March 16, 1866.

404 – In 1866, Vermont was home: e-mail from Vincent Feeney to the author, January 4, 2009.

407 – The reporter attending the celebration: *Free Press*, March 19, 1866.

Chapter 20

409 – Killian, O'Mahony's treasurer: Walker, pp. 81-82.

409 – There Stephens met Gustave Cluseret: ibid, pp. 86-87.

410 – Even as the Burlington Fenians: *Free Press*, March 19, 1866.

410n - McGee had reportedly also written prominent Fenians in the United States to suggest that they use their funds to transport all the Irish from their homeland to settle the American West. Killian had worked for McGee in New York, but they appear to have parted ways over the question of Irish nationalism.

411 – A U.S. Navy warship, the *Winooski*: Walker, pp. 83-84.

412 – Michael Murphy in Toronto: Senior, p. 52.

412 – Reportedly, one group stormed: Walker, p. 84.

413 – Regular steamship navigation opened: *Free Press*, April 20, 1866.

413 – On April 30, delegates: Walker, p. 85.

414 – Upon arrival in New York: ibid, pp. 87-89.

414 – On May 15, some 6,000 Fenians: *Free Press*, May 16, 1866.

415 – When John Mitchel learned: Walker, p. 89.

416 – Sufficient quantities of arms and ammunition: ibid, p. 93.

417 – O'Neill brought with him: Morgan, p. 32.

417 – The Canadian authorities had already: Senior, p. 71.

418 – Meade arrived in Buffalo: Walker, p. 99.

418 – At a meeting in Montreal: *Free Press*, June 8, 1866.

419 – The property was brought to Burlington: ibid, May 31, 1866.

421 – A collection of funds was made: ibid, June 4, 1866.

422 – Even as the newspapers: ibid, June 2, 1866.

422 – The Burlington Fenian Hall: ibid, June 5, 1866.

424 – A brief item titled: ibid, June 7, 1866.

425 – Back in St. Albans: ibid.

425 – Spear was at the same hotel: ibid, June 8, 1866.

425 – Spear appeared before them: ibid, June 7, 1866.

426 – At Frelighsburg that evening: ibid, June 12, 1866.

426 – The British flag from the: ibid, June 8, 1866.

426 – Another flag displayed: ibid, June 9, 1866.

427 – A detachment of twenty-five men: ibid.

428 – Even with the overwhelming: Senior, pp. 123-126.

429 – Safely back across the border: *Free Press*, June 11, 1866.

430 – The only confirmed fatality: Senior, p. 126.

431 – Other spots along the border: *Free Press*, June 12, 1866.

431 – The regular U.S. troops: ibid, June 22, 1866.

432 – The one-armed general was confirmed: Maharay, pp. 267-268.

433 – When O'Neill visited him: Walker, p. 101.

434 – After casting his lot with the Roberts wing: *Free Press*, July 10, 1866.

Chapter 21

438 – Twenty-two prisoners had already: Walker, pp. 123, 129.

438 – Setting the example by: ibid, pp. 127-128.

438 – The Catholic Church, ever hostile: *Free Press*, July 17, 1866.

439 – Roberts himself stayed in jail: Walker, p. 105.

439 – The Roberts faction held: ibid, p. 112.

439 – The convention voted to appoint: ibid, p. 131.

439 – Late in October, Stephens: ibid, p. 135.

440 – Although no toast was offered: *Reunion Society*, p. 61.

441 – In any case, the General Assembly: *Acts*

and Resolves passed by the General Assembly of the State of Vermont at the Annual Session 1866, Montpelier, Freeman Steam Printing, 1866, p. 288.

441 – The bitter factional fights: Walker, pp. 135-136.

442 – An uprising in Ireland: ibid, pp. 137-138. The castle armory held 9,000 stand of arms with ammunition, 4,000 swords, and powder in bulk stored in the arsenal.

444 – However, on Saturday morning: *Free Press*, March 16, 1867.

445 – John Lonergan forcefully rejected: ibid, March 18, 1867.

446 – Suspicion as to who wrote this obituary for the Fenian movement in Vermont falls on the editor of the *Free Press*, Benedict, as having the newspaper contacts and the attitude that would slant the article against the Fenians. He was a conservative, wealthy Republican with deep roots in Vermont whose writings show prejudice against John Lonergan, the upstart Irish Catholic Democrat and immigrant. Benedict's official history of Vermont's role in the Civil War gives scant recognition to Lonergan and presents the disbanding of his Emmets Guards in an unfavorable light. In his numerous lectures on the battle of Gettysburg, Benedict's accounts of the climatic flank attack of July 3 focused on that rare Irish Republican, James Scully, rather than the company commander.

447 – Sailors off Her Majesty's steamer: *Free Press*, March 21, 1867.

447 – The Fenians in the Ogdensburg area: ibid, March 25, 1867.

447 – A correspondent from the New York: ibid, March 29, 1867.

448 – That spring, the Fenians purchased: Walker, pp. 144-146.

448 – Following the collapse of the planned: ibid, pp. 154-155.

449 – During the night, he fell: Keneally, pp. 454-455. Meagher's life had recently been threatened and there was speculation that he might have been killed by vigilantes or Fenians, though suicide or an accident were not ruled out. The body was never found.

449 – On October 30, he attended: *Reunion Society*, pp. 63-78.

449 – Burlington's Irish community celebrated: Howard Coffin, *An Inland See: A Brief History of the Roman Catholic Diocese of Burlington*, Burlington, The Roman Catholic Diocese of Burlington, 2001, p. 22.

450 – That same month, Lonergan embarked: Sturtevant, p. 433.

450 – On reading the second issue: *Free Press*, February 25, 1868.

451 – The day before the first issue: City Hall Records, Burlington, Vol. 4, p. 209.

451 – The next St. Patrick's Day: ibid, Vol. 4, p. 103.

451 – Lonergan no longer had any: *Free Press*, March 18, 1868.

453 – After a futile effort to close: Walker, p. 150.

453 – During the Civil War: Senior, p. 133.

454 – In the early hours of April 7: Keneally, pp. 476-477.

454 – In May, Lonergan "suspended" publication: *Free Press*, May 30, 1868.

455 – Activity was supposedly taking place: ibid.

456 – Based at least in part: Senior, p. 135.

457 – The next afternoon, a Fenian convention: *Free Press*, June 22, 1868.

457 – In Burlington on the following Monday: Sturtevant, p. 753.

458 – Yet the only marching: Walker, p. 175.

458 – The chairman of the Committee: ibid, p. 177.

459 – Instead, the largest event of this nature: *Free Press*, March 19, 1869.

460 – Three months later, John Lonergan: ibid, June 22, 1869.

461 – When the pardons were granted: Keneally, pp. 423, 485, 491-492.

Chapter 22

467 – The Fenians received a severe blow: The Official Catholic Encyclopedia, www.oce.catholic.com.

468 – The Burlington Democrats met: *Free Press*, February 26, 1870.

468 – In the heavily Irish South Ward: ibid, February 28, 1870.

469 – The Hibernians were said to have: ibid.

471 – The mayor was instructed to communicate: ibid, March 9, 1870.

472 – Despite the threat of continuing snow: ibid, March 18, 1870.

476n – The captain of Co. G had been wounded: Peck, p. 494.

478 – In announcing the lecture at City Hall: *Free Press*, April 6, 1870.

478 – In the spring of 1870: ibid, April 9, 1870.

478 – Upon his return to New York City: ibid, April 13, 1870.

478n – Lonergan might take pride: ibid, April 15, 1870.

480 – In reaction, Canadian volunteers: Senior, p. 144.

480 – O'Neill had even borrowed: Walker, p. 183.

481 – The Montreal *Witness* speculated: *Free Press*, April 19, 1870.

481 – O'Neill was reported to have: ibid, April 25, 1870.

483 – Instead of Fenian developments: ibid, May 23, 1870.

485 – The Canadian Governor General claimed: Senior, p. 143.

488 – The first of O'Neill's units: *Free Press*, May 26, 1870.

488 – Teamsters were being given: ibid, May 25, 1870.

489 – News that a company of Canadian militia: ibid, May 26, 1870.

489 – With Col. Lewis in charge: ibid, May 27, 1870.

489 – The marshal immediately informed: ibid, May 26, 1870.

491 – Westover captained a group: Senior, p. 140.

492 – Around 3:00 AM on May 25: *Free Press*, May 28, 1870.

493 – Foster turned his horse: Senior, p. 160.

Chapter 23

495 – O'Neill spoke to the Fenians: *Free Press*, May 26, 1870.

496 – The Vermonters moved at double-time: Senior, pp. 160-161.

496 – An aide to O'Neill: *Free Press*, May 30, 1870.

497 – O'Neill berated his soldiers: ibid, May 26, 1870.

498 – O'Neill withdrew from the battle line: ibid, May 26, 1870.

499 – After observing O'Neill's arrest: Keneally, pp. 503-504.

499 – Although Lonergan had never: ibid, p. 505.

500 – Benedict—the editor of the *Free Press*: *Free Press*, May 27, 1870.

501 – The Canadian forces hurried them: Senior, p. 163.

502 – The raid on Canada not only faced: *Free Press*, May 27, 1870.

504 – The authorities in St. Albans: ibid, May 28, 1870.

505 – Spared during the 1866 attacks: Senior, pp. 164-172.

508 – The funeral for the two Fenians: *Free Press*, July 1, 1970.

508 – Rowe's uniform reportedly had been stripped: Senior, p. 163.

510 – Despite the generally negative reaction: *Free Press*, June 20, 1870.

511n – Ignoring this pledge, a year later: Walker, p. 190.

512 – In 1880 and again the following year: NARA, Lonergan records.

516 – An item under "Vermont Personals": *Free Press*, November 13, 1893.

SELECTED BIBLIOGRAPHY

A LARGE NUMBER OF BOOKS PROVIDED general background for this story, along with each author's own perspective of the history of Ireland, Canada, or the United States—particularly the American Civil War. Far fewer comprehensive sources were found on more specific aspects, such as Vermont's history or that of the Fenian Brotherhood.

GENERAL

Of those books covering more than one of the three divisions used here—Ireland, America, and Canada—the following were particularly useful:

Cavanagh, Michael. *Memoirs of Gen. Thomas Francis Meagher,* Worcester, Massachusetts, The Messenger Press, 1892

Kee, Robert. *The Green Flag: A History of Irish Nationalism,* New York, Penguin Books, 1972

Keneally, Thomas. *The Great Shame,* New York, Anchor Books, 2000

Rossa, Jeremiah O'Donovan. *Rossa's Recollections, 1838 to 1898: Memoirs of an Irish Revolutionary,* Guilford, Connecticut, The Lyons Press, 2004

IRELAND

Ellis, Peter Berresford. *Celtic Myths and Legends,* New York, Carroll & Graf, 2002

Laxton, Edward. *The Famine Ships: The Irish Exodus to America,* New York, Henry Holt and Company, 1996

MacManus, Seumas. *The Story of the Irish Race,* The Devin-Adair Company, New York, 1921

Ó Néill, Eoghan. *The Golden Vale of Ivowen: Between Slievenamon and Suir,* Dublin, Geography Publications, 2001

Power, Patrick C. *Carrick-on-Suir and its People,* Dun Laoghaire, Anna Livia Books, 1976

Slater, Isaac. *Commercial Directory of Ireland,* Manchester, 1846

AMERICA

Frequently consulted to help put Lonergan's story into the overall political and military developments at the time of the American Civil War, these two works also served as models of clear writing and concise summaries of sweeping events.

Goodwin, Doris Kearns. *Team of Rivals: The Political Genius of Abraham Lincoln*, Simon & Schuster, New York, 2005

McPherson, James M. *The Illustrated Battle Cry of Freedom*, Oxford University Press, New York, 2003

Vermont

Feeney, Vincent E. *Finnigans, Slaters, and Stonepeggers: A History of the Irish in Vermont*, Bennington, Vermont, Images from the Past, 2009

Sherman, Michael; Sessions, Gene; and Potash, P. Jeffery. *Freedom and Unity – A History of Vermont*, Barre, Vermont, Vermont Historical Society, 2004

Vermont in the Civil War

Benedict, George G. *Vermont in the Civil War*, 2 vols, Burlington, Vermont, The Free Press Association, 1886, Vol. 1

Coffin, Howard. *Nine Months to Gettysburg*, Woodstock, Vermont, The Countryman Press, 1997
————. *Full Duty: Vermonters in the Civil War*, Woodstock, Vermont, The Countryman Press, 1993

Collective of authors, *Proceedings of the Reunion Society of Vermont Officers*, Burlington, Free Press Association, 1885

Peck, Theodore S. *Revised Roster of Vermont Volunteers and Lists of Vermonters Who Served in the Army and Navy of the United States During the War of the Rebellion, 1861-66*, 2 vols., Montpelier, Vermont, Watchman Publishing Company, 1892

Sturtevant, Ralph Orson. *History of the 13th Regiment Vermont Volunteers*, [no publisher given], 1910

Ward, Eric. *Army Life in Virginia: The Civil War Letters of George G. Benedict*, Mechanicsburg, Pennsylvania, Stackpole Books, 2002

Zeller, Paul G. *The Second Vermont Volunteer Infantry Regiment, 1861-1865*, Jefferson, North Carolina, McFarland & Company, 2002

Daily Free Press, Burlington, Vermont. By 1870, it had added "*and Times*" to the masthead after buying up the defunct *Burlington Times*.

Web site: Vermont in the Civil War, http://www.vermontcivilwar.org/ is an amazingly comprehensive collection of information placed on line by Tom Ledoux.

SELECTED BIBLIOGRAPHY

Gettysburg

Hess, Earl J. *Pickett's Charge—The Last Attack at Gettysburg*, Chapel Hill, North Carolina, The University of North Carolina Press, 2001

Sears, Stephen W. *Gettysburg*, Boston/New York, Houghton Mifflin, 2004

Trudeau, Noah Andre. *Gettysburg: A Testing of Courage*, New York, HarperCollins, 2002

Wert, Jeffry D. *Gettysburg: Day* Three, New York, Simon & Schuster, 2001

FENIANS

Morgan, Jack. *Through American and Irish Wars: The Life and Times of General Thomas W. Sweeney, 1820-1892,* Irish Academic Press, Dublin and Portland, Oregon

Senior, Hereward. *The Last Invasion of Canada: The Fenian Raids, 1866-1870,* Toronto, Dundurn Press, 1991

Walker, Mabel Gregory. *The Fenian Movement*, Colorado Springs, Colorado, Ralph Myles Publisher, 1969

INDEX

1798 uprising 32, 73, 77, 452
1848 rebellion in France 51
1848 uprising, Ireland, xvi, 72–93
1st Regiment of Vermont Volunteer Infantry 158–159
    returns home 177
1st Virginia 235, 238, 307, 326
2nd Vermont Regiment 164, 167, 168, 169, 171, 172, 175, 176, 178, 179, 181, 182, 191, 199, 203, 209, 217, 218, 225, 231, 268, 338, 343, 382
    in Battle of Bull Run 177
    in Virginia 178
    3rd Vermont Regiment 162, 166, 171, 176, 177, 179, 197
    in battle at Lee's Mills 197
4th Vermont Regiment 197
6th Vermont Regiment 189, 197
7th Vermont Regiment 190
8th Vermont Regiment 190
9th NYSM Regiment 130
    See also 69th New York
9th Vermont Regiment 198, 206, 213 allowed to resume active duty 263
    guards prisoners at Camp Douglas 213
    mustered in 199
    surrenders at Harper's Ferry 213
10th Vermont Regiment 206
    Chittenden County to provide a company for, 1862 204
    mustered in 200
11th Vermont Regiment 206
    converted to Heavy Artillery 200
    mustered in 200
12th Vermont Regiment 200, 220, 229, 232, 342
    assigned to guard prisoners from Gettysburg 333
    march to Wolf Shoals 248–250
    mustered out 343
    (note) 341
    reviewed and inspected by Gov. Holbrook 222
    selected to guard baggage train 293
    term of service expires 333
13th Vermont Regiment 200, 217, 228, 232, 270, 290, 293, 297, 307, 316, 331
    arrival at battlefield at Gettysburg 294
    begin the march home 337–339
    camps on the Occoquan 266
    capture rebels at Codori house 305
    celebrates New Year's Day, 1863 246
    departs for Brattleboro 221
    fires on Pickett's Charge 321
    first days at Wolf Shoals 250
    helps construct pontoon bridge across the Occoquan 279
    in Washington, D.C. October, 1861 228
    leads brigade, July 1, 1863 293
    leaves Wolf Run Shoals 266
    low desertion rate of 334
    march to Centreville 283
    march to Wolf Shoals 248–250
    mustered out 345
    rescues Union Cannon 304
    six men captured by Mosby's Rangers 274
    Sturtevant's history of 232
    sworn into U.S. Army 223
    target for sharpshooters 314
    travel to Washington, D.C. 227
    under bombardment at Battle of Gettysburg 311
    veterans arrive at Marine Hospital, Burlington, Vermont 258
14th Vermont Regiment 200, 217, 229, 230, 293, 298, 303, 308, 312, 316, 328, 344
    casualties, July 3, 1863 314
    fires on Pickett's Charge 321
    sent to join 12th & 13th on the Occoquan 264
15th Vermont Regiment 200, 217, 229, 230, 344
    and suppression of draft riots 344

ordered to Gettysburg but then returned to guard duty 298
selected to guard baggage train 293
sent to Union Mills Station 264
16th Vermont Regiment 200, 217, 229, 293, 295, 303, 312, 321, 324, 328, 344
and suppression of draft riots 344
on picket duty 308
sent to Union Mills Station 264
17th Vermont Regiment 200, 381
members of 13th Vermont recruited for 342
veterans of 2nd Vermont Brigade recruited for 353
28th Massachusetts Regiment 124, 239
at battle of Fredericksburg 238–239
37th New York Regiment 130
63rd New York Regiment 214
69th New York Regiment 129, 145, 159–160, 187, 197, 358, 365, 366 in battle of Fredericksburg 239
88th New York Regiment 301
99th NYSM Regiment 367, 414
116th Pennsylvania Regiment
in Battle of Fredericksburg 188, 238, 240

Adams, Charles F., U.S. Ambassador to Ireland 387
Adams, Sullivan 348
Albert Edward, Prince of Wales See Edward VII
Alexandria, Virginia 212, 232, 233, 235, 236, 243, 244, 245, 258, 264, 267, 277, 279, 285, 340
Allen, Ethan 110–111, 460
Allen Grays (Vermont militia) 142, 144, 151
make-up of 151, 151–152
Allen, Heman, Pvt. 317, 322
Allen, Ira 112–113
American Hotel, Burlington, Vermont 361, 365, 366, 373, 379, 445, 457, 459, 460
Antietam, Battle of 214

anti-Irish sentiment in Vermont 119–121
Appomattox Court House, Surrender at 381
Army of the Potomac 175, 189, 195, 196, 201, 212, 213, 233, 251, 252, 270, 275, 284, 287, 288, 290, 292, 336, 365, 368, 381, 382
defeated at Fredericksburg 240
demoralized under Burnside 247
Fenian officers in, given leave 356
in Battle of Gettysburg 297, 307, 309
morale improved under Hooker 269
pursues Lee north 277, 279, 280
Second Vermont Brigade
expect to join 255, 262-263
joins 278
Arthur, J.A., Deputy U.S. Marshall 420, 427
"A" tents 232, 236, 279
Austine, Maj. William 223, 343, 345
Ayers, Joseph, Pvt. 248

Balfe, John (informant) 72
Ballingary 83, 84, 85, 86, 89, 90, 91, 92,94
Baltimore, Maryland 228, 339
Banks, Nathaniel P., Gen. 196
Battery Park, Burlington, Vermont 105,165, 215
Baxter, H. Henry, Vermont AIG 154, 155–156, 158, 162, 163–164, 166, 167
and disbanding of Emmet Guard 172
refuses to swear in Emmet Guard 170
Benedict, George G. 216, 257, 289, 293, 294, 323, 324, 333, 361–362, 373, 472, 484, 500, 509, 516, 518
aide to commander, St. Albans Raid 371
and Burlington Free Press (newspaper) 249, 368
becomes aide-de-camp to Blunt 257n
description of wounded at Gettysburg 308
lectures on role of 2nd Vermont at Gettysburg 354
Benedict, George W. 205
Big Bethel, Battle of 177
Bigelow, George H. 380, 452, 477
Blake, Thomas, Sgt. 326

INDEX

Blunt, Asa P., Col. , 12 Vermont Regiment 245, 342
  commander of 2nd Vermont Brigade 230, 255
Blunt, Mary, wife of Asa P. 260
Boleyn, Anne, connection to Carrick 24
Boru, Brian 22–23
Boyne, Battle of 27
Boyton, Joseph J., Capt. 271, 273
Brandon Company, (Vermont militia) 142, 144, 151, 152, 158, 177. See also Allen Grays
Brandy Station, Battle of 278
Brattleboro, Vermont 207,219,220, 221, 222, 227, 230, 258, 265, 340, 341, 342, 346
Brenan, Joseph (Irish writer and revolutionary) 127, 130,153
Brooks, Isaac, Pvt. 230
Brooks, W.T.H., Gen. First Vermont Brigade 196
Brown, Andrew, Lt. Col. 218, 225, 271
Brown, John 147, 149
Brown, Stephen F., Lt. 290, 315, 327
Brophy, J.B. (Fenian) 459
Buchanan, James, President 148,149
Buford, John, Brig. Gen. 278, 292, 297
Bull Run, Battle of 175, 187, 236
  2nd Vermont in 177
  tour of battleground by 2nd Vermont Brigade 278
Burlington, Vermont 101, 108
  arrival of Lonergans in 101, 107
  Cathedral of the Immaculate Conception 449
  emigration route to 107
  Fenian movement in 138
  Fourth of July, 1862 203
  Hawthorne comments on Irish during visit 118
  Irish community when Lonergans arrived 118
  quota of volunteers for 1862 206
Burnham, William T. , Capt. 168–169, 172, 178, 181
Burnside, Ambrose E., Maj. Gen. 234, 247
  flawed attack on Fredericksburg 238
  orders "mud march" 247–248
  removed from command 248
  replaces McClellan 233
Butler family, Carrick 4
  Duke of Ormonde 25
Butt, Isaac 462
Byrne, Patrick, parish priest, Carrick 58, 79, 81, 96

Cameron, Simon 148, 195
  Lonergan pleads case with 179
  Secretary of War 149, 178
Camp Carusi 274n
Camp Casey 229, 231
Camp Lincoln, Brattleboro, Vermont 219, 220, 221, 222, 340, 342, 344
Camp Underwood, Burlington 167
Camp Vermont 233, 235, 236, 237
Canada rebellion in 114–115
  Dominion of Canada 448, 454, 455, 463
  invasions by Fenians See Fenian Brotherhood, attacks on Canada
Cappoquin 127, 130
Carleton, Charles, Maj., (Fenian) 496
Carpenter, B. Walter 371, 440–441
Carrick on Suir, 389n, 398, 443, 521,
  1848 uprising in xvi, 76–79, 87
  history of 3–11
Casey, Silas, Gen. 229
  Casey's Division 229, 230, 231, 251, 264
Catlett's Station, Virginia 275
Catholic chaplains, with Irish units 241, 261
Catholic emancipation 40
Cavalry, Fenian 425, 426, 488, 495-496
Cavanagh, Michael 75–76, 90, 91, 159, 201
Cemetery Hill, Gettysburg 294, 296, 297, 298, 299, 300, 302, 317, 321
Cemetery Ridge, Gettysburg 294, 297, 298, 299, 301, 303, 305, 311, 318, 336
Chancellorsville, Virginia 270
Clan na Gael 511, 524
Clapp, William, Collector of Customs,

Burlington, Vermont 432
Clarendon, Lord, (representative of the crown) 60, 68
Clarke, Albert, Lt. 315, 335–336
    editor, St. Albans Messenger 476–477, 484, 500, 509
Clark, Henry J., the Hon., friend of Thomas D'Arcy McGee 444, 445
Clarke, Lawrence D., Capt. 218, 265
Clark, Martin, Pvt. 265, 266 and 266n
Cleveland, Grover 515
Clonmel 4, 6, 8, 11, 26, 29, 33, 66, 75, 77, 83, 88, 92, 93, 94, 96, 102, 116, 127, 139, 389, 443
Clontarf 22, 41, 56
Cluseret, Gustave 409, 439, 440, 442, 443
Coburn, Lewis C., Capt. 218, 273
Codori house 301, 305, 516
Company A, 13th Vermont Regiment xv, 166, 219, 225, 460. See also Irish Company (Lonergan's) described as Emmet Guards in Rutland Herald (1863) 346
    fires on Pickett's forces 321, 325
    position on July 3, 1863 313
    discontent with Protestant services 242
Company G, 2nd Vermont 315, 327
Company H, 2nd Vermont Regiment 168, 171, 178
    Burnham elected captain of 169
Company K, 2nd Vermont Regiment 164, 166, 191, 290. See also Emmet Guards (original)
    officially disbanded 172
    ordered to disband 170
Confederate Clubs 71, 86, 96
    Carrick 57, 64, 78
    Cork 63
    Dublin 54, 56, 75, 83
    established by Young Ireland 45
Confederation of Kilkenny 25
Considine, Owen 134
Continental (steamboat) 227
Contri, Col. (Fenian) 426
Copperhead, (Democrats) 366, 368

Corcoran, Michael 159, 184, 187, 365
    authorized to raise "Irish Legion" 202
    captured by Confederate Forces 176
    charges dropped 159
    court martial of 145
    death of 358
    named commander of Fenian forces 139
    persuades O'Mahony not to enlist 160
    released in prisoner exchange 201
Corey, James A., Pvt. 229
    death at Gettysburg 326
Cornwallis, Lord 33, 36
Crime and Outrage (Ireland) Bill
    See Treason-Felony Act 55
Crimean War 132–133
Cromwell, Oliver, crushes Irish independence 26–27
Cronan, P.W. 472, 473, 474
    presents Robert Emmet's story in Burlington 477
Cronan, William, Capt. (Fenian) 488, 495, 500, 503, 508
Cuchulain (legendary hero) 14
Cullen, Paul, (Archbishop, Cardinal) 128, 467
    denounces Irish People (newspaper) 358
Culp's Hill, Gettysburg 294, 300, 306, 311, 331
Customs House, Burlington, Vermont 420, 422, 424, 426, 427, 430, 432, 464

Davis, George, Vermont Quartermaster General 155, 222
Davis, Jefferson, president of Confederacy 150, 151, 387
Davis, Thomas xiii, 40, 42
Deasy, Timothy, Capt. 448, 522
Death Feast at Fredericksburg 240
Decoration Day 483
DeGoesbriand, Louis, Bishop of Burlington, 360, 450
Denieffe, Joseph 133, 134
Denison, Dudley C., District Attorney 421
Desmond, Cornelius, Pvt. 231

INDEX

Dillingham, Paul 440
   Governor 423
   Lt. Governor 373, 392
Dillon, John Blake 40, 61, 68, 72, 74, 83
   flight after Ballingary 90
Dix, John A., Maj. Gen. 354, 374, 376, 387
Dobbyn, James (informant) 72
Doheny, Michael 46, 62, 63, 65, 134
   childhood 10
   co-creator of Emment Monument Ass'n 132
   fistfight with McGee 133
   flees Ireland 91
   founds Phoenix (newspaper) 138
   organizes funeral service for MacManus 184
   rising of 1848 83, 90
Doherty, Michael 129
Dolan, Christopher M., 1st Lt. in Emmet Guards 203, 419
Donnelly, John J. 489, 500, 510
   takes command of Fenian forces 499
   wounded 501
Dooley, John (journalist) 238
Dooley, John, Lt. (son of John Dooley) 238, 307, 320, 326
Doubleday, Abner, Maj. Gen. 292, 293, 294, 302
   approves 13th Vermont attack on Pickett 322
   praise for Green Mountain Boys 325
Douglas, Stephen, Democratic candidate for president, 1860 148
   votes received in Vermont 149
draft
   1862 204
   1863 344
   riots, 1863 344
Drew, John T. Capt., Vermont Guards 163, 164, 176
Drogheda, massacre at 26
Duffy, Charles Gavan 40, 43, 52, 54, 57, 58, 60, 61, 62, 63, 75, 76
   arrested 62
   co-founder of The Nation (newspaper) 40
Duggan, James, Bishop of Chicago 363

Dullahan, John, Hibernian Society, Burlington, Vermont 444, 445, 451, 459, 473, 474, 508
Dunne, Peter (Fenian) 388
Dyer, Charles, Pvt. 260

Eaton, Solon, Capt., Vergennes Company 172, 177
Eccles Hill, Quebec 430, 485, 490, 491, 492, 495, 496, 501, 503, 504, 508
Edward VII 144–145, 518
Edwards Ferry, Virginia 285
Eleventh Corps (Union) 236, 277, 278, 292, 293, 294, 297, 299
Emancipation Proclamation 215, 247
Emigration from Ireland during the Famine 99–102
Emmet Guards (2nd organization) 280
   See Irish Company (Lonergan's)
Emmet Guards (original) 158, 166, 168, 180, 181, 183, 191, 195, 202, 211, 217, 218, 372
   accepted for service 168
   formation of 152–153
   offered for service, April 1861 161
   still listed as Uniformed Militia 206
Emmet Monument Association 128, 132, 133, 134, 135, 138
Emmet, Robert 36–38, 474, 477, 481
Emmet, Thomas 32, 34, 36
Emmitsburg, Maryland 291, 334, 335
Emmitsburg Road, Gettysburg 294, 296, 298, 301, 302, 304, 308, 312, 321, 324, 327
"E Pluribus Erin Union go bragh" 210, 362, 450
Ewell, Richard, Maj. Gen., Second Corps (Confederate) 276, 288
Excelsior Brigade (New York) 261
   led by Sickles 241

Fairbanks, Erastus, Gov. 120, 121–122, 153–154, 156, 195, 338
   farewell address to General Assembly 182
   orders Emmet Guard disbanded 170

orders organization of 4th and 5th
regiments 176
receives status report from Baxter 163
Fairfax Court House 237, 240, 242, 244, 245,
248, 249, 253, 266, 281, 358
Fairfax Station 243, 253, 254, 255, 258, 264,
268, 274, 279, 281
Fairfield, Vermont, Irish population 116
Fair Grounds, Burlington, Vermont 143, 215
Fair Oaks, Battle of 197, 201
famine in Ireland 38, 44, 49, 234
Faugh a ballagh 198, 214, 239, 304
Fenian banner 124, 135, 239, 349
Fenian Brotherhood 183, 186, 191, 201, 349,
353, 356, 401, 434, 510
 adopts new constitution 390
 agent visits Vermont, 1864 376
 attack on Canada 397, 398, 399, 402
  1866 417–432
  1870 495–500
  Queen's Birthday 415
  rumors of 397, 401–402, 447, 455,
  480–483
  U.S. takes measures to prevent 402-
  403, 487
 attempt to seize Campobello Island
 409–412
 banned by Church 467
 capture schooner Wentworth 412
 condemned by Church 357
 establishment of 135–136
 fund-raising 134, 136, 184, 388, 390,
 391, 404, 457
 growing dissatisfaction with
 O'Mahony 385
 hopes for U.S. support of cause 183,
 354, 383, 433
 in New York City 138, 159, 184, 201,
 388, 400
 in Vermont 138, 152, 404
 leaders released on bail, 1866
 438–439

losses in battle of Fredericksburg 240
organizes public associations 359
prepares to invade Canada, 1867 447
purchase of armaments 386
Senate faction holds convention 398
trials in Canada for captured invaders
437–438
Fenian Brotherhood, Burlington 397, 405
 declared by Lonergan independent of
 political parties 434
 meeting, June 4, 1866 422
 parade before St. Patrick's Day, 1867 444
Fenian Cavalry See Cavalry, Fenian
Fenian Convention 511
 Chicago, 1863 356–357
 Chicago, 1870 (Senate) 480
 Cincinnati, 1865 380
 New York, 1870 (O'Neill) 480
 Philadelphia, 1865 390–391
Fenian Fair, Chicago, 1864 363, 363–364
Fenian Hall, Burlington 400, 421, 422, 455
Fenians in Confederacy 234–235
Fenian, derivation of 16
Fenian Regiments 439, 488
Fenian Sisterhood 390, 405, 406, 407
Finn McCool See McCool, Finn
First Corps (Confederate) 276–278, 288
 led by Longstreet 276
 see also Longstreet's Corps
First Corps (Union) 278, 280, 283, 284, 285,
289, 290, 292, 293, 294, 295, 298, 302, 303,
313
First Vermont Brigade 179, 189, 217, 220, 230,
238, 269, 270, 276, 283, 284, 285, 334,
381, 460
 and attack on Richmond, April 1862 196
 at Antietam 214
 at Fairfax Station 279
 encounters 2nd Brigade at Middletown,
 Md. 336–337, 338
 praise for 2nd Brigade at Gettysburg 306
Fiske, Joshua, Pvt. 237

INDEX

FitzGerald, J.E. 361
Foster, George P., Brevet Brig. Gen. 382, 449
    U.S. Marshall 483, 489, 493, 498, 511
Fletcher Company. See Company H, 2nd Vermont Regiment
Fletcher, Ryland, Gov. of Vermont 142
Floyd, John, Secretary of War 149
Fort Lyon, Virginia 235
Fort Sumter, South Carolina 150, 154, 156
Frederick, Maryland 213, 288, 289, 290, 337
    reception of 13th Vermont in 338
Fredericksburg, Virginia Battle of 237
Free Press (newspaper) 143, 154, 158, 162, 164, 207, 211, 258, 259, 349, 360, 361, 362, 368, 373, 376, 379, 401, 410, 411, 414, 422, 424, 426, 430, 432, 442, 443, 446, 469, 471, 472, 476, 478, 483, 499, 500, 509, 512, 530
    editorials on Fenians 413, 423, 429, 482
    failure to refer to Emmet Guards 347
    letter from "Erin" 402
    Lonergan posts notices in 158, 208, 364, 434,
    on Fenian attacks on Canada 397, 399, 403, 420, 481, 486–487, 503, 507
    on Lonergan 157, 164, 165n, 171, 258, 450, 502, 508, 518, 519
    political affiliation 121, 368
    prints Fenian appeal 1866 399,
Fremont, John C., Maj. Gen. 187
French, William, Gen. 214, 238
Frontier Cavalry, Vermont 376–378
    mustered out 382

Gaelic (language) 14
Garnett, Robert B., Brig. Gen. 320, 326
Gettysburg, Battle of xv–xvi
    July 1, 1863 292
    July 2, 1863 297–306
    July 3, 1863 311–329
Gettysburg, Pennsylvania 288, 289, 290
Gibson, Augustus, Maj. 431, 456
    arrests Sweeney 425

Gladstone, William Ewart, British Prime Minister 458, 461, 463, 508
Gleason, John H., Gen. (Fenian) 447, 503, 507
    arrested 507
Gleason, Rollo, Maj. 362
Grant, Ulysses S.
    General 195, 275
    President, 458, 475, 482, 504, 510
    and 1870 Fenian attack 487, 493
Gray, Phillip 126–127, 131, 133
Great Britain
    displeased with U.S. support of Fenians 356
    support of Confederacy 183, 354, 458, 475
    strained relationship with U.S. 356, 383, 386, 438, 458
Green Mountain Guards (Vermont militia)
    Bellows Falls 142
    Swanton 158, 218
Green Mountain Rangers. See Emmet Guards (original)
Green Mountain Rangers (Vermont militia) 111
    Burlington 168, 171, 172
    Granville 142,
Grosse Île (quarantine station) 101, 522–523
Guilford Station, Virginia 285
Gibbon, James (Fenian) 502

Hall, Nathaniel B., Maj. 393, 440, 449
Halleck, Henry, Maj. Gen. 212, 276
Halpine, William G., Gen. 388, 396
Hanlin, John, Pvt. 326, 512, 514
Hancock, Winfield Scott, Maj. Gen. 238, 261, 290, 318, 354, 376, 456
    orders Meagher to command retreat from Chancellorsville 270
    wounded at Gettysburg 324
    Lonergan petitions for a commission 374
Harper's Ferry, Virginia 147, 213, 338
    9th Vermont sent to defend 213
harp, uncrowned (Fenian symbol) 54, 124, 188, 349
    on Lonergan's uniform 299
Harrisburg, Pennsylvania 287, 288

Hawthorne, Nathaniel, visits Burlington, 1832 118
Hearn, John D. 140
Heintzelman, Samuel P., Maj. Gen. 231, 247, 251, 262
    command converted to Twenty-second Corps 251
    given command of defenses around Washington 231
Henry II of England 23–24
Henry VIII of England 24, 25
Henry, Alvin H. 211, 280
    enlists with Lonergan 209
    serves as First Sergeant 209, 216
    in hospital, June 1863 273
Henry, Hugh H., U.S. Marshal 421, 432, 483
Herndon Station, Virginia 285
Hibernian Society, Burlington, Vermont, 364, 365, 397, 405, 444, 445, 446, 459, 468, 469, 471, 472
    organization of 359
    celebration of St. Patrick's Day, 1865 379–380
Hill, A.P., Maj. Gen. (Confederate) 288
    commander of Third Corps 276
Holbrook, Frederick, Gov. 198, 222, 342
    authorizes recruitment of veterans 353
    establishes Vermont hospital for soldiers 258
    elected governor of Vermont, 1861 180
    illness delays taking office 182
    petitioned by Second Vermont Brigade 264
    telegraph to Edwin M. Stanton 199
Hollywood, Edward 52, 55
    arrest of 63
    flight after Ballingary 90
Hooker, Joseph., Maj. Gen., 419, 423
    Battle of Chancellorsville 270–271
    in dispute with Meagher 261
    introduces practice of wearing badge 263n
    mobilizes Army 270
    nicknamed "Fighting Joe" 255
    possible replacement for McClellan 234
    reorganizes Army of the Potomac 262
    replaced as Army commander by Meade 289
    rides past 2nd Vermont 289
    sends cavalry north into Pennsylvania 291
    takes command from Burnside 248
    withdraws from 2nd assault on Fredericksburg 270
Hopkins, Gen., Ass't AG, Vermont Militia 163
Howard Guards, (Vermont militia) 141, 142, 143, 151, 152, 156, 157, 158, 211, 220
    assigned as Company C of 12th Vermont 220
Howard Hotel, Burlington, Vermont 215
Howard, Oliver O., Maj. Gen. 292
Hoyt, W.H., editor of Sentinel (newspaper) 365, 368, 450
Hunter, S.N. (informant) 491
Hyde, Breed, Col. 197

illness, in camp 230, 236, 248
"Ireland Boys, Hurrah" (song) 240
    Irish attitude toward
        preservation of the Union 147
        slavery 148
        draft 344
        Emancipation Proclamation 215
    in New York 125
    in Vermont 112, 115–120
    Militia units 125, 129
        See also individual units (69th New York, etc.)
Irish Brigade 188, 193, 196, 197, 201, 234, 241, 269, 270, 271, 280, 301, 362, 365, 366, 373, 380, 388, 389, 440, 460, 503, 506
    assigned to Army of the Potomac 189
    at Antietam 214
    at Gettysburg 299
    celebrates St. Patrick's Day, 1863 261–262
    in battle of Fredericksburg 238–240
    in Seven Days' Retreat 198
Irish Citizen (newspaper) 130

INDEX

Irish Company (Lonergan's) 209, 218, 234, 248, 259, 295, 309, 331, 362, 476. See also Company A, 13th Vermont Regiment
 as Emmet Guard becomes Company A 219
 fighting at Gettysburg, July 2, 1863 304–306
 fighting at Gettysburg, July 3, 1863 316–325, 327–328
 departs for Brattleboro 220–221
 departure from Brattleboro 224
 election of officers 216
 escorts Howard Guards to Union Station, Burlington, Vermont 220
 leaves Camp Vermont 236
 pivot point for attack on Pickett's flank 323
 rejects petition for change of terms of enlistment 264–265
 sworn into U.S. Army 223
 welcome home 346, 347–348
Irish Felon, The (newspaper) 62, 64, 73
Irish Land Act, 1870 462
Irish League 62, 71
Irish Legion (Corcoran) 358, 359, 365, 389
Irish People (newspaper) 357, 389, 400
Irish Republican Brotherhood (IRB) 381, 389, 437, 462, 525
 arranges for O'Donovan Rossa's burial 524
 condemned by Church 357
 establishment of 134–135
 uprising of 1867 442–443
Irish Watchman (newspaper) 450, 451, 454, 476

Jackman, Alonzo, Brig. Gen. , Vermont Militia 143, 157, 219, 370
 and organization of 13th Vermont 218
Jackson, Thomas J., "Stonewall," Maj. Gen. (Confederate) 196, 270
 mortally wounded 275
 outflanks Pope's forces 212
 recalled from Shenandoah Valley by Lee 197
Jericho Cornet Band 348, 360, 361, 404
Jersey City, New Jersey 227, 341
Johnson, Andrew, President 381, 382, 383, 386, 392, 402, 411, 426, 433, 439n, 458, 487
 and Fenian attack, 1866 421, 423, 426, 427–428, 438
Johnston, Joseph E., Maj. Gen. (Confederate) 196, 197
Jones, Nathaniel, Lt. 230
Joyce, Charles H., Maj. 167, 172, 371, 440, 457, 460

Kelly, Patrick, Col. 299
 assumes command of Irish Brigade 271
Kelly, Thomas J. 381, 388, 414, 440
 arrested 448
 escapes Dublin 409
 takes control of IRB after Stephens' arrest 394
Kemper, James L., Brig. Gen. (Confederate) 320, 321, 326
Kenyon, Father 61, 74
Kickham, Charles 355, 357, 363, 389–390
 arrested 391
 attends Fenian convention in Chicago 356
 writes for Irish People (newspaper) 358
Kiernan, Lawrence D. 405
Kilkenny 4, 6, 25, 26, 45, 59, 65, 68, 73, 74, 75, 76, 77, 82, 83, 84, 90
Killian, B. Doran, Fenian treasurer 393, 411, 414
Know Nothing party 120, 125

Lalor, James Fintan 62, 73, 127
Leavenworth Block, Burlington, Vermont 165, 190, 191
Le Caron, Henri, Maj. (British secret agent) 453, 454, 455, 456, 479, 480, 484, 485, 488, 489
 with O'Neill during 1870 invasion 489
Lee, Robert E., Gen. (Confederate) 197, 198, 213, 279, 381
 commander of Army of Northern Virginia 203, 212
 demonstrates generalship 213, 287
Limerick, Treaty of 28
Lincoln, Abraham, President 148, 183, 355, 356,

368, 372, 376, 439
 1861 inaugural address 149
 allows Union officers to attend Fenian
  convention 356
 and McClellan 214
 assassination of 381
 calls for add'l volunteers 362
 comments on Stoughton's capture 255
 declares amnesty for deserters 263
 and Emancipation Proclamation 215, 247
 levy of July 1862 198
 mobilizes militia 151, 156–157
 visits 2nd Vermont Regiment 178
Lincoln, Vermont 512, 514, 527
Lindsey, Daniel C. 468, 469, 474, 477
Little Round Top, Gettysburg 301
Lonergan, Edward 10, 445, 446, 452, 453, 460
Lonergan, Ellen, (child of Thomas and Mary) 10
Lonergan, Jane (child of John and Roseanna) 512
Lonergan, John xv, 8, 45, 46, 65, 67, 148, 157, 205, 224, 255, 452, 503, 507
 1866 invasion of Canada 421, 424, 430
 1870 invasion of Canada 486, 488, 495, 499, 501, 502
 accused of giving preference to Irish volunteers 163
 active in local Democratic politics 367, 468, 469
 applies for increase in disability pension 514
 appointed to U.S. Customs in Montreal 515
 arrested 242, 273
 and "mud march" 248
 and Reunion Society 373, 440, 449, 457, 460, 511
 and Thomas Francis Meagher 57, 359–361, 364–366
 attempts to take command of 13th Vermont 273
 awarded Medal of Honor 518
 baptism 10
 birth of children 380, 451, 512
 captures Confederates at Codori house 305

 Christmas leave 241
 claims right flank position for Irish Company 316
 confused with Capt. Lewis C. Coburn in records 218
 cooper 122, 132, 182, 190, 202, 512
 death of 518
 education of 11–12
 elected captain 164, 155, 216
 emigration of 97
 enlists in Allen Grays (Brandon) 144
 fall into the Monocacy 286, 373, 449, 510, 511, 514
 Fenian activities 358, 390, 397, 399, 400, 413, 463
 General Orders of 249, 251-252
 grocer 154, 392, 413, 449, 459, 464
 in St. Patrick's Day in Burlington 361, 404
 lead attack on Pickett 322–324
 marriage of 222
 on furlough in Vermont, March 1863 258–260
 passed over for promotion 1863 271
 pension 514, 515
 presented with sword 272, 273
 publishes Irish Watchman (newspaper) 450
 recruiting officer 162, 202, 206
 reimbursement by Vermont 182, 440, 441
 refuses field promotion 333
 scolded by Stannard 306
 speech at homecoming in Burlington 348
 unauthorized trip to Virginia 178–183, 231
 with U.S. Customs 392, 413, 459, 515
Lonergan, John Patrick (child of John and Roseanna) 451, 464
Lonergan, Mary (child of Thomas and Mary) 10
Lonergan, Mary Nolan (wife of Thomas the elder) 9, 97, 119, 512
Lonergan, Roseanna (child of John and Roseanna) 512, 527

INDEX

Lonergan, Roseanna Sorrigan 371, 441, 451, 512, 526

Lonergan, Sarah Ellen (child of John and Roseanna) 441, 464

Lonergan, Thomas (father) ix, x, xiii, xv, xvi, 3, 6, 7, 8, 9, 10, 11, 12, 14, 18, 19, 21, 22, 26, 28, 31, 33, 37, 38, 45, 46, 51, 57, 58, 65, 67, 68, 69, 77, 79, 81, 87, 91, 92, 96, 97, 99, 100, 101, 103, 108, 259, 380, 413, 441, 449, 459

Lonergan, Thomas (child of Thomas and Mary) 10, 97, 98, 119, 378, 451

Lonergan, Thomas Francis (child of John and Roseanna) 380, 464

Lonergan, Thomas Francis (second child by that name, of John and Roseanna) 465, 519, 526

Longstreet, James, Lt. Gen. (Confederate) 239, 276, 288, 301

Luby, Thomas Clark 139, 140, 358, 363

Lynch, Father 471, 472, 473, 475

Lyon, Matthew 112–113

Macdonald, John A., Prime Minister of Canada 398, 455, 480

Mahan, John W., Gen. (Fenian) 425, 426, 429, 431

Malone, New York 417, 418, 422, 427, 428, 430, 431, 434, 437, 447, 455, 481, 485, 502, 503, 504, 505, 507

Manassas Junction, Virginia 175, 213, 232, 279

Manassas, Second Battle of 213

Manchester Martyrs 448, 522

Marine Hospital 258, 259

Marsh, George P. 120

Martin, John 50, 52, 62

Marye's Heights, Fredericksburg, Virginia 238, 270

Mason-Dixon Line 147, 287

McAllister, Ziba, Pvt. 302

McClellan, George B., Maj. Gen. 179, 195, 196, 197, 198, 203, 212, 243, 262, 269, 270

    Democratic candidate for president 368

hesitancy 214

    replaced by Burnside 233

    Union forces consolidated under 213

McCool, Finn (legendary hero) 14, 16–18, 189, 311, 521

    banner of 34

McCormack, The Widow 84

McDermot, James "Red" (informer) 394, 410

McDevitt, David, 2nd Lt. 216, 312, 324, 340

    elected 2nd Lt. of Irish Company 216

McDowell, Irvin, Gen. 175

McEnerny, Michael, Corp. 229

    death at Gettysburg 326

McGee, Thomas D'Arcy 59, 62, 72, 395, 419–419, 445, 454

    assassinated 454

    elected to Revolutionary Committee 68

    rising of 1848 84

    moves to Canada 133

McGrath, John, Treasurer, Burlington Fenian Brotherhood 397n

McHale, John, Archbishop of Tuam 128

    presides over MacManus funeral in Dublin 185

McInnerny, John, Secretary of Hibernian Society 469, 473, 474, 475

MacManus, Terence Bellew 75, 83

    arrest of 90

    battle at Ballangary 84–85

    Van Dieman's Land (Tasmania) 102, 128, 129

    funeral of 54n, 184–185

    trial after 1848 uprising 94

McMicken, Gilbert 394, 453, 454, 455, 479, 480

    and Le Caron 454

McNamara, John, Secretary, Burlington Fenian Brotherhood 397n, 434, 469

Meade, George, Lt., (son of George G.) 302

Meade, George G., Maj. Gen. 277, 292, 297, 411, 418, 423, 427–428, 433, 456n, 502, 507

    in St. Albans following 1866 invasion 430–431

    takes command of Army of Potomac 289

Meagher, Thomas Francis 42, 45, 52, 53, 56, 60, 61, 72, 126, 136, 186, 197, 198, 201, 272
   arrested 63, 90
   death of 449, 452
   initiated into Fenian Brotherhood 359
   Irish Brigade 188, 238, 270–271
   military secretary of Montana 388
   orator 43, 66, 86
   charged with sedition 53
   description of Carrick 79
   elected to Revolutionary Committee 68
   homecoming parade for 69th New York 187
   "Meagher of the Sword" 43, 160, 186
   organizes funeral service for MacManus 184
   rising of 1848 83, 94–95
   runs for Parliament 50
   St. Patrick's Day celebration in Virginia, 1863 261
   "Sword Speech" 43
   trial 94–95
   in U.S. Civil War, 160, 176, 187, 188, 189, 214, 261, 269, 387
   Van Dieman's Land (Tasmania) 102, 128, 129
   visits Burlington, Vermont 359, 364
   visits Carrick 57
   visits Corcoran's Irish Legion 358
Medal of Honor 197, 304, 516–518, 517, 527
Meehan, James, Col. 388, 390, 427, 439
Michel, Sir John, Lt. Gen., British commander 402, 428
militia, in Vermont 140–144, 374
Millen, F.B., Gen. (Fenian) 381, 388, 393
Mitchel, James, (son of John), company commander, 1st Virginia 235, 366
Mitchel, John 50, 54, 56, 126, 130, 136, 184, 235, 366, 391, 414, 415
   charged with sedition 53
   imprisoned by U.S. government 387
   leaves Confederation, Ireland 45
   observes battle of Fredericksburg 238
   replaces Davis as editor of The Nation 43
   starts United Irishman (newspaper) 45
   trial in Ireland 59–61
   Van Dieman's Land (Tasmania) 128, 129–130
Mitchel, John, (son of John) 150, 366
Mitchell, Willy, (son of John) 235, 238, 307, 320
   death at Gettysburg 326
Monahan, John J. 361, 404, 406, 452, 456, 457, 472, 504, 519
   in Fenian attack on Canada, 1870 486
   second in command in Sarsfield Circle 421
Monocacy Junction, Maryland 337, 339
Monocacy River, Maryland 286, 288, 335, 337, 339
   John Lonergan's fall into 286
Montpelier Company, (Vermont militia) 169, 218, 225
   "monster meetings" 41, 42, 64
   on Slievenamon 64, 355
Mosby, John Singleton, Capt. (Confederate) 252, 255, 263, 269, 279, 287. See also Mosby's Rangers
Mosby's Rangers 252, 253, 255, 263, 269, 274, 275, 279, 287.
   capture 13th Vermont supply wagons 274
   capture Stoughton 253
   raid on Catlett's Station 275
Mount Vernon 232, 233
Moylan, Michael, Pvt. 326
"mud march" 247
Mullagh 8, 80, 92
Mullaghmast 25, 41
Mullinahone 33, 82, 355, 363
Munson, William D., Lt. Col. 300, 302, 306, 333, 368
   promoted 271
   receives command of 13th Vermont 329
Murphy Hotel, Burlington, Vermont 215
Murphy, John, (Fenian) 159
Murphy, Edward 378, 379, 471
Murphy, Michael, Fenian, Toronto 359, 395, 410, 412, 422

INDEX

Murphy, Thomas 378, 492, 519

Nagle, Pierce (informer) 389
Nation, The, (newspaper) 40, 42, 62
New Haven, Connecticut 227
New Year's Day, 1863, celebration 246
Nichols, William T., Col., 14th Vermont Regiment 314, 344, 373, 374
Nine Year's War (1594-1603) 25
"No Irish Need Apply" 115, 186, 528
Noyes, Carolus, lawyer and politician 164, 182, 440

O'Brien, William (Fenian) 496, 504, 505
    funeral of 508–509
O'Brien, William Smith 41–42, 52, 53, 55, 61, 63, 72, 72–74, 78, 126, 131, 496, 505
    arrest of 89
    charged with sedition 53
    in battle at Ballingary 83–85
    jailed as MP 43
    pardoned 129
    trial after 1848 uprising 93–94
    trial for sedition 59–61
    Van Dieman's Land (Tasmania) 102, 128, 129
O'Connell, Daniel 38–43, 44
O'Doherty, Kevin 62–63, 128
O'Donoghue, Patrick 82, 83, 86
    arrest of 90
    trial after 1848 uprising 94
    Van Dieman's Land (Tasmania) 102, 128, 129
Ogdensburg, New York 401, 417, 419, 422, 431, 434, 447, 455, 482
O'Gorman, Richard 59, 60, 61, 68, 72
    flight after Ballingary 90
    rising of 1848 84
O'Leary, John 92, 127, 137, 138, 363, 414
    editor of Irish People (newspaper) 358
    sentenced 395
O'Mahony, Ellen, Fenian Sisterhood 390
O'Mahony, John 46, 77–82, 87, 127, 131, 133, 134, 136, 160, 186, 309, 357, 358, 359, 363, 388, 393, 411, 511
    1860 tour of Ireland 139–140
    abolishes Senate 396
    and arrested men in Carrick 66–67
    attack on Canada 399, 407, 409
    calls for national convention of Fenians 356
    co-creator of Emmet Monument Ass'n 132
    disputes with Stephens 137, 385
    elected Fenian president, 1865 391
    Fenian dissatisfaction with 380, 385, 413
    funeral service for MacManus 184
    head centre of Fenian Brotherhood 188, 357, 396
    letter to William Sullivan 137
    musters clubs, 1848 79
    neighbor of Lonergans in Carrick 58
    organizer of Carrick Confederate Club 65
    raises 99th New York 366–367
    resigns as Head Centre 414
    rising of 1848 79, 83, 90–92
    visits 69th New York in Virginia 161
O'Neill, John, Col. (Fenian) 433, 453, 456, 457, 458, 463, 480, 482, 484, 485, 487, 488, 489, 492, 493, 495, 504, 509, 511
    appointed Inspector General of Fenian army 439
    hands over command to Boyle O'Reilly 498
    in attack on Canada, 1866 417–418, 419, 420, 421, 431
    on the field, 1870 496–497
O'Reilly, John Boyle 461, 489
    assigned command by O'Neill 498
    relinquishes command to Donnelly 499

Page, Lemuel W., Capt. 220
"Pat Malloy" (Irish ballad) 393, 440, 449, 506
Patten, John, Corp. 322
Pavilion Hotel, Montpelier 373
Peck, James S., Adjutant, 13th Vermont 273

refusal to obey Lonergan's commands 273
Penal Laws (Ireland) 3, 10, 28, 128
Philadelphia, Pennsylvania 201, 341
    13th Vermont stops in 228
    69th New York cheered in 187
    Fenian populations in 202
    Meagher gives speech in 188
    reception of 13th Vermont in 340
Phoenix movement 128, 132
Pickett, George, Maj. Gen. (Confederate) 307
"Pickett's Charge" 319–321
Pigeon Hill, Quebec 426, 428, 429, 430, 485
Pingree, Samuel E., Capt. 196
Pitt, William 34, 36
Pius IX 468, 475
    declares Fenians subject to excommunication 467
Pleasanton, Alfred, Maj. Gen. 277, 279
Pope, John, Maj. Gen. 212, 213
potato blight 42–43,
Potomac River 160, 229, 231, 233, 235, 252, 255, 277, 281, 283
    Robert E. Lee
        crosses 1862 213-214
        crosses, 1863 279, 281
        retreat blocked by 335, 336, 338, 353
    2nd Vermont Brigade
        camps on 232, 266, 267
        crosses 285, 286
Proctor, Redfield, Col., 15th Vermont Regiment 264, 298, 370, 373, 393, 516
    praise for Lonergan 517

Queen's Birthday 480, 486
Queen's Own Rifles 417

Rains, Gabriel J., Lt. Col. 159, 168
Randall, Charles (son of Francis V.), in Lonergan's Company 266
Randall, Francis V., Col. 223, 236, 237, 245, 251, 267, 278, 295, 306, 319, 322, 338, 343, 392, 510

appointed commander of 17th Vermont 354
chosen commander of 13th Vermont 217
commands 2nd Vermont Brigade at Gettysburg 300, 302–303, 321, 324, 329, 333-334, 337
departure of 13th Vermont from Brattleboro 225
farewell to 13th Vermont 345
has Lonergan and Coburn arrested 273
leads 13th at Battle of Gettysburg
    July 2 302-306
    July 3 315, 316, 319-322, 324-325
protests conditions of boxcars sent to transport 13th Vermont 339
senior officer of 12th and 13th Vermont 232, 255
writes letter confirming Lonergan's deeds at Gettysburg 516
Randall, Francis V., Jr., (son of Francis V., Col.) drummer 302
Ransom Guards (Vermont militia) 141, 142
"Reaping of Mullagh, The" (ballad) 92
Red River Valley, Canada, unrest in 463
Reilly, Thomas Devin 61, 62, 68, 75, 76, 82
    flight after Ballingary 90
    rising of 1848 83
Repeal Association 40–43, 49
reunion, Second Vermont 460, 510
Reunion Society of Vermont 373, 392, 440, 449, 457, 460
Revolutionary Committee 68, 71, 72
Reynolds, John F., Maj. Gen. 277, 289, 290, 292–293
Reynolds, Lawrence (Fenian) 262, 290, 292, 293
Richardson, Alden, Pvt. 248
Richardson, Israel, Gen. 214
Richelieu River 107, 113, 114, 116, 399, 420, 485
Ripley, Edward H. Col. 373
Roberts, William F. 400, 402, 413, 415, 416, 444
    arrested 427

INDEX

supports invasion of Canada 394, 396
favors Republican party 439
leader of Fenian "Senate" faction 390, 391, 393, 414, 453
released on bail 439
Robinson, John C., Brig. Gen. 292
Rorty, James McKay, Capt. 309, 313, 316, 317
Rossa, Jeremiah O'Donovan 128, 132, 140, 185, 462
    arrested, 1865 389
    business manager of Irish People (newspaper) 358
    death of 524
    sentenced 395
Rowe, John (Fenian) 496, 505, 508–509
Rowley, Thomas A., Brig. Gen. 292
Royal Guides (Canadian militia) 428, 429
Rutland Daily Herald (newspaper) 204, 265, 272, 413
    description of Lonergan's sword 272
Rutland, Vermont 119, 152, 159, 164, 180, 204, 209-211, 216, 361, 368, 404, 413, 469, 510
    celebration of 15th Amendment in 483
    center of Irish population 116
    distribution of bounty by selectmen of 224
    draft riot in 344
    Fenians involved in invasion of Canada 486
    recruitment of volunteers 1862 206, 207
    return of 13th Vermont to 346
Ryan, Father 360, 361, 365

Sarsfield Circle 397, 405, 421, 455. See also Fenian Brotherhood, Burlington
Sarsfield Club, Limerick 57
Sarsfield, Patrick 27, 28
Sargent, Joseph, chaplain for 13th Vermont 241, 267
Savage, John (Fenian) 453, 463
Scott, Julian (drummer) 197
Scott, Thomas A., Ass't Secretary of War 188
Scott, Winfred, Gen. 419
Scully, James B. 273, 322, 452, 484, 519

ass't marshal in 1st St. Patrick's Day Parade, Burlington 361
elected 2nd sergeant of Irish Company 216
enlists with Lonergan 209, 378
injured 326
Republican, Centre Ward, Burlington 469
pivot point for "change front forward" 324
Second Corps (Confederate) 276, 277
Second Corps (Union) 214, 238, 279, 290, 299, 301, 308, 313, 317, 318
Second Vermont Brigade 216, 217, 219, 229, 231, 235, 236, 241, 253, 255, 256, 257, 259, 262, 263, 264, 268, 270, 277, 278, 279, 284, 289, 341, 344, 348, 358, 460
    at Gettysburg 294, 295, 297, 298, 334, 294, 300, 302, 312, 314, 316,
    faces Stuart's cavalry 243–246
    formed by GO 230
    Hooker wants to reassign 276
    marches north 280n, 283–289, 290, 292, 293
    ordered to Virginia 231
    outnumbered by Pickett's force 322
    part of "Defenses of Washington" 247
    petitions Gov. Holbrook re terms of enlistment 264
    receives orders to march north 278
    redeployed to Fairfax Court House 240
    remains assigned to Casey's Division 251
Sedgwick, John, Maj. Gen. 214, 269, 270
Seminary Ridge, Gettysburg 294, 297, 318, 319
Sentinel, The (newspaper) 121, 153, 190, 191, 195, 264, 365, 373, 450, 476
Seven Days' Battles 197, 198
Seward, William H. 148, 387, 398, 433
Shenandoah Valley 176, 196, 197, 213, 277
Sherbrooke, Quebec 420
Sheridan, Phillip H., Maj. Gen. 439, 449
Shields, James, Maj. Gen. 189, 196
Sickles, Daniel E., Maj. Gen. 290, 292, 298, 301, 314
    See also Excelsior Brigade (New York)
Sigel, Franz, Maj. Gen., Reserve Corps 236, 240

Sinn Fein 525
Sinnott, John xiv, 229, 312, 313, 328, 329, 362, 460
    death of (note) 346
    elected first lieutenant of Irish Company 216
    presents sword to Lonergan 272
    recruiting officer, 209-210
    wounded at Gettysburg xv, 318
Sinnott, Patrick A. 400, 409, 410
Sir John's Road, Carrick 8–9, 13, 65, 87, 92
Sixth Corps 269, 270, 284, 285, 334
"skedaddle rangers" (draft dodgers) 207–208, 419
Skibbereen 128, 132, 140, 185
Skinner's Lane, Burlington, Vermont 190, 349
Sligo 72, 139, 396, 448
Slievenamon, (mountain) 14, 15, 33, 58, 108, 185, 193, 291, 299,
    rally on 64
Smith, Henry, Sgt. Maj. 319, 324, 328
Smith, James C. 162
Smith, John 54n
Smith, John G., Gov. 373, 381–382
Smith, William F., "Baldy", Brig. Gen. 179, 181, 182, 196, 371,460
    gives Lonergan pass to visit Cameron 179
Smyth, Patrick 72, 76, 82, 83, 129
    flight after Ballingary 90
Sorrigan, Roseanna. See Lonergan, Roseanna Sorrigan
Spear, Samuel B., Gen. (Fenian) 419, 422, 425, 439, 491, 503
    appointed Secretary of War (Fenian) 439
    leads 1866 invasion 425–426, 428–429
Speed, James, U.S. Attorney General 423
Spring Bank estate, Virginia 232
Springfield, Massachusetts 227, 341
St. Albans Messenger (newspaper) 422, 476, 500
St. Albans Raid, 1864 369–371, 374, 386, 402
St. Albans, Vermont 115, 141, 142, 143, 221, 228, 372, 378, 380, 401, 434, 438, 443, 481, 484, 498
    Fenian circle in 404, 405,

    base for Fenian attack on Canada 398, 417, 420–431, 455–458, 485–502
Stannard, George J., Col. 143, 144, 152, 155, 156, 157, 158, 166, 167, 182, 199, 213, 263, 268, 269, 271, 275, 278, 279, 280, 284, 285, 289, 290, 292, 293, 294, 295, 297, 298, 300, 302, 306, 307, 308, 313, 314, 315, 316, 318, 319, 321, 322, 323, 324, 325, 326, 327, 328, 333, 341, 349, 354, 371, 392, 440,452, 457, 459, 460, 483, 510
    appointed Collector of Customs, Burlington, Vermont 432
    appointed to replace Stoughton 263
    honored at first Reunion Society gathering 373
    named commander of Army forces on northern border 374
    official report on Gettysburg 321, 354
    rebukes Randall 306
    joins 2nd Vermont Brigade at Wolfe Run Shoals 268
    takes command of 9th Vermont 199
    visits 13th Vermont 271, 275
    wounded 328
    writes endorsement for Lonergan 372
Stanton, Edwin M. 189, 195, 198, 205 207, 228
Stephens, James 85, 87, 131–133, 133, 185, 186, 356, 381, 389–390, 427
    arrested 391
    attempts to revitalize Fenian support for IRB 437
    becomes Head Centre for Fenian Brortherhood 414–415
    Chief Organizer of Irish Republic 134
    demands money for revolution 391
    disputes with O'Mahony and U.S. branch 385, 388, 390
    escapes 394, 409
    flight after Ballingary 90
    "Supreme Organizer of the Irish race" 357
    publishes Irish People (newspaper) 357

INDEX

ours of America 136, 363, 414
urges support for Democratic party 439
with Young Irelanders 82
Stephens, William H., Capt. 405
St. Mary's Church and Hall, Burlington, Vermont 359, 360, 444, 452, 471, 474
Stoughton, Edwin H., Col. 197, 219, 222, 243
    appointed brigadier general 230
    captured by Mosby's Rangers 253
    in command of 2nd Vermont Brigade 237
    orders Lonergan released from arrest 242
    replaced by Stannard 263
St. Patrick 18, 22, 35
St. Patrick's Benevolent Society of Winooski 360, 361, 405, 444, 459
St. Patrick's Day 42, 53, 130, 134, 153, 193, 259, 260, 261, 262, 263
    celebrated by Army of Potomac 260, 261
    Burlington, Vermont, celebrations 359–362, 379, 397, 401, 403–407, 444, 451–453, 459, 472–478
    Irish Republican Brotherhood established on 134
    New York City, 1854 130
    not celebrated in Burlington 153, 259
Stuart, J.E.B. Maj. Gen. (Confederate) 243, 276, 279, 285, 288
Sturtevant, Ralph O. 227, 232, 245, 266, 273, 285, 295, 303, 311, 314, 322, 328, 334
    account of 13th firing in two directions 327
    author of unofficial history of 13th Vermont Regiment 216, 300n
Sturtevant, Wesley C., Corp. 315–316, 333
Sullivan, William (Fenian) 137–138
Sumner, Edwin B., Gen. 189, 197, 214
sunburst (Fenian symbol) 17, 18, 34, 41, 56, 124, 135, 188, 216, 291, 299, 349
Sweeney, Thomas W., Gen. (Fenian) 393, 396, 398, 402, 410, 427, 433
    arrested in St. Albans 425
    moves north with Fenian forces 419
    plans multiple attacks on Canada 415
    released on bail 439
    resigns as commander in chief of Irish army 439

Taneytown Road, Gettysburg 298, 302, 308, 331
Tara 17, 21, 22, 41
Temperance movement in Vermont 121–122
Tenants' League 127
Third Corps (Confederate) 276, 277,
Third Corps (Union) 290, 292, 293, 298, 301, 306, 314, 336n
    on Cemetery Ridge 298
Tir na nOg 1, 18, 21, 216, 240, 291
Tone, Wolfe 32, 34
Train, George Francis, candidate for president, 1872 478–479
Treason-Felony Act 55
Tuatha De Danna 15
Tunbridge Light Infantry (Vermont militia) 142
Twenty-second Corps 251, 278, 290

Ulster, Rising of 1641 25
Underwood, Levi, Lt. Gov., recommends Emmet Guards for service 161
Union, Act of, 1801 35
Union Mills Station, Virginia 236, 264, 279, 281, 283
United Irishman (newspaper) 45, 50, 62
United Irishmen 32–34, 36
U.S. relationship with Great Britain.
    See Great Britain

Veazey, Wheelock G., Col., 16th Vermont 308, 312, 318, 337, 373, 374
Vermont
    history of 109–115
    Irish settlement in 116–120
    railroads in 119–120
Vermont Cavalry 204, 228
Vermont militia 140–144, 153–154
Vermont, raising troops in 198,

bounties 199, 200, 203, 204, 205, 224, 353, 362, 368, 378
draft 200, 202, 204, 205, 206, 207, 208, 211, 215, 379
    draft riot 344, 349, 362, 368,
militia 157, 158–159, 161, 162, 166, 200, 206, 207
recruiting 162, 163, 164, 177, 187, 189, 190, 191, 198, 199, 203, 206, 223
troop levy 161, 199, 205, 206,
volunteers 161, 162, 163, 200
war meetings 157, 204, 209, 219n
Vicksburg, Mississippi, 247, 275, 353
Victoria, Queen 94, 96,126, 127n, 145, 415, 508, 518
Vikings 22
Vincent, Margaret, casualty of 1866 invasion 430
Vinegar Hill, Ireland 32, 73, 74

Wadsworth, James S., Brig. Gen. 292
Ward, Bob 68, 76
Washburn, Peter T. 148, 205, 222, 342, 373, 423
    replaces Baxter as AIG 180
Washington, D.C., 13th Vermont arrives in 228–229
Weeks, Timothy, Sgt. 237
Weir, Gulian, Lt. 301, 325
Wells, William, Gen. 516
Westford Drum Corps 348
Westford, Vermont 204, 206, 209, 211, 215, 216, 225, 248, 346, 347, 348
    Lonergan recruits in 209
Westover, Asa, Canadian Home Guard 491, 492
West Windsor Guards (Vermont militia) 211
White, Marvin, Capt. 236
Whiting, Henry, Col. 173, 181, 182
    commissioned and commander of 2nd Vermont 167
Wilderness, The. Battle of 270
Wilder, Orcas B. , Capt. 274, 335
    presents Randall with captured horse 274
Williams, Merrit B., Capt. 300, 335

Winooski, U.S. warship 411, 412
Winooski, Vermont 109, 110, 155, 156, 157, 164, 165, 166, 168, 169, 171, 220, 249, 266
    citizens opposed to Lonergan raising a company 163
    Irish settlement in 120
    Lonergan recruiting officer for 162
    Lonergan recruits in 209
    Lonergan works as grocer in 154
Winooski Volunteers, (Vermont militia). See Company K, 2nd Vermont Regiment
Wolf Run Shoals, Virginia 243, 248, 249, 250, 252, 255, 259, 260, 264, 266, 268, 279, 281, 313
Wood, Fernando (mayor of New York) 145
Woodstock Light Infantry, (Vermont militia) 211
Wright, Ambrose R., Brig. Gen. (Confederate) 301–303

Young Ireland 43, 71, 77, 89, 128, 184
Young Irelanders 125, 126, 129, 388
    organize Confederation for Legislative Independence 45

INDEX

THE
BREWSTER RIVER PRESS
ASSISTS AUTHORS
WHO WANT TO RETAIN CONTROL OF
THEIR BOOKS THROUGH SELF-PUBLISHING.
OUR PROFESSIONALS CAN HELP WITH
THE DESIGN, EDITING, AND PRODUCTION OF BOOKS,
SPECIALIZING IN HISTORICAL SUBJECTS.

BREWSTER RIVER PRESS